CONSTITUTIONAL
LAW
AND POLITICS

VOLUME ONE

CONSTITUTIONAL LAW AND POLITICS

VOLUME ONE

*Struggles for Power
and Governmental Accountability*

DAVID M. O'BRIEN

UNIVERSITY OF VIRGINIA

W · W · NORTON & COMPANY · *New York*

Printed in the United States of America.

The text of this book is composed in New Baskerville,
with the display set in New Baskerville.
Composition by Arcata Graphics/Kingsport.
Manufacturing by Arcata Graphics/Halliday.
Book design by Jacques Chazaud.

First Edition.
Library of Congress Cataloging-in-Publication Data

O'Brien, David M.
    Constitutional law and politics/David M. O'Brien.
        p.   cm.
    Includes indexes.
    Contents: v. 1. Struggles for power and governmental
accountability—v. 2. Civil rights and civil liberties.
    1. United States—Constitutional law—Interpretation and
construction—History—Cases.   2. United States—Constitutional
history—Cases.   3. Political questions and judicial power—United
States—History—Cases.   4. Civil rights—United States—History—
Cases.   5. United States—Politics and government.   I. Title.
KF4541.A7027   1991
342.73—dc20
[347.302]   90–7878

ISBN 0-393-96034-X

W. W. Norton & Company, Inc., 500 Fifth Avenue, New York, N.Y. 10110
W. W. Norton & Company, Ltd., 10 Coptic Street, London WC1A 1PU

1 2 3 4 5 6 7 8 9 0

For
Claudine, Benjamin and Sara

CONTENTS

Cases within brackets are discussed and extensively quoted in the topic intro-
ductions.

ILLUSTRATIONS

PREFACE

Because there is no dearth of casebooks, the introduction of a new one perhaps needs a defense, or at least an explanation of how it differs from others. What distinguishes this casebook is its treatment and incorporation of material on constitutional history and American politics. Few casebooks pay adequate attention to the forces of history and politics on the course of constitutional law. Yet constitutional law, history, and politics are intimately intertwined.

The Constitution and Bill of Rights, of course, are political documents. Rooted in historic struggles and based on political compromises, their provisions and guarantees continue to invite competing interpretations and political contests over, for example, the separation of powers between Congress and the president, federalism, and civil rights and liberties. Because the Constitution says nothing about *who* should interpret it or about *how* it should be interpreted, constitutional law is animated by the politics of interpretation and the interpretation of politics. Neither do we have a single accepted theory of constitutional interpretation, nor do the justices write on a clean slate. Instead, we face constitutional choices and competing judicial and political philosophies.

The Supreme Court's decisions do not occur in a political vaccuum, standing apart from history and the political struggles within the Court and the country. Virtually every major political controversy raises questions of constitutional law, no less than do technological changes and social movements and economic forces. The development and direction of constitutional law also shifts (more or less quickly) with the Court's changing composition. Members of the Court, just as other citizens, differ in their readings of the Constitution. Moreover, major confrontations in constitutional law and politics, such as those over the powers of the national government, or slavery, school desegregation, and abortion, involve continuing struggles that run from one generation to another. In the course of those struggles, constitutional law evolves with changes in the Court and the country. The Constitution and the Bill of Rights bind the Court, other political institutions, and the people in an ongoing dialogue over the exercise of and limitations on governmental power.

By providing the historical context and explaining the political contests among the justices and between the Court and the country, this casebook aims to make constitutional law more accessible for students. History and politics are also important for students' analyzing of particular decisions and their relation to developments and changes in constitutional law and politics. They are crucial as well for students trying to critically evaluate competing interpretations and to appreciate the political consequences of alternative interpretations. And they are essential if students are to engage in the dialogue of constitutional law, confront constitutional choices, and come to terms with their and others' views of the Constitution and the Bill of Rights.

This casebook is different in several ways. First, it comes in two volumes. Volume I, *Struggles for Power and Governmental Accountability*, deals with separation of powers, federalism, and the democratic process. Volume II, *Civil Rights and Civil Liberties* is devoted to the enduring struggles to limit governmental power and guarantee civil rights and liberties. As a two-volume set, it is more comprehensive in its coverage than other casebooks. This permits both more introductory background material and a larger selection of cases. Instructors, therefore, have greater flexibility when assigning cases, and students will find useful the additional cases and guides to other cases and resources.

Second, two chapters dealing with the politics of constitutional interpretation and Supreme Court decision making contain material not usually found in casebooks. Chapter 1 goes beyond dealing with the establishment of the power of judicial review, and political criticisms of the Court's exercise of that power, to examining rival theories of constitutional interpretation. Students are introduced to differing judicial and political philosophies and referred to cases and opinions found in subsequent chapters that illustrate these different positions on constitutional interpretation. Chapter 2 combines an introduction to jurisdictional matters, such as standing, with a discussion of how the Court operates as an institution and in relation to other political institutions, which may help promote compliance with and implementation of its rulings, or thwart and even reverse them. In short, Chapter 1 prepares students for critically evaluating competing interpretations of constitutional provisions in subsequent chapters. And Chapter 2 prepares them for understanding the political struggles that take place within the Court as well as between the Court and other political institutions over its decisions. While the volumes are designed for a two-semester course, both of these chapters are included in each volume for the convenience of teachers and students who have only a one-semester course in constitutional law.

As already noted, each chapter and subsection contains a lengthy introductory essay. These essays focus on particular provisions of the Constitution and the Bill of Rights, why they took the form they did, and what controversies surrounded them during the Founding period and later. Most begin with the debates at the Constitutional Convention of 1787 and those between the Federalists and Anti-Federalists during the ratification period, and then review subsequent cases and controversies. Besides providing a historical and political context for the cases in each chapter, the essays highlight the continuity and changes in the debates over constitutional law and politics that run from the Founding period to recent rulings of the Rehnquist Court.

Something should also be said about the case excerpts. Most are preceded by "headnotes," short explanations of the facts and why the case was appealed to the Court. But, unlike the brief (and usually dry) headnotes typically found in casebooks, these reveal something about the personal and political struggles of those who appeal to the Court. Throughout, there is an attempt to help students understand the judicial and political process and appreciate how questions of constitutional law are embedded in everyday life. For this reason, students will also find excerpts from oral arguments before the Court and other materials bearing on the political struggles that they represent. Along with excerpts of the opinion announcing the decision of the Court, students will frequently encounter excerpts from separate concurring and dissenting opinions. These are included to help students appreciate the choices that the Court and they must make when interpreting the Constitution and the Bill of Rights.

In addition, each volume contains three types of boxes, which include materials that further place constitutional interpretation and law in historical and political perspective. One set of boxes, *Constitutional History,* presents important background material, such as excerpts from John Locke on the connection between property and liberty and explanatory notes on the "Watergate crisis" and the battle over the Equal Rights Amendment. Another set, *The Development of Law,* shows changes and patterns in constitutional law and refers students to other cases on topics of special interest. The third, *Inside the Court,* illustrates the internal dynamics of the Court when engaged in the process of constitutional interpretation and deciding cases. These boxes are indicated by ☐ in the contents.

Finally, each volume begins with the Constitution of the United States. What follows will, it is hoped, enrich students' understanding of constitutional law, politics, and history, as well as open them to the possibilities in interpreting the Constitution and the Bill of Rights. But the Constitution is where students should begin their study, and it is assuredly where they will return again and again.

D. M. O.

ACKNOWLEDGMENTS

I am indebted to my students and colleagues, but I owe a larger debt to Claudine, my wife, for giving me the freedom to work as I do and to enjoy life's pleasures with Benjamin and Sara. I continue to be grateful for the inspiration and support of my teacher C. Herman Pritchett, University of California, Santa Barbara, and my colleague at the University of Virginia Henry J. Abraham. They along with Ira Carmen, University of Illinois; Phillip Cooper, SUNY at Albany; Jerome Hanus, The American University; and Gerald Rosenberg, University of Chicago, read and made very helpful suggestions on various parts of the manuscript for which I am grateful. Also, I thank Thomas Baker, Texas Tech University; Sue Davis, University of Delaware; Susan Fino, Wayne State University; Christine Harrington, New York University; and H. N. Hirsch, University of California, San Diego, for offering comments that helped shape the project early on in its development. The generous support of the American Philosophical Society and the Earhart Foundation contributed to this project as well. Stephen Bragaw was a faithful and meticulous research assistant; Candace Levy copyedited the manuscript with the utmost care. Once again, I appreciate the understanding and assistance of Donald Fusting, a patient and wise editor at Norton.

I am grateful as well for permission to reproduce materials here granted by the following individuals and organizations:

Justices William J. Brennan, Jr., and Antonin Scalia; Ronald K. L. Collins; the curator of the Supreme Court of the United States; Peter Galie; the Library of Congress; Justice Hans Linde of the Oregon State Supreme Court; the Supreme Court Historical Society; the National Portrait Gallery/Smithsonian Institution; *The New York Times;* the Roosevelt Library; Sygma/*New York Times Magazine;* Paula Okamoto; and Wide World Photos.

CONSTITUTIONAL
LAW
AND POLITICS

VOLUME ONE

THE UNITED STATES CONSTITUTION AND AMENDMENTS

W E THE PEOPLE of the United States, in Order to form a more perfect Union, establish Justice, insure domestic Tranquility, provide for the common defence, promote the general Welfare, and secure the Blessings of Liberty to ourselves and our Posterity, do ordain and establish this Constitution for the United States of America.

ARTICLE I

SECTION 1. All legislative Powers herein granted shall be vested in a Congress of the United States, which shall consist of a Senate and House of Representatives.

SECTION 2. The House of Representatives shall be composed of Members chosen every second Year by the People of the several States, and the Electors in each State shall have the Qualifications requisite for Electors of the most numerous Branch of the State Legislature.

No Person shall be a Representative who shall not have attained to the Age of twenty five Years, and been seven Years a Citizen of the United States, and who shall not, when elected, be an Inhabitant of that State in which he shall be chosen.

[Representatives and [direct Taxes] shall be apportioned

among the several States [which may be included within this Union,] according to their respective Numbers, which shall be determined by adding to the whole Number of free Persons, including those bound to Service for a Term of Years, and excluding Indians not taxed, three fifths of all other Persons. *(This clause was changed by section 2 of the Fourteenth Amendment.)*] The actual Enumeration shall be made within three Years after the first Meeting of the Congress of the United States, and within every subsequent Term of ten Years, in such Manner as they shall by Law direct. The Number of Representatives shall not exceed one for every thirty Thousand, but each State shall have at Least one Representative; and until such enumeration shall be made, the State of New Hampshire shall be entitled to chuse three, Massachusetts eight, Rhode-Island and Providence Plantations one, Connecticut five, New-York six, New Jersey four, Pennsylvania eight, Delaware one, Maryland six, Virginia ten, North Carolina five, South Carolina five, and Georgia three.

When vacancies happen in the Representation from any State, the Executive Authority thereof shall issue Writs of Election to fill such Vacancies.

The House of Representatives shall chuse their Speaker and other Officers; and shall have the sole Power of Impeachment.

SECTION 3. The Senate of the United States shall be composed of two Senators from each State, [chosen by the Legislature thereof, *(This provision was changed by section 1 of the Seventeenth Amendment.)*] for six Years; and each Senator shall have one Vote.

Immediately after they shall be assembled in Consequence of the first Election, they shall be divided as equally as may be into three Classes. The Seats of the Senators of the first Class shall be vacated at the Expiration of the second Year, of the second Class at the Expiration of the fourth Year, and of the third Class at the Expiration of the sixth Year, so that one third may be chosen every second Year; [and if Vacancies happen by Resignation, or otherwise, during the Recess of the Legislature of any State, the Executive thereof may make temporary Appointments until the next Meeting of the Legislature, which shall then fill such Vacancies. *(This clause was changed by section 2 of the Seventeenth Amendment.)*]

No Person shall be a Senator who shall not have attained to the Age of thirty Years, and been nine Years a Citizen of the United States, and who shall not, when elected, be an Inhabitant of that State for which he shall be chosen.

The Vice President of the United States shall be President of the Senate, but shall have no Vote, unless they be equally divided.

The Senate shall chuse their other Officers, and also a President pro tempore, in the Absence of the Vice President, or when he shall exercise the Office of President of the United States.

The Senate shall have the sole Power to try all Impeachments. When sitting for that Purpose, they shall be on Oath or Affirmation. When the President of the United States is tried, the Chief Justice shall preside: And no Person shall be convicted without the Concurrence of two thirds of the Members present.

Judgment in Cases of Impeachment shall not extend further than to removal from Office, and disqualification to hold and enjoy any Office of honor, Trust or Profit under the United States: but the Party convicted shall nevertheless be liable and subject to Indictment, Trial, Judgment and Punishment, according to Law.

SECTION 4. The Times, Places and Manner of holding Elections for Senators and Representatives, shall be prescribed in each State by the Legislature thereof; but the Congress may at any time by Law make or alter such Regulations, except as to the Places of chusing Senators.

The Congress shall assemble at least once in every Year, and such Meeting shall be [on the first Monday in December, *(This provision was changed by section 2 of the Twentieth Amendment.)*] unless they shall by Law appoint a different Day.

SECTION 5. Each House shall be the Judge of the Elections, Returns and Qualifications of its own Members, and a Majority of each shall constitute a Quorum to do Business; but a smaller Number may adjourn from day to day, and may be authorized to compel the Attendance of absent Members, in such Manner, and under such Penalties as each House may provide.

Each House may determine the Rules of its Proceedings, punish its Members for disorderly Behaviour, and, with the Concurrence of two thirds, expel a Member.

Each House shall keep a Journal of its Proceedings, and from time to time publish the same, excepting such Parts as may in their Judgment require Secrecy; and the Yeas and Nays of the Members of either House on any question shall, at the Desire of one fifth of those Present, be entered on the Journal.

Neither House, during the Session of Congress, shall, without the Consent of the other, adjourn for more than three days, nor to any other Place than that in which the two Houses shall be sitting.

SECTION 6. The Senators and Representatives shall receive a Compensation for their Services, to be ascertained by Law, and paid out of the Treasury of the United States. They shall in all Cases, except Treason, Felony and Breach of the Peace, be privileged from Arrest during their Attendance at the Session of their respective Houses, and in going to and returning from the same; and for any Speech or Debate in either House, they shall not be questioned in any other Place.

No Senator or Representative shall, during the Time for which he was elected, be appointed to any civil Office under the Authority of the United States, which shall have been created, or the Emoluments whereof shall have been encreased during such time; and no Person holding any Office under the United States, shall be a Member of either House during his Continuance in Office.

SECTION 7. All Bills for raising Revenue shall originate in the House of Representatives; but the Senate may propose or concur with Amendments as on other Bills.

Every Bill which shall have passed the House of Representatives and the Senate, shall, before it become a Law, be presented to the President of the United States; If he approve he shall sign it, but if not he shall return it, with his Objections to that House in which it shall have originated, who shall enter the Objections at large on their Journal, and proceed to reconsider it. If after such Reconsideration two thirds of that House shall agree to pass the Bill, it shall be sent, together with the Objections, to the other House, by which it shall likewise be reconsidered, and if approved by two thirds of that House, it shall become a Law. But in all such Cases the Votes of both Houses shall be determined by yeas and Nays, and the Names of the Persons voting for and against the Bill shall be entered on the Journal of each House respectively. If any bill shall not be returned by the President within ten Days (Sundays excepted) after it shall have been presented to him, the Same shall be a Law, in like Manner as if he had signed it, unless the Congress by their Adjournment prevent its Return, in which Case it shall not be a Law.

Every Order, Resolution, or Vote to which the Concurrence of the Senate and House of Representatives may be necessary (except on a question of Adjournment) shall be presented to the President of the United States; and before the Same shall take Effect, shall be approved by him, or being disapproved by him, shall be repassed by two thirds of the Senate and House of Representatives, according to the Rules and Limitations prescribed in the Case of a Bill.

SECTION 8. The Congress shall have Power To lay and collect Taxes, Duties, Imposts and Excises, to pay the Debts and provide for the common Defence and general Welfare of the United

States; but all Duties, Imposts and Excises shall be uniform throughout the United States;

To borrow Money on the credit of the United States;

To regulate Commerce with foreign Nations, and among the several States, and with the Indian tribes;

To establish an uniform Rule of Naturalization, and uniform Laws on the subject of Bankruptcies throughout the United States;

To coin Money, regulate the Value thereof, and of foreign Coin, and fix the Standard of Weights and Measures;

To provide for the Punishment of counterfeiting the Securities and current Coin of the United States;

To establish Post Offices and post Roads;

To promote the Progress of Science and useful Arts, by securing for limited Times to Authors and Inventors the exclusive Right to their respective Writings and Discoveries;

To constitute Tribunals inferior to the supreme Court;

To define and punish Piracies and Felonies committed on the high Seas, and Offences against the Law of Nations;

To declare War, grant Letters of Marque and Reprisal, and make Rules concerning Captures on Land and Water;

To raise and support Armies, but no Appropriation of Money to that Use shall be for a longer Term than two Years;

To provide and maintain a Navy;

To make Rules for the Government and Regulation of the land and naval Forces;

To provide for calling forth the Militia to execute the Laws of the Union, suppress Insurrections and repel Invasions;

To provide for organizing, arming, and disciplining, the Militia, and for governing such Part of them as may be employed in the Service of the United States, reserving to the States respectively, the Appointment of the Officers, and the Authority of training the Militia according to the discipline prescribed by Congress;

To exercise exclusive Legislation in all Cases whatsoever, over such District (not exceeding ten Miles square) as may, by Cession of particular States, and the Acceptance of Congress, become the Seat of the Government of the United States, and to exercise like Authority over all Places purchased by the Consent of the Legislature of the State in which the Same shall be, for the Erection of Forts, Magazines, Arsenals, dock-Yards, and other needful Buildings;—And

To make all Laws which shall be necessary and proper for carrying into Execution the foregoing Powers, and all other Powers vested by this Constitution in the Government of the United States, or in any Department or Officer thereof.

SECTION 9. The Migration or Importation of such Persons as any of the States now existing shall think proper to admit, shall not be prohibited by the Congress prior to the Year one thousand eight hundred and eight, but a Tax or duty may be imposed on such Importation, not exceeding ten dollars for each Person.

The Privilege of the Writ of Habeas Corpus shall not be suspended, unless when in Cases of Rebellion or Invasion the public Safety may require it.

No Bill of Attainder or ex post facto Law shall be passed.

No Capitation, or other direct, Tax shall be laid, unless in Proportion to the Census or Enumeration herein before directed to be taken.

No Tax or Duty shall be laid on Articles exported from any State.

No Preference shall be given by any Regulation of Commerce or Revenue to the Ports of one State over those of another: nor shall Vessels bound to, or from, one State, be obliged to enter, clear, or pay Duties in another.

No Money shall be drawn from the Treasury, but in Consequence of Appropriations made by Law; and a regular Statement and Account of the Receipts and Expenditures of all public Money shall be published from time to time.

No Title of Nobility shall be granted by the United States: And no Person holding any Office of Profit or Trust under them, shall, without the Consent of the Congress, accept of any present, Emolument, Office, or Title, of any kind whatever, from any King, Prince, or foreign State.

SECTION 10. No State shall enter into any Treaty, Alliance, or Confederation; grant Letters of Marque and Reprisal; coin Money; emit Bills of Credit; make any Thing but gold and silver Coin a Tender in Payment of Debts; pass any Bill of Attainder, ex post facto Law, or Law impairing the Obligation of Contracts, or grant any Title of Nobility.

No State shall, without the Consent of the Congress, lay any Imposts or Duties on Imports or Exports, except what may be absolutely necessary for executing it's inspection Laws: and the net Produce of all Duties and Imposts, laid by any State on Imports or Exports, shall be for the Use of the Treasury of the United States; and all such Laws shall be subject to the Revision and Controul of the Congress.

No State shall, without the Consent of Congress, lay any Duty of Tonnage, keep Troops, or Ships of War in time of Peace, enter into any Agreement or Compact with another State, or with a foreign Power, or engage in War, unless actually invaded, or in such imminent Danger as will not admit of delay.

ARTICLE II

SECTION 1. The executive Power shall be vested in a President of the United States of America. He shall hold his Office during the Term of four Years, and, together with the Vice President, chosen for the same Term, be elected, as follows

Each State shall appoint, in such Manner as the Legislature thereof may direct, a Number of Electors, equal to the whole Number of Senators and Representatives to which the State may be entitled in the Congress: but no Senator or Representative, or Person holding an Office of Trust or Profit under the United States, shall be appointed an Elector.

[The Electors shall meet in their respective States, and vote by Ballot for two Persons, of whom one at least shall not be an inhabitant of the same State with themselves. And they shall make a List of all the Persons voted for, and of the Number of Votes for each; which List they shall sign and certify, and transmit sealed to the Seat of the Government of the United States, directed to the President of the Senate. The President of the Senate shall, in the Presence of the Senate and House of Representatives, open all the Certificates, and the Votes shall then be counted. The Person having the greatest Number of Votes shall be the President, if such Number be a Majority of the whole Number of Electors appointed; and if there be more than one who have such Majority, and have an equal Number of Votes, then the House of Representatives shall immediately chuse by Ballot one of them for President; and if no Person have a Majority, then from the five highest on the List the said House shall in like Manner chuse the President. But in chusing the President, the Votes shall be taken by States, the Representation from each State having one Vote; A quorum for this purpose shall consist of a Member or Members from two thirds of the States, and a Majority of all the States shall be necessary to a Choice. In every Case, after the Choice of the President, the Person having the greatest Number of Votes of the Electors shall be the Vice President. But if there should remain two or more who have equal Votes, the Senate shall chuse from them by Ballot the Vice President. *(This clause was superseded by the Twelfth Amendment.)*]

The Congress may determine the Time of chusing the Electors, and the Day on which they shall give their Votes; which Day shall be the same throughout the United States.

No Person except a natural born Citizen, or a Citizen of the United States, at the time of the Adoption of this Constitution, shall be eligible to the Office of President; neither shall any Person be eligible to that Office who shall not have attained to the Age of thirty five Years, and been fourteen Years a Resident within the United States.

[In Case of the Removal of the President from Office, or of his Death, Resignation, or Inability to discharge the Powers and Duties of the said Office, the Same shall devolve on the Vice President, and the Congress may by Law provide for the Case of Removal, Death, Resignation or Inability, both of the President and Vice President, declaring what Officer shall then act as President, and such Officer shall act accordingly, until the Disability be removed, or a President shall be elected. *(This clause was modified by the Twenty-Fifth Amendment.)*]

The President shall, at stated Times, receive for his Services, a Compensation, which shall neither be encreased nor diminished during the Period for which he shall have been elected, and he shall not receive within that Period any other Emolument from the United States, or any of them.

Before he enter on the Execution of his Office, he shall take the following Oath or Affirmation:—"I do solemnly swear (or affirm) that I will faithfully execute the Office of President of the United States, and will to the best of my Ability, preserve, protect and defend the Constitution of the United States."

SECTION 2. The President shall be Commander in Chief of the Army and Navy of the United States, and of the Militia of the several States, when called into the actual Service of the United States; he may require the Opinion, in writing, of the principal Officer in each of the executive Departments, upon any Subject relating to the Duties of their respective Offices, and he shall have Power to grant Reprieves and Pardons for Offences against the United States, except in Cases of Impeachment.

He shall have Power, by and with the Advice and Consent of the Senate, to make Treaties, provided two thirds of the Senators present concur; and he shall nominate, and by and with the Advice and Consent of the Senate, shall appoint Ambassadors, other public Ministers and Consuls, Judges of the supreme Court, and all other Officers of the United States, whose Appointments are not herein otherwise provided for, and which shall be established by Law: but the Congress may by Law vest the Appointment of such inferior Officers, as they think proper, in the President alone, in the Courts of Law, or in the Heads of Departments.

The President shall have Power to fill up all Vacancies that may happen during the Recess of the Senate, by granting Commissions which shall expire at the End of their next Session.

Section 3. He shall from time to time give to the Congress Information of the State of the Union, and recommend to their Consideration such Measures as he shall judge necessary and expedient; he may, on extraordinary Occasions, convene both Houses, or either of them, and in Case of Disagreement between them, with Respect to the Time of Adjournment, he may adjourn them to such Time as he shall think proper; he shall receive Ambassadors and other public Ministers; he shall take Care that the Laws be faithfully executed, and shall Commission all the Officers of the United States.

Section 4. The President, Vice President and all civil Officers of the United States, shall be removed from Office on Impeachment for, and Conviction of, Treason, Bribery, or other high Crimes and Misdemeanors.

ARTICLE III

Section 1. The judicial Power of the United States, shall be vested in one supreme Court, and in such inferior Courts as the Congress may from time to time ordain and establish. The Judges, both of the supreme and inferior Courts, shall hold their Offices during good Behaviour, and shall, at stated Times receive for their Services, a Compensation, which shall not be diminished during their Continuance in Office.

Section 2. The judicial Power shall extend to all Cases, in Law and Equity, arising under this Constitution, the Laws of the United States, and Treaties made, or which shall be made, under their Authority;—to all Cases affecting Ambassadors, other public Ministers and Consuls;—to all Cases of admiralty and maritime Jurisdiction;—to Controversies to which the United States shall be a Party;—to Controversies between two or more States;—between a State and Citizens of another State;—between Citizens of different States,—between Citizens of the same State claiming Lands under Grants of different States, and between a State, or the Citizens thereof, and foreign States, Citizens or Subjects.

In all Cases affecting Ambassadors, other public Ministers and Consuls, and those in which a State shall be Party, the supreme Court shall have original Jurisdiction. In all the other Cases before mentioned, the supreme Court shall have appellate Jurisdiction, both as to Law and Fact, with such Exceptions, and under such Regulations as the Congress shall make.

The Trial of all Crimes, except in Cases of Impeachment,

shall be by Jury; and such Trial shall be held in the State where the said Crimes shall have been committed; but when not committed within any State, the Trial shall be at such Place or Places as the Congress may by Law have directed.

SECTION 3. Treason against the United States, shall consist only in levying War against them, or in adhering to their Enemies, giving them Aid and Comfort. No Person shall be convicted of Treason unless on the Testimony of two Witnesses to the same overt Act, or on Confession in open Court.

The Congress shall have Power to declare the Punishment of Treason, but no Attainder of Treason shall work Corruption of Blood, or Forfeiture except during the Life of the Person attainted.

ARTICLE IV

SECTION 1. Full Faith and Credit shall be given in each State to the public Acts, Records, and judicial Proceedings of every other State; And the Congress may by general Laws prescribe the Manner in which such Acts, Records and Proceedings shall be proved, and the Effect thereof.

SECTION 2. The Citizens of each State shall be entitled to all Privileges and Immunities of Citizens in the several States.

A Person charged in any State with Treason, Felony, or other Crime, who shall flee from Justice, and be found in another State, shall on Demand of the executive Authority of the State from which he fled, be delivered up, to be removed to the State having Jurisdiction of the Crime.

[No Person held to Service or Labour in one State, under the Laws thereof, escaping into another, shall, in Consequence of any Law or Regulation therein, be discharged from such Service or Labour, but shall be delivered up on Claim of the Party to whom such Service or Labour may be due. *(This clause was superseded by the Thirteenth Amendment.)*]

SECTION 3. New States may be admitted by the Congress into this Union; but no new State shall be formed or erected within the Jurisdiction of any other State; nor any State be formed by the Junction of two or more States, or Parts of States, without the Consent of the Legislatures of the States concerned as well as of the Congress.

The Congress shall have Power to dispose of and make all needful Rules and Regulations respecting the Territory or other Property belonging to the United States; and nothing in this

Constitution shall be so construed as to Prejudice any Claims of the United States, or of any particular State.

SECTION 4. The United States shall guarantee to every State in this Union a Republican Form of Government, and shall protect each of them against Invasion; and on Application of the Legislature, or of the Executive (when the Legislature cannot be convened) against domestic Violence.

ARTICLE V

The Congress, whenever two thirds of both Houses shall deem it necessary, shall propose Amendments to this Constitution, or, on the Application of the Legislatures of two thirds of the several States, shall call a Convention for proposing Amendments, which, in either Case, shall be valid to all Intents and Purposes, as Part of this Constitution, when ratified by the legislatures of three fourths of the several States, or by Conventions in three fourths thereof, as the one or the other Mode of Ratification may be proposed by the Congress; Provided that no Amendment which may be made prior to the Year One thousand eight hundred and eight shall in any Manner affect the first and fourth Clauses in the Ninth Section of the first Article; and that no State, without its Consent, shall be deprived of it's equal Suffrage in the Senate.

ARTICLE VI

All Debts contracted and Engagements entered into, before the Adoption of this Constitution, shall be as valid against the United States under this Constitution, as under the Confederation.

This Constitution, and the Laws of the United States which shall be made in Pursuance thereof; and all Treaties made, or which shall be made, under the Authority of the United States, shall be the supreme Law of the Land; and the Judges in every State shall be bound thereby, any Thing in the Constitution or Laws of any State to the Contrary notwithstanding.

The Senators and Representatives before mentioned, and the Members of the several State Legislatures, and all executive and judicial Officers, both of the United States and of the several States, shall be bound by Oath or Affirmation, to support this Constitution; but no religious Test shall ever be required as a Qualification to any Office or public Trust under the United States.

ARTICLE VII

The Ratification of the Conventions of nine States, shall be sufficient for the Establishment of this Constitution between the States so ratifying the Same.

DONE in Convention by the Unanimous Consent of the States present the Seventeenth Day of September in the Year of our Lord one thousand seven hundred and Eighty seven and of the Independance of the United States of America the Twelfth.

IN WITNESS whereof We have hereunto subscribed our Names.

AMENDMENT I

[The first ten amendments (the Bill of Rights) were ratified December 15, 1791.]

Congress shall make no law respecting an establishment of religion, or prohibiting the free exercise thereof; or abridging the freedom of speech, or of the press, or the right of the people peaceably to assemble, and to petition the Government for a redress of grievances.

AMENDMENT II

A well regulated Militia, being necessary to the security of a free State, the right of the people to keep and bear Arms, shall not be infringed.

AMENDMENT III

No Soldier shall, in time of peace be quartered in any house, without the consent of the Owner, nor in time of war, but in a manner to be prescribed by law.

AMENDMENT IV

The right of the people to be secure in their persons, houses, papers, and effects, against unreasonable searches and seizures, shall not be violated, and no Warrants shall issue, but upon probable cause, supported by Oath or affirmation, and particularly describing the place to be searched, and the persons or things to be seized.

AMENDMENT V

No person shall be held to answer for a capital, or otherwise infamous crime, unless on a presentment or indictment of a Grand Jury, except in cases arising in the land or naval forces, or in the Militia, when in actual service in time of War or public danger; nor shall any person be subject for the same offence to be twice put in jeopardy of life or limb, nor shall be compelled in any criminal case to be a witness against himself, nor be deprived of life, liberty, or property, without due process of law; nor shall private property be taken for public use, without just compensation.

AMENDMENT VI

In all criminal prosecutions, the accused shall enjoy the right to a speedy and public trial, by an impartial jury of the State and district wherein the crime shall have been committed; which district shall have been previously ascertained by law, and to be informed of the nature and cause of the accusation; to be confronted with the witnesses against him; to have compulsory process for obtaining Witnesses in his favor, and to have the assistance of counsel for his defence.

AMENDMENT VII

In Suits at common law, where the value in controversy shall exceed twenty dollars, the right of trial by jury shall be preserved, and no fact tried by a jury, shall be otherwise re-examined in any Court of the United States, than according to the rules of the common law.

AMENDMENT VIII

Excessive bail shall not be required, nor excessive fines imposed, nor cruel and unusual punishments inflicted.

AMENDMENT IX

The enumeration in the Constitution, of certain rights, shall not be construed to deny or disparage others retained by the people.

AMENDMENT X

The powers not delegated to the United States by the Constitution, nor prohibited by it to the States, are reserved to the States respectively, or to the people.

AMENDMENT XI

[Ratified February 7, 1795.]

The Judicial power of the United States shall not be construed to extend to any suit in law or equity, commenced or prosecuted against one of the United States by Citizens of another State, or by Citizens or Subjects of any Foreign State.

AMENDMENT XII

[Ratified June 15, 1804.]

The Electors shall meet in their respective states, and vote by ballot for President and Vice-President, one of whom, at least, shall not be an inhabitant of the same state with themselves; they shall name in their ballots the person voted for as President, and in distinct ballots the person voted for as Vice-President, and they shall make distinct lists of all persons voted for as President, and of all persons voted for as Vice-President, and of the number of votes for each, which lists they shall sign and certify, and transmit sealed to the seat of the government of the United States, directed to the President of the Senate;— The President of the Senate shall, in the presence of the Senate and House of Representatives, open all the certificates and the votes shall then be counted;—The person having the greatest number of votes for President, shall be the President, if such number be a majority of the whole number of Electors appointed; and if no person have such majority, then from the persons having the highest numbers not exceeding three on the list of those voted for as President, the House of Representatives shall choose immediately, by ballot, the President. But in choosing the President, the votes shall be taken by states, the representation from each state having one vote; a quorum for this purpose shall consist of a member or members from two-thirds of the states, and a majority of all the states shall be necessary to a choice. [And if the House of Representatives shall not choose a President whenever the right of choice shall devolve upon them, before the fourth day of March next following, then the Vice-

President shall act as President, as in the case of the death or other constitutional disability of the President— *(This clause was superseded by section 3 of the Twentieth Amendment.)]*. The person having the greatest number of votes as Vice-President, shall be the Vice-President, if such number be a majority of the whole number of Electors appointed, and if no person have a majority, then from the two highest numbers on the list, the Senate shall choose the Vice-President; a quorum for the purpose shall consist of two-thirds of the whole number of Senators, and a majority of the whole number shall be necessary to a choice. But no person constitutionally ineligible to the office of President shall be eligible to that of Vice-President of the United States.

AMENDMENT XIII

[Ratified December 6, 1865.]

SECTION 1. Neither slavery nor involuntary servitude, except as a punishment for crime whereof the party shall have been duly convicted, shall exist within the United States, or any place subject to their jurisdiction.

SECTION 2. Congress shall have power to enforce this article by appropriate legislation.

AMENDMENT XIV

[Ratified July 9, 1868.]

SECTION 1. All persons born or naturalized in the United States, and subject to the jurisdiction thereof, are citizens of the United States and of the State wherein they reside. No State shall make or enforce any law which shall abridge the privileges or immunities of citizens of the United States; nor shall any State deprive any person of life, liberty, or property, without due process of law; nor deny to any person within its jurisdiction the equal protection of the laws.

SECTION 2. Representatives shall be apportioned among the several States according to their respective numbers, counting the whole number of persons in each State, excluding Indians not taxed. But when the right to vote at any election for the choice of electors for President and Vice President of the United States, Representatives in Congress, the Executive and Judicial officers of a State, or the members of the Legislature thereof, is denied to any of the male inhabitants of such State, being twenty-one years of age, and citizens of the United States, or in any way abridged, except for participation in rebellion, or other crime, the basis of representation therein shall be reduced in the proportion which the number of such male citizens shall bear to the whole number of male citizens twenty-one years of age in such State.

SECTION 3. No person shall be a Senator or Representative in Congress, or elector of President and Vice President, or hold any office, civil or military, under the United States, or under any State, who, having previously taken an oath, as a member of Congress, or as an officer of the United States, or as a member of any State legislature, or as an executive or judicial officer of any State, to support the Constitution of the United States, shall have engaged in insurrection or rebellion against the same, or given aid or comfort to the enemies thereof. But Congress may by a vote of two-thirds of each House, remove such disability.

SECTION 4. The validity of the public debt of the United States, authorized by law, including debts incurred for payment of pensions and bounties for services in suppressing insurrection or rebellion, shall not be questioned. But neither the United States nor any State shall assume or pay any debt or obligation incurred in aid of insurrection or rebellion against the United States, or any claim for the loss or emancipation of any slave; but all such debts, obligations and claims shall be held illegal and void.

SECTION 5. The Congress shall have power to enforce, by appropriate legislation, the provisions of this article.

AMENDMENT XV

[Ratified February 3, 1870.]

SECTION 1. The right of citizens of the United States to vote shall not be denied or abridged by the United States or by any State on account of race, color, or previous condition of servitude.

SECTION 2. The Congress shall have power to enforce this article by appropriate legislation.

AMENDMENT XVI

[Ratified February 3, 1913.]

The Congress shall have power to lay and collect taxes on incomes, from whatever source derived, without apportionment among the several States, and without regard to any census or enumeration.

AMENDMENT XVII

[Ratified April 8, 1913.]

The Senate of the United States shall be composed of two Senators from each State, elected by the people thereof, for six years; and each Senator shall have one vote. The electors in each State shall have the qualifications requisite for electors of the most numerous branch of the State legislatures.

When vacancies happen in the representation of any State in the Senate, the executive authority of such State shall issue writs of election to fill such vacancies: *Provided,* That the legislature of any State may empower the executive thereof to make temporary appointments until the people fill the vacancies by election as the legislature may direct.

This amendment shall not be so construed as to affect the election or term of any Senator chosen before it becomes valid as part of the Constitution.

AMENDMENT XVIII

[Ratified January 16, 1919.]

SECTION 1. After one year from the ratification of this article the manufacture, sale, or transportation of intoxicating liquors within, the importation thereof into, or the exportation thereof from the United States and all territory subject to the jurisdiction thereof for beverage purposes is hereby prohibited.

SECTION 2. The Congress and the several States shall have concurrent power to enforce this article by appropriate legislation.

SECTION 3. This article shall be inoperative unless it shall have been ratified as an amendment to the Constitution by the legislatures of the several States, as provided in the Constitution, within seven years from the date of the submission hereof to the States by the Congress.

AMENDMENT XIX

[Ratified August 18, 1920.]

The right of citizens of the United States to vote shall not be denied or abridged by the United States or by any State on account of sex.

Congress shall have power to enforce this article by appropriate legislation.

AMENDMENT XX

[Ratified January 23, 1933.]

SECTION 1. The terms of the President and Vice President shall end at noon on the 20th day of January, and the terms of Senators and Representatives at noon on the 3d day of January, of the years in which such terms would have ended if this article had not been ratified; and the terms of their successors shall then begin.

SECTION 2. The Congress shall assemble at least once in every year, and such meeting shall begin at noon on the 3d day of January, unless they shall by law appoint a different day.

SECTION 3. If, at the time fixed for the beginning of the term of the President, the President elect shall have died, the Vice President elect shall become President. If a President shall not have been chosen before the time fixed for the beginning of his term, or if the President elect shall have failed to qualify, then the Vice President elect shall act as President until a President shall have qualified; and the Congress may by law provide for the case wherein neither a President elect nor a Vice President elect shall have qualified, declaring who shall then act as President, or the manner in which one who is to act shall be selected, and such person shall act accordingly until a President or Vice President shall have qualified.

SECTION 4. The Congress may by law provide for the case of the death of any of the persons from whom the House of Representatives may choose a President whenever the right of choice shall have devolved upon them, and for the case of the death of any of the persons from whom the Senate may choose a Vice President whenever the right of choice shall have devolved upon them.

SECTION 5. Sections 1 and 2 shall take effect on the 15th day of October following the ratification of this article.

SECTION 6. This article shall be inoperative unless it shall have been ratified as an amendment to the Constitution by the legislatures of three-fourths of the several States within seven years from the date of its submission.

AMENDMENT XXI

[Ratified December 5, 1933.]

SECTION 1. The eighteenth article of amendment to the Constitution of the United States is hereby repealed.

SECTION 2. The transportation or importation into any State, Territory, or possession of the United States for delivery or use therein of intoxicating liquors, in violation of the laws thereof, is hereby prohibited.

SECTION 3. This article shall be inoperative unless it shall have been ratified as an amendment to the Constitution by conventions in the several States, as provided in the Constitution, within seven years from the date of the submission hereof to the States by the Congress.

AMENDMENT XXII

[Ratified February 27, 1951.]

SECTION 1. No person shall be elected to the office of the President more than twice, and no person who has held the office of President, or acted as President, for more than two years of a term to which some other person was elected President shall be elected to the office of the President more than once. But this Article shall not apply to any person holding the office of President when this Article was proposed by the Congress, and shall not prevent any person who may be holding the office of President, or acting as President, during the term within which this Article becomes operative from holding the office of President or acting as President during the remainder of such term.

SECTION 2. This article shall be inoperative unless it shall have been ratified as an amendment to the Constitution by the legislatures of three-fourths of the several States within seven years from the date of its submission to the States by the Congress.

AMENDMENT XXIII

[Ratified March 29, 1961.]

SECTION 1. The District constituting the seat of Government of the United States shall appoint in such manner as the Congress may direct:

A number of electors of President and Vice President equal to the whole number of Senators and Representatives in Congress to which the District would be entitled if it were a State, but in no event more than the least populous State; they shall be in addition to those appointed by the States, but they shall be considered, for the purposes of the election of President and Vice President, to be electors appointed by a State; and they shall meet in the District and perform such duties as provided by the twelfth article of amendment.

SECTION 2. The Congress shall have power to enforce this article by appropriate legislation.

AMENDMENT XXIV

[Ratified January 23, 1964.]

SECTION 1. The right of citizens of the United States to vote in any primary or other election for President or Vice President, for electors for President or Vice President, or for Senator or Representatives in Congress, shall not be denied or abridged by the United States or any State by reason of failure to pay any poll tax or other tax.

SECTION 2. The Congress shall have power to enforce this article by appropriate legislation.

AMENDMENT XXV

[Ratified February 10, 1967.]

SECTION 1. In case of the removal of the President from office or of his death or resignation, the Vice President shall become President.

SECTION 2. Whenever there is a vacancy in the office of the Vice President, the President shall nominate a Vice President who shall take office upon confirmation by a majority vote of both Houses of Congress.

SECTION 3. Whenever the President transmits to the President pro tempore of the Senate and the Speaker of the House of Representatives his written declaration that he is unable to discharge the powers and duties of his office, and until he transmits to them a written declaration to the contrary, such powers and duties shall be discharged by the Vice President as Acting President.

SECTION 4. Whenever the Vice President and a majority of either the principal officers of the executive departments or of such other body as Congress may by law provide, transmit to the President pro tempore of the Senate and the Speaker of the House of Representatives their written declaration that the President is unable to discharge the powers and duties of his office, the Vice President shall immediately assume the powers and duties of the office as Acting President.

Thereafter, when the President transmits to the President pro tempore of the Senate and the Speaker of the House of Representatives his written declaration that no inability exists, he shall resume the powers and duties of his office unless the Vice President and a majority of either the principal officers of the executive department or of such other body as Congress may by law provide, transmit within four days to the President pro tempore of the Senate and the Speaker of the House of Representatives their written declaration that the President is unable to discharge the powers and duties of his office. Thereupon Congress shall decide the issue, assembling within forty-eight hours for that purpose if not in session. If the Congress, within twenty-one days after receipt of the latter written declaration, or, if Congress is not in session, within twenty-one days after Congress is required to assemble, determines by two-thirds vote of both Houses that the President is unable to discharge the powers and duties of his office, the Vice President shall continue to discharge the same as Acting President; otherwise, the President shall resume the powers and duties of his office.

AMENDMENT XXVI

[Ratified July 1, 1971.]

SECTION 1. The right of citizens of the United States, who are eighteen years of age or older, to vote shall not be denied or abridged by the United States or by any State on account of age.

SECTION 2. The Congress shall have power to enforce this article by appropriate legislation.

1

THE SUPREME COURT, JUDICIAL REVIEW, AND CONSTITUTIONAL POLITICS

J UDICIAL REVIEW IS one of the greatest and most controversial contributions of the Constitution to the law and politics of government. Article III of the Constitution simply provides that "[t]he judicial Power of the United States, shall be vested in one supreme Court, and in such inferior Courts as the Congress may from time to time ordain and establish." Remarkably, that power is not further defined in the Constitution. But in the course of constitutional politics, *judicial review* has come to be the power of the Supreme Court and the federal judiciary to consider and overturn any congressional and state legislation or other official governmental action deemed inconsistent with the Constitution, Bill of Rights, or federal law.

Like other provisions of the Constitution, the three brief sections in Article III register compromises forged during the Constitutional Convention; the Constitution, as the renowned historian and editor of *The Records of the Federal Convention of 1787*, Max Farrand, observed, is "a bundle of compromises."[1] The first section of Article III makes clear that the Supreme Court is the only federal court constitutionally required. The convention left it for the First Congress to establish a system of lower federal courts, which it did with the Judiciary Act of 1789. Both the convention and the First Congress rejected proposals that would have left the administration of justice entirely in the hands of state courts (with appeals to the Supreme Court). Also rejected was a proposal to join justices and executive branch officials in a "council of revision" with a veto power over congressional legislation. Agreement on the importance of guaranteeing judicial independence resulted in the first section of Article III also providing that federal judges "hold their Offices during good Behaviour," subject only to impeachment, and forbidding the diminution of their salaries. That guarantee reflects colonial opposition to royalist judges under the English Crown. One of the grievances listed in the Declaration of Independence as a justification for the Revolutionary War was that King George III had "made Judges dependent on his Will alone."[2] The two remaining sections of Article III specify the kinds of cases and controversies that the federal judiciary may hear (that is, jurisdiction) (see Chapter 2) and empower Congress to punish individuals for treason.

The Framers, it is fair to say, failed to think through the power of judicial review and its ramifications for constitutional politics. "[T]he framers anticipated some sort of judicial review," noted political scientist Edward S. Corwin, but he added that "it is equally without question that the ideas generally current in 1787 were far from presaging the present role of the Court."[3] In a letter to Corwin, Max Farrand also concluded that "[t]he framers of the Constitution did not realize it themselves [how markedly different their conceptions of judicial review were]: they were struggling to express an idea and their experience was as yet insufficient."[4]

The Constitutional Convention left the power of the judiciary (and much else set forth in the Constitution) to be worked out in practice. As John Mercer, a delegate to the Constitutional Convention from Maryland, observed, "It is a great mistake to suppose that the paper we are to propose will govern the United States. It is the men whom it will bring into the government and interest in maintaining it that is to govern them. The paper will only mark out the mode and the form."[5] The Constitution, of course, is not self-interpreting and crucial principles—such as judicial review, separation of powers, and federalism—are presupposed rather than spelled out. Moreover, in creating separate institutions that share specific and delegated powers, the Constitution amounts to a prescription for political struggle and an invitation for an ongoing debate about enduring constitutional principles.

Almost immediately following the convention in 1787, controversy erupted over the powers granted the national government and in particular to the federal judiciary. Those opposed to the states' ratification of the Constitution, the Anti-Federalists, warned that "[t]here are no well defined limits of the Judiciary Powers, they seem to be left as a boundless ocean."[6] Fears that "the powers of the judiciary may be extended to any degree short of Almighty" were echoed by Thomas Tredwell, among others, during New York's convention.[7] Robert Yates, one of the most articulate Anti-Federalists writing under the name of Brutus, attacked both the independence and the power of federal judges:

There is no authority that can remove them, and they cannot be controuled by the laws of the legislature. In short, they are independent of the people, of the legislature, and of every power under heaven. Men placed in this situation will generally soon feel themselves independent of heaven itself. . . .

And in their decisions they will not confine themselves to any fixed or established rules, but will determine, according to what appears to them, the reason and spirit of the constitution. The opinions of the supreme court, whatever they may be, will have the force of law; because there is no power provided in the constitution, that can correct their errors, or controul their adjudiciations. From this court there is no appeal.[8]

"This power in the judicial," charged Brutus, "will enable them to mould the government, into almost any shape they please."
Defenders of the Constitution countered that "the powers given the Supreme Court are not only safe, but constitute a wise and valuable part of the system."[9] In North Carolina's convention, Governor Johnston observed that "[i]t is obvious to every one that there ought to be one Supreme Court for national purposes."[10] During the fight for New York's ratification, Alexander Hamilton provided the classic defense of the judiciary as "the least dangerous branch." Responding to Brutus in *The Federalist*, No. 78, Hamilton argued,

Whoever attentively considers the different departments of power must perceive, that in a government in which they are separated from each other, the judiciary, from the nature of its functions, will always be the least dangerous to the political rights of the constitution; because it will be least in a capacity to annoy or injure them. The executive not only dispenses the honors, but holds the sword of the community. The legislature not only commands the purse, but prescribes the rules by which the duties and rights of every citizen are to be regulated. The judiciary on the contrary has no influence over either the sword or the purse, no direction either of the strength or of the wealth of the society, and can take no active resolution whatever. It may truly be said to have neither Force nor Will, but merely judgment; and must ultimately depend upon the aid of the executive arm even for the efficacy of its judgments.

If it be said that the legislative body are themselves the constitutional judges of their own powers, and that the construction they put upon them is conclusive upon other departments, it may be answered, that this cannot be the natural presumption, where it is not to be collected from any particular provisions in the constitution. It is not otherwise to be supposed that the constitution could intend to enable the representatives of the people to substitute their *will* to that of their constituents. It is far more rational to suppose that the courts were designed to be an intermediate body between the people and the legislature, in order, among other things, to keep the latter within the limits assigned to their authority. The interpretation of the laws is the proper and peculiar province of the courts. A constitution is in fact, and must be, regarded by the judges as a fundamental law. It therefore belongs to them as to ascertain its meaning as well as the meaning of any particular act proceeding from the legislative body. If there should happen to be an irreconcilable variance between the two, that which has the superior obligation and validity ought of course to be preferred; or in other words, the constitution ought to be preferred to the statute, the intention of the people to the intention of their agents.

Nor does this conclusion by any means suppose a superiority of the judicial to the legislative power. It only supposes that the power of the people is superior to both; and that where the will of the legislature declared in its statutes, stands in opposition to that of the people declared in the constitution, the judges ought to be governed by the latter, rather than the former. . . .

If then the courts of justice are to be considered as the bulwarks of a limited constitution against legislative encroachments, this consideration will afford a strong argument for the permanent tenure of judicial offices, since nothing will contribute so much as this to that independent spirit in the judges, which must be essential to the faithful performance of so arduous a duty.

The Federalists' interpretation of Article III was advanced by others in the effort to win ratification. In Pennsylvania's convention, James Wilson, who was one of the first justices appointed by President George Washington, argued that

under this Constitution, the legislature may be restrained, and kept within its prescribed bounds, by the interposition of the judicial department. . . . [T]he power of the Constitution [is] paramount to the power of the legislature acting under that Constitution; for it is possible that the legislature, when acting in that capacity, may transgress the bounds assigned to it, and an act may pass, in the usual *mode,* notwithstanding that transgression; but when it comes to be discussed before *the judges,*— when they consider its principles, and find it to be incompatible with the superior power of the Constitution,—it is their duty to pronounce it *void.*[11]

In Connecticut, Oliver Ellsworth, another who was later appointed to the Court, declared, "If the general legislature should at any time overleap their limits, the judicial department is a constitutional check."[12]

Even among the Federalists, however, there were differing

views of the judiciary's power. Alexander Hamilton and James Madison agreed that the Court would exercise some checking power over the states. The Court, in Madison's words, was "the surest expositor of . . . the [constitutional] boundaries . . . between the Union and its members."[13] But they were in less agreement on whether the Court had the power to check coequal branches, the Congress and the president. In *The Federalist*, Madison called the judiciary an "auxiliary precaution" against the possible domination of one branch of government over another.

HOW TO LOCATE DECISIONS
OF THE SUPREME COURT

The decisions of the Supreme Court are published in the *United States Reports* by the U.S. Government Printing Office. Each decision is referred to by the names of the appellant, the person bringing the suit, and the appellee, the respondent: hence, *McCulloch v. Maryland*. After the name of the case is the volume number in which it appears in the *United States Reports* and the page number on which the Court's opinion begins, followed by the year of the decision. *McCulloch v. Maryland*, 17 U.S. 316 (1819), thus may be found in volume 17 of the *United States Reports* beginning on page 316.

Prior to the publication of the *United States Reports* in 1875, the Court's opinions used to be cited according to the name of the reporter of the Court, who published the Court's opinions at his own expense. Decisions thus would originally be cited as follows:

1789–1800	Dallas	(1–4 Dall., 1–4 U.S.)
1801–1815	Cranch	(1–9 Cr., 5–13 U.S.)
1816–1827	Wheaton	(1–12 Wheat., 14–25 U.S.)
1828–1842	Peters	(1–16 Pet., 26–41 U.S.)
1843–1860	Howard	(1–24 How., 42–65 U.S.)
1861–1862	Black	(1–2 Bl., 66–67 U.S.)
1863–1874	Wallace	(1–23 Wall., 68–90 U.S.)
1875–		(91– , U.S.)

The full citation for *McCulloch v. Maryland* is 4 Wheat. (17 U.S.) 316 (1819). But with volume 91 in 1875, the reporters' names were dropped, and decisions were then cited only by the volume number and the designation "U.S."

In addition, two companies print editions of the Court's decisions. There is the *Lawyers' Edition*, published by the Lawyer's Cooperative, and *The Supreme Court Reporter*, published by West Publishing Company. The *Lawyers' Edition* is cited as L.Ed. (e.g., 91 L.Ed. 575), and *The Supreme Court Reporter* is cited as S.Ct. (e.g., 104 S.Ct. 3005).

Later, during a debate in the First Congress in 1789, he observed that "in the ordinary course of Government, . . . the exposition of the laws and Constitution devolves upon the Judiciary." Still, Madison doubted that the Court's interpretation of the Constitution was superior to that given by Congress. "Nothing has been offered to invalidate the [view]," he argued, "that the meaning of the Constitution may as well be ascertained by the legislative as by the judicial authority."[14] The Court stood as a forum of last resort, Madison explained, but "this resort must necessarily be deemed the last in relation to the authorities of the other departments of the government; not in relation to the rights of the parties to the constitutional compact, from which the judicial, as well as the other departments, hold their delegated trusts."[15]

From the initial debate in the Constitutional Convention in 1787 to those between the Federalists and the Anti-Federalists over state ratification of the Constitution and into the First Congress, the power of judicial review and the meaning of other key provisions and principles of the Constitution has remained a continuing source of controversy in constitutional politics. And the Supreme Court has remained, as Justice Oliver Wendell Holmes observed, a "storm center" of political controversy.

A. ESTABLISHING AND CONTESTING THE POWER OF JUDICIAL REVIEW

In its first decade, the Supreme Court had little business, frequent turnover in personnel, no chambers or staff, no fixed customs, and no institutional identity. When the Court initially convened on February 1, 1790, only Chief Justice John Jay and two other justices arrived at the Exchange Building in New York City. They adjourned until the next day when Justice John Blair arrived; the two other justices never arrived. With little to do other than admit attorneys to practice before its bar, the Court concluded its first sessions in less than two weeks.

When the capital moved from New York City to Philadelphia in the winter of 1790, the Court met in Independence Hall and in the Old City Hall, until the capital again moved to Washington, D.C., in 1800. Most of the first justices' time was spent riding circuit. That is, each would travel throughout a particular area, or circuit, in the country. Under the Judiciary Act of 1789, they were required twice a year to hold court, in the company of local district judges, in a circuit to hear appeals from the federal district courts. Hence, the justices resided primarily in their circuits, rather than in Washington, and felt a greater allegiance to their circuits than to the Court.

The Court's uncertain status was reflected in the first justices' exercise of their power of judicial review. Although in its initial years the Court had few important cases, *Chisholm v. Georgia*, 2 Dall. (2 U.S.) 419 (1793) (see Vol. 1, Ch. 7), precipitated the country's first constitutional crisis. In that case, Justice James Wilson, who had been a delegate to the Constitutional Convention and Pennsylvania's ratifying convention, ruled that citizens of one state could sue another state in federal courts. That provoked an angry dissent from Justice James Iredell, a southerner who had attended North Carolina's ratifying convention and a strong proponent of "states' rights." His dissent invited the adoption by Congress of the Eleventh Amendment in 1795, overturning *Chisholm* and guaranteeing sovereign immunity for states from lawsuits brought by citizens of other states. The outcry over *Chisholm* convinced Chief Justice John Jay that the Court would remain "the least dangerous branch." He resigned in 1795 to become an envoy to England and later declined reappointment as chief justice.

The Court, though, in *Ware v. Hylton*, 3 Dall. (3 U.S.) 199 (1796), upheld the provisions of a federal treaty, the 1783 peace treaty with England, over state law. And *Hylton v. United States*, 3 Dall. (3 U.S.) 171 (1796), affirmed, over objections raised by the states, Congress's power to levy a carriage tax (and thus implicitly asserted the Court's power to nullify acts of Congress).

Still, two years later, *Calder v. Bull*, 3 Dall. (3 U.S.) 386 (1798) illustrates how uncertain and divided the justices were about exercising their power of judicial review. There the Court declined to assert its power when ruling that conflicts between state laws and state constitutions are matters for state, not federal, courts to resolve. But Justice Iredell maintained that a state law might run against principles of "natural justice" and the Court still have no power to strike it down. By contrast, Justice Samuel Chase contended that the Court had the power to overturn laws that violate fundamental principles, explaining,

I cannot subscribe to the omnipotence of a State legislature, or that it is absolute and without controul; although its authority should not be expressly restrained by the Constitution, or fundamental laws of the State. The people of the United States erected their Constitution . . . to establish justice, to promote the general welfare, to secure the blessings of liberty; and to protect their persons and property from violence. . . . There are acts which the Federal, or State, Legislature cannot do. . . . It is against all reason and justice to entrust a Legislature with SUCH [despotic] powers; and therefore, it cannot be presumed that they have done it. The genius, the nature, and the spirit of our State Governments, amount to a prohibition of such [unlimited] acts of legislation; and the general principles of law and reason forbid them.

The uncertainty and controversy over the power of judicial review was further underscored in 1798 with the passage of the Virginia and Kentucky Resolutions (see p. 41), in response to Congress's enactment of the Alien and Sedition Acts. Drafted by James Madison and Thomas Jefferson, the Virginia and Kentucky Resolutions not only contended that Congress had violated the First Amendment but claimed that state legislatures had the power to judge the constitutionality of federal laws. Jefferson went so far as to assert that states could nullify federal laws that they deemed unconstitutional. The "sovereign and independent" states, in his words, "have the unquestionable right to judge . . . and, that a nullification [by] those sovereignties, of all unauthorized acts done under the color of that instrument is the rightful remedies."

Jefferson remained opposed to the power of judicial review and the view that the Supreme Court's interpretation of the Constitution was binding on the other branches of government. In a 1819 letter to Spencer Roane, a Virginia state judge, Jefferson explained,

My construction of the Constitution is . . . that each department is truly independent of the others, and has an equal right to decide for itself what is the meaning of the Constitution in the cases submitted to its action most especially where it is to act ultimately and without appeal. . . . Each of the three departments has equally the right to decide for itself what is its duty under the Constitution, without any regard to what the others may have decided for themselves under a similar question.[16]

Although less strident than Jefferson, Madison thought that the "true and safe construction" of the Constitution would emerge with the "uniform sanction of successive legislative bodies; through a period of years and under the varied ascendency of parties."[17]

Chief Justice John Marshall provided the classic justification for the power of judicial review in the landmark ruling in *Marbury v. Madison* (1803) (see p. 45). Notice that Marshall's arguments draw on both general principles and the text of the Constitution and are not unassailable. In an otherwise unimportant state case, *Eakin v. Raub* (Pa., 1825) (see p. 55), for example, Pennsylvania Supreme Court Justice John Gibson expressly refutes Marshall's arguments. It does not inexorably follow from Marshall's claim that the Constitution created a limited government that *only* the judiciary should enforce those limitations. No more persuasive is the argument that judges have the power to authoritatively interpret the Constitution based on their taking an oath to uphold the document, because all federal and state officers take an oath to support the Constitution. Like Madison and Jefferson, Justice Gibson rejects *Marbury*'s implication that the judiciary has a monopoly (or supremacy) over interpretating the Constitution or, as Chief Justice Charles Evans Hughes's later put it, "We are under a Constitution but the Constitution is what the judges say it is."[18] In providing a rationale for judicial self-restraint, Gibson embraces a theory of *tripartie* constitutional interpretation—namely, that each branch has the authority to interpret the Constitution.

Chief Justice Marshall's arguments based on the text of the Constitution fare better. In specifying that the "judicial Power shall extend to" cases and controversies "arising under this Constitution," Article III implies that constitutional questions may be decided by the judiciary. And, as Marshall points out, the Supremacy Clause of Article III makes it clear that the Constitution is "the supreme Law of the Land." Judicial review is thus a logical implication of the Constitution, for as Justice Joseph Story observed,

The laws and treaties, and even the constitution, of the United States, would become a dead letter with out it. Indeed, in a complicated government, like ours, where there is an assemblage of republics, combined under a common head, the necessity of some controlling judicial power, to ascertain and enforce the powers of the Union is, if possible, still more striking. The laws of the whole would otherwise be in continual danger of being contravened by the laws of the parts. The national government would be reduced to a servile dependence upon the states; and the same scenes would be again acted over in solemn mockery, which began in the neglect, and ended in the ruin, of the confederation.[19]

Still and undeniably, the power of judicial review is not expressly provided for in the Constitution and its exercise remains a continuing source of controversy.

The immediate political controversy over the exercise of judicial review in *Marbury* in striking down a section of the Judiciary Act of 1789 was defused by Chief Justice Marshall's conclusion that the Court had no power to order the delivery of Marbury's commission. Though outraged by Marshall's assertion of judicial review, Madison and Jefferson had not been compelled by the Court to do anything. Jefferson continued to maintain that each branch of government could interpret the Constitution and to deny that the Court's interpretations were binding on the president's exercise of executive powers. In a letter to Mrs. John Adams in 1804, explaining his decision to pardon those tried and convicted under the Sedition Act of 1798, Jefferson wrote,

The Judges, believing the law constitutional, had a right to pass a sentence of fine and imprisonment; because that power was placed in their hands by the Constitution. But the Executive, believing the law to be unconstitutional, was bound to remit the execution of it; because that power has been confided to him by the Constitution. The instrument meant that its co-ordinate branches should be checks on each other. But the opinion which gives to the Judges the right to decide what Laws are constitutional, and what not, not only for themselves in their own sphere of action, but for the Legislative and Executive also in their spheres, would make the Judiciary a despotic branch.[20]

Jefferson was not the last president to contest the authority of the Court. An irate President Andrew Jackson, on hearing of the decision in *Worcester v. Georgia*, 31 U.S. 515 (1832), holding that states could not pass laws affecting federally recognized Indian nations, reportedly declared, "John Marshall has made his decision, now let him enforce it."[21] Jackson elaborated his view in his Veto Message of 1832 (see p. 60), explaining his vetoing of legislation recharting the national bank (see Vol. 1, Ch. 6). Besides contending that *McCulloch v. Maryland*, 17 U.S. 316 (1819) (see Vol. 1, Ch. 6) was not binding on his actions, Jackson reiterated the position that

[t]he Congress, the Executive, and the Court must each for itself be guided by its own opinion of the Constitution. Each public officer who takes an oath to support the Constitution swears that he will support it as he understands it, and not as it is understood by others. . . . The opinion of the judges has no more authority over Congress than the opinion of Congress has over the judges, and on that point the President is independent of both.[22]

Jackson's Veto Message drew an impassioned response from Senator Daniel Webster, who thundered in the halls of Congress that

[t]he President is as much bound by the law as any private citizen. . . . He may refuse to obey the law, and so may a private citizen; but both do it at their own peril, and neither of them can settle the question of its validity. The President may say a law is unconstitutional, but he is not the judge. . . . If it were otherwise, there would be no government of laws; but we should all live under the government, the rule, the caprices of individuals. . . .

[President Jackson's] message . . . converts a constitutional limitation of power into mere matters of opinion, and then strikes the judicial department, as an efficient department, out of our system. . . .

[The message] denies first principles. It contradicts truths heretofore received as indisputable. It denies to the judiciary the interpretation of law.

Controversy over judicial review continues, but it bears emphasizing that Jefferson, Jackson, and subsequent presidents concede that the Court's rulings are binding for the actual cases decided and handed down. Technically, a decision of the Court is final only for the parties involved in the case. Yet, because the justices in their opinions give general principles for deciding a case and because they generally adhere to precedents (or tend to do so until the composition of the bench markedly changes), the Court's rulings are usually considered controlling for other similar cases and the larger political controversy they represent. But in major confrontations in constitutional politics—like those over the creation of a national bank, slavery, school desegregation, and abortion—the Court alone cannot lay those controversies to rest.

What presidents, Congress, the states, and others occasionally deny is *judicial supremacy* or the finality of the Court's interpretation of broad constitutional principles for resolving major political controversies. In his famous debates with Stephen Douglas, for instance, Abraham Lincoln denounced the Court's ruling in *Dred Scott v. Sandford,* 60 U.S. 393 (1857) (see Vol. 2, Ch. 12), that blacks were not citizens of the United States. While Lincoln doubted that "we, as a mob, will decide [Dred Scott] to be free," he exclaimed that

we nevertheless do oppose that decision as a political rule which shall be binding on the voter, to vote for nobody who thinks it wrong, which shall be binding on the members of Congress or the President to favor no measure that does not actually concur with the principles of that decision. . . . We propose so resisting it as to have it reversed if we can, and a new judicial rule established upon this subject.[23]

Later, in his first Inaugural Address in 1861, Lincoln elaborated,

I do not forget the position assumed by some, that constitutional questions are to be decided by the Supreme Court; nor do I deny that such decisions must be binding in any case, upon the parties to a suit, as to the object of that suit, while they are also entitled to a very high respect and consideration, in all parallel cases, by all other departments of government. And while it is obviously possible that such decision may be erroneous in any given case, still the evil effect following it, being limited to that particular case, with the chance that it may be over-ruled, and never become a precedent for other cases, can better be borne than could the evils of a different practice. At the same time the candid citizen must confess that if the policy of the government, upon vital questions, affecting the whole people, is to be irrevocably fixed by the decisions of the Supreme Court, the instant they are made, in ordinary litigation between parties, in personal actions, the people will have ceased, to be their own rulers, having to that extent, practically resigned their government, into the hands of that eminent tribunal. Nor is there, in this view, any assault upon the court, or the judges. It is a duty, from which they may not shrink, to decide cases properly brought before them; and it is no fault of theirs, if others seek to turn their decisions to political purposes.

In major confrontations with the Court, other presidents have taken similar positions to that of President Lincoln. During the constitutional crisis of 1937, resulting from the Court's invalidation of much of the early New Deal progressive economic legislation, President Franklin D. Roosevelt proposed that Congress expand the size of the Court from nine to fifteen justices, and thereby enable him to secure a majority sympathetic to his programs and policies. And in a "Fireside Chat" in March 1937 (see p. 63), FDR followed the footsteps of Jefferson, Jackson, and Lincoln in attacking the Court for becoming a "super-legislature."

Judicial supremacy over interpreting the Constitution remains controversial. In *Marbury*, however, Chief Justice Marshall did not lay claim to judicial supremacy, only that the Court, no less than the president and Congress, has the authority and duty to interpret the Constitution.[24] By contrast, in this century justices have often asserted the supremacy of their decisions. In *United States v. Butler*, 297 U.S. 1 (1936), Justice (and later Chief Justice) Harlan Stone claimed that "While unconstitutional exercise of power by the executive and legislative branches of government is subject to judicial restraint, the only check upon our own exercise of power is our own sense of self-restraint." In the wake of massive resistence to the Court's watershed ruling on school desegregation, in *Brown v. Board of Education*, 347 U.S. 483 (1954) (see Vol. 2, Ch. 12), all nine justices took the unusual step of signing the opinion announcing *Cooper v. Aaron*, 358 U.S. 1 (1958) (see Vol. 2, Ch. 12), which ordered the desegregation of schools in Little Rock, Arkansas. And they interpreted *Marbury* to have

declared the basic principle that the federal judiciary is supreme in the exposition of the law of the Constitution. . . . It follows that the interpretation of the Fourteenth Amendment enunciated by this Court in the *Brown* case is the supreme law of the land, and Article VI of the Constitution makes it binding effect on the States. . . . Every state legislator and executive and judicial officer is solemnly committed by oath taken pursuant to Article VI, 3 "to support this Constitution."

The Court likewise proclaimed itself the "ultimate interpreter of the Constitution" in *Baker v. Carr*, 369 U.S. 186 (1962) (see page 131), when holding that courts could decide disputes over the malapportionment of state legislatures. And again citing *Marbury* in *Powell v. McCormack*, 395 U.S. 486 (1969) (see Vol. 1, Ch. 5), involving a controversy over the House of Representatives' exclusion of a duely elected representative, the Court declared that "it is the responsibility of this Court to act as the ultimate interpreter of the Constitution."

Despite the Court's occasional claims of judicial supremacy, the president, Congress, and the states may in various ways undercut and thwart compliance with, if not ultimately overturn, the Court's rulings (see Chapter 2). By deciding only immediate cases, the Court infuses constitutional meaning into the larger surrounding political controversies by bringing them within the language, structure, and spirit of the Constitution. The Court may thus raise a controversial issue, as it did with school desegregation in *Brown* and with the right to abortion in *Roe,* to the national political agenda. But by itself the Court cannot lay those controversies to rest because its power, in Chief Justice Edward White's words, rests "solely upon the approval of a free people."[25] In areas of major and continuing political controversy, constitutional law is a kind of dialogue between the Court and the country over the meaning of the Constitution, and judicial review is more provisional than final.[26]

Even more than Chief Justice Marshall's arguments in *Marbury,* the establishment of judicial review turned on public acceptance and the forces of history. That is not to gainsay Marshall's contributions. He had a keen understanding of the malleable nature of the young republic and the important role that the first generation would play in establishing the power of the national government. Marshall's long tenure (1801–1835) and that of others who served with him may have contributed as well. After *Marbury,* moreover, the Court did not again strike down another act of Congress or challenge a coequal branch of government until the 1857 ill-fated ruling in *Dred Scott,* which left the Court at low ebb for two decades. Instead, the Marshall Court buttressed its own power by defending the interests of the national government against the states and striking down state laws.

Finally, social forces have shaped the Court's role in the kinds of cases and controversies brought to it for review. As already noted, the Court had little important business during its first decade. Over 40 percent of its business consisted in admiralty and prize cases (disputes over captured property at sea). About 50 percent raised issues of common law, and the remaining 10 percent dealt with matters like equity, including one probate case. By the late nineteenth century, the Court's business gradually changed in response to developments in American society. The number of admiralty cases, for instance, had by 1882 dwindled to less than 4 percent of the total. Almost 40 percent of the Court's decisions still dealt with either disputes of common law or questions of jurisdiction and procedure in federal courts. More than 43 percent of the Court's business, however, involved interpreting congressional statutes. Less than 4 percent of the cases raised issues of constitutional interpretation. The decline in admiralty and common law litigation and the increase in statutory interpretation reflected the impact of the Industrial Revolution and the growing governmental regulation of social and economic relations. In the twentieth century, the trend has continued. In the 1980s, about 47 percent of the cases annually decided by the Court involved matters of constitutional law. Another 38 percent dealt with the interpretation of congressional legislation. The remaining 15 percent resolved issues of administrative law, taxation, patents, and claims.

The Court is no longer "the least dangerous branch" or primarily concerned with correcting the errors of lower courts. In response to growing and changing litigation, the Court more frequently overturns prior rulings, congressional legislation, and state and local laws. The Court takes only "hard cases," involving major issues of legal policy and "not primarily to preserve the rights of the litigants," in the words of Chief Justice William Howard Taft: "The Supreme Court's function is for the purpose of expounding and stabilizing principles of law for the benefit of the people of the country, passing upon constitutional questions and other important questions of law for the public benefit."[27]

The Court and the country have changed with constitutional politics. From 1789 to the Civil War, the major controversies confronting the Court involved disputes between the national government and the states, and the Court employed its power to preserve the Union (see Vol. 1, Ch. 6 and 7). Between 1865 and 1937, during the Reconstruction and the Industrial Revolution, the dominant political controversy revolved around balancing regulatory interests and those of businesses, and the Court defended the interests of American capitalism and private enterprise (see Vol. 2, Ch. 3). Only after 1937 did the Court begin to assume the role of "a guardian for civil liberties and civil rights" in defending the rights of minorities (see Vol. 2, Chs. 4–12). The Court's role has changed with constitutional politics, as Harvard Law School professor Paul Freund nicely expressed by analogy, "As Hamlet is to one generation a play of revenge, to another a conflict between will and conscience, and to another a study in mother-fixation, so the Constitution has been to one generation a means of cementing the Union, to another a protectorate of burgeoning property, and to another a safeguard of basic human rights and equality before the law."[28]

CONSTITUTIONAL HISTORY

Decisions of the Supreme Court Overruled
and Acts of Congress Held Unconstitutional,
and State Laws and Municipal Ordinances Overturned,
1789–1989*

Year	Supreme Court Decision Overruled	Acts of Congress Overturned	State Laws Overturned	Ordinances Overturned
1789–1800, Pre-Marshall				
1801–1835, Marshall Court	3	1	18	
1836–1864, Taney Court	6	1	21	
1865–1873, Chase Court	3	10	33	
1874–1888, Waite Court	11	9	7	
1889–1910, Fuller Court	4	14	73	15
1910–1921, White Court	6	12	107	18
1921–1930, Taft Court	5	12	131	12
1930–1940, Hughes Court	14	14	78	5
1941–1946, Stone Court	24	2	25	7
1947–1952, Vinson Court	11	1	38	7
1953–1969, Warren Court	46	25	150	16
1969–1986, Burger Court	50	34	192	15
1986– , Rehnquist Court	5	4	31	4

* Note that in *Immigration and Naturalization Service v. Chadha* (1983), the Burger Court struck down a provision for a "one-house" legislative veto in the Immigration and Naturalization Act but effectively declared all one- and two-house legislative vetoes unconstitutional. While 212 statutes containing provisions for legislative vetoes were implicated by the Court's decision, *Chadha* is here counted as a single declaration of the unconstitutionality of congressional legislation. Note also that the Court's ruling in *Texas v. Johnson* (1989), striking down a Texas law making it a crime to desecrate the American flag, invalidated laws in forty-eight states and a federal statute. It is counted here, however, only once.

NOTES

1. See Max Farrand, *The Framing of the Constitution* (New Haven, CT: Yale University Press, 1913); Max Farrand, ed., *The Records of the Federal Convention of 1787*, 4 vols. (New Haven, CT: Yale University Press, 1911); and John P. Roche, "The Founding Fathers: A Reform Caucus in Action," 55 *American Political Science Review* 799 (1961).

2. The Supreme Court has enforced the tenure and salary provisions

in *Ex parte Milligan*, 4 Wall. 2 (1867) (see Vol. 1, Ch. 3), holding that civilians cannot be tried before military tribunals; in *O'Donoghue v. United States*, 289 U.S. 516 (1933), holding that judicial salaries cannot be reduced, even during the Great Depression; and *Northern Pipe Line Construction Co. v. Marathon Pipe Line Co.*, 458 U.S. 50 (1982), striking down a statute expanding the power of bankruptcy judges.

3. Edward S. Corwin, "The Constitution as Instrument and as Symbol," 30 *American Political Science Review* 1078 (1936).

4. Letter from Max Farrand to Edward Corwin, Jan. 3, 1939, in Edward Samuel Corwin Papers, Box 3, Princeton University Library, Princeton, NJ.

5. Quoted in James Madison, *Notes of Debates in the Federal Convention of 1787* (Athens: Ohio University Press, 1966), 455–456.

6. A Columbia Patriot, in *The Complete Anti-Federalist*, Vol. 4, ed. Herbert J. Storing (Chicago: University of Chicago Press, 1981), 276.

7. Thomas Tredwell, in *The Debates in the Several State Conventions on the Adoption of the Federal Constitution*, Vol. 4, ed., Jonathan Elliot (New York: Burt Franklin, 1974), 401.

8. Brutus, in *The Complete Anti-Federalist*, Vol. 2, ed. Storing, 438–439, 420, 422.

9. James Wilson, in *The Debates*, Vol. 2, ed. Elliot, 494.

10. Governor Johnston, in *The Debates*, Vol. 4, ed. Elliot, 142.

11. James Wilson, in *The Debates*, Vol. 2, ed. Elliot, 445–446.

12. Oliver Ellsworth, in *The Debates*, Vol. 2, ed. Elliot, 196.

13. Letter from James Madison to an unidentified person, Aug. 1834, reprinted in *Letters and Other Writings of James Madison*, Vol. 4 (Philadelphia, 1865), 350.

14. James Madison, in *Annals of Congress*, Vol. 1 (Washington, DC: Gales & Seaton, 1789), 500, 546–547.

15. James Madison, "Report on the Virginia Resolutions," in *The Debates*, Vol. 5, ed. Elliot, 549.

16. Thomas Jefferson, *The Works of Thomas Jefferson*, Vol. 12, ed. Paul Ford (New York: G. P. Putnam's Sons, 1904–1905), 137–138.

17. Quoted in Robert J. Morgan, *James Madison on the Constitution and the Bill of Rights* (Westport, CT: Greenwood Press, 1988), 196. For more on Jefferson's and Madison's views, see the discussion of the controversy over Congress's creating a national bank and *McCulloch v. Maryland*, 17 U.S. 316 (1819) (see page 447).

18. Charles Evans Hughes, *Address and Papers of Charles Evans Hughes* (New York: Columbia University Press, 1908), 139.

19. Joseph Story, *Commentaries on the Constitution*, (Durham, NC: Carolina Academic Press, 1987), reprint of 1833 ed.

20. Thomas Jefferson, Letter to John Adams, Sept. 11, 1804, as quoted in Charles Warren, *The Supreme Court in United States History*, Vol. 1 (Boston: Little, Brown, 1922), 265.

21. Quoted in Edward Corwin, *The Doctrine of Judicial Review* (Princeton, NJ: Princeton University Press, 1914), 22.

22. President's Veto Message (July 10, 1832), *A Compilation of the Messages and Papers of the Presidents*, Vol. 2, ed. J. Richardson (New

York: Bureau of National Literature, 1917), 582.

23. Abraham Lincoln, *The Collected Works of Abraham Lincoln,* Vol. 2, ed. Roy Basler (New Brunswick, NJ: Rutgers University Press, 1953), 401.

24. See David M. O'Brien, "Judicial Review and Constitutional Politics: Theory and Practice," 48 *University of Chicago Law Review* 1070 (1981).

25. Quoted in David M. O'Brien, *Storm Center: The Supreme Court in American Politics,* 2nd ed. (New York: W. W. Norton, 1990), 22.

26. See Paul Diamond, *The Supreme Court and Judicial Choice* (Ann Arbor: University of Michigan Press, 1989).

27. William H. Taft, *Hearings before the House Committee on the Judiciary,* 67th Cong., 2d sess., 1922, 2.

28. Paul Freund, "My Philosophy of Law," 39 *Connecticut Bar Journal* 220 (1965).

SELECTED BIBLIOGRAPHY

Cannon, Mark, and O'Brien, David, eds. *Views from the Bench: The Judiciary and Constitutional Politics.* Chatham, NJ: Chatham House, 1985.

Corwin, Edward S. *The Doctrine of Judicial Review.* Princeton, NJ: Princeton University Press, 1914.

———. *Constitutional Revolution, Ltd.* Claremont, CA: Claremont Colleges, 1941.

Diamond, Paul R. *The Supreme Court & Judicial Choice.* Ann Arbor: University of Michigan, 1989.

Fisher, Louis. *Constitutional Dialogues.* Princeton, NJ: Princeton University Press, 1988.

Freund, Paul A. *The Supreme Court of the United States.* Cleveland, OH: World Publishing, 1961.

Lasser, William. *The Limits of Judicial Power.* Chapel Hill: University of North Carolina Press, 1988.

Levy, Leonard, ed. *American Constitutional History.* New York: Macmillan, 1989.

———. *Judicial Review, History and Democracy.* New York: Harper & Row, 1967.

Nagel, Robert F. *Constitutional Cultures.* Berkeley: University of California, 1989.

Steamer, Robert. *The Supreme Court in Crisis: A History of Conflict.* Amherst: University of Massachusetts Press, 1971.

Warren, Charles. *The Supreme Court in United States History,* 3 vols. Boston: Little, Brown, 1922.

The Virginia and Kentucky
Resolutions of 1798

In the spring of 1798, President John Adams and his Federalist-dominated Congress enacted the Alien and Sedition Acts, regulating immigration and making criticism of the government a crime of seditious libel. The laws aimed at silencing partisan criticism of the Adams's administration's pro-British policies by Jeffersonian-Republicans. Although Jeffersonian-Republicans were prosecuted under the laws, often receiving stiff penalties, no court ruled on the constitutionality of the laws or whether they violated the First Amendment's guarantee for freedom of speech and press. The Kentucky legislature adopted a resolution secretly written by Thomas Jefferson, and Virginia adopted a similar resolution drafted by James Madison. Prosecutions for seditious libel ended in 1801, when the laws expired and Jefferson became president. Over 160 years later, the Supreme Court in a landmark ruling on libel, in The *New York Times Company v. Sullivan*, 376 U.S. 254 (1964) (see Vol. 2, Ch. 5), declared the Sedition Act and seditious libel unconstitutional and inconsistent with the First Amendment.

VIRGINIA RESOLUTIONS, DECEMBER 21, 1798

1. *Resolved*, That the General Assembly of Virginia doth unequivocally express a firm resolution to maintain and defend the Constitution of the United States, and the Constitution of this State, against every aggression, either foreign or domestic, and that it will support the government of the United States in all measures warranted by the former. . . .

3. That this Assembly doth explicitly and peremptorily declare that it views the powers of the Federal Government as resulting from the compact to which the States are parties, as limited by the plain sense and intention of the instrument constituting that compact; as no further valid than they are authorized by the grants enumerated in that compact; and that in case of a deliberate, palpable, and dangerous exercise of other powers not granted by the said compact, the States, who are the parties thereto, have the right, and are in duty bound, to interpose for arresting the progress of the evil, and for maintaining within their respective limits, the authorities, rights, and liberties appertaining to them.

4. That the General Assembly doth also express its deep regret that a spirit has in sundry instances been manifested by the Federal Government, to enlarge its powers by forced constructions of the constitutional charter which defines them; and that indications have appeared of a design to expound certain general phrases

(which, having been copied from the very limited grant of powers in the former articles of confederation, were the less liable to be misconstrued), so as to destroy the meaning and effect of the particular enumeration, which necessarily explains and limits the general phrases, and so as to consolidate the States by degrees into one sovereignty, the obvious tendency and inevitable result of which would be to transform the present republican system of the United States into an absolute, or at best, a mixed monarchy.

5. That the General Assembly doth particularly protest against the palpable and alarming infractions of the Constitution, in the two late cases of the "alien and sedition acts," passed at the last session of Congress, the first of which exercises a power nowhere delegated to the Federal Government; and which by uniting legislative and judicial powers to those of executive, subverts the general principles of free government, as well as the particular organization and positive provisions of the federal Constitution; and the other of which acts exercises in like manner a power not delegated by the Constitution, but on the contrary expressly and positively forbidden by one of the amendments thereto; a power which more than any other ought to produce universal alarm, because it is levelled against that right of freely examining public characters and measures, and of free communication among the people thereon, which has ever been justly deemed the only effectual guardian of every other right.

6. That this State having by its convention which ratified the federal Constitution, expressly declared, "that among other essential rights, the liberty of conscience and of the press cannot be cancelled, abridged, restrained, or modified by any authority of the United States," and from its extreme anxiety to guard these rights from every possible attack of sophistry or ambition, having with other States recommended an amendment for that purpose, which amendment was in due time annexed to the Constitution, it would mark a reproachful inconsistency and criminal degeneracy, if an indifference were now shown to the most palpable violation of one of the rights thus declared and secured, and to the establishment of a precedent which may be fatal to the other.

KENTUCKY RESOLUTIONS, NOVEMBER 10, 1798

1. *Resolved,* That the several states composing the United States of America, are not united on the principle of unlimited submission to their general government; but that by compact, under the style and title of a Constitution for the United States, and of amendments thereto, they constituted a general government for special purposes, delegated to that government certain definite powers, reserving, each state to itself, the residuary mass of right to their own self-government; and that whensoever the general government assumes undelegated powers, its acts are unauthorita-

tive, void, and of no force: That to this compact each state acceded as a state, and is an integral party, its co-states forming as to itself, the other party: That the government created by this compact was not made the exclusive or final *judge* of the extent of the powers delegated to itself; since that would have made its discretion, and not the Constitution, the measure of its powers; but that, as in all other cases of compact among parties having no common judge, each party has an equal right to judge for itself, as well of infractions, as of the mode and measure of redress.

2. *Resolved,* That the Constitution of the United States having delegated to Congress a power to punish treason, counterfeiting the securities and current coin of the United States, piracies and felonies committed on the high seas, and offences against the laws of nations, and no other crimes whatever, . . . all other [of] their acts which assume to create, define, or punish crimes other than those enumerated in the Constitution, are altogether void, and of no force, and that the power to create, define, and punish such other crimes is reserved, and of right appertains, solely and exclusively, to the respective states, each within its own territory.

3. *Resolved,* That it is true as a general principle, and is also expressly declared by one of the amendments to the Constitution, that "the powers not delegated to the United States by the Constitution, nor prohibited by it to the states, are reserved to the states respectively, or to the people"; and that no power over the freedom of religion, freedom of speech, or freedom of the press, being delegated to the United States by the Constitution, nor prohibited by it to the states, all lawful powers respecting the same did of right remain, and were reserved to the states, or to the people; that thus was manifested their determination to retain to themselves the right of judging how far the licentiousness of speech and of the press may be abridged without lessening their useful freedom, and how far those abuses which cannot be separated from their use, should be tolerated rather than the use be destroyed; and thus also they guarded against all abridgment by the United States of the freedom of religious opinions and exercises, and retained to themselves the right of protecting the same, as this state by a law passed on the general demand of its citizens, had already protected them from all human restraint or interference: and that in addition to this general principle and express declaration, another and more special provision has been made by one of the amendments to the Constitution, which expressly declares, that "Congress shall make no law respecting an establishment of religion, or prohibiting the free exercise thereof, or abridging the freedom of speech, or of the press," thereby guarding in the same sentence, and under the same words, the freedom of religion, of speech, and of the press, insomuch, that whatever violates either, throws down the sanctuary which

covers the others, and that libels, falsehoods, and defamations, equally with heresy and false religion, are withheld from the cognizance of federal tribunals: that therefore the act of the Congress of the United States, passed on the 14th day of July, 1798, entitled, "an act in addition to the act for the punishment of certain crimes against the United States," which does abridge the freedom of the press, is not law, but is altogether void and of no effect.

4. *Resolved,* That alien-friends are under the jurisdiction and protection of the laws of the state wherein they are; that no power over them has been delegated to the United States, nor prohibited to the individual states distinct from their power over citizens; and it being true as a general principle, and one of the amendments to the Constitution having also declared, that "the powers not delegated to the United States by the Constitution, nor prohibited by it to the states, are reserved to the states respectively, or to the people," the act of the Congress of the United States, passed on the 22d day of June, 1798, entitled "an act concerning aliens," which assumes power over alien-friends not delegated by the Constitution, is not law, but is altogether void and of no force. . . .

6. *Resolved,* That the imprisonment of a person under the protection of the laws of this commonwealth, on his failure to obey the simple *order* of the President, to depart out of the United States, as is undertaken by the said act, entitled "an act concerning aliens," is contrary to the Constitution, one amendment to which has provided, that "no person shall be deprived of liberty without due process of law," and that another having provided, "that in all criminal prosecutions, the accused shall enjoy the right to a public trial by an impartial jury, to be informed of the nature and cause of the accusation, to be confronted with the witnesses against him, to have compulsory process for obtaining witnesses in his favour, and to have the assistance of counsel for his defence," the same act undertaking to authorize the President to remove a person out of the United States, who is under the protection of the law, on his own suspicion, without accusation, without jury, without public trial, without confrontation of the witnesses against him, without having witnesses in his favour, without defence, without counsel, is contrary to these provisions, also, of the Constitution, is therefore not law, but utterly void and of no force.

That transferring the power of judging any person who is under the protection of the laws, from the courts to the President of the United States, as is undertaken by the same act, concerning aliens, is against the article of the Constitution which provides, that "the judicial power of the United States shall be vested in courts, the judges of which shall hold their offices during good behaviour," and that the said act is void for that reason also;

and it is further to be noted, that this transfer of judiciary power is to that magistrate of the General Government, who already possesses all the executive, and a qualified negative in all the legislative powers.

Marbury v. Madison
1 Cr. (5 U.S.) 137 (1803)

This case grew out of one of the great early struggles over the course of constitutional politics. Shortly after the ratification of the Constitution, two rival political parties emerged with widely different views of the Constitution and governmental power. The Federalists who, since the Constitutional Convention, supported a strong national government, including the power of the federal courts to interpret the Constitution. Their opponents, the Anti-Federalists and later the Jeffersonian-Republicans (who after the 1832 election became known as Democrats), remained distrustful of the national government and continued to favor the states and state courts. The struggle between the Federalists and the Jeffersonian-Republicans finally came to a head with the election of 1800. The Jeffersonians defeated the Federalists, who had held office since the creation of the republic and feared what the Jeffersonian-Republicans might do once in office.

Before leaving office, President John Adams and his Federalist-dominated Congress vindictively created a number of new judgeships and appointed all Federalists in the hope that they would counter the Jeffersonians once in office. But with time running out before the inauguration of Thomas Jefferson as president in 1801, not all of the commissions for the new judgeships were delivered. John Marshall, whom Adams had just appointed as chief justice, continued to work as secretary of state, delivering the commissions. But he failed to deliver seventeen commissions before Adams's term expired and left them for his successor as secretary of state, James Madison, to deliver. The Federalists' attempt to pack the courts infuriated the Jeffersonian-Republicans. And President Jefferson instructed Madison not to deliver the rest of the commissions.

William Marbury was one whose commission went undelivered. He decided to sue to force Madison to give him his commission. Specifically, he sought a *writ of mandamus*, which is simply a court order directing a government official (Madison) to perform a certain act (hand over the commission). Marbury argued that Section 13 of the Judiciary Act of 1789 had authorized the Supreme Court to issue such writs. He saw this as a way of getting back his commission and for the Marshall Court to take a stand against the Jeffersonians.

Marbury v. Madison was a politically explosive case for the Court and the country over the still-untested power of judicial review. The Court faced a major dilemma. On the one hand, if the Marshall Court ordered Marbury's commission, it was likely that Jefferson would refuse to comply. The Court would then be powerless, perhaps permanently. On the other hand, if the Court refused to issue the writ, it would appear weak and that would confirm the Jeffersonian argument that the courts had no power to intrude on the executive branch. Chief Justice Marshall's opinion, handed down on February 24, 1803, however, shrewdly asserted the power of judicial review and for the first time overturned part of an act of Congress, but gave Jefferson no opportunity to retaliate and thus helped to defuse the political controversy surrounding the case. While Jeffersonians fervently disagreed with Marshall's ruling, there was little for them to do because Marshall had not ordered the delivery of Marbury's commission.

Chief Justice MARSHALL delivers the opinion of the Court.

At the last term on the affidavits then read and filed with the clerk, a rule was granted in this case, requiring the secretary of state to show cause why a mandamus should not issue, directing him to deliver to William Marbury his commission as a justice of the peace for the county of Washington, in the District of Columbia.

No cause has been shown, and the present motion is for a *mandamus.* The peculiar delicacy of this case, the novelty of some of its circumstances, and the real difficulty attending the points which occur in it, require a complete exposition of the principles on which the opinion to be given by the court is founded.

These principles have been, on the side of the applicant very ably argued at the bar. In rendering the opinion of the court, there will be some departure in form, though not in substance, from the points stated in that argument.

In the order in which the court has viewed this subject, the following questions have been considered and decided.

1st. Has the applicant a right to the commission he demands?

2d. If he has a right, and that right has been violated, do the laws of his country afford him a remedy?

3d. If they do afford him a remedy, is it a *mandamus* issuing from this court?

The first object of inquiry is,

1st. Has the applicant a right to the commission he demands?

His right originates in an act of congress passed in February, 1801, concerning the District of Columbia.

After dividing the district into two counties, the 11th section of this law enacts, "that there shall be appointed in and for each of the said counties, such number of discreet persons to be justices of the peace as the president of the United States shall, from time to time, think expedient, to continue in office for five years."

It appears, from the affidavits, that in compliance with this law, a commission for William Marbury, as a justice of the peace for the county of Washington, was signed by John Adams, then President of the United States; after which the seal of the United States was affixed to it; but the commission has never reached the person for whom it was made out.

In order to determine whether he is entitled to this commission, it becomes necessary to inquire whether he has been appointed to the office. For if he has been appointed, the law continues him in office for five years, and he is entitled to the possession of those evidences of office, which, being completed, became his property.

The 2d section of the 2d article of the constitution declares, that "the president shall nominate, and, by and with the advice and consent of the senate, shall appoint, ambassadors, other public ministers and consuls, and all other officers of the United States, whose appointments are not otherwise provided for."

The 3d section declares, that "he shall commission all the officers of the United States."

An act of congress directs the secretary of state to keep the seal of the United States, "to make out and record, and affix the said seal to all civil commissions to officers of the United States, to be appointed by the president, by and with the consent of the senate, or by the president alone; provided, that the said seal shall not be affixed to any commission before the same shall have been signed by the President of the United States."

These are the clauses of the constitution and laws of the United States, which affect this part of the case. They seem to contemplate three distinct operations:

1st. The nomination. This is the sole act of the president, and is completely voluntary.

2d. The appointment. This is also the act of the president, and is also a voluntary act, though it can only be performed by and with the advice and consent of the senate.

3d. The commission. To grant a commission to a person appointed, might, perhaps, be deemed a duty enjoined by the constitution. "He shall," says that instrument, "commission all the officers of the United States." . . .

The last act to be done by the president is the signature of the commission. He has then acted on the advice and consent of the senate to his own nomination. The time for deliberation has then passed. He has decided. His judgment, on the advice and consent of the senate concurring with his nomination, has been made, and the officer is appointed. . . .

It is . . . decidedly the opinion of the court, that when a commission has been signed by the president, the appointment is made; and that the commission is complete when the seal of the United States has been affixed to it by the secretary of state.

Where an officer is removable at the will of the executive, the circumstance which completes his appointment is of no concern; because the act is at any time revocable; and the commission may be arrested, if still in the office. But when the officer is not removable at the will of the executive, the appointment is not revocable, and cannot be annulled. It has conferred legal rights which cannot be resumed. . . .

Mr. Marbury, then, since his commission was signed by the president, and sealed by the secretary of state, was appointed; and as the law creating the office, gave the officer a right to hold for five years, independent of the executive, the appointment was not revocable, but vested in the officer legal rights, which are protected by the laws of his country.

To withhold his commission, therefore, is an act deemed by the court not warranted by law, but violative of a vested legal right.

This brings us to the second inquiry; which is,

2d. If he has a right, and that right has been violated, do the laws of this country afford him a remedy?

The very essence of civil liberty certainly consists in the right of every individual to claim the protection of the laws, whenever he receives an injury. One of the first duties of government is to afford that protection. In Great Britain the king himself is sued in the respectful form of a petition, and he never fails to comply with the judgment of his court. . . .

By the constitution of the United States, the president is invested with certain important political powers, in the exercise of which he is to use his own discretion, and is accountable only to his country in his political character and to his own conscience. To aid him in the performance of these duties, he is authorized to appoint certain officers, who act by his authority, and in conformity with his orders.

In such cases, their acts are his acts; and whatever opinion may be entertained of the manner in which executive discretion may be used, still there exists, and can exist, no power to control that discretion. The subjects are political. They respect the nation, not individual rights, and being intrusted to the executive, the decision of the executive is conclusive. . . .

But when the legislature proceeds to impose on that officer other duties; when he is directed peremptorily to perform certain acts; when the rights of individuals are dependent on the performance of those acts; he is so far the officer of the law; is amenable to the laws for his conduct; and cannot at his discretion sport away the vested rights of others.

The conclusion from this reasoning is, that where the heads of departments are the political or confidential agents of the executive, merely to execute the will of the president, or rather to act in cases in which the executive possesses a constitutional or legal discretion, nothing can be more perfectly clear than that their acts are only politically examinable. But where a specific duty is assigned by law, and individual rights depend upon the performance of that duty, it seems equally clear that the individual who considers himself injured, has a right to resort to the laws of his country for a remedy. . . .

It is, then, the opinion of the Court,

1st. That by signing the commission of Mr. Marbury, the President of the United States appointed him a justice of peace for the county of Washington, in the District of Columbia; and that the seal of the United States, affixed thereto by the secretary of state, is conclusive testimony of the verity of the signature, and of the completion of the appointment; and that the appointment conferred on him a legal right to the office for the space of five years.

2d. That, having this legal title to the office, he has a consequent right to the commission; a refusal to deliver which is a plain violation of that right, for which the laws of his country afford him a remedy.

It remains to be inquired whether,

3d. He is entitled to the remedy for which he applies. This depends on,

1st. The nature of the writ applied for; and,

2d. The power of this court.

1st. The nature of the writ. . . .

[T]o render the *mandamus* a proper remedy, the officer to whom it is to be directed, must be one to whom, on legal principles, such writ may be directed; and the person applying for it must be without any other specific and legal remedy.

1st. With respect to the officer to whom it would be directed. The intimate political relation subsisting between the President of the United States and the heads of departments, necessarily renders any legal investigation of the acts of one of those high officers peculiarly irksome, as well as delicate; and excites some hesitation with respect to the propriety of entering into such investigation. Impressions are often received without much reflection or examination, and it is not wonderful that in such a case as this the assertion, by an individual, of his legal claims in a court of justice, to which claims it is the duty of that court to attend, should at first view be considered by some, as an attempt to intrude into the cabinet, and to intermeddle with the prerogatives of the executive.

It is scarcely necessary for the court to disclaim all pretensions to such jurisdiction. An extravagance, so absurd and excessive, could not have been entertained for a moment. The province of the court is, solely, to decide on the rights of individuals, not to inquire how the executive, or executive officers, perform duties in which they have a discretion. Questions in their nature political, or which are, by the constitution and laws, submitted to the executive, can never be made in this court.

But, if this be not such a question; if, so far from being an intrusion into the secrets of the cabinet, it respects a paper which, according to law, is upon record, and to a copy of which the law gives a right. . . .

If one of the heads of departments commits any illegal act, under colour of his office, by which an individual sustains an injury, it cannot be pretended that his office alone exempts him from being sued in the ordinary mode of proceeding, and being compelled to obey the judgment of the law. How, then, can his office exempt him from this particular mode of deciding on the legality of his conduct if the case be such a case as would, were any other individual the party complained of, authorize the process?

It is not by the office of the person to whom the writ is directed, but the nature of the thing to be done, that the propriety or impropriety of issuing a *mandamus* is to be determined. . . .

This, then, is a plain case for a *mandamus,* either to deliver the commission, or a copy of it from the record; and it only remains to be inquired,

Whether it can issue from this court.

The act to establish the judicial courts of the United States authorizes the Supreme Court "to issue writs of *mandamus* in cases warranted by the principles and usages of law, to any courts appointed, or persons holding office, under the authority of the United States."

The secretary of state, being a person holding an office under the authority of the United States, is precisely within the letter of the description, and if this court is not authorized to issue a writ of mandamus to such an officer, it must be because the law is unconstitutional, and therefore absolutely incapable of conferring the authority, and assigning the duties which its words purport to confer and assign.

The constitution vests the whole judicial power of the United States in one supreme court, and such inferior courts as congress shall, from time to time, ordain and establish. This power is expressly extended to all cases arising under the laws of the United States; and, consequently, in some form, may be exercised over the present case; because the right claimed is given by a law of the United States.

In the distribution of this power it is declared that "the supreme court shall have original jurisdiction in all cases affecting ambassa-

dors, other public ministers and consuls, and those in which a
state shall be a party. In all other cases, the supreme court shall
have appellate jurisdiction."

It has been insisted, at the bar, that as the original grant of
jurisdiction, to the supreme and inferior courts, is general, and
the clause, assigning original jurisdiction to the supreme court,
contains no negative or restrictive words, the power remains to
the legislature, to assign original jurisdiction to that court in other
cases than those specified in the article which has been recited;
provided those cases belong to the judicial power of the United
States.

If it had been intended to leave it in the discretion of the
legislature to apportion the judicial power between the supreme
and inferior courts according to the will of that body, it would
certainly have been useless to have proceded further than to
have defined the judicial power, and the tribunals in which it
should be vested. The subsequent part of the section is mere
surplusage, is entirely without meaning, if such is to be the construction. If congress remains at liberty to give this court appellate
jurisdiction, where the constitution has declared their jurisdiction
shall be original; and original jurisdiction where the constitution
has declared it shall be appellate; the distribution of jurisdiction,
made in the constitution, is form without substance.

Affirmative words are often, in their operation, negative of
other objects than those affirmed; and in this case, a negative
or exclusive sense must be given to them, or they have no operation
at all.

It cannot be presumed that any clause in the constitution is
intended to be without effect; and, therefore, such a construction
is inadmissible, unless the words require it.

If the solicitude of the convention, respecting our peace with
foreign powers, induced a provision that the supreme court
should take original jurisdiction in cases which might be supposed
to affect them; yet the clause would have proceeded no further
than to provide for such cases, if no further restriction on the
powers of congress had been intended. That they should have
appellate jurisdiction in all other cases, with such exceptions as
congress might make, is no restriction; unless the words be deemed
exclusive of original jurisdiction.

When an instrument organizing fundamentally a judicial system, divides it into one supreme, and so many inferior courts
as the legislature may ordain and establish; then enumerates its
powers, and proceeds so far to distribute them, as to define the
jurisdiction of the supreme court by declaring the cases in which
it shall take original jurisdiction, and that in others it shall take
appellate jurisdiction; the plain import of the words seems to
be, that in one class of cases its jurisdiction is original, and not
appellate; in the other it is appellate, and not original. If any

other construction would render the clause inoperative, that is an additional reason for rejecting such other construction, and for adhering to their obvious meaning.

To enable this court, then, to issue a *mandamus,* it must be shown to be an exercise of appellate jurisdiction, or to be necessary to enable them to exercise appellate jurisdiction.

It has been stated at the bar that the appellate jurisdiction may be exercised in a variety of forms, and that if it be the will of the legislature that a *mandamus* should be used for that purpose, that will must be obeyed. This is true, yet the jurisdiction must be appellate, not original.

It is the essential criterion of appellate jurisdiction, that it revises and corrects the proceedings in a cause already instituted, and does not create that cause. Although, therefore, a mandamus may be directed to courts, yet to issue such a writ to an officer for the delivery of a paper, is in effect the same as to sustain an original action for that paper, and, therefore, seems not to belong to appellate, but to original jurisdiction. Neither is it necessary in such a case as this, to enable the court to exercise its appellate jurisdiction.

The authority, therefore, given to the supreme court, by the act establishing the judicial courts of the United States, to issue writs of *mandamus* to public officers, appears not to be warranted by the constitution; and it becomes necessary to inquire whether a jurisdiction so conferred can be exercised.

The question, whether an act, repugnant to the constitution, can become the law of the land, is a question deeply interesting to the United States; but, happily, not of an intricacy proportioned to its interest. It seems only necessary to recognize certain principles, supposed to have been long and well established, to decide it.

That the people have an original right to establish, for their future government, such principles, as, in their opinion, shall most conduce to their own happiness is the basis on which the whole American fabric has been erected. The exercise of this original right is a very great exertion; nor can it, nor ought it, to be frequently repeated. The principles, therefore, so established, are deemed fundamental. And as the authority from which they proceed is supreme, and can seldom act, they are designed to be permanent.

This original and supreme will organizes the government, and assigns to different departments their respective powers. It may either stop here, or establish certain limits not to be transcended by those departments.

The government of the United States is of the latter description. The powers of the legislature are defined and limited; and that those limits may not be mistaken, or forgotten, the constitution is written. To what purpose are powers limited, and to what purpose is that limitation committed to writing, if these limits may, at any time, be passed by those intended to be restrained? The distinction between a government with limited and unlimited powers is abolished, if those limits do not confine the persons on whom they are imposed, and if acts prohibited and acts allowed, are of equal obligation. It is a proposition too plain to be contested, that the constitution controls any legislative act repugnant to it; or, that the legislature may alter the constitution by an ordinary act.

Between these alternatives there is no middle ground. The constitution is either a superior paramount law, unchangeable by ordinary means, or it is on a level with ordinary legislative acts, and, like other acts, is alterable when the legislature shall please to alter it.

If the former part of the alternative be true, then a legislative act contrary to the constitution is not law: if the latter part be true, then written constitutions are absurd attempts, on the part of the people, to limit a power in its own nature illimitable.

Certainly all those who have framed written constitutions contemplate them as forming the fundamental and paramount law of the nation, and, consequently, the theory of every such government must be, that an act of the legislature, repugnant to the constitution, is void.

This theory is essentially attached to a written constitution, and, is consequently, to be considered, by this court, as one of the fundamental principles of our society. It is not therefore to be lost sight of in the further consideration of this subject.

If an act of the legislature, repugnant to the constitution, is void, does it, notwithstanding its invalidity, bind the courts, and oblige them to give it effect? Or, in other words, though it be not law, does it constitute a rule as operative as if it was a law? This would be to overthrow in fact what was established in theory; and would seem, at first view, an absurdity too gross to be insisted on. It shall, however, receive a more attentive consideration.

It is emphatically the province and duty of the judicial department to say what the law is. Those who apply the rule to particular cases, must of necessity expound and interpret that rule. If two laws conflict with each other, the courts must decide on the operation of each.

So if a law be in opposition to the constitution; if both the law and the constitution apply to a particular case, so that the court must either decide that case conformably to the law, disregarding the constitution; or conformably to the constitution, disregarding the law; the court must determine which of these conflicting rules governs the case. This is of the very essence of judicial duty.

If, then, the courts are to regard the constitution, and the constitution is superior to any ordinary act of the legislature, the constitution, and not such ordinary act, must govern the case to which they both apply.

Those, then, who controvert the principle that the constitution is to be considered, in court, as a paramount law, are reduced to the necessity of maintaining that courts must close their eyes on the constitution, and see only the law.

This doctrine would subvert the very foundation of all written constitutions. It would declare that an act which, according to the principles and theory of our government, is entirely void, is yet, in practice, completely obligatory. It would declare that if the legislature shall do what is expressly forbidden, such act, notwithstanding the express prohibition, is in reality effectual. It would be given to the legislature a practical and real omnipotence, with the same breath which professes to restrict their powers within narrow limits. It is prescribing limits, and declaring that those limits may be passed at pleasure.

That it thus reduces to nothing what we have deemed the greatest improvement on political institutions, a written constitution, would of itself be sufficient, in America, where written constitutions have been viewed with so much reverence, for rejecting the construction. But the peculiar expressions of the constitution of the United States furnish additional arguments in favour of its rejection.

The judicial power of the United States is extended to all cases arising under the constitution.

Could it be the intention of those who gave this power, to say that in using it the constitution should not be looked into? That a case arising under the constitution should be decided without examining the instrument under which it arises?

This is too extravagant to be maintained.

In some cases, then, the constitution must be looked into by the judges. And if they can open it at all, what part of it are they forbidden to read or to obey?

There are many other parts of the constitution which serve to illustrate this subject.

It is declared that "no tax or duty shall be laid on articles exported from any state." Suppose a duty on the export of cotton, of tobacco, or of flour; and a suit instituted to recover it. Ought judgment to be rendered in such a case? Ought the judges to close their eyes on the constitution, and only see the law?

The constitution declares "that no bill of attainder or *ex post facto* law shall be passed."

If, however, such a bill should be passed, and a person should be prosecuted under it; must the court condemn to death those victims whom the constitution endeavors to preserve?

"No person," says the constitution, "shall be convicted of treason unless on the testimony of two witnesses to the same overt act, or on confession in open court."

Here the language of the constitution is addressed especially to the courts. It prescribes, directly for them, a rule of evidence not to be departed from. If the legislature should change that rule, and declare one witness, or a confession out of court, sufficient for conviction, must the constitutional principle yield to the legislative act?

From these, and many other selections which might be made, it is apparent, that the framers of the constitution contemplated that instrument as a rule for the government of courts, as well as of the legislature.

Why otherwise does it direct the judges to take an oath to support it? This oath certainly applies in an especial manner, to their conduct in their official character. How immoral to impose it on them, if they were to be used as the instruments, and the knowing instruments, for violating what they swear to support!

The oath of office, too, imposed by the legislature, is completely demonstrative of the legislative opinion on this subject. It is in these words: "I do solemnly swear that I will administer justice without respect to persons, and do equal right to the poor and to the rich; and that I will faithfully and impartially discharge all the duties incumbent on me as ———, according to the best of my abilities and understanding agreeably to the constitution and laws of the United States."

Why does a judge swear to discharge his duties agreeably to the constitution of the United States, if that constitution forms no rule for his government? if it is closed upon him, and cannot be inspected by him?

If such be the real state of things, this is worse than solemn mockery. To prescribe, or to take this oath, becomes equally a crime.

It is also not entirely unworthy of observation, that in declaring what shall be the *supreme law* of the land, *the constitution* itself is first mentioned; and not the laws of the United States generally, but those only which shall be made in *pursuance* of the constitution, have that rank.

Thus, the particular phraseology of the constitution of the United States confirms and strengthens the principle, supposed to be essential to all written constitutions, that a law repugnant to the constitution is void; and that *courts*, as well as other departments, are bound by that instrument.

The rule must be discharged.

Eakin v. Raub

12 Sargeant & Rawle 330 (Pa., 1825)

In this case involving the power of the Pennsylvania Supreme Court to invalidate a state law, Justice John Bannister Gibson wrote a dissenting opinion aimed at refuting Chief Justice John Marshall's arguments for judicial review in *Marbury v. Madison*

(1803) (see p. 45). Note that Justice Gibson's criticism of *Marbury* was limited to the exercise of judicial review over coequal branches of government. While he contended that state courts had no power to overturn state laws deemed to violate the state constitution, Justice Gibson did not deny that state courts could strike down state laws that were inconsistent with federal law or the Constitution. Moreover, twenty years later, Justice Gibson repudiated the position taken in his opinion here. In *Norris v. Clymer*, 2 Pa. 277 (1845), he explained his change in "opinion for two reasons. The late convention (which drafted Pennsylvania's state constitution), by their silence, sanctioned the pretensions of the courts to deal freely with the Acts of the Legislature; and from experience of the necessity of the case."

Justice GIBSON dissenting.

I am aware, that a right [in the judiciary] to declare all unconstitutional acts void . . . is generally held as a professional dogma, but, I apprehend, rather as a matter of faith than of reason. I admit that I once embraced the same doctrine, but without examination, and I shall therefore state the arguments that impelled me to abandon it, with great respect for those by whom it is still maintained. But I may premise, that it is not a little remarkable, that although the right in question has all along been claimed by the judiciary, no judge has ventured to discuss it, except Chief Justice MARSHALL, and if the argument of a jurist so distinguished for the strength of his ratiocinative powers be found inconclusive, it may fairly be set down to the weakness of the position which he attempts to defend. . . .

I begin, then, by observing that in this country, the powers of the judiciary are divisible into those that are POLITICAL and those that are purely civil. Every power by which one organ of the government is enabled to control another, or to exert an influence over its acts, is a political power. . . .

The constitution and the right of the legislature to pass the act, may be in collision. But is that a legitimate subject for judicial determination? If it be, the judiciary must be a peculiar organ, to revise the proceedings of the legislature, and to correct its mistakes; and in what part of the constitution are we to look for this proud pre-eminence? Viewing the matter in the opposite direction, what would be thought of an act of assembly in which it should be declared that the supreme court had, in a particular case, put a wrong construction on the constitution of the United States, and that the judgment should therefore be reversed? It would doubtless be thought a usurpation of judicial power. But it is by no means clear, that to declare a law void which has been enacted according to the forms prescribed in the constitution, is not a usurpation of legislative power. . . .

But it has been said to be emphatically the business of the judiciary, to ascertain and pronounce what the law is; and that this necessarily involves a consideration of the constitution. It does so: but how far? If the judiciary will inquire into anything besides the form of enactment, where shall it stop? . . .

In theory, all the organs of the government are of equal capacity; or, if not equal, each must be supposed to have superior capacity only for those things which peculiarly belong to it; and as legislation peculiarly involves the consideration of those limitations which are put on the law-making power, and the interpretation of the laws when made, involves only the construction of the laws themselves, it follows that the construction of the constitution in this particular belongs to the legislature, which ought therefore to be taken to have superior capacity to judge of the constitutionality of its own acts. But suppose all to be of equal capacity in every respect, why should one exercise a controlling power over the rest? That the judiciary is of superior rank, has never been pretended, although it has been said to be co-ordinate. It is not easy, however, to comprehend how the power which gives law to all the rest, can be of no more than equal rank with one which receives it, and is answerable to the former for the observance of its statutes. Legislation is essentially an act of sovereign power; but the execution of the laws by instruments that are governed by prescribed rules and exercise no power of volition, is essentially otherwise. . . . It may be said, the power of the legislature, also, is limited by prescribed rules. It is so. But it is nevertheless, the power of the people, and sovereign as far as it extends. It cannot be said, that the judiciary is co-ordinate merely because it is established by the constitution. If that were sufficient, sheriffs, registers of wills, and recorders of deeds, would be so too. Within the pale of their authority, the acts of these officers will have the power of the people for their support; but no one will pretend, they are of equal dignity with the acts of the legislature. Inequality of rank arises not from the manner in which the organ has been constituted, but from its essence and the nature of its functions; and the legislative organ is superior to every other, inasmuch as the power to will and to command, is essentially superior to the power to act and to obey. . . .

Everyone knows how seldom men think exactly alike on ordinary subjects; and a government constructed on the principle of assent by all its parts, would be inadequate to the most simple operations. The notion of a complication of counter checks has been carried to an extent in theory, of which the framers of the constitution never dreamt. When the entire sovereignty was separated into its elementary parts, and distributed to the appropriate branches, all things incident to the exercise of its powers were committed to each branch exclusively. The negative which each part of the legislature may exercise, in regard to the acts of the other, was thought sufficient to prevent material infractions of the restraints which were put on the power of the whole; for, had it been intended to interpose the judiciary as an additional barrier, the matter would surely not have been left in doubt. The judges would not have been left to stand on the insecure and ever shifting ground of public opinion as to constructive powers; they would have been placed on the impregnable ground of an express grant. They would not have been compelled to resort to debates in the convention, or the opinion that was generally entertained at the time. . . .

The power is said to be restricted to cases that are free from doubt or difficulty. But the abstract existence of a power cannot depend on the clearness or obscurity of the case in which it is to be exercised; for that is a consideration that cannot present itself, before the question of the existence of the power shall have been determined; and, if its existence be conceded, no considerations of policy arising from the obscurity of the particular case, ought to influence the exercise of it. . . .

To say, therefore, that the power is to be exercised but in perfectly clear cases, is to betray a doubt of the propriety of exercising it at all. Were the same caution used in judging of the existence of the power that is inculcated as to the exercise of it, the profession would perhaps arrive at a different conclusion. The grant of a power so extraordinary ought to appear so plain, that he who should run might read. . . .

What I have in view in this inquiry, is the supposed right of the judiciary to interfere, in cases where the constitution is to be carried into effect through the instrumentality of the legislature, and where that organ must necessarily first decide on the constitutionality of its own act. The oath to support the constitution is not peculiar to the judges, but is taken indiscriminately by every officer of the government, and is designed rather as a test of the political principles of the man, than to bind the officer in the discharge of his duty; otherwise it is difficult to determine what operation it is to have in the case of a recorder of deeds, for instance, who, in the execution of his office, has nothing to do with the constitution. But granting it to relate to the official conduct of the judge, as well as every other officer, and not to his political principles, still it must be understood in reference to supporting the constitution, *only as far as that may be involved in his official duty;* and, consequently, if his official duty does not comprehend an inquiry into the authority of the legislature, neither does his oath. . . .

But do not the judges do a positive act in violation of the constitution, when they give effect to an unconstitutional law? Not if the law has been passed according to the forms established in the constitution. The fallacy of the question is, in supposing that the judiciary adopts the acts of the legislature as its own; whereas the enactment of a law and the interpretation of it are not concurrent acts, and as the judiciary is not required to concur in the enactment, neither is it in the breach of the constitution which may be the consequence of the enactment. The fault is imputable to the legislature, and on it the responsibility exclusively rests. . . .

But it has been said, that this construction would deprive the citizen of the advantages which are peculiar to a written constitution, by at once declaring the power of the legislature in practice to be illimitable. . . . But there is no magic or inherent power in parchment and ink, to command respect and protect principles from violation. In the business of government a recurrence to first principles answers the end of an observation at sea with a view to correct the dead reckoning; and for this purpose, a written constitution is an instrument of inestimable value. It is of inestimable value, also, in rendering its first principles familiar to the mass of people; for, after all, there is no effectual guard against legislative usurpation but public opinion, the force of which, in this country is inconceivably great. . . . Once let public opinion be so corrupt as to sanction every misconstruction of the constitution and abuse of power which the temptation of the moment may dictate, and the party which may happen to be predominant, will laugh at the puny efforts of a dependent power to arrest it in its course.

For these reasons, I am of [the] opinion that it rests with the people, in whom full and absolute sovereign power resides, to correct abuses in legislation, by instructing their representatives to repeal the obnoxious act. What is wanting to plenary power in the government, is reserved by the people for their own immediate use; and to redress an infringement of their rights in this respect, would seem to be an accessory of the power thus reserved. It might, perhaps, have been better to vest the power in the judiciary; as it might be expected that its habits of deliberation, and the aid derived from the arguments of counsel, would more frequently lead to accurate conclusions. On the other hand, the judiciary is not infallible; and an error by it would admit of no remedy but a more distinct expression of the public will, through the extraordinary medium of a convention; whereas, an error by the legislature admits of a remedy by an exertion of the same will, in the ordinary exercise of the right of suffrage—a mode better calculated to attain the end, without popular excitement. It may be said, the people would probably not notice an error of their representatives. But they would as probably do so, as notice an error of the judiciary; and, besides, it is a postulate in the theory of our government, and the very basis of the superstructure, that the people are wise, virtuous, and competent to manage their own affairs; and if they are not so, in fact, still every question of this sort must be determined according to the principles of the constitution, as it came from the hands of the framers, and the existence of a defect which was not foreseen, would not justify those who administer the government, in applying a corrective in practice, which can be provided only by convention. . . .

But in regard to an act of [a state] assembly, which is found to be in collision with the constitution, laws, or treaties of the *United States,* I take the duty of the judiciary to be exactly the reverse. By becoming parties to the federal constitution, the states have agreed to several limitations of their individual sovereignty, to enforce which, it was thought to be absolutely necessary to prevent them from giving effect to laws in violation of those limitations, through the instrumentality of their own judges. Accordingly, it is declared in the sixth article and second section of the federal constitution, that "This constitution, and the laws of the *United States* which shall be made in pursuance thereof, and all treaties made, or which shall be made under the authority of the *United States,* shall be the *supreme* law of the land; and the *judges* in every *state* shall be BOUND thereby: anything in the *laws* or *constitution* of any *state* to the contrary notwithstanding."

President Jackson's Veto Message of 1832

President Andrew Jackson distrusted banks and, as a westerner, opposed the policies of the Bank of the United States which limited credit for land speculation. When Congress rechartered the Bank in 1832, Jackson vetoed the bill with this message,[*] drafted by Secretary of Treasury (and later appointed as chief justice) Roger B. Taney. The controversy over the establishment of the national bank and its importance in shaping constitutional politics is dealt with further in Vol. 1, Ch. 6.

To the Senate:

The bill "to modify and continue" the act entitled "An act to incorporate the subscribers to the Bank of the United States" was presented to me on the 4th July instant. Having considered it with that solemn regard to the principles of the Constitution which the day was calculated to inspire, and come to the conclusion that it ought not to become a law, I herewith return it to the Senate, in which it originated, with my objections.

* From James D. Richardson, ed., *A Compilation of the Messages and Papers of the Presidents,* (Washington, DC: Bureau of National Literature and Act, 1908), Vol. 2, 581–582.

It is maintained by the advocates of the bank that its constitutionality in all its features ought to be considered as settled by precedent and by the decision of the Supreme Court. To this conclusion I can not assent. Mere precedent is a dangerous source of authority, and should not be regarded as deciding questions of constitutional power except where the acquiescence of the people and the States can be considered as well settled. So far from this being the case on this subject, an argument against the bank might be based on precedent. One Congress, in 1791, decided in favor of a bank; another in 1811, decided against it. One Congress, in 1815, decided against a bank, another, in 1816, decided in its favor. Prior to the present Congress, therefore, the precedents drawn from that source were equal. If we resort to the States, the expressions of legislative, judicial, and executive opinions against the bank have been probably to those in its favor as 4 to 1. There is nothing in precedent, therefore, which, if its authority were admitted, ought to weigh in favor of the act before me.

If the opinion of the Supreme Court covered the whole ground of this act, it ought not to control the coordinate authorities of this Government. The Congress, the Executive, and the Court must each for itself be guided by its own opinion of the Constitution. Each public officer who takes an oath to support the Constitution swears that he will support it as he understands it, and not as it is understood by others. It is as much the duty of the House of Representatives, of the Senate, and of the President to decide upon the constitutionality of any bill or resolution which may be presented to them for passage or approval as it is of the supreme judges when it may be brought before them for judicial decision. The opinion of the judges has no more authority over Congress than the opinion of Congress has over the judges, and on that point the President is independent of both. The authority of the Supreme Court must not, therefore, be permitted to control the Congress or the Executive when acting in their legislative capacities, but to have only such influence as the force of their reasoning may deserve.

But in the case relied upon the Supreme Court have not decided that all the features of this corporation are compatible with the Constitution. It is true that the court have said that the law incorporating the bank is a constitutional exercise of power by Congress; but taking into view the whole opinion of the court and the reasoning by which they have come to that conclusion, I understand them to have decided that inasmuch as a bank is an appropriate means for carrying into effect the enumerated powers of the General Government, therefore the law incorporating it is in accordance with that provision of the Constitution which declares that Congress shall have power "to make all laws which shall be necessary and proper for carrying those powers into execution."

Having satisfied themselves that the word *"necessary"* in the Constitution means *"needful," "requisite," "essential," "conducive to,"* and that "a bank" is a convenient, a useful, and essential instrument in the prosecution of the Government's "fiscal operations," they conclude that to "use one must be within the discretion of Congress" and that "the act to incorporate the Bank of the United States is a law made in pursuance of the Constitution"; "but," say they, *"where the law is not prohibited and is really calculated to effect any of the objects intrusted to the Government, to undertake here to inquire into the degree of its necessity would be to pass the line which circumscribes the judicial department and to tread on legislative ground."*

The principle here affirmed is that the "degree of its necessity," involving all the details of a banking institution, is a question exclusively for legislative consideration. A bank is constitutional, but it is the province of the Legislature to determine whether this or that particular power, privilege, or exemption is "necessary and proper" to enable the bank to discharge its duties to the Government, and from their decision there is no appeal to the courts of justice. Under the decision of the Supreme Court, therefore, it is the exclusive province of Congress and the President to decide whether the particular features of this act are *necessary* and *proper* in order to enable the bank to perform conveniently and efficiently the public duties assigned to it as a fiscal agent, and therefore constitutional, or *unnecessary* and *improper,* and therefore unconstitutional. . . .

The bank is professedly established as an agent of the executive branch of the Government, and its constitutionality is maintained on that ground. Neither upon the propriety of present action nor upon the provisions of this act was the Executive consulted. It has had no opportunity to say that it neither needs nor wants an agent clothed with such powers and favored by such exemptions. There is nothing in its legitimate functions which makes it necessary or proper. Whatever interest or influence, whether public or private, has given birth to this act, it can not be found either in the wishes or necessities of the executive department, by which present action is deemed premature, and the powers conferred upon its agent not only unnecessary, but dangerous to the Government and country. . . .

Nor is our Government to be maintained or our Union preserved by invasions of the rights and powers of the several States. In thus attempting to make our General Government strong we make it weak. Its true strength consists in leaving individuals and States as much as possible to themselves—in making itself felt, not in its power, but in its beneficence; not in its control, but in its protection; not in binding the States more closely to the center, but leaving each to move unobstructed in its proper orbit.

Experience should teach us wisdom. Most of the difficulties

our Government now encounters and most of the dangers which impend over our Union have sprung from an abandonment of the legitimate objects of Government by our national legislation, and the adoption of such principles as are embodied in this act. Many of our rich men have not been content with equal protection and equal benefits, but have besought us to make them richer by act of Congress. By attempting to gratify their desires we have in the results of our legislation arrayed section against section, interest against interest, and man against man, in a fearful commotion which threatens to shake the foundations of our Union. It is time to pause in our career to review our principles, and if possible revive that devoted patriotism and spirit of compromise which distinguished the sages of the Revolution and the fathers of our Union. If we can not at once, in justice to interests vested under improvident legislation, make our Government what it ought to be, we can at least take a stand against all new grants of monopolies and exclusive privileges, against any prostitution of our Government to the advancement of the few at the expense of the many, and in favor of compromise and gradual reform in our code of laws and system of political economy.

I have now done my duty to my country. If sustained by my fellow-citizens, I shall be grateful and happy; if not, I shall find in the motives which impel me ample grounds for contentment and peace.

President Roosevelt's Radio Broadcast, March 9, 1937

During President Franklin D. Roosevelt's first term (1933–1937), the Supreme Court by a vote of five to four invalidated much of his New Deal program and plan for the country's economic recovery from the Great Depression. After his landslide reelection in November 1936, FDR proposed in February 1937 that Congress expand the size of the Court from nine to fifteen justices, and thereby give him the chance to secure a majority sympathetic to his policies. On March 9, 1937, the Democratic president made the following radio address in an effort to marshal public support for his "Court-packing plan." But that same month, while the Senate Judiciary Committee was considering his proposal, Justice Owen Roberts, who had previously cast the crucial vote for overturning progressive economic legislation, switched sides and voted to uphold New Deal legislation. The Court's proverbial

---

* From 1937 *Public Papers and Addresses of Franklin D. Roosevelt* (1941), 122.

"switch-in-time-that-saved-nine" then contributed to the Democrat-dominated Senate's defeat of FDR's proposal. The constitutional crisis that loomed over the Court and the country in 1937 is discussed further in Vol. 1, Ch. 6 and in Vol. 2, Ch. 3.

Tonight, sitting at my desk in the White House, I make my first radio report to the people in my second term of office.

I am reminded of that evening in March, four years ago, when I made my first radio report to you. We were then in the midst of the great banking crisis.

Soon after, with the authority of the Congress, we asked the Nation to turn over all of its privately held gold, dollar for dollar, to the Government of the United States.

Today's recovery proves how right that policy was.

But when, almost two years later, it came before the Supreme Court its constitutionality was upheld only by a five-to-four vote. The change of one vote would have thrown all the affairs of this great Nation back into hopeless chaos. In effect, four Justices ruled that the right under a private contract to exact a pound of flesh was more sacred than the main objectives of the Constitution to establish an enduring Nation.

In 1933 you and I knew that we must never let our economic system get completely out of joint again—that we could not afford to take the risk of another great depression.

We also became convinced that the only way to avoid a repetition of those dark days was to have a government with power to prevent and to cure the abuses and the inequalities which had thrown that system out of joint.

We then began a program of remedying those abuses and inequalities—to give balance and stability to our economic system—to make it bomb-proof against the causes of 1929.

Today we are only part-way through that program—and recovery is speeding up to a point where the dangers of 1929 are again becoming possible, not this week or month perhaps, but within a year or two.

National laws are needed to complete that program. Individual or local or state effort alone cannot protect us in 1937 any better than ten years ago.

It will take time—and plenty of time—to work out our remedies administratively even after legislation is passed. To complete our program of protection in time, therefore, we cannot delay one moment in making certain that our National Government has power to carry through.

Four years ago action did not come until the eleventh hour. It was almost too late.

If we learned anything from the depression we will not allow ourselves to run around in new circles of futile discussion and debate, always postponing the day of decision.

The American people have learned from the depression. For in the last three national elections an overwhelming majority of them voted a mandate that the Congress and the President begin the task of providing that protection—not after long years of debate, but now.

The Courts, however, have cast doubts on the ability of the elected Congress to protect us against catastrophe by meeting squarely our modern social and economic conditions.

We are at a crisis in our ability to proceed with that protection. It is a quiet crisis. There are no lines of depositors outside closed banks. But to the far-sighted it is far-reaching in its possibilities of injury to America.

I want to talk with you very simply about the need for present action in this crisis—the need to meet the unanswered challenge of one-third of a Nation ill-nourished, ill-clad, ill-housed.

Last Thursday I described the American form of Government as a three horse team provided by the Constitution to the American people so that their field might be plowed. The three horses are, of course, the three branches of government—the Congress, the Executive and the Courts. Two of the horses are pulling in unison today; the third is not. Those who have intimated that the President of the United States is trying to drive that team, overlook the simple fact that the President, as Chief Executive, is himself one of the three horses.

It is the American people themselves who are in the driver's seat.

It is the American people themselves who want the furrow plowed.

It is the American people themselves who expect the third horse to pull in unison with the other two.

I hope that you have re-read the Constitution of the United States. Like the Bible, it ought to be read again and again.

It is an easy document to understand when you remember that it was called into being because the Articles of Confederation under which the original thirteen States tried to operate after the Revolution showed the need of a National Government with power enough to handle national problems. In its Preamble, the Constitution states that it was intended to form a more perfect Union and promote the general welfare; and the powers given to the Congress to carry out those purposes can be best described by saying that they were all the powers needed to meet each and every problem which then had a national character and which could not be met by merely local action.

But the framers went further. Having in mind that in succeeding generations many other problems then undreamed of would become national problems, they gave to the Congress the ample broad powers "to levy taxes . . . and provide for the common defense and general welfare of the United States."

That, my friends, is what I honestly believe to have been the clear and underlying purpose of the patriots who wrote a Federal Constitution to create a National Government with national power, intended as they said, "to form a more perfect union . . . for ourselves and our posterity."

For nearly twenty years there was no conflict between the Congress and the Court. Then, in 1803, Congress passed a statute which the Court said violated an express provision of the Constitution. The Court claimed the power to declare it unconstitutional and did so declare it. But a little later the Court itself admitted that it was an extraordinary power to exercise and through Mr. Justice Washington laid down this limitation upon it: "It is but a decent respect due to the wisdom, the integrity and the patriotism of the Legislative body, by which any law is passed, to presume in favor of its validity until its violation of the Constitution is proved beyond all reasonable doubt."

But since the rise of the modern movement for social and economic progress through legislation, the Court has more and more often and more and more boldly asserted a power to veto laws passed by the Congress and State Legislatures in complete disregard of this original limitation.

In the last four years the sound rule of giving statutes the benefit of all reasonable doubt has been cast aside. The Court has been acting not as a judicial body, but as a policy-making body.

When the Congress has sought to stabilize national agriculture, to improve the conditions of labor, to safeguard business against unfair competition, to protect our national resources, and in many other ways, to serve our clearly national needs, the majority of the Court has been assuming the power to pass on the wisdom of these Acts of the Congress—and to approve or disapprove the public policy written into these laws.

That is not only my accusation. It is the accusation of most distinguished Justices of the present Supreme Court. I have not the time to quote to you all the language used by dissenting Justices in many of these cases. But in the case holding the Railroad Retirement Act unconstitutional, for instance, Chief Justice Hughes said in a dissenting opinion that the majority opinion was "a departure from sound principles," and placed "an unwarranted limitation upon the commerce clause." And three other Justices agreed with him.

In the case holding the A.A.A. unconstitutional, Justice Stone said of the majority opinion that it was a "tortured construction of the Constitution." And two other Justices agreed with him.

In the case holding the New York Minimum Wage Law unconstitutional, Justice Stone said that the majority were actually reading into the Constitution their own "personal economic predilections," and that if the legislative power is not left free to choose the methods of solving the problems of poverty, subsistence and health of large numbers in the community, then "government is to be rendered impotent." And two other Justices agreed with him.

In the face of these dissenting opinions, there is no basis for the claim made by some members of the Court that something in the Constitution has compelled them regretfully to thwart the will of the people.

In the face of such dissenting opinions, it is perfectly clear, that as Chief Justice Hughes has said: "We are under a Constitution but the Constitution is what the Judges say it is."

The Court in addition to the proper use of its judicial functions has improperly set itself up as a third House of the Congress— a super-legislature, as one of the Justices has called it—reading into the Constitution words and implications which are not there, and which were never intended to be there.

We have, therefore, reached the point as a Nation where we must take action to save the Constitution from the Court and the Court from itself. We must find a way to take an appeal from the Supreme Court to the Constitution itself. We want a Supreme Court which will do justice under the Constitution— not over it. In our Courts we want a government of laws and not of men.

I want—as all Americans want—an independent judiciary as proposed by the framers of the Constitution. That means a Supreme Court that will enforce the Constitution as written—that will refuse to amend the Constitution by the arbitrary exercise of judicial power—amendment by judicial say-so. It does not mean a judiciary so independent that it can deny the existence of facts universally recognized.

How then could we proceed to perform the mandate given us? It was said in last year's Democratic platform "If these problems cannot be effectively solved within the Constitution, we shall seek such clarifying amendment as will assure the power to enact those laws, adequately to regulate commerce, protect public health and safety, and safeguard economic security." In other words, we said we would seek an amendment only if every other possible means by legislation were to fail.

When I commenced to review the situation with the problem squarely before me, I came by a process of elimination to the conclusion that short of amendments the only method which was clearly constitutional, and would at the same time carry out other much needed reforms, was to infuse new blood into all our Courts. We must have men worthy and equipped to carry out impartial justice. But, at the same time, we must have Judges who will bring to the Courts a present-day sense of the Constitution—Judges who will retain in the Courts the judicial functions of a court, and reject the legislative powers which the Courts have today assumed. . . .

What is my proposal? It is simply this: whenever a Judge or Justice of any Federal Court has reached the age of seventy and does not avail himself of the opportunity to retire on a pension, a new member shall be appointed by the President then in office, with the approval, as required by the Constitution, of the Senate of the United States.

That plan has two chief purposes. By bringing into the Judicial system a steady and continuing stream of new and younger blood, I hope, first, to make the administration of all Federal justice speedier and, therefore, less costly; secondly, to bring to the decision of social and economic problems younger men who have had personal experience and contact with modern facts and circumstances under which average men have to live and work. This plan will save our national Constitution from hardening of the judicial arteries.

The number of Judges to be appointed would depend wholly on the decision of present Judges now over seventy, or those who would subsequently reach the age of seventy.

If, for instance, any one of the six Justices of the Supreme Court now over the age of seventy should retire as provided under the plan, no additional place would be created. Consequently, although there never can be more than fifteen, there may be only fourteen, or thirteen, or twelve. And there may be only nine.

There is nothing novel or radical about this idea. It seeks to maintain the Federal bench in full vigor. It has been discussed and approved by many persons of high authority ever since a similar proposal passed the House of Representatives in 1869.

Why was the age fixed at seventy? Because the laws of many States, the practice of the Civil Service, the regulations of the Army and Navy, and the rules of many of our Universities and of almost every great private business enterprise, commonly fix the retirement age at seventy years or less.

The statute would apply to all the Courts in the Federal system. There is general approval so far as the lower Federal courts are concerned. The plan has met opposition only so far as the Supreme Court of the United States itself is concerned. If such a plan is good for the lower courts it certainly ought to be equally good for the highest Court from which there is no appeal.

Those opposing this plan have sought to arouse prejudice and fear by crying that I am seeking to "pack" the Supreme Court and that a baneful precedent will be established.

What do they mean by the words "packing the Court"?

Let me answer this question with a bluntness that will end all *honest* misunderstanding of my purposes.

If by that phrase "packing the Court" it is charged that I wish to place on the bench spineless puppets who would disregard the law and would decide specific cases as I wished them to be decided, I make this answer—that no President fit for his office would appoint, and no Senate of honorable men fit for their office would confirm, that kind of appointees to the Supreme Court.

But if by that phrase the charge is made that I would appoint and the Senate would confirm Justices worthy to sit beside present members of the Court who understand those modern conditions—that I will appoint Justices who will not undertake to override the judgment of the Congress on legislative policy—that I will appoint Justices who will act as Justices and not as legislators—if the appointment of such Justices can be called "packing the Courts," then I say that I and with me the vast majority of the American people favor doing just that thing—now.

Is it a dangerous precedent for the Congress to change the number of the Justices? The Congress has always had, and will have, that power. The number of Justices has been changed several times before—in the Administrations of John Adams and Thomas Jefferson,—both signers of the Declaration of Independence—Andrew Jackson, Abraham Lincoln and Ulysses S. Grant.

I suggest only the addition of Justices to the bench in accordance with a clearly defined principle relating to a clearly defined age limit. Fundamentally, if in the future, America cannot trust the Congress it elects to refrain from abuse of our Constitutional usages, democracy will have failed far beyond the importance to it of any kind of precedent concerning the Judiciary. . . .

It is the clear intention of our public policy to provide for a constant flow of new and younger blood into the Judiciary. Normally every President appoints a large number of District and Circuit Judges and a few members of the Supreme Court. Until my first term practically every President of the United States had appointed at least one member of the Supreme Court. President Taft appointed five members and named a Chief Justice—President Wilson three—President Harding four including a Chief Justice—President Coolidge one—President Hoover three including a Chief Justice.

Such a succession of appointments should have provided a Court well-balanced as to age. But chance and the disinclination of individuals to leave the Supreme bench have now given us a Court in which five Justices will be over seventy-five years of age before next June and one over seventy. Thus a sound public policy has been defeated.

I now propose that we establish by law an assurance against any such ill-balanced Court in the future. I propose that hereafter, when a Judge reaches the age of seventy, a new and younger Judge shall be added to the Court automatically. In this way I propose to enforce a sound public policy by law instead of leaving the composition of our Federal Courts, including the highest, to be determined by chance or the personal decision of individuals.

If such a law as I propose is regarded as establishing a new precedent—is it not a most desirable precedent?

Like all lawyers, like all Americans, I regret the necessity of this controversy. But the welfare of the United States, and indeed of the Constitution itself, is what we all must think about first. Our difficulty with the Court today rises not from the Court as an institution but from human beings within it. But we cannot yield our constitutional destiny to the personal judgment of a few men who, being fearful of the future, would deny us the necessary means of dealing with the present.

This plan of mine is no attack on the Court; it seeks to restore the Court to its rightful and historic place in our system of Constitutional Government and to have it resume its high task of building anew on the Constitution "a system of living law."

B. THE POLITICS OF CONSTITUTIONAL INTERPRETATION

Constitutional interpretation and law, Justice Felix Frankfurter observed, "is not at all a science, but applied politics."[1] The Constitution, of course, is a political document and as a written document is not self-interpreting; its interpretation is political. *How* the Constitution should be interpreted is thus as controversial as the ongoing debate over *who* should interpret it.

For much of the nineteenth century, theories of constitutional interpretation were generally not debated.[2] The Court's interpretation of the Constitution, of course, remained politically controversial. Yet, the great debates between Jeffersonian-Republicans and Federalists centered on disagreements over fundamental principles of constitutional politics (the power and structure of government and guarantees for civil rights and liberties), rather than competing interpretative theories. Their struggle was over rival political philosophies and interpretations of the political system created by the Constitution. That struggle continues except that contemporary debates, within the Court and the legal community, tend to be more complex and linked to rival theories of constitutional interpretation that aim to justify or criticize the Court's exercise of judicial review.

In 1833, for example, Justice Joseph Story in his influential *Commentaries on the Constitution of the United States* saw no need to offer a theory of constitutional interpretation, explaining that,

[t]he reader must not expect to find in these pages any novel views and novel constructions of the Constitution. I have not the ambition to be the author of any new plan of interpreting the theory of the Constitution, or of enlarging or narrowing its powers by ingenious subtleties and learned doubts. . . . Upon subjects of government, it has always appeared to me, that metaphysical refinements are out of place. A constitution of government is addressed to the common sense of the people, and never was designed for trials of logical skill or visionary speculation.[3]

Story assumed that "The first and fundamental rule in the interpretation of all instruments is, to construe them according to the sense of the terms and the intention of the parties."[4] This "plain meaning rule" was set forth by Chief Justice John Marshall in *Struges v. Crowninshield*, 17 U.S. 122 (1819):

[A]lthough the spirit of an instrument, especially of a constitution, is to be respected not less than its letter, yet the spirit is to be collected chiefly from its words. . . . [I]f, in any case, the plain meaning of a provision, not contradicted by any other provision in the same instrument, is to be disregarded, because we believe the framers of that instrument could not intend what they say, it must be one in which the absurdity and injustice of applying the provision to the case, would be so monstrous that all mankind would, without hesitation, unite in rejecting the application.

While the plain meaning of the Constitution for Story and Marshall was derived from a commonsense, rather than a literal, reading of the Constitution, Jeffersonian-Republicans nevertheless charged them with distorting the plain meaning of the document to advance their nationalistic political vision.

One reason political struggles in the nineteenth century did not invite debates over competing theories of constitutional interpretation is that Federalists and Jeffersonian-Republicans largely professed acceptance of the English declaratory theory of law. This theory, or philosophy, of legal positivism holds that judges have no discretion, make no law, but simply discover and "declare" the law.[5] According to one of the most widely read English jurists, Sir William Blackstone, in his *Commentaries on the Laws of England* (1765–1768), judges were merely the "depositories of the laws; the living oracles" of law. Hamilton and Marshall considered themselves Blacktonians; judges, Hamilton wrote in *The Federalist*, No. 78, "may truly be said to have neither FORCE nor WILL, but merely judgment."

By the late nineteenth century, the Blackstonian theory of law was under sharp attack. Oliver Wendell Holmes (1841–1935) was one of the first to debunk the idea that law is "a brooding omnipresence in the sky."[6] In his words, "The life of the law has not been logic; it has been experience. The felt necessities of the time, the prevalent moral and political theories, intuitions of public policy, avowed or unconscious, even the prejudices which judges share with their fellow-men, have had a good deal more to do than the syllogism in determining the rules by which men should be governed."[7] Holmes took it for granted that judges make law and pointed toward the empirical study of law: "The prophecies of what the courts will do in fact, and nothing more pretentious, are what I mean by the law."[8] Nor was Holmes alone in the revolt against legal formalism and the "mechanical jurisprudence" associated with the declaratory theory of judicial decision making.[9] Roscoe Pound (1870–1964), the founder of "sociological jurisprudence" and dean of Harvard Law School, encouraged the use of sociology and the study of law in relation to changing social forces. Unlike Holmes, though, Pound also encouraged judges to creatively mold law to the needs of society; judges should become "social engineers."[10]

One immediate consequence of this revolt against legal formalism was the innovation in legal argumentation that became known as "the Brandeis brief," after its author, a progressive legal reformer and later justice, Louis D. Brandeis. In 1908, in support of Oregon's law limiting working hours for women, Brandeis filed a brief in *Muller v. Oregon*, 208 U.S. 412 (1908), which included only two pages of legal argumentation, followed by ninety-seven pages of statistics and other social science data documenting the health risks for women working long hours. Drawing on social science in legal argumentation was necessary, claimed Brandeis, if law was to keep "pace with the rapid development of our political, economic, and social ideals."[11]

In the 1920s and 1930s a diverse group of law professors, political scientists, economists and sociologists, emerged calling themselves "American legal realists."[12] They further questioned the determinancy of formal legal rules and the facts of cases for judicial decision making, thereby underscoring that judges interpret (and manipulate) both legal rules and the facts when deciding cases.[13] Karl Llewellyn, one of the most influential legal realists, brought these insights to bear on constitutional interpretation when calling for a "jurisprudence of a living Constitution":

A "written constitution" is a system of unwritten practices in which the Document in question, by virtue of men's attitudes, has *a little influence. Where it makes no important difference which way the decision goes,* the Text—in the absence of countervailing practice—is an excellent traffic light. . . . The view advanced here *sounds* unorthodox. It sounds unorthodox only because it puts into words the *tacit* doing of the Court, and draws from that doing conclusions not to be avoided by a candid child. . . . Whatever the Court has *said*, it has repeatedly turned to established governmental practice in search of norms. What the Court has *said*, it has shaped the living Constitution to the needs of the day as it felt them. The whole expansion of the due process clause has been an enforcement of the majority's ideal of government-as-it-should-be, running free of the language of the Document.[14]

The Supreme Court was not immune from this change in legal thinking. On the bench sat Holmes (1902–1932), Brandeis (1916–1939), Benjamin Cardozo (1932–1938),[15] and Felix Frankfurter (1939–1962), among other legal progressives. Moreover, even judicial conservatives on the Court no longer denied that the process of interpreting the Constitution involves making law. As Chief Justice Harlan F. Stone, a political and judicial conservative, reflected in a letter to Edward Corwin, "I always thought the real villain in the play was Blackstone, who gave to both lawyers and judges artificial notions of the law which, when applied to constitutional interpretation made the Constitutional a mechanical and inadequate instrument of government."[16] Justice Frankfurter, a former liberal professor at Harvard Law School who became an advocate of judicial self-restraint on the bench, elaborated his view in a letter to Justice Hugo Black:

> I think one of the evil features, a very evil one, about all this assumption that judges only find the law and don't make it, often becomes the evil of a lack of candor. By covering up the law-making function of judges, we miseducate the people and fail to bring out into the open the real responsibility of judges for what they do. . . .

> That phrase "judicial legislation" has become ever since a staple of a term of condemnation. I, too, am opposed to judicial legislation in its invidious sense; but I deem equally mischievous—because founded on an untruth and an impossible aim—the notion that judges merely announce the law which they find and do not themselves inevitably have a share in the law-making. Here, as elsewhere, the difficulty comes from arguing in terms of absolutes when the matter at hand is conditioned by circumstances, is contingent upon the everlasting problem of how far is too far and how much is too much. Judges as you well know, cannot escape the responsibility of filling in gaps which the finitude of even the most imaginative legislation renders inevitable. . . .

> So the problem is not whether judges make the law, but when and how and how much. Holmes put it in his highbrow way, that "they can do so only interstitially; they are confined from molar to molecular motions." I used to say to my students that legislatures make law wholesale, judges retail.[17]

Once constitutional interpretation was candidly conceded to be a lawmaking process, the Court and its commentators squarely faced what has been called the Madisonian dilemma and "the countermajoritarian difficulty" for judicial review. As former judge and unsuccessful 1987 Supreme Court nominee Robert Bork explains,

The United States was founded as what we now call a Madisonian system, one which allows majorities to rule in wide areas of life simply because they are majorities, but which also holds that individuals have some freedoms that must be exempt from majority control. The dilemma is that neither the majority nor the minority can be trusted to define the proper spheres of democratic authority and individual liberty. The first would court tyranny by the majority; the second tyranny by the minority.[18]

When overturning legislation, the Court exercises a countermajoritarian power and substitutes its interpretation of the Constitution for that of elected representatives. Theories or rationalizations of the Court's interpretation of the Constitution thus appear necessary to justify the Court's countermajoritarian role in American politics, especially in the last fifty years as the Court increasingly overturned legislation in defense of civil rights and liberties.

In addition, in the aftermath of the American legal realist movement, legal scholarship became more pluralistic and interdisciplinary. Again quoting Judge Bork:

The fact is that the law has little intellectual or structural resistence to outside influences, influences that should properly remain outside. The striking, and peculiar, fact . . . is that the law possesses very little theory about itself. . . . This theoretical emptiness at its center makes law, particularly constitutional law, unstable, a ship with a great deal of sail but a very shallow keel, vulnerable to the winds of intellectual or moral fashion, which it then validates as the commands of our most basic compact.[19]

Since World War II, legal scholars have turned not only toward moral and political philosophy as a guide for constitutional interpretation and the Court's exercise of judicial review, they have also called for the development of a "political jurisprudence," combining normative theory with empirical studies;[20] an economic approach to law, which would make rights turn on cost-risk-benefit analysis;[21] and drawn on theories of literary criticism.[22] Still others in the Critical Legal Studies movement attack theories of liberal legalism in an effort to deconstruct legal reasoning and law to show its drawbacks for minorities, women, and the poor.[23]

The rest of this section surveys and illustrates various theories of constitutional interpretation in terms of two broad approaches that have come to be known as *interpretivism* and *noninterpretivism*. Broadly speaking, interpretivists hold that constitutional interpretation should be limited solely to the text and historical context of particular provisions of the Constitution and Bill of Rights. By contrast, noninterpretivists maintain that constitutional interpretation frequently requires going beyond the text and historical context of specific provisions to articulate and apply broader principles of constitutional politics. Neither approach is inextricably linked to either a liberal or a conservative political philosophy; for example, a predominately conservative Court in the late nineteenth century invented and wrote into constitutional law a "liberty of contract" to strike down progressive economic legislation (see Vol. 2, Ch. 3), while in the twentieth century a more liberal Court proclaimed and enforced a "right of privacy" to overturn legislation restricting the use of contraceptives and the availability of abortions (see Vol. 2, Ch. 11).

NOTES

1. Felix Frankfurter, in *Law and Politics,* ed. E. Prichard, Jr., and Archibald Macleish (New York: Harcourt, Brace, 1939), 6.

2. See Robert H. Bork, "Styles in Constitutional Theory," 1984 *Supreme Court Historical Society Yearbook* 53 (1985).

3. Joseph Story, *Commentaries on the Constitution of the United States* (Durham, NC: Carolina Academic Press, 1987), vi, reprint of 1833 ed.

4. Ibid., 135.

5. See, generally, Lord Lloyd, *Lloyd's Introduction to Jurisprudence,* 5th ed. (London: Stevens & Sons, 1985); H. L. A. Hart, *Essays in Jurisprudence and Philosophy* (Oxford, UK: Claredon Press, 1983), Chs. 1–5, 13; William Nelson, *Americanization of the Common Law* (Cambridge: Harvard University Press, 1975); and Morton Horwitz, *The Transformation of American Law, 1780–1860* (Cambridge: Harvard University Press, 1977).

6. *Southern Pacific Co. v. Jensen,* 244 U.S. 205 (1916).

7. Oliver W. Holmes, *The Common Law* (Boston: Little, Brown, 1881), 1.

8. Oliver W. Holmes, "The Path of Law," 10 *Harvard Law Review* 39 (1897).

9. See, generally, Morton White, *Social Thought in America: The Revolt against Formalism* (New York: Viking Press, 1949); and Benjamin Twiss, *Lawyers and the Constitution* (Princeton, NJ: Princeton University Press, 1942).

10. See Roscoe Pound, *An Introduction to the Philosophy of Law* (New Haven, CT: Yale University Press, 1922).

11. Louis Brandeis, "The Living Law," 10 *Illinois Law Review* 461 (1916).

12. See Wilfred Rumble, *American Legal Realism* (Ithica, NY: Cornell University Press, 1968).

13. See Jerome Frank, *Law and the Modern Mind* (New York: Coward-McCann, 1930), and *Courts on Trial* (Princeton, NJ: Princeton University Press, 1949).

14. Karl Llewellyn, "The Constitution As an Institution," 34 *Columbia Law Review* 39–40 (1934).

15. See Benjamin Cardozo's highly acclaimed *The Nature of the Judicial Process* (New York: Yale University Press, 1921).

16. Letter to E. Corwin, November 5, 1942, in Harlan F. Stone Papers, Box 10, Library of Congress, Washington, DC

17. Letter to Justice Black, December 15, 1939, in Stone Papers, Box 13.

18. Bork, "Styles in Constitutional Theory," 53.

19. Robert H. Bork, "Tradition and Morality in Constitutional Law," in *Views from the Bench: The Judiciary and Constitutional Politics*, ed. Mark Cannon and David M. O'Brien (Chatham, NJ: Chatham House, 1985), 166.

20. See Martin Shapiro, "Political Jurisprudence," 52 *Kentucky Law Review* 294 (1964); Harry Stumpf, Martin Shapiro, David Danelski, Austin Sarat, and David O'Brien, "Whither Political Jurisprudence?: A Symposium," 36 *Western Political Quarterly* 533 (1984); and Rogers Smith, "Political Jurisprudence, The 'New Institutionalism,' and the Future of Public Law," 82 *American Political Science Review* 89 (1988).

21. See, for example, Richard Posner, *Economic Analysis of Law*, 2d ed. (Boston: Little, Brown, 1977).

22. See William Bishin and Christopher Stone, *Law, Language and Ethics* (Mineola, NY: Foundation Press, 1972); John Brigham, *Constitutional Language* (Westport, CT: Greenwood Press, 1978); Leif Carter, *Contemporary Constitutional Lawmaking* (New York: Pergamon, 1985); James White, *The Legal Imagination* (Chicago: University of Chicago Press, 1973); James White, *When Words Lose Their Meaning* (Chicago: Chicago University Press, 1984); Richard Posner, *Law and Literature: A Misunderstood Relation* (Cambridge: Harvard University Press, 1988); and James White, *Justice as Translation* (Chicago: University of Chicago Press, 1990).

23. See David Kairys, ed., *The Politics of Law* (New York: Pantheon, 1982); and Editors of the Harvard Law Review, *Essays on Critical Legal Studies* (Cambridge: Harvard Law Review Association, 1986).

(1) The Text and Historical Context

The Supreme Court has been criticized by presidents from Thomas Jefferson to Ronald Reagan and George Bush for departing from a "strict" or "literal" interpretation of the Constitution. During the 1968 presidential election campaign, for instance, Republican nominee Richard Nixon attacked the "liberal jurisprudence" of the Warren Court (1953–1969) and promised to appoint only strict constructionists to the bench. *Strict constructionists* hold that constitutional interpretation should be confined to the "four corners" of the document, the literal language of the text of the Constitution.

Within the Court, Chief Justice Roger Taney expressed a strong version of strict constructionism in *Dred Scott v. Sandford,* 60 U.S. 393 (1857) (see Vol. 2, Ch. 12), when holding that blacks were not citizens of the United States within the meaning of "citizens" in Article III:

No one, we presume, supposes that any change in public opinion or feeling, in relation to this unfortunate race [of blacks], in the civilized nations of Europe or in this country, should induce the court to give to the words of the Constitution a more liberal construction in their favor than they were intended to bear when the instrument was framed and adopted. . . .

It [the Constitution] speaks not only in the same words, but with the same meaning and intent with which it spoke when it came from the hands of its framers, and was voted on and adopted by the people of the United States. Any other rule of construction would abrogate the judicial character of this Court and make it the mere reflex of the popular opinion or passion of the day.

This version of strict constructionism unrealistically (or disingenuously) denies the basic choices involved in constitutional interpretation. For example, much turns on whether the Court analyzes church-state controversies from the perspective of the First Amendment's free exercise clause or its establishment clause (see Vol. 2, Ch. 6). When applying the Fourth Amendment's guarantee against "unreasonable searches and seizures," the Warren Court chose to enforce strictly the requirements specified in that amendment's warrants and probable cause clauses. By contrast, the Burger Court (1969–1986), and the Rehnquist Court (1986–), tended to give less force to those requirements by relying instead on the justices' reading of what is "reasonable" under the amendment's reasonableness clause. Whether the Fourth Amendment is enforced primarily in terms of its reasonableness clause or its warrants and probable cause clauses represents a basic constitutional choice with important consequences for individual rights and law enforcement interests (see Vol. 2, Ch. 7).

Justice Hugo Black claimed to be an "absolutist," a "literalist." In his words:

My view is, without deviation, without exception, without any if's, but's, or whereas, that freedom of speech means that government shall not do anything to people, or, in the words of the Magna Carta, move against people, either for the views they have or the views they express or the words they speak or write. Some people would have you believe that this is a very radical position, and maybe it is. But all I am doing is following what to me is the clear wording of the First Amendment that "Congress shall make no law . . . abridging the freedom of speech or of the press."[1]

However, Justice Black acknowledged that the Constitution presents some interpretive problems and constitutional choices. In the controversy over the Court's application of the Bill of Rights to the states under the Fourteenth Amendment, for instance, Black became convinced that those guarantees were included in the amendment's privileges or immunities clause, whereas other justices contended that they were included in the Fourteenth Amendment's due process clause (see Vol. 2, Ch. 4).

Justice Black's absolutism was in response to the Court's *balancing* of First Amendment freedoms against governmental interests in national security in cases like *Dennis v. United States*, 341 U.S. 494 (1951) (see Vol. 2, Ch. 5), under the guise of the "clear and present danger" test. He opposed the Court's invention and use of such tests and metaphors. Still, much of constitutional law consists in metaphors created by the Court when explaining and applying constitutional provisions; consider the debates over executive privilege (see Vol. 1, Ch. 4), states' sovereignty (see Vol. 1, Ch. 4), the liberty of contract (see Vol. 2, Ch. 3), the high wall of separation between church and state (see Vol. 2, Ch. 6), or the controversy over whether the Constitution is colorblind (see Vol. 2, Ch. 12).

Interpretivism is usually only the beginning, not the end, of constitutional interpretation. The most frequently contested guarantees of the Constitution are neither unambiguous nor amenable to a literal or strict interpretation. What is the literal meaning of the reasonableness clause of the Fourth Amendment or of the due process and equal protection clauses of the Fourteenth Amendment? Nor do interpretivists, like Justice Black, deny First Amendment protection for posters and songs on the ground that they are not strictly speaking "speech"; although Black drew a line at extending protection to speech-plus-conduct and "symbolic speech" (see Vol. 2, Ch. 5).

Crucial provisions in the Constitution have what philosophers call an "open texture."[2] They are framed in general terms that are nonexhaustive of all future applications and have an essential incompleteness in dictating unforeseeable applications. The commerce clause in Article I, for example, gives Congress the power to regulate interstate commerce but fails to define *interstate commerce*. No one today, though, contends that interstate commerce should include only the methods of transportation available in 1787 or exclude modes of commerce, such as telecommunications, that were unforeseen by the Constitutional Convention.

These are only some of the problems with strict constructionism, as federal court of appeals Judge Richard Posner notes in an essay titled, "What Am I? A Potted Plant? The Case against

Strict Constructionism." Moreover, Posner underscores that nothing in the Constitution commands the Court to construe either "strictly" or "broadly" the document:

> Even the decision to read the Constitution narrowly, and thereby "re-strain" judicial interpretation, is not a decision that can be read directly from the text. The Constitution does not say, "Read me broadly," "Read me narrowly." That decision must be made a matter of political theory, and will depend on such things as one's view of the springs of judicial legitimacy and of the relative competence of courts and legislatures in dealing with particular types of issues.[3]

Strict constructionism is incomplete as a theory of interpretation and inadequately deals with the fact that the Constitution was framed in generalities in order to express general principles. Because this is so, interpretivists often turn to the historical context of the Constitution. Consider, for example, the 1985 call for a *jurisprudence of original intention* by Ronald Reagan's attorney general, Edwin Meese III:

> As the "faithful guardians of the Constitution," the judges were expected to resist any political effort to depart from the literal provisions of the Constitution. The test of the document and the original intention of those who framed it would be the judicial standard in giving effect to the Constitution. . . . [But] it seems fair to conclude that far too many of the court's opinions are, on the whole, more policy choices than articulations of constitutional principle. The voting blocs, the arguments, all reveal a greater allegiance to what the court thinks constitutes sound public policy than a deference to what the Constitution—its text and intention—demand.[4]

Meese was not the first to contend that the text and the Framers' intent should solely guide constitutional interpretation.[5] Nonetheless, he sparked considerable debate and provoked Justice William J. Brennan to respond in a speech, observing,

> In its most doctrinaire incarnation, this view demands that Justices discern exactly what the Framers thought about the question under consideration and simply follow that intention in resolving the case before them. It is a view that feigns self-effacing deference to the specific judgments of those who forged our original social compact. But in truth it is little more than arrogance cloaked as humility. It is arrogant to pretend that from our vantage we can gauge accurately the intent of the Framers on application of principle to specific, contemporary questions. All too often, sources of potential enlightenment such as records of the ratification debates provide sparse or ambiguous evidence of the original intention. Typically, all that can be gleaned is that the Framers themselves did not agree about the application or meaning of particular constitutional provisions, and hid their differences in cloaks of generality. Indeed, it is far from clear whose intention is relevant—that of the drafters, the congressional disputants, or the ratifiers in

the states?—or even whether the idea of an original intention is a coherent way of thinking about a jointly drafted document drawing its authority from a general assent of the states. And apart from the problematic nature of the sources, our distance of two centuries cannot but work as a prism refracting all we perceive. . . .

We current Justices read the Constitution in the only way that we can: as Twentieth Century Americans. We look to the history of the time of framing and to the intervening history of interpretation. But the ultimate question must be, what do the words of the text mean in our time. For the genius of the Constitution rests not in any static meaning it might have had in a world that is dead and gone, but in the adaptability of its great principles to cope with current problems and current needs. What the Constitution's fundamentals meant to the wisdom of other times cannot be their measure to the vision of our time. Similarly, what those fundamentals mean for us, our descendants will learn, cannot be the measure to the vision of their time.[6]

As Justice Brennan suggests, there are methodological difficulties with a "jurisprudence of original intention." For one thing, determining "intent" is a subjective enterprise; it proposes to discover what the Framers had in mind when drafting and ratifying the Constitution. But as already noted, the Framers often disagreed and were forced to compromise on the language of the Constitution. At best, this approach considers the intentions of the drafters and ratifiers of the Constitution. And, who are "the Framers"? Should the views of only the thirty-nine signers of the document be considered, or should those of the other sixteen delegates who left before the Constitutional Convention concluded or refused to sign the document be considered as well? There are also compelling reasons for including the views of delegates to the thirteen state ratifying conventions, for as a result of those conventions the Bill of Rights was immediately added to the Constitution (see Vol. 2, Ch. 4).

Problems with discovering the intentions of the Framers also arise because the proceedings of the Constitutional Convention were conducted in secrecy and records of that convention and those in the states are far from complete and reliable. Moreover, it is debatable that the Framers intended their intentions to limit or guide constitutional interpretation.[7] Not until 1819 were speeches, resolutions, and votes of the delegates to the Constitutional Convention published. Almost another decade passed before Jonathan Elliot began publishing his collection of the debates in the state ratifying conventions. James Madison, who took notes of the debates at the Constitutional Convention and whose notes provide the only full record, refused to allow the publication of his notes until 1840, after his death. Madison insisted that the intent and literal reading of the text would be a "hard rule of construction." Instead, among the "obvious and just guides applicable to the Constn. of the U.S.," he listed:

1. the evils & defects for curing which the Constitution was called for & introduced. 2. The comments prevailing at the times it was adopted. 3. The early, deliberate & continued practice under the Constitution as preferable to constructions adopted on the spur of occasions, and subject to the vicissitudes of party or personal considerations.[8]

In addition, it bears noting that in its first fifty years the Supreme Court infrequently cited works such as *The Federalist Papers* in its opinions. Between 1790 and 1839, *The Federalist Papers* were cited in only fifteen decisions; by comparison, between 1950 and 1984 they were cited in 108 cases.[9]

Because of these difficulties, Chief Justice William Rehnquist, Justice Antonin Scalia, Judge Bork, and others associated with interpretivism and the "originalist" approach to constitutional interpretation more modestly contend that the Court should remain faithful to the "original understanding" or "original meaning"[10] of the governing principles or political philosophy of the Framers. They do not claim to be uncovering the Framers' subjective intentions but rather limiting the interpretation of constitutional provisions to those principles that the Framers might be fairly said to have embraced when drafting and ratifying the Constitution. Judge Bork explains that

[a] major problem with the idea of original intention is that the Framers articulated their principles in light of the world they knew, a world very different in important respects from that in which judges must decide cases today. . . . In order to protect the freedoms the Framers envisaged, the judge must discern a principle in the applications the Framers thought of and then apply that principle to circumstances they did not foresee.[11]

Nor do Chief Justice Rehnquist, Justice Scalia, and Judge Bork claim that originalism eliminates the burden of making basic constitutional choices. Rather, they argue that this approach is superior to other noninterpretativist approaches because it ostensibly sharply limits the exercise of judicial review and thus proves more responsive to criticisms of the Court's countermajoritarian power. In Justice Scalia words,

The principal theoretical defect of nonoriginalism, in my view, is its incompatibility with the very principle that legitimizes judicial review of constitutionality. Nothing in the text of the Constitution confers upon the courts the power to inquire into, rather than passively assume, the constitutionality of federal statutes. . . . Quite to the contrary, the legislature would seem a much more appropriate expositor of social values, and *its* determination that a statute is compatible with the Constitution should, as in England, prevail.[12]

Justice Scalia concedes that originalism poses methodological problems in practice, but nonetheless claims that it is "the lesser evil" in constitutional interpretation:

[It] *is* true that it is often exceedingly difficult to plumb the original understanding of an ancient text. Properly done, the task requires the consideration of an enormous mass of material—in the case of the Constitution and its Amendments, for example, to mention only one element, the records of the ratifying debates in all the states. Even beyond that, it requires an evaluation of the reliability of that material—many of the reports of the ratifying debates, for example, are thought to be quite unreliable. And further still, it requires immersing oneself in the political and intellectual atmosphere of the time—somehow placing out of mind knowledge that we have which an earlier age did not, and putting on beliefs, attitudes, philosophies, prejudices and loyalties that are not those of our day. It is, in short, a task sometimes better suited to the historian than the lawyer. . . .

I can be much more brief in describing what seems to me the second most serious objection to originalism. In its undiluted form, at least, it is medicine that seems too strong to swallow. Thus, almost every originalist would adulterate it with the doctrine of *stare decisis* [which holds that prior decisions should be respected]. . . . But *stare decisis* alone is not enough to prevent originalism from being what many would consider too bitter a pill. What if some state should enact a new law providing public lashing, or branding of the right hand, as punishment for certain criminal offenses? Even if it could be demonstrated unequivocally that these were not cruel and unusual measures [which are forbidden under the Eighth Amendment] in 1791, and even though no prior Supreme Court decision has specifically disapproved them, I doubt whether any federal judge—even among the many who consider themselves originalists—would sustain them against an eighth amendment challenge. It may well be . . . that this cannot legitimately be reconciled with originalist philosophy—that it represents the unrealistic view of the Constitution as a document intended to create a perfect society for all ages to come, whereas in fact it was a political compromise that did not pretend to create a perfect society even for its own age (as its toleration of slavery, which a majority of the founding generation recognized as an evil, well enough demonstrates). Even so, I am confident that public flogging and hand-branding would not be sustained by our courts, and any espousal of originalism as a practical theory of exegesis must somehow come to terms with that reality.[13]

Justice Scalia's discussion of public flogging and the Eighth Amendment is revealing not only in indicating that he is (in his words) "a faint-hearted originalist," because he would hold public flogging unconstitutional despite the fact that the Framers permitted that practice. The original understanding of constitutional guarantees, as Justice Anthony Kennedy observed during his 1987 Senate confirmation hearings, is a "necessary starting point," not an "adequate methodology" or "mechanical process" that "tells us how to decide a case."

What Scalia's discussion also points out is that crucial *concepts* in the Constitution give rise to competing *conceptions* and political philosophies.[14] Scalia would not limit the concept of cruel and unusual punishment in the Eighth Amendment to the Framers' conception of that punishment in 1791. Nor would Scalia go as far as Justice Brennan in interpreting the Eighth Amendment to bar capital punishment based on his "constitutional vision of human dignity" (see Vol. 2, Ch. 10). But, why not? What divides justices like Scalia and Brennan is their underlying judicial and political philosophies of the Constitution and the exercise of judicial review. So too, just as the Federalists and Anti-Federalists had competing political visions of the separation of powers and federalism, for example, even originalists such as Chief Justice Rehnquist and Justice Scalia may have rival conceptions and interpretations of the separation of powers; see, for instance, *Morrison v. Olson,* 108 S.Ct. 2597 (1988) (see Vol. 1, Ch. 4).

An underlying problem for interpretivists and noninterpretivists is how broadly or narrowly they conceive and express the concept or principle of a constitutional provision. Consider, for example, the constitutional choices presented in interpreting and applying the Fourth Amendment and the equal protection clause of the Fourteenth Amendment.

The Fourth Amendment guarantees the people a right "to be secure in their persons, houses, papers, and effects against unreasonable searches and seizures." That guarantee was interpreted in *Olmstead v. United States,* 277 U.S. 438 (1928) (see Vol. 2, Ch. 7), not to cover wiretaps because a majority of the Court limited the amendment's application to Framers' conception of "unreasonable searches and seizures," giving the lowest level of generality to the amendment's principle, so as to bar only actual physical trespass by police. By contrast, dissenting Justice Louis Brandeis argued for a broader conception of the amendment and a more general principle of privacy in the home that would have extended the guarantees of the amendment to cover electronic surveillance. Almost forty years later, in *Katz v. United States,* 389 U.S. 347 (1967) (see Vol. 2, Ch. 7), the Court finally embraced the broader principle of Fourth Amendment–protected privacy.

The Fourteenth Amendment guarantees "the equal protection of the laws." The principle of equality embodied there might be interpreted to bar only discrimination against blacks, because in the historical context of the post–Civil War period the Thirty-ninth Congress was indisputably primarily concerned with ensuring that states did not deny certain rights of newly freed blacks. However, the principle of equality has been given broader application and a higher level of generality so as to bar other kinds of racial discrimination against, for example, Hispanics and Asians. Even more broadly (as further discussed in Vol. 2, Ch. 12), the amendment has been construed to forbid forms of nonracial discrimination against women, children, and aliens. But how and on what basis may this broader application of the equal protection clause be defended and the Court's exercise of judicial review in this way justified?

In sum and in Judge Bork's words, "The question is always the level of generality the judge chooses when he states the idea or object of the Framers."[15] Interpretivists, no less than noninterpretivists, cannot evade making basic constitutional choices in their conceptions and formulations of the underlying principles of constitutional provisions.

NOTES

1. Hugo Black, *A Constitutional Faith* (New York: Knopf, 1968), 45.

2. See H. L. A. Hart, *The Concept of Law* (Oxford, UK: Clarendon Press, 1961), 124–132.

3. Richard Posner, "What Am I? A Potted Plant?" *The New Republic,* Sept. 28, 1987, 23.

4. Edwin Meese, "The Attorney General's View of the Supreme Court: Toward a Jurisprudence of Original Intention," in *Special Issue, Law and Public Affairs,* ed. Charles Wise and David O'Brien, 45 *Public Administration Review* 701 (1985).

5. See also Raoul Berger, *Government by Judiciary* (Cambridge: Harvard University Press, 1977); and Walter Berns, *Taking the Constitution Seriously* (New York: Simon & Schuster, 1987).

6. William J. Brennan, Jr., "The Constitution of the United States: Contemporary Ratification," Georgetown University, Washington, DC (Oct. 12, 1985).

7. See H. Jefferson Powell, "The Original Understanding of Original Intent," 98 *Harvard Law Review* 885 (1985); and James Hutson, "The Creation of the Constitution: The Integrity of the Documentary Record," 65 *Texas Law Review* 1 (1986).

8. Quoted in Robert Morgan, *James Madison on the Constitution and the Bill of Rights* (Westport, CT: Greenwood Press, 1988), 196–197.

9. See James Wilson, "The Most Sacred Text: The Supreme Court's Use of *The Federalist Papers,*" 1985 *Brigham Young University Law Review* 65 (1985).

10. See Antonin Scalia, "Originalism: The Lesser Evil," 57 *Cincinnati Law Review* 849 (1989).

11. Robert Bork, "Foreword" to Gary McDowell, *The Constitution and Contemporary Constitutional Theory* (Cumberland, VA: Center for Judicial Studies, 1985), x.

12. Scalia, "Originalism," 854.

13. Scalia, "Originalism," 856–857.

14. On the distinction between concepts and conceptions, see Ronald Dworkin, *Taking Rights Seriously* (Cambridge: Harvard University Press, 1977), 135–137.

15. Bork, "Foreword," x.

SELECTED BIBLIOGRAPHY

Berger, Raoul. *Government by Judiciary: The Transformation of the Fourteenth Amendment.* Cambridge: Harvard University Press, 1977.

Berns, Walter. *Taking the Constitution Seriously.* New York: Simon & Schuster, 1987.

Bickel, Alexander. *The Morality of Consent.* New Haven, CT: Yale University Press, 1975.

Black, Hugo. *A Constitutional Faith.* New York: Knopf, 1968.

Bork, Robert. *The Tempting of America.* New York: Free Press, 1989.

Gabin, Sanford. *Judicial Review and the Reasonable Doubt Test.* Port Washington, NY: Kennikat Press, 1980.

Jacobson, Gary. *Pragmatism, Statesmanship, and the Supreme Court.* Ithaca, NY: Cornell University Press, 1977.

Levy, Leonard. *Original Intent and The Framers' Constitution.* New York: Macmillan, 1988.

Nagel, Robert. *Constitutional Cultures.* Berkeley: University of California Press, 1989.

Thayer, Bradley. *Thayer's Legal Essays.* Boston: Boston Book Company, 1908.

(2) In and Beyond the Text

Noninterpretivism differs from interpretivism in the sources and kinds of argumentation marshaled in support of giving broader scope or higher levels of generality to constitutional principles. Whereas interpretivists confine analysis to the text and historical context of a provision, noninterpretivists tend to formulate more broadly the underlying principle of a constitutional provision. Noninterpretivists may turn to history and social science, for example, or appeal to natural law, natural rights, and moral or political philosophy, or call on process-oriented theories of judicial review and arguments about the structure of the Constitution.

Historical, economic, technological, and political changes are obviously relevant to constitutional interpretation. Yet, when and how should the Court use *history*? The Sixth Amendment, for instance, guarantees criminal defendants the right to a jury trial but does not define *jury*. When confronted with the question of whether juries must consist of twelve members, in *Thompson v. Utah*, 170 U.S. 343 (1882), the Court simply ruled that the Sixth Amendment incorporated the traditional common-law practice of twelve-member juries because that practice was firmly rooted in English history and familiar to the Framers of the Bill of Rights. The Court may also take *judicial notice* of historical events without the benefit of their being adjudicated, such as the fact that there was an economic depression in the 1930s. Chief Justice Morrison Waite drew heavily on history as a guide when upholding under the commerce clause the power of Congress, over that of the states, to regulate interstate telegraph lines, in *Pensacola Telegraph Co. v. Western Union Telegraph, Co.,* 96 U.S. 1 (1877):

> The powers thus granted are not confined to the instrumentalities of commerce . . . known or in use when the Constitution was adopted, but they keep pace with the progress of the country, and adapt themselves to the new developments of time and circumstance. They extend from the horse with its rider to the stage-coach, from the sailing-vessel to the steamboat . . . and from the railroad to the telegraph, as these new agencies are successively brought into use to meet the demands of increasing population and wealth. . . . As they were intrusted to the general government for the good of the nation, it is not only the right, but the duty, of Congress to see to it that intercourse among the States and the transmission of intelligence are not obstructed or unnecessarily encumbered by State legislation.

Justice Holmes took an even more expansive view of the use of history in the famous case dealing with the national government's treaty-making power. In *Missouri v. Holland,* 252 U.S. 416 (1920) (see Vol. 1, Ch. 3). Note his observation that "[t]he case before us must be considered in light of our whole experience and not merely in that of what was said a hundred years ago."

The Court's reliance on history is not unproblematic, however.[1] Justices are not trained as historians and they may confront problems in evaluating different schools of history and the works of revisionist historians. More fundamentally, Chief Justice William Rehnquist, among others, cautions against turning to history because it encourages the notion that the "Constitution is a living document" and that the Court ought to keep the Constitution in "tune with the times." In Rehnquist's view, there are three serious flaws with the notion of a living Constitution:

> First, it misconceives the nature of the Constitution, which was designed to enable the popularly elected branches of government, not the judicial branch, to keep the country abreast of the times. Second, [it] ignores the Supreme Court's disasterous experiences when in the past it embraced contemporary, fashionable notions of what a living Constitution should contain. Third, however socially desirable the goals to be advanced, . . . advancing them through a free-wheeling, non-elected judiciary is quite unacceptable in a democratic society.[2]

Social science may prove a no less controversial source of support for the Court's decisions. In the landmark school desegregation ruling in *Brown v. Board of Education,* 347 U.S. 483 (1954) (see Vol. 2, Ch. 12), for example, the Court cited in footnote 11 several social science studies in support of overturning the racial doctrine of "separate but equal facilities." Among those studies was the Swedish economist and sociologist Gunner Myrdal's book *An American Dilemma* (1944), the premier work on race relations in America. The Court's mention of *An American Dilemma* intensified the antagonism of powerful southerners, such as the South Carolina governor and former Supreme Court justice James F. Byrnes and Mississippi senator James O. Eastland. They and others attacked the Court for citing the work of "foreign sociologists," bad social science research, and, most of all, for drawing on social science in the first place, instead of simply sticking to the text and historical context of the Constitution.

The Court's use of social science materials may raise questions about judicial competence and the legitimacy of basing decisions on social science evidence.[3] Consider *Williams v. Florida,* 399 U.S. 78 (1970) (see Vol. 2, Ch. 9), upholding juries composed of less than twelve members, despite history and the ruling in *Thompson v. Utah* that the Sixth Amendment jury consisted "as it was at common law, of twelve persons, neither more nor less." *Williams* proved controversial because the Court held on the basis of psychological and sociological studies of small-group behavior that juries of less than twelve members were "functionally equivalent" to traditional twelve-member juries.

Natural law and *natural rights,* or what Edward Corwin termed, the "higher law" background of the Constitution, is an older tradition and source of constitutional interpretation.[4] The Framers took seriously natural law and natural rights in maintaining that individuals enjoy certain rights prior to the establishment of government and which may not be denied by government. Federalists, though, contended that the Constitution adequately safeguarded natural rights by creating a government of limited and specifically delegated powers. But the Anti-Federalists pushed for the addition of a bill of rights containing a statement of natural rights (see Vol. 2, Ch. 4).

Although the natural rights tradition runs throughout much of constitutional law, controversy has ensnarled appeals to natural law and rights ever since Justices Iredell and Chase debated, in *Calder v. Bull,* 3 Dall. 398, (1798), whether the Court has the power to strike down legislation based on principles of natural justice. Chief Justice John Marshall faced the problem of enforcing his own acceptance of natural rights against the claims of Spanish and Portuguese slave traders in *The Antelope Case,* 23 U.S. 66 (1825). Slaves had been seized by pirates, who were later captured by an American naval ship, and the slave traders and owners sued to recover their "property." Of slavery and the slave trade, Chief Justice Marshall observed "[t]hat it is contrary to the law of nature will scarcely be denied. That every man has a natural right to the fruits of his own labor, is generally admitted, and [that] no other person can rightfully deprive him of those fruits, and appropriate them against his will, seems to be the necessary result of this admission." But Marshall concluded that

> [w]hatever might be the answer of a moralist to this question, a jurist must search for its legal solution, in those principles of action which are sanctioned by the usages, the national acts, and the general assent, of that portion of the world of which he considers himself as a part, and to whose law the appeal is made. If we resort to this standard as the test of international law, the question . . . is decided in favor of the legality of the [slave] trade.

Other members of the Court, though, have sided with Justice Chase's position in *Calder* that with respect to "certain vital principles . . . [a]n act of the Legislature (for I cannot call it a *law*) contrary to the *great first principles* of the social compact, cannot be considered a *rightful exercise* of legislative authority" and, therefore, must be overturned. Consider the debate over fundamental rights and the formulations and standards used by the Court when interpreting the Fourteenth Amendment's due process clause (see Vol. 2, Ch. 4). In *Hurtado v. California*, 110 U.S. 516 (1884) (see Vol. 2, Ch. 4), for example, Justice Stanley Matthews speaks of the "wellsprings of justice." In *Adamson v. California*, 332 U.S. 46 (1947) (see Vol. 2, Ch. 4), and *Rochin v. California*, 342 U.S. 165 (1952) (see Vol. 2, Ch. 4), Justice Frankfurter invokes "the shocks the conscious test" and "fundamental fairness standard" for determining what process is due under the due process clause.

The principal criticism of "natural law formulations" is levied in opinions by Justice Hugo Black, particularly in his dissent from the Court's recognition of a right of privacy in *Griswold v. Connecticut*, 381 U.S. 481 (1965) (see Vol. 2, Ch. 4), where he observes that

> [o]ne of the most effective ways of diluting or expanding a constitutionally guaranteed right is to substitute for the crucial word or words of a constitutional guarantee another word for the word or words, more or less flexible and more or less restricted in meaning. . . . Use of any such broad, unbounded judicial authority would make this Court's members a day-to-day constitutional convention.

This criticism of the Court for imposing its own substantive value choices applies as well to those arguing that the Court should draw on *moral* and *political philosophy.* Yet Professor Ronald Dworkin and other contemporary legal scholars call for "a fusion of constitutional law and moral theory" or political philosophy.[5] Contemporary legal scholarship is indeed marked by a proliferation of expressly normative theories that would rationalize and guide constitutional interpretation according to "abstract beliefs about morality and justice,"[6] the "voice of reason,"[7] "a moral patrimony" implicit in "our common heritage,"[8] "the circumstances and values of the present generation,"[9] "conventional morality,"[10] "public morality,"[11] "constitutional morality,"[12] "fundamental values,"[13] and the "essential principles of justice,"[14] or "the idea of progress."[15] But this movement toward more specialized and abstract theories of constitutional interpretation raises the ante for reaching consensus within the Supreme Court and the country.[16]

Interpretivists counter that the turn to moral and political philosophy only exacerbates the problems of constitutional interpretation and the countermajoritarian difficulty of judicial review. As Stanford University Law School professor John Hart Ely cleverly put it, "The Constitution may follow the flag, but is it really supposed to keep up with the *New York Review of Books?*"[17] Judge Bork raises other concerns:

The abstract, universalistic style of legal thought has a number of dangers. For one thing, it teaches disrespect for the actual institutions of the American polity. These institutions are designed to achieve compromise, to slow change, to dilute absolutisms. They embody wholesome inconsistencies. They are designed, in short, to do things that abstract generalizations about the just society tend to bring into contempt.[18]

Interpreting the Constitution, nevertheless, presupposes a judicial and political philosophy and poses inescapable questions of substantive value choices. As Justice Brennan explains,

Faith in democracy is one thing, blind faith quite another. Those who drafted our Constitution understood the difference. One cannot read the text without admitting that it embodies substantive choices; it places certain values beyond the power of any legislature. . . .

To remain faithful to the content of the Constitution, therefore, an approach to interpreting the text must account for the existence of these substantive value choices, and must accept the ambiguity inherent in the effort to apply them to modern circumstances. The Framers discerned fundamental principles through struggles against particular malefactions of the Crown; the struggle shapes the particular contours of the articulated principles. But our acceptance of the fundamental principles has not and should not bind us to those precise, at times anachronistic, contours. Successive generations of Americans have continued to respect these fundamental choices and adopt them as their

own guide to evaluating quite different historical practices. Each generation has the choice to overrule or add to the fundamental principles
enunciated by the Framers; the Constitution can be amended or it
can be ignored. Yet with respect to its fundamental principles, the
text has suffered neither fate. . . .

The Constitution on its face is, in large measure, a structuring text, a
blueprint for government. And when the text is not prescribing the
form of the government it is limiting the powers of that government.
The original document, before addition of any of the amendments,
does not speak primarily of the rights of man, but of the abilities and
disabilities of government. When one reflects upon the text's preoccupa-
tion with the scope of government as well as its shape, however, one
comes to understand that what this text is about is the relationship of
the individual and the state. The text marks the metes and bounds of
official authority and individual autonomy. When one studies the boundary that the text marks out, one gets a sense of the vision of the individual
embodied in the Constitution.

As augmented by the Bill of Rights and the Civil War Amendments,
this text is a sparking vision of the supremacy of the human dignity
of every individual. This vision is reflected in the very choice of democratic self-governance: the supreme value of a democracy is the presumed worth of each individual. . . . It is a vision that has guided us
as a people throughout our history, although the precise rules by which
we have protected fundamental human dignity have been transformed
over time in response to both transformations of social conditions and
evolution of our concepts of human dignity.[19]

Neither do alternative theories and modes of constitutional
interpretation elude a dependence on political philosophy. Interpreting the Constitution frequently requires, as Professor Charles
L. Black, Jr., argues, "inference from the structure and relationships created by the constitution in all its parts or in some principal part."[20] Chief Justice Marshall's watershed opinion in *McCulloch v. Maryland*, 4 Wheat. (17 U.S.) 316 (1819) (see Vol. 1,
Ch. 6), illustrates the role of *structural analysis* of the Constitution.
There, Marshall upheld the constitutionality of the national bank
as a necessary and proper exercise of Congress's powers based
on inferences from the structure of federalism, instead of relying
on the necessary and proper clause per se. Still, Jeffersonian-
Republicans disagreed with the infusion of Marshall's nationalistic political philosophy into constitutional law. Moreover, differences rooted in rival political philosophies over the structure
of federalism persist in the Court and the country (see Vol. 1,
Ch. 6).

Nor do attempts to reconcile the exercise of the Court's power
with majoritarian democracy in terms of what has become known
as *process-oriented theory of judicial review* fare much better.[21] Justice
Harlan Stone initially suggested that the Court's role ought to
be limited to policing the political process and ensuring that it
does not discriminate against "discrete insular minorities," in

footnote 4 of *United States v. Carolene Products Co.*, 304 U.S. 144 (1938) (see Vol. 2, Ch. 12). In a book titled *Democracy and Distrust*, Professor Ely further developed the theory that the Court's role should be limited to policing the democratic process and facilitating the representation of minorities in the electoral process: "[T]he general theory is one that bounds judicial review under the Constitution's open-ended provisions by insisting that it can appropriately concern itself only with questions of participation, and not with the substantive merits of the political choice under attack."[22] In this way, Ely aims to justify the Court's supervision of the electoral process (see Vol. 1, Ch. 8) and reconcile judicial review with democratic theory. But Ely fails to provide a general theory in saying nothing about how the Court should handle cases involving disputes over presidential power and federalism, for example.[23] Moreover, the process-oriented theory of judicial review has been criticized for too sharply limiting the Court's role in protecting civil liberties and civil rights. As Justice Robert Jackson in *West Virginia State Board of Education v. Barnett*, 319 U.S. 624 (1943) (see Vol. 2, Ch. 6), observes, "The very purpose of a Bill of Rights was to withdraw certain subjects from the vicissitudes of political controversy, to place them beyond the reach of majorities and officials and to establish them as legal principles to be applied by the courts" (see also Vol. 2, Ch. 4).

Ultimately, what divides the justices, and sometimes the Court and the country, has less to do with interpretivism and noninterpretivism than fundamentally rival political philosophies and views of the role of the Court in American politics. It is not just that constitutional interpretation draws on the text, structure, history, doctrines, practices, and moral and political philosophy that is important, but how these sources and modes of analysis are employed. Admittedly, as Justice Scalia has noted, there may be a "sense of dissatisfaction" with finding that we "do not yet have an agreed-upon theory" of constitutional interpretation. "But it should come as no surprise."[24] Indeed, in constitutional politics there are no simple solutions but instead an invitation for reflection and enduring political struggles.

NOTES

1. See Willard Hurst, "The Role of History," in *Supreme Court and Supreme Law*, ed. Edmond Cahn, *(New York: Clarion Book, 1971);* and Charles Miller, *The Supreme Court and the Uses of History* (Cambridge: Harvard University Press, 1969).

2. William Rehnquist, "The Notion of a Living Constitution," in

Views from the Bench: The Judiciary and Constitutional Politics, ed. Mark Cannon and David O'Brien (Chatham, NJ: Chatham House, 1985), 191.

3. See Paul Rosen, *The Supreme Court and Social Science* (Urbana: University of Illinois Press, 1972); Wallace Loh, ed., *Social Research in the Judicial Process* (New York: Russell Sage Foundation, 1984); and David O'Brien, "The Seduction of the Judiciary: Social Science and the Courts," 64 *Judicature* 8 (1980).

4. See Edward S. Corwin, *The "Higher Law" Background of American Constitutional Law* (Ithaca, NY: Cornell University Press, 1955); Thomas Grey, "Do We Have an Unwritten Constitution," 27 *Stanford Law Review* 703 (1975); Robert Goldwin and William Schambra, eds., *How Does the Constitution Secure Rights?* (Washington, DC: American Enterprise Institute, 1985); Morton White, *The Philosophy of the American Revolution* (New York: Oxford University Press, 1978); and Symposium, "The Framers' Intent: An Exchange," 10 *University of Puget Sound Law Review* 343–369 (1987).

5. See Ronald Dworkin, *Taking Rights Seriously* (Cambridge: Harvard University Press, 1977), 149; Ronald Dworkin, *A Matter of Principle* (Harvard University Press, 1985); and Ronald Dworkin, *Law's Empire* (Cambridge: Harvard University Press, 1986).

6. See G. Edward White, "Reflections on the Role of the Supreme Court: The Contemporary Debate and the Lessons of History," 63 *Judicature* 162 (1979); and Philip Bobbit, *Constitutional Fate* (New York: Oxford University Press, 1982).

7. Henry Hart, "Foreword: The Time Chart of the Justices," 73 *Harvard Law Review* 84 (1959).

8. Charles Black, "Old and New Ways in Judicial Review," address given at Bowdoin College, 1957.

9. Terrance Sandalow, "Constitutional Interpretation," 79 *Michigan Law Review* 1033 (1981). See also Joseph Grano, "Judicial Review and a Written Constitution in a Democratic Society," 28 *Wayne Law Review* 1 (1981); and Paul Brest, "The Misconceived Quest for the Original Understanding," 60 *Boston University Law Review* 204 (1980).

10. Harry Wellington, "Common Law Rules and Constitutional Double Standards: Some Notes on Adjudication," 83 *Yale Law Journal* 221 (1973). See also Michael Perry, *The Constitution, the Courts, and Human Rights* (New Haven, CT: Yale University Press, 1982); and Michael Perry, *Morality, Politics & Law* (New York: Oxford University Press, 1988).

11. Owen Fiss, "Objectivity and Interpretation," 34 *Stanford Law Review* 739 (1982).

12. Dworkin, *Taking Rights Seriously,* 149.

13. Kenneth Karst, "The Freedom of Intimate Association," 89 *Yale Law Journal* 624 (1980); and Richard Richards, "Human Rights As the Unwritten Constitution: The Problem of Change and Stability in Constitutional Interpretation," 4 *University of Dayton Law Review* 295 (1979).

14. Michael Michelman, "In Pursuit of Constitutional Welfare Rights: One View of Rawl's Theory of Justice," 121 *University of Pennsylvania Law Review* 962 (1979).

15. Alexander Bickel, *The Supreme Court and the Idea of Progress* (New York: Harper & Row, 1970).

16. See David O'Brien, " 'The Imperial Judiciary:' Of Paper Tigers and Socio-Legal Indicators," 2 *Journal of Law & Politics* 1 (1985); and William Van Alstyne, "Interpreting *This* Constitution: The Unhelpful Contributions of Special Theories of Judicial Review," 35 *University of Florida Law Review* 209 (1983).

17. John Ely, *Democracy and Distrust* (Cambridge: Harvard University Press, 1980), 58.

18. Robert Bork, "Tradition and Morality in Constitutional Law," in *Views from the Bench,* ed. Cannon and O'Brien, 169.

19. William Brennan, Jr., "The Constitution of the United States: Contemporary Ratification," speech given at Georgetown University, Oct. 12, 1985.

20. Charles Black, Jr., *Structure and Relationship in Constitutional Law* (Baton Rouge: Louisiana University Press, 1969).

21. See Laurence Tribe, "The Puzzling Persistence of Process-Based Constitutional Theories," 89 *Yale Law Journal* 1063 (1980); and Mark Tushnet, "Darkness on the Edge of Town: The Contributions of John Hart Ely," 89 *Yale Law Journal* 1037 (1980).

22. Ely, *Democracy and Distrust,* 181.

23. See David O'Brien, "Judicial Review and Constitutional Politics: Theory and Practice," 48 *University of Chicago Law Review* 1052 (1981).

24. Antonin Scalia, "Originalism: The Lesser Evil," 57 *Cincinnati Law Review* 850 (1989), 865.

SELECTED BIBLIOGRAPHY

Barber, Sotirios. *On What the Constitution Means.* Baltimore, MD: Johns Hopkins University Press, 1984.

Bickel, Alexander. *The Supreme Court and the Idea of Progress.* New York: Harper & Row, 1970.

———. *The Least Dangerous Branch.* New York: Bobbs-Merrill, 1961.

Black, Charles, Jr. *Decision According to Law.* New York: W. W. Norton, 1981.

———. *Structure and Relationship in Constitutional Law.* Baton Rouge: Louisiana State University Press, 1969.

Bobbitt, Philip. *Constitutional Fate.* New York: Oxford University Press, 1982.

Carter, Leif. *Contemporary Constitutional Lawmaking.* New York. Pergamon, 1985.

Choper, Jesse. *Judicial Review and the National Political Process.* Chicago: University of Chicago Press, 1980.

Corwin, Edward. *The "Higher Law" Background of American Constitutional Law.* Ithaca, NY: Cornell University Press, 1955.

Dworkin, Ronald. *Taking Rights Seriously.* Cambridge: Harvard University Press, 1977.

———. *Law's Empire.* Cambridge: Harvard University Press, 1986.

Ely, John. *Democracy and Distrust*. Cambridge: Harvard University Press, 1980.

Harmon, M. Judd, ed., *Essays on the Constitution of the United States*. Port Washington, NY: Kennikat Press, 1978.

Kairys, David. *The Politics of Law*. New York: Pantheon Books, 1982.

Levinson, Sanford. *Constitutional Faith*. Princeton, NJ: Princeton University Press, 1988.

Loh, Wallace, ed., *Social Research in the Judicial Process*. New York: Russell Sage Foundation, 1984.

Lusky, Louis. *By What Right? A Commentary on the Supreme Court's Power to Revise the Constitution*, Charlottesville, VA: Michie, 1975.

Miller, Charles. *The Supreme Court and the Uses of History*, Cambridge: Harvard University Press, 1969.

Perry, Michael. *Morality, Politics & Law*. New York: Oxford University Press, 1988.

———. *The Constitution, the Courts, and Human Rights*. New Haven, CT: Yale University Press, 1982.

Posner, Richard. *The Problems of Jurisprudence*. Cambridge: Harvard University Press, 1990.

Rosen, Paul. *The Supreme Court and Social Science*. Urbana: University of Illinois Press, 1972.

Smith, Rogers. *Liberalism and American Constitutional Law*. Cambridge: Harvard University Press, 1985.

Tribe, Laurence. *Constitutional Choices*. Cambridge: Harvard University Press, 1985.

Tushnet, Mark. *Red, White, and Blue: A Critical Analysis of Constitutional Law*. Cambridge: Harvard University Press, 1988.

White, James. *Justice as Translation*. Chicago: University of Chicago Press, 1990.

———. *When Words Lose Their Meaning*. Chicago: University of Chicago Press, 1984.

2

LAW AND POLITICS IN THE SUPREME COURT: JURISDICTION AND DECISION-MAKING PROCESS

T HE SUPREME COURT is the only federal court in the United States to have complete power to decide what to decide, that is, which cases to hear. This power enables the Court to set its own agenda as well as to manage its docket. Like other courts, the Supreme Court, however, must await issues brought by lawsuits; it does not initiate its own. Also, like other social institutions, it is affected by social change. One hundred and fifty years ago, the Court's docket did not include issues of personal privacy raised by electronic surveillance and computer data banks, for instance, or controversies over abortion and the patenting of organic life-forms. As technology develops and society changes, courts respond. Law evolves more or less quickly in response to social change. Another change occurring over the past several decades has been a substantial increase in the number of cases, the caseload, sent to the Court. Unable to hear them all, the Court assumed the power to pick which issues it will decide. The Court now functions like a roving commission in responding to social forces.

A. JURISDICTION AND JUSTICIABLE CONTROVERSIES

Jurisdiction is the authorized power of a court to hear a case and to exercise judicial review. The Court's jurisdiction derives from three sources: (1) Article III of the Constitution, which defines the Court's original jurisdiction; (2) congressional legislation, providing the basis for hearing appeals of lower courts' decisions, or appellate jurisdiction; and (3) the Court's own interpretation of 1 and 2 together with its own rules for accepting cases.

Article III of the Constitution provides that the judicial power extends to all federal questions, that is, "all Cases, in Law and Equity, arising under this Constitution, the Laws of the United States, and Treaties." The Court also has original jurisdiction over specific kinds of "cases or controversies": those affecting ambassadors and other public ministers and consuls, disputes to which the United States is a party, disputes between two or more states, disputes between a state and a citizen of another state, and disputes between a state (or its citizens) and foreign countries. The Court today has only about ten cases each term (the first Monday in October through June) coming on original jurisdiction. Most involve states suing each other over land and water rights, and they tend to be rather complex and carried over for several terms before they are finally decided.

Congress establishes (and may change) the appellate jurisdiction of the federal judiciary, including the Supreme Court. Most cases used to come as direct appeals, requiring obligatory review. But as the caseload increased, Congress expanded the Court's discretionary jurisdiction by replacing appeals with petitions for *certiorari* (a petition asking a court to inspect the proceedings and decision of a lower court), which the Court may in its discretion grant or deny. Prior to the Judiciary Act of 1925, which broadened the Court's discretionary jurisdiction, appeals amounted to 80 percent of the docket and petitions for *certiorari*, less than 20 percent. Today, well over 95 percent of the docket comes on *certiorari*.

Although most cases now come as *certiorari* (*cert.*) petitions, Congress provides that appellate courts may submit a writ of certification to the Court, requesting the justices to clarify or "make more certain" a point of federal law. The Court receives only a handful of such cases each term. Congress also gave the Court the power to issue certain extraordinary writs, or orders. In a few cases, the Court may issue writs of *mandamus* and prohibition, ordering lower courts or public officials to either do something or refrain from some action. In addition, the Court has the power to grant writs of *habeas corpus* ("produce the body"), enabling it to review cases by prisoners who claim that their constitutional rights have been violated and they are unlawfully imprisoned.

FIGURE 2.1

Avenues of appeal:
The two main routes to the Supreme Court.

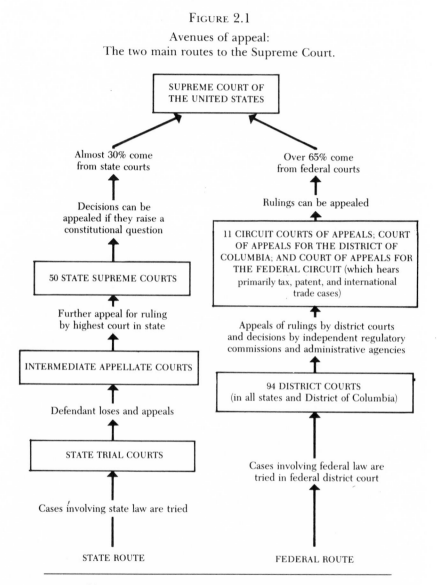

Note: In addition, some cases come directly to the Supreme Court from trial courts when they involve reapportionment or civil rights disputes. Appeals from the Court of Military Appeals also go directly to the Supreme Court. A few cases come on "original jurisdiction" and involve disputes between state governments.

Congress also established the practice of giving the poor, or the indigent, the right to file without the payment of fees. When filing an appeal or petition for certiorari, indigents may file an affidavit requesting that they be allowed to proceed *in forma pauperis* ("in the manner of a pauper,") without the usual filing fees and forms. The Court sets both the rules governing filing fees and the form that appeals, cert. petitions, and other documents must take. Except for indigents, the Court requires $200 for filing any case and another $100 if a case is granted oral argument. Indigents are exempt as well from the Court's rules specifying particular colors and lengths of paper for various kinds of filings. All cert. petitions, for instance, must have a white color, whereas opposing briefs are light orange. Any document filed by the federal government has a gray cover. No petition or appeal may exceed thirty pages, and for those few cases granted oral argument, briefs on the merits of cases are limited to fifty pages.

The Constitution and Congress thus stipulate the kinds of cases and controversies the Court may consider. Yet, as Charles Evans Hughes, who later became chief justice (1930–1941), candidly remarked, "We are under the Constitution, but the Constitution is what the Judges say it is."[1] The Court has developed its own doctrines for denying a large number of case reviews and for setting its own agenda. Specifically, the Court considers whether it has jurisdiction over a "case or controversy," and then whether that dispute is justiciable, or capable of judicial resolution. Justices thus may, or may not, deny a case if it (1) lacks adverseness or (2) is brought by parties who lack "standing to sue," or poses issues that either (3) are not "ripe," (4) have become "moot," or (5) involve a "political question." What all this means is discussed below.

Adverseness and Advisory Opinions

The Court generally maintains that litigants, those involved in a lawsuit, must be real and adverse in seeking a decision that will resolve their dispute and not some hypothetical issue. The requirement of real and adverse parties means that the Court will not decide so-called friendly suits, (when the parties do not have adverse interests in the outcome of a case). Nor will the Court give "advisory opinions" on issues not raised in an actual lawsuit. The Jay Court denied two requests for advisory opinions: one in 1790 by Secretary of Treasury Alexander Hamilton on the national government's power to assume state Revolutionary War debts, and the other in 1793 by Secretary of State Thomas Jefferson for an interpretation of certain treaties and international law. Chief Justice John Jay held that it would be improper for the Court to judge such matters, because the president may call on cabinet heads for advice. The Court continues to maintain that it is inappropriate "to give opinions in the nature of advice concerning legislative action, a function never conferred upon it by the Constitution and against the exercise of which this court has steadily set its face from the beginning."[2]

Historically, justices have nevertheless extrajudicially advised attorneys, congressmen, and presidents. They occasionally even accuse each other of including in opinions *dicta* (statements of personal opinion or philosophy not necessary to the decision handed down) that is tantamount to "giving legal advice."[3] The Court, furthermore, upheld the constitutionality of the Declaratory Judgment Act authorizing federal courts to declare, or make clear, rights and legal relationships even before a legislature has mandated a law to take effect, although only in "cases of actual controversy."[4]

Standing to Sue

Standing, like adverseness, is a threshold requirement for getting into court. "Generalizations about standing to sue," as Justice William O. Douglas discouragingly, but candidly, put it, "are largely worthless as such."[5] Nonetheless, the basic requirement is that individuals show injury to a legally protected interest or right and demonstrate that other opportunities for defending that claim (before an administrative tribunal or a lower court) have been exhausted. The claim of an injury "must be of a personal and not official nature" and of "some specialized interest of [the individual's] own to vindicate, apart from political concerns which belong to it."[6] The interest must be real as opposed to speculative or hypothetical.

The injuries and legal interests claimed traditionally turned on a showing of personal or proprietary damage. Typically, plaintiffs had suffered some "pocketbook" or monetary injury. But in the last thirty years, individuals have sought standing to represent nonmonetary injuries and "the public interest."

The law of standing is a combination of judge-made law and congressional legislation, as interpreted by the Court. During Earl Warren's tenure as chief justice (1953–1969) the Court substantially lowered the threshold for standing and permitted more litigation of public policy issues. *Frothingham v. Mellon*, 262 U.S. 447 (1923), was the leading case on taxpayer suits until it was overturned in *Flast v. Cohen* (1968) (see page 116). In *Frothingham*, the Taft Court had denied taxpayers standing to challenge the constitutionality of federal legislation. Mrs. Frothingham, a tax-

Figure 2.2

Jurisdictional map of the U.S. courts of appeal and U.S. district courts.

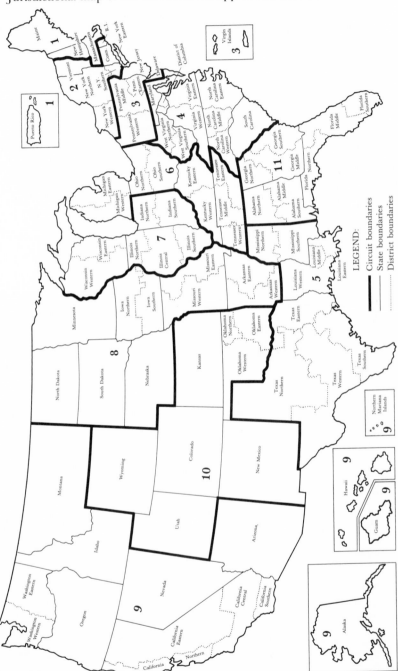

Note: The court of appeals for the federal circuit is located in the District of Columbia.
Source: Administrative Office of the U.S. Courts, Washington, D.C.

payer, had attacked Congress's appropriation of federal funds to the states for a maternal and infant care program. She claimed that Congress exceeded its power and intruded on "the reserved rights of the states" under the Tenth Amendment of the Constitution. Writing for the Court, Justice George Sutherland avoided confronting the merits of her claim by denying standing. He did so on the grounds that an individual taxpayer's interest in the financing of federal programs is "comparatively minute and indeterminable," when viewed in light of all taxpayers. Frothingham's "injury" was neither direct nor immediate and the issue raised was basically "political, not judicial." As Sutherland put it,

[T]he relation of a taxpayer of the United States to the Federal Government is very different [from that relationship with state and local governments]. His interest in the moneys of the Treasury—partly realized from taxation and partly from other sources—is shared with millions of others; is comparatively minute and indeterminable; and the effect upon future taxation, or any payment out of the funds, so remote, fluctuating and uncertain, that no basis is afforded for an appeal to the preventive powers of a court of equity.

To gain standing, according to Sutherland, a taxpayer "must be able to show not only that the statute is invalid but that he has sustained . . . some direct injury as the result of its enforcement, and not merely that he suffers in some indefinite way in common with people generally."

Frothingham's "direct injury" test was met in *Pierce v. Society of Sisters,* 268 U.S. 510 (1925). There, a religious school won a court order barring the enforcement of Oregon's 1922 constitutional amendment requiring children between the ages of eight and sixteen to attend public schools. The Court affirmed on the grounds that the law directly damages the business and property interests of the school and because it "unreasonably interferes with the liberty of parents and guardians to direct the upbringing and education of children under their control."

The federal government relied on *Frothingham* to provide an absolute barrier to subsequent taxpayer suits until the Warren Court repudiated that view in *Flast v. Cohen* (1968) (see page 116). In his opinion for the Court, Chief Justice Warren created a two-pronged standard for granting standing to taxpayers: Taxpayers must show a logical relationship between their status as taxpayers and the challenged legislative statute as well as a connection between that status and the "precise nature of the constitutional infringement alleged."

The Burger Court (1969–1986) and the current Rehnquist Court tightened the requirements for standing in some cases, but relaxed it in others. In 1972, in two sharply divided decisions,

CONSTITUTIONAL HISTORY
Major Legislation Affecting the Jurisdiction and Business of the Supreme Court

Legislation	Commentary
Judiciary Act of 1789	Provided basic appellate jurisdiction; a 3-tier judiciary system staffed by justices and district court judges; and required circuit riding.
Acts of 1793, 1801, 1802, and 1803	Provided rotation system for circuit riding, then eliminated the responsibilities, only to have Jeffersonians reinstate circuit-riding duties.
Act of 1807	Added 7th circuit and justice.
Act of 1837	Divided country into 9 circuits and brought number of justices to 9. (Court's jurisdiction was also expanded to include appeals from new states and territories in 1825, 1828, and 1848.)
Acts of 1855 and 1863	California added as 10th circuit and 10th justice added to the Court.
Acts of 1866, 1867, 1869, and 1871	Expanded federal jurisdiction over civil rights; reorganized country into 9 circuits and reduced number of justices to 7, and later fixed the number at 9; as well as expanded jurisdiction over habeas corpus and state court decisions.
Act of 1875	Greatly expanded jurisdiction over civil disputes, and gave power to review of writs of error, and granted full federal question review from state courts.
Act of 1887	Curbed access by raising amount of dispute in diversity cases; and provided writ of error in all capital cases.
Circuit Court of Appeals Act of 1891	Established 9 circuit courts, and judgeships; broadened review of criminal cases and provided for limited discretionary review via writs of *certiorari*.

Legislation	Commentary
Act of 1892	Provided for *in forma pauperis* filings.
Act of 1893	Created District of Columbia Circuit.
Acts of 1903 and 1907	Provided direct appeal under antitrust and interstate commerce acts; granted government right of direct appeal in dismissals of criminal prosecutions.
Acts of 1910, 1911, and 1913	Altered federal injunctive power; established 3-judge courts because of abuses by single judges in enjoining state economic regulation; and later extended the jurisdiction of 3-judge courts and direct appeals to the Court.
Acts of 1914, 1915, and 1916	Jurisdiction over some state cases made discretionary and eliminated right to review in bankruptcy, trademark, and Federal Employer's Liability Act (FELA).
Judiciary Act of 1925	Greatly extended the Court's discretionary jurisdiction by replacing mandatory appeals with petitions for certiorari.
Act of 1928	Appeals became the sole method of mandatory appellate review.
Act of 1939	Expanded review of decisions by Court of Claims over both law and fact.
Act of 1948	Judicial code revised, codified, and enacted into law; 11th circuit established.
Act of 1950 (Hobbes Act)	Eliminated 3-judge court requirement in certain areas.
Voting Rights Act of 1965	Provided direct appeal over decisions of 3-judge courts in area of voting rights.
Acts of 1970, 1971, 1974, 1975, and 1976	Reorganized District of Columbia courts; expanded Court's discretionary review; repealed direct government appeals under Act of 1907; eliminated direct appeals in antitrust and Interstate Commerce Commission (ICC) cases; further cut back jurisdiction and direct appeals from 3-judge courts, with the exception of areas of voting rights and reapportionment.

Legislation	Commentary
Federal Courts Improvement Act of 1982	Created Court of Appeals for the Federal Circuit, by joining the court of claims with the court of customs and patent appeals.
Act to Improve the Administration of Justice of 1988	Eliminated virtually all of the Court's non-discretionary appellate jurisdiction, except for appeals in reapportionment cases, cases under the Civil Rights Act and Voting Rights Act, antitrust laws, and the Presidential Election Campaign Fund Act.

the Burger Court denied standing to a group challenging military surveillance of lawful political protests in public places and to the Sierra Club when challenging the construction of a ski resort in Mineral King National Park. In both *Laird v. Tatum*, 408 U.S. 1 (1972), and *Sierra Club v. Morton*, 405 U.S. 727 (1972), a bare majority found that the groups failed to show a "personal stake in the outcome" of the litigation. The following year, however, standing was granted to a group of law students attacking a proposed surcharge on railroad freight. The students contended that the surcharge would discourage the recycling of bottles and cans, and thus contribute to environmental pollution. In *United States v. Students Challenging Regulatory Agency Procedure (SCRAP)*, 412 U.S. 669 (1973), the Burger Court granted standing, observing that "[a]esthetic and environmental well-being, like economic well-being, are important ingredients of the quality of life in our society, and the fact that particular environmental interests are shared by the many rather than the few does not make them less deserving of legal protection through the judicial process."

Plaintiffs, those bringing suit, must still claim a personal injury, but they now can act as surrogates for special interest groups. The personal injuries claimed thus embrace a public injury. Congress at the same time expanded the principle even more by providing that any individual "adversely affected or aggrieved" may challenge administrative decisions. Health, safety, and environmental legislation passed in the 1970s mandated such "citizen suits" and right to judicial review of regulatory action. Even when legislation does not provide for the citizen suits, individuals may claim personal injuries, or a "private cause of action," to gain access to the courts and to force agency compliance with the law.

The more conservative Burger and Rehnquist courts have restricted standing requirements in several ways. First, they have refused to recognize new interests and injuries in granting standing. In *Linda R. S. v. Richard D.*, 410 U.S. 614 (1973), an unwed mother sought enforcement of child support under the Texas Penal Code because the local prosecutor refused to enforce the statute against fathers of illegitimate children. A majority of the Court ruled that she had no recognizable injury and no standing because she could not prove that payments stopped because that particular statute was unenforced. Justices Byron White and William Douglas, in dissent, argued that unwed mothers and illegitimate children were thus rendered nonpersons: "Texas prosecutes fathers of legitimate children on the complaint of the mother asserting nonsupport and refuses to entertain like complaints from the mother of an illegitimate child. [We] see no basis for saying that the latter mother has no standing to demand that the discrimination be ended, one way or another."

In *Paul v. Davis*, 424 U.S. 693 (1976), the Court's majority rejected a claim of injury to personal reputation by an individual who objected to the circulation of a flyer to local merchants that carried his photograph along with that of other alleged "active shoplifters." Rehnquist dismissed the claim out-of-hand. But, Justice William Brennan in dissent responded that, "The Court by mere fiat and with no analysis wholly excludes personal interest in reputation from the ambit of 'life, liberty, or property' under the Fifth and Fourteenth Amendments, thus rendering due process concerns *never* applicable to the official stigmatization, however, arbitrary." The Court went even further with its reinterpretation of the application of *Flast*'s test for taxpayer suits in *Valley Forge Christian College v. Americans United for Separation of Church and State, Inc.* (1982) (see page 125).

Ripeness and Mootness

With these doctrines the Court wields a double-edged sword. Appellants, those appealing a lower court ruling, may discover that a case is dismissed because it was brought too early or because the issues are moot and the case was brought too late. Cases are usually rejected as not ripe if the injury claimed has not yet been realized, or if other avenues of appeal have not yet been exhausted. Alternatively, a case may be dismissed if pertinent facts or laws change so that there is no longer real adverseness or an actual case or controversy. The issue becomes moot because "there is no subject matter on which the judgement of the court can operate," and hence a ruling would not prove "conclusive" and final.[7] In practice both doctrines bend to the Court's will, because the requirement of ripeness permits the Court to avoid or delay deciding certain issues.

THE DEVELOPMENT OF LAW
Other Important Recent Rulings on Standing

Case	Vote	Ruling
Schlesinger v. Reservists Committee to Stop the War, 418 U.S. 208 (1974)	6:3	Members of an organization of present and past members of the military reserves opposed to the Vietnam War had no standing to file a class action suit against the secretary of defense, attacking the constitutionality of members of Congress holding commissions in the reserves and voting on appropriations for the war, as an alleged violation of Article I, Section 6, Clause 2, which declares that "no person holding any office under the United States, shall be a Member of either House during his continuance in office."
United States v. Richardson, 418 U.S. 166 (1974)	5:4	Denied taxpayer standing to bring suit against Congress's secret funding for the Central Intelligence Agency, as an alleged violation of Article I, Section 9, Clause 7, which provides that "no Money shall be drawn from the Treasury, but in Consequence of Appropriations made by Law; and a regular Statement of Account of the Receipts and Expenditures of all public money shall be published from time to time."
Warth v. Seldin, 422 U.S. 490 (1975)	5:4	Denied standing to various organizations in Rochester, New York, seeking to sue officials of the suburban town of Penfield, claiming that the latter's zoning ordinance excluded low- and moderate-income persons from living in the town and violated their rights under the Bill of Rights. The Court held that the individuals and organizations failed to show that they had been "personally" injured.

Case	Vote	Ruling
Simon v. Eastern Kentucky Welfare Rights Organization, 426 U.S. 26 (1976)	9:0	Denied standing to indigents seeking to challenge federal tax regulations reducing the amount of free medical care hospitals must provide in order to receive certain tax benefits.
City of Los Angeles v. Lyons, 461 U.S. 95 (1983)	5:4	Held that an arrestee had standing to sue the city for damages incurred as a result of police subjecting him to a "choke hold," but that he had no standing to seek an injunction against the police practice of using choke holds, because he failed to show that he might ever be subjected to a choke hold again.
Allen v. Wright, 468 U.S. 737 (1984)	5:3	Denied standing to parents of black children, attending public schools in districts around the country that were in the process of desegregation, to sue various government officials and present their contention that the IRS failed to fulfill its obligation under the law to deny tax-exempt status to private schools engaged in racial discrimination.

A finding of mootness likewise enables the Court to avoid, if not escape, deciding controversial political issues. *DeFunis v. Odegaard*, 416 U.S. 312 (1974), for example, involved a white student, who was denied admission to the University of Washington Law School. The student claimed that the school's affirmative action program discriminated against him and allowed the entrance of minorities with lower LSAT test scores. After the trial judge ruled in his favor, he was admitted into law school but by the time his case reached the Supreme Court he was completing his final year and assured of graduation. Over four dissenters, the majority held that the case was moot. Yet, as the dissenters predicted, the issue would not go away. Within four years, the Burger Court reconsidered the issue of reverse discrimination in university affirmative action programs in *Regents of the University of California v. Bakke*, 438 U.S. 265 (1978) (see Vol. 2, Ch. 12). In *Bakke*, Justice Lewis Powell held that quota systems for minorities in college admissions are unconstitutional, but also that the Constitution is not "color-blind" and affirmative action programs are permissible to achieve a diverse student body in colleges and universities.

THE DEVELOPMENT OF LAW
Class Action Suits

The Federal Rules of Civil Procedure provide for "class action" suits—suits filed by an individual for himself and for all others who have suffered the same injury. This rule enables individuals who have suffered small monetary damages to bring lawsuits that they might not otherwise have because of the prohibitively high cost of litigation. Specifically, Rule 23 provides in that,

One or more members of a class may use or be sued as representative parties on behalf of all only if (1) the class is so numerous that joinder of all members is impracticable, (2) there are questions of law or fact common to the class, (3) the claims or defenses of the representative parties are typical of the claims or defenses of the class, and (4) the representative parties will fairly and adequently protect the interests of the class. . . .

   In any class action maintained under [this Rule], the court shall direct to the members of the class the best notice practicable under the circumstances, including individual notice to all members who can be identified.

The scope of this rule, however, was limited by *Eisen v. Carlisle & Jacquelin*, 417 U.S. 156 (1974), holding that when a representative of a class action suit refuses to pay the cost of giving actual notice to all reasonably identiable class members, federal courts are required to dismiss the suit. Here, representatives would have had to notify 2,250,000 class members at a cost of $225,000.

The issue of mootness could have presented a problem when the Burger Court ruled on abortion in *Roe v. Wade,* 410 U.S. 113 (1973) (see Vol. 2, Ch. 11). There the Court struck down Texas's criminal statute prohibiting abortions, except when necessary to save a mother's life. When defending the law, the state's attorney general argued that the plaintiff was a single woman whose pregnancy had already resulted in birth by the time the case reached the Court, and hence her claim was moot. However, Justice Harry Blackmun, writing for the Court, rejected that view out of hand:

[W]hen, as here, pregnancy is a significant fact in the litigation, the normal 266-day human gestation period is so short that the pregnancy will come to term before the usual appellate process is complete. If that termination makes a case moot, pregnancy litigation seldom will survive much beyond the trial stage, and appellate review will be effectively denied. Our law should not be that rigid. Pregnancy often comes more than once to the same woman, and in the general population, if man is to survive, it will always be with us. Pregnancy provides a classic justification for a conclusion of nonmootness. It truly could be "capable of repetition, yet evading review."

INSIDE THE COURT

Standing and the Connecticut Birth Control Cases

Between 1943 and 1965, the Court continually refused standing to individuals attacking the constitutionality of a late nineteenth-century Connecticut statute. The law prohibited virtually all single and married individuals from using contraceptives and physicians from giving advice about their use. In *Tileston v. Ullman,* 318 U.S. 44 (1943), a doctor sued charging that the statute prevented him from giving information to patients. But the Court ruled that he had no real interest or personal injury because he had not been arrested, observing that

[w]e are of the opinion that the proceedings in the state courts present no constitutional question which appellant has standing to assert. The sole constitutional attack upon the statutes under the Fourteenth Amendment is confined to their deprivation of life—obviously not appellant's but his patients'. There is no allegation or proof that appellant's life is in danger. His patients are not parties to this preceeding and there is no basis on which we can say that has standing to secure an adjudication of his patient's constitutional right to life, which they do not assert in their own behalf.

More than a decade later in *Poe v. Ullman,* 367 U.S. 497 (1961), a doctor, Buxton, and a patient were likewise denied standing on the ground that the law had not been enforced for more than eighty years, even though the state had begun to close birth control clinics. This time the justices split five to four and only Chief Justice Warren and Justices Clark and Whittaker joined Justice Frankfurter's opinion for the Court (Justice Brennan concurred in the decision but not in the opinion). There, Frankfurter observed that

[t]he Connecticut law prohibiting the use of contraceptives has been on the State's books since 1879. . . . During more than three-quarters of a century since its enactment, a prosecution for its violation seems never to have been initiated, save in [one] case. . . . Neither counsel nor our own researches have discovered any other attempt to enforce the prohibition of distribution or use of contraceptive devices by criminal process. The unreality of these law suits is illuminated by another circumstance. We were advised by counsel for appellants that contraceptives are commonly and notoriously sold in Connecticut drug stores. Yet no prosecutions are recorded. . . .

The restriction of our jurisdiction to cases and controversies within the meaning of Article III of the Constitution . . . is not the sole limitation on the exercise of our appellate powers, especially in cases raising constitutional questions. . . .

The various doctrines of "standing," "ripeness," and "mootness," which this Court has evolved with particular, though not exclusive, reference to such cases are but several manifestations—each having its own "varied application"—of the primary conception that federal judicial power is to be exercised to strike down legislation, whether state or federal, only at the instance of one who is himself immediately harmed, or immediately threatened with harm, by the challenged action. . . .

Nor does the allegation by the Poes and Doe that they are unable to obtain information concerning contraceptive devices from Dr. Buxton, "for the sole reason that the delivery and use of such information and advice may or will be claimed by the defendant's State's Attorney to constitute offenses," disclose a necessity for present constitutional decision. It is true that this Court has several times passed upon criminal statutes challenged by persons who claimed that the effects of the statutes were to deter others from maintaining profitable or advantageous relations with the complainants. . . . But in these cases the deterrent effect complained of was one which was grounded in a realistic fear of prosecution. We cannot agree that if Dr. Buxton's compliance with these statutes is uncoerced by the risk of their enforcement, his patients are entitled to a declaratory judgment concerning the statute's validity.

Finally, after Dr. Buxton and Estelle Griswold, executive director of Planned Parenthood League of Connecticut, were found guilty of prescribing contraceptives to a married couple, the Court in *Griswold v. Connecticut* (1965) (see Vol. 2, Ch. 3) struck down what Justice Potter Stewart called Connecticut's "uncommonly silly law." In his opinion announcing the Court's ruling, Justice Douglas explained why Griswold and Buxton were now being granted standing:

They gave information, instruction, and medical advice to *married persons* as to the means of preventing conception. They examined the wife and prescribed the best contraceptive device or material for her use. Fees were usually charged, although some couples were serviced free. . . .

The appellants were found guilty as accessories and fined $100 each, against the claim that the accessory statute as so applied violated the Fourteenth Amendment. . . .

We think that appellants have standing to raise the constitutional rights of the married people with whom they had a professional relationship. *Tileston v. Ullman*, is different, for there the plaintiff seeking to represent others asked for a declaratory judgment. In that situation, we thought that the requirements of standing should be strict, lest the standards of "case or controversy" in Article III of the Constitution become blurred. Here those doubts are removed by reason of a criminal conviction for serving married couples in violation of an aiding-and-abetting statute. Certainly the accessory should have standing to assert that the offense which he is charged with assisting is not, or cannot constitutionally be a crime.

Griswold was limited to the privacy and marital decisions of couples. Consequently, in *Eisenstadt v. Baird*, 405 U.S. 438 (1972), to gain standing to claim that single individuals also have a right to acquire and use contraceptives, a doctor arranged to be arrested after delivering a public lecture on contraceptives and handing out samples to single women in the audience. The Court accepted the case and ruled that single women also have the right to acquire and use contraceptives.

Political Questions

Even when the Court has jurisdiction over a properly framed suit, it may decline to rule because it decides that a case raises a "political question" that should be resolved by other political branches. Like other jurisdictional doctrines, the political question doctrine means what the justices say it means.

The doctrine has its origin in Chief Justice Marshall's observation in *Marbury v. Madison,* 5 U.S. 137 (1803) (see Chapter 1), that "[t]he province of the Court, is, solely, to decide on the rights of individuals. . . . Questions in the nature political, or which are, by the constitution and laws, submitted to the executive can never be made in this Court." Yet as the French commentator Alexis de Tocqueville noted in the 1830s, "Scarcely any political question arises in the United States that is not resolved, sooner or later, into a judicial question."[8] Litigation that reaches the Court is political, and the justices for political reasons decide what and how to decide cases on their docket.

The Taney Court first developed the doctrine in *Luther v. Borden,* 7 How. [48 U.S.] 1 (1849). There, the Court held that whether Rhode Island had a "republican form of government," as guaranteed by Article IV of the Constitution, was a question for Congress, not the Court, to decide. Subsequent rulings elaborated other reasons for the doctrine besides deference to separation of powers. The Court may lack information and resources needed for a ruling. In some areas, as in foreign policy and international relations, the Court lacks both adequate standards for resolving disputes and the means to enforce its decisions.

For many decades the Court relied on the doctrine to avoid entering the "political thicket" of state representation and apportionment, that is, the ways by which a state is divided geographically as a basis for representation in state and federal elections. When declining to rule on the malapportionment of Illinois's congressional districts in *Colegrove v. Green,* 328 U.S. 549 (1946), Justice Felix Frankfurter explained,

We are of opinion that the petitioners ask of this Court what is beyond its competence to grant. This is one of those demands on judicial power which cannot be met by verbal fencing about "jurisdiction." It must be resolved by considerations on the basis of which this Court, from time to time, has refused to intervene in controversies. It has refused to do so because due regard for the effective working of our Government revealed this issue to be of a peculiarly political nature and therefore not meet for judicial determination.

This is not an action to recover for damages because of the discriminatory exclusion of a plaintiff from rights enjoyed by other citizens. The basis for the suit is not a private wrong, but a wrong suffered by Illinois as a polity. . . . In effect this is an appeal to the federal courts to reconstruct the electoral process of Illinois in order that it may be adequately represented in the councils of the Nation. Because the Illinois legislature has failed to revise its Congressional Representative districts in order to reflect great changes, during more than a generation, in the distribution of its population, we are asked to do this, for Illinois. . . .

Of course no court can affirmatively remap the Illinois districts so as to bring them more in conformity with the standards of fairness for a representative system. At best we could only declare the existing electoral system invalid. The result would be to leave Illinois undistricted and to bring into operation, if the Illinois legislature chose not to act, the choice of members for the House of Representatives on a state-wide ticket. The last stage may be worse than the first. . . .

Nothing is clearer than that this controversy concerns matters that bring courts into immediate and active relations with party contests. From the determination of such issues this Court has traditionally held aloof. It is hostile to the democratic system to involve the judiciary in the politics of the people. And it is not less pernicious if such judicial intervention in an essentially political contest be dressed up in the abstract phrases of the law.

The one stark fact that emerges from the study of the history of Congressional apportionment is its enrollment in politics, in the sense of party contests and party interests. The Constitution enjoins upon Congress the duty of apportioning Representatives "among the several States . . . according to their respective Numbers. . . ." Article I, Sec. 2. Yet, Congress has at times been heedless of this command and not apportioned according to the requirements of the Census. It never occurred to anyone that this Court could issue mandamus to compel Congress to perform its mandatory duty to apportion.

Still, blacks and other minorities in urban areas were often denied equal representation until the Court reversed itself in *Baker v. Carr* (1962) (see page 131).

In *Goldwater v. Carter* (1979) (see page 145), the Court issued an order vacating (overturning) a lower court decision in a dispute between several congressmen, headed by conservative Senator Barry Goldwater, and Democratic President James Carter over the termination of a defense treaty with Taiwan. There, Justices Lewis F. Powell and William Rehnquist took quite different views of the application of the "political questions" doctrine in controversies between Congress and the president.

The doctrine's logic is admittedly circular. "Political questions are matters not soluble by the judicial process; matters not soluble by the judicial process are political questions. As an early dictionary explained," political scientist John Roche says, "violins are small cellos, and cellos are large violins."[9] Still, Columbia Law professor Louis Henkin points out, even when denying review because of a political question, "the court does not refuse judicial review; it exercises it. It is not dismissing the case or the issue as nonjusticiable; it adjudicates it. It is not refusing to pass on the power of the political branches; it passes upon it, only to affirm that they had the power which had been challenged and that nothing in the Constitution prohibited the particular exercise of it."[10]

Stare Decisis and Other Policies

The justices occasionally rely on other self-denying policies to avoid reaching issues as well. They, for example, may invoke what has been called the doctrine of *strict necessity*, and thereupon formulate and decide only the narrowest possible issue.

Another doctrine, *stare decisis* ("let the prior decision stand"), is also not a mechanical formula. It is rather a judicial policy that promotes "the certainty, uniformity, and stability of the law." Even conservative Justice George Sutherland recognized that members of the Court "are not infallible, and when convinced that a prior decision was not originally based on, or that conditions have so changed as to render the decision no longer in accordance with, sound reason, [they] should not hesitate to say so."[11] "*Stare decisis* is usually the wise policy," Justice Louis Brandeis remarked, "because in most matters it is more important that the applicable rule of law be settled than that it be settled right."[12] On constitutional matters, however, Justice Douglas among others emphasizes, "*stare decisis*—that is, established law— was really no sure guideline because what did . . . the judges who sat there in 1875 know about, say, electronic surveillance? They didn't know anything about it."[13] At the time of his ill-fated nomination to the Court in 1987, former Court of Appeals Judge Robert Bork agreed and raised serious questions about the value of judicial precedents, although for somewhat different reasons than Douglas. Bork contended that "the real meaning of the Constitution ought to prevail over a prior mistake by the Court" and "the Court ought to be always open to rethink constitutional problems." But he also maintained that "certain precedents [are] so fixed, some issues so settled, that regardless of how you felt about them you shouldn't vote to overrule them." Bork gave as an example nineteenth-century cases dealing with Congress's power under the commerce clause, which however wrongly decided should be upheld. By contrast, he did "not include *Roe v. Wade* in that category."[14] Even without Bork on the high bench, the Rehnquist Court has made clear that it pays much less deference to decisions handed down by the Warren and Burger courts in the area of civil liberties and civil rights.

In sum, *stare decisis* and the precedential value of the Court's jurisdictional doctrines and policies, as Justice Jackson in half-jest quipped, "are accepted only at their current valuation and have a mortality rate as high as their authors."[15]

Formal Rules and Practices

Except for government attorneys and members of the practicing bar, few people pay any attention to the technical Rules of the Court. Yet, they are an exercise of political power and determine the nation's access to justice. The rules govern the admission and activities of attorneys in filing appeals, petitions, and motions, and conducting oral arguments. They stipulate the fees, forms, and length of filings. Most important, they explain the Court's formal grounds for granting and disposing of cases.

To expedite the process of deciding what to decide, the Court periodically revises its rules. For example, even after the Judiciary Act of 1925 expanded the Court's discretionary jurisdiction, the justices still felt burdened by mandatory appeals. Accordingly, in 1928 the Court required the filing of a jurisdictional statement, explaining the circumstances of an appeal, the questions presented, and why the Court should grant review. The requirement also allowed the justices to screen appeals just like petitions for *certiorari*.

One of the reasons for granting *certiorari* given in the Court's rules is whether "a federal court of appeals has rendered a decision in conflict with the decision of another federal court of appeals on the same matter." This rule is especially advantageous for the federal government. The Department of Justice has a relitigation policy. If it receives an adverse ruling from circuit court of appeals, it will relitigate the issue in other circuits to obtain favorable decisions and generate a conflict among the circuits, which then may be brought to the Court. One function of the Court, in Chief Justice Fred Vinson's words, has become the resolution of "conflicts of opinion on federal questions that have arisen among lower courts."[16] The rule for granting circuit conflicts, however important, does not control the justices' actual practice of granting *certiorari*. The government and individuals often allege circuit conflicts simply in an effort to get their cases accepted. But most circuit conflicts are "tolerable" and need not be immediately decided. The justices often feel that conflicts should percolate in the circuits before they take them. Sometimes, a majority may want to avoid or delay addressing an issue that has created a conflict among the circuits. Most crucial in granting *certiorari* is simply the majority's agreement on the importance of the issue presented.

NOTES

1. Charles E. Hughes, *Addresses of Charles Evans Hughes* (New York: Putnam's, 1916), 185–186.

2. *Muskrat v. United States*, 219 U.S. 346 (1911).

3. See *Duke Power Co. v. Carolina Environmental Study Group*, 438 U.S. 59 (1978); and *Bellotti v. Baird*, 443 U.S. 622 (1979).

4. *Aetna Life Insurance Co. v. Haworth*, 300 U.S. 277 (1937).

5. *Data Processing Service v. Camp*, 397 U.S. 150, 151 (1970).

6. *Braxton County Court v. West Virginia*, 208 U.S. 192 (1908); and *Coleman v. Miller*, 307 U.S. 433 (1931) (Frankfurter, J., dissenting opinion).

7. *Ex parte Baez*, 177 U.S. 378 (1900).

8. Alexis de Tocqueville, *Democracy in America*, Vol. 1, ed. P. Bradley (New York: Vintage, 1945), 288.

9. John Roche, "Judicial Self-Restraint," 49 *American Political Science Review* 768 (1955).

10. Louis Henkin, "Is There a 'Political Question' Doctrine?" 85 *Yale Law Journal* 606 (1976).

11. Draft of an opinion, George Sutherland Papers, Manuscript Room, Library of Congress.

12. *Burnet v. Coronado Oil*, 285 U.S. 393 (1932) (Brandeis, J., dissenting opinion).

13. William O. Douglas, interview on *CBS Reports*, Sept. 6, 1972, CBS News, transcript p. 13.

14. See Ronald Collins and David M. O'Brien, "Just Where Does Judge Bork Stand?" *The National Law Journal* 13 (Sept. 7, 1987).

15. Robert Jackson, "The Task of Maintaining Our Liberties: The Role of the Judiciary," 39 *American Bar Association Journal* 962 (1953).

16. Fred Vinson, address before the American Bar Association, Sept. 7, 1949, reprinted in 69 S.Ct. vi (1949).

SELECTED BIBLIOGRAPHY

Cannon, Mark, and O'Brien, David M. *Views from the Bench: The Judiciary and Constitutional Politics*. Chatham, NJ: Chatham House, 1985.

Carp, Robert. *Policymaking and Politics in the Federal District Courts*. Knoxville: University of Tennessee Press, 1983.

Goldman, Sheldon, and Sarat, Austin, eds. *American Court Systems,* 2nd ed. New York: Longman's, 1989.

Howard, J. Woodford. *Courts of Appeals in the Federal Judicial System*. Princeton, N.J.: Princeton University Press, 1981.

Stern, Robert, and Gressman, Eugene *Supreme Court Practice*, 6th ed. Washington, DC: Bureau of National Affairs, 1987.

Strum, Philippa. *The Supreme Court and "Political Questions": A Study in Judicial Evasion*. Birmingham: University of Alabama Press, 1974.

Flast v. Cohen
392 U.S. 83, 88 S.Ct. 1942 (1968)

Florance Flast and several other taxpayers sought standing to challenge the constitutionality of the Elementary and Secondary Education Act of 1965. The act provided funding for the instruction and purchase of textbooks for religious schools. Flast contended that the act violated the First Amendment's ban on the establishment of religion and guarantee for the free exercise of religion. In a federal district court in New York, she filed suit against Wilbur Cohen, the secretary of health, education, and welfare, to enjoin the spending of funds authorized for religious schools. The district court denied standing and Flast appealed to the Supreme Court.

Chief Justice WARREN delivers the opinion of the Court.

In *Frothingham v. Mellon* [262 U.S. 447] (1923), this Court ruled that a federal taxpayer is without standing to challenge the constitutionality of a federal statute. That ruling has stood for 45 years as an impenetrable barrier to suits against Acts of Congress brought by individuals who can assert only the interest of federal taxpayers. In this case, we must decide whether the *Frothingham* barrier should be lowered when a taxpayer attacks a federal statute on the ground that it violates the Establishment and Free Exercise Clauses of the First Amendment. . . .

This Court first faced squarely the question whether a litigant asserting only his status as a taxpayer has standing to maintain a suit in a federal court in *Frothingham v. Mellon*, supra, and that decision must be the starting point for analysis in this case. The taxpayer in *Frothingham* attacked as unconstitutional the Maternity Act of 1921, 42 Stat. 224, which established a federal program of grants to those States which would undertake programs to reduce maternal and infant mortality. . . . The Court noted that a federal taxpayer's "interest in the moneys of the Treasury . . . is comparatively minute and indeterminable" and that "the effect upon future taxation, of any payment out of the [Treasury's] funds, . . . [is] remote, fluctuating and uncertain." As a result, the Court ruled that the taxpayer had failed to allege the type of "direct injury" necessary to confer standing.

Although the barrier *Frothingham* erected against federal taxpayer suits has never been breached, the decision has been the source of some confusion and the object of considerable criticism. The confusion has developed as commentators have tried to determine whether *Frothingham* establishes a constitutional bar to taxpayer suits or whether the Court was simply imposing a rule of self restraint which was not constitutionally compelled. The conflicting viewpoints are reflected in the arguments made to this Court by the parties in this case. The Government has pressed upon us the view that *Frothingham* announced a constitutional rule, compelled by the Article III limitations on federal court jurisdiction and grounded in considerations of the doctrine of separation of powers. Appellants, however, insist that *Frothingham* expressed no more than a policy of judicial self-restraint which can be disregarded when compelling reasons for assuming jurisdiction over a taxpayer's suit exist. The opinion delivered in *Frothingham* can be read to support either position. . . .

To the extent that *Frothingham* has been viewed as resting on policy considerations, it has been criticized as depending on assumptions not consistent with modern conditions. For example, some commentators have pointed out that a number of corporate taxpayers today have a federal tax liability running into hundreds of millions of dollars, and such taxpayers have a far greater monetary stake in the Federal Treasury than they do in any municipal treasury. To some degree, the fear expressed in *Frothingham* that allowing one taxpayer to sue would inundate the federal courts with countless similar suits has been mitigated by the ready availability of the devices of class actions and joinder under the Federal Rules of Civil Procedure, adopted subsequent to the decision in *Frothingham*. . . .

The jurisdiction of federal courts is defined and limited by Article III of the Constitution. In terms relevant to the question for decision in this case, the judicial power of federal courts is constitutionally restricted to "cases" and "controversies." As is so often the situation in constitutional adjudication, those two words have an iceberg quality, containing beneath their surface simplicity submerged complexities which go to the very heart of our constitutional form of government. Embodied in the words "cases" and "controversies" are two complementary but somewhat different limitations. In part those words limit the business of federal courts to questions presented in an adversary context and in a form historically viewed as capable of resolution through the judicial process. And in part those words define the role assigned to the judiciary in a tripartite allocation of power to assure that the federal courts will not intrude into areas committed to the other branches of government. Justiciability is the term of art employed to give expression to this dual limitation placed upon federal courts by the case-and-controversey doctrine.

Justiciability is itself a concept of uncertain meaning and scope. Its reach is illustrated by the various grounds upon which questions sought to be adjudicated in federal courts have been held not to be justiciable. Thus, no justiciable controversy is presented when the parties seek adjudication of only a political question, when the parties are asking for an advisory opinion, when the question sought to be adjudicated has been mooted by subsequent developments, and when there is no standing to maintain the action. Yet it remains true that "[j]usticiability is . . . not a legal concept with a fixed content or susceptible of scientific verification. Its utilization is the resultant of many subtle pressures," *Poe v. Ullman* [367 U.S. 497 (1961)].

Part of the difficulty in giving precise meaning and form to the concept of justiciability stems from the uncertain historical antecedents of the case-and-controversy doctrine. For example, Justice FRANKFURTER twice suggested that historical meaning could be imparted to the concepts of justiciability and case and controversy by reference to the practices of the courts of Westminster when the Constitution was adopted. . . .

However, the power of English judges to deliver advisory opinions was well established at the time the Constitution was drafted. And it is quite clear that "the oldest and most consistent thread in the federal law of justiciability is that the federal courts will not give advisory opinions." Thus, the implicit policies embodied in Article III, and not history alone, impose the rule against advisory opinions on federal courts. When the federal judicial power is invoked to pass upon the validity of actions by the Legislative and Executive Branches of the Government, the rule against advisory opinions implements the separation of powers prescribed by the Constitution and confines federal courts to the role assigned them by Article III. However, the rule against advisory opinions also recognizes that such suits often "are not pressed before the Court with that clear concreteness provided when a question emerges precisely framed and necessary for decision from a clash of adversary argument exploring every aspect of a multifaced situation embracing conflicting and demanding interests." Consequently, the Article III prohibition against advisory opinions reflects the complementary constitutional considerations expressed by the justiciability doctrine: Federal judicial power is limited to those disputes which confine federal courts to a rule consistent with a system of separated powers and which are traditionally thought to be capable of resolution through the judicial process.

Additional uncertainty exists in the doctrine of justiciability because that doctrine has become a blend of constitutional requirements and policy considerations. And a policy limitation is "not always clearly distinguished from the constitutional limitation.". . . The "many subtle pressures" which cause policy considerations to blend into the constitutional limitations of Article III make the justiciability doctrine one of uncertain and shifting contours.

It is in this context that the standing question presented by this case must be viewed and that the Government's argument on that question must be evaluated. As we understand it, the Government's position is that the constitutional scheme of separation of powers, and the deference owed by the federal judiciary to the other two branches of government within that scheme, present an absolute bar to taxpayer suits challenging the validity of federal spending programs. The Government views such suits as involving no more than the mere disagreement by the taxpayer "with the uses to which tax money is put."According to the Government, the resolution of such disagreements is committed to other branches of the Federal Government and not to the judiciary. Consequently, the Government contends that, under no circumstances, should standing be conferred on federal taxpayers to challenge a federal taxing or spending program. An analysis of the function served by standing limitations compels a rejection of the Government's position.

Standing is an aspect of justiciability and, as such, the problem of standing is surrounded by the same complexities and vagaries that inhere in justiciability. . . .

Despite the complexities and uncertainties, some meaningful form can be given to the jurisdictional limitations placed on federal court power by the concept of standing. The fundamental aspect of standing is that it focuses on the party seeking to get his complaint before a federal court and not on the issues he wishes to have adjudicated. The "gist of the question of standing" is whether the party seeking relief has "alleged such a personal stake in the outcome of the controversy as to assure that concrete adverseness which sharpens the presentation of issues upon which the court so largely depends for illumination of difficult constitutional questions." *Baker v. Carr,* [369 U.S. 186] (1962). In other words, when standing is placed in issue in a case, the question is whether the person whose standing is challenged is a proper party to request an adjudication of a particular issue and not whether the issue itself is justiciable. Thus, a party may have standing in a particular case, but the federal court may nevertheless decline to pass on the merits of the case because, for example, it presents a political question. A proper party is demanded so that federal courts will not be asked to decide "ill-defined controversies over constitutional issues," *United Public Workers of America v. Mitchell,* 330 U.S. 75, (1947), or a case which is of "a hypothetical or abstract character," . . . So stated, the standing requirement is closely related to, although more general than, the rule that federal courts will not entertain friendly suits. . . .

When the emphasis in the standing problem is placed on whether the person invoking a federal court's jurisdiction is a proper party to maintain the action, the weakness of the Government's argument in this case becomes apparent. The question whether a particular person is a proper party to maintain the action does not, by its own force, raise separation of powers problems related to improper judicial interference in areas committed to other branches of the Federal Government. Such problems arise, if at all, only from the substantive issues the individual seeks to have adjudicated. Thus, in terms of Article III limitations on federal court jurisdiction, the question of standing is related only to whether the dispute sought to be adjudicated will be presented in an adversary context and in a form historically viewed as capable of judicial resolution. It is for that reason that the emphasis in standing problems is on whether the party invoking federal court jurisdiction has "a personal stake in the outcome of the controversy," *Baker v. Carr,* and whether the dispute touches upon "the legal relations of parties having adverse legal interests." A taxpayer may or may not have the requisite personal stake in the outcome, depending upon the circumstances of the particular case. Therefore, we find no absolute bar in Article III to suits by federal taxpayers challenging allegedly unconstitutional federal taxing and spending programs. There remains, however, the problem of determining the circumstances under which a federal taxpayer will be deemed to have the personal stake and interest that impart the necessary concrete adverseness to such litigation so that standing can be conferred on the taxpayer *qua* taxpayer consistent with the constitutional limitations of Article III. . . .

Whether such individuals have standing to maintain that form of action turns on whether they can demonstrate the necessary stake as taxpayers in the outcome of the litigation to satisfy Article III requirements.

The nexus demanded of federal taxpayers has two aspects to it. First, the taxpayer must establish a logical link between that status and the type of legislative enactment attacked. Thus, a taxpayer will be a proper party to allege the unconstitutionality only of exercises of congressional power under the taxing and spending clause of Art. I, § 8, of the Constitution. It will not be sufficient to allege an incidental expenditure of tax funds in the administration of an essentially regulatory statute. . . . Secondly, the taxpayer must establish a nexus between that status and the precise nature of the constitutional infringement alleged. Under this requirement, the taxpayer must show that the challenged enactment exceeds specific constitutional limitations imposed upon the exercise of the congressional taxing and spending power and not simply that the enactment is generally beyond the powers delegated to Congress by Art. I, § 8. When both nexuses are established, the litigant will have shown a taxpayer's stake in the outcome of the controversy and will be a proper and appropriate party to invoke a federal court's jurisdiction.

The taxpayer-appellants in this case have satisfied both nexuses to support their claim of standing under the test we announce today. Their constitutional challenge is made to an exercise by Congress of its power under Art. I, § 8, to spend for the general welfare, and the challenged program involves a substantial expenditure of federal tax funds. In addition, appellants have alleged that the challenged expenditures violate the Establishment and

Free Exercise Clauses of the First Amendment. Our history vividly illustrates that one of the specific evils feared by those who drafted the Establishment Clause and fought for its adoption was that the taxing and spending power would be used to favor one religion over another or to support religion in general. James Madison, who is generally recognized as the leading architect of the religion clauses of the First Amendment, observed in his famous Memorial and Remonstrance Against Religious Assessments that "the same authority which can force a citizen to contribute three pence only of his property for the support of any one establishment, may force him to conform to any other establishment in all cases whatsoever." 2 Writings of James Madison 183, 186 (Hunt ed. 1901). The concern of Madison and his supporters was quite clearly that religious liberty ultimately would be the victim if government could employ its taxing and spending powers to aid one religion over another or to aid religion in general. The Establishment Clause was designed as a specific bulwark against such potential abuses of governmental power, and that clause of the First Amendment operates as a specific constitutional limitation upon the exercise by Congress of the taxing and spending power conferred by Art. I, § 8.

The allegations of the taxpayer in *Frothingham v. Mellon*, supra, were quite different from those made in this case, and the result in *Frothingham* is consistent with the test of taxpayer standing announced today. The taxpayer in *Frothingham* attacked a federal spending program and she, therefore, established the first nexus required. However, she lacked standing because her constitutional attack was not based on an allegation that Congress, in enacting the Maternity Act of 1921, had breached a specific limitation upon its taxing and spending power. The taxpayer in *Frothingham* alleged essentially that Congress, by enacting the challenged statute, had exceeded the general powers delegated to it by Art. I, § 8, and that Congress had thereby invaded the legislative province reserved to the States by the Tenth Amendment. To be sure, Mrs. Frothingham made the additional allegation that her tax liability would be increased as a result of the allegedly unconstitutional enactment, and she framed that allegation in terms of a deprivation of property without due process of law. However, the Due Process Clause of the Fifth Amendment does not protect taxpayers against increases in tax liability, and the taxpayer in *Frothingham* failed to make any additional claim that the harm she alleged resulted from a breach by Congress of the specific constitutional limitations imposed upon an exercise of the taxing and spending power. In essence, Mrs. Frothingham was attempting to assert the States' interest in their legislative prerogatives and not a federal taxpayer's interest in being free of taxing and spending in contravention of specific constitutional limitations imposed upon Congress' taxing and spending power.

We have noted that the Establishment Clause of the First Amendment does specifically limit the taxing and spending power conferred by Art. I, § 8. Whether the Constitution contains other specific limitations can be determined only in the context of future cases. However, whenever such specific limitations are found, we believe a taxpayer will have a clear stake as a taxpayer in assuring that they are not breached by Congress. Consequently, we hold that a taxpayer will have standing consistent with Article III to invoke federal judicial power when he alleges that congressional action under the taxing and spending clause is in derogation of those constitutional provisions which operate to restrict the exercise of the taxing and spending power. The taxpayer's allegation in such cases would be that his tax money is being extracted and spent in violation of specific constitutional protections against such abuses of legislative power. Such an injury is appropriate for judicial redress, and the taxpayer has established the necessary nexus between his status and the nature of the allegedly unconstitutional action to support his claim of standing to secure judicial review. Under such circumstances, we feel confident that the questions will be framed with the necessary specificity, that the issues will be contested with the necessary adverseness and that the litigation will be pursued with the necessary vigor to assure that the constitutional challenge will be made in a form traditionally thought to be capable of judicial resolution. We lack that confidence in cases such as *Frothingham* where a taxpayer seeks to employ a federal court as a forum in which to air his generalized grievances about the conduct of government or the allocation of power in the Federal System.

Justice DOUGLAS concurring.

While I have joined the opinion of the Court, I do not think that the test it lays down is a durable one for the reasons stated by my Brother HARLAN. . . . It would therefore be the part of wisdom, as I see the problem, to be rid of *Frothingham* here and now. . . .

Most laws passed by Congress do not contain even a ghost of a constitutional question. The "political" decisions, as distinguished from the "justiciable" ones, occupy most of the spectrum of congressional action. The case or controversy requirement comes into play only when the Federal Government does something that affects a person's life, his liberty, or his property. The wrong may be slight or it may be grievous. . . .

We have a Constitution designed to keep government out of private domains. But the fences have often been broken down; and *Frothingham* denied effective machinery to restore them. The Constitution even with the judicial gloss it has acquired plainly is not adequate to protect the individual against the growing bureaucracy in the Legislative and Executive Branches. He faces a formidable opponent in government, even when he is endowed with funds and with courage. The individual is almost certain to be plowed under, unless he has a well-organized active political group to speak for him. The church is one. The press is another. The union is a third. But if a powerful sponsor is lacking, individual liberty withers—in spite of glowing opinions and resounding constitutional phrases.

I would not be niggardly therefore in giving private attorneys general standing to sue. I would certainly not wait for Congress to give its blessing to our deciding cases clearly within our Article III jurisdiction. To wait for a sign from Congress is to allow important constitutional questions to go undecided and personal liberty unprotected.

Justice STEWART concurring.

I join the judgment and opinion of the Court, which I understand to hold only that a federal taxpayer has standing to assert that a specific expenditure of federal funds violates the Establishment Clause of the First Amendment. Because that clause plainly prohibits taxing and spending in aid of religion, every taxpayer can claim a personal constitutional right not to be taxed for the support of a religious institution. The present case is thus readily distinguishable from *Frothingham v. Mellon,* where the taxpayer did not rely on an explicit constitutional prohibition but instead questioned the scope of the powers delegated to the national legislature by Article I of the Constitution. . . .

In concluding that the appellants therefore have standing to sue, we do not undermine the salutary principle, established by *Frothingham* and reaffirmed today, that a taxpayer may not "employ a federal court as a forum in which to air his generalized grievances about the conduct of government or the allocation of power in the Federal System."

Justice FORTAS concurring.

I would confine the ruling in this case to the proposition that a taxpayer may maintain a suit to challenge the validity of a federal expenditure on the ground that the expenditure violates the Establishment Clause. As the Court's opinion recites, there is enough in the constitutional history of the Establishment Clause to support the thesis that this Clause includes a *specific* prohibition upon the use of the power to tax to support an establishment of religion. There is no reason to suggest, and no basis in the logic of this decision for implying, that there may be other types of congressional expenditures which may be attacked by a litigent solely on the basis of his status as a taxpayer.

Justice HARLAN dissenting.

The problems presented by this case are narrow and relatively abstract, but the principles by which they must be resolved involve nothing less than the proper functioning of the federal courts, and so run to the roots of our constitutional system. The nub of my view is that the end result of *Frothingham v. Mellon* was correct, even though, like others, I do not subscribe to all of its reasoning and premises. Although I therefore agree with certain of the conclusions reached today by the Court, I cannot accept the standing doctrine that it substitutes for *Frothingham,* for it seems to me that this new doctrine rests on premises that do not withstand analysis. Accordingly, I respectfully dissent. . . .

The lawsuits here and in *Frothingham* are fundamentally different. They present the question whether federal taxpayers *qua* taxpayers may, in suits in which they do not contest the validity of their previous or existing tax obligations, challenge the constitutionality of the uses for which Congress has authorized the expenditure of public funds. These differences in the purposes of the cases are reflected in differences in the litigants' interests. An action brought to contest the validity of tax liabilities assessed to the plaintiff is designed to vindicate interests that are personal and proprietary. The wrongs alleged and the relief sought by such a plaintiff are unmistakably private; only secondarily are his interests representative of those of the general population. I take it that the Court, although it does not pause to examine the question, believes that the interests of those who as taxpayers challenge the constitutionality of public expenditures may, at least in certain circumstances, be similar. Yet this assumption is surely mistaken. . . .

Presumably the Court recognizes at least certain . . . hazards, else it would not have troubled to impose limitations upon the situations in which, and purposes for which, such suits may be brought. Nonetheless, the limitations adopted by the Court are, as I have endeavored to indicate, wholly untenable. This is the more unfortunate because there is available a resolution of this problem that entirely satisfies the demands of the principle of separation of powers. This Court has previously held that individual litigants have standing to represent the public interest, despite their lack of economic or other personal interests, if Congress has appropriately authorized such suits. Any hazards to the proper allocation of authority among the three branches of the Government would be substantially diminished if public actions had been pertinently authorized by Congress and the President. I appreciate that this Court does not ordinarily await the mandate of other branches of the Government, but it seems to me that the extraordinary character of public actions, and of the mischievous, if not dangerous, consequences they involve for the proper functioning of our constitutional system, and in particular of the federal courts, makes such judicial forbearance the part of wisdom. It must be emphasized that the implications of these questions of judicial policy are of fundamental significance for the other branches of the Federal Government.

Such a rule could readily be applied to this case. Although various efforts have been made in Congress to authorize public actions to contest the validity of federal expenditures in aid of religiously affiliated schools and other institutions, no such authorization has yet been given.

This does not mean that we would, under such a rule, be enabled to avoid our constitutional responsibilities, or that we would confine to limbo the First Amendment or any other constitutional command. The question here is not, despite the Court's unarticulated premise, whether the religious clauses of the First Amendment are hereafter to be enforced by the federal courts; the issue is simply whether plaintiffs of an *additional* category, heretofore excluded from those courts, are to be permitted to maintain suits. The recent history of this Court is replete with illustrations, including even one announced today that questions involving the religious clauses will not, if federal taxpayers are prevented from contesting federal expenditures, be left "unacknowledged, unresolved, and undecided."

Accordingly, for the reasons contained in this opinion, I would affirm the judgment of the District Court.

Valley Forge Christian College v. Americans United for Separation of Church and State, Inc.
454 U.S. 464, 102 S.Ct. 752 (1982)

Americans United for Separation of Church and State, an organization dedicated to the separation of religion from government, filed a suit in federal district court in Pennsylvania to stop the Department of Health, Education and Welfare (now the Department of Education) from conveying as "surplus property" a closed and former army hospital to Valley Forge Christian College. Under the Federal Property and Administrative Services Act of 1949, the department has authority to sell surplus government property for educational use to nonprofit, tax-exempt educational institutions. Congress has the power to "dispose of and make all needful Rules and Regulations respecting the . . . Property belonging to the United States," under Article IV, Section 3, Clause 2. But Americans United for Separation of Church

and State contended that the department's conveyance here
abridged its members First Amendment rights to religious freedom and "deprived [them] of the fair and constitutional use of
[their] tax dollars." The district court dismissed the suit but the
Court of Appeals for the Third Circuit reversed. Thereupon,
Valley Forge Christian College appealed to the Supreme Court.

Justice REHNQUIST delivers the opinion of the Court.

We need not mince words when we say that the concept of
"Art. III standing" has not been defined with complete consistency
in all of the various cases decided by this Court which have discussed it, nor when we say that this very fact is probably proof
that the concept cannot be reduced to a one-sentence or one-
paragraph definition. But of one thing we may be sure: Those
who do not possess Art. III standing may not litigate as suitors
in the courts of the United States. Article III, which is every bit
as important in its circumscription of the judicial power of the
United States as in its granting of that power, is not merely a
troublesome hurdle to be overcome if possible so as to reach
the "merits" of a lawsuit which a party desires to have adjudicated;
it is a part of the basic charter promulgated by the Framers of
the Constitution at Philadelphia in 1787, a charter which created
a general government, provided for the interaction between that
government and the governments of the several States, and was
later amended so as to either enhance or limit its authority with
respect to both States and individuals. . . .

[I]n *Flast v. Cohen,* [392 U.S. 83 (1968)], [t]he Court developed
a two-part test to determine whether the plaintiffs had standing
to sue. First, because a taxpayer alleges injury only by virtue of
his liability for taxes, the Court held that "a taxpayer will be a
proper party to allege the unconstitutionality only of exercises
of congressional power under the taxing and spending clause
of Art. I, § 8, of the Constitution." Second, the Court required
the taxpayer to "show that the challenged enactment exceeds
specific constitutional limitations upon the exercise of the taxing
and spending power and not simply that the enactment is generally
beyond the powers delegated to Congress by Art. I, § 8."

Unlike the plaintiffs in *Flast,* respondents fail the first prong
of the test for taxpayer standing. Their claim is deficient in two
respects. First, the source of their complaint is not a congressional
action, but a decision by HEW to transfer a parcel of federal
property. *Flast* limited taxpayer standing to challenges directed
"only [at] exercises of congressional power." See *Schlesinger v.
Reservists Committee to Stop the War,* [418 U.S. 208 (1974)] (denying
standing because the taxpayer plaintiffs "did not challenge an

enactment under Art. I, § 8, but rather the action of the Executive Branch").

Second, and perhaps redundantly, the property transfer about which respondents complain was not an exercise of authority conferred by the Taxing and Spending Clause of Art. I, § 8. The authorizing legislation, the Federal Property and Administrative Services Act of 1949, was an evident exercise of Congress' power under the Property Clause, Art. IV, § 3, cl. 2. Respondents do not dispute this conclusion, and it is decisive of any claim of taxpayer standing under the *Flast* precedent.

Justice BRENNAN, with whom Justice MARSHALL and Justice BLACKMUN join, dissenting.

The opinion of the Court is a stark example of this unfortunate trend of resolving cases at the "threshold" while obscuring the nature of the underlying rights and interests at stake. The Court waxes eloquent on the blend of prudential and constitutional considerations that combine to create our misguided "standing" jurisprudence. *But not one word is said about the Establishment Clause right that the plaintiff seeks to enforce.* And despite its pat recitation of our standing decisions, the opinion utterly fails, except by the sheerest form of *ipse dixit*, to explain why this case is unlike *Flast v. Cohen* (1968), and is controlled instead by *Frothingham v. Mellon* (1923). . . .

It is at once apparent that the test of standing formulated by the Court in *Flast* sought to reconcile the developing doctrine of taxpayer "standing" with the Court's historical understanding that the Establishment Clause was intended to prohibit the Federal Government from using tax funds for the advancement of religion, and thus the constitutional imperative of taxpayer standing in certain cases brought pursuant to the Establishment Clause. The two-pronged "nexus" test offered by the Court, despite its general language, is best understood as "a determinant of standing of plaintiffs alleging only injury as taxpayers who challenge alleged violations of the Establishment and Free Exercise Clauses of the First Amendment," and not as a general statement of standing principles. The test explains what forms of governmental action may be attacked by someone alleging *only* taxpayer status, and, without ruling out the possibility that history might reveal another similarly founded provision, explains why an Establishment Clause claim is treated differently from any other assertion that the Federal Government has exceeded the bounds of the law in allocating its largesse. . . .

The nexus test that the Court "announced," sought to maintain necessary continuity with prior cases, and set forth principles to guide future cases involving taxpayer standing. But *Flast* did not depart from the principle that no judgment about standing should be made without a fundamental understanding of the rights at issue. The two-part *Flast* test did not supply the rationale for the Court's decision, but rather is exposition: That rationale was supplied by an understanding of the nature of the restrictions on government power imposed by the Constitution and the intended beneficiaries of those restrictions.

It may be that Congress can tax for *almost* any reason, or for no reason at all. There is, so far as I have been able to discern, but one constitutionally imposed limit on that authority. Congress cannot use tax money to support a church, or to encourage religion. That is "*the* forbidden exaction." *Everson v. Board of Education* [330 U.S. 1 (1947)]. In absolute terms the history of the Establishment Clause of the First Amendment makes this clear. History also makes it clear that the federal taxpayer is a singularly "proper and appropriate party to invoke a federal court's jurisdiction" to challenge a federal bestowal of largesse as a violation of the Establishment Clause. Each, and indeed every, federal taxpayer suffers precisely the injury that the Establishment Clause guards against when the Federal Government directs that funds be taken from the pocketbooks of the citizenry and placed into the coffers of the ministry.

A taxpayer cannot be asked to raise his objection to such use of his funds at the time he pays his tax. Apart from the unlikely circumstance in which the Government announced in advance that a particular levy would be used for religious subsidies, taxpayers could hardly assert that they were being injured until the Government actually lent its support to a religious venture. Nor would it be reasonable to require him to address his claim to those officials charged with the collection of federal taxes. Those officials would be without the means to provide appropriate redress—there is no practical way to segregate the complaining taxpayer's money from that being devoted to the religious purpose. Surely, then, a taxpayer must have standing at the time that he learns of the Government's alleged Establishment Clause violation to seek equitable relief in order to halt the continuing and intolerable burden on his pocketbook, his conscience, and his constitutional rights.

Blind to history, the Court attempts to distinguish this case from *Flast* by wrenching snippets of language from our opinions, and by perfunctorily applying that language under color of the first prong of *Flast*'s two-part nexus test. The tortuous distinctions thus produced are specious, at best: at worst, they are pernicious to our constitutional heritage.

First, the Court finds this case different from *Flast* because here the "source of [plaintiffs'] complaint is not a *congressional* action, but a decision by HEW to transfer a parcel of federal property." This attempt at distinction cannot withstand scrutiny. *Flast* involved a challenge to the actions of the Commissioner of Education, and other officials of HEW, in disbursing funds under the Elementary and Secondary Education Act of 1965 to "religious and sectarian" schools. Plaintiffs disclaimed "any intent[ion] to challenge . . . all programs under . . . the Act." Rather, they claimed that defendant-administrators' approval of such expenditures was not authorized by the Act, or alternatively, to the extent the expenditures were authorized, the Act was "unconstitutional and void." In the present case, respondents challenge HEW's grant of property pursuant to the Federal Property and Administrative Services Act of 1949, seeking to enjoin HEW "from making a grant of this and other property to the [defendant] so long as such a grant will violate the Establishment Clause." It may be that the Court is concerned with the adequacy of respondents' pleading; respondents have not, in so many words, asked for a declaration that the "Federal Property and Administrative Services Act is unconstitutional and void to the extent that it authorizes HEW's actions." I would not construe their complaint so narrowly.

More fundamentally, no clear division can be drawn in this context between actions of the Legislative Branch and those of the Executive Branch. To be sure, the First Amendment is phrased as a restriction on Congress' legislative authority; this is only natural since the Constitution assigns the authority to legislate and appropriate only to the Congress. But it is difficult to conceive of an expenditure for which the last governmental actor, either implementing directly the legislative will, or acting within the scope of legislatively delegated authority, is not an Executive Branch official. The First Amendment binds the Government as a whole, regardless of which branch is at work in a particular instance.

The Court's second purported distinction between this case and *Flast* is equally unavailing. The majority finds it "decisive" that the Federal Property and Administrative Services Act of 1949 "was an evident exercise of Congress' power under the Property Clause, Art. IV, § 3, cl. 2," while the Government action in *Flast* was taken under Art. I, § 8. The Court relies on *United States v. Richardson*, 418 U.S. [166] (1974), and *Schlesinger v. Reservists Committee to Stop the War*, 418 U.S. 208 (1974), to support the distinction between the two Clauses, noting that those cases involved alleged deviations from the requirements of Art. I, § 9, cl. 7, and Art. I, § 6, cl. 2, respectively. The standing defect in each case was *not*, however, the failure to allege a violation of the Spending Clause; rather, the taxpayers in those cases had not complained of the distribution of Government largesse, and thus failed to meet the essential requirement of taxpayer standing recognized in *Doremus* [*v. Board of Education*, 342 U.S. 429 (1952)].

It can make no constitutional difference in the case before us whether the donation to the petitioner here was in the form of a cash grant to build a facility, see *Tilton v. Richardson*, 403 U.S. 672 (1971), or in the nature of a gift of property including a facility already built. That this is a meaningless distinction is illustrated by *Tilton*. In that case, taxpayers were afforded standing to object to the fact that the Government had not received adequate assurance that if the property that it financed for use as an educational facility was later converted to religious uses, it would receive full value for the property, as the Constitution requires. The complaint here is precisely that, although the property at issue is actually being used for a sectarian purpose, the Government has not received, nor demanded, full value payment. Whether undertaken pursuant to the Property Clause or the Spending Clause, the breach of the Establishment Clause, and the relationship of the taxpayer to that breach, is precisely the same.

Plainly hostile to the Framers' understanding of the Establishment Clause, and *Flast*'s enforcement of that understanding, the Court vents that hostility under the guise of standing, "to slam the courthouse door against plaintiffs who [as the Framers intended] are entitled to full consideration of their [Establishment Clause] claims on the merits." *Barlow v. Collins*, 397 U.S. 159 (1970) (BRENNAN, J., concurring in result and dissenting). Therefore, I dissent.

Justice STEVENS dissenting.

For the Court to hold that plaintiffs' standing depends on whether the Government's transfer was an exercise of its power to spend money, on the one hand, or its power to dispose of tangible property, on the other, is to trivialize the standing doctrine. . . .

Today the Court holds, in effect, that the Judiciary has no greater role in enforcing the Establishment Clause than in enforcing other "norm[s] of conduct which the Federal Government is bound to honor," such as the Accounts Clause, *United States v. Richardson*, and the Incompatibility Clause, *Schlesinger v. Reservists Committee to Stop the War*. Ironically, however, its decision rests on the premise that the difference between a disposition of funds pursuant to the Spending Clause and a disposition of realty pursuant to the Property Clause is of fundamental jurisprudential significance. With all due respect, I am persuaded that the essential holding of *Flast v. Cohen* attaches special importance to the Establishment Clause and does not permit the drawing of a tenuous distinction between the Spending Clause and the Property Clause.

Baker v. Carr

369 U.S. 186, 82 S.Ct. 691 (1962)

In 1901, the Tennessee legislature apportioned both houses and provided for subsequent reapportionment every ten years on the basis of the number of voters in each of the state's counties as reported in the census. But for more than sixty years proposals to redistribute legislative seats failed to pass, while the state's population shifted from rural to urban areas. Charles Baker and several other citizens and urban residents sued various Tennessee officials. Baker claimed that as an urban resident he was being denied the equal protection of the law under the Fourteenth Amendment. He asked the court to order state officials to either hold an at-large election or an election in which legislators would be selected from constituencies in accordance with the 1960 federal census. The federal district court dismissed the suit, conceding that Baker's civil rights were being denied but holding that the court could offer no remedy. Baker made a further appeal to the Supreme Court.

When the Supreme Court granted review in *Baker v. Carr,* it faced two central issues: first, whether the malapportionment of a state legislature is a "political question" for which courts have no remedy and second, the merits of Baker's claim that individuals have a right to equal votes and equal representation. With potentially broad political consequences, the case was divisive for the Court and was carried over and reargued for a term. Allies on judicial self-restraint, Justices Frankfurter and Harlan were committed to their view, expressed in *Colegrove v. Green,* 328 U.S. 549 (1948), that the "Court ought not to enter this political thicket." At conference, Justices Clark and Whittaker supported their view that the case presented a nonjusticiable political question. By contrast, Chief Justice Warren and Justices Black, Douglas, and Brennan thought that the issue was justiciable. They were also prepared to address the merits of the case. The pivotal justice, Potter Stewart, considered the issue justiciable, but he refused to address the merits of the case. He voted to reverse the lower court ruling only if the Court's decision was limited to holding that courts have jurisdiction to decide such disputes. He did not want the Court to take on the merits of reapportionment in this case.

Assigned the task of drafting the opinion, Brennan had to hold on to Stewart's vote and dissuade Black and Douglas from writing opinions on the merits that would threaten the loss of the crucial fifth vote. After circulating his draft and incorporating suggested changes, he optimistically wrote Black, "Potter Stewart was satisfied with all of the changes. The Chief also is agreed. It, therefore, looks as though we have a court agreed upon this as circulated." It appeared that the decision would come down on the original five to four vote.

Clark, however, had been pondering the fact that in this case the population ratio for the urban and rural districts in Tennessee was more than nineteen to one. As he put it, "city slickers" had been "too long deprive[d] of a constitutional form of government." Clark concluded that citizens denied equal voting power had no political recourse; their only recourse was to the federal judiciary. Clark thus wrote an opinion abandoning Frankfurter and going beyond the majority to address the merits of the claim.

Brennan faced the dilemma of how to bring in Clark without losing Stewart, and thereby enlarge the consensus. Further negotiations were necessary but limited. Brennan wrote his brethren:

> The changes represent the maximum to which Potter will subscribe. We discussed much more elaborate changes which would have taken over a substantial part of Tom Clark's opinion. Potter felt that if they were made it would be necessary for him to dissent from that much of the revised opinion. I therefore decided it was best not to press for the changes but to hope that Tom will be willing to join the Court opinion but say he would go further as per his separate opinion.

Even though there were five votes for deciding the merits, the final opinion was limited to the jurisdictional question. Douglas refrained from addressing the merits in his concurring opinion. Stewart joined with an opinion emphasizing how limited he deemed the ruling. Clark filed his opinion discussing the merits of the case. Whittaker withdrew from the case, retiring from the Court two weeks later because of poor health. Only Frankfurter and Harlan were left dissenting, resulting in a six-to-two majority.*

Justice BRENNAN delivers the opinion of the Court.

[W]e hold today only (a) that the court possessed jurisdiction of the subject matter: (b) that a justiciable cause of action is stated upon which appellants would be entitled to appropriate relief; and (c) because appellees raise the issue before this Court, that the appellants have standing to challenge the Tennessee apportionment statutes. Beyond noting that we have no cause at this

---

* Sources of quotations are internal Court memos, located in the William J. Brennan, Jr., Papers, Library of Congress; and the Tom C. Clark Papers, University of Texas Law School.

stage to doubt the District Court will be able to fashion relief if violations of constitutional rights are found, it is improper now to consider what remedy would be most appropriate if appellants prevail at the trial.

JURISDICTION OF THE SUBJECT MATTER

The District Court was uncertain whether our cases withholding federal judicial relief rested upon a lack of federal jurisdiction or upon the inappropriateness of the subject matter for judicial consideration—what we have designated "nonjusticiability." The distinction between the two grounds is significant. In the instance of nonjusticiability, consideration of the cause is not wholly and immediately foreclosed: rather, the Court's inquiry necessarily proceeds to the point of deciding whether the duty asserted can be judicially identified and its breach judicially determined, and whether protection for the right asserted can be judicially molded. In the instance of lack of jurisdiction the cause either does not "arise under" the Federal Constitution, laws or treaties (or fall within one of the other enumerated categories of Art. III, § 2), or is not a "case or controversy" within the meaning of that section; or the cause is not one described by any jurisdictional statute. Our conclusion that this cause presents no nonjusticiable "political question" settles the only possible doubt that it is a case or controversy. . . .

The appellees refer to *Colegrove v. Green,* 328 U.S. 549 [1946], as authority that the District Court lacked jurisdiction of the subject matter. Appellees misconceive the holding of that case. The holding was precisely contrary to their reading of it. Seven members of the Court participated in the decision. Unlike many other cases in this field which have assumed without discussion that there was jurisdiction, all three opinions filed in Colegrove discussed the question. Two of the opinions expressing the views of four of the Justices, a majority, flatly held that there was jurisdiction of that subject matter. Justice BLACK joined by Justice DOUGLAS and Justice MURPHY stated: "It is my judgment that the District Court had jurisdiction. . . ." Justice RUTLEDGE, writing separately, expressed agreement with this conclusion. . . . Indeed, it is even questionable that the opinion of Justice FRANK-FURTER, joined by Justices REED and BURTON, doubted jurisdiction of the subject matter. . . .

JUSTICIABILITY

In holding that the subject matter of this suit was not justiciable, the District Court relied on *Colegrove v. Green,* supra, and subsequent *per curiam* cases. The court stated: "From a review of these decisions there can be no doubt that the federal rule . . . is that the federal courts . . . will not intervene in cases of this type to compel legislative reapportionment." We understand the District

Court to have read the cited cases as compelling the conclusion that since the appellants sought to have a legislative apportionment held unconstitutional, their suit presented a "political question" and was therefore nonjusticiable. We hold that this challenge to an apportionment presents no nonjusticiable "political question." The cited cases do not hold the contrary.

Of course the mere fact that the suit seeks protection of a political right does not mean it presents a political question. Such an objection "is little more than a play upon words." Rather, it is argued that apportionment cases, whatever the actual wording of the complaint, can involve no federal constitutional right except one resting on the guaranty of a republican form of government, and that complaints based on that clause have been held to present political questions which are nonjusticiable.

We hold that the claim pleaded here neither rests upon nor implicates the Guaranty Clause and that its justiciability is therefore not foreclosed by our decisions of cases involving that clause. . . . To show why we reject the argument based on the Guaranty Clause, we must examine the authorities under it. But because there appears to be some uncertainty as to why those cases did present political questions, and specifically as to whether this apportionment case is like those cases, we deem it necessary first to consider the contours of the "political question" doctrine.

Our discussion, even at the price of extending this opinion, requires review of a number of political question cases, in order to expose the attributes of the doctrine—attributes which, in various settings, diverge, combine, appear, and disappear in seeming disorderliness. . . .

We have said that "In determining whether a question falls within [the political question] category, the appropriateness under our system of government of attributing finality to the action of the political departments and also the lack of satisfactory criteria for a judicial determination are dominant considerations." *Coleman v. Miller* [307 U.S. 433 (1939)]. The nonjusticiability of a political question is primarily a function of the separation of powers. Much confusion results from the capacity of the "political question" label to obscure the need for case-by-case inquiry. Deciding whether a matter has in any measure been committed by the Constitution to another branch of government, or whether the action of that branch exceeds whatever authority has been committed, is itself a delicate exercise in constitutional interpretation, and is a responsibility of this Court as ultimate interpreter of the Constitution. To demonstrate this requires no less than to analyze representative cases and to infer from them the analytical threads that make up the political question doctrine. We shall then show that none of those threads catches this case.

Foreign relations: There are sweeping statements to the effect that all questions touching foreign relations are political questions. Not only does resolution of such issues frequently turn on standards that defy judicial application, or involve the exercise of a discretion demonstrably committed to the executive or legislature; but many such questions uniquely demand single-voiced statement of the Government's views. Yet it is error to suppose that every case or controversy which touches foreign relations lies beyond judicial cognizance. Our cases in this field seem invariably to show a discriminating analysis of the particular question posed, in terms of the history of its management by the political branches, of its susceptibility to judicial handling in the light of its nature and posture in the specific case, and of the possible consequences of judicial action. . . .

Dates of duration of hostilities: Though it has been stated broadly that the power which declared the necessity is the power to declare its cessation, and what the cessation requires," *Commercial Trust Co. v. Miller,* 262 U.S. 51 [1923], here too analysis reveals isolable reasons for the presence of political questions, underlying this Court's refusal to review the political departments' determination of when or whether a war has ended. Dominant is the need for finality in the political determination, for emergency's nature demands "A prompt and unhesitating obedience." *Martin v. Mott,* 12 Wheat. [(256 U.S.) 19 (1827)] [Calling up of militia.] . . . Further, clearly definable criteria for decision may be available. In such case the political question barrier falls away. . . .

Validity of enactments: In *Coleman v. Miller,* supra, this Court held that the questions of how long a proposed amendment to the Federal Constitution remained open to ratification, and what effect a prior rejection had on a subsequent ratification, were committed to congressional resolution and involved criteria of decision that necessarily escaped the judicial grasp. Similar considerations apply to the enacting process: "The respect due to coequal and independent departments," and the need for finality and certainty about the status of a statute contribute to judicial reluctance to inquire whether, as passed, it complied with all requisite formalities. *Field v. Clark,* 143 U.S. 649 [1892]. . . .

Republican form of government: Luther v. Borden, 7 How. 1 [1848], though in form simply an action for damages for trespass was, as Daniel Webster said in opening the argument for the defense, "an unusual case." The defendants, admitting an otherwise tortious breaking and entering, sought to justify their action on the ground that they were agents of the established lawful government of Rhode Island, which State was then under martial law to defend itself from active insurrection; that the plaintiff was engaged in that insurrection; and that they entered under orders to arrest the plaintiff. The case arose "out of the unfortunate political differences which agitated the people of Rhode Island in 1841 and 1842," and which had resulted in a situation wherein two groups laid competing claims to recognition as the lawful government. . . .

Chief Justice TANEY's opinion for the Court reasoned as follows: (1) If a court were to hold the defendants' acts unjustified because the charter government had no legal existence during the period in question, it would follow that all of that government's actions—laws enacted, taxes collected, salaries paid, accounts settled, sentences passed—were of no effect; and that "the officers who carried their decisions into operation [were]answerable as trespassers, if not in some cases as criminals." There was, of course, no room for application of any doctrine of *de facto* status to uphold prior acts of an officer not authorized *de jure,* for such would have defeated the plaintiff's very action. A decision for the plaintiff would inevitably have produced some significant measure of chaos, a consequence to be avoided if it could be done without abnegation of the judicial duty to uphold the Constitution.

(2) No state court had recognized as a judicial responsibility settlement of the issue of the locus of state governmental authority. Indeed, the courts of Rhode Island had in several cases held that "it rested with the political power to decide whether the charter government had been displaced or not," and that that department had acknowledged no change.

(3) Since "[t]he question relates, altogether, to the constitution and laws of [the] . . . State," the courts of the United States had to follow the state courts' decisions unless there was a federal constitutional ground for overturning them.

(4) No provision of the Constitution could be or had been invoked for this purpose except Art. IV, § 4, the Guaranty Clause. Having already noted the absence of standards whereby the choice between governments could be made by a court acting independently, Chief Justice TANEY now found further textual and practical reasons for concluding that, if any department of the United States was empowered by the Guaranty Clause to resolve the issue, it was not the judiciary:

"Under this article of the Constitution it rests with Congress to decide what government is the established one in a State. For as the United States guarantee to each State a republican government, Congress must necessarily decide what government is established in the State before it can determine whether it is a republican or not. And when the senators and representatives of a State are admitted into the councils of the Union, the authority of the government under which they are appointed, as well as its republican character, is recognized by the proper constitutional authority. And its decision is binding on every other department of the government, and could not be questioned in a judicial tribunal. It is true that the contest in this case did not last long enough to bring the matter to this issue; and . . . Congress was not called upon to decide the controversy. Yet the right to decide is placed there, and not in the courts.

"So, too, as relates to the clause in the above-mentioned article of the Constitution, providing for cases of domestic violence. It rested with Congress, too, to determine upon the means proper to be adopted to fulfill this guarantee. . . . [B]y the act of February 28, 1795, [Congress] provided, that, 'in case of an insurrection in any State against the government thereof, it shall be lawful for the President of the United States, on application of the legislature of such State or of the executive (when the legislature cannot be convened) to call forth such number of the militia of any other State or States, as may be applied for, as he may judge sufficient to suppress such insurrection.'

"By this act, the power of deciding whether the exigency had arisen upon which the government of the United States is bound to interfere, is given to the President" [*Luther v. Borden*].

Clearly, several factors were thought by the Court in *Luther* to make the question there "political": the commitment to the other branches of the decision as to which is the lawful state government; the unambiguous action by the President, in recognizing the charter government as the lawful authority; the need for finality in the executive's decision; and the lack of criteria by which a court could determine which form of government was republican. . . .

But the only significance that *Luther* could have for our immediate purposes is in its holding that the Guaranty Clause is not a repository of judicially manageable standards which a court could utilize independently in order to identify a State's lawful government. The Court has since refused to resort to the Guaranty Clause—which alone had been invoked for the purpose—as the source of a constitutional standard for invalidating state action. . . .

We come, finally, to the ultimate inquiry whether our precedents as to what constitutes a nonjusticiable "political question" bring the case before us under the umbrella of that doctrine. A natural beginning is to note whether any of the common characteristics which we have been able to identify and label descriptively are present. We find none: The question here is the consistency of state action with the Federal Constitution. We have no question decided, or to be decided, by a political branch of government coequal with this Court. Nor do we risk embarrassment of our government abroad, or grave disturbance at home if we take issue with Tennessee as to the constitutionality of her action here challenged. Nor need the appellants, in order to succeed in this action, ask the Court to enter upon policy determinations for which judicially manageable standards are lacking. Judicial standards under the Equal Protection Clause are well developed and familiar, and it has been open to courts since the enactment of the Fourteenth Amendment to determine, if on the particular facts they must, that a discrimination reflects *no* policy, but simply arbitrary and capricious action.

This case does, in one sense, involve the allocation of political power within a State, and the appellants might conceivably have added a claim under the Guaranty Clause. Of course, as we have seen, any reliance on that clause would be futile. But because any reliance on the Guaranty Clause could not have succeeded it does not follow that appellants may not be heard on the equal protection claim which in fact they tender. . . .

We conclude that the complaint's allegations of a denial of equal protection present a justiciable constitutional cause of action upon which appellants are entitled to a trial and a decision. The right asserted is within the reach of judicial protection under the Fourteenth Amendment.

The judgment of the District Court is reversed and the cause is remanded for further proceedings consistent with this opinion.

Reversed and remanded.

Justice WHITTAKER did not participate in the decision of this case.

Justice DOUGLAS concurring.

While I join the opinion of the Court and, like the Court, do not reach the merits, a word of explanation is necessary. I put to one side the problems of "political" questions involving the distribution of power between this Court, the Congress, and the Chief Executive. We have here a phase of the recurring problem of the relation of the federal courts to state agencies. More particularly, the question is the extent to which a State may weight one person's vote more heavily than it does another's.

So far as voting rights are concerned, there are large gaps in the Constitution. Yet the right to vote is inherent in the republican form of government envisaged by Article IV, Section 4 of the Constitution. . . .

Race, color, or previous condition of servitude is an impermissible standard by reason of the Fifteenth Amendment, and that alone is sufficient to explain *Gomillion v. Lightfoot*, 364 U.S. 339 [1960].

Sex is another impermissible standard by reason of the Nineteenth Amendment.

There is a third barrier to a State's freedom in prescribing qualifications of voters and that is the Equal Protection Clause of the Fourteenth Amendment, the provision invoked here. And so the question is, may a State weight the vote of one county or one district more heavily than it weights the vote in another?

The traditional test under the Equal Protection Clause has been whether a State has made "an invidious discrimination," as it does when it selects "a particular race or nationality for oppressive treatment." Universal equality is not the test; there is room for weighting. . . .

I agree with my Brother CLARK that if the allegations in the complaint can be sustained a case for relief is established. We are told that a single vote in Moore County, Tennessee, is worth 19 votes in Hamilton County, that one vote in Stewart or in Chester County is worth nearly eight times a single vote in Shelby or Knox County. The opportunity to prove that an "invidious discrimination" exists should therefore be given the appellants.

Justice CLARK concurring.

One emerging from the rash of opinions with their accompanying clashing of views may well find himself suffering a mental blindness. The Court holds that the appellants have alleged a cause of action. However, it refuses to award relief here—although the facts are undisputed—and fails to give the District Court any guidance whatever. One dissenting opinion, bursting with words that go through so much and conclude with so little, contemns the majority action as "a massive repudiation of the experience of our whole past." Another describes the complaint as merely asserting conclusory allegations that Tennessee's apportionment is "incorrect," "arbitrary," "obsolete," and "unconstitutional." I believe it can be shown that this case is distinguishable from earlier cases dealing with the distribution of political power by a State, that a patent violation of the Equal Protection Clause of the United States Constitution has been shown, and that an appropriate remedy may be formulated. . . .

The truth is that—although this case has been here for two years and has had over six hours' argument (three times the ordinary case) and has been most carefully considered over and over again by us in Conference and individually—no one, not even the State nor the dissenters, has come up with any rational basis for Tennessee's apportionment statute. . . .

Although I find the Tennessee apportionment statute offends the Equal Protection Clause, I would not consider intervention by this Court into so delicate a field if there were any other relief available to the people of Tennessee. But the majority of the people of Tennessee have no "practical opportunities for exerting their political weight at the polls" to correct the existing "invidious discrimination." Tennessee has no initiative and referendum. I have searched diligently for other "practical opportunities" present under the law. I find none other than through the federal courts. The majority of the voters have been caught up in a legislative strait jacket. Tennessee has an "informed, civically militant electorate" and "an aroused popular conscience," but it does not sear "the conscience of the people's representatives." This is because the legislative policy has riveted the present seats in the Assembly to their respective constituencies, and by the votes of their incumbents a reapportionment of any kind is prevented. The people have been rebuffed at the hands of the Assembly; they have tried the constitutional convention route, but since the call must originate in the Assembly it, too, has been fruitless. They have tried Tennessee courts with the same result, and Governors have fought the tide only to flounder. It is said that there is recourse in Congress and perhaps that may be, but from a practical standpoint this is without substance. To date Congress has never undertaken such a task in any State. We therefore must conclude that the people of Tennessee are stymied and without judicial intervention will be saddled with the present discrimination in the affairs of their state government.

Justice STEWART concurring.

The separate writings of my dissenting and concurring Brothers stray so far from the subject of today's decision as to convey, I think, a distressingly inaccurate impression of what the Court decides. For that reason, I think it appropriate, in joining the opinion of the Court, to emphasize in a few words what the opinion does and does not say.

The Court today decides three things and no more: "(a) that the court possessed jurisdiction of the subject matter; (b) that a justiciable cause of action is stated upon which appellants would be entitled to appropriate relief; and (c) . . . that the appellants have standing to challenge the Tennessee apportionment statutes.". . .

Justice FRANKFURTER, with whom Justice HARLAN joins, dissenting.

The Court today reverses a uniform course of decision established by a dozen cases, including one by which the very claim now sustained was unanimously rejected only five years ago. The impressive body of rulings thus cast aside reflected the equally uniform course of our political history regarding the relationship between population and legislative representation—a wholly different matter from denial of the franchise to individuals because of race, color, religion or sex. Such a massive repudiation of the experience of our whole past in asserting destructively novel judicial power demands a detailed analysis of the role of this Court in our constitutional scheme. Disregard of inherent limits in the effective exercise of the Court's "judicial Power" not only presages the futility of judicial intervention in the essentially political conflict of forces by which the relation between population and representation has time out of mind been and now is determined. It may well impair the Court's position as the ultimate organ of "the supreme Law of the Land" in that vast range of legal problems, often strongly entangled in popular feeling, on which this Court must pronounce. The Court's authority—possessed of neither the purse nor the sword—ultimately rests on sustained public confidence in its moral sanction. Such feeling must be nourished by the Court's complete detachment, in fact and in appearance, from political entanglements and by abstention from injecting itself into the clash of political forces in political settlements.

A hypothetical claim resting on abstract assumptions is now for the first time made the basis for affording illusory relief for a particular evil even though it foreshadows deeper and more pervasive difficulties in consequence. The claim is hypothetical and the assumptions are abstract because the Court does not vouchsafe the lower courts—state and federal—guidelines for formulating specific, definite, wholly unprecedented remedies for the inevitable litigations that today's umbrageous disposition is bound to stimulate in connection with politically motivated reapportionments in so many States. In such a setting, to promulgate jurisdiction in the abstract is meaningless. It is as devoid of reality as "a brooding omnipresence in the sky," for it conveys no intimation what relief, if any, a District Court is capable of affording that would not invite legislatures to play ducks and drakes with the judiciary. For this Court to direct the District Court to enforce a claim to which the Court has over the years consistently found itself required to deny legal enforcement and at the same time to find it necessary to withhold any guidance to the lower court how to enforce this turnabout, new legal claim, manifests an odd—indeed an esoteric—conception of judicial propriety. One of the Court's supporting opinions, as elucidated by commentary, unwittingly affords a disheartening preview of the mathematical quagmire (apart from divers judicially inappropriate and elusive determinants) into which this Court today catapults the lower courts of the country without so much as adumbrating the basis for a legal calculus as a means of extrication. Even assuming the indispensable intellectual disinterestedness on the part of judges in such matters, they do not have accepted legal standards or criteria or even reliable analogies to draw upon for making judicial judgments. To charge courts with the task of accommodating the incommensurable factors of policy that underlie these mathematical puzzles is to attribute, however flatteringly, omnicompetence to judges. . . .

We were soothingly told at the bar of this Court that we need not worry about the kind of remedy a court could effectively fashion once the abstract constitutional right to have courts pass on a state-wide system of electoral districting is recognized as a matter of judicial rhetoric, because legislatures would heed the Court's admonition. This is not only a euphoric hope. It implies a sorry confession of judicial impotence in place of a frank acknowledgment that there is not under our Constitution a judicial remedy for every political mischief, for every undesirable exercise of legislative power. The Framers carefully and with deliberate forethought refused so to enthrone the judiciary. In this situation, as in others of like nature, appeal for relief does not belong here. Appeal must be to an informed, civically militant electorate. In a democratic society like ours, relief must come through an aroused popular conscience that sears the conscience of the people's representatives. In any event there is nothing judicially more unseemly nor more self-defeating than for this Court to make *in terrorem* pronouncements, to indulge in merely empty rhetoric, sounding a word of promise to the ear, sure to be disappointing to the hope. . . .

From its earliest opinions this Court has consistently recognized a class of controversies which do not lend themselves to judicial standards and judicial remedies. To classify the various instances as "political questions" is rather a form of stating this conclusion than revealing of analysis. Some of the cases so labelled have no relevance here. But from others emerge unifying considerations that are compelling.

1. The cases concerning war or foreign affairs, for example, are usually explained by the necessity of the country's speaking with one voice in such matters. While this concern alone undoubtedly accounts for many of the decisions, others do not fit the pattern. It would hardly embarrass the conduct of war were this Court to determine, in connection with private transactions between litigants, the date upon which war is to be deemed terminated. But the Court has refused to do so. A controlling factor in such cases is that, decision respecting these kinds of complex matters of policy being traditionally committed not to courts but to the political agencies of government for determination by criteria of political expediency, there exists no standard ascertainable by settled judicial experience or process by reference to which a political decision affecting the question at issue between the parties can be judged. . . .

2. The Court has been particularly unwilling to intervene in matters concerning the structure and organization of the political institutions of the States. The abstention from judicial entry into such areas has been greater even than that which marks the Court's ordinary approach to issues of state power challenged under broad federal guarantees. . . .

3. The cases involving Negro disfranchisement are no exception to the principle of avoiding federal judicial intervention into matters of state government in the absence of an explicit and clear constitutional imperative. For here the controlling command of Supreme Law is plain and unequivocal. An end of discrimination against the Negro was the compelling motive of the Civil War Amendments. . . .

4. The Court has refused to exercise its jurisdiction to pass on "abstract questions of political power, of sovereignty, of government." *Massachusetts v. Mellon,* 262 U.S. 447 [1923]. The "political question" doctrine, in this aspect, reflects the policies underlying the requirement of "standing": that the litigant who would challenge official action must claim infringement of an interest particular and personal to himself, as distinguished from a cause of dissatisfaction with the general frame and functioning of government—a complaint that the political institutions are awry. . . . What renders cases of this kind non-justiciable is not necessarily the nature of the parties to them, for the Court has resolved other issues between similar parties; nor is it the nature of the legal question involved, for the same type of question has been adjudicated when presented in other forms of controversy. The crux of the matter is that courts are not fit instruments of decision where what is essentially at stake is the composition of those large contests of policy traditionally fought out in non-judicial forums, by which governments and the actions of governments are made and unmade. . . .

5. The influence of these converging considerations—the caution not to undertake decision where standards meet for judicial judgment are lacking, the reluctance to interfere with matters of state government in the absence of an unquestionable and effectively enforceable mandate, the unwillingness to make courts arbiters of the broad issues of political organization historically committed to other institutions and for whose adjustment the judicial process is ill-adapted—has been decisive of the settled line of cases, reaching back more than a century, which holds that Art. IV, § 4, of the Constitution, guaranteeing to the States "a Republican Form of Government," is not enforceable through the courts. . . .

The present case involves all of the elements that have made the Guarantee Clause cases non-justiciable. It is, in effect, a Guarantee Clause claim masquerading under a different label. But it cannot make the case more fit for judicial action that appellants invoke the Fourteenth Amendment rather than Art. IV, § 4, where, in fact, the gist of their complaint is the same—unless it can be found that the Fourteenth Amendment speaks with greater particularity to their situation. We have been admonished to avoid "the tyranny of labels." Art. IV, § 4, is not committed by express constitutional·terms to Congress. It is the nature of the controversies arising under it, nothing else, which has made it judicially unenforceable. Of course, if a controversy falls within judicial power, it depends "on how he [the plaintiff] casts his action," whether he brings himself within a jurisdictional statute. But where judicial competence is wanting, it cannot be created by invoking one clause of the Constitution rather than another. . . .

Appellants invoke the right to vote and to have their votes counted. But they are permitted to vote and their votes are counted. They go to the polls, they cast their ballots, they send their representatives to the state councils. Their complaint is simply that the representatives are not sufficiently numerous or powerful—in short, that Tennessee has adopted a basis of representation with which they are dissatisfied. . . . What is actually asked of the Court in this case is to choose among competing bases of representation—ultimately, really, among competing theories of political philosophy—in order to establish an appropriate frame of government for the State of Tennessee and thereby for all the States of the Union. . . .

To find such a political conception legally enforceable in the broad and unspecific guarantee of equal protection is to rewrite the Constitution. See *Luther v. Borden,* supra. Certainly, "equal protection" is no more secure a foundation for judicial judgment of the permissibility of varying forms of representative government than is "Republican Form.". . .

The notion that representation proportioned to the geographic spread of population is so universally accepted as a necessary element of equality between man and man that it must be taken to be the standard of a political equality preserved by the Fourteenth Amendment—that it is, in appellants' words "the basic principle of representative government"—is, to put it bluntly, not true. However desirable and however desired by some among the great political thinkers and framers of our government, it has never been generally practiced, today or in the past. It was not the English system, it was not the colonial system, it was not the system chosen for the national government by the Constitution, it was not the system exclusively or even predominantly practiced by the States at the time of adoption of the Fourteenth Amendment, it is not predominantly practiced by the States today. Unless judges, the judges of this Court, are to make their private views of political wisdom the measure of the Constitution—views which in all honesty cannot but give the appearance, if not reflect the reality, of involvement with the business of partisan politics so inescapably a part of apportionment controversies—the Fourteenth Amendment, "itself a historical product," *Jackman v. Rosenbaum Co.,* 260 U.S. 22 [1922], provides no guide for judicial oversight of the representation problem.

Justice HARLAN, with whom Justice FRANKFURTER joins, dissenting.

I can find nothing in the Equal Protection Clause or elsewhere in the Federal Constitution which expressly or impliedly supports the view that state legislatures must be so structured as to reflect with approximate equality the voice of every voter. Not only is that proposition refuted by history, as shown by my Brother FRANKFURTER, but it strikes deep into the heart of our federal system. Its acceptance would require us to turn our backs on the regard which this Court has always shown for the judgment of state legislatures and courts on matters of basically local concern.

In the last analysis, what lies at the core of this controversy is a difference of opinion as to the function of representative government. It is surely beyond argument that those who have the responsibility for devising a system of representation may permissibly consider that factors other than bare numbers should be taken into account. The existence of the United States Senate is proof enough of that. To consider that we may ignore the Tennessee Legislature's judgment in this instance because that body was the product of an asymmetrical electoral apportionment would in effect be to assume the very conclusion here disputed. Hence we must accept the present form of the Tennessee Legislature as the embodiment of the State's choice," or, more realistically, its compromise, between competing political philosophies. The federal courts have not been empowered by the Equal Protection Clause to judge whether this resolution of the State's internal political conflict is desirable or undesirable, wise or unwise.

Goldwater v. Carter
444 U.S. 996, 100 S.Ct. 533 (1979)

In 1979, Senator Barry Goldwater and several other senators filed suit against President James ("Jimmy") Carter, challenging the constitutionality of Carter's termination of a defense treaty with Taiwan without the approval of the Senate. Underlying the case was the enduring support that the nation's conservative leadership extended toward Taiwan. A tiny island, Taiwan housed the Chinese nationalist government after it was forced out of the China mainland by the new communist government. Granting a petition for *certiorari* but without hearing oral arguments, the Court vacated a court of appeals ruling and remanded the case to a federal district court with directions to dismiss the complaint. In separate concurring opinions, Justice Powell rejects the application of the "political questions" doctrine here, while Justice Rehnquist contends that it applies here and in other controversies over foreign policy. In his dissenting opinion, Justice Brennan rejects the idea that the question presented here is "political" and further discusses the scope of the judicial power.

Justice POWELL concurring.

Although I agree with the result reached by the Court, I would dismiss the complaint as not ripe for judicial review.

This Court has recognized that an issue should not be decided if it is not ripe for judicial review. Prudential considerations persuade me that a dispute between Congress and the President is not ready for judicial review unless and until each branch has taken action asserting its constitutional authority. Differences between the President and the Congress are commonplace under our system. The differences should, and almost invariably do, turn on political rather than legal considerations. The Judicial Branch should not decide issues affecting the allocation of power between the President and Congress until the political branches reach a constitutional impasse. Otherwise, we would encourage small groups or even individual Members of Congress to seek judicial resolution of issues before the normal political process has the opportunity to resolve the conflict.

In this case, a few Members of Congress claim that the President's action in terminating the treaty with Taiwan has deprived them of their constitutional role with respect to a change in the supreme law of the land. Congress has taken no official action. In the present posture of this case, we do not know whether there ever will be an actual confrontation between the Legislative and Executive Branches. Although the Senate has considered a resolution declaring that Senate approval is necessary for the termination of any mutual defense treaty, no final vote has been taken on the resolution. Moreover, it is unclear whether the resolution would have retroactive effect. It cannot be said that either the Senate or the House has rejected the President's claim. If the Congress chooses not to confront the President, it is not our task to do so. I therefore concur in the dismissal of this case.

Justice REHNQUIST suggests, however, that the issue presented by this case is a nonjusticiable political question which can never be considered by this Court. I cannot agree. In my view, reliance upon the political-question doctrine is inconsistent with our precedents. As set forth in the seminal case of *Baker v. Carr*, [369 U.S. 186] (1962), the doctrine incorporates three inquiries: (i) Does the issue involve resolution of questions committed by the text of the Constitution to a coordinate branch of Government? (ii) Would resolution of the question demand that a court move beyond areas of judicial expertise? (iii) Do prudential considerations counsel against judicial intervention? In my opinion the answer to each of these inquiries would require us to decide this case if it were ready for review. . . .

In my view, the suggestion that this case presents a political question is incompatible with this Court's willingness on previous occasions to decide whether one branch of our Government has impinged upon the power of another. Under the criteria enunciated in *Baker v. Carr,* we have the responsibility to decide whether both the Executive and Legislative Branches have constitutional roles to play in termination of a treaty. If the Congress, by appropriate formal action, had challenged the President's authority to terminate the treaty with Taiwan, the resulting uncertainty could have serious consequences for our country. In that situation, it would be the duty of this Court to resolve the issue.

JUSTICE REHNQUIST, with whom the Chief Justice, Justice STEWART, and Justice STEVENS join, concurring.

I am of the view that the basic question presented by the petitioners in this case is "political" and therefore nonjusticiable because it involves the authority of the President in the conduct of our country's foreign relations and the extent to which the Senate or the Congress is authorized to negate the action of the President. In *Coleman v. Miller,* 307 U.S. 433 (1939), a case in which members of the Kansas Legislature brought an action attacking a vote of the State Senate in favor of the ratification of the Child Labor Amendment, Chief Justice HUGHES wrote in what is referred to as the "Opinion of the Court":

> We think that . . . the question of the efficacy of ratifications by state legislatures, in the light of previous rejection or attempted withdrawal, should be regarded as a political question pertaining to the political departments, with the ultimate authority in the Congress in the exercise of its control over the promulgation of the adoption of the Amendment.
>
> The precise question as now raised is whether, when the legislature of the State, as we have found, has actually ratified the proposed amendment, the Court should restrain the state officers from certifying the ratification to the Secretary of State, because of an earlier rejection, and thus prevent the question from coming before the political departments. We find no basis in either Constitution or statute for such judicial action. Article V, speaking solely of ratification, contains no provision as to rejection.

Thus, Chief Justice HUGHES' opinion concluded that "Congress in controlling the promulgation of the adoption of a constitutional amendment has the final determination of the question whether by lapse of time its proposal of the amendment had lost its vitality prior to the required ratifications.". . .

I believe it follows a *fortiori* from *Coleman* that the controversy in the instant case is a nonjusticiable political dispute that should be left for resolution by the Executive and Legislative Branches of the Government. Here, while the Constitution is express as to the manner in which the Senate shall participate in the ratification of a treaty, it is silent as to that body's participation in the abrogation of a treaty. . . .

I think that the justification for concluding that the question here is political in nature are even more compelling than in *Coleman* because it involves foreign relations—specifically a treaty commitment to use military force in the defense of a foreign government if attacked. In *United States v. Curtiss-Wright Corp.*, 299 U.S. 304 (1936), this Court said:

> Whether, if the Joint Resolution had related solely to internal affairs it would be open to the challenge that it constituted an unlawful delegation of legislative power to the Executive, we find it unnecessary to determine. The whole aim of the resolution is to affect a situation entirely external to the United States, and falling within the category of foreign affairs.

The present case differs in several important respects from *Youngstown Sheet & Tube Co. v. Sawyer*, 343 U.S. 579 (1952), cited by petitioners as authority both for reaching the merits of this dispute and for reversing the Court of Appeals. In *Youngstown*, private litigants brought a suit contesting the President's authority under his war powers to seize the Nation's steel industry, an action of profound and demonstrable domestic impact. Here, by contrast, we are asked to settle a dispute between coequal branches of our Government, each of which has resources available to protect and assert its interests, resources not available to private litigants outside the judicial forum. Moreover, as in *Curtiss-Wright*, the effect of this action, as far as we can tell, is "entirely external to the United States, and [falls] within the category of foreign affairs." Finally, as already noted, the situation presented here is closely akin to that presented in *Coleman*, where the Constitution spoke only to the procedure for ratification of an amendment, not to its rejection.

Justice BLACKMUN, with whom Justice WHITE joins, dissenting in part.

In my view, the time factor and its importance are illusory; if the President does not have the power to terminate the treaty (a substantial issue that we should address only after briefing and oral argument), the notice of intention to terminate surely has no legal effect. It is also indefensible, without further study, to pass on the issue of justiciability or on the issues of standing or ripeness. While I therefore join in the grant of the petition for certiorari, I would set the case for oral argument and give it the plenary consideration it so obviously deserves.

Justice BRENNAN dissenting.

I respectfully dissent from the order directing the District Court to dismiss this case, and would affirm the judgment of the Court of Appeals insofar as it rests upon the President's well-established authority to recognize, and withdraw recognition from, foreign governments.

In stating that this case presents a non-justiciable "political question," Justice REHNQUIST, in my view, profoundly misapprehends the political-question principle as it applies to matters of foreign relations. Properly understood, the political-question doctrine restrains courts from reviewing an exercise of foreign policy judgment by the coordinate political branch to which authority to make that judgment has been "constitutional[ly] commit[ted]." *Baker v. Carr.* But the doctrine does not pertain when a court is faced with the *antecedent* question whether a particular branch has been constitutionally designated as the repository of political decisionmaking power. The issue of decisionmaking authority must be resolved as a matter of constitutional law, not political discretion; accordingly, it falls within the competence of the courts.

The constitutional question raised here is prudently answered in narrow terms. Abrogation of the defense treaty with Taiwan was a necessary incident to Executive recognition of the Peking Government, because the defense treaty was predicated upon the now-abandoned view that the Taiwan Government was the only legitimate political authority in China. Our cases firmly establish that the Constitution commits to the President alone the power to recognize, and withdraw recognition from, foreign regimes. That mandate being clear, our judicial inquiry into the treaty rupture can go no further.

B. THE COURT'S DOCKET AND SCREENING CASES

The justices' interpretation of their jurisdiction and rules governs access to the Court. But they also need flexible procedures for screening cases and deciding what to decide. This is because the Court's docket has grown phenomenally (see Figure 2.3).

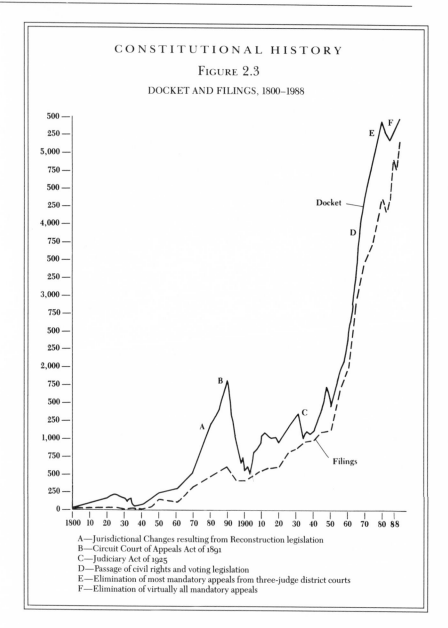

CONSTITUTIONAL HISTORY

FIGURE 2.3

DOCKET AND FILINGS, 1800–1988

A—Jurisdictional Changes resulting from Reconstruction legislation
B—Circuit Court of Appeals Act of 1891
C—Judiciary Act of 1925
D—Passage of civil rights and voting legislation
E—Elimination of most mandatory appeals from three-judge district courts
F—Elimination of virtually all mandatory appeals

When any appeal or cert. petition arrives at the Court it immediately goes to the clerk's office. Staff look at whether it satisfies
requirements as to form, length, and fees and if the filing is
from an indigent whether there is an affidavit stating that the
petitioner is too poor to pay fees. All unpaid cases are assigned

a number, in the order they arrive, and placed on what is called the Miscellaneous Docket. Paid cases are also assigned a number, but placed on the Appellate Docket. The clerk then notifies the other party, or respondent, in each case that they must file a brief in response within thirty days. After receiving briefs from respondents, the clerk circulates to the justices' chambers a list of cases ready for consideration and a set of briefs for each case.

For much of the Court's history every justice was responsible for reviewing each case. The justices did not work by panels or delegate responsibility for screening cases to others. That is no longer true. In 1972 the *"cert.* pool" was established. Seven of the justices now share their collective law clerks' memos on all paid and unpaid cases. The memos explain the facts, issues raised, and lower court ruling as well as recommend whether the case should be granted or denied. Those justices not joining the pool—Marshall and Stevens—receive copies of unpaid cases along with other filings. Brennan examined each case himself, when he had time to do so. Stevens has his clerks screen all the cases and write memos on only those they think are important enough for him to consider.

C. THE RULE OF FOUR AND AGENDA SETTING

When Congress gave the Court discretionary jurisdiction in the Judiciary Act of 1925, by substituting petitions for *certiorari* for mandatory appeals, the justices developed the informal "rule of four" to decide which petitions they would grant. During conference, at least four justices must agree that a case warrants oral argument and consideration by the full Court.

The rule of four operates in a fraction of cases due to the increasing caseload, which is a result of a number of factors. Most important, institutional norms promote a shared conception of the role of the Court as a tribunal for resolving only issues of national importance. Justices agree that the overwhelming proportion of cases are "frivolous," and that there is a limited number of cases to which they may give full consideration. "As a rule of thumb," Byron White, among others on the current Court, said, "the Court should not be expected to produce more than 150 opinions per term in argued cases."[1]

The caseload and institutional norms push toward limiting the operation of the rule of four. But the rule remains useful, particularly if there is a bloc of justices who share the same ideological orientation. The rule of four thus enables a bloc of justices to work together in picking cases they want the Court to rule on.

Denial of *certiorari* is an important technique for managing the Court's caseload. But its meaning in particular cases may be far from clear. The Court has few fixed rules and even the rule of four is not "an absolutely inflexible rule."[2] In two capital punishment cases, *Drake v. Zant* and *Westbrook v. Balkcom,* 449 U.S. 999 (1980), *four* justices issued dissenting opinions from the denial of review of both cases. Each justice indicated but for one more vote, they would have granted the case, vacated the ruling below, and remanded the case to the lower court.

Although enabling the Court to manage its business, denials invite confusion and the suspicion, as Justice Jackson once observed, "that this Court no longer respects impersonal rules of law but is guided in these matters by personal impression which from time to time may be shared by a majority of the justices."[3]

NOTES

1. Byron White, "The Work of the Supreme Court: Nuts and Bolts Description," 54 *New York State Bar Journal* 346 (1982).
2. Potter Stewart, "Inside the Supreme Court," *The New York Times,* Oct. 1, 1979, p. 17A, col. 2.
3. *Brown v. Allen,* 344 U.S. 443, 535 (1953) (Jackson, J., concurring opinion).

D. SUMMARILY DECIDED CASES

Even before the 1988 Act to Improve the Administration of Justice, which eliminated virtually all mandatory appeals, the distinction between mandatory and discretionary review of appeals and *cert.* petitions had largely disappeared in the Court's process of deciding what to decide. The Court annually received only about 250 appeals and the overwhelming majority were summarily decided (without hearing oral arguments and full consideration). They simply dismissed them for want of jurisdiction or failure to present a substantial federal question, or they ordered the lower court ruling affirmed or reversed.

Summarily decided cases enable the Court to cut down on its workload. But they also engender confusion among the lower courts. Summary decisions take the form of rather cryptic orders or *per curiam* (unsigned) opinions. Like denials of *cert.* petitions, they invite confusion over how the Court views the merits of a case and the lower court ruling. The problem is one of the Court's own making. The Court holds that summarily decided cases do not have the same precedential weight as plenary decisions, but they are nonetheless binding on lower courts "until such time as the Court informs [them] that [they] are not."[1]

Another problem is that occasionally cases that some justices think deserve full consideration are summarily decided. "No specter of increasing caseload can possibly justify today's summary disposition of this case," Brennan charged in *Roe v. Locke*, 423 U.S. 48 (1975), holding a Tennessee statute forbidding "crimes against nature" was not vague as claimed by an individual convicted of forcibly performing cunnilingus. Stewart sounded the refrain the next term in *United States v. Jacobs*, 429 U.S. 909 (1975). "While our heavy caseload necessarily leads us sometimes to dispose of cases summarily, it must never lead us to dispose of any case irresponsibly. Yet I fear precisely that has happened here." These are the words of dissenters in cases that they thought merited full consideration, but were outvoted by a majority who simply did not want to bother with hearing oral arguments and giving cases full consideration. *Goldwater v. Carter* (1979) (see page 145) is another example. There, Justices Blackmun and White viewed the majority's summary disposition and decision "indefensible" in failing to "set the case for oral argument and giv[ing] it the plenary consideration it so obviously deserved." Later that term, Stevens, Brennan, and Marshall dissented in *Snepp v. United States* (1980) (see page 154), which they thought raised important First Amendment issues. *Florida v. Meyers* (1984) (see page 156) illustrates the Court's continued practice of summarily deciding cases, even those that come as petitions for *certiorari*, when a majority wants to decide a case but does not want to bother with hearing oral arguments on the case.

NOTE

1. *Hicks v. Miranda*, 422 U.S. 322 (1975).

Snepp v. United States
444 U.S. 507, 100 S.Ct. 763 (1980)

The United States government sought an injunction (an order) against Frank Snepp, a former agent for the Central Intelligence Agency (CIA), requiring him to submit all of his future fiction and nonfiction writings for prepublication review by the CIA and ordering the creation of a government trust from the royalties he earned from his book *Decent Interval,* which he published without CIA approval as required in his CIA contract. The district court decided for the government and Snepp appealed, contending that the CIA's prepublication review and the lower court's ruling abridged his First Amendment freedoms of speech and press. Without hearing oral arguments, the Court in a *per curiam* opinion held that Snepp had breached his fiduciary obligations by failing to submit his manuscript for review and upheld the lower court's ruling denying him royalties from his book. Justice Stevens's dissenting opinion discusses some additional facts and objects to the Court's summary disposition of this case.

Justice STEVENS, with whom Justice BRENNAN and Justice MARSHALL join, dissenting.

In this case Snepp admittedly breached his duty to submit the manuscript of his book, Decent Interval, to the CIA for prepublication review. However, the Government has conceded that the book contains no classified, nonpublic material. Thus, by definition, the interest in confidentiality that Snepp's contract was designed to protect has not been compromised. Nevertheless, the Court today grants the Government unprecedented and drastic relief in the form of a constructive trust over the profits derived by Snepp from the sale of the book. Because that remedy is not authorized by any applicable law and because it is most inappropriate for the Court to dispose of this novel issue summarily on the Government's conditional cross-petition for certiorari, I respectfully dissent. . . .

The Court's decision to dispose of this case summarily on the Government's conditional cross-petition for certiorari is just as unprecedented as its disposition of the merits.

Snepp filed a petition for certiorari challenging the Fourth Circuit's decision insofar as it affirmed the entry of an injunction requiring him to submit all future manuscripts for prepublication review and remanded for a determination of whether punitive damages would be appropriate for his failure to submit Decent Interval to the Agency prior to its publication. The Government filed a brief in opposition as well as a cross petition for certiorari, the Government specifically stated, however, that it was cross-petitioning only to bring the entire case before the Court in the event that the Court should decide to grant Snepp's petition. The Government explained that "[b]ecause the contract remedy provided by the court of appeals appears to be sufficient in this case to protect the Agency's interest, the government has not independently sought review in this Court.". . .

Given the Government's position, it would be highly inappropriate, and perhaps even beyond this Court's jurisdiction, to grant the Government's petition while denying Snepp's. Yet that is in essence what has been done. The majority obviously does not believe that Snepp's claims merit this Court's consideration, for they are summarily dismissed in a footnote. . . .

It is clear that Snepp's petition would not have been granted on its own merits.

The Court's opinion is a good demonstration of why this Court should not reach out to decide a question not necessarily presented to it, as it has done in this case. Despite the fact that the Government has specifically stated that the punitive damages remedy is "sufficient" to protect its interests, the Court forges ahead and summarily rejects that remedy on the grounds that (a) it is too speculative and thus would not provide the Government with a "reliable deterrent against similar breaches of security." and (b) it might require the Government to reveal confidential information in court, the Government might forego damages rather than make such disclosures, and the Government might thus be left with "no remedy at all." It seems to me that the Court is foreclosed from relying upon either ground by the Government's acquiescence in the punitive damages remedy. Moreover, the second rationale is entirely speculative and, in this case at least, almost certainly wrong. The Court states that

> [p]roof of the tortious conduct necessary to sustain an award of punitive damages might force the Government to disclose some of the very confidences that Snepp promised to protect. . . .

Yet under the Court of Appeals' opinion the Government would be entitled to punitive damages simply by proving that Snepp deceived it into believing that he was going to comply with his duty to submit the manuscript for prepublication review and that the Government relied on these misrepresentations to its detriment. I fail to see how such a showing would require the Government to reveal any confidential information or to expose itself to "probing discovery into the Agency's highly confidential affairs.". . .

The uninhibited character of today's exercise in lawmaking is highlighted by the Court's disregard of two venerable principles that favor a more conservative approach to this case.

First, for centuries the English-speaking judiciary refused to grant equitable relief unless the plaintiff could show that his remedy at law was inadequate. Without waiting for an opportunity to appraise the adequacy of the punitive damages remedy in this case, the Court has jumped to the conclusion that equitable relief is necessary.

Second, and of greater importance, the Court seems unaware of the fact that its drastic new remedy has been fashioned to enforce a species of prior restraint on a citizen's right to criticize his government. Inherent in this prior restraint is the risk that the reviewing agency will misuse its authority to delay the publication of a critical work or to persuade an author to modify the contents of his work beyond the demands of secrecy. The character of the covenant as a prior restraint on free speech surely imposes an especially heavy burden on the censor to justify the remedy it seeks. It would take more than the Court has written to persuade me that that burden has been met.

I respectfully dissent.

Florida v. Meyers

466 U.S. 380, 104 S.Ct. 1852 (1984)

The pertinent facts are discussed in the *per curiam* opinion announcing the Court's decision. Justice Stevens's dissenting opinion raises issues about the Court's summary disposition of cases.

PER CURIAM.

Respondent was charged with sexual battery. At the time of his arrest, police officers searched his automobile and seized several items. The vehicle was then towed to Sunny's Wrecker, where it was impounded in a locked, secure area. Approximately eight hours later, a police officer went to the compound and, without obtaining a warrant, searched the car for a second time. Additional evidence was seized. At the subsequent trial, the court denied respondent's motion to suppress the evidence seized during the second search, and respondent was convicted.

On appeal, the Florida District Court of Appeal for the Fourth District reversed the conviction, holding that even though respondent conceded that the initial search of the automobile was valid, the second search violated the Fourth Amendment. . . . The Florida Supreme Court denied the State's petition for discretionary review, and the State filed the present petition for certiorari. We reverse.

The District Court of Appeal either misunderstood or ignored our prior rulings with respect to the constitutionality of the warrantless search of an impounded automobile. In *Michigan v. Thomas*, 458 U.S. 259 (1982), we upheld a warrantless search of an automobile even though the automobile was in police custody and even though a prior inventory search had already been made. That ruling controls the disposition of this case. . . . The petition for certiorari is therefore granted, the judgment of the District Court of Appeal is reversed, and the case is remanded to that court for further proceedings not inconsistent with this opinion.

It is so ordered.

Justice STEVENS, with whom Justice BRENNAN and Justice MARSHALL join, dissenting.

No judicial system is perfect. In this case the Florida District Court of Appeal for the Fourth District appears to have made an error. In the exercise of its discretion, the Florida Supreme Court elected not to correct that error. No reasons were given for its denial of review and since the record is not before us, we cannot know what discretionary factors may have prompted the Florida Supreme Court's decision. This Court, however, finds time to correct the apparent error committed by the intermediate appellate court, acting summarily without benefit of briefs on the merits or argument. . . .

For three other reasons I believe the Court should deny certiorari in cases of this kind. First, our pronouncements concerning our confidence in the ability of the state judges to decide Fourth Amendment questions, are given a hollow ring when we are found peering over their shoulders after every misreading of the Fourth Amendment. Second, our ability to perform our primary responsibilities can only be undermined by enlarging our self-appointed role as supervisors of the administration of justice in the state judicial systems. Dispositions such as that today can only encourage prosecutors to file in increasing numbers petitions for certiorari in relatively routine cases, and if we take it upon ourselves to review and correct every incorrect disposition of a federal question by every intermediate state appellate court, we will soon become so busy that we will either be unable to discharge our primary responsibilities effectively, or else be forced to make still another adjustment in the size of our staff in order to process cases effectively. We should focus our attention on methods of using our scarce resources wisely rather than laying another course of bricks in the building of a federal judicial bureaucracy.

Third, and perhaps most fundamental, this case and cases like it pose disturbing questions concerning the Court's conception of its role. Each such case, considered individually, may be regarded as a welcome step forward in the never-ending war against crime. Such decisions are certain to receive widespread approbation, particularly by members of society who have been victimized by lawless conduct. But we must not forget that a central purpose of our written Constitution, and more specifically of its unique creation of a life-tenured federal judiciary, was to ensure that certain rights are firmly secured *against* possible oppression by the Federal or State Governments. As I wrote last Term: "I believe that in reviewing the decisions of state courts, the primary role of this Court is to make sure that persons who seek to *vindicate* federal rights have been fairly heard." *Michigan v. Long,* 463 U.S. 1032 (1983) (emphasis in original) (dissenting opinion). Yet the Court's recent history indicates that, at least with respect to its summary dispositions, it has been primarily concerned with vindicating the will of the majority and less interested in its role as protector of the individual's constitutional rights. Since the beginning of the October 1981 Term, the Court has decided in summary fashion 19 cases, including this one, concerning the constitutional rights of persons accused or convicted of crime. All 19 were decided on the petition of the warden or prosecutor, and in all he was successful in obtaining reversal of a decision upholding a claim of constitutional right. I am not saying that none of these cases should have been decided summarily. But I am saying that this pattern of results, and in particular the fact that in its last two and one-half Terms the Court has been unwilling in even a single criminal case to employ its discretionary power of summary disposition in order to uphold a claim of constitutional right, is quite striking. It may well be true that there have been times when the Court overused its power of summary disposition to protect the citizen against government overreaching. Nevertheless, the Court must be ever mindful of its primary role as the protector of the citizen and not the warden or the prosecutor. The Framers surely feared the latter more than the former.

I respectfully dissent.

E. THE ROLE OF ORAL ARGUMENT

The Court grants a full hearing—that is, oral argument—to less than 180 of the more than 5,000 cases on the docket each term. When cases are granted full consideration, attorneys for each side submit briefs setting forth their arguments and how they think the case should be decided. The clerk of the Court circulates the briefs to each chamber and sets a date for the attorneys to orally argue their views before the justices. After hearing oral arguments, in private conference the justices vote on how to decide the issues presented in a case.

For fourteen weeks each term, from the first Monday in October until the end of April, the Court hears arguments from ten to twelve o'clock and from one to three o'clock on Monday, Tuesday, and Wednesday about every two weeks. The importance of oral argument, Chief Justice Hughes observed, lies in the fact that often "the impression that a judge has at the close of a full oral argument accords with the conviction which controls his final vote."[1] The justices hold conference and take their initial, often decisive, vote on cases within a day or two after hearing arguments. Oral arguments come at a crucial time. They focus the minds of the justices and present the possibility for fresh perspectives on a case. It is the only opportunity for attorneys to communicate directly with the justices. Two basic factors appear to control the relative importance of oral argument. As Justice Wiley Rutledge observed, "One is brevity. The other is the preparation with which the judge comes to it."[2] When the Court revised its rules in 1980, the justices underscored that *"[t]he Court looks with disfavor on any oral argument that is read from a prepared text."* Central to preparation and delivery is a bird's-eye view of the case, the issues and facts, and the reasoning behind legal developments. Crisp, concise, and conversational presentations are what the justices want. An attorney must never forget, in Chief Justice Rehnquist's words, that "[h]e is not, after all, presenting his case to some abstract, platonic embodiment of appellate judges as a class, but . . . nine flesh and blood men and women." Oral argument is definitely not a "brief with gestures."[3]

NOTES

1. Charles E. Hughes, *The Supreme Court of the United States* (New York: Columbia University Press, 1928), 61.

2. Wiley Rutledge, "The Appellate Brief," 28 *American Bar Association Journal* 251 (1942).

3. William Rehnquist, "Oral Advocacy: A Disappearing Art," Brainerd Currie Lecture, Mercer University School of Law, Oct. 20, 1983, msp. 4.

F. CONFERENCE DELIBERATIONS

The justices meet alone in conference to decide which cases to accept and to discuss the merits of those few cases on which they hear oral arguments. Throughout the term during the weeks in which the Court hears oral arguments, conferences are held on Wednesday afternoons to take up the four cases argued on Monday, and then on Fridays to discuss new filings and the eight cases for which oral argument was heard on Tuesday and Wednesday. In May and June, when the Court does not hear oral arguments, conferences are held on Thursdays, from ten in the morning until four or four-thirty in the afternoon, with the justices breaking for a forty-five-minute lunch around twelve-thirty. A majority may vote to hold a special session during the summer months, when extraordinarily urgent cases arise.

Summoned by a buzzer five minutes before the hour, the justices meet in the conference room, located directly behind the courtroom itself and next to the chief justice's chamber. The oak-paneled room is lined with *United States Reports* (containing the Court's decisions). Over the mantle of an exquisite fireplace at one end hangs a portrait of Chief Justice Marshall. Next to the fireplace stands a large rectangular table where the justices sit. The chief justice sits at the one end and the senior associate justice at the other. Along the right-hand side of the chief justice, next to the fireplace, sit Marshall, Blackmun, and Stevens; on the left-hand side, sit O'Connor, Scalia, Kennedy, and Souter, the most junior justice. The seating of the justices traditionally has been on the basis of seniority. But variations occur due to individual justices' preferences.

Members of the Burger Court, in the tradition begun by Chief Justice Melville Fuller, shaking hands in the robing room prior to going on the bench to hear oral arguments. *Yoichi Okamoto*

Two conference lists are circulated to each chamber by noon on Wednesday prior to the Friday conference. They structure conference discussion and enable the justices to get through their caseload. On the first list—Special List I, or the Discuss List—are jurisdictional statements, petitions for certiorari and motions that are ready and worth discussing. The Discuss List typically includes between forty and fifty cases for each conference. Attached is a second list—Special List II or what was called the Dead List—containing those cases considered unworthy of discussion. Any justice may request that a case be put on the Discuss List, and only after the chief's conference secretary has heard from all chambers do the lists become final. Over 70 percent of the cases on the conference lists are automatically denied without discussion and most of those that do make the Discuss List are denied as well. The conference lists are an important

---

INSIDE THE COURT

On the Tentativeness of Votes
and the Importance of Opinion Writing

In two other controversial cases, involving claims by the press to a First Amendment right of access to visit and interview prisoners, Burger switched his vote after conference. During the conference discussion of *Pell v. Procunier* 417 U.S. 817 (1974) and *Saxbe v. Washington Post* 417 U.S. 843 (1974), the vote went five to four for recognizing that the press has a First Amendment right of access. But Burger later changed his mind and explained that the final outcome of the cases depended on how the opinions were written:

This difficult case has few very clear cut and fixed positions but my further study over the weekend leads me to see my position as closer for those who would sustain the authority of the corrections administrators than those who would not! I would therefore reverse in 73–754, affirm in 73–918 and reverse in 73–1265.

This is another one of those cases that will depend a good deal on "how it is written." The solution to the problem must be allowed time for experimentation and I fear an "absolute" constitutional holding adverse to administrators will tend to "freeze" progress.

The Court ultimately divided five to four, but held that the press does not have a First Amendment right of access to interview inmates of prisons. Like *Roe v. Wade* 410 U.S. 113 (1973), these examples illustrate how important postconference deliberations and communications among the chambers have become for the Court's decision making.

Source: William J. Brennan, Jr., Papers, Manuscripts Room, Library of Congress.

technique for saving time and focusing attention on the few cases deemed worthy of consideration.

The significance of conference discussions has changed with the increasing caseload. Conference discussions do not play the role that they once did. When the docket was smaller in the nineteenth century, conferences were integral to the justices' collective deliberations. As the caseload grew, conferences became largely symbolic of past collective deliberations. They now serve only to discover consensus. There is no longer time to reach agreement and compromise on opinions for the Court. "In fact," Justice Antonin Scalia claims, "to call our discussion of a case a conference is really something of a misnomer. It's much more a statement of the views of each of the nine Justices."[1] More discussion, however, he admits would probably not contribute much or lead justices to change their minds when voting on cases. This is because the justices confront similar issues year after year and, as Chief Justice Rehnquist notes, "it would be surprising if [justices] voted differently than they had the previous time."[2]

The justices' votes are always tentative until the day the Court hands down its decision and opinion. Before, during, and after conference justices may use their votes in strategic ways to influence the disposition of a case.

NOTES

1. Antonin Scalia, comments at George Washington National Law Center, Feb. 16, 1988, quoted in "Ruling Fixed Opinions," *The New York Times*, Feb. 22, 1988, p. 16A.
2. William H. Rehnquist, quoted in David M. O'Brien, *Storm Center: The Supreme Court in American Politics*, 2d ed., (New York: W. W. Norton, 1990).

G. POSTCONFERENCE WRITING AND CIRCULATION OF OPINIONS

Opinions justify or explain votes at conference. The opinion for the Court is the most important and most difficult to write because it represents a collective judgment. Because conference votes are tentative, the assignment, drafting, and circulation of opinions is crucial to the Court's rulings. At each stage justices compete for influence in determining the Court's final decision and opinion.

By tradition, when the chief justice is in the majority, he assigns the Court's opinion. If the chief justice did not vote with the majority, then the senior associate justice who was in the majority either writes the opinion or assigns it to another. Chief justices may keep cases for themselves. This is in the tradition of Chief Justice Marshall, but as modified by the workload and other justices' expectations of equitable opinion assignments. In unanimous decisions and landmark cases the chief justice often self-assigns the Court's opinion.

Parity in opinion assignment now generally prevails. But the practice of immediately assigning opinions after conference as Hughes did, or within a day or two as Stone did, was gradually abandoned by the end of Vinson's tenure as chief justice. Warren and Burger adopted the practice of assigning opinions after each two-week session of oral arguments and conferences. With more assignments to make at any given time, they thus acquired greater flexibility in distributing the workload. They also enhanced their own opportunities for influencing the final outcome of cases through their assignment of opinions.

Writing opinions is the most difficult and time-consuming task of the justices. Justices differ in their styles and approaches to opinion writing. They now more or less delegate responsibility to their clerks for assisting in the preparation of opinions. Chief Justice Rehnquist, for example, usually has one of his clerks do a first draft, without bothering about style, and gives him about ten days to prepare it. Before having the clerk begin work, Rehnquist goes over the conference discussion with the clerk and explains how he thinks "an opinion can be written supporting the result reached by the majority."

Only after a justice is satisfied with an initial draft does the opinion circulate to the other justices for their reactions. The practice of circulating draft opinions is pivotal in the Court's decision-making process because all votes are tentative until the final opinion is handed down.

Final published opinions for the Court are the residue of conflicts and compromises among the justices. But they also reflect changing institutional norms. In historical perspective, changes in judicial norms have affected trends in opinion writing, the value of judicial opinions and the Court's contributions to public law.

"The business of the Court," Justice Stewart once observed, "is to give institutional opinions for its decisions." The opinion for the Court serves to communicate an institutional decision. For much of the Court's history, there were few concurring opinions (those in which a justice agrees with the Court's ruling but not the reasons given in its opinion) and dissenting opinions (those in which justices disagree with the Court's ruling and give an alternative interpretation). It was also rare for a justice to write a separate opinion in which he or she concurred and dissented from parts of the opinion for the Court. But in the last forty years there has been a dramatic increase in the total number of opinions issued each term, as depicted in Figure 2.4.

The increase in the number of opinions reflects in part that the justices are now more interested in merely the tally of votes than arriving at an institutional decision and opinion. The number of cases decided by a bare majority has thus grown in the

CONSTITUTIONAL HISTORY

Comparison of Dissent Rates

Justice	Number of Dissenting Opinions	Average Per Term
The Great Dissenters		
W. Johnson (1804–1834)	30	1.0
J. Catron (1837–1865)	26	0.9
N. Clifford (1858–1881)	60	2.6
J. Harlan (1877–1911)	119	3.5
O. Holmes (1902–1932)	72	2.4
L. Brandeis (1915–1939)	65	2.9
H. Stone (1925–1946)	93	4.6
H. Black (1937–1971)	310	9.1
F. Frankfurter (1939–1962)	251	10.9
J. Harlan (1955–1971)	242	15.1
The Burger and Rehnquist Courts		
W. Douglas (1969–1974)	231	38.5
J. Stevens (1975–1990)	318	21.2
W. Brennan, Jr. (1969–1990)	379	18.0
T. Marshall (1969–1990)	322	15.3
W. Rehnquist (1971–1990)	250	13.1
P. Stewart (1969–1981)	130	10.8
B. White (1969–1990)	217	10.6
H. Blackmun (1971–1990)	203	10.5
A. Scalia (1986–1990)	32	8.3
L. Powell, Jr. (1971–1987)	159	9.9
S. O'Connor (1981–1990)	64	7.0
W. Burger (1969–1986)	111	6.5
A. Kennedy (1987–1990)	17	5.6

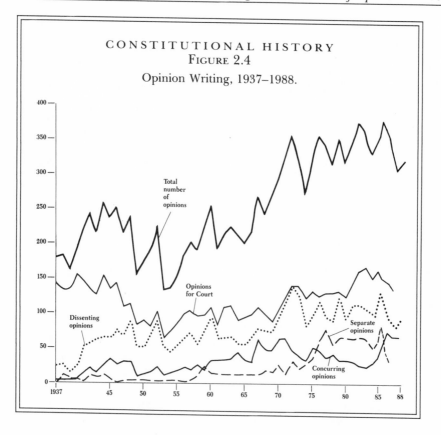

CONSTITUTIONAL HISTORY
FIGURE 2.4
Opinion Writing, 1937–1988.

last few decades. In addition, sometimes a bare majority for deciding a case a certain way cannot agree on an opinion for the Court's decision and the author of the opinion announcing the Court's decision must write for only a plurality.

In contrast to the author of an opinion for the Court, a justice writing separate concurring or dissenting opinions does not carry the burden of massing other justices. Dissenting opinions are more understandable and defensible. Dissenting opinions in the view of Chief Justice Charles Evans Hughes, who rarely wrote dissents, appeal "to the brooding spirit of the law, to the intelligence of a future day, when a later decision may possibly correct the error into which the dissenting judge believes the Court to have been betrayed."[1] The first Justice John M. Harlan's dissent from the doctrine of "separate but equal" in *Plessy v. Ferguson,* 163 U.S. 537 (1896) (see Vol. 2, Ch. 12) was eventually vindicated in *Brown v. Board of Education* (1954). Dissents may also appeal for more immediate legislative action: Justice James Iredell's dissent in *Chisholm v. Georgia,* 2 U.S. 419 (1793), invited the adoption of the Eleventh Amendment overturning the Court's

decision; and the dissenters' arguments in *Dred Scott v. Sandford,*
60 U.S. 393 (1857) (see Vol. 2, Ch. 12), lent support to the
passage of the Thirteenth, Fourteenth, and Fifteenth Amendments after the Civil War. A dissenting opinion is a way of
undercutting the Court's decision and opinion. The threat of a
dissent may thus be useful when trying to persuade the majority
to narrow its holding or tone down the language of its opinion.

NOTE

1. Charles Evans Hughes, *The Supreme Court of the United States* (New
York: Columbia University Press, 1928).

H. OPINION DAYS AND COMMUNICATING DECISIONS

The justices announce their decisions in the courtroom, typically crowded with reporters, anxious attorneys, and curious
spectators. When several decisions are to be handed down, the
justices delivering the Court's opinions make their announce-
ments in reverse order of seniority. Authors of concurring or
dissenting opinions are free to give their views orally as well.
By tradition there is no prior announcement as to when cases
will be handed down. Most opinions are now announced in two
to four minutes with justices merely stating the result in each
case. In especially controversial cases, for example, *Webster v.
Reproductive Health Services* (1989) (see Vol. 2, Ch. 11) concerning
restrictions on abortion, justices may read portions of their opinions and, sometimes, dissents.

Justices appreciate that compliance with their decisions depends on public understanding of their opinions. And media
coverage of the Court has grown in the last thirty years. On
"Opinion Days," journalists now receive copies of the headnotes—prepared by the reporter of decisions—summarizing the
main points of a decision. The Court now has a public information office as well. The office serves primarily reporters (not
members of the general public, whose inquiries are typically
handled by the offices of the clerk, marshal, or curator) and
provides space for a pressroom with sixteen assigned cubicles.
The public information officer makes available all filings and
briefs for cases on the docket, the Court's conference lists and
final opinions, and speeches made by the justices.

The justices' private conference room. *Supreme Court Historical Society.*

I. THE IMPACT OF SUPREME COURT DECISIONS: COMPLIANCE AND IMPLEMENTATION

"By itself," political scientist Robert Dahl observed, "the Court is almost powerless to affect the course of national policy."[1] This is because the Court's rulings are not self-executing. Enforcement and implementation required the cooperation and coordination of all three branches of government.

Brown v. Board of Education (1954) (see Vol. 2, Ch. 12), the public school desegregation case, dramatically altered the course of American life, but also reflected the justices' awareness that their decisions are not self-executing. When striking down the "separate but equal" doctrine, which was practised in segregated public school systems, the Warren Court waited a year after *Brown I* (1954) before issuing in *Brown II* its mandate for "all deliberate speed" in ending racial segregation in public education. The Court knew that there would be substantial public resistence to the social policy announced in *Brown I*. A rigid time table for desegregation would have only intensified opposition. President Dwight Eisenhower refused to endorse the ruling for some time. Hence, implementation of *Brown* was deliberately slow and uneven. The Department of Justice had little role in ending school segregation before the passage of the Civil Rights

Act of 1964 during Lyndon B. Johnson's presidency. For over three decades problems of implementing and achieving compliance with *Brown* persisted. Litigation by civil rights groups forced change, but it was piecemeal, costly, and modest. The judiciary alone could not achieve desegregation.

Public opinion serves to curb the Court when it threatens to go too far or too fast in its rulings. The Court has usually been in line with major political movements, except during transitional periods or critical elections.[2] Life in the marble temple is not immune from shifts in public opinion. But justices deny being directly influenced by public opinion. The Court's prestige rests on preserving the public's view that justices base their decisions on interpretations of the law, rather than on their personal policy preferences. Yet complete indifference to public opinion would be the height of judicial arrogance.

Most of the Court's decisions do not attract widespread public attention. Most people find the Court remote and confusing or identify with its institutional symbols. The public perceives the Court as a temple of law rather than of politics—impartial and removed from the pressures of special partisan interests.[3] Issues such as school desegregation, school prayer, and abortion focus public attention and may mobilize public support or opposition for the Court. But those issues are also the most divisive within the country as well. Public opinion, therefore, tends to be diffuse and indirectly expressed by public officials and elected representatives.

Less concerned about public opinion than elected public officials, justices are sensitive to the attitudes of the Court's immediate constituents: the solicitor general, the attorney general and the Department of Justice, counsel for federal agencies, states' attorneys general, and the legal profession. Their responses to the Court's rulings help shape public understanding and determine the extent of compliance.

The solicitor general, attorney general, and agency counsel interpret the Court's decisions and advise the White House and agencies on compliance. Justices may find a favorable or unfavorable reception from the executive branch. The solicitor general decides which and what kinds of cases to take to the Court. In selecting cases he tries to offer the Court (or a majority) opportunities for pursuing their policy goals and those of the president.

The attorney general, cabinet heads, and agency counsel may likewise extend or thwart the Court's policies. They do so through their advisory opinions, litigation strategies, and development of agency policy and programs. The reactions of the fifty state attorneys general are no less important. Each has a pivotal role in advising governors, mayors, police chiefs, and others in his or her state. Their responses tend to reflect state and local reactions to the Court's rulings. Regional differences were evident in responses to the 1962 and 1963 school prayer decisions. In upholding separation of church and state, the Court struck down a state-composed prayer in *Engel v. Vitale,* 370 U.S. 421 (1962), and the reciting of the Lord's Prayer in public schools in *Abington School District v. Schempp,* 374 U.S. 203 (1963) (see Vol. 2, Ch. 6). Long-standing practices of school prayer in the East and South were not to be easily relinquished. Voluntary school prayer, silent meditation, and "the objective study of the Bible and of religion" were viewed as still permissible. Where school prayer received support in state constitutions or legislation, state and local officials denied the legitimacy of the Court's decrees and refused to obey.

The justices do consider anticipated reactions of the immediate audience of the Court's rulings. One example is that of Chief Justice Warren's opinion in *Miranda v. Arizona,* 384 U.S. 436 (1966) (see Vol. 2, Ch. 8), which held that police must read suspects their rights, granted them by the Fifth and Sixth Amendments, to remain silent and to consult and have the presence of an attorney during police questioning. A former attorney general in California, Chief Justice Warren knew full well that not all state attorneys general and police supported the Court's rulings on criminal procedure. He, therefore, strove to outline in *Miranda* a code for police procedures governing the interrogation of criminal suspects that police could not easily evade.

The Court's decisions have traditionally applied retroactively, permitting individuals to have retrials. In *Linkletter v. Walker* (1965) (see page 178), however, the Court refused to apply retroactively its controversial ruling in *Mapp v. Ohio,* 367 U.S. 643 (1961) (see Vol. 2, Ch. 7), which extended to the states the Fourth Amendment exclusionary rule, forbidding the use at trial of evidence obtained in violation of the requirements for a proper search and seizure. The Court subsequently developed what became known as its *ambulatory-retroactively doctrine* in other areas of criminal law as well. "That doctrine," Justice Harlan explained, "was the product of the Court's disquietude with the impacts of its fast-moving pace in constitutional innovation in the criminal field." But he also objected that the doctrine merely rationalizes the Court's freedom "to act, in effect, like a legislature, making its new constitutional rules wholly or partially retroactive or only prospective as it deems wise."[4] In *Griffith v. Kentucky* (1987) (see page 183), Justice Blackmun further explains the Court's application of the doctrine of ambulatory retroactivity.

The Court directly and indirectly encourages interest groups and the government to litigate issues of public policy. The Court selects and decides "only those cases which present questions whose resolution will have immediate importance far beyond the particular facts and parties involved." Attorneys whose cases are accepted by the Court, Chief Justice Fred Vinson emphasized, "are, in a sense, prosecuting or defending class actions; that you represent your clients, but [more crucially] tremendously important principles, upon which are based the plans, hopes and aspirations of a great many people throughout the country."[5]

Interest groups from the entire political spectrum look to the Court to decide issues of public policy: from business organizations and corporations in the late nineteenth century to the Jehovah's Witnesses in the 1930s, to the ACLU and NAACP in the 1950s and 1960s, and to "liberal" women's rights groups and consumer and environmental protection groups—like the National Organization of Women (NOW), Common Cause, "Nader's Raiders," the Sierra Club, the Environmental Defense Fund, and the Natural Resources Defense Council—as well as to a growing number of conservative "public interest" law firms like the Pacific Legal Foundation, the Mountain States Legal Foundation, and the Washington Legal Foundation. "This is government by lawsuit," Justice Robert Jackson declared, "these constitutional lawsuits are the stuff of power politics in America."[6]

Interest group activities and public interest law firms offer a number of advantages for litigating policy disputes. They command greater financial resources than the average individual. A single suit may settle a large number of claims, and the issues are not as likely to be compromised or settled out of court. Interest group law firms typically specialize in particular kinds of lawsuits. They are, therefore, able to litigate more skillfully and over a longer period of time. There are also tactical opportunities. Litigants may be chosen to bring test cases, and those cases may be coordinated with other litigation and the activities of other organizations.

The Court is an instrument of political power, but the justices remain dependent on the attitudes and actions of their immediate constitutents, elected officials, and the dynamics of pressure-group politics and public opinion. Implementation and compliance largely depends on lower courts, Congress, and the president.

Compliance with the Court's decisions by lower courts is invariably uneven. They may extend or limit decisions in anticipation of later rulings by the high Court. Following the watershed ruling on privacy in *Griswold v. Connecticut*, 381 U.S. 479 (1965) (see Vol. 2, Ch. 4), lower courts interpreted the newfound constitutional right of privacy to strike down a wide range of laws, from those limiting the length of male employees' and students' hair to ones forbidding certain sexual acts between consenting adults and the use of marijuana, to laws requiring psychological tests of applicants for government jobs, and to laws governing access to financial and medical records. The Court reversed or would not approve the extension of the right of privacy in many of these areas.

A simple model of compliance is not very useful: Decisions handed down by the Court are not necessarily or readily applied by lower courts. Ambiguity and plurality or five-to-four decisions invite lower courts to pursue their own policy goals. Crucial language in an opinion may be treated as *dicta*. Differences between the facts on which the Court ruled and the circumstances of a case at hand may be emphasized so as to distinguish or reach the opposite result of the Court's decision. Lower courts may thus effectively delay implementation and compliance.

Open defiance is infrequent but not unprecedented. *Jaffree v. Board of School Commissioners* (1983) (see page 187) is extreme but illustrative of lower court defiance. There, a federal district court judge in Alabama directly challenged the legitimacy of the Court in its public school prayer rulings. A majority of the Court rebuffed the lower court when it decided an appeal of the ruling and struck down the "moment of silence" law in *Wallace v. Jaffree*, 472 U.S. 38 (1985) (see Vol. 2, Ch. 6).

Major confrontations between Congress and the Court have occurred a number of times. With the election of Thomas Jefferson in 1800, Republicans gained control of Congress. Defeated President John Adams and the outgoing Federalists in Congress passed the Judiciary Act of 1801, creating new circuit court judgeships and stipulating that when the next vacancy on the Court occurred it should go unfilled. That attempt to maintain influence in the judiciary was quickly countered. In 1802, the Republican Congress repealed the Act of 1801, abolishing the judgeships and returning the number of justices to six. Congress also postponed the Court's next term to preclude it from immediately hearing a challenge, in *Stuart v. Laird*, 5 U.S. 299 (1803), to its repealing legislation. When the Court decided *Stuart*, it upheld Congress's power to repeal the Judiciary Act of 1801. The Jeffersonian-Republicans then impeached Justice Samuel Chase for expounding federalist doctrine. Although the Senate acquitted him, it would not confirm nominees for federal judgeships unless they were Republicans.

The Marshall Court approved the expansion of national governmental power, but in response Congress in the 1820s and 1830s threatened to remove the Court's jurisdiction over disputes involving states' rights. After the Civil War, Congress succeeded in repealing the Court's jurisdiction over certain denials of writs of *habeas corpus*—orders commanding that a prisoner be brought before a judge and cause shown for his imprisonment. In *Ex parte McCardle*, 74 U.S. 506 (1869), the Court upheld the repeal of its jurisdiction and thus avoided deciding a controversial case attacking the constitutionality of Reconstruction legislation.

At the turn of the century, Progressives in Congress unsuccessfully sought to pressure the Court—dominated at the time by advocates of laissez-faire social and economic policy. They proposed requiring a two-thirds vote by the justices when striking down federal statutes and permitting Congress to overrule the Court's decisions by a two-thirds majority. The confrontation escalated with the Court's invalidation of President Franklin D. Roosevelt's early New Deal program passed by Congress in the 1930s. FDR retaliated by attempting to pack the Court by increasing the number of justices. Even though it was upset by the Court's invalidation of the New Deal, Congress would not accept FDR's Court-packing plan. It did, though pass legislation allowing justices to retire, after ten years of service at age seventy, with full- rather than half-salary. Congress thus made retirement more financially attractive and gave FDR opportunities to appoint justices who shared his political philosophy.

Congress may pressure the Court in a number of ways. The Senate may try to influence judicial appointments and justices may be impeached. More often, institutional and jurisdictional changes are used as weapons against the Court. Congress has tried to pressure the Court when setting its terms and size, and when authorizing appropriations for salaries, law clerks, secretaries, and office technology. Only once, in 1802 when repealing the Judiciary Act of 1801 and abolishing a session for a year, did Congress actually set the Court's term to delay and influence a particular decision.

The size of the Court is not preordained and changes generally reflect attempts to control the Court. The Jeffersonian-Republicans' quick repeal of the act passed by the Federalists in 1801, reducing the number of justices, was the first of several attempts to influence the Court. Presidents James Madison, James Monroe, and John Adams all claimed that the country's geographical expansion warranted enlarging the size of the Court. But Congress refused to do so until the last day of Andrew Jackson's term in 1837. During the Civil War, the number of justices increased to ten ostensibly due to the creation of a tenth circuit in the West. This gave Abraham Lincoln his fourth appointment and a chance to secure a pro-Union majority on the bench. Antagonism toward President Andrew Johnson's Reconstruction policies following the Civil War led to a reduction from ten to seven justices. After General Ulysses S. Grant was elected president, Congress again authorized nine justices—the number that has prevailed. In the nineteenth century at least, Congress rather successfully denied presidents additional appointments to preserve the Court's policies and increased the number of justices as a way to change the ideological composition of the Court.

Although Article III of the Constitution forbids reducing justices' salaries, Congress may withhold salary increases as punishment, especially in times of high inflation. More direct attacks are possible. Under Article III, Congress is authorized "to make exceptions" to the appellate jurisdiction of the Court. That authorization has been viewed as a way of denying the Court review of certain kinds of cases. But Congress succeeded only once, with the 1868 repeal of jurisdiction over writs of *habeas corpus,* which the Court upheld in *Ex parte McCardle,* 7 Wall. (74 U.S.) 506 (1869).

Court-curbing legislation is not a very viable weapon. Rather than limiting judicial review, Congress has given the Court the power to set its own agenda and decide major issues of public law and policy—precisely the kinds of issues that Congress then seeks to deny the Court review. The Court has also suggested that it would not approve repeals of its jurisdiction that are merely attempts to dictate how particular kinds of cases should be decided.[7] Most proposals to curb the Court, of course, are simply that. During the McCarthy era, for instance, Republican Senator William Jenner spearheaded a drive to forbid review of cases challenging legislative committees investigating un-American activities. Another unsuccessful attempt was made in 1968 to amend the Omnibus Crime Control and Safe Streets Act so as to prevent the Court from reviewing state criminal cases raising *Miranda* issues.

Congress has had somewhat greater success in reversing the Court by constitutional amendment. Congress must pass a constitutional amendment that three-fourths of the states must then ratify. The process is cumbersome and thousands of amendments to overrule the Court have failed. But four decisions have been overturned by constitutional amendment. *Chisholm v. Georgia,* 2 U.S. 419 (1793), holding that citizens of one state could sue in federal courts another state, was reversed by the Eleventh Amendment, guaranteeing sovereign immunity for states from suits by citizens of another state. The Thirteenth and Fourteenth Amendments, abolishing slavery and making blacks citizens of the United States, technically overturned the ruling in *Dred Scott v. Sanford* (1857) that blacks were not persons under the Constitution. With the ratification in 1913 of the Sixteenth Amendment, Congress reversed *Pollock v. Farmers' Loan and Trust Company*, 157 U.S. 429 (1895), which had invalidated a federal income tax. In 1970 an amendment to the Voting Rights Act of 1965 lowered the voting age to eighteen years for all elections. Although signing the act into law, President Richard Nixon had his attorney general challenge the validity of lowering the voting age by simple legislation, rather than by constitutional amendment. Within six months in *Oregon v. Mitchell*, 400 U.S. 112 (1970), a bare majority of the Court held that Congress exceeded its power by lowering the voting age for state and local elections. Less than a year later the Twenty-sixth Amendment was ratified extending the franchise to eighteen year olds in all elections.

More successful than Court-curbing and amending the Constitution are congressional enactments and rewriting of legislation in response to the Court's rulings. Congressional reversals usually relate to nonstatutory matters involving administrative policies. *Zurcher v. The Stanford Daily*, 436 U.S. 547 (1978) (see Vol. 2, Ch. 5), held that there was no constitutional prohibition against police searching newsrooms for "mere evidence," photographs, of a crime. Congress subsequently reversed that holding by passing the Privacy Protection Act of 1980 prohibiting unannounced searches of newsrooms and requiring that such evidence be obtained by a subpoena.

Congress cannot overturn the Court's interpretations of the Constitution by mere legislation. But Congress can enhance or thwart compliance with the Court's rulings. After the Warren Court's landmark decision in *Gideon v. Wainwright*, 372 U.S. 335 (1963) (see Vol. 2, Ch. 9), that indigents have a right to counsel, Congress provided attorneys for indigents charged with federal offenses. By contrast, in the Crime Control and Safe Streets Act of 1968, Congress permitted federal courts to use evidence obtained from suspects who had not been read their *Miranda* rights, if their testimony appeared voluntary based on the "totality of the circumstances" surrounding their interrogation. Congress thus attempted to return to a pre-*Miranda* standard for police questioning of criminal suspects.

Congress indubitably has the power to delay and undercut implementation of the Court's rulings. On major issues of public policy Congress is likely to prevail or, at least, temper the impact of the Court's rulings. But the Court forges public policy not only when invalidating federal legislation. No less importantly, the Court makes policy by overturning state and local laws and practices. The continuing controversies over decisions striking down state laws on school desegregation, school prayer, and abortion are a measure of the Court's influence on American life.

Charged with the responsibility of taking "care that the laws be faithfully executed," the president is the chief executive officer under the Constitution. As the only nationally elected public official, the president represents the views of the dominant national political coalition. A president's obligation to faithfully execute the laws, including decisions of the Court, thus may collide with his own perceived electoral mandate.

The Court has often been the focus of presidential campaigns and power struggles. But presidents rarely openly defy particular decisions by the Court. Presidential defiance is, perhaps, symbolized by the famous remark attributed to Andrew Jackson: "John Marshall has made his decision, now let him enforce it." Jackson's refusal to enforce the decision in *Worcester v. Georgia,* 31 U.S. 515 (1832), which denied state courts jurisdiction over crimes committed on Indian lands, in fact simply left enforcement problems up to the courts and legislatures. During the Civil War however, Lincoln ordered his military commanders to refuse to obey writs of habeas corpus issued by Chief Justice Taney.

In major confrontations, presidents generally yield to the Court. Richard Nixon complied with the ruling in *New York Times Co. v. United States,* 403 U.S. 713 (1971) (see Vol. 1, Ch. 4) (page 273), which struck down, as a prior restraint on freedom of the press, an injunction against the publication of the Pentagon Papers—a top secret report detailing the history of America's involvement in Vietnam. Then, during the Watergate scandal in 1974, Nixon submitted to the Court's decision in *United States v. Nixon,* 418 U.S. 683 (1974) (see Vol. 1, Ch. 4) (page 373) ordering the release of White House tape recordings pertinent to the trial of his former attorney general John Mitchell and other presidential aides for conspiracy and obstruction of justice.

Although seldom directly defying the Court, in the short and long run they may undercut Supreme Court policymaking. By contradictory directives to federal agencies and assigning low priority for enforcement by the Department of Justice, presidents may limit the Court's decisions. Presidents may also make broad moral appeals in response to the Court's rulings, and those appeals may transcend their limited time in office. The Court put school desegregation and abortion on the national agenda. But President John F. Kennedy's appeal for civil rights captivated a generation and encouraged public acceptance of the Court's rulings. Similarly, President Ronald Reagan's opposition to abortion focused attention on "traditional family values" and served to legitimate resistence to the Court's decisions.

Presidential influence over the Court in the long run remains contingent on appointments to the Court. Vacancies occur on the average of one every twenty-two months. Four presidents—including Jimmy Carter—had no opportunity to appoint members of the Court. There is no guarantee how a justice will vote or whether that vote will prove sufficient in limiting or reversing past rulings with which a president disagrees. But through their appointments presidents may leave their mark on Supreme Court policymaking and possibly align the Court and the country or precipitate later confrontations.

For much of the Court's history, the work of the justices has not involved major issues of public policy. In most areas of public law and policy, the fact that the Court decides an issue is more important than what it decides. Relatively few of the major issues of public policy that arise in government reach the Court. When the Court does decide major questions of public policy, its rulings decide only the instant case and not the larger surrounding political controversies. Major confrontations in constitutional politics, like those over school desegregation and abortion, are determined as much by what is possible in a system of free government and pluralistic society as by what the Court says about the meaning of the Constitution. And on those controversial issues of public policy, constitutional law frames the political debate in the ongoing dialogue between the Court and the country. The Court's rulings and interpretation of the Constitution rests, in Chief Justice Edward White's words, "solely upon the approval of a free people."[8]

NOTES

1. Robert Dahl, "Decision-Making in a Democracy: The Supreme Court as a National Policy-Maker," 6 *Journal of Public Law* 293 (1957).

2. See Richard Funston, "The Supreme Court and Critical Elections," 69 *American Political Science Review* 795 (1975).

3. See, for example, Walter Murphy, J. Tananhaus and D. Kastner, *Public Evaluations of Constitutional Courts* (Beverly Hills, CA: Sage, 1973).

4. Williams v. United States, 401 U.S. 675 (1971).

5. Fred Vinson, speech given before the American Bar Association, Sept. 7, 1949, reprinted in 69 S.Ct. vi (1949).

6. Robert Jackson, *The Struggle for Judicial Supremacy* (New York: Knopf, 1951), 287.

7. *United States v. Klein,* 80 U.S. 128 (1872).

8. Edward White, "The Supreme Court of the United States," 7 *American Bar Association Journal* 341 (1921).

SELECTED BIBLIOGRAPHY

Abraham, Henry J. *The Judicial Process,* 6th ed. New York: Oxford University Press, 1991.

Baum, Lawrence. *The Supreme Court.* Washington, DC, Congressional Quarterly, 1989.

Becker, Ted, and Feeley, Malcolm, eds. *The Impact of Supreme Court Decisions,* 2nd ed. New York: Oxford University Press, 1973.

Blandford, Linda, and Evans, Patricia. *Supreme Court of the United States 1789–1980: An Index to Opinions Arranged by Justice,* 2 vols. New York: Kraus International, 1983.

Cannon, Mark, and O'Brien, David M. *Views from the Bench: The Judiciary and Constitutional Politics.* Chatham: Chatham House, 1985.

Cardozo, Benjamin. *The Nature of the Judicial Process.* New Haven, CT: Yale University Press, 1921.

Cooper, Phillip. *Hard Judicial Choices.* New York: Oxford University Press, 1988.

Friedman, Leon, and Israel, Fred. *The Justices of the United States Supreme Court 1789–1978: Their Lives and Major Opinions,* 5 vols. New York: Chelsea House, 1980.

Goldman, Sheldon, and Jahnige, Thomas P. *The Federal Courts as a Political System,* 3rd ed. New York: Harper & Row, 1985.

Horwitz, Donald. *The Courts and Social Policy.* Washington, DC: Brookings Institution, 1977.

Johnson, Charles, and Canon, Bradley. *Judicial Policies: Implementation and Impact.* Washington, DC: Congressional Quarterly, 1984.

Lawrence, Susan. *The Poor in Court.* Princeton, NJ: Princeton University Press, 1990.

Murphy, Walter. *Elements of Judicial Strategy.* Chicago: University of Chicago Press, 1964.

Murphy, Walter, and Pritchett, C. Herman, eds. *Courts, Judges, and Politics,* 4th ed. New York: Random House, 1985.

O'Brien, David M. *Storm Center: The Supreme Court in American Politics,* 2nd ed. New York: W. W. Norton, 1990.

O'Connor, Karen, and Epstein, Lee. *Woman's Organizations' Use of the Courts.* Lexington, MA: Lexington Books, 1980.

Pritchett, C. Herman. *The Roosevelt Court.* New York: Macmillan, 1947.

Provine, Doris. *Case Selection in the United States Supreme Court.* Chicago: University of Chicago Press, 1980.

Schubert, Glendon. *The Judicial Mind.* Chicago: Northwestern University Press, 1965.

_____, ed. *Judicial Behavior: A Reader in Theory and Research.* Chicago: Rand McNally, 1964.

_____. *The Constitutional Polity.* Boston: Boston University, 1970.

_____. *Judicial Policymaking,* 2nd ed. New York: Scott, Foresman, 1974.

Shapiro, Martin. *Law and Politics in the Supreme Court.* New York: Free Press, 1964.

Sheldon, Charles. *The Judicial Process: Models and Approaches.* New York: Dodd, Mead, 1974.

Supreme Court Historical Society. *Yearbook.* Washington, DC: SCHS, 1976–present.

Linkletter v. Walker

381 U.S. 618, 85 S.Ct. 1731 (1965)

Victor Linkletter was tried and convicted in state court on evidence illegally obtained by police prior to *Mapp v. Ohio*, 367 U.S. 643 (1961) (see Vol. 2, Ch. 7), which barred states from using illegally obtained evidence at trial under the Fourth Amendment's exclusionary rule. Linkletter contended that *Mapp* should apply retroactively and he should be retried with the illegally obtained evidence excluded. A federal district court disagreed and after a court of appeals affirmed that ruling, Linkletter appealed to the Supreme Court.

Justice CLARK delivers the opinion of the Court.

In *Mapp v. Ohio*, 367 U.S. 643 (1961), we held that the exclusion of evidence seized in violation of the search and seizure provisions of the Fourth Amendment was required of the States by the Due Process Clause of the Fourteenth Amendment. In so doing we overruled *Wolf v. People of State of Colorado*, 338 U.S. 25 (1949), to the extent that it failed to apply the exclusionary rule to the States. This case presents the question of whether this requirement operates retrospectively upon cases finally decided in the period prior to *Mapp*. The Court of Appeals for the Fifth Circuit held that it did not, and we granted certiorari in order to settle what has become a most troublesome question in the administration of justice. We agree with the Court of Appeals. . . .

At common law there was no authority for the proposition that judicial decisions made law only for the future. Blackstone stated the rule that the duty of the court was not to "pronounce a new law, but to maintain and expound the old one." 1 Blackstone, Commentaries 69 (15th ed. 1809). . . .

In the case of the overruled decision, *Wolf v. People of State of Colorado,* supra, here, it was thought to be only a failure at true discovery and was consequently never the law; while the overruling one, Mapp, was not "new law but an application of what is, and theretofore had been, the true law.". . .

On the other hand, [the late-nineteenth century legal philosopher John] Austin maintained that judges do in fact do something more than discover law; they make it interstitially by filling in with judicial interpretation the vague, indefinite, or generic statutory or common-law terms that alone are but the empty crevices of the law. Implicit in such an approach is the admission when a case is overruled that the earlier decision was wrongly decided. However, rather than being erased by the later overruling decision it is considered as an existing juridical fact until overruled, and intermediate cases finally decided under it are not to be disturbed.

The Blackstonian view ruled English jurisprudence and cast its shadow over our own. . . . However, some legal philosophers continued to insist that such a rule was out of tune with actuality largely because judicial repeal ofttime did "work hardship to those who [had] trusted to its existence." Cardozo, Address to the N. Y. Bar Assn. (1932). . . .

It is true that heretofore, without discussion, we have applied new constitutional rules to cases finalized before the promulgation of the rule. Petitioner contends that our method of resolving those prior cases demonstrates that an absolute rule of retroaction prevails in the area of constitutional ad judication. However, we believe that the Constitution neither prohibits nor requires retrospective effect. As Justice CARDOZO said, "We think the Federal Constitution has no voice upon the subject.". . .

Once the premise is accepted that we are neither required to apply, nor prohibited from applying, a decision retrospectively, we must then weigh the merits and demerits in each case by looking to the prior history of the rule in question, its purpose and effect, and whether retrospective operation will further or retard its operation. We believe that this approach is particularly correct with reference to the Fourth Amendment's prohibitions as to unreasonable searches and seizures. Rather than "disparaging" the Amendment we but apply the wisdom of Justice HOLMES that "[t]he life of the law has not been logic: it has been experience." Holmes, The Common Law 5 (Howe ed. 1963).

Since *Weeks v. United States,* 232 U.S. 383 (1914) this Court has adhered to the rule that evidence seized by federal officers in violation of the Fourth Amendment is not admissible at trial in a federal court. In 1949 in *Wolf v. People of State of Colorado,* supra, the Court decided that while the right to privacy—"the core of the Fourth Amendment"—was such a basic right as to be implicit in "the concept of ordered liberty" and thus enforceable against the States through the Fourteenth Amendment, "the ways of enforcing such a basic right raise questions of a different order. How such arbitrary conduct should be checked, what remedies against it should be afforded, the means by which the right should be made effective, are all questions that are not to be so dogmatically answered as to preclude the varying solutions which spring from an allowable range of judgment on issues not susceptible of quantitative solution."

Mapp was announced in 1961. The Court in considering "the current validity of the factual grounds upon which Wolf was based" pointed out that prior to *Wolf* "almost two-thirds of the States were opposed to the use of the exclusionary rule, now, despite the *Wolf* case, more than half of those since passing upon it . . . have wholly or partly adopted or adhered to the *Weeks* rule.". . .

We believe that the existence of the *Wolf* doctrine prior to *Mapp* is "an operative fact and may have consequences which cannot justly be ignored. The past cannot always be erased by a new judicial declaration." The thousands of cases that were finally decided on *Wolf* cannot be obliterated. The "particular conduct, private and official," must be considered. Here "prior determinations deemed to have finality and acted upon accordingly" have "become vested." And finally, "public policy in the light of the nature both of the [*Wolf* doctrine] and of its previous application" must be given its proper weight. In short, we must look to the purpose of the *Mapp* rule; the reliance placed upon the *Wolf* doctrine; and the effect on the administration of justice of a retrospective application of *Mapp*.

It is clear that the *Wolf* Court, once it had found the Fourth Amendment's unreasonable Search and Seizure Clause applicable to the States through the Due Process Clause of the Fourteenth Amendment, turned its attention to whether the exclusionary rule was included within the command of the Fourth Amendment. This was decided in the negative. It is clear that based upon the factual considerations heretofore discussed the *Wolf* Court then concluded that it was not necessary to the enforcement of the Fourth Amendment for the exclusionary rule to be extended to the States as a requirement of due process. *Mapp* had as its prime purpose the enforcement of the Fourth Amendment through the inclusion of the exclusionary rule within its rights. This, it was found, was the only effective deterrent to lawless police action. Indeed, all of the cases since *Wolf* requiring the exclusion of illegal evidence have been based on the necessity for an effective deterrent to illegal police action. We cannot say that this purpose would be advanced by making the rule retrospective. The misconduct of the police prior to *Mapp* has already occurred and will not be corrected by releasing the prisoners involved. Nor would it add harmony to the delicate state-federal relationship of which we have spoken as part and parcel of the purpose of *Mapp*. Finally, the ruptured privacy of the victims' homes and effects cannot be restored. Reparation comes too late. . . .

Finally, there are interests in the administration of justice and the integrity of the judicial process to consider. To make the rule of *Mapp* retrospective would tax the administration of justice to the utmost. Hearings would have to be held on the excludability of evidence long since destroyed, misplaced or deteriorated. If it is excluded, the witnesses available at the time of the original trial will not be available or if located their memory will be dimmed. To thus legitimate such an extraordinary procedural weapon that has no bearing on guilt would seriously disrupt the administration of justice. . . .

All that we decide today is that though the error complained of might be fundamental it is not of the nature requiring us to overturn all final convictions based upon it. After full consideration of all the factors we are not able to say that the *Mapp* rule requires retrospective application.

Affirmed.

Justice BLACK, with whom Justice DOUGLAS joins, dissenting.

The Court offers no defense based on any known principle of justice for discriminating among defendants who were similarly convicted by use of evidence unconstitutionally seized. It certainly cannot do so as between Linkletter and Miss Mapp. The crime with which she was charged took place more than a year before his, yet the decision today seems to rest on the fanciful concept that the Fourth Amendment protected her 1957 offense against conviction by use of unconstitutional evidence but denied its protection to Linkletter for his 1958 offense. In making this ruling the Court assumes for itself the virtue of acting in harmony with a comment of Justice HOLMES that "[t]he life of the law has not been logic: it has been experience." Justice HOLMES was not there talking about the Constitution; he was talking about the evolving judge-made law of England and of some of our States whose judges are allowed to follow in the common law tradition. It should be remembered in this connection that no member of this Court has ever more seriously criticized it than did Justice HOLMES for reading its own predilections into the "vague contours" of the Due Process Clause. But quite apart from that, there is no experience of the past that justifies a new Court-made rule to perpetrate a grossly invidious and unfair discrimination against Linkletter simply because he happened to be prosecuted in a State that was evidently well up with its criminal court docket. If this discrimination can be excused at all it is not because of experience but because of logic—sterile and formal at that—not, according to Justice HOLMES, the most dependable guide in lawmaking. . . .

As the Court concedes, this is the first instance on record where this Court, having jurisdiction, has ever refused to give a previously convicted defendant the benefit of a new and more expansive Bill of Rights interpretation. I am at a loss to understand why those who suffer from the use of evidence secured by a search and seizure in violation of the Fourth Amendment should be treated differently from those who have been denied other guarantees of the Bill of Rights. . . .

One reason—perhaps a basic one—put forward by the Court for its refusal to give Linkletter the benefit of the search and seizure exclusionary rule is the repeated statement that the purpose of that rule is to deter sheriffs, policemen, and other law officers from making unlawful searches and seizures. The inference I gather from these repeated statements is that the rule is not a right or privilege accorded to defendants charged with crime but is a sort of punishment against officers in order to keep them from depriving people of their constitutional rights. In passing I would say that if that is the sole purpose, reason, object and effect of the rule, the Court's action in adopting it sounds more like law making than construing the Constitution. . . . [T]he undoubted implication of today's opinion that the rule is not a safeguard for defendants but is a mere punishing rod to be applied to law enforcement officers is a rather startling departure from many past opinions, and even from *Mapp* itself. *Mapp* quoted from the Court's earlier opinion in *Weeks v. United States,* supra, certainly not with disapproval, saying that the Court "in that case clearly stated that use of the seized evidence involved 'a denial of the constitutional rights of the accused.' " I have read and reread the *Mapp* opinion but have been unable to find one word in it to indicate that the exclusionary search and seizure rule should be limited on the basis that it was intended to do nothing in the world except to deter officers of the law. . . .

The Court says that the exclusionary rule's purpose of preventing law enforcement officers from making lawless searches and seizures "will not at this late date be served by the wholesale release of the guilty victims." It has not been the usual thing to cut down trial protections guaranteed by the Constitution on the basis that some guilty persons might escape. There is probably no one of the rights in the Bill of Rights that does not make it more difficult to convict defendants. But all of them are based on the premise, I suppose, that the Bill of Rights' safeguards should be faithfully enforced by the court without regard to a particular judge's judgment as to whether more people could be convicted by a refusal of courts to enforce the safeguards. Such has heretofore been accepted as a general maxim. . . .

The plain facts here are that the Court's opinion cuts off many defendants who are now in jail from any hope of relief from unconstitutional convictions. . . . No State should be considered to have a vested interest in keeping prisoners in jail who were convicted because of lawless conduct by the State's officials. Careful analysis of the Court's opinion shows that it rests on the premise that a State's assumed interest in sustaining convictions obtained under the old, repudiated rule outweighs the interests both of that State and of the individuals convicted in having wrongful convictions set aside. It certainly offends my sense of justice to say that a State holding in jail people who were convicted by unconstitutional methods has a vested interest in keeping them there that outweighs the right of persons adjudged guilty of crime to challenge their unconstitutional convictions at any time. . . .

Griffith v. Kentucky
479 U.S. 314, 107 S.Ct. 708 (1987)

Justice Blackmun's opinion for the Court discusses the issues presented here.

Justice BLACKMUN delivers the opinion of the Court.

These cases, one state and one federal, concern the retrospective application of *Batson v. Kentucky,* [476 U.S. 79] (1986).

In *Batson,* this Court ruled that a defendant in a state criminal trial could establish a prima facie case of racial discrimination violative of the Fourteenth Amendment, based on the prosecution's use of peremptory challenges to strike members of the defendant's race from the jury venire, and that, once the defendant had made the prima facie showing, the burden shifted to the prosecution to come forward with a neutral explanation for those challenges. In the present cases we consider whether that ruling is applicable to litigation pending on direct state or federal review or not yet final when *Batson* was decided. We answer that question in the affirmative. . . .

Twenty-one years ago, this Court adopted a three-pronged analysis for claims of retroactivity of new constitutional rules of criminal procedure. See *Linkletter v. Walker,* 381 U.S. 618 (1965). In *Linkletter,* the Court held that *Mapp v. Ohio* [367 U.S. 643 (1961)], which extended the Fourth Amendment exclusionary rule to the States, would not be applied retroactively to a state conviction that had become final before *Mapp* was decided. The Court explained that "the Constitution neither prohibits nor requires retrospective effect" of a new constitutional rule, and that a determination of retroactivity must depend on "weigh[ing] the merits and demerits in each case." The Court's decision not to apply *Mapp* retroactively was based on "the purpose of the *Mapp* rule; the reliance placed upon the [previous] doctrine; and the effect on the administration of justice of a retrospective application of *Mapp*.". . .

Shortly after the decision in *Linkletter*, the Court held that the three-pronged analysis applied both to convictions that were final and to convictions pending on direct review. . . .

In *United States v. Johnson*, 457 U.S. 537 (1982), however, the Court shifted course. In that case, we reviewed at some length the history of the Court's decisions in the area of retroactivity and concluded, in the words of Justice HARLAN: " '[R]etroactivity' must be rethought." Specifically, we concluded that the retroactivity analysis for convictions that have become final must be different from the analysis for convictions that are not final at the time the new decision is issued. We observed that, in a number of separate opinions since *Linkletter*, various Members of the Court "have asserted that, at a minimum, all defendants whose cases were still pending on direct appeal at the time of the law-changing decision should be entitled to invoke the new rule." The rationale for distinguishing between cases that have become final and those that have not, and for applying new rules retroactively to cases in the latter category, was explained at length by Justice HARLAN in *Desist v. United States*, 394 U.S. [244 (1969)] (dissenting opinion), and in *Mackey v. United States*, 401 U.S. 667 (1971) (opinion concurring in judgments). In *United States v. Johnson*, we embraced to a significant extent the comprehensive analysis presented by Justice HARLAN in those opinions.

In Justice HARLAN's view, and now in ours, failure to apply a newly declared constitutional rule to criminal cases pending on direct review violates basic norms of constitutional adjudication. First, it is a settled principle that this Court adjudicates only "cases" and "controversies." See U.S. Const., Art. III, § 2. Unlike a legislature, we do not promulgate new rules of constitutional criminal procedure on a broad basis. Rather, the nature of judicial review requires that we adjudicate specific cases, and each case usually becomes the vehicle for announcement of a new rule. But after we have decided a new rule in the case selected, the integrity of judicial review requires that we apply that rule to all similar cases pending on direct review. . . .

As a practical matter, of course, we cannot hear each case pending on direct review and apply the new rule. But we fulfill our judicial responsibility by instructing the lower courts to apply the new rule retroactively to cases not yet final. . . .

Second, selective application of new rules violates the principle of treating similarly situated defendants the same. . . .

In *United States v. Johnson*, our acceptance of Justice HARLAN's views led to the holding that "subject to [certain exceptions], a decision of this Court construing the Fourth Amendment is to be applied retroactively to all convictions that were not yet final at the time the decision was rendered." The exceptions to which we referred related to three categories in which we concluded that existing precedent established threshold tests for the retroactivity analysis. In two of these categories, the new rule already was retroactively applied: (1) when a decision of this Court did nothing more than apply settled precedent to different factual situations, and (2) when the new ruling was that a trial court lacked authority to convict a criminal defendant in the first place. . . .

The third category—where a new rule is a "clear break" with past precedent—is the one at issue in these cases. . . .

Under this exception, a new constitutional rule was not applied retroactively, even to cases on direct review, if the new rule explicitly overruled a past precedent of this Court, or disapproved a practice this Court had arguably sanctioned in prior cases, or overturned a longstanding practice that lower courts had uniformly approved. . . .

For the same reasons that persuaded us in *United States v. Johnson* to adopt different conclusions as to convictions on direct review from those that already had become final, we conclude that an engrafted exception based solely upon the particular characteristics of the new rule adopted by the Court is inappropriate.

First, the principle that this Court does not disregard current law, when it adjudicates a case pending before it on direct review, applies regardless of the specific characteristics of the particular new rule announced. . . .

Second, the use of a "clear break" exception creates the same problem of not treating similarly situated defendants the same. . . .

We therefore hold that a new rule for the conduct of criminal prosecutions is to be applied retroactively to all cases, state or federal, pending on direct review or not yet final, with no exception for cases in which the new rule constitutes a "clear break" with the past. Accordingly, in No. 85–5221, the judgment of the Supreme Court of Kentucky is reversed, and the case is remanded to that court for further proceedings not inconsistent with this opinion. In No. 85–5731, the judgment of the United States Court of Appeals for the Tenth Circuit is reversed, and the case is remanded to that court for further proceedings consistent with this opinion.

Justice POWELL concurring.

I join the Court's opinion, and consider it an important step toward ending the confusion that has resulted from applying *Linkletter v. Walker* on a case by case basis.

Chief Justice REHNQUIST dissenting.

In Justice HARLAN's view, new constitutional rules governing criminal prosecutions should apply retroactively for cases pending on direct appeal when the rule is announced, and, with narrow exceptions, should not apply in collateral proceedings challenging convictions that become final before the rule is announced. The majority today adopts only a portion of this approach. I therefore join Justice WHITE's dissent. . . .

Justice WHITE, with whom the Chief Justice and Justice O'CONNOR join, dissenting.

Last Term this Court decided that the rule announced in *Batson v. Kentucky* (1986), should not apply on collateral review of convictions that became final before the decision in *Batson* was announced. *Allen v. Hardy* [478 U.S. 255] (1986). In reaching this judgment, the Court weighed the three factors that it has traditionally considered in deciding the retroactivity of a new rule of criminal procedure: " '(a) the purpose to be served by the new standards, (b) the extent of the reliance by law enforcement authorities on the old standards, and (c) the effect on the administration of justice of a retroactive application of the new standards.' " No Justice suggested that this test is unworkable. The question, then, is why the Court feels constrained to fashion a different rule for cases on direct review. The reasons the Court offers are not new, and I find them as unpersuasive today as I have in the past. . . .

The Court has already recognized that *Batson* constitutes "an explicit and substantial break with prior precedent," and that "prosecutors, trial judges, and appellate courts throughout our state and federal systems justifiably have relied on the standard of *Swain*." *Allen v. Hardy*. The reasons that the Court gave in *Allen v. Hardy* for concluding that "retroactive application of the *Batson* rule on collateral review of final convictions would seriously disrupt the administration of justice" apply equally to retroactive application of the *Batson* rule on direct review.

The majority knows that it is penalizing justifiable reliance on *Swain*, and in doing so causing substantial disruption in the administration of justice; yet the majority acts as if it has no principled alternative.

Jaffree v. Board of School Commissioners of Mobile County
554 F.Supp. 1104 (1983)

Ishmael Jaffree challenged the constitutionality of Alabama's law authorizing teachers to lead students in a moment of "silent mediation or voluntary prayer" as a violation of the First Amendment guarantees for religious freedom. Federal District Court Judge Brevard Hand rejected Jaffree's complaint in an opinion sharply critical of the Supreme Court's rulings on the First Amendment establishment clause. His ruling was subsequently appealed by Jaffree and overturned by a court of appeals. Governor George Wallace then appealed that ruling to the Supreme Court in *Wallace v. Jaffree*, 472 U.S. 38 (1985) (see Vol. 2, Ch. 6).

MEMORANDUM OPINION

Chief Judge BREVARD HAND.

The United States Supreme Court has previously addressed itself in many cases to the practice of prayer and religious services in the public schools. As courts are wont to say, this court does not write upon a clean slate when it addresses the issue of school prayer.

Viewed historically, three decisions have lately provided general rules for school prayer. In *Engel v. Vitale*, 370 U.S. 421 [1962], *Abington v. Schempp*, 374 U.S. 203 (1963), and *Murray v. Curlett*, 374 U.S. 203 (1963) the Supreme Court established the basic considerations. As stated, the rule is that "[t]he First Amendment has erected a wall between church and state. That wall must be kept high and impregnable. We could not approve the slightest breach." *Everson v. Board of Education*, 330 U.S. 1 (1947).

The principles enunciated in *Engel v. Vitale, Abington v. Schempp*, and *Murray v. Curlett* have been distilled to this: "To pass muster under the Establishment Clause, the governmental activity must, first, reflect a clearly secular governmental purpose; second, have a primary effect that neither advances nor inhibits religion; and third, avoid excessive government entanglement with religion. *Committee for Public Education & Religious Liberty v. Nyquist*, 413 U.S. 756 (1973).". . .

In sum, under present rulings the use of officially-authorized prayers or Bible readings for motivational purposes constitutes a direct violation of the establishment clause. Through a series of decisions, the courts have held that the establishment clause was designed to avoid any official sponsorship or approval of religious beliefs. Even though a practice may not be coercive, active support of a particular belief raises the danger, under the rationale of the Court, that state-approved religious views may be eventually established. . . .

In the face of this precedent the defendants argue that school prayers as they are employed are constitutional. The historical argument which they advance takes two tacks. First, the defendants urge that the first amendment to the U.S. Constitution was intended only to prohibit the *federal government* from establishing a *national* religion. Read in its proper historical context, the defendants contend that the first amendment has no application to the states. The intent of the drafters and adoptors of the first amendment was to prevent the establishment of a national church or religion, and to prevent any single religious sect or denomination from obtaining a preferred position under the auspices of the federal government. . . .

Second, the defendants argue that whatever prohibitions were initially placed upon the federal government by the first amendment that those prohibitions were not incorporated against the states when the fourteenth amendment became law on July 19, 1868. The defendants have introduced the Court to a mass of historical documentation which all point to the intent of the Thirty-ninth Congress to narrowly restrict the scope of the fourteenth amendment. In particular, these historical documents, according to the defendants, clearly demonstrate that the first amendment was never intended to be incorporated through the fourteenth amendment to apply against the states. The Court [subsequently] examine[d] each historical argument in turn. . . .

[The Court concluded that] the establishment clause, as ratified in 1791, was intended only to prohibit the federal government from establishing a national religion. The function of the establishment clause was two-fold. First, it guaranteed to each individual that Congress would not impose a national religion. Second, the establishment clause guaranteed to each state that the states were free to define the meaning of religious establishment under their own constitutions and laws.

The historical record clearly establishes that when the fourteenth amendment was ratified in 1868 that its ratification did not incorporate the first amendment against the states. . . .

What is a court to do when faced with a direct challenge to settled precedent? In most types of cases "it is more important that the applicable rule of law be settled than that it be settled right." *Burnet v. Coronado Oil & Gas Co.*, 285 U.S. 393 (1932) (BRANDEIS, J., dissenting). This general rule holds even where the court is persuaded that it has made a serious error of interpretation in cases involving a statute. However, in cases involving the federal constitution, where correction through legislative action is practically impossible, a court should be willing to examine earlier precedent and to overrule it if the court is persuaded that the earlier precedent was wrongly decided. . . .

"[T]he ultimate touchstone of constitutionality is the Constitution itself and not what we have said about it." *Graves v. O'Keefe,* 306 U.S. 466 (1939) (FRANKFURTER, J., concurring). "By placing a premium on 'recent cases' rather than the language of the Constitution, the Court makes it dangerously simple for future Courts using the technique of interpretation to operate as a 'continuing Constitutional Convention.' " *Coleman v. Alabama,* 399 U.S. 1 (1970) (BURGER, C.J.). . . .

This Court's review of the relevant legislative history surrounding the adoption of both the first amendment and of the fourteenth amendment, together with the plain language of those amendments, leaves no doubt that those amendments were not intended to forbid religious prayers in the schools which the states and their political subdivisions mandate. . . .

If the appellate courts disagree with this Court in its examination of history and conclusion of constitutional interpreation thereof, then this Court will look again at the record in this case and reach conclusions which it is not now forced to reach.

3

PRESIDENTIAL POWER, THE RULE OF LAW, AND FOREIGN AFFAIRS

Article II of the Constitution establishes the basis for presidential power. It does so in both general and specific terms. "The executive Power shall be vested in a President" and "he shall take Care that the Laws be faithfully executed" are broad authorizations. In contrast with the lengthy enumeration of Congress's specific powers in Article I, those granted the president are few in number. The president is given, for example, power to veto legislation, power to pardon individuals of crimes, and power to act as commander in chief of the military. In addition, other powers—such as that of making treaties and appointing federal judges and other governmental officers—are shared with the Senate and their exercise, subject to Senate approval.

A. OFFICE AND POWERS: THE TWO PRESIDENCIES

The powers exercised by the contemporary presidency would have surprised those of the Founding generation. They expected, as James Madison put it in *Federalist,* No. 51, that "in republican government, the legislative authority necessarily predominates." Alexander Hamilton, however, prophetically championed the cause of a vigorous chief executive and maintained that the enumerated powers were not exhaustive of the powers of the president. In *Federalist,* No. 70 he set forth the principal arguments for a strong independent president (see page 195).

The basis for broad presidential power was laid by the Constitutional Convention in 1787. Although many delegates distrusted executive power, there was agreement that the Articles of Confederation, which failed to provide for a separate executive, had proven disastrous. Accordingly, the executive power is lodged in a single individual, elected for a four-year term and eligible for reelection. Notably, election to the office is also based on the vote of the electoral college. That resulted as a compromise between congressional selection and direct popular election. And it reflects both a fear that Congress might overshadow the president as well as a distrust of direct democracy. Finally, certain powers—such as that of vetoing legislation—were granted to further ensure presidential independence from Congress.

"[T]he history of the presidency is a history of aggrandizement, but the story is a highly discontinuous one," observed Edward S. Corwin. "That is to say, what the presidency is at any particular moment depends in important measure on who is the President."[1] Undeniably, presidential character and understanding of the powers of the Oval Office are crucial. But presidential power has also grown enormously with the emergence of the United States as a world power and is due to the acquiescence of Congress, the courts, and the American people. Moreover, the power vested in the executive branch now resides in an institutionalized presidency, with more than 3 million employees, thousands of whom wield significant power.

The growth of the institutional presidency makes questions about the limitations imposed on the office of the president more pressing. For in keeping faith with the theory of our written Constitution, "[a]ll the officers of the Government, from the highest to the lowest, are creatures of the law and are bound to obey it."[2] However, in times of emergency and national crisis, presidents have asserted unauthorized power, even ignored constitutional constraints and suspended basic rights.

A central issue in constitutional politics thus involves whether the authority granted in Article II exhausts the powers of the president. To what extent does the president enjoy inherent power and extraordinary powers in times of emergency?

One classic theory is that the president, like the old English Crown, enjoys the sovereign's "prerogative" of asserting, when necessary, unauthorized power in pursuit of the public interest. Eighteenth-century English philosopher John Locke, in his *Two Treatises of Government,* described this prerogative as "the power to act according to discretion for the public good, *without the prescription of law and sometimes even against it"* (emphasis added). Periodically, throughout our history presidents have made similar claims. President Thomas Jefferson did so in 1803 when purchasing the Louisiana Territory, despite doubts about the authority to acquire new lands. At the outset of the Civil War, Abraham Lincoln took extraordinary measures—calling up state militias, spending unappropriated funds, and blockading Southern ports—without authorization. He later defended his actions as essential to preserving the Union:

I [understood] my oath to preserve the constitution to the best of my ability, imposed upon me the duty of preserving, by every indispensable means, that government—that nation—of which that constitution was the organic law. Was it possible to lose the nation, and yet preserve the constitution? . . . I felt that measures, otherwise unconstitutional, might become lawful, by becoming indispensable to the preservation of the constitution, through the preservation of the nation.[3]

Franklin D. Roosevelt likewise claimed extensive powers during World War II. And as we will see later in this chapter, Harry S. Truman claimed the power to seize steel mills during the undeclared Korean War and, in 1971, Richard M. Nixon sought to suppress publication of the "Pentagon Papers," a history of the U.S. involvement in the Vietnam War.

During emergencies and national strife, Madison and Hamilton agreed that the national government enjoys extraordinary power. "It is in vain to oppose constitutional barriers to the impulse of self-preservation," Madison cautioned in *Federalist* No. 41. Hamilton (in *Federalist* No. 23) was even more emphatic about the powers that could be marshaled for national defense. They "ought to exist without limitation," he argued, *"because it is impossible to forsee or to define the extent and variety of the means which may be necessary to satisfy them"* (emphasis in original).

Still, how far presidents may go, without congressional authorization, when responding to perceived threats to national security remains a fundamental issue in constitutional politics. In *Ex parte Milligan* (1866) (see page 225), the Court rejected Lincoln's suspension of the right of *habeas corpus* and order for trials of civilians by military commissions, with the poignant observation that "[t]he Constitution of the United States is a law for rulers and people, equally in war and in peace, and covers with the shield of its protection all classes of men, at all times, and under all circumstances." However, in *Korematsu v. United States* (1944) (see page 232), the internment of Japanese-American citizens during World War II was upheld under legislation that made it a crime for persons of Japanese ancestry to be in "military zones" as designated by a commander under the secretary of war.

There are two rival theories of the nature and scope of the inherent presidential power; both are more restrictive than Locke's theory of the prerogative but also more generous than a rigid adherence to constitutional theory. Theodore Roosevelt took the position that inherent power extends to doing anything not expressly forbidden, so long as it serves the public interest and does not conflict with existing legislation. According to him,

The executive power was limited only by specific restrictions and prohibitions appearing in the Constitution or imposed by the Congress under its Constitutional powers. . . . I declined to adopt the view that what was imperatively necessary for the Nation could not be done by the President unless he could find some specific authorization to do it. My belief was that it was not only his right but his duty to do anything that the needs of the Nation demanded unless such action was forbidden by the Constitution or by the laws.[4]

By contrast, President (and later Chief Justice) William Howard Taft contended that inherent powers are limited and must be

Chief Justice William Howard Taft, the only president (1909–1913) also to serve on the Supreme Court (1921–1930). *Library of Congress.*

traceable to specific grants of power in the Constitution or legislation. In his words,

The true view of the Executive function is, as I conceive it, that the President can exercise no power which cannot be fairly and reasonably traced to some specific grant of power or justly implied and included within such express grant as proper and necessary to its exercise. Such specific grant must be either in the Federal Constitution or in an act of Congress passed in pursuance thereof. There is no undefined residuum of power which he can exercise because it seems to him to be in the public interest.[5]

In addition, a distinction is usually drawn between the inherent powers of the president in domestic and in foreign affairs. As political scientist Aaron Wildavsky remarked, "The United States has one President, but it has two presidencies; one presidency is for domestic affairs, and the other is concerned with defense and foreign policy."[6] In the domestic area, claims to inherent presidential power are usually limited and sharply criticized, whereas Congress and the Court generally acknowledge presidential dominance in foreign affairs. The scope of presidential powers in this area, as Clinton Rossiter noted, have historically "been presidentially, not judicially, shaped; their exercise is for Congress and the people, not the Court, to oversee."[7]

This chapter examines the express and inherent powers of the president in foreign affairs. It does so in terms of basic interpretative choices that give rise to conflicts in constitutional politics. In addressing the president's powers as commander in chief and in foreign affairs, specific attention is given to the treaty-making and war-making powers. Chapter 4 examines the president's powers in domestic affairs.

NOTES

1. E. Corwin, *The President,* 5th ed.(New York: New York University Press, 1984), 29–30.

2. *United States v. Lee,* 106 U.S. 196 (1882).

3. John Nicolay and John Hay, eds., *The Complete Works of Abraham Lincoln,* Vol. 10 (New York: Francis D. Tandy, 1894), 65–68.

4. T. Roosevelt, *Autobiography* (New York: Macmillan, 1931), 38.

5. W. Taft, *Our Chief Magistrate and His Powers* (New York: Columbia University, 1916), 139–140.

6. A. Wildavsky, "The Two Presidencies," 4 *Trans-Action* 230 (Dec. 1969).

7. C. Rossiter, *The Supreme Court and the Commander in Chief* (Ithaca, NY: Cornell University Press, 1976), 126.

SELECTED BIBLIOGRAPHY

Bessette, Joseph, and Tulis, Jeffrey. *The Presidency in the Constitutional Order.* Baton Rouge: Louisiana University Press, 1981.
Crovitz, L. Godron, and Rabkin, Jeremy, eds. *The Fettered Presidency.* Washington, DC: American Enterprise Institute, 1989.
Corwin, Edward. *The President: Office and Powers,* 5th rev. ed. New York: New York University Press, 1984.
Henkin, Louis. *Constitutionalism, Democracy, and Foreign Affairs.* New York: Columbia University Press, 1989.

CONSTITUTIONAL HISTORY

Alexander Hamilton,
The Federalist, No. 70

Energy in the executive is a leading character in the definition of good government. It is essential to the protection of the community against foreign attacks; it is not less essential to the steady administration of the laws; to the protection of property against those irregular and high-handed combinations which sometimes interrupt the ordinary course of justice; to the security of liberty against the enterprises and assaults of ambition, of faction, and of anarchy. Every man the least conversant in Roman history knows how often that republic was obliged to take refuge in the absolute power of a single man, under the formidable title of dictator, as well against the intrigues of ambitious individuals who aspired to the tyranny, and the seditions of whole classes of the community whose conduct threatened the existence of all government, as against the invasions of external enemies who menaced the conquest and destruction of Rome. . . .

The ingredients which constitute energy in the executive are unity; duration; an adequate provision for its support; and competent powers.

The ingredients which constitute safety in the republican sense are a due dependence on the people, and a due responsibility.

Those politicians and statesmen who have been the most celebrated for the soundness of their principles and for the justness of their views have declared in favor of a single executive and a numerous legislature. They have, with great propriety, considered energy as the most necessary qualification of the former, and have regarded this as most applicable to power in a single hand; while they have, with equal propriety, considered the latter as best adapted to deliberation and wisdom, and best calculated to conciliate the confidence of the people and to secure their privileges and interests.

That unity is conducive to energy will not be disputed. Decision, activity, secrecy, and dispatch will generally characterize the proceedings of one man in a much more eminent degree than the proceedings of any greater number; and in proportion as the number is increased, these qualities will be diminished. . . . In the legislature, promptitude of decision is oftener an evil than a benefit. The differences of opinion, and the jarring of parties in that department of the government, though they may sometimes obstruct salutary plans, yet often promote deliberation and circumspection, and serve to check excesses in the majority. When a resolution too is once taken, the opposition must be at an end. That resolution is a law, and resistance to it punishable. But no favorable circumstances palliate or atone for the disadvantages of dissention in the executive department. Here they are pure and unmixed. There is no point at which they cease to operate. They serve to embarrass and weaken the execution of the plan or measure to which they relate, from the first step to the final conclusion of it. They constantly counteract those qualities in the executive which are the most necessary ingredients in its composition—vigor and expedition, and this without any counterbalancing good. In the conduct of war, in which the energy of the executive is the bulwark of the national security, everything would be to be apprehended from its plurality.

B. AS COMMANDER IN CHIEF AND IN FOREIGN AFFAIRS

The president's powers in foreign affairs flow from being commander in chief of the military and from specific powers (shared with the Senate) to make treaties and appoint ambassadors. Numerous other powers have developed in practice, from appointing diplomatic corps and negotiating with foreign governments, to using military forces to implement foreign policy independent of congressional authorization. Congressional legislation and treaties have also expanded presidential power. And presidents may defend controversial actions as necessary under their obligation to "take Care that the Laws be faithfully executed." In addition, as Justice Frankfurter once noted, "Past practice does not, by itself, create power, but 'long-continued practice, known to and acquiesced in by Congress, would raise a presumption that the [action] has been [taken] in pursuance of its consent.'"

A principal justification—which has come to be known as the "sole organ theory"—for presidential independence in foreign affairs was offered by John Marshall in the House of Representatives in 1799. When defending President John Adams's extradition of a fugitive under the Jay Treaty, he proclaimed, "The President is the sole organ of the nation in its external relations, and its sole representative with foreign nations." Although Marshall contended that the president was the sole organ in communicating and negotiating with other countries, the theory has been expanded to include unilaterial military action as well. Such a broad view of inherent powers runs back to Alexander Hamilton, who warned in *Federalist* No. 23, "The circumstances that endanger the safety of nations is infinite, and for this reason no constitutional shackles can wisely be imposed on the power to which the care of it is committed."

The Supreme Court in *United States v. Curtiss-Wright Export Corporation* (1936) (see page 198) wrote the sole organ theory into constitutional law. In upholding a delegation of power by Congress to the president that the Court would have invalidated had it been in the area of domestic—rather than foreign—affairs, Justice Sutherland agreed with Wildavsky that there are indeed two presidencies. And in the area of foreign affairs the president enjoys a large reservoir of inherent power. Notably, though, the opinion rests in part on a dubious reading of history: Sutherland maintains that sovereignty—including control over foreign affairs—passed directly from the English Crown to the national government, despite the fact that during the postindependence period the original thirteen states each acted on their own in foreign affairs and Article 2 of the Articles of Confederation recognized the sovereignty of the states (see Chapter 7).

Curtiss-Wright also exemplifies the Court's deference to the president in foreign affairs in recognition of the fact that Congress, not the judiciary, provides the most effective check. Congress is more effective because it has the power of authorization and appropriation of funds for the executive branch. Thus in *Goldwater v. Carter,* (1979) (see page 145), the Court refused to consider the merits of suit filed by senators challenging President Jimmy Carter's termination, without congressional approval, of a Mutual Defense Treaty with Taiwan (an island off the coast of the Peoples' Republic of China in which Chinese nationalists and non-Communists established a government-in-exile after the Chinese Communist revolution). Other cases also demonstrate the Court's recurrent deference. *Haig v. Agee,* 453 U.S. 280 (1981), for instance, held that "the President, acting through the Secretary of State, has authority to revoke a passport on the ground that the holder's activities in foreign countries are causing or are likely to cause serious damage to the national security or foreign policy of the United States." Subsequently, *Regan v. Wald,* 468 U.S. 222 (1984), upheld the Reagan administration's restrictions on travel to Cuba.

The Court's deference to, and recognition of, congressional acquiescence in the assertion of broad presidential powers in foreign affairs is further underscored by the ruling affirming President Carter's financial actions during the 1979 Iranian Hostage crisis, in *Dames & Moore v. Regan* (1981) (see page 201).

SELECTED BIBIOGRAPHY

Henkin, Louis. *Foreign Affairs and the Constitution*. Mineola, NY: Foundation Press, 1972.

Irons, Peter. *Justice at War: The Story of the Japanese American Internment Cases*. New York: Oxford University Press, 1983.

May, Christopher. *In the Name of War: Judicial Review and the War Powers Since 1918*. Cambridge, MA: Harvard University Press, 1989.

Rossiter, Clinton. *The Supreme Court and the Commander in Chief*, rev. ed. Ithaca, NY: Cornell University Press 1976.

Wormuth, Francis, and Firmage, Edwin B. *To Chain the Dog of War: The War Power of Congress in History and Law,* 2nd ed. Urbana: University of Illinois Press, 1989.

United States v. Curtiss-Wright Corporation
299 U.S. 304, 57 S.Ct. 216 (1936)

In 1934 Congress passed a joint resolution authorizing the president to prohibit the sale of munitions to two South American nations—Paraguay and Bolivia—who were embattled over the disputed land of Chaco, for as long as he believed that such an embargo would contribute to peace. President Roosevelt immediately issued a proclamation ordering an embargo on arms sales to the countries. Subsequently, the Curtiss-Wright Corporation was indicted for selling fifty machine guns to Bolivia. In the district court, the corporation contended that the president's actions were illegal because Congress had unconstitutionally delegated legislative powers to the executive. The district judge agreed and the government appealed directly to the Supreme Court, which reversed the lower court's ruling.

Justice SUTHERLAND delivers the opinion of the Court.

First. It is contended that by the Joint Resolution the going into effect and continued operation of the resolution was conditioned (a) upon the President's judgment as to its beneficial effect upon the re-establishment of peace between the countries engaged in armed conflict in the Chaco; (b) upon the making of a proclamation, which was left to his unfettered discretion, thus constituting an attempted substitution of the President's will for that of Congress; (c) upon the making of a proclamation putting an end to the operation of the resolution, which again was left to the President's unfettered discretion; and (d) further, that the extent of its operation in particular cases was subject to limitation and exception by the President, controlled by no standard. in each of these particulars, appellees urge that Congress abdicated its essential functions and delegated them to the Executive.

Whether, if the Joint Resolution had related solely to internal affairs, it would be open to the challenge that it constituted an unlawful delegation of legislative power to the Executive, we find it unnecessary to determine. The whole aim of the resolution is to affect a situation entirely external to the United States, and falling within the category of foreign affairs. The determination which we are called to make, therefore, is whether the Joint Resolution, as applied to that situation, is vulnerable to attack under the rule that forbids a delegation of the lawmaking power. In other words, assuming (but not deciding) that the challenged delegation, if it were confined to internal affairs, would be invalid, may it nevertheless be sustained on the ground that its exclusive aim is to afford a remedy for a hurtful condition within foreign territory?

It will contribute to the elucidation of the question if we first consider the differences between the powers of the federal government in respect of foreign or external affairs and those in respect of domestic or internal affairs. That there are differences between them, and that these differences are fundamental, may not be doubted.

The two classes of powers are different, both in respect of their origin and their nature. The broad statement that the federal government can exercise no powers except those specifically enumerated in the Constitution, and such implied powers as are necessary and proper to carry into effect the enumerated powers, is categorically true only in respect of our internal affairs. In that field, the primary purpose of the Constitution was to carve from the general mass of legislative powers *then possessed by the states* such portions as it was thought desirable to vest in the federal government, leaving those not included in the enumeration still in the states. That this doctrine applies only to powers which the states had is self-evident. And since the states severally never possessed international powers, such powers could not have been carved from the mass of state powers but obviously were transmitted to the United States from some other source. During the Colonial period, those powers were possessed exclusively by and were entirely under the control of the Crown. By the Declaration of Independence, "the Representatives of the United States of America" declared the United (not the several) Colonies to be free and independent states, and as such to have "full Power to levy War, conclude Peace, contract Alliances, establish Commerce and to do all other Acts and Things which Independent States may of right do."

As a result of the separation from Great Britain by the colonies, acting as a unit, the powers of external sovereignty passed from the Crown not to the colonies severally, but to the colonies in their collective and corporate capacity as the United States of

America. Even before the Declaration, the colonies were a unit in foreign affairs, acting through a common agency—namely, the Continental Congress, composed of delegates from the thirteen colonies. That agency exercised the powers of war and peace, raised an army, created a navy, and finally adopted the Declaration of Independence. Rulers come and go; governments end and forms of government change; but sovereignty survives. A political society cannot endure without a supreme will somewhere. Sovereignty is never held in suspense. When, therefore, the external sovereignty of Great Britain in respect of the colonies ceased, it immediately passed to the Union. . . .

It results that the investment of the federal government with the powers of external sovereignty did not depend upon the affirmative grants of the Constitution. The powers to declare and wage war, to conclude peace, to make treaties, to maintain diplomatic relations with other sovereignties, if they had never been mentioned in the Constitution, would have vested in the federal government as necessary concomitants of nationality. . . .

Not only, as we have shown, is the federal power over external affairs in origin and essential character different from that over internal affairs, but participation in the exercise of the power is significantly limited. In this vast external realm, with its important, complicated, delicate and manifold problems, the President alone has the power to speak or listen as a representative of the nation. He *makes* treaties with the advice and consent of the Senate; but he alone negotiates. Into the field of negotiation the Senate cannot intrude; and Congress itself is powerless to invade it. As Marshall said in his great argument of March 7, 1800, in the House of Representatives, "The President is the sole organ of the nation in its external relations, and its sole representative with foreign nations.". . .

The marked difference between foreign affairs and domestic affairs in this respect is recognized by both houses of Congress in the very form of their requisitions for information from the executive departments. In the case of every department except the Department of State, the resolution *directs* the official to furnish the information. In the case of the State Department, dealing with foreign affairs, the President is *requested* to furnish the information "if not incompatible with the public interest." A statement that to furnish the information is not compatible with the public interest rarely, if ever, is questioned.

When the President is to be authorized by legislation to act in respect of a matter intended to affect a situation in foreign territory, the legislator properly bears in mind the important consideration that the form of the President's action—or, indeed, whether he shall act at all—may well depend, among other things, upon the nature of the confidential information which he has or may thereafter receive, or upon the effect which his action may have upon our foreign relations. This consideration, in connection with what we have already said on the subject discloses the unwisdom of requiring Congress in this field of governmental power to lay down narrowly definite standards by which the President is to be governed. . . . It is enough to summarize by saying that, both upon principle and in accordance with precedent, we conclude there is sufficient warrant for the broad discretion vested in the President to determine whether the enforcement of the statute will have a beneficial effect upon the re-establishment of peace in the affected countries; whether he shall make proclamation to bring the resolution into operation; whether and when the resolution shall cease to operate and to make proclamation accordingly; and to prescribe limitations and exceptions to which the enforcement of the resolution shall be subject. . . .

The judgment of the court below must be reversed and the cause remanded for further proceedings in accordance with the foregoing opinion.

It is so ordered.

Justice McREYNOLDS does not agree. He is of opinion that the court below reached the right conclusion and its judgment ought to be affirmed.

Justice STONE took no part in the consideration or decision of this case.

Dames & Moore v. Regan
453 U.S. 654, 101 S.Ct. 2972 (1981)

After the seizure of the U.S. Embassy in Tehran, Iran, in November 1979 and the taking of diplomatic personnel as hostages, President Carter invoked the International Emergency Economic Powers Act (IEEPA) and ordered a freeze on Iranian assets within the United States. On January 20, 1981, the hostages were released by Iran on the basis of an agreement that the government would "terminate all legal proceedings in the United States courts involving claims of United States persons and institutions against Iran and its state enterprises, to nullify all attachments and judgments obtained therein, [and] to prohibit future litigation based on these claims." Various executive orders implementing the agreement issued by Carter were subsequently reaffirmed by the Reagan administration. Dames & Moore sought to regain over $3 million owed to it under a contract for services performed for the Iranian government. In the trial court, the company claimed that the executive orders went beyond the president's statutory and constitutional powers. After the district court held against Dames & Moore, the company appealed to the Supreme Court, which granted *certiorari* on an expedited basis and upheld the actions of the president.

Justice REHNQUIST delivers the opinion of the Court.

The questions presented by this case touch fundamentally upon the matter in which our Republic is to be governed. Throughout the nearly two centuries of our Nation's existence under the Constitution, this subject has generated considerable debate. We have had the benefit of commentators such as John Jay, Alexander Hamilton, and James Madison writing in The Federalist Papers at the Nation's very inception, the benefit of astute foreign observers of our system such as Alexis deTocqueville and James Bryce writing during the first century of the Nation's existence, and the benefit of many other treatises as well as more than 400 volumes of reports of decisions of this Court. As these writings reveal it is doubtless both futile and perhaps dangerous to find any epigrammatical explanation of how this country has been governed. . . .

Our decision today will not dramatically alter this situation, for the Framers "did not make the judiciary the overseer of our government." We are confined to a resolution of the dispute presented to us. That dispute involves various Executive Orders and regulations by which the President nullified attachments and liens on Iranian assets in the United States, directed that these assets be transferred to Iran, and suspended claims against Iran that may be presented to an International Claims Tribunal. This action was taken in an effort to comply with an Executive Agreement between the United States and Iran. . . .

[T]he decisions of the Court in this area have been rare, episodic, and afford little precedential value for subsequent cases. The tensions present in any exercise of executive power under the tripartite system of Federal Government established by the Constitution have been rejected in opinions by Members of this Court more than once. . . . Justice JACKSON in his concurring opinion in *Youngstown* [*Sheet & Tube Co. v. Sawyer*, 343 U.S. 579 (1952)], which both parties agree brings together as much combination of analysis and common sense as there is in this area, focused not on the "plenary and exclusive power of the President" but rather responded to a claim of virtually unlimited powers for the Executive by noting:

"The example of such unlimited executive power that must have most impressed the forefathers was the prerogative exer-

cised by George III, and the description of its evils in the Declaration of Independence leads me to doubt that they were creating their new Executive in his image.". . .

As we now turn to the factual and legal issues in this case, we
freely confess that we are obviously deciding only one more episode in the never-ending tension between the President exercising
the executive authority in a world that presents each day some
new challenge with which he must deal and the Constitution
under which we all live and which no one disputes embodies
some sort of system of checks and balances.

I

On November 4, 1979, the American Embassy in Tehran was
seized and our diplomatic personnel were captured and held hostage. In response to that crisis, President Carter, acting pursuant
to the International Emergency Economic Powers Act. (hereinafter "IEEPA"), declared a national emergency on November
14, 1979, and blocked the removal or transfer of "all property
and interests in property of the Government of Iran, its instrumentalities and controlled entities and the Central Bank of Iran which
are or become subject to the jurisdiction of the United States.". . .
On November 15, 1979, the Treasury Department's Office of
Foreign Assets Control issued a regulation providing that "[u]nless
licensed or authorized . . . any attachment, judgment, decree,
lien, execution, garnishment, or other judicial process is null and
void with respect to any property in which on or since [November
14, 1979] there existed an interest of Iran.". . .
On December 19, 1979, petitioner Dames & Moore filed suit
in the United States District Court for the Central District of
California against the Government of Iran, the Atomic Energy
Organization of Iran, and a number of Iranian banks. In its complaint, petitioner alleged that its wholly owned subsidiary, Dames
& Moore International, S. R. L., was a party to a written contract
with the Atomic Energy Organization, and that the subsidiary's
entire interest in the contract had been assigned to petitioner.
. . . Petitioner contended . . . that it was owed $3,436,694.30
plus interest for services performed under the contract prior to
the date of termination. The District Court issued orders of attachment directed against property of defendants, and the property
of certain Iranian banks was then attached to secure any judgment
that might be entered against them.
On January 20, 1981, the Americans held hostage were released
by Iran pursuant to an Agreement entered into the day before.
. . . The Agreement stated that "it is the purpose of [the United
States and Iran] . . . to terminate all litigation as between the
Government of each party and the nationals of the other, and
to bring about the settlement and termination of all such claims

through binding arbitration." In furtherance of this goal, the Agreement called for the establishment of an Iran-United States Claims Tribunal which would arbitrate any claims not settled within 6 months. Awards of the Claims Tribunal are to be "final and binding" and "enforceable . . . in the courts of any nation in accordance with its law." . . . Under the Agreement, the United States is obligated:

> "to terminate all legal proceedings in United States courts involving claims of United States persons and institutions against Iran and its state enterprises, to nullify all attachments and judgments obtained therein, to prohibit all further litigation based on such claims, and to bring about the termination of such claims through binding arbitration." . . .

In addition, the United States must "act to bring about the transfer" by July 19, 1981, of all Iranian assets held in this country by American banks. One billion dollars of these assets will be deposited in a security account in the Bank of England, to the account of the Algerian Central Bank, and used to satisfy awards rendered against Iran by the Claims Tribunal. . . .

On January 19, 1981, President Carter issued a series of Executive Orders implementing the terms of the Agreement. . . .

On February 24, 1981, President Reagan issued an Executive Order in which he "ratified" the January 19th Executive Orders. Moreover, he "suspended" all "claims which may be presented to the . . . Tribunal" and provided that such claims "shall have no legal effect in any action now pending in any court of the United States." The suspension of any particular claim terminates if the Claims Tribunal determines that it has no jurisdiction over that claim; claims are discharged for all purposes when the Claims Tribunal either awards some recovery and that amount is paid, or determines that no recovery is due. . . .

The parties and the lower courts confronted with the instant questions have all agreed that much relevant analysis is contained in *Youngstown Sheet & Tube Co. v. Sawyer* (1952) (see page 255). Justice BLACK's opinion for the Court in that case, recognized that "[t]he President's power, if any, to issue the order must stem either from an act of Congress or from the Constitution itself." Justice JACKSON's concurring opinion elaborated in a general way the consequences of different types of interaction between the two democratic branches in assessing presidential authority to act in any given case. When the President acts pursuant to an express or implied authorization from Congress, he exercises not only his powers but also those delegated by Congress. In such a case the executive action "would be supported by the strongest of presumptions and the widest latitude of judicial interpretation, and the burden of persuasion would rest heavily upon any who might attack it." When the President acts in the absence of congressional authorization he may enter "a zone of twilight in which he and Congress may have concurrent authority, or in which its distribution is uncertain." In such a case the analysis becomes more complicated, and the validity of the President's action, at least so far as separation of powers principles are concerned, hinges on a consideration of all the circumstances which might shed light on the views of the Legislative Branch toward such action, including "congressional inertia, indifference or quiescence." Finally, when the President acts in contravention of the will of Congress, "his power is at its lowest ebb," and the Court can sustain his actions "only by disabling the Congress from acting upon the subject." . . .

Although we have in the past and do today find Justice JACKSON's classification of executive actions into three general categories analytically useful. . . . Justice JACKSON himself recognized that his three categories represented "a somewhat over-simplified grouping," and it is doubtless the case that executive action in any particular instance falls, not neatly in one of three pigeonholes, but rather at some point along a spectrum running from explicit congressional authorization to explicit congressional prohibition. This is particularly true as respects cases such as the one before us, involving responses to international crises the nature of which Congress can hardly have been expected to anticipate in any detail. . . .

The Government . . . has principally relied on § 1702 of IEEPA as authorization for these actions. [It] provides in part:

> "At the times and to the extent specified in section 1701 of this title, the President may, . . . nullify, void, prevent or prohibit, any acquisition, holding, withholding, use, transfer, withdrawal, transportation, importation or exportation of, or dealing in, or exercising any right, power or privilege with respect to, or transactions involving, any property in which any foreign country or a national thereof has any interest; by any person, or with respect to any property, subject to the jurisdiction of the United States."

The Government contends that the acts of "nullifying" the attachments and ordering the "transfer" of the frozen assets are specifically authorized by the plain language of the above statute. . . .

Petitioner contends that we should ignore the plain language of this statute because an examination of its legislative history as well as the history of § 5(b) of the Trading With the Enemy Act (hereinafter "TWEA"), 50 U.S.C. App. § 5(b), from which the pertinent language of § 1702 is directly drawn, reveals that the statute was not intended to give the President such extensive power over the assets of a foreign state during times of national emergency. . . .

We do not agree and refuse to read out of § 1702 all meaning to the words "transfer," "compel," or "nullify." Nothing in the legislative history of either § 1702 or § 5(b) of the TWEA requires such a result. To the contrary, we think both the legislative history and cases interpreting the TWEA fully sustain the broad authority of the Executive when acting under this congressional grant of power. . . .

Because the President's action in nullifying the attachments and ordering the transfer of the assets was taken pursuant to specific congressional authorization, it is "supported by the strongest of presumptions and the widest latitude of judicial interpretation, and the burden of persuasion would rest heavily upon any who might attack it." *Youngstown* (JACKSON, J., concurring). Under the circumstances of this case, we cannot say that petitioner has sustained that heavy burden. A contrary ruling would mean that the Federal Government as a whole lacked the power exercised by the President, and that we are not prepared to say.

Although we have concluded that the IEEPA constitutes specific congressional authorization to the President to nullify the attachments and order the transfer of Iranian assets, there remains the question of the President's authority to suspend claims pending in American courts. Such claims have, of course, an existence apart from the attachments which accompanied them. In terminating these claims through Executive Order No. 12294 the President purported to act under authority of both the IEEPA and 22 U.S.C. § 1732, the so-called "Hostage Act.". . .

We conclude that although the IEEPA authorized the nullification of the attachments, it cannot be read to authorize the suspension of the claims. . . .

Concluding that neither the IEEPA nor the Hostage Act constitutes specific authorization of the President's action suspending claims, however, is not to say that these statutory provisions are entirely irrelevant to the question of the validity of the President's action. We think both statutes highly relevant in the looser sense of indicating congressional acceptance of a broad scope for executive action in circumstances such as those presented in this case. . . . [T]he IEEPA delegates broad authority to the President to act in times of national emergency with respect to property of a foreign country. The Hostage Act similarly indicates congressional willingness that the President have broad discretion when responding to the hostile acts of foreign sovereigns. . . .

Although we have declined to conclude that the IEEPA or the Hostage Act directly authorizes the President's suspension of claims for the reasons noted, we cannot ignore the general tenor of Congress' legislation in this area in trying to determine whether the President is acting alone or at least with the acceptance of Congress. . . . Congress cannot anticipate and legislate with regard to every possible action the President may find it necessary to take or every possible situation in which he might act. Such failure of Congress specifically to delegate authority does not, "especially . . . in the areas of foreign policy and national security," imply "congressional disapproval" of action taken by the Executive. *Haig v. Agee*, [453 U.S. 280] (1981). On the contrary, the enactment of legislation closely related to the question of the President's authority in a particular case which evinces legislative intent to accord the President broad discretion may be considered to "invite" "measures on independent presidential responsibility," *Youngstown* (JACKSON, J., concurring). At least this is so where there is no contrary indication of legislative intent and when, as here, there is a history of congressional acquiescence in conduct of the sort engaged in by the President. It is to that history which we now turn.

Not infrequently in affairs between nations, outstanding claims by nationals of one country against the government of another country are "sources of friction" between the two sovereigns. To resolve these difficulties, nations have often entered into agreements settling the claims of their respective nationals. . . .

Under such agreements, the President has agreed to renounce or extinguish claims of United States nationals against foreign governments in return for lump sum payments or the establishment of arbitration procedures. . . .

Crucial to our decision today is the conclusion that Congress has implicitly approved the practice of claim settlement by executive agreement. This is best demonstrated by Congress' enactment of the International Claims Settlement Act of 1949. . . .

In light of all of the foregoing—the inferences to be drawn from the character of the legislation Congress has enacted in the area, such as the IEEPA and the Hostage Act, and from the history of acquiescence in executive claims settlement—we conclude that the President was authorized to suspend pending claims pursuant to Executive Order No. 12294. As Justice FRANKFURTER pointed out in *Youngstown*, "a systematic, unbroken executive practice, long pursued to the knowledge of Congress and never before questioned . . . may be treated as a gloss on 'Executive Power' vested in the President by § 1 of Art. II." Past practice does not, by itself, create power, but "long-continued practice, known to and acquiesced in by Congress, would raise a presumption that the [action] has been [taken] in pursuance of its consent. . . ."

Our conclusion is buttressed by the fact that the means chosen by the President to settle the claims of American nationals provided an alternate forum, the Claims Tribunal, which is capable of providing meaningful relief. . . .

Just as importantly, Congress has not disapproved of the action taken here. Though Congress has held hearings on the Iranian Agreement itself, Congress has not enacted legislation, or even passed a resolution, indicating its displeasure with the Agreement. Quite the contrary, the relevant Senate Committee has stated that the establishment of the Tribunal is "of vital importance to the United States." We are thus clearly not confronted with a situation in which Congress has in some way resisted the exercise of presidential authority.

Finally, we re-emphasize the narrowness of our decision. We do not decide that the President possesses plenary power to settle claims, even as against foreign governmental entities. . . . But where, as here, the settlement of claims has been determined to be a necessary incident to the resolution of a major foreign policy dispute between our country and another, and where, as here, we can conclude that Congress acquiesced in the President's action, we are not prepared to say that the President lacks the power to settle such claims.

Justice STEVENS concurred, and Justice POWELL concurred and dissented in part in a separate opinion.

C. THE TREATY-MAKING POWER AND EXECUTIVE INDEPENDENCE

The president makes treaties "by and with the Advice and Consent of the Senate." Although President George Washington initially sought Senate consultation when negotiating an Indian treaty in 1789, presidents since him have tended to negotiate treaties independently and only later to obtain ratification by a two-thirds vote of the Senate. There are times, though, when senators become involved in negotiations, dealing with trade or especially controversial agreements like the Strategic Arms Limitations Treaty (SALT) II treaty in 1979. Presidential dominance nevertheless is now the norm.

Treaties are on a par with federal legislation and considered part of the supreme law of the land. Moreover, in the *Missouri v. Holland* (1920) (see page 210), the Court ruled that a treaty on migratory birds gave Congress the authority to pass regulations forbidding the killing of such birds. Treaties thus may be a source of law and a basis of power that neither the president nor Congress had before their adoption. They often serve, for example, as the basis for presidents making *executive agreements* with foreign countries in order to implement treaty provisions.

Independent of treaties and congressional authorization, presidents increasingly enter into executive agreements with other countries. In *United States v. Belmont,* 301 U.S. 324 (1937), the Court upheld such agreements as valid international compacts and then ruled that they have the same legal effect as treaties in *United States v. Pink* (1942) (see page 213).

As a result of the rulings in *Belmont* and *Pink,* presidents may circumvent the treaty-making provision and executive agreements now outnumber treaties. Many of the most sensitive agreements were not even made known to Congress until it passed the Case Act in 1972, requiring notification within sixty days of "any international agreement." After Congress discovered that the Ford and Carter administrations had not fully complied and made a number of secret "executive arrangements," the act was amended to require notification within twenty days of any "oral international agreement, which shall be reduced to writing."[1]

In general, the Court defers to the president and tries to avoid deciding issues arising from the independence of the executive branch in the conduct of foreign affairs. Questions thus remain over the president's unilateral termination of treaties, see *Goldwater v. Carter* (1979) (see page 145), and reinterpretation of the language of treaties over Senate opposition.

However, the Court has, albeit infrequently and reluctantly,

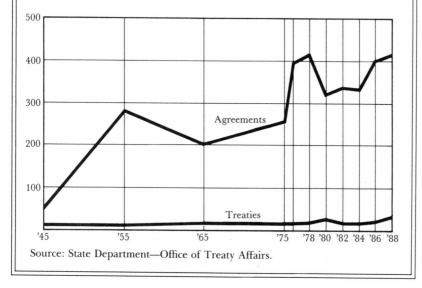

CONSTITUTIONAL HISTORY
FIGURE 3.1

Alternatives to treaties: The rise of
executive agreements and arrangements

Since 1945, U.S. presidents have increasingly used executive agreements, which do not require Senate approval, as substitutes for traditional treaties.

Source: State Department—Office of Treaty Affairs.

recognized constitutional limitations on the scope of treaties and executive agreements. In *Geofroy v. Riggs,* 133 U.S. 258 (1890), the Court rejected the contention that the treaty power "extends so far as to authorize what the Constitution forbids, or a change in the character of the government." But Justice Holmes's sweeping opinion in *Missouri v. Holland* (see page 210) raised anew questions about the scope of treaties and executive agreements. The Court finally qualified that ruling in *Reid v. Covert,* 354 U.S. 1 (1957), holding that executive agreements could not deprive individuals of the guarantees of the Bill of Rights. At issue in *Reid v. Covert* was the constitutionality of an executive agreement permitting dependents of American military residing in Great Britian to be tried for crimes committed there by military courts under the Uniform Code of Military Justice, which does not extend the same guarantees as those in the Bill of Rights to criminal trials. Notably, when invalidating the executive agreement the Court was bitterly divided and forced to overrule a five-to-four decision one year earlier, in *Reid v. Covert,* 351 U.S. 487 (1956), that had reached the opposite conclusion.

NOTES

1. For further discussion, see Louis Fisher, *Constitutional Conflicts between Congress and the President* (Princeton, NJ: Princeton University Press, 1985), ch. 8; and Arthur Bestor, "Separation of Powers in the Domain of Foreign Affairs: The Original Intent of the Constitution Historically Examined," 5 *Seton Hall Law Review* 527 (1974).

SELECTED BIBLIOGRAPHY

Goldwater, Barry. "Treaty Termination Is a Shared Power," 65 *American Bar Association Journal* 198 (1979).
Kennedy, Edward. "Normal Relations with China: Good Law, Good Policy," 7 *Policy Review* 125 (1979).

Missouri v. Holland
252 U.S. 416, 40 S.Ct. 382 (1920)

Pursuant to treaty between the United States and Great Britian in 1916 for the protection of birds migrating between Canada and the United States, legislation and regulations were adopted in 1918 to establish closed hunting seasons and to prevent the killing of certain migratory birds. The state of Missouri contended that the treaty and regulations violated the Tenth Amendment's provision that "powers not delegated by to the United States by the Constitution . . . are reserved to the States." After unsuccessfully seeking in a federal district court a bill of equity to stop a U.S. game warden from enforcing the regulations, the state appealed to the Supreme Court, which then affirmed the lower court's ruling.

Justice HOLMES delivers the opinion of the Court.

This is a bill in equity brought by the State of Missouri to prevent a game warden of the United States from attempting to enforce the Migratory Bird Treaty Act of July 3, 1918, c. 128, 40 Stat. 755, and the regulations made by the Secretary of Agriculture in pursuance of the same. The ground of the bill is that the statute is an unconstitutional interference with the rights reserved to the States by the Tenth Amendment. . . . It is unnecessary to go into any details, because, as we have said, the question raised is the general one whether the treaty and statute are void as an interference with the rights reserved to the States.

To answer this question it is not enough to refer to the Tenth Amendment, reserving the powers not delegated to the United States, because by Article 2, Section 2, the power to make treaties is delegated expressly, and by Article 6 treaties made under the authority of the United States along with the Constitution and laws of the United States made in pursuance thereof, are declared the supreme law of the land. If the treaty is valid there can be no dispute about the validity of the statute under Article 1, Section 8, as a necessary and proper means to execute the powers of the Government. The language of the Constitution as to the supremacy of treaties being general, the question before us is narrowed to an inquiry into the ground upon which the present supposed exception is placed.

It is said that a treaty cannot be valid if it infringes the Constitution, that there are limits, therefore, to the treaty-making power, and that one such limit is that what an act of Congress could not do unaided, in derogation of the powers reserved to the States, a treaty cannot do. An earlier act of Congress that attempted by itself and not in pursuance of a treaty to regulate the killing of migratory birds within the States had been held bad in the District Court. *United States v. Shauver,* [214 F.Supp. 154 (1914)]; *United States v. McCullagh,* [221 F.Supp. 288(1915)]. Those decisions were supported by arguments that migratory birds were owned by the States in their sovereign capacity for the benefit of their people, and that under cases like *Geer v. Connecticut,* 161 U.S. 519 [1896], this control was one that Congress had no power to displace. The same argument is supposed to apply now with equal force.

Whether the two cases cited were decided rightly or not they cannot be accepted as a test of the treaty power. Acts of Congress are the supreme law of the land only when made in pursuance of the Constitution, while treaties are declared to be so when made under the authority of the United States. It is open to question whether the authority of the United States means more than the formal acts prescribed to make the convention. We do not mean to imply that there are no qualifications to the treaty-making power; but they must be ascertained in a different way. It is obvious that there may be matters of the sharpest exigency for the national well being that an act of Congress could not deal with but that a treaty followed by such an act could, and it is not lightly to be assumed that, in matters requiring national action, "a power which must belong to and somewhere reside in every civilized government" is not to be found, *Andrews v. Andrews,* 188 U. S. 14 [1903]. What was said in that case with regard to the powers of the States applies with equal force to the powers of the nation in cases where the States individually are incompetent to act. We are not yet discussing the particular case before us but only are considering the validity of the test proposed. With regard to that we may add that when we are dealing with words that also are a constituent act, like the Constitution of the United States, we must realize that they have called into life a being the development of which could not have been foreseen completely by the most gifted of its begetters. It was enough for them to realize or to hope that they had created an organism; it has taken a century and has cost their successors much sweat and blood to prove that they created a nation. The case before us must be considered in the light of our whole experience and not merely in that of what was said a hundred years ago. The treaty in question does not contravene any prohibitory words to be found in the Constitution. The only question is whether it is forbidden by some invisible radiation from the general terms of the Tenth Amendment. We must consider what this country has become in deciding what that amendment has reserved.

The State as we have intimated founds its claim of exclusive authority upon an assertion of title to migratory birds, an assertion that is embodied in statute. No doubt it is true that as between a State and its inhabitants the State may regulate the killing and sale of such birds, but it does not follow that its authority is exclusive of paramount powers. To put the claim of the State upon title is to lean upon a slender reed. Wild birds are not in the possession of anyone; and possession is the beginning of ownership. The whole foundation of the State's rights is the presence within their jurisdiction of birds that yesterday had not arrived, tomorrow may be in another State and in a week a thousand miles away. If we are to be accurate we cannot put the case of the State upon higher ground than that the treaty deals with creatures that for the moment are within the state borders, that it must be carried out by officers of the United States within the same territory, and that but for the treaty the State would be free to regulate this subject itself. . . .

Here a national interest of very nearly the first magnitude is involved. It can be protected only by national action in concert with that of another power. The subject matter is only transitorily within the State and has no permanent habitat therein. But for the treaty and the statute there soon might be no birds for any powers to deal with. We see nothing in the Constitution that compels the Government to sit by while a food supply is cut off and the protectors of our forests and our crops are destroyed. It is not sufficient to rely upon the States. The reliance is vain, and were it otherwise, the question is whether the United States is forbidden to act. We are of opinion that the treaty and statute must be upheld. . . . Decree affirmed.

Justice VAN DEVANTER and Justice PITNEY dissent.

United States v. Pink
315 U.S. 203, 62 S.Ct. 552 (1942)

Following diplomatic recognition of Soviet Russia in 1933 President Franklin Roosevelt negotiated the "Litvinov Assignment," under which it was stipulated that instead of each government prosecuting claims for recovery of assets against citizens of the other, the Soviet Union would give title to claims to assets in America to the U.S. government and vice versa. In *United States v. Belmont,* 301 U.S. 324 (1937), a New York banker, August Belmont, contended that funds deposited in his bank by the Petrograd Metal Works prior to the Russian Revolution in 1918 were subject to New York laws and thus could not be confiscated by the federal government. Justice Sutherland, relying on his earlier opinion in *United States v. Curtiss-Wright Export Corporation* (1936) (see page 198), however, upheld the agreement as a valid international compact that superseded the laws of New York. Subsequently, the federal government sought to recover the assets of the New York branch of the First Russian Insurance Company and sued Louis H. Pink, Superintendent of Insurance for the state of New York. The state supreme court dismissed the government's complaint and a federal court of appeals affirmed, whereupon the government appealed to the Supreme Court.

Justice DOUGLAS delivers the opinion of the Court.

This Court, speaking through Justice SUTHERLAND, held [in *United States v. Belmont* (1937)] that the conduct of foreign relations is committed by the Constitution to the political departments of the Federal Government; that the propriety of the exercise of that power is not open to judicial inquiry; and that recognition of a foreign sovereign conclusively binds the courts and "is retroactive and validates all actions and conduct of the government so recognized from the commencement of its existence." If further held that recognition of the Soviet Government, the establishment of diplomatic relations with it, and the Litvinov Assignment were "all parts of one transaction, resulting in an international compact between the two governments." After stating that "in respect of what was done here, the Executive had authority to speak as the sole organ" of the national government, it added, "The assignment and the agreements in connection therewith did not, as in the case of treaties, as that term is used in the treaty making clause of the Constitution (Art. 2, § 2), require the advice and consent of the Senate." It held that the "external powers of the United States are to be exercised without regard to state laws or policies. The supremacy of a treaty in this respect has been recognized from the beginning." And it added that "all international compacts and agreements" are to be treated with similar dignity for the reason that "complete power over international affairs is in the national government and is not and cannot be subject to any curtailment or interference on the part of the several states.". . .

The holding in the *Belmont* case is therefore determinative of the present controversy unless the stake of the foreign creditors in this liquidation proceeding and the provision which New York has provided for their protection call for a different result. . . .

We recently stated in *Hines v. Davidowitz*, 312 U.S. 52 [1941], that the field which affects international relations is "the one aspect of our government that from the first has been most generally conceded imperatively to demand broad national authority"; and that any state power which may exist "is restricted to the narrowest of limits." There we were dealing with the question as to whether a state statute regulating aliens survived a similar federal statute. We held that it did not. Here we are dealing with an exclusive federal function. If state laws and policies did not yield before the exercise of the external powers of the United States, then our foreign policy might be thwarted. These are delicate matters. If state action could defeat or alter our foreign policy, serious consequences might ensue. The nation as a whole would be held to answer if a State created difficulties with a foreign power. . . .

The action of New York in this case amounts in substance to a rejection of a part of the policy underlying recognition by this nation of Soviet Russia. Such power is not accorded a State in our constitutional system. To permit it would be to sanction a dangerous invasion of Federal authority. For it would "imperil the amicable relations between governments and vex the peace of nations." *Octjen v. Central Leather Co.*, [246 U.S. 297 (1918)]. It would tend to disturb that equilibrium in our foreign relations which the political departments of our national government had diligently endeavored to establish.

We repeat that there are limitations on the sovereignty of the States. No State can rewrite our foreign policy to conform to its own domestic policies. Power over external affairs is not shared by the States; it is vested in the national government exclusively. It need not be so exercised as to conform to state laws or state policies whether they be expressed in constitutions, statutes, or judicial decrees. And the policies of the States become wholly irrelevant to judicial inquiry, when the United States, acting within its constitutional sphere, seeks enforcement of its foreign policy in the courts. . . .

We hold that the right to the funds or property in question became vested in the Soviet Government as the successor to the First Russian Insurance Co.; that this right has passed to the United States under the Litvinov Assignment; and that the United States is entitled to the property as against the corporation and the foreign creditors.

The judgment is reversed. . . .

It is so ordered.

Justice REED and Justice JACKSON did not participate in the consideration or decision of this case.

Justice FRANKFURTER.

The nature of the controversy makes it appropriate to add a few observations to my Brother DOUGLAS' opinion. . . .

That the President's control of foreign relations includes the settlement of claims is indisputable. Thus, referring to the adhesion of the United States to the Dawes Plan, Secretary of State Hughes reported "that this agreement was negotiated under the long-recognized authority of the President of the United States to arrange for the payment of claims in favor of the United States and its nationals. The exercise of this authority has many illustrations, one of which is the Agreement of 1901 for the so-called Boxer Indemnity." (Secretary Hughes to President Coolidge, February 3, 1925, MS., Department of State, quoted in 5 Hackworth, Digest of Int. Law, c. 16, § 514.) The President's power to negotiate such a settlement is the same whether it is an isolated transaction between this country and a friendly nation, or is part of a complicated negotiation to restore normal relations, as was the case with Russia.

That the power to establish such normal relations with a foreign country belongs to the President is equally indisputable. Recognition of a foreign country is not a theoretical problem or an exercise in abstract symbolism. It is the assertion of national power directed towards safeguarding and promoting our interests and those of civilization. Recognition of a revolutionary government normally involves the removal of areas of friction. As often as not, areas of friction are removed by the adjustment of claims pressed by this country on behalf of its nationals against a new régime. . . .

The controlling history of the Soviet régime and of this country's relations with it must be read between the lines of the Roosevelt-Litvinov Agreement. One needs to be no expert in Russian law to know that the expropriation decrees intended to sweep the assets of Russian companies taken over by that government into Russia's control no matter where those assets were credited. Equally clear is it that the assignment by Russia meant to give the United States as part of the comprehensive settlement everything that Russia claimed under its laws against Russians. It does violence to the course of negotiations between the United States and Russia and to the scope of the final adjustment to assume that a settlement thus made on behalf of the United States—to settle both money claims and to soothe feelings—was to be qualified by the variant notions of the courts of the forty-eight states regarding "situs" or "jurisdiction" over intangibles or the survival of extinct Russian corporations. In our dealings with the outside world the United States speaks with one voice and acts as one, unembarrassed by the complications as to domestic issues which are inherent in the distribution of political power between the national government and the individual states.

Chief Justice STONE dissented.

Goldwater v. Carter
444 U.S. 996, 100 S.Ct. 533, (1979).

This case, arising from President Carter's termination of a defense treaty with Taiwan, is reprinted in Chapter 2 (see page 145).

D. WAR-MAKING AND EMERGENCY POWERS

An enduring struggle between the president and Congress over the power to wage war took root at the Constitutional Convention. Delegates initially gave Congress the power "to make war," but finally settled on giving it the power "to declare war" in Article I, Section 8. This reflected a recognition that the president as commander in chief may need "to repel sudden attacks," but also that the nation must be safeguarded against unchecked presidential power to wage or initiate war. The war-making power is thus a shared power. The president oversees all military operations in peace and war time, yet Congress has the power to "raise and support Armies" as well as to "provide for calling forth the Militia to execute the Laws of the Union, suppress Insurrections and repel Invasions."

Although Congress has the power to declare war, the president's power to order the military into conflict in foreign countries and to wage war has been firmly demonstrated. In fact, just five wars have been "declared" and only with the War of 1812 did Congress actively debate the merits of entering the conflict. As earlier noted, at the outset of the Civil War, Lincoln asserted expansive powers before seeking congressional approval. During World Wars I and II, Congress simply recognized a state of war when passing broad legislation delegating vast discretionary powers to the president. Moreover, every twentieth-century president from Theodore Roosevelt to George Bush has ordered troops into foreign conflicts without congressional assent and with little or no prior notification.

In historical perspective, restraints on the president's power to wage war remain almost entirely in the hands of Congress. The Court is especially reluctant to question the wisdom of a president's military decisions. It also recognizes the potential futility of declaring unconstitutional presidential actions during wartime and international emergencies. The Court tends to agree with the view expressed by Charles Evans Hughes, before becoming chief justice, that "[t]he power to wage war is the power to wage war successfully. . . . That is, there are constantly new applications of unchanged powers. . . . So, also, we have a *fighting* Constitution."[1]

A basic constitutional dilemma in enforcing constraints on presidential power to wage war nevertheless remains. Thomas Jefferson, the renowned "strict constructionist," posed the problem of, on the one hand, adhering to constitutional constraints and guarantees and, on the other hand, of taking unauthorized action deemed necessary to preserve the country. In the Kentucky Resolutions of 1798, he argued in opposition to the Alien and Sedition acts and partisan prosecution of critics of the Federalists that "[i]n questions of power then let no more be heard of confidence in man, but bind him down by the chains of the Constitution." Yet Jefferson later took a broad view of the government's power to respond to national emergencies, "A strict observance of the written laws is doubtless *one* of the high duties of a good citizen, but it is not *the highest*. The laws of necessity, of self-preservation, of saving our country when in danger, are of higher obligation."[2] The dilemma of preserving the Constitution and the country was put well in 1967 by Chief Justice Earl Warren: " '[N]ational defense' cannot be deemed an end in itself. . . . Implicit in the term . . . is the notion of defending those values and ideas which set this Nation apart. . . . It would indeed be ironic if, in the name of national defense, we would sanction the subversion of one of those liberties . . . which makes the defense of the Nation worthwhile."[3]

Justices no less than others are often sharply divided over ignoring or enforcing and broadly or narrowly interpreting constraints on the president's war-making powers. The Court's rulings in controversies arising from Lincoln's actions at the start of the Civil War are illustrative. The full Court never ruled on Lincoln's orders suspending the writ of habeas corpus. But Chief Justice Taney in *Ex parte Merryman,* 17 Fed. Cases 144 (1861), declared them unconstitutional on the ground that Article I, Section 9 gives Congress, not the president, the power to suspend the writ "when in Cases of Rebellion or Invasion the public Safety may require it." Lincoln nonetheless disregarded Taney's opinion and continued to contend that the president shares with Congress the power to suspend the writ. The president's military orders for a blockade of Confederate ports was subsequently upheld by a bare majority in *The Prize Cases* (1863) (see page 221). Four dissenters, though, point out that the Constitution grants only Congress the power to call up the militia to suppress insurrections. Three years later and notably after the end of the Civil War, however, a unanimous Court ruled in *Ex parte Milligan* (1866) (see page 225) that Lincoln's orders for the trial of civilians by military courts were unconstitutional.[4]

During World War II the Court again proved reluctant to enforce constitutional guarantees against claims of broad emergency powers. The forced evacuation of over 100,000 Japanese and Japanese-Americans from the West Coast was based on both congressional legislation and executive orders. The Court initially avoided ruling on the questions arising from the denial of civil liberties and property rights by the evacuation and internment program. *Hirabayshi v. United States,* 320 U.S. 91 (1943), upheld a curfew imposed on Japanese-Americans but avoided ruling on their evacuation. The next year, in *Korematsu v. United States* (1944) (see page 232), one of the most libertarian justices, Hugo Black, handed down an opinion finding the evacuation program constitutional. The three dissenters all disagreed on different grounds, but notably Justice Robert Jackson sharply criticized the sanctioning of "a military expedient that has no place in law under the Constitution." To partially deflect some of the criticism of *Korematsu,* on the same day as that ruling came down

Japanese-Americans in an internment camp during World War II.
AP/Wide world.

Justice Douglas announced the decision in *Ex parte Endo,* 323
U.S. 283 (1944). In that case the Court upheld the right of a
loyal Japanese-American woman to a writ of *habeas corpus* releasing her from a relocation camp, but again refused to address
the constitutionality of the detention program. Despite the outcry
over these rulings, Justices Black and Douglas never regreted
their decisions and the latter once explained, "The decisions
were extreme and went to the verge of wartime power; and
they have been severely criticized. It is, however, easy in retro-
spect to denounce what was done, as there actually was no invasion of our country. . . . But those making plans for defense
of the nation had no such knowledge and were planning for
the worst."[5] Over forty years later in 1988, President Reagan
signed legislation providing reparations for those interned in
relocation camps during World War II.

Controversies arising from the undeclared war in Vietnam
were evaded as well by the Court, even though several of the
justices maintained that it ought to consider cases challenging
the constitutionality of the war.[6] Presidents from Eisenhower
to Nixon justified their sending military advisers and troops to
Vietnam on their power as commander in chief. In addition,
Johnson and Nixon defended their escalation of the war and
bombing of North Vietnam on a joint resolution passed by Congress in 1964 after an alleged torpedo boat attack on two U.S.
destroyers in the Gulf of Tonkin. The Gulf of Tonkin Resolution,

---

CONSTITUTIONAL HISTORY

The State Department's Justification for President Lyndon Johnson's War Efforts in Vietnam

There can be no question in present circumstances of the President's authority to commit United States forces to the defense of South Viet-Nam. The grant of authority to the President in Article II of the Constitution extends to the actions of the United States currently undertaken in Viet-Nam. . . .

Under the Constitution, the President, in addition to being Chief Executive, is Commander in Chief of the Army and Navy. He holds the prime responsibility for the conduct of the United States foreign relations. These duties carry very broad powers, including the power to deploy American forces abroad and commit them to military operations when the President deems such action necessary to maintain the security and defense of the United States.

Leonard Meeker, "The Legality of United States Participation in the Defense of Viet-Nam," 54 *Department of State Bulletin* 484 (1966).

---

as it was called, supported "the determination of the President, as commander in chief, to take all necessary measures to repel any armed attack against the forces of the United States and to prevent further aggression." Both the Johnson and Nixon administrations claimed that the resolution gave the president as much power as a declaration of war. But as military involvement increased and opposition to the war grew, Congress tried to curb the president with legislation—prohibiting the use of funds for combat forces in Cambodia and Laos, and repealing the Gulf of Tonkin Resolution. These limitations proved unavailing because continued military presence in Vietnam could be justified as necessary to protect troops there until they could be safely withdrawn. One major result of the struggle between Congress and the president over the Vietnam War was the passage in 1973 of the War Powers Resolution, over Nixon's veto (see page 243).

NOTES

1. C. E. Hughes, "War Powers under the Constitution," 62 *American Bar Association Reports* 238 (1917).
2. T. Jefferson, Letter to J. B. Colvin, in *The Writings of Thomas Jefferson*, Vol. 12, ed. Andrew A. Lipscomb (Washington, DC: The Tho-

mas Jefferson Memorial Association, 1903), 418.

3. *United States v. Robel,* 389 U.S. 258 (1967).

4. Military trials of captured saboteurs and enemies during World War II, however, were upheld in *Ex parte Quirin,* 317 U.S. 1 (1942), and *In re Yamashita,* 327 U.S. 1 (1946). But the Court has maintained that citizens and military dependents may not be tried by military courts either for capital offenses, in *Reid v. Covert,* 351 U.S. 487 (1957), or noncapital offenses, in *Kinsella v. United States ex rel. Singleton,* 361 U.S. 234 (1960), and *McElroy v. United States ex rel. Guagliardo,* 361 U.S. 281 (1960). In some cases the Court has also questioned the safeguards afforded military personnel in courts-martial under the Uniform Code of Military Justice, see Joseph W. Bishop, Jr., *Justice under Fire: A Study of Military Law* (New York: Charterhouse, 1974).

5. *De Funis v. Odegaard,* 416 U.S. 312 (1973).

6. See *Mora v. McNamara,* 389 U.S. 934 (1967); *Massachusetts v. Laird,* 400 U.S. 886 (1970); and *Sarnoff v. Schultz,* 409 U.S. 929 (1972).

SELECTED BIBLIOGRAPHY

Berman, Larry. *The New American Presidency.* Boston: Little, Brown, 1987.

Franck, Thomas, and Weisband, Edward. *Foreign Policy by Congress.* New York: Oxford University Press, 1979.

Irons, Peter. *Justice at War.* New York: Oxford University Press, 1983.

The Prize Cases

2 Bl. (67 U.S.) 935, 17 L.Ed. 459 (1863)

After the outbreak of the Civil War in April 1861 but before convening a special session of Congress, President Abraham Lincoln declared the Southern states in rebellion and ordered a blockade of their ports. Congress subsequently passed legislation authorizing his actions, yet Lincoln maintained that his actions were justifiable given his inherent powers as commander in chief and legislation in 1795 and 1807 that had delegated certain war powers to the president. The owners of several ships, which had been seized and confiscated in the blockade, unsuccessfully challenged the legality of the blockade in federal district courts and then appealed to the Supreme Court. Justice Robert Grier's opinion for the Court affirming the actions of the president prompted dissenting Justice Samuel Nelson to issue a sharply worded reminder of the importance the rule of law and constitutional constraints on the president.

Justice GRIER delivers the opinion of the Court.

Had the President a right to institute a blockade of ports in possession of persons in armed rebellion against the government, on the principles of international law, as known and acknowledged among civilized States? . . .

That the President, as the Executive Chief of the Government and Commander-in-Chief of the Army and Navy, was the proper person to make such notification, has not been, and cannot be disputed.

The right of prize and capture has its origin in the *"jus belli,"* and is governed and adjudged under the laws of nations. To legitimate the capture of a neutral vessel or property on the high seas, a war must exist *de facto,* and the neutral must have a knowledge or notice of the intention of one of the parties belligerent to use this mode of coercion against a port, city or territory, in possession of the other.

Let us inquire whether, at the time this blockade was instituted, a state of war existed which would justify a resort to these means of subduing the hostile force.

War has been well defined to be, "That state in which a nation prosecutes its right by force." . . .

By the Constitution, Congress alone has the power to declare a national or foreign war. It cannot declare war against a State or any number of States, by virtue of any clause in the Constitution. The Constitution confers on the President the whole executive power. He is bound to take care that the laws be faithfully executed. He is Commander-in-Chief of the Army and Navy of the United States, and of the militia of the several States when called into the actual service of the United States. He has no power to initiate or declare a war either against a foreign nation or a domestic State. But by the Acts of Congress of Feb. 28th, 1795, ch. 36 (1 Stat. at L., 424), and 3d of March 1807, ch. 39 (1 Stat. at L., 443), he is authorized to call out the militia and use military and naval forces of the United States in case of invasion by foreign nations, and to suppress insurrection against the government of a State or of the United States.

If a war be made by invasion of a foreign Nation, the President is not only authorized but bound to resist force, by force. He does not initiate the war, but is bound to accept the challenge without waiting for any special legislative authority. And whether the hostile party be a foreign invader, or States organized as rebellion, it is none the less a war, although the declaration of it be *"unilateral."*. . .

Whether the President in fulfilling his duties, as Commander-in-Chief, in suppressing an insurrection, has met with such armed hostile resistence, and a civil war of such alarming proportions as will compel him to accord to them the character of belligerents, is a question to be decided by him, and this court must be governed by the decisions and acts of the Political Department of the government to which this power was intrusted. "He must determine what degree of force the crisis demands." The proclamation of blockade is, itself, official and conclusive evidence to the court that a state of war existed which demanded and authorized a recourse to such a measure, under the circumstances peculiar to the case.

Justice NELSON dissenting.

[W]e are asked: what would become of the peace and integrity of the Union, in case of an insurrection at home or invasion from abroad, if this power could not be exercised by the President in the recess of Congress, and until that body could be assembled?

The framers of the Constitution fully comprehended this question, and provided for the contingency. Indeed, it would have been surprising if they had not, as a rebellion had occurred in the State of Massachusetts while the Convention was in session, and which had become so general that it was quelled only by calling upon the military power of the State. The Constitution declares that Congress shall have power "to provide for calling forth the militia to execute the laws of the Union, suppress insurrections, and repel invasions." Another clause, "that the President shall be Commander-in-chief of the Army and Navy of the United States, and of the Militia of the several States when called into the actual service of the United States;" and, again: "He shall take care that the laws shall be faithfully executed." Congress passed laws on this subject in 1792 and 1795. 1 United States Laws, pp. 264, 424.

The last Act provided that whenever the United States shall be invaded or be in imminent danger of invasion from a foreign nation, it shall be lawful for the President to call forth such number of the militia most convenient to the place of danger, and in case of insurrection in any State against the government thereof, it shall be lawful for the President, on the application of the Legislature of such State, if in session, or if not, of the Executive of the State to call forth such number of militia of any other State or States, as he may judge sufficient to suppress such insurrection. . . .

It has also been argued that this power of the President from necessity should be construed as vesting him with the war power, or the Republic might greatly suffer or be in danger from the attacks of the hostile party before the assembling of Congress. But we have seen that the whole military and naval forces are in his hands under the municipal laws of the country. He can meet the adversary upon land and water with all the forces of the government. The truth is, this idea of the existence of any necessity for clothing the President with the war power, under the Act of 1795, is simply a monstrous exaggeration; for, besides having the command of the whole of the army and navy, Congress can be assembled within any thirty days, if the safety of the country requires that the war power shall be brought into operation. . . .

So the war carried on by the President against the insurrectionary districts in the Southern States, as in the case of the King of Great Britain in the American Revolution, was a personal war against those in rebellion, and with encouragement and support of loyal citizens with a view to their co-operation and aid in suppressing the insurgents, with this difference, as the war making power belonged to the King, he might have recognized or declared the war at the beginning to be a civil war which would draw after it all the rights of a belligerent, but in the case of the President no such power existed; the war, therefore, from necessity, was a personal war, until Congress assembled and acted upon this state of things.

Down to this period the only enemy recognized by the government was the persons engaged in the rebellion, all others were peaceful citizens, entitled to all the privileges of citizens under the Constitution. Certainly it cannot rightfully be said that the President has the power to convert a loyal citizen into a belligerent enemy or confiscate his property as enemy's property.

Congress assembled on the call for an extra session the 4th July, 1861, and among the first Acts passed was one in which the President was authorized by proclamation to interdict all trade and intercourse between all the inhabitants of States in insurrection and rest of the United States, subjecting vessel and cargo to capture and condemnation as prize, and also to direct the capture of any ship or vessel belonging in whole or in part to any inhabitant of a State whose inhabitants are declared by the proclamation to be in a state of insurrection, found at sea or in any part of the rest of the United States. Act of Congress of 13 July, 1861, secs. 5, 6. The 4th section also authorized the President to close any port in a Collection District obstructed so that the revenue could not be collected and provided for the capture and condemnation of any vessel attempting to enter.

The President's Proclamation was issued on the 16th August following, and embraced Georgia, North and South Carolina, part of Virginia, Tennessee, Alabama, Louisiana, Texas, Arkansas, Mississippi and Florida.

This Act of Congress, we think, recognized a state of civil war between the government and the Confederate States. . . .

Upon the whole, after the most careful consideration of this case which the pressure of other duties has admitted, I am compelled to the conclusion that no civil war existed between this

Government and the States in insurrection till recognized by the Act of Congress 13th July, 1861; that the President does not possess the power under the Constitution to declare war or recognize its existence within the meaning of the law of nations, which carries with it belligerent rights, and thus change the country and all its citizens from a state of peace to a state of war; that this power belongs exclusively to the Congress of the United States and, consequently, that the President had no power to set on foot a blockade under the law of nations, and the capture of the vessel and cargo in this case, and in all cases before us in which the capture occurred before the 13th July, 1861, for breach of blockade, or as enemies' property, are illegal and void, and that the decrees of condemnation should be reversed and the vessel and cargo restored.

Ex parte Milligan
4 Wall. (71 U.S.) 2, 18 L.Ed. 281 (1866)

In 1862, President Abraham Lincoln ordered the suspension of the writ of *habeas corpus* and that all persons disloyal to the Union should be tried and punished by court-martial or military commissions. In 1863, Congress passed legislation suspending the writ. A year later, Lambdin P. Milligan, a lawyer sympathizing with the Confederacy, was seized and tried by a military commission in Indiana. He appealed to the federal circuit court for a writ of *habeas corpus* and challenged the commission's jurisdiction, because Indiana was not a state in insurrection and had functioning civil courts. The circuit judges were sharply divided and decided to certify certain questions—pertaining to the issuance of a writ of *habeas corpus* and the jurisdiction of the military commission—to the Supreme Court for decision. The Court unanimously ruled against the president's actions on the grounds that Congress had not authorized the use of courts-martial in an opinion by Justice David Davis, an appointee of President Lincoln. But Chief Justice Salmon Chase, in a separate opinion joined by three other justices, took strong exception to Justice Davis's opinion, also holding that it is not within Congress's power to establish military commissions.

Justice DAVIS delivers the opinion of the Court.

The controlling question in the case is this: Upon the *facts* stated in Milligan's petition, and the exhibits filed, had the military commission mentioned in it *jurisdiction*, legally, to try and sentence him? Milligan, not a resident of one of the rebellious states, or a prisoner of war, but a citizen of Indiana for twenty years past, and never in the military or naval service, is, while at his home, arrested by the military power of the United States, imprisoned, and, on certain criminal charges preferred against him, tried, convicted, and sentenced to be hanged by a military commission, organized under the direction of the military commander of the military district of Indiana. Had this tribunal the *legal* power and authority to try and punish this man?

No graver question was ever considered by this court, nor one which more nearly concerns the rights of the whole people; for it is the birthright of every American citizen when charged with crime, to be tried and punished according to law. The power of punishment is, alone through the means which the laws have provided for that purpose, and if they are ineffectual, there is an immunity from punishment, no matter how great an offender the individual may be, or how much his crimes may have shocked the sense of justice of the country, or endangered its safety. By the protection of the law human rights are secured; withdraw that protection, and they are at the mercy of wicked rulers, or the clamor of an excited people. If there was law to justify this military trial, it is not our province to interfere; if there was not, it is our duty to declare the nullity of the whole proceedings. The decision of this question does not depend on argument or judicial precedents, numerous and highly illustrative as they are. These precedents inform us of the extent of the struggle to preserve liberty and to relieve those in civil life from military trials. The founders of our government were familiar with the history of that struggle; and secured in a written constitution every right which the people had wrested from power during a contest of ages. By that Constitution and the laws authorized by it this question must be determined. The provisions of that instrument on the administration of criminal justice are too plain and direct, to leave room for misconstruction or doubt of their true meaning. Those applicable to this case are found in that clause of the original Constitution which says, "That the trial of all crimes, except in case of impeachment, shall be by jury"; and in the fourth, fifth, and sixth articles of the amendments. . . .

Have any of the rights guaranteed by the Constitution been violated in the case of Milligan? and if so, what are they?

Every trial involves the exercise of judicial power; and from what source did the military commission that tried him derive their authority? Certainly no part of the judicial power of the country was conferred on them; because the Constitution expressly vests it "in one supreme court and such inferior courts as the Congress may from time to time ordain and establish," and it is not pretended that the commission was a court ordained and established by Congress. They cannot justify on the mandate of the President; because he is controlled by law, and has his appropriate sphere of duty, which is to execute, not to make, the laws; and there is "no unwritten criminal code to which resort can be had as a source of jurisdiction."

But it is said that the jurisdiction is complete under the "laws and usages of war."

It can serve no useful purpose to inquire what those laws and usages are, whence they originated, where found, and on whom they operate; they can never be applied to citizens in states which have upheld the authority of the government, and where the courts are open and their process unobstructed. This court has judicial knowledge that in Indiana the Federal authority was always unopposed, and its courts always open to hear criminal accusations and redress grievances; and no usage of war could sanction a military trial there for any offence whatever of a citizen in civil life, in nowise connected with the military service. Congress could grant no such power; and to the honor of our national legislature be it said, it has never been provoked by the state of the country even to attempt its exercise. One of the plainest constitutional provisions was, therefore, infringed when Milligan was tried by a court not ordained and established by Congress, and not composed of judges appointed during good behavior.

Why was he not delivered to the Circuit Court of Indiana to be proceeded against according to law? No reason of necessity could be urged against it; because Congress had declared penalties against the offences charged, provided for their punishment, and directed that court to hear and determine them. And soon after this military tribunal was ended, the Circuit Court met, peacefully transacted its business, and adjourned. It needed no bayonets to protect it, and required no military aid to execute its judgments. It was held in a state, eminently distinguished for patriotism, by judges commissioned during the Rebellion, who were provided with juries, upright, intelligent, and selected by a marshal appointed by the President. The government had no right to conclude that Milligan, if guilty, would not receive in that court merited punishment; for its records disclose that it was constantly engaged in the trial of similar offences, and was never interrupted in its administration of criminal justice. If it was dangerous, in the distracted condition of affairs, to leave Milligan unrestrained of his liberty, because he "conspired against the government, afforded aid and comfort to rebels, and incited the people to insurrection," the *law* said arrest him, confine him closely, render him powerless to do further mischief; and then present his case to the grand jury of the district, with proofs of his guilt, and, if indicted, try him according to the course of the common law. If this had been done, the Constitution would have been vindicated, the law of 1863 enforced, and the securities for personal liberty preserved and defended.

Another guarantee of freedom was broken when Milligan was

denied a trial by jury. The great minds of the country have differed on the correct interpretation to be given to various provisions of the Federal Constitution; and judicial decision has been often invoked to settle their true meaning; but until recently no one ever doubted that the right of trial by jury was fortified in the organic law against the power of attack. It is *now* assailed; but if ideas can be expressed in words, and language has any meaning, *this right*—one of the most valuable in a free country—is preserved to every one accused of crime who is not attached to the army, or navy, or militia in actual service. The sixth amendment affirms that "in all criminal prosecutions the accused shall enjoy the right to a speedy and public trial by an impartial jury," language broad enough to embrace all persons and cases; but the fifth, recognizing the necessity of an indictment, or presentment, before any one can be held to answer for high crimes, "*excepts* cases arising in the land or naval forces, or in the militia, when in actual service, in time of war or public danger"; and the framers of the Constitution, doubtless, meant to limit the right of trial by jury, in the sixth amendment, to those persons who were subject to indictment or presentment in the fifth. . . .

It is claimed that martial law covers with its broad mantle the proceedings of this military commission. The proposition is this: that in a time of war the commander of an armed force (if in his opinion the exigencies of the country demand it, and of which he is to judge), has the power, within the lines of his military district, to suspend all civil rights and their remedies, and subject citizens as well as soldiers to the rule of *his will;* and in the exercise of his lawful authority cannot be restrained, except by his superior officer or the President of the United States.

If this position is sound to the extent claimed, then when war exists, foreign or domestic, and the country is subdivided into military departments for mere convenience, the commander of one of them can, if he chooses, within his limits, on the plea of necessity, with the approval of the Executive, substitute military force for and to the exclusion of the laws, and punish all persons, as he thinks right and proper, without fixed or certain rules.

The statement of this proposition shows its importance; for, if true, republican government is a failure, and there is an end of liberty regulated by law. Martial law, established on such a basis, destroys every guarantee of the Constitution, and effectually renders the "military independent of and superior to the civil power"—the attempt to do which by the King of Great Britain was deemed by our fathers such an offence, that they assigned it to the world as one of the causes which impelled them to declare their independence. Civil liberty and this kind of martial law cannot endure together; the antagonism is irreconcilable; and, in the conflict, one or the other must perish.

This nation, as experience has proved, cannot always remain at peace, and has no right to expect that it will always have wise and humane rulers, sincerely attached to the principles of the Constitution. Wicked men, ambitious of power, with hatred of liberty and contempt of law, may fill the place once occupied by Washington and Lincoln; and if this right is conceded, and the calamities of war again befall us, the dangers to human liberty are frightful to contemplate. If our fathers had failed to provide for just such a contingency, they would have been false to the trust reposed in them. They knew—the history of the world told them—the nation they were founding, be its existence short or long, would be involved in war; how often or how long continued, human foresight could not tell; and that unlimited power, wherever lodged at such a time, was especially hazardous to freemen. For this, and other equally weighty reasons, they secured the inheritance they had fought to maintain, by incorporating in a written constitution the safeguards which *time* had proved were essential to its preservation. Not one of these safeguards can the President, or Congress, or the Judiciary disturb, except the one concerning the writ of *habeas corpus.*

It is essential to the safety of every government that, in a great crisis, like the one we have just passed through, there should be a power somewhere of suspending the writ of *habeas corpus.* In every war, there are men of previously good character, wicked enough to counsel their fellow-citizens to resist the measures deemed necessary by a good government to sustain its just authority and overthrow its enemies; and their influence may lead to dangerous combinations. In the emergency of the times, an immediate public investigation according to law may not be possible; and yet, the peril to the country may be too imminent to suffer such persons to go at large. Unquestionably, there is then an exigency which demands that the government, if it should see fit in the exercise of a proper discretion to make arrests, should not be required to produce the persons arrested in answer to a writ of *habeas corpus.* The Constitution goes no further. It does not say after a writ of *habeas corpus* is denied a citizen, that he shall be tried otherwise than by the course of the common law; if it had intended this result, it was easy by the use of direct words to have accomplished it. The illustrious men who framed that instrument were guarding the foundations of civil liberty against the abuses of unlimited power; they were full of wisdom, and the lessons of history informed them that a trial by an established court, assisted by an impartial jury, was the only sure way of protecting the citizen against oppression and wrong. Knowing this, they limited the suspension to one great right, and left the rest to remain forever inviolable. But, it is insisted that the safety of the country in time of war demands that this broad claim for martial law shall be sustained. If this were true, it could be well said that a country, preserved at the sacrifice of all the cardinal principles of liberty, is not worth the cost of preservation. Happily, it is not so.

It will be borne in mind that this is not a question of the power to proclaim martial law, when war exists in a community and the courts and civil authorities are overthrown. Nor is it a question what rule a military commander, at the head of his army, can impose on states in rebellion to cripple their resources and quell the insurrection. The jurisdiction claimed is much more extensive. The necessities of the service, during the late Rebellion, required that the loyal states should be placed within the limits of certain military districts and commanders appointed in them; and, it is urged, that this, in a military sense, constituted them the theatre of military operations; and, as in this case, Indiana had been and was again threatened with invasion by the enemy, the occasion was furnished to establish martial law. The conclusion does not follow from the premises. If armies were collected in Indiana, they were to be employed in another locality, where the laws were obstructed and the national authority disputed. On *her* soil there was no hostile foot; if once invaded, that invasion was at an end, and with it all pretext for martial law. Martial law cannot arise from a *threatened* invasion. The necessity must be actual and present; the invasion real, such as effectually closes the courts and deposes the civil administration.

It is difficult to see how the *safety* of the country required martial law in Indiana. If any of her citizens were plotting treason, the power of arrest could secure them, until the government was prepared for their trial, when the courts were open and ready to try them. It was as easy to protect witnesses before a civil as a military tribunal; and as there could be no wish to convict, except on sufficient legal evidence, surely an ordained and established court was better able to judge of this than a military tribunal composed of gentlemen not trained to the profession of the law.

It follows, from what has been said on this subject, that there are occasions when martial rule can be properly applied. If, in foreign invasion or civil war, the courts are actually closed, and it is impossible to administer criminal justice according to law, *then,* on the theatre of active military operations, where war really prevails, there is a necessity to furnish a substitute for the civil authority, thus overthrown, to preserve the safety of the army and society; and as no power is left but the military, it is allowed to govern by martial rule until the laws can have their free course. As necessity creates the rule, so it limits its duration; for, if this government is continued *after* the courts are reinstated, it is a gross usurpation of power. Martial rule can never exist where the courts are open, and in the proper and unobstructed exercise of their jurisdiction. It is also confined to the locality of actual war. Because, during the late Rebellion it could have been enforced in Virginia, where the national authority was overturned and the courts driven out, it does not follow that it should obtain in Indiana, where that authority was never disputed, and justice was always administered. And so in the case of a foreign invasion, martial rule may become a necessity in one state, when, in another, it would be "mere lawless violence." . . .

The two remaining questions in this case must be answered in the affirmative. The suspension of the privilege of the writ of *habeas corpus* does not suspend the writ itself. The writ issues as a matter of course; and on the return made to in the court decides whether the part applying is denied the right of proceeding any further with it.

If the military trial of Milligan was contrary to law, then he was entitled, on the facts stated in his petition, to be discharged from custody by the terms of the act of Congress of March 3d, 1863.

Chief Justice CHASE delivers the following opinion.

[T]he opinion which has just been read . . . asserts not only that the Military Commission held in Indiana was not authorized by Congress, but that it was not in the power of Congress to authorize it; from which it may be thought to follow, that Congress had no power to indemnify the officers who composed the commission against liability in civil courts for acting as members of it.

We cannot agree to this. . . .

We think that Congress had power, though not exercised, to authorize the Military Commission which was held in Indiana.

Congress has the power not only to raise and support and govern armies, but to declare war. It has, therefore, the power to provide by law for carrying on war. This power necessarily extends to all legislation essential to the prosecution of war with vigor and success, except such as interferes with the command of the forces and conduct of campaigns. That power and duty belong to the President as Commander-in-Chief. Both these powers are derived from the Constitution, but neither is defined by that instrument. Their extent must be determined by their nature, and by the principles of our institutions. . . .

We think that the power of Congress, in such times and in such localities, to authorize trials for crimes against the security and safety of the national forces, may be derived from its constitutional authority to raise and support armies and to declare war, if not from its constitutional authority to provide for governing the national forces. . . .

Justice WAYNE, Justice SWAYNE and Justice MILLER concur with me in these views.

Korematsu v. United States
323 U.S. 214, 65 S.Ct. 193 (1944)

Following the Japanese attack on Pearl Harbor in December 1941 and amid growing fears that the West Coast might be invaded, President Franklin D. Roosevelt issued in February 1942 an executive order authorizing the creation of "military zones" in which military commanders could impose curfews and exclude individuals to prevent espionage and sabotage. Congress a month later passed legislation approving these orders and providing criminal penalties for their violation. Tens of thousands of Japanese-Americans along the West Coast were subsequently subjected to curfews, evacuations, and internment in "relocation camps," which were set up farther inland. The constitutionality of these orders were immediately challenged. In *Hirabayashi v. United States*, 320 U.S. 81 (1943), the orders for curfews were upheld, but the Court avoided ruling on the evacuation program. The Court then squarely confronted a challenge to the latter when Toyosaburo Korematsu, a citizen of Japanese ancestry, refused to leave his home in California and was convicted in district court for violating the exclusion order. The Supreme Court granted his petition for *certiorari* after a court of appeals upheld his conviction. Justice Hugo Black's opinion for the Court affirming the lower court's decision drew three sharp dissents from Justices Owen Roberts, Frank Murphy, and Robert Jackson.

Justice BLACK delivers the opinion of the Court.

The 1942 Act was attacked in the *Hirabayashi* case [320 U.S. 81] as an unconstitutional delegation of power; it was contended that the curfew order and other orders on which it rested were beyond the war powers of the Congress, the military authorities and of the President, as Commander in Chief of the Army; and finally that to apply the curfew order against none but citizens of Japanese ancestry amounted to a constitutionally prohibited discrimination solely on account of race. To these questions, we gave the serious consideration which their importance justified. We upheld the curfew order as an exercise of the power of the government to take steps necessary to prevent espionage and sabotage in an area threatened by Japanese attack.

In the light of the principles we announced in the *Hirabayashi* case, we are unable to conclude that it was beyond the war power of Congress and the Executive to exclude those of Japanese ancestry from the West Coast war area at the time they did. True, exclusion from the area in which one's home is located is a far greater deprivation than constant confinement to the home from 8 P.M. to 6 A.M. Nothing short of apprehension by the proper military authorities of the gravest imminent danger to the public safety can constitutionally justify either. But exclusion from a threatened area, no less than curfew, has a definite and close relationship to the prevention of espionage and sabotage. The military authorities, charged with the primary responsibility of defending our shores, concluded that curfew provided inadequate protection and ordered exclusion. They did so, as pointed out in our *Hirabayashi* opinion, in accordance with Congressional authority to the military to say who should, and who should not, remain in the threatened areas.

In this case the petitioner challenges the assumptions upon which we rested our conclusions in the *Hirabayashi* case. He also urges that by May 1942, when Order No. 34 was promulgated, all danger of Japanese invasion of the West Coast had disappeared. After careful consideration of these contentions we are compelled to reject them.

Here, as in the *Hirabayashi* case, "we cannot reject as unfounded the judgment of the military authorities and of Congress that there were disloyal members of that population, whose number and strength could not be precisely and quickly ascertained. We cannot say that the war-making branches of the Government did not have ground for believing that in a critical hour such persons could not readily be isolated and separately dealt with, and constituted a menace to the national defense and safety, which demanded that prompt and adequate measures be taken to guard against it."

Like curfew, exclusion of those of Japanese origin was deemed necessary because of the presence of an unascertained number of disloyal members of the group, most of whom we have no doubt were loyal to this country. It was because we could not reject the finding of the military authorities that it was impossible to bring about an immediate segregation of the disloyal from the loyal that we sustained the validity of the curfew order as applying to the whole group. In the instant case, temporary exclusion of the entire group was rested by the military on the same ground. The judgment that exclusion of the whole group was for the same reason a military imperative answers the contention that the exclusion was in the nature of group punishment based on antagonism to those of Japanese origin. That there were members of the group who retained loyalties to Japan has been confirmed by investigations made subsequent to the exclusion. Approximately five thousand American citizens of Japanese ancestry refused to swear unqualified allegiance to the United States and to renounce allegiance to the Japanese Emperor, and several thousand evacuees requested repatriation to Japan.

We uphold the exclusion order as of the time it was made and when the petitioner violated it. . . . In doing so, we are not unmindful of the hardships imposed by it upon a large group of American citizens. . . . But hardships are part of war, and war is an aggregation of hardships. All citizens alike, both in and out of uniform, feel the impact of war in greater or lesser measure. Citizenship has its responsibilities as well as its privileges, and in time of war the burden is always heavier. Compulsory exclusion of large groups of citizens from their homes, except under circumstances of direst emergency and peril, is inconsistent with our basic governmental institutions. But when under conditions of modern warfare our shores are threatened by hostile forces, the power to protect must be commensurate with the threatened danger. . . .

Since the petitioner has not been convicted of failing to report or to remain in an assembly or relocation center, we cannot in this case determine the validity of those separate provisions of the order. It is sufficient here for us to pass upon the order which petitioner violated. To do more would be to go beyond the issues raised, and to decide momentous questions not contained within the framework of the pleadings or the evidence in this case. It will be time enough to decide the serious constitutional issues which petitioner seeks to raise when an assembly or relocation order is applied or is certain to be applied to him, and we have its terms before us.

Some of the members of the Court are of the view that evacuation and detention in an Assembly Center were inseparable. After May 3, 1942, the date of Exclusion Order No. 34, Korematsu was under compulsion to leave the area not as he would choose but via an Assembly Center. The Assembly Center was conceived as a part of the machinery for group evacuation. The power to exclude includes the power to do it by force if necessary. And any forcible measure must necessarily entail some degree of detention or restraint whatever method of removal is selected. But whichever view is taken, it results in holding that the order under which petitioner was convicted was valid.

It is said that we are dealing here with the case of imprisonment of a citizen in a concentration camp solely because of his ancestry, without evidence or inquiry concerning his loyalty and good disposition towards the United States. Our task would be simple, our duty clear, were this a case involving the imprisonment of a loyal citizen in a concentration camp because of racial prejudice. Regardless of the true nature of the assembly and relocation centers—and we deem it unjustifiable to call them concentration camps with all the ugly connotations that term implies—we are dealing specifically with nothing but an exclusion order. To cast this case into outlines of racial prejudice, without reference to the real military dangers which were presented; merely confuses the issue. Korematsu was not excluded from the Military Area because of hostility to him or his race. He was excluded because we are at war with the Japanese Empire, because the properly constituted military authorities feared an invasion of our West Coast and felt constrained to take proper security measures, because they decided that the military urgency of the situation demanded that all citizens of Japanese ancestry be segregated from the West Coast temporarily, and finally, because Congress, reposing its confidence in this time of war in our military leaders—as inevitably it must—determined that they should have the power to do just this. There was evidence of disloyalty on the part of some, the military authorities considered that the need for action was great, and time was short. We cannot—by availing ourselves of the calm perspective of hindsight—now say that at that time these actions were unjustified.

Affirmed.

Justice FRANKFURTER concurring.

According to my reading of Civilian Exclusion Order No. 34, it was an offense for Korematsu to be found in Military Area No. 1, the territory wherein he was previously living, except within the bounds of the established Assembly Center of that area. Even though the various orders issued by General DeWitt be deemed a comprehensive code of instructions, their tenor is clear and not contradictory. They put upon Korematsu the obligation to leave Military Area No. 1, but only by the method prescribed in the instructions, i.e., by reporting to the Assembly Center. I am unable to see how the legal considerations that led to the decision in *Kiyoshi Hirabayashi v. United States* fail to sustain the military order which made the conduct now in controversy a crime. And so I join in the opinion of the Court, but should like to add a few words of my own.

The provisions of the Constitution which confer on the Congress and the President powers to enable this country to wage war are as much part of the Constitution as provisions looking to a nation at peace. And we have had recent occasion to quote approvingly the statement of former Chief Justice HUGHES that the war power of the Government is "the power to wage war successfully." *Hirabayashi v. United States.* Therefore, the validity of action under the war power must be judged wholly in the context of war. That action is not to be stigmatized as lawless because like action in times of peace would be lawless. To talk about a military order that expresses an allowable judgment of war needs by those entrusted with the duty of conducting war as "an unconstitutional order" is to suffuse a part of the Constitution with an atmosphere of unconstitutionality. The respective spheres of action of military authorities and of judges are of course very different. But within their sphere, military authorities are no more outside the bounds of obedience to the Constitution than are judges within theirs. "The war power of the United States, like its other powers . . . is subject to applicable constitutional limitations," *Hamilton v. Kentucky Distilleries Co.,* 251 U.S. 146 [1919]. To recognize that military orders are "reasonably expedient military precautions" in time of war and yet to deny them constitutional legitimacy makes of the the Constitution an instrument for dialectic subtleties not reasonably to be attributed to the hard-headed Framers, of whom a majority had had actual participation in war. If a military order such as that under review does not transcend the means appropriate for conducting war, such action by the military is as constitutional as would be any authorized action by the Interstate Commerce Commission within the limits of the constitutional power to regulate commerce. And being an exercise of the war power explicitly granted by the Constitution for safeguarding the national life by prosecuting war effectively, I find nothing in the Constitution which denies to Congress the power to enforce such a valid military order by making its violation an offense triable in the civil courts. . . . To find that the Constitution does not forbid the military measures now complained of does not carry with it approval of that which Congress and the Executive did. That is their business, not ours.

Justice ROBERTS dissenting.

I dissent, because I think the indisputable facts exhibit a clear violation of Constitutional rights.

This is not a case of keeping people off the streets at night as was *Kiyoshi Hirabayashi v. United States,* nor a case of temporary exclusion of a citizen from an area for his own safety or that of the community, nor a case of offering him an opportunity to go temporarily out of an area where his presence might cause danger to himself or to his fellows. On the contrary, it is the case of convicting a citizen as a punishment for not submitting to imprisonment in a concentration camp, based on his ancestry, and solely because of his ancestry, without evidence or inquiry concerning his loyalty and good disposition towards the United States. If this be a correct statement of the facts disclosed by this record, and facts of which we take judicial notice, I need hardly labor the conclusion that Constitutional rights have been violated.

Justice MURPHY dissenting.

This exclusion of "all persons of Japanese ancestry, both alien and non-alien," from the Pacific Coast area on a plea of military necessity in the absence of martial law ought not to be approved. Such exclusion goes over "the very brink of constitutional power" and falls into the ugly abyss of racism.

In dealing with matters relating to the prosecution and progress of a war, we must accord great respect and consideration to the judgments of the military authorities who are on the scene and who have full knowledge of the military facts. The scope of their discretion must, as a matter of necessity and common sense, be wide. And their judgments ought not to be overruled lightly by those whose training and duties ill-equip them to deal intelligently with matters so vital to the physical security of the nation.

At the same time, however, it is essential that there be definite limits to military discretion, especially where martial law has not been declared. Individuals must not be left impoverished of their constitutional rights on a plea of military necessity that has neither substance nor support. Thus, like other claims conflicting with the asserted constitutional rights of the individual, the military claim must subject itself to the judicial process of having its reasonableness determined and its conflicts with other interests reconciled. "What are the allowable limits of military discretion, and whether or not they have been overstepped in a particular case, are judicial questions." *Sterling v. Constantin*, 287 U.S. 378 [1932].

The judicial test of whether the Government, on a plea of military necessity, can validly deprive an individual of any of his constitutional rights is whether the deprivation is reasonably related to a public danger that is so "immediate, imminent, and impending" as not to admit of delay and not to permit the intervention of ordinary constitutional processes to alleviate the danger. Civilian Exclusion Order No. 34, banishing from a prescribed area of the Pacific Coast "all persons of Japanese ancestry, both alien and non-alien," clearly does not meet that test. Being an obvious racial discrimination, the order deprives all those within its scope of the equal protection of the laws as guaranteed by the Fifth Amendment. It further deprives these individuals of their constitutional rights to live and work where they will, to establish a home where they choose and to move about freely. In excommunicating them without benefit of hearings, this order also deprives them of all their constitutional rights to procedural due process. Yet no reasonable relation to an "immediate, imminent, and impending" public danger is evident to support this racial restriction which is one of the most sweeping and complete deprivations of constitutional rights in the history of this nation in the absence of martial law. . . .

The military necessity which is essential to the validity of the evacuation order thus resolves itself into a few intimations that certain individuals actively aided the enemy, from which it is inferred that the entire group of Japanese Americans could not be trusted to be or remain loyal to the United States. No one denies, of course, that there were some disloyal persons of Japanese descent on the Pacific Coast who did all in their power to aid their ancestral land. Similar disloyal activities have been engaged in by many persons of German, Italian and even more pioneer stock in our country. But to infer that examples of individual disloyalty prove group disloyalty and justify discriminatory action against the entire group is to deny that under our system of law individual guilt is the sole basis for deprivation of rights. Moreover, this inference, which is at the very heart of the evacuation orders, has been used in support of the abhorrent and despicable treatment of minority groups by the dictatorial tyrannies which this nation is now pledged to destroy. To give constitutional sanction to that inference in this case, however well-intentioned may have been the military command on the Pacific Coast, is to adopt one of the cruelest of the rationales used by our enemies to destroy the dignity of the individual and to encourage and open the door to discriminatory actions against other minority groups in the passions of tomorrow. . . .

Moreover, there was no adequate proof that the Federal Bureau of Investigation and the military and naval intelligence services did not have the espionage and sabotage situation well in hand during this long period. Nor is there any denial of the fact that not one person of Japanese ancestry was accused or convicted of espionage or sabotage after Pearl Harbor while they were still free, a fact which is some evidence of the loyalty of the vast majority of these individuals and of the effectiveness of the established methods of combatting these evils. It seems incredible that under these circumstances it would have been impossible to hold loyalty hearings for the mere 112,000 persons involved—or at least for the 70,000 American citizens—especially when a large part of this number represented children and elderly men and women. Any inconvenience that may have accompanied an attempt to conform to procedural due process cannot be said to justify violations of constitutional rights of individuals.

I dissent, therefore, from this legalization of racism. Racial discrimination in any form and in any degree has no justifiable part whatever in our democratic way of life. It is unattractive in any setting but it is utterly revolting among a free people who have embraced the principles set forth in the Constitution of the United States.

Justice JACKSON dissenting.

Korematsu was born on our soil, of parents born in Japan. The Constitution makes him a citizen of the United States by nativity and a citizen of California by residence. No claim is made that he is not loyal to this country. There is no suggestion that apart from the matter involved here he is not law-abiding and well disposed. Korematsu, however, has been convicted of an act not commonly a crime. It consists merely of being present in the state whereof he is a citizen, near the place where he was born, and where all his life he has lived.

Even more unusual is the series of military orders which made this conduct a crime. They forbid such a one to remain, and they also forbid him to leave. They were so drawn that the only way Korematsu could avoid violation was to give himself up to the military authority. This meant submission to custody, examination, and transportation out of the territory, to be followed by indeterminate confinement in detention camps.

A citizen's presence in the locality; however, was made a crime only if his parents were of Japanese birth. Had Korematsu been one of four—the others being, say, a German alien enemy, an Italian alien enemy, and a citizen of American-born ancestors, convicted of treason but out on parole—only Korematsu's presence would have violated the order. The difference between their innocence and his crime would result, not from anything he did, said, or thought, different than they, but only in that he was born of different racial stock.

Now, if any fundamental assumption underlies our system, it is that guilt is personal and not inheritable. Even if all of one's antecedents had been convicted of treason, the Constitution forbids its penalties to be visited upon him, for it provides that "no Attainder of Treason shall work Corruption of Blood, or Forfeiture except during the Life of the Person attained." Article 3, § 3, cl. 2. But here is an attempt to make an otherwise innocent act a crime merely because this prisoner is the son of parents as to whom he had no choice, and belongs to a race from which there is no way to resign. If Congress in peace-time legislation should enact such a criminal law, I should suppose this Court would refuse to enforce it.

But the "law" which this prisoner is convicted of disregarding is not found in an act of Congress, but in a military order. Neither the Act of Congress nor the Executive Order of the President, nor both together, would afford a basis for this conviction. It rests on the orders of General DeWitt. And it is said that if the military commander had reasonable military grounds for promulgating the orders, they are constitutional and become law, and the Court is required to enforce them. There are several reasons why I cannot subscribe to this doctrine.

It would be impracticable and dangerous idealism to expect or insist that each specific military command in an area of probable operations will conform to conventional tests of constitutionality. When an area is so beset that it must be put under military control at all, the paramount consideration is that its measures be successful, rather than legal. The armed services must protect a society, not merely its Constitution. The very essence of the military job is to marshal physical force, to remove every obstacle to its effectiveness, to give it every strategic advantage. Defense measures will not, and often should not, be held within the limits that bind civil authority in peace. No court can require such a commander in such circumstances to act as a reasonable man; he may be unreasonably cautious and exacting. Perhaps he should be. But a commander in temporarily focusing the life of a community on defense is carrying out a military program; he is not making law in the sense the courts know the term. He issues orders, and they may have a certain authority as military commands, although they may be very bad as constitutional law.

But if we cannot confine military expedients by the Constitution, neither would I distort the Constitution to approve all that the military may deem expedient. That is what the Court appears to be doing, whether consciously or not. I cannot say, from any evidence before me, that the orders of General DeWitt were not reasonably expedient military precautions, nor could I say that they were. But even if they were permissible military procedures, I deny that it follows that they are constitutional. If, as the Court holds, it does follow, then we may as well say that any military order will be constitutional and have done with it.

The limitation under which courts always will labor in examining the necessity for a military order are illustrated by this case. How does the Court know that these orders have a reasonable basis in necessity? No evidence whatever on that subject has been taken by this or any other court. There is sharp controversy as to the credibility of the DeWitt report. So the Court, having no real evidence before it, has no choice but to accept General DeWitt's own unsworn, self-serving statement, untested by any cross-examination, that what he did was reasonable. And thus it will always be when courts try to look into the reasonableness of a military order.

In the very nature of things military decisions are not susceptible of intelligent judicial appraisal. They do not pretend to rest on evidence, but are made on information that often would not be admissible and on assumptions that could not be proved. Information in support of an order could not be disclosed to courts without danger that it would reach the enemy. Neither can courts act on communications made in confidence. Hence courts can never have any real alternative to accepting the mere declaration of the authority that issued the order that it was reasonably necessary from a military viewpoint.

Much is said of the danger to liberty from the Army program for deporting and detaining these citizens of Japanese extraction. But a judicial construction of the due process clause that will sustain this order is a far more subtle blow to liberty than the promulgation of the order itself. A military order, however unconstitutional, is not apt to last longer than the military emergency. Even during that period a succeeding commander may revoke it all. But once a judicial opinion rationalizes such an order to show that it conforms to the Constitution, or rather rationalizes the Constitution to show that the Constitution sanctions such an order, the Court for all time has validated the principle of racial discrimination in criminal procedure and of transplanting American citizens. The principle then lies about like a loaded weapon ready for the hand of any authority that can bring forward a plausible claim of an urgent need. Every repetition imbeds that principle more deeply in our law and thinking and expands it to new purposes. All who observe the work of courts are familiar with what Judge CARDOZO described as "the tendency of a principle to expand itself to the limit of its logic." A military commander may overstep the bounds of constitutionality, and it is an incident. But if we review and approve, that passing incident becomes the doctrine of the Constitution. There it has a generative power of its own, and all that it creates will be in its own image. Nothing better illustrates this danger than does the Court's opinion in this case.

It argues that we are bound to uphold the conviction of Korematsu because we upheld one in *Kiyshi Hirabayashi v. United States.* when we sustained these orders in so far as they applied a curfew requirement to a citizen of Japanese ancestry. I think we should learn something from that experience.

In that case we were urged to consider only the curfew feature, that being all that technically was involved, because it was the only count necessary to sustain Hirabayashi's conviction and sentence. We yielded, and the CHIEF JUSTICE guarded the opinion as carefully as language will do. He said: "Our investigation here does not go beyond the inquiry whether, in the light of all the relevant circumstances preceding and attending their promulgation, the challenged orders and statute *afforded a reasonable basis for the action taken in imposing the curfew."* . . . "We decide only the issue as we have defined it—we decide only that the *curfew order* as applied, and at the time it was applied, was within the boundaries of the war power." And again: "It is unnecessary to consider whether or to what extent *such findings would support orders differing from the curfew order."* [Italics supplied.] However, in spite of our limiting words we did validate a discrimination on the basis of ancestry for mild and temporary deprivation of liberty. Now the principle of racial discrimination is pushed from support of mild measures to very harsh ones, and from temporary deprivations to indeterminate ones. And the precedent which it is said requires us to do so is *Hirabayashi*. The Court is now saying that in *Hirabayashi* we did decide the very things we there said we were not deciding. Because we said that these citizens could be made to stay in their homes during the hours of dark, it is said we must require them to leave home entirely; and if that, we are told they may also be taken into custody for deportation; and if that, it is argued they may also be held for some undetermined time in detention camps. How far the principle of this case would be extended before plausible reasons would play out, I do not know.

I should hold that a civil court cannot be made to enforce an order which violates constitutional limitations even if it is a reasonable exercise of military authority. The courts can exercise only the judicial power, can apply only law, and must abide by the Constitution, or they cease to be civil courts and become instruments of military policy.

Of course the existence of a military power resting on force, so vagrant, so centralized, so necessarily heedless of the individual, is an inherent threat to liberty. But I would not lead people to rely on this Court for a review that seems to me wholly delusive. The military reasonableness of these orders can only be determined by military superiors. If the people ever let command of the war power fall into irresponsible and unscrupulous hands, the courts wield no power equal to its restraint. The chief restraint upon those who command the physical forces of the country, in the future as in the past, must be their responsibility to the political judgments of their contemporaries and to the moral judgments of history.

My duties as a justice as I see them do not require me to make a military judgment as to whether General DeWitt's evacuation and detention program was a reasonable military necessity. I do not suggest that the courts should have attempted to interfere with the Army in carrying out its task. But I do not think they may be asked to execute a military expedient that has no place in law under the Constitution. I would reverse the judgment and discharge the prisoner.

War Powers Resolution
87 Stat. 555 (1973)

During the height of the Vietnam War in 1973, Congress passed the War Powers Resolution. It imposed a number of limitations on presidential commitment of troops abroad without specific congressional authorization and requires the president to notify and consult with Congress before sending armed forces into actual or potential hostilities. The act remains controversial and its constitutionality a matter of dispute.[*]

There are those who defend Congress's power to limit the president's war-making powers. For example, S. Carter argues that

[t]he "inherent" powers to which opponents of the War Powers Resolution make reference are really [powers] thought to be inherent because the President has historically exercised them. But they are powers the President has exercised in the absence of any congressional objection. . . . [Moreover,] historical acquiescence by Congress in the President's exercise of a particular power does not by itself prove that Congress lacks the authority to limit the exercise of that power when it gathers the wisdom and courage to do so.[†]

Contrariwise, others contend that the act is far too broad and a congressional intrusion on inherent presidential powers. Among them Eugene V. Rostow points out,

The pattern against which the [War Powers Resolution] protests is old, familiar, and rooted in the nature of things. There is nothing constitutionally illegitimate or even dubious about "undeclared" wars. We and other nations fought them frequently in the eighteenth and nineteenth centuries, as well as in the twentieth. . . . [This act] would turn the clock back to the Articles of Confederation, and destroy the Presidency which it was one of the chief aims of the men of Annapolis and Philadelphia to create.[‡]

Resolved by the Senate and House of Representatives of the United States of America in Congress assembled, That:

Section 1. This joint resolution may be cited as the "War Powers Resolution."

---

[*] See Robert Scigliano, "The War Powers Resolution and the War Powers," in *The Presidency in the Constitutional Order*, ed. Joseph M. Bissette and Jeffrey Tulis (Baton Rouge: Louisiana State University Press, 1981).
[†] S. Carter, "The Constitutionality of the War Powers Resolution," 70 *Virginia Law Review* 101 (1984).
[‡] Eugene V. Rostow, "Great Cases Make Bad Law: The War Powers Act," 50 *Texas Law Review* 833 (1972).

Sec. 2. (a) It is the purpose of this joint resolution to fulfill the intent of the framers of the Constitution of the United States and insure that the collective judgment of both the Congress and the President will apply to the introduction of United States Armed Forces into hostilities, or into situations where imminent involvement in hostilities is clearly indicated by the circumstances, and to the continued use of such forces in hostilities or in such situations.

(b) Under article I, section 8, of the Constitution, it is specifically provided that the Congress shall have the power to make all laws necessary and proper for carrying into execution, not only its own powers but also all other powers vested by the Constitution in the Government of the United States, or in any department or officer thereof.

(c) The constitutional powers of the President as Commander-in-Chief to introduce United States Armed Forces into hostilities, or into situations where imminent involvement in hostilities is clearly indicated by the circumstances, are exercised only pursuant to (1) a declaration of war, (2) specific statutory authorization, or (3) a national emergency created by attack upon the United States, its territories or possessions, or its armed forces.

Sec. 3. The President in every possible instance shall consult with Congress before introducing United States Armed Forces into hostilities or into situations where imminent involvement in hostilities is clearly implicated by the circumstances, and after every such introduction shall consult regularly with the Congress until United States Armed Forces are no longer engaged in hostilities or have been removed from such situations.

Sec. 4. (a) In the absence of a declaration of war, in any case in which United States Armed Forces are introduced—

(1) into hostilities or into situations where imminent involvement in hostilities is clearly indicated by the circumstances;

(2) into the territory, airspace or waters of a foreign nation, while equipped for combat, except for deployments which relate solely to supply, replacement, repair, or training of such forces; or

(3) in numbers which substantially enlarge United States Armed Forces equipped for combat already located in a foreign nation; the President shall submit within 48 hours to the Speaker of the House of Representatives and to the President pro tempore of the Senate a report, in writing, setting forth—

(A) the circumstances necessitating the introduction of United States Armed Forces;

(B) the constitutional and legislative authority under which such introduction took place; and

(C) the estimated scope and duration of the hostilities or involvement.

(b) The President shall provide such other information as the

Congress may request in the fulfillment of its constitutional responsibilities with respect to committing the Nation to war and to the use of United States Armed Forces abroad.

(c) Whenever United States Armed Forces are introduced into hostilities or into any situation described in subsection (a) of this section, the President shall, so long as such armed forces continue to be engaged in such hostilities or situation, report to the Congress periodically on the status of such hostilities or situation as well as on the scope and duration of such hostilities or situation, but in no event shall he report to the Congress less often than once every six months.

Sec. 5. (a) Each report submitted pursuant to section 4(a)(1) shall be transmitted to the Speaker of the House of Representatives and to the President pro tempore of the Senate on the same calendar day. Each report so transmitted shall be referred to the Committee on Foreign Affairs of the House of Representatives and to the Committee on Foreign Relations of the Senate for appropriate action. If, when the report is transmitted, the Congress has adjourned sine die or has adjourned for any period in excess of three calendar days, the Speaker of the House of Representatives and the President pro tempore of the Senate, if they deem it advisable (or if petitioned by at least 30 percent of the membership of their respective Houses) shall jointly request the President to convene Congress in order that it may consider the report and take appropriate action pursuant to this section.

(b) Within sixty calendar days after a report is submitted or is required to be submitted pursuant to section 4(a)(1), whichever is earlier, the President shall terminate any use of United States Armed Forces with respect to which such report was submitted (or required to be submitted), unless the Congress (1) has declared war or has enacted a specific authorization for such use of United States Armed Forces, (2) has extended by law such sixty-day period, or (3) is physically unable to meet as a result of an armed attack upon the United States. Such sixty-day period shall be extended for not more than an additional thirty days if the President determines and certifies to the Congress in writing that unavoidable military necessity respecting the safety of United States Armed Forces requires the continued use of such armed forces in the course of bringing about a prompt removal of such forces.

(c) Notwithstanding subsection (b), at any time that United States Armed Forces are engaged in hostilities outside the territory of the United States, its possessions and territories without a declaration of war or specific statutory authorization, such forces shall be removed by the President if the Congress so directs by concurrent resolution.

Sec. 6. (a) Any joint resolution or bill introduced pursuant to section 5(b) at least thirty calendar days before the expiration of the sixty-day period specified in such section shall be referred to the Committee on Foreign Affairs of the House of Representatives or the Committee on Foreign Relations of the Senate, as the case may be, and such committee shall report one such joint resolution or bill, together with its recommendations, not later than twenty-four calendar days before the expiration of the sixty-day period specified in such section, unless such House shall otherwise determine by the yeas and nays.

(b) Any joint resolution or bill so reported shall become the pending business of the House in question (in the case of the Senate the time for debate shall be equally divided between the proponents and the opponents), and shall be voted on within three calendar days thereafter, unless such House shall otherwise determine by yeas and nays.

(c) Such a joint resolution or bill passed by one House shall be referred to the committee of the other House named in subsection (a) and shall be reported out not later than fourteen calendar days before the expiration of the sixty-day period specified in section 5(b). The joint resolution or bill so reported shall become the pending business of the House in question and shall be voted on within three calendar days after it has been reported, unless such House shall otherwise determine by yeas and nays.

(d) In the case of any disagreement between the two Houses of Congress with respect to a joint resolution or bill passed by both Houses, conferees shall be promptly appointed and the committee of conference shall make and file a report with respect to such resolution or bill not later than four calendar days before the expiration of the sixty-day period specified in section 5(b). In the event the conferees are unable to agree within 48 hours, they shall report back to their respective Houses in disagreement. Notwithstanding any rule in either House concerning the printing of conference reports in the Record or concerning any delay in the consideration of such reports, such report shall be acted on by both Houses not later than the expiration of such sixty-day period.

Sec. 7. (a) Any concurrent resolution introduced pursuant to section 5(c) shall be referred to the Committee on Foreign Affairs of the House of Representatives or the Committee on Foreign Relations of the Senate, as the case may be, and one such concurrent resolution shall be reported out by such committee together with its recommendations within fifteen calendar days, unless such House shall otherwise determine by the yeas and nays.

(b) Any concurrent resolution so reported shall become the pending business of the House in question (in the case of the Senate the time for debate shall be equally divided between the proponents and the opponents) and shall be voted on within three calendar days thereafter, unless such House shall otherwise determine by yeas and nays.

(c) Such a concurrent resolution passed by one House shall

be referred to the committee of the other House named in subsection (a) and shall be reported out by such committee together with its recommendations within fifteen calendar days and shall thereupon become the pending business of such House and shall be voted upon within three calendar days, unless such House shall otherwise determine by yeas and nays.

(d) In the case of any disagreement between the two Houses of Congress with respect to a concurrent resolution passed by both Houses, conferees shall be promptly appointed and the committee of conference shall make and file a report with respect to such concurrent resolution within six calendar days after the legislation is referred to the committee of conference. Notwithstanding any rule in either House concerning the printing of conference reports in the Record or concerning any delay in the consideration of such reports, such report shall be acted on by both Houses not later than six calendar days after the conference report is filed. In the event the conferees are unable to agree within 48 hours, they shall report back to their respective Houses in disagreement.

Sec. 8. (a) Authority to introduce United States Armed Forces into hostilities or into situations wherein involvement in hostilities is clearly indicated by the circumstances shall not be inferred—

(1) from any provision of law (whether or not in effect before the date of the enactment of this joint resolution), including any provision contained in any appropriation Act, unless such provision specifically authorizes the introduction of United States Armed Forces into hostilities or into such situations and states that it is intended to constitute specific statutory authorization within the meaning of this joint resolution; or

(2) from any treaty heretofore or hereafter ratified unless such treaty is implemented by legislation specifically authorizing the introduction of United States Armed Forces into hostilities or into such situations and stating that it is intended to constitute specific statutory authorization within the meaning of this joint resolution.

(b) Nothing in this joint resolution shall be construed to require any further specific statutory authorization to permit members of United States Armed Forces to participate jointly with members of the armed forces of one or more foreign countries in the headquarters operations of high-level military commands which were established prior to the date of enactment of this joint resolution and pursuant to the United Nations Charter or any treaty ratified by the United States prior to such date.

(c) For purposes of this joint resolution, the term "introduction of United States Armed Forces" includes the assignment of members of such armed forces to command, coordinate, participate in the movement of, or accompany the regular or irregular military forces of any foreign country or government when such military forces are engaged, or there exists an imminent threat that such forces will become engaged, in hostilities.

(d) Nothing in this joint resolution—

(1) is intended to alter the constitutional authority of the Congress or of the President, or the provisions of existing treaties; or

(2) shall be construed as granting any authority to the President with respect to the introduction of United States Armed Forces into hostilities or into situations wherein involvement in hostilities is clearly indicated by the circumstances which authority he would not have had in the absence of this joint resolution.

Sec. 9. If any provision of this joint resolution or the application thereof to any person or circumstance is held invalid, the remainder of the joint resolution and the application of such provision to any other person or circumstance shall not be affected thereby.

Sec. 10. This joint resolution shall take effect on the date of its enactment.

[Passed over Presidential veto November 7, 1973.]

4

THE PRESIDENT AS CHIEF EXECUTIVE IN DOMESTIC AFFAIRS

THE GROWTH IN the legislative powers of the president might appear paradoxical given the principle of separation of powers. Article I vests "[a]ll legislative powers" in Congress, while Article II provides that "[t]he executive Power shall be vested in a President." Yet the Constitution provides the president with certain legislative powers as well. He has the power to inform Congress about "the State of the Union," to convene both houses of Congress on extraordinary occasions, and to veto legislation. As chief executive, the president also has the power to appoint subordinate officers in the government and thereby influence the development and implementation of legislation.

The legislative and administrative role of the president has nonetheless grown enormously with the development of White House staff and the institutionalized presidency. The state of the union address, for instance, has become an occasion for presidents to announce their own broad legislative programs. Even more important, Congress has delegated vast legislative powers to the executive branch. As a result, administrative agencies, under the control and supervision of the president, are responsible for developing and implementing the overwhelming majority of all federal regulations. Besides these statutory grants of power to the executive branch, presidents may assert legislative powers through executive orders, presidential proclamations, and White House oversight of regulatory rule making. In addition, presidents may claim inherent or implied powers as chief executive and under their obligation to "take Care that the Laws be faithfully executed."

This chapter examines the president's powers as chief executive in regard to controversies over national security, the appointment and removal of federal officials, and the legislative role of the presidency in the administrative state. The chapter concludes by taking up issues involving presidential immunity and accountability, dealing particularly with claims to executive privilege and the impeachment of the president.

SELECTED BIBLIOGRAPHY

Barber, Sotirios. *The Constitution and the Delgation of Congressional Power.* Chicago: University of Chicago Press, 1975.

Fisher, Louis. *The Politics of Shared Power: Congress and the Executive.* Washington, DC: Congressional Quarterly Press, 1981.

Marcus, Maeva. *Truman and the Steel Seizure Case.* New York: Columbia University Press, 1977.

Pyle, Christopher, and Pious, Richard M., eds. *The President, Congress and the Constitution.* New York: Free Press, 1984.

Rohr, John. *To Run a Constitution: The Legitimacy of the Administrative State.* Lawrence: University of Kansas, 1986.

A. NATIONAL SECURITY AND INHERENT AND EMERGENCY POWERS

In times of emergency and in response to perceived threats to national security, presidents claim inherent or implied powers over domestic as well as foreign affairs. They do so as chief executive and as empowered to "take Care that the Laws be faithfully executed." But the Court has been more troubled by claims to inherent presidential powers in domestic, as opposed to foreign, affairs. As Chief Justice Hughes observed in *Home Building & Loan Association v. Blaisdell*, 290 U.S. 398 (1934) (see Vol. 2, Ch. 3);

Emergency does not create power. Emergency does not increase granted power or remove or diminish the restrictions imposed upon power granted or reserved. The Constitution was adopted in a period of grave emergency. Its grants of power to the federal government and its limitations of the power of the States were determined in the light of emergency, and they are not altered by emergency. . . .

While emergency does not create power, emergency may furnish the occasion for the exercise of power. . . . The constitutional question presented in the light of an emergency is whether the power possessed embraces the particular exercise of it in response to particular conditions.

The Court first confronted claims of inherent presidential powers in domestic affairs in *In re Neagle,* 135 U.S. 546 (1890). David Neagle, a U.S. marshal, had been assigned by the attorney general to protect Justice Stephen Field, after a disgruntled litigant threatened his life, while riding circuit in California. Neagle subsequently shot and killed the litigant and was charged with murder by state authorities. The federal government sought his release, contending that he was simply performing his duties as a marshal, even though there was no statutory authority for the president to assign bodyguards to federal judges. Over the dissent of Chief Justice Fuller and Justice Lamar, the Court ruled that the president's power to faithfully execute the laws was not "limited to the enforcement of acts of Congress." According to the majority it was unthinkable that the president should not have "within the domain of [his] powers no means of protecting . . . judges."

In another late-nineteenth century case, the Court underscored that the president's obligation to faithfully execute the laws conveyed certain inherent powers as well. In *In re Debs,* 158 U.S. 564 (1895), the Court unanimously upheld the contempt conviction of Eugene Debs, a prominent Socialist and labor leader, for violating an injunction against a labor union strike aimed at preventing the operation of certain railroads. Although there was no express authority for the government's injunction, Justice Brewer upheld the convictions and injunction on the grounds that "[t]he national government, given by the Constitution power to regulate interstate commerce, has by express statute assumed jurisdiction over such commerce when carried on railroads. It is charged, therefore, with the duty of keeping those highways of interstate free from obstruction."

By contrast in this century the Court has rejected broad claims of inherent presidential powers in domestic affairs. In the famous "Steel Seizure case," *Youngstown Sheet & Tube v. Sawyer* (1952) (see page 255), the justices divided six to three in striking down President Harry Truman's order for the secretary of commerce to seize and operate the nation's steel mills so as to avert a nationwide strike that might have jeopardized an undeclared war in Korea. However, only Justices Black and Douglas took the position that the president has no such inherent powers. The four others in the majority took more pragmatic approaches, emphasizing that Congress contemplated but rejected passing legislation authorizing the president to seize steel mills in the event of labor strikes. While contending that in different circumstances such an exercise of power might be justified, these justices found the president's actions in this case too drastic. Chief Justice Fred Vinson, along with two other dissenters, nevertheless adhered to the view advanced by *Neagle* in maintaining that Truman was simply "faithfully execut[ing] the laws by acting in an emergency to maintain the status quo, thereby preventing collapse of the legislative programs until Congress could act."

INSIDE THE COURT

The Argument for Inherent and Emergency Presidential Powers in "the Steel Seizure Case"

During oral arguments before federal district court Judge David A. Pine, Assistant Attorney General Holmes Baldridge contended in the following exchange that the president enjoys inherent and unreviewable powers in times of national emergency.

THE COURT: Now, Mr. Attorney General . . . I wonder if you would give me such assistance as you can . . . as to your power or as to your client's power.
    As I understand it you do not assert any statutory power.

MR. BALDRIDGE: That is correct.

THE COURT: And you do not assert any express constitutional power.

MR. BALDRIDGE: Well, your Honor, we base the President's power on Sections 1, 2 and 3 of Article II of the Constitution, and whatever inherent, implied or residual powers may flow therefrom. . . .
    We say that when an emergency situation in this country arises that is of such importance to the entire welfare of the country that something has to be done about it and has to be done now, and there is no statutory provision for handling the matter, that it is the duty of the Executive to step in and protect the national security and the national interests. . . .

THE COURT: So you contend the Executive has unlimited power in time of an emergency?

MR. BALDRIDGE: He has the power to take such action as is necessary to meet the emergency.

THE COURT: If the emergency is great, it is unlimited, isn't it?

MR. BALDRIDGE: I suppose if you carry it to its logical conclusion, that is true. But I do want to point out that there are limitations on the Executive power. One is the ballot box and the other is impeachment. . . .

THE COURT: And that the Executive determines the emergencies and the Courts cannot even review whether it is an emergency.

MR. BALDRIDGE: That is correct.

During the Nixon presidency, the Court once again confronted claims to inherent presidential powers invoked to protect national security interests. In the "Pentagon Papers" case, *New York Times Co. v. United States* (1971) (see page 273), a bitterly divided Court agreed only on a brief *per curiam* opinion rejecting, as a prior restraint on freedom of the press, the administration's efforts to enjoin the publication of a history of America's involvement in Vietnam that was prepared by a California think tank, the Rand Corporation, for the Department of Defense and classified top secret. Although all nine justices issued separate opinions in the six to three decision, five justices—Black, Douglas, Stewart, White, and Marshall—indicated that the president has no power, without prior congressional authorization, to suppress the publication of classified documents in the interests of national security.[1]

The following year in *United States v. United States District Court,* 407 U.S. 297 (1972), the Court dealt another blow to claims of inherent power by the Nixon presidency. The administration had wiretapped the offices of a number of domestic organizations to gather intelligence information in the interests of national security. The justices (eight to zero) ruled that such domestic security surveillance, conducted without congressional guidelines or judicially issued search warrants, ran afoul of the Fourth Amendment's guarantee against unreasonable searches and seizures. Subsequently, Congress passed the Foreign Intelligence Surveillance Act of 1978, requiring the government to obtain a warrant prior to undertaking electronic surveillance for the purpose of obtaining foreign intelligence information.

Despite these rulings, the permissible scope of presidential power that may be invoked in the interests of national security remains a matter of considerable contention, especially when supported by congressional legislation but challenged as infringing on First Amendment freedoms.[2] Although the Court has not squarely addressed this controversy, note that five justices in the "Pentagon Papers" case suggest that the president may enjoin the publication of documents in the interest of "national security" when expressly authorized to do so by Congress. Also, in *Snepp v. United States* (1980) (see page 154), the Court upheld over First Amendment objections the Central Intelligence Agency's (CIA) requirements, based in part on statutory authority, that employees and former employees submit any writing related to the agency for prepublication review to safeguard interests in foreign affairs and national security.

In *United States v. The Progressive, Inc.,* 467 F.Supp. 990 (1979), the government sought and obtained from a federal district court a temporary injunction against the publication of an article titled

"The H-Bomb Secret: How We Got It, Why We're Telling It."
It did so under the Atomic Energy Act, which authorizes the
government to obtain a temporary or permanent injunction
against the dissemination of any "restricted data" concerning
the construction of atomic weapons. Judge Robert W. Warren
found "no plausible reason why the public needs to know the
technical details about hydrogen bomb construction to carry on
an informed debate" about nuclear proliferation. And he distinguished this case from *The New York Times* case, observing,

> In the first place, the study involved in the *New York Times* case contained
> historical data relating to events that occurred some three to twenty
> years previously. Secondly, the Supreme Court agreed with the lower
> court that no cogent reasons were advanced by the government as to
> why the article affected national security except that publication might
> cause some embarrassment to the United States. A final and most vital
> difference between these two cases is the fact that a specific statute is
> involved here. Section 2274 of The Atomic Energy Act prohibits anyone
> from communicating, transmitting or disclosing any restricted data to
> any person "with reason to believe such data will be utilized to injure
> the United States or to secure an advantage to any foreign nation."

But when a similar article appeared in another publication, the
government abandoned its efforts to permanently enjoin *The
Progressive* magazine's article. The Supreme Court thus did not
rule on the government's actions and whether the Atomic Energy
Act is overly broad or so vague as to infringe on First Amendment
freedoms.[3]

NOTES

1. See Peter Junger, "Down Memory Lane: The Case of the Pentagon
Papers," 23 *Case Western Reserve Law Review* 3 (1971).

2. In *Laird v. Tatum,* 408 U.S. 1 (1972), the Court (six to three)
denied standing to a groups of citizens challenging the army's domestic
surveillance program, undertaken at the direction of the White House
but without congressional authorization, of activists political groups,
including the Southern Christian Leadership Conference and the National Association for the Advancement of Colored People. The majority
held that they had failed to show direct injury and a "chilling effect"
on their First Amendment freedoms resulting from the army's use of
undercover agents to infiltrate their organizations and collect data on
their activities.

3. For further discussion, see David M. O'Brien, *The Public's Right
to Know: The Supreme Court and the First Amendment* (New York: Praeger,
1981), Ch. 5.

SELECTED BIBLIOGRAPHY

Hoffman, Daniel. *Government Secrecy and the Founding Fathers.* Westport, CT: Greenwood, 1981.

Randall, James. *Constitutional Problems under Lincoln.* Urbana: University of Illinois Press, 1964.

Westin, Alan. *Anatomy of a Constitutional Law Case.* New York: Macmillan, 1958.

Youngstown Sheet & Tube Co. v. Sawyer

343 U.S. 579, 72 S.Ct. 863 (1952)

A labor dispute that began in 1951 during the "police action" (undeclared war) in Korea eventually led the United Steel Workers to call a strike to shut down steel mills in April 1952. Instead of invoking provisions of the Taft-Hartley Act, which passed over a presidential veto and provided for a cooling-off period in labor-management disputes, hours before the strike President Harry S. Truman issued Executive Order 10340. It directed Secretary of Commerce Charles Sawyer to seize and operate the steel mills. The steel companies immediately sought an injunction in a federal district court to restrain Sawyer from seizing the mills. Judge David Pine ruled against the president, observing,

There is no express grant of power in the Constitution authorizing the President to direct this seizure. There is no grant of power from which it reasonably can be implied. There is no enactment of Congress authorizing it. . . .

The President therefore must derive this broad "residuum of power" or "inherent" power from the Constitution itself, more particularly Article II thereof, which contains that grant of Executive power. . . .

[But, t]here is no undefined residuum of power which he can exercise because it seems to him to be in the public interest, and there is nothing in the *Neagle* case and its definition of a law of the United States, or in other precedents, warranting such an inference.

When the labor unions then called another strike, the government obtained from an appellate court a stay on Judge Pine's order pending direct appeal to the Supreme Court. The Court expedited the case, granting *certiorari* on May 3, hearing oral arguments on May 12, and handing down its decision within a month, on June 12, 1952. President Truman was angered by the six-to-three ruling that he had exceeded his powers, particularly because the majority included two of his own appointees, Justices Tom Clark and Harold Burton, and Clark, earlier as attorney general, had advised Truman that he had the power to deal with such emergences. Chief Justice Fred Vinson and Justice Sherman Minton, two other appointees of Truman, dissented along with Justice Stanley Reed.

Justice BLACK delivers the opinion of the Court.

We are asked to decide whether the President was acting within his constitutional power when he issued an order directing the Secretary of Commerce to take possession of and operate most of the Nation's steel mills. The mill owners argue that the President's order amounts to lawmaking, a legislative function which the Constitution has expressly confided to the Congress and not to the President. The Government's position is that the order was made on findings of the President that his action was necessary to avert a national catastrophe which would inevitably result from a stoppage of steel production, and that in meeting this grave emergency the President was acting within the aggregate of his constitutional powers as the Nation's Chief Executive and the Commander in Chief of the Armed Forces of the United States. The issue emerges here from the following series of events:

In the latter part of 1951, a dispute arose between the steel companies and their employees over terms and conditions that should be included in new collective bargaining agreements. Long-continued conferences failed to resolve the dispute. On December 18, 1951, the employees' representative, United Steelworkers of America, C. I. O., gave notice of an intention to strike when the existing bargaining agreements expired on December 31. The Federal Mediation and Conciliation Service then intervened in an effort to get labor and management to agree. This failing, the President on December 22, 1951, referred the dispute to the Federal Wage Stabilization Board to investigate and make recommendations for fair and equitable terms of settlement. This Board's report resulted in no settlement. On April 4, 1952, the Union gave notice of a nation-wide strike called to begin at 12:01 A.M. April 9. The indispensability of steel as a component of substantially all weapons and other war materials led the President to believe that the proposed work stoppage would immediately jeopardize our national defense and that governmental seizure of the steel mills was necessary in order to assure the continued availability of steel. Reciting these considerations for his action, the President, a few hours before the strike was to begin, issued Executive Order 10340. The order directed the Secretary of Commerce to take possession of most of the steel mills and keep

them running. The Secretary immediately issued his own possessory orders, calling upon the presidents of the various seized
companies to serve as operating managers for the United States.
They were directed to carry on their activities in accordance with
regulations and directions of the Secretary. The next morning
the President sent a message to Congress reporting his action.
Cong. Rec., April 9, 1952, p. 3962. Twelve days later he sent a
second message. Cong. Rec., April 21, 1952, p. 4192. Congress
has taken no action.

Obeying the Secretary's orders under protest, the companies
brought proceedings against him in the District Court. Their
complaints charged that the seizure was not authorized by an
act of Congress or by any constitutional provisions. The District
Court was asked to declare the orders of the President and the
Secretary invalid and to issue preliminary and permanent injunctions restraining their enforcement. Opposing the motion for
preliminary injunction, the United States asserted that a strike
disrupting steel production for even a brief period would so endanger the well-being and safety of the Nation that the President
had "inherent power" to do what he had done—power "supported
by the Constitution, by historical precedent, and by court decisions." The Government also contended that in any event no
preliminary injunction should be issued because the companies
had made no showing that their available legal remedies were
inadequate or that their injuries from seizure would be irreparable.
Holding against the Government on all points, the District Court
on April 30 issued a preliminary injunction restraining the Secretary from "continuing the seizure and possession of the plant
. . . and from acting under the purported authority of Executive
Order No. 10340." On the same day the Court of Appeals stayed
the District Court's injunction. Deeming it best that the issues
raised be promptly decided by this Court, we granted certiorari
on May 3 and set the cause for argument on May 12. . . .

The President's power, if any, to issue the order must stem
either from an act of Congress or from the Constitution itself.
There is no statute that expressly authorizes the President to
take possession of property as he did here. Nor is there any act
of Congress to which our attention has been directed from which
such a power can fairly be implied. Indeed, we do not understand
the Government to rely on statutory authorization for this seizure.
There are two statutes which do authorize the President to take
both personal and real property under certain conditions. However, the Government admits that these conditions were not met
and that the President's order was not rooted in either of the
statutes. The Government refers to the seizure provisions of one
of these statutes (§ 201 (b) of the Defense Production Act) as
"much too cumbersome, involved, and time-consuming for the
crisis which was at hand."

Moreover, the use of the seizure technique to solve labor disputes in order to prevent work stoppages was not only unauthorized by any congressional enactment; prior to this controversy, Congress had refused to adopt that method of settling labor disputes. When the Taft-Hartley Act was under consideration in 1947, Congress rejected an amendment which would have authorized such governmental seizures in cases of emergency. Apparently it was thought that the technique of seizure, like that of compulsory arbitration, would interfere with the process of collective bargaining. Consequently, the plan Congress adopted in that Act did not provide for seizure under any circumstances. Instead, the plan sought to bring about settlements by use of the customary devices of mediation, conciliation, investigation by boards of inquiry, and public reports. In some instances temporary injunctions were authorized to provide cooling-off periods. All this failing, unions were left free to strike after a secret vote by employees as to whether they wished to accept their employers' final settlement offer.

It is clear that if the President had authority to issue the order he did, it must be found in some provisions of the Constitution. And it is not claimed that express constitutional language grants this power to the President. The contention is that presidential power should be implied from the aggregate of his powers under the Constitution. Particular reliance is placed on provisions in Article II which say that "the executive Power shall be vested in a President . . ."; that "he shall take Care that the Laws be faithfully executed"; and that he "shall be Commander in Chief of the Army and Navy of the United States."

The order cannot properly be sustained as an exercise of the President's military power as Commander in Chief of the Armed Forces. The Government attempts to do so by citing a number of cases upholding broad powers in military commanders engaged in day-to-day fighting in a theater of war. Such cases need not concern us here. Even though "theater of war" [is] an expanding concept, we cannot with faithfulness to our constitutional system hold that the Commander in Chief of the Armed Forces has the ultimate power as such to take possession of private property in order to keep labor disputes from stopping production. This is a job for the Nation's lawmakers, not for its military authorities.

Nor can the seizure order be sustained because of the several constitutional provisions that grant executive power to the President. In the framework of our Constitution, the President's power to see that the laws are faithfully executed refutes the idea that he is to be a lawmaker. The Constitution limits his functions in the lawmaking process to the recommending of laws he thinks wise and the vetoing of laws he thinks bad. And the Constitution is neither silent nor equivocal about who shall make laws which the President is to execute. The first section of the first article says that "All legislative Powers herein granted shall be vested in a Congress of the United States. . . ." After granting many powers to the Congress, Article I goes on to provide that Congress may "make all Laws which shall be necessary and proper for carrying into Execution the foregoing Powers and all other Powers vested by this Constitution in the Government of the United States, or in any Department or Officer thereof."

The President's order does not direct that a congressional policy be executed in a manner prescribed by Congress—it directs that a presidential policy be executed in a manner prescribed by the President. The preamble of the order itself, like that of many statutes, sets out reasons why the President believes certain policies should be adopted, proclaims these policies as rules of conduct to be followed, and again, like a statute, authorizes a government official to promulgate additional rules and regulations consistent with the policy proclaimed and needed to carry that policy into execution. The power of Congress to adopt such public policies as those proclaimed by the order is beyond question. It can authorize the taking of private property for public use. It can make laws regulating the relationships between employers and employees, prescribing rules designed to settle labor disputes, and fixing wages and working conditions in certain fields of our economy. The Constitution did not subject this law-making power of Congress to presidential or military supervision or control.

It is said that other Presidents without congressional authority have taken possession of private business enterprises in order to settle labor disputes. But even if this be true, Congress has not thereby lost its exclusive constitutional authority to make laws necessary and proper to carry out the powers vested by the Constitution "in the Government of the United States, or in any Department or Officer thereof."

The Founders of this Nation entrusted the law making power to the Congress alone in both good and bad times. It would do no good to recall the historical events, the fears of power and the hopes for freedom that lay behind their choice. Such a review would but confirm our holding that this seizure order cannot stand.

The judgment of the District Court is affirmed.

Affirmed.

Justice JACKSON concurring.

That comprehensive and undefined presidential powers hold both practical advantages and grave dangers for the country will impress anyone who has served as legal adviser to a President in time of transition and public anxiety. While an interval of detached reflection may temper teachings of that experience, they probably are a more realistic influence on my views than the conventional materials of judicial decision which seem unduly to accentuate doctrine and legal fiction. But as we approach the question of presidential power, we half overcome mental hazards by recognizing them. The opinions of judges, no less than executives and publicists, often suffer the infirmity of confusing the issue of a power's validity with the cause it is invoked to promote, of confounding the permanent executive office with its temporary occupant. The tendency is strong to emphasize transient results upon policies—such as wages or stabilization—and lose sight of enduring consequences upon the balanced power structure of our Republic.

A judge, like an executive adviser, may be surprised at the poverty of really useful and unambiguous authority applicable to concrete problems of executive power as they actually present themselves. Just what our forefathers did envision, or would have envisioned had they foreseen modern conditions, must be divined from materials almost as enigmatic as the dreams Joseph was called upon to interpret for Pharaoh. A century and a half of partisan debate and scholarly speculation yields no net result but only supplies more or less apt quotations from respected sources on each side of any question. They largely cancel each other. And court decisions are indecisive because of the judicial practice of dealing with the largest questions in the most narrow way.

The actual art of governing under our Constitution does not and cannot conform to judicial definitions of the power of any of its branches based on isolated clauses or even single Articles torn from context. While the Constitution diffuses power the better to secure liberty, it also contemplates that practice will integrate the dispersed powers into a workable government. It enjoins upon its branches separateness but interdependence, autonomy but reciprocity. Presidential powers are not fixed but fluctuate, depending upon their disjunction or conjunction with those of Congress. We may well begin by a somewhat over-simplified grouping of practical situations in which a President may doubt, or others may challenge, his powers, and by distinguishing roughly the legal consequences of this factor of relativity.

1. When the President acts pursuant to an express or implied authorization of Congress, his authority is at its maximum, for it includes all that he possesses in his own right plus all that Congress can delegate. In these circumstances, and in these only, may he be said (for what it may be worth), to personify the federal sovereignty. If his act is held unconstitutional under these circumstances, it usually means that the Federal Government as an undivided whole lacks power. A seizure executed by the President pursuant to an Act of Congress would be supported by the strongest of presumptions and the widest latitude of judicial interpreta-

tion, and the burden of persuasion would rest heavily upon any who might attack it.

2. When the President acts in absence of either a congressional grant or denial of authority, he can only rely upon his own independent powers, but there is a zone of twilight in which he and Congress may have concurrent authority, or in which its distribution is uncertain. Therefore, congressional inertia, indifference or quiescence may sometimes, at least as a practical matter, enable, if not invite, measures on independent presidential responsibility. In this area, any actual test of power is likely to depend on the imperatives of events and contemporary imponderables rather than on abstract theories of law.

3. When the President takes measures incompatible with the expressed or implied will of Congress, his power is at its lowest ebb, for then he can rely only upon his own constitutional powers minus any constitutional powers of Congress over the matter. Courts can sustain exclusive Presidential control in such a case only by disabling the Congress from acting upon the subject. Presidential claim to a power at once so conclusive and preclusive must be scrutinized with caution, for what is at stake is the equilibrium established by our constitutional system.

Into which of these classifications does this executive seizure of the steel industry fit? It is eliminated from the first by admission, for it is conceded that no congressional authorization exists for this seizure. That takes away also the support of the many precedents and declarations which were made in relation, and must be confined, to this category.

Can it then be defended under flexible tests available to the second category? It seems clearly eliminated from that class because Congress has not left seizure of private property an open field but has covered it by three statutory policies inconsistent with this seizure. In cases where the purpose is to supply needs of the Government itself, two courses are provided: one, seizure of a plant which fails to comply with obligatory orders placed by the Government, another, condemnation of facilities, including temporary use under the power of eminent domain. The third is applicable where it is the general economy of the country that is to be protected rather than exclusive governmental interests. None of these were invoked. In choosing a different and inconsistent way of his own, the President cannot claim that it is necessitated or invited by failure of Congress to legislate upon the occasions, grounds and methods for seizure of industrial properties.

This leaves the current seizure to be justified only by the severe tests under the third grouping, where it can be supported only by any remainder of executive power after subtraction of such powers as Congress may have over the subject. In short, we can sustain the President only by holding that seizure of such strikebound industries is within his domain and beyond control by

Congress. Thus, this Court's first review of such seizures occurs under circumstances which leave Presidential power most vulnerable to attack and in the least favorable of possible constitutional postures.

I did not suppose, and I am not persuaded, that history leaves it open to question, at least in the courts, that the executive branch, like the Federal Government as a whole, possesses only delegated powers. The purpose of the Constitution was not only to grant power, but to keep it from getting out of hand. However, because the President does not enjoy unmentioned powers does not mean that the mentioned ones should be narrowed by a niggardly construction. Some clauses could be made almost unworkable, as well as immutable, by refusal to indulge some latitude of interpretation for changing times. I have heretofore, and do now, give to the enumerated powers the scope and elasticity afforded by what seem to be reasonable practical implications instead of the rigidity dictated by a doctrinaire textualism. . . .

Loose and irresponsible use of adjectives colors all non-legal and much legal discussion of presidential powers. "Inherent" powers, "implied" powers, "incidental" powers, "plenary" powers, "war" powers and "emergency" powers are used, often interchangeably and without fixed or ascertainable meanings.

The vagueness and generality of the clauses that set forth presidential powers afford a plausible basis for pressures within and without an administration for presidential action beyond that supported by those whose responsibility it is to defend his actions in court. The claim of inherent and unrestricted presidential powers has long been a persuasive dialectical weapon in political controversy. While it is not surprising that counsel should grasp support from such unadjudicated claims of power, a judge cannot accept self-serving press statements of the attorney for one of the interested parties as authority in answering a constitutional question, even if the advocate was himself. But prudence has counseled that actual reliance on such nebulous claims stop short of provoking a judicial test.

The Solicitor General, acknowledging that Congress has never authorized the seizure here, says practice of prior Presidents has authorized it. He seeks color of legality from claimed executive precedents, chief of which is President Roosevelt's seizure on June 9, 1941, of the California plant of the North American Aviation Company. Its superficial similarities with the present case, upon analysis, yield to distinctions so decisive that it cannot be regarded as even a precedent, much less an authority for the present seizure.

The appeal, however, that we declare the existence of inherent powers *ex necessitate* to meet an emergency asks us to do what many think would be wise, although it is something the forefathers omitted. They knew what emergencies were, knew the pressures they engender for authoritative action, knew, too, how they afford a ready pretext for usurpation. We may also suspect that they suspected that emergency powers would tend to kindle emergencies. Aside from suspension of the privilege of the writ of habeas corpus in time of rebellion or invasion, when the public safety may require it, they made no express provision for exercise of extraordinary authority because of a crisis. I do not think we rightfully may so amend their work, and, if we could, I am not convinced it would be wise to do so, although many modern nations have forthrightly recognized that war and economic crises may upset the normal balance between liberty and authority. Their experience with emergency powers may not be irrelevant to the argument here that we should say that the Executive, of his own volition, can invest himself with undefined emergency powers. . . .

In view of the ease, expedition and safety with which Congress can grant and has granted large emergency powers, certainly ample to embrace this crisis, I am quite unimpressed with the argument that we should affirm possession of them without statute. Such power either has no beginning or it has no end. If it exists, it need submit to no legal restraint. I am not alarmed that it would plunge us straightway into dictatorship, but it is at least a step in that wrong direction.

As to whether there is imperative necessity for such powers, it is relevant to note the gap that exists between the President's paper powers and his real powers. The Constitution does not disclose the measure of the actual controls wielded by the modern presidential office. That instrument must be understood as an Eighteenth-Century sketch of a government hoped for, not as a blueprint of the Government that is. Vast accretions of federal power, eroded from that reserved by the States, have magnified the scope of presidential activity. Subtle shifts take place in the centers of real power that do not show on the face of the Constitution.

Executive power has the advantage of concentration in a single head in whose choice the whole Nation has a part, making him the focus of public hopes and expectations. In drama, magnitude and finality his decisions so far overshadow any others that almost alone he fills the public eye and ear. No other personality in public life can begin to compete with him in access to the public mind through modern methods of communications. By his prestige as head of state and his influence upon public opinion he exerts a leverage upon those who are supposed to check and balance his power which often cancels their effectiveness.

Moreover, rise of the party system has made a significant extra-constitutional supplement to real executive power. No appraisal of his necessities is realistic which overlooks that he heads a political system as well as a legal system. Party loyalties and interests, sometimes more binding than law, extend his effective control into branches of government other than his own and he often may win, as a political leader, what he cannot command under the Constitution. Indeed, Woodrow Wilson, commenting on the President as leader both of his party and of the Nation, observed, "If he rightly interpret the national thought and boldly insist upon it, he is irresistible. . . . His office is anything he has the sagacity and force to make it." I cannot be brought to believe that this country will suffer if the Court refuses further to aggrandize the presidential office, already so potent and so relatively immune from judicial review, at the expense of Congress.

But I have no illusion that any decision by this Court can keep power in the hands of Congress if it is not wise and timely in meeting its problems. A crisis that challenges the President equally, or perhaps primarily, challenges Congress. If not good law, there was worldly wisdom in the maxim attributed to Napoleon that "The tools belong to the man who can use them." We may say that power to legislate for emergencies belongs in the hands of Congress, but only Congress itself can prevent power from slipping through its fingers.

The essence of our free Government is "leave to live by no man's leave, underneath the law"—to be governed by those impersonal forces which we call law. Our Government is fashioned to fulfill this concept so far as humanly possible. The Executive, except for recommendation and veto, has no legislative power. The executive action was have here originates in the individual will of the President and represents an exercise of authority without law. No one, perhaps not even the President, knows the limits of the power he may seek to exert in this instance and the parties affected cannot learn the limit of their rights. We do not know today what powers over labor or property would be claimed to flow from Government possession if we should legalize it, what rights to compensation would be claimed or recognized, or on what contingency it would end. With all its defects, delays and inconveniences, men have discovered no technique for long preserving free government except that the Executive be under the law, and that the law be made by parliamentary deliberations.

Such institutions may be destined to pass away. But it is the duty of the Court to be last, not first, to give them up.

Justice BURTON concurring.

My position may be summarized as follows:
The validity of the President's order of seizure is at issue and ripe for decision. Its validity turns upon its relation to the constitutional division of governmental power between Congress and the President.

The Constitution has delegated to Congress power to authorize action to meet a national emergency of the kind we face. Aware of this responsibility, Congress has responded to it. It has provided at least two procedures for the use of the President. . . .

The controlling fact here is that Congress, within its constitutionally delegated power, has prescribed for the President specific procedures, exclusive of seizure, for his use in meeting the present type of emergency. Congress has reserved to itself the right to determine where and when to authorize the seizure of property in meeting such an emergency. Under these circumstances, the President's order of April 8 invaded the jurisdiction of Congress. It violated the essence of the principle of the separation of governmental powers. Accordingly, the injunction against its effectiveness should be sustained.

Justice CLARK concurring.

The limits of presidential power are obscure. However, Article II, no less than Article I, is part of "a constitution intended to endure for ages to come, and, consequently, to be adapted to the various crises of human affairs." Some of our Presidents, such as Lincoln, "felt that measures otherwise unconstitutional might become lawful by becoming indispensable to the preservation of the Constitution through the preservation of the nation." Others, such as Theodore Roosevelt, thought the President to be capable, as a "steward" of the people, of exerting all power save that which is specifically prohibited by the Constitution or the Congress. In my view—taught me not only by the decision of Chief Justice Marshall in *Little v. Barreme,* 2 Cranch 170 [1804], but also by a score of other pronouncements of distinguished members of this bench—the Constitution does grant to the President extensive authority in times of grave and imperative national emergency. In fact, to my thinking, such a grant may well be necessary to the very existence of the Constitution itself. As Lincoln aptly said, "[is] it possible to lose the nation and yet preserve the Constitution?" In describing this authority I care not whether one calls it "residual," "inherent," "moral," "implied," "aggregate," "emergency," or otherwise. I am of the conviction that those who have had the gratifying experience of being the President's lawyer have used one or more of these adjectives only with the utmost of sincerity and the highest of purpose.

I conclude that where Congress has laid down specific procedures to deal with the type of crisis confronting the President, he must follow those procedures in meeting the crisis; but that in the absence of such action by Congress, the President's independent power to act depends upon the gravity of the situation confronting the nation. I cannot sustain the seizure in question because . . . Congress had prescribed methods to be followed by the President in meeting the emergency at hand.

Justice DOUGLAS concurring.

There can be no doubt that the emergency which caused the President to seize these steel plants was one that bore heavily on the country. But the emergency did not create power; it merely marked an occasion when power should be exercised. And the fact that it was necessary that measures be taken to keep steel in production does not mean that the President, rather than the Congress, had the constitutional authority to act. The Congress as well as the President, is trustee of the national welfare. The President can act more quickly than the Congress. The President with the armed services at his disposal can move with force as well as with speed. All executive power—from the reign of ancient kings to the rule of modern dictators—has the outward appearance of efficiency.

Legislative power, by contrast, is slower to exercise. There must be delay while the ponderous machinery of committees, hearings, and debates is put into motion. That takes time; and while the Congress slowly moves into action, the emergency may take its toll in wages, consumer goods, war production, the standard of living of the people, and perhaps even lives. Legislative action may indeed often be cumbersome, time-consuming, and apparently inefficient. . . .

We therefore cannot decide this case by determining which branch of government can deal most expeditiously with the present crisis. The answer must depend on the allocation of powers under the Constitution. . . .

The legislative nature of the action taken by the President seems to me to be clear. When the United States takes over an industrial plant to settle a labor controversy, it is condemning property. The seizure of the plant is a taking in the constitutional sense. A permanent taking would amount to the nationalization of the industry. A temporary taking falls short of that goal. But though the seizure is only for a week or a month, the condemnation is complete and the United States must pay compensation for the temporary possession. . . .

The power of the Federal Government to condemn property is well established. *Kohl v. United States*, 91 U.S. 367 [1876]. It can condemn for any public purpose; and I have no doubt but that condemnation of a plant, factory, or industry in order to promote industrial peace would be constitutional. But there is a duty to pay for all property taken by the Government. The command of the Fifth Amendment is that no "private property be taken for public use, without just compensation." That constitutional requirement has an important bearing on the present case.

The President has no power to raise revenues. That power is in the Congress by Article I, Section 8 of the Constitution. The President might seize and the Congress by subsequent action might ratify the seizure. But until and unless Congress acted, no condemnation would be lawful. The branch of government that has the power to pay compensation for a seizure is the only one able to authorize a seizure or make lawful one that the President had effected. That seems to me to be the necessary result of the condemnation provision in the Fifth Amendment. It squares with the theory of checks and balances expounded by Justice BLACK in the opinion of the Court in which I join.

If we sanctioned the present exercise of power by the President, we would be expanding Article II of the Constitution and rewriting it to suit the political conveniences of the present emergency. . . .

We pay a price for our system of checks and balances, for the distribution of power among the three branches of government. It is a price that today may seem exorbitant to many. Today a kindly President uses the seizure power to effect a wage increase and to keep the steel furnaces in production. Yet tomorrow another President might use the same power to prevent a wage increase, to curb trade unionists, to regiment labor as oppressively as industry thinks it has been regimented by this seizure.

Justice FRANKFURTER concurring.

Before the cares of the White House were his own, President Harding is reported to have said that government after all is a very simple thing. He must have said that, if he said it, as a fleeting inhabitant of fairyland. The opposite is the truth. A constitutional democracy like ours is perhaps the most difficult of man's social arrangements to manage successfully. Our scheme of society is more dependent than any other form of government on knowledge and wisdom and self-discipline for the achievement of its aims. For our democracy implies the reign of reason on the most extensive scale. The Founders of this Nation were not imbued with the modern cynicism that the only thing that history teaches is that it teaches nothing. They acted on the conviction that the experience of man sheds a good deal of light on his nature. It sheds a good deal of light not merely on the need for effective power, if a society is to be at once cohesive and civilized, but also on the need for limitations on the power of governors over the governed. . . .

The pole-star for constitutional adjudications is John MARSHALL's greatest judicial utterance that "it is *a constitution* we are expounding." *McCulloch v. Maryland*, 4 Wheat. 316 [1819]. That requires both a spacious view in applying an instrument of government "made for an undefined and expanding future," *Hurtado v. People of State of California*, 110 U.S. 516 [1884], and as narrow a delimitation of the constitutional issues as the circumstances permit. Not the least characteristic of great statesmanship which the Framers manifested was the extent to which they did not attempt to bind the future. It is no less incumbent upon this Court to avoid putting fetters upon the future by needless pronouncements today.

MARSHALL's admonition that "it is *a constitution* we are expounding" is especially relevant when the Court is required to give legal sanctions to an underlying principle of the Constitution—that of separation of powers. . . .

The issue before us can be met, and therefore should be, without attempting to define the President's powers comprehensively. I shall not attempt to delineate what belongs to him by virtue of his office beyond the power even of Congress to contract; what authority belongs to him until Congress acts; what kind of problems may be dealt with either by the Congress or by the President or by both, what power must be exercised by the Congress and cannot be delegated to the President. It is as unprofitable to lump together in an undiscriminating hotch-potch past presidential actions claimed to be derived from occupancy of the office, as it is to conjure up hypothetical future cases. The judiciary may, as this case proves, have to intervene in determining where authority lies as between the democratic forces in our scheme of government. But in doing so we should be wary and humble. Such is the teaching of this Court's role in the history of the country.

It is in this mood and with this perspective that the issue before the Court must be approached. We must therefore put to one side consideration of what powers the President would have had if there had been no legislation whatever bearing on the authority asserted by the seizure, or if the seizure had been only for a short, explicitly temporary period, to be terminated automatically unless Congressional approval were given. These and other questions, like or unlike, are not now here. I would exceed my authority were I to say anything about them.

The question before the Court comes in this setting. Congress has frequently—at least 16 times since 1916—specifically provided for executive seizure of production, transportation, communications, or storage facilities. In every case it has qualified this grant of power with limitations and safeguards. This body of enactments—summarized in tabular form in Appendix I—demonstrates that Congress deemed seizure so drastic a power as to require that it be carefully circumscribed whenever the President was vested with this extraordinary authority. The power to seize has uniformly been given only for a limited period or for a defined emergency, or has been repealed after a short period. Its exercise has been restricted to particular circumstances such as "time of war or when war is imminent," the needs of "public safety" or of "national security or defense," or "urgent and impending need." The period of governmental operation has been limited, as, for instance, to "sixty days after the restoration of productive efficiency." Seizure statutes usually make executive action dependent on detailed conditions: for example, (a) failure or refusal of the owner of a plant to meet governmental supply needs or (b) failure of voluntary negotiations with the owner for the use of a plant necessary for great public ends. Congress often has specified the particular executive agency which should seize or operate the plants or whose judgment would appropriately test the need for seizure. Congress also has not left to implication that just compensation be paid; it has usually legislated in detail regarding enforcement of this litigation-breeding general requirement. . . .

In adopting the provisions which it did, by the Labor Management Relations Act of 1947, for dealing with a "national emergency" arising out of a breakdown in peaceful industrial relations, Congress was very familiar with Government seizure as a protective measure. On a balance of considerations Congress chose not to lodge this power in the President. It chose not to make available in advance a remedy to which both industry and labor were fiercely hostile. In deciding that authority to seize should be given to the President only after full consideration of the particular situation should show such legislation to be necessary, Congress presumably acted on experience with similar industrial conflicts in the past. It evidently assumed that industrial shutdowns in basic industries are not instances of spontaneous generation, and that danger warnings are sufficiently plain before the event to give ample opportunity to start the legislative process into action.

In any event, nothing can be plainer than that Congress made a conscious choice of policy in a field full of perplexity and peculiarly within legislative responsibility for choice. In formulating legislation for dealing with industrial conflicts, Congress could not more clearly and emphatically have withheld authority than it did in 1947. Perhaps as much so as is true of any piece of modern legislation, Congress acted with full consciousness of what it was doing and in the light of much recent history. Previous seizure legislation had subjected the powers granted to the President to restrictions of varying degrees of stringency. Instead of giving him even limited powers, Congress in 1947 deemed it wise to require the President, upon failure of attempts to reach a voluntary settlement, to report to Congress if he deemed the power of seizure a needed shot for his locker. The President could not ignore the specific limitations of prior seizure statutes. No more could he act in disregard of the limitation put upon seizure by the 1947 Act. . . .

By the Labor Management Relations Act of 1947, Congress

said to the President, "You may not seize. Please report to us and ask for seizure power if you think it is needed in a specific situation.". . .

It is not a pleasant judicial duty to find that the President has exceeded his powers and still less so when his purposes were dictated by concern for the Nation's well-being, in the assured conviction that he acted to avert danger. But it would stultify one's faith in our people to entertain even a momentary fear that the patriotism and the wisdom of the President and the Congress, as well as the long view of the immediate parties in interest, will not find ready accommodation for differences on matters which, however close to their concern and however intrinsically important, are overshadowed by the awesome issues which confront the world.

Chief Justice VINSON, with whom Justice REED and Justice MINTON join, dissenting.

Those who suggest that this is a case involving extraordinary powers should be mindful that these are extraordinary times. A world not yet recovered from the devastation of World War II has been forced to face the threat of another and more terrifying global conflict.

Accepting in full measure its responsibility in the world community, the United States was instrumental in securing adoption of the United Nations Charter, approved by the Senate by a vote of 89 to 2. The first purpose of the United Nations is to "maintain international peace and security, and to that end: to take effective collective measures for the prevention and removal of threats to the peace, and for the suppression of acts of aggression or other breaches of the peace.". . . In 1950, when the United Nations called upon member nations "to render every assistance" to repel aggression in Korea, the United States furnished its vigorous support. For almost two full years, our armed forces have been fighting in Korea, suffering casualties of over 108,000 men. Hostilities have not abated. The "determination of the United Nations to continue its action in Korea to meet the aggression" has been reaffirmed. Congressional support of the action in Korea has been manifested by provisions for increased military manpower and equipment and for economic stabilization. . . .

One is not here called upon even to consider the possibility of executive seizure of a farm, a corner grocery store or even a single industrial plant. Such considerations arise only when one ignores the central fact of this case—that the Nation's entire basic steel production would have shut down completely if there had been no Government seizure. Even ignoring for the moment whatever confidential information the President may possess as "the Nation's organ for foreign affairs," the uncontroverted affidavits in this record amply support the finding that "a work stoppage would immediately jeopardize and imperil our national defense.". . .

In passing upon the grave constitutional question presented in this case, we must never forget, as Chief Justice MARSHALL admonished, that the Constitution is "intended to endure for ages to come, and consequently, to be adapted to the various *crises* of human affairs," and that "[i]ts means are adequate to its ends." Cases do arise presenting questions which could not have been foreseen by the Framers. In such cases, the Constitution has been treated as a living document adaptable to new situations. But we are not called upon today to expand the Constitution to meet a new situation. For, in this case, we need only look to history and time-honored principles of constitutional law—principles that have been applied consistently by all branches of the Government throughout our history. It is those who assert the invalidity of the Executive Order who seek to amend the Constitution in this case.

A review of executive action demonstrates that our Presidents have on many occasions exhibited the leadership contemplated by the Framers when they made the President Commander in Chief, and imposed upon him the trust to "take Care that the Laws be faithfully executed." With or without explicit statutory authorization, Presidents have at such times dealt with national emergencies by acting promptly and resolutely to enforce legislative programs, at least to save those programs until Congress could act. Congress and the courts have responded to such executive initiative with consistent approval. . . .

The President reported to Congress the morning after the seizure that he acted because a work stoppage in steel production would immediately imperil the safety of the Nation by preventing execution of the legislative programs for procurement of military equipment. And, while a shutdown could be averted by granting the price concessions requested by plaintiffs, granting such concessions would disrupt the price stabilization program also enacted by Congress. Rather than fail to execute either legislative program, the President acted to execute both. . . .

The absence of a specific statute authorizing seizure of the steel mills as a mode of executing the laws—both the military procurement program and the anti-inflation program—has not until today been thought to prevent the President from executing the laws. . . .

There is no statute prohibiting seizure as a method of enforcing legislative programs. Congress has in no wise indicated that its legislation is not to be executed by the taking of private property (subject of course to the payment of just compensation) if its legislation cannot otherwise be executed. Indeed, the Universal

Military Training and Service Act authorizes the seizure of *any* plant that fails to fill a Government contract or the properties of *any* steel producer that fails to allocate steel as directed for defense production. And the Defense Production Act authorizes the President to requisition equipment and condemn real property needed without delay in the defense effort. Where Congress authorizes seizure in instances not necessarily crucial to the defense program, it can hardly be said to have disclosed an intention to prohibit seizures where essential to the execution of that legislative program.

Whatever the extent of Presidential power on more tranquil occasions, and whatever the right of the President to execute legislative programs as he sees fit without reporting the mode of execution to Congress, the single Presidential purpose disclosed on this record is to faithfully execute the laws by acting in an emergency to maintain the status quo, thereby preventing collapse of the legislative programs until Congress could act. The President's action served the same purposes as a judicial stay entered to maintain the status quo in order to preserve the jurisdiction of a court. In his Message to Congress immediately following the seizure, the President explained the necessity of his action in executing the military procurement and anti-inflation legislative programs and expressed his desire to cooperate with any legislative proposals approving, regulating or rejecting the seizure of the steel mills. Consequently, there is no evidence whatever of any Presidential purpose to defy Congress or act in any way inconsistent with the legislative will. . . .

The diversity of views expressed in the six opinions of the majority, the lack of reference to authoritative precedent, the repeated reliance upon prior dissenting opinions, the complete disregard of the uncontroverted facts showing the gravity of the emergency and the temporary nature of the taking all serve to demonstrate how far afield one must go to affirm the order of the District Court.

The broad executive power granted by Article II to an officer on duty 365 days a year cannot, it is said, be invoked to avert disaster. Instead, the President must confine himself to sending a message to Congress recommending action. Under this messenger-boy concept of the Office, the President cannot even act to preserve legislative programs from destruction so that Congress will have something left to act upon. There is no judicial finding that the executive action was unwarranted because there was in fact no basis for the President's finding of the existence of an emergency for, under this view, the gravity of the emergency and the immediacy of the threatened disaster are considered irrelevant as a matter of law. . . .

As the District Judge stated, this is no time for "timorous" judicial action. But neither is this a time for timorous executive action. Faced with the duty of executing the defense programs which Congress had enacted and the disastrous effects that any stoppage in steel production would have on those programs, the President acted to preserve those programs by seizing the steel mills. There is no question that the possession was other than temporary in character and subject to congressional direction— either approving, disapproving or regulating the manner in which the mills were to be administered and returned to the owners. The President immediately informed Congress of his action and clearly stated his intention to abide by the legislative will. No basis for claims of arbitrary action, unlimited powers or dictatorial usurpation of congressional power appears from the facts of this case. On the contrary, judicial, legislative and executive precedents throughout our history demonstrate that in this case the President acted in full conformity with his duties under the Constitution. Accordingly, we would reverse the order of the District Court.

New York Times Co. v. United States
403 U.S. 670, 91 S.Ct. 2140 (1971)

In 1971, amid growing opposition to the undeclared Vietnam War, the Nixon administration sought to enjoin *The New York Times* and the *Washington Post* from publishing a series of articles based on a forty-seven-volume study, *History of U.S. Decision Making Process on Viet Nam Policy.* The study was prepared in 1968 and was classified top secret—sensitive. *The New York Times* received duplicates of the study from Daniel Ellsberg, who had secretly copied them while working for a think tank and after his unsuccessful efforts to persuade leading politicians to publicize the study.

After several months of reviewing the documents, *The New York Times* commenced publication of selected items on June 13, 1971. Following the third installment the Department of Justice sought an injunction against publication of the balance of the series and obtained a temporary restraining order prohibiting further publication until June 19. On June 18 the *Washington Post* also printed two articles based on the study, and by five o'clock that day the government had filed a similar suit against its further publication of the material.

The next morning a district court denied the government's request for a preliminary injunction, but later in the day a circuit court judge extended the temporary restraining order until noon, June 21, to give a panel of the Court of Appeals for the District of Columbia Circuit in the opportunity to consider the government's application. On June 22, the circuit court remanded the case to the district court to determine whether any of the other materials posed "such grave and immediate danger" to the security of the country as to warrant prior restraint and a continued stay on publication until June 25. *The New York Times* promptly appealed to the Supreme Court to vacate the stay on publication and to expedite consideration of the case. On June 25 the Court granted *certiorari* and heard arguments the next day. Remarkably, four days later the Court issued no less than ten opinions: one brief *per curiam* opinion, six concurring and three dissenting opinions.

Per Curiam

We granted certiorari in these cases in which the United States seeks to enjoin the New York Times and the Washington Post from publishing the contents of a classified study entitled "History of U.S. Decision-Making Process on Viet Nam Policy."

"Any system of prior restraints of expression comes to this Court bearing a heavy presumption against its constitutional validity." *Bantam Books, Inc. v. Sullivan*, 372 U.S. 58 (1963); see also *Near v. Minnesota ex rel. Olson*, 283 U.S. 697 (1931). The Government "thus carries a heavy burden of showing justification for the imposition of such a restraint." *Organization for a Better Austin v. Keefe*, 402 U.S. 415 (1971). The District Court for the Southern District of New York in the *New York Times* case, 328 F.Supp. 324, and the District Court for the District of Columbia and the Court of Appeals for the District of Columbia Circuit, 446 F.2d 1327, in the *Washington Post* case held that the Government had not met that burden. We agree.

The judgment of the Court of Appeals for the District of Columbia Circuit is therefore affirmed. The order of the Court of Appeals for the Second Circuit is reversed and the case is remanded with directions to enter a judgment affirming the judgment of the District Court for the Southern District of New York. The stays entered June 25, 1971, by the Court are vacated.

Justice BLACK, with whom Justice DOUGLAS joins, concurring.

I believe that every moment's continuance of the injunctions against these newspapers amounts to a flagrant, indefensible, and continuing violation of the First Amendment. . . . In my view it is unfortunate that some of my Brethren are apparently willing to hold that the publication of news may sometimes be enjoined. Such a holding would make a shambles of the First Amendment. . . .

In seeking injunctions against these newspapers and in its presentation to the Court, the Executive Branch seems to have forgotten the essential purpose and history of the First Amendment. When the Constitution was adopted, many people strongly opposed it because the document contained no Bill of Rights to safeguard certain basic freedoms. They especially feared that the new powers granted to a central government might be interpreted to permit the government to curtail freedom of religion, press, assembly, and speech. . . . Madison and the other Framers of the First Amendment, able men that they were, wrote in language they earnestly believed could never be misunderstood: "Congress shall make no law . . . abridging the freedom . . . of the press. . . ." Both the history and language of the First Amendment support the view that the press must be left free to publish news, whatever the source, without censorship, injunctions, or prior restraints. . . .

The Government's case here is based on premises entirely different from those that guided the Framers of the First Amendment. The Solicitor General has carefully and emphatically stated:

> "Now, Justice [BLACK], your construction of . . . [the First Amendment] is well known, and I certainly respect it. You say that no law means no law, and that should be obvious. I can only say, Mr. Justice, that to me it is equally obvious that 'no law' does not mean 'no law,' and I would seek to persuade the Court that that is true. . . . [T]here are other parts of the Constitution that grant powers and responsibilities to the Executive, and . . . the First Amendment was not intended to make it impossible for the Executive to function or to protect the security of the United States."

And the Government argues in its brief that in spite of the First Amendment, "[t]he authority of the Executive Department to protect the nation against publication of information whose disclosure would endanger the national security stems from two interrelated sources: the constitutional power of the President over the conduct of foreign affairs and his authority as Commander-in-Chief."

In other words, we are asked to hold that despite the First Amendment's emphatic command, the Executive Branch, the Congress, and the Judiciary can make laws enjoining publication of current news and abridging freedom of the press in the name of "national security." The Government does not even attempt to rely on any act of Congress. Instead it makes the bold and dangerously farreaching contention that the courts should take it upon themselves to "make" a law abridging freedom of the press in the name of equity, presidential power and national security. . . . To find that the President has "inherent power" to halt the publication of news by resort to the courts would wipe out the First Amendment and destroy the fundamental liberty and security of the very people the Government hopes to make "secure." No one can read the history of the adoption of the First Amendment without being convinced beyond any doubt that it was injunctions like those sought here that Madison and his collaborators intended to outlaw in this Nation for all time.

The word "security" is a broad, vague generality whose contours should not be invoked to abrogate the fundamental law embodied in the First Amendment. The guarding of military and diplomatic secrets at the expense of informed representative government provides no real security for our Republic. The Framers of the First Amendment, fully aware of both the need to defend a new nation and the abuses of the English and Colonial Governments, sought to give this new society strength and security by providing that freedom of speech, press, religion, and assembly should not be abridged.

Justice DOUGLAS, with whom Justice BLACK joins, concurring.

The Government says that it has inherent powers to go into court and obtain an injunction to protect the national interest, which in this case is alleged to be national security.

Near v. Minnesota ex rel. Olson, 283 U.S. 697 [1931], repudiated that expansive doctrine in no uncertain terms. . . .

Secrecy in government is fundamentally anti-democratic, perpetuating bureaucratic errors. Open debate and discussion of public issues are vital to our national health. On public questions there should be "uninhibited, robust, and wide-open" debate.

Justice BRENNAN concurring.

I write separately in these cases only to emphasize what should be apparent that our judgments in the present cases may not be taken to indicate the propriety, in the future, of issuing temporary stays and restraining orders to block the publication of material sought to be suppressed by the Government. So far as I can determine, never before has the United States sought to enjoin a newspaper from publishing information in its possession. The relative novelty of the questions presented, the necessary haste with which decisions were reached, the magnitude of the interests asserted, and the fact that all the parties have concentrated their arguments upon the question whether permanent restraints were proper may have justified at least some of the restraints heretofore imposed in these cases. . . . But even if it be assumed that some of the interim restraints were proper in the two cases before us, that assumption has no bearing upon the propriety of similar judicial action in the future. . . . More important, the First Amendment stands as an absolute bar to the imposition of judicial restraints in circumstances of the kind presented by these cases.

Justice STEWART, with whom Justice WHITE joins, concurring.

In the governmental structure created by our Constitution, the Executive is endowed with enormous power in the two related areas of national defense and international relations. This power, largely unchecked by the Legislative and Judicial branches, has been pressed to the very hilt since the advent of the nuclear missile age. For better or for worse, the simple fact is that a President of the United States possesses vastly greater constitutional independence in these two vital areas of power than does, say, a prime minister of a country with a parliamentary form of government.

In the absence of the governmental checks and balances present in other areas of our national life, the only effective restraint upon executive policy and power in the areas of national defense and international affairs may lie in an enlightened citizenry—in an informed and critical public opinion which alone can here protect the values of democratic government. For this reason, it is perhaps here that a press that is alert, aware, and free most vitally serves the basic purpose of the First Amendment. For without an informed and free press there cannot be an enlightened people.

Yet it is elementary that the successful conduct of international diplomacy and the maintenance of an effective national defense require both confidentiality and secrecy. Other nations can hardly deal with this Nation in an atmosphere of mutual trust unless they can be assured that their confidences will be kept. And within our own executive departments, the development of considered and intelligent international policies would be impossible if those charged with their formulation could not communicate with each other freely, frankly, and in confidence. In the area of basic national defense the frequent need for absolute secrecy is, of course, self-evident.

I think there can be but one answer to this dilemma, if dilemma it be. The responsibility must be where the power is. If the Constitution gives the Executive a large degree of unshared power in the conduct of foreign affairs and the maintenance of our national defense, then under the Constitution the Executive must have the largely unshared duty to determine and preserve the degree of internal security necessary to exercise that power successfully. It is an awesome responsibility, requiring judgment and wisdom of a high order. I should suppose that moral, political, and practical considerations would dictate that a very first principle of that wisdom would be an insistence upon avoiding secrecy for its own sake. For when everything is classified, then nothing is classified, and the system becomes one to be disregarded by the cynical or the careless, and to be manipulated by those intent on self-protection or self-promotion. I should suppose, in short, that the hallmark of a truly effective internal security system would be the maximum possible disclosure, recognizing that secrecy can best be preserved only when credibility is truly maintained. But be that as it may, it is clear to me that it is the constitutional duty of the Executive—as a matter of sovereign prerogative and not as a matter of law as the courts know law—through the promulgation and enforcement of executive regulations, to protect the confidentiality necessary to carry out its responsibilities in the fields of international relations and national defense.

This is not to say that Congress and the courts have no role to play. Undoubtedly Congress has the power to enact specific and appropriate criminal laws to protect government property and preserve government secrets. . . . Moreover, if Congress should pass a specific law authorizing civil proceedings in this field, the courts would likewise have the duty to decide the constitutionality of such a law as well as its applicability to the facts proved.

But in the cases before us we are asked neither to construe specific regulations nor to apply specific laws. We are asked, instead, to perform a function that the Constitution gave to the Executive, not the Judiciary. We are asked, quite simply, to prevent the publication by two newspapers of material that the Executive Branch insists should not, in the national interest, be published. I am convinced that the Executive is correct with respect to some of the documents involved. But I cannot say that disclosure of any of them will surely result in direct, immediate, and irreparable damage to our Nation or its people. That being so, there can under the First Amendment be but one judicial resolution of the issues before us. I join the judgments of the Court.

Justice WHITE, with whom Justice STEWART joins, concurring.

I concur in today's judgments, but only because of the concededly extraordinary protection against prior restraints enjoyed by the press under our constitutional system. I do not say that in no circumstances would the First Amendment permit an injunction against publishing information about government plans or operations. Nor, after examining the materials the Government characterizes as the most sensitive and destructive, can I deny that revelation of these documents will do substantial damage to public interests. Indeed, I am confident that their disclosure will have that result. But I nevertheless agree that the United States has not satisfied the very heavy burden that it must meet to warrant an injunction against publication in these cases, at least in the absence of express and appropriately limited congressional authorization for prior restraints in circumstances such as these.

The Government's position is simply stated: The responsibility of the Executive for the conduct of the foreign affairs and for the security of the Nation is so basic that the President is entitled to an injunction against publication of a newspaper story whenever he can convince a court that the information to be revealed threatens "grave and irreparable" injury to the public interest; and the injunction should issue whether or not the material to be published is classified, whether or not publication would be lawful under relevant criminal statutes enacted by Congress, and regardless of the circumstances by which the newspaper came into possession of the information.

At least in the absence of legislation by Congress, based on its own investigations and findings, I am quite unable to agree that the inherent powers of the Executive and the courts reach so far as to authorize remedies having such sweeping potential for inhibiting publications by the press. Much of the difficulty inheres in the "grave and irreparable danger" standard suggested by the United States. If the United States were to have judgment under such a standard in these cases, our decision would be of little guidance to other courts in other cases, for the material at issue here would not be available from the Court's opinion or from public records, nor would it be published by the press. Indeed, even today where we hold that the United States has not met its burden, the material remains sealed in court records and it is properly not discussed in today's opinions. Moreover, because the material poses substantial dangers to national interests and because of the hazards of criminal sanctions, a responsible press may choose never to publish the more sensitive materials. To sustain the Government in these cases would start the courts down a long and hazardous road that I am not willing to travel, at least without congressional guidance and direction.

Justice MARSHALL concurring.

The problem here is whether in these particular cases the Executive Branch has authority to invoke the equity jurisdiction of the courts to protect what it believes to be the national interest. See *In re Debs*, 158 U.S. 564 (1895). The Government argues that in addition to the inherent power of any government to protect itself, the President's power to conduct foreign affairs and his position as Commander in Chief give him authority to impose censorship on the press to protect his ability to deal effectively with foreign nations and to conduct the military affairs of the country. Of course, it is beyond cavil that the President has broad powers by virtue of his primary responsibility for the conduct of our foreign affairs and his position as Commander in Chief. . . .

It would, however, be utterly inconsistent with the concept of separation of powers for this Court to use its power of contempt to prevent behavior that Congress has specifically declined to prohibit. There would be a similar damage to the basic concept of these co-equal branches of Government if when the Executive Branch has adequate authority granted by Congress to protect "national security" it can choose instead to invoke the contempt power of a court to enjoin the threatened conduct. The Constitution provides that Congress shall make laws, the President execute laws, and courts interpret laws. It did not provide for government by injunction in which the courts and the Executive Branch can "make law" without regard to the action of Congress. It may be more convenient for the Executive Branch if it need only convince a judge to prohibit conduct rather than ask the Congress to pass a law, and it may be more convenient to enforce a contempt order than to seek a criminal conviction in a jury trial. Moreover, it may be considered politically wise to get a court to share the responsibility for arresting those who the Executive Branch has probable cause to believe are violating the law. But convenience and political considerations of the moment do not justify a basic departure from the principles of our system of government.

Chief Justice BURGER dissenting.

I suggest . . . these cases have been conducted in unseemly haste. . . .

Here, moreover, the frenetic haste is due in large part to the manner in which the Times proceeded from the date it obtained the purloined documents. It seems reasonably clear now that the haste precluded reasonable and deliberate judicial treatment of these cases and was not warranted. . . .

The newspapers make a derivative claim under the First Amendment; they denominate this right as the public "right to know"; by implication, the Times asserts a sole trusteeship of that right by virtue of its journalistic "scoop." The right is asserted as an absolute. Of course, the First Amendment right itself is not an absolute, as Justice HOLMES so long ago pointed out in his aphorism concerning the right to shout "fire" in a crowded theater if there was no fire. There are other exceptions, some of which Chief Justice HUGHES mentioned by way of example in *Near v. Minnesota ex rel. Olson*. There are no doubt other exceptions no one has had occasion to describe or discuss. . . .

It is not disputed that the Times has had unauthorized possession of the documents for three to four months, during which it has had its expert analysts studying them, presumably digesting them and preparing the material for publication. During all of this time, the Times, presumably in its capacity as trustee of the public's "right to know," has held up publication for purposes it considered proper and thus public knowledge was delayed. No doubt this was for a good reason; the analysis of 7,000 pages of complex material drawn from a vastly greater volume of material would inevitably take time and the writing of good news stories takes time. But why should the United States Government, from whom this information was illegally acquired by someone, along with all the counsel, trial judges, and appellate judges be placed under needless pressure? After these months of deferral, the alleged "right to know" has somehow and suddenly become a right that must be vindicated instanter.

Would it have been unreasonable, since the newspaper could anticipate the Government's objections to release of secret material, to give the Government an opportunity to review the entire collection and determine whether agreement could be reached on publication? Stolen or not, if security was not in fact jeopardized, much of the material could no doubt have been declassified, since it spans a period ending in 1968. With such an approach— one that great newspapers have in the past practiced and stated editorially to be the duty of an honorable press—the newspapers and Government might well have narrowed the area of disagreement as to what was and was not publishable, leaving the remainder to be resolved in orderly litigation, if necessary. To me it is hardly believable that a newspaper long regarded as a great institution in American life would fail to perform one of the basic and simple duties of every citizen with respect to the discovery or possession of stolen property or secret government documents. That duty, I had thought—perhaps naively—was to report forthwith, to responsible public officers. This duty rests on taxi drivers, Justices, and the New York Times. The course followed by the Times, whether so calculated or not, removed any possibility of orderly litigation of the issues. If the action of the judges up to now has been correct, that result is sheer happenstance.

Justice HARLAN, with whom THE CHIEF JUSTICE and Justice BLACKMUN join, dissenting.

With all respect, I consider that the Court has been almost irresponsibly feverish in dealing with these cases.

Both the Court of Appeals for the Second Circuit and the Court of Appeals for the District of Columbia Circuit rendered judgment on June 23. The New York Times' petition for certiorari, its motion for accelerated consideration thereof, and its application for interim relief were filed in this Court on June 24 at about 11 A.M. The application of the United States for interim relief in the *Post* case was also filed here on June 24 at about 7:15 P.M. This Court's order setting a hearing before us on June 26 at 11 A.M., a course which I joined only to avoid the possibility of even more peremptory action by the Court, was issued less than 24 hours before. The record in the *Post* case was filed with the Clerk shortly before 1 P.M. on June 25; the record in the *Times* case did not arrive until 7 or 8 o'clock that same night. The briefs of the parties were received less than two hours before argument on June 26.

This frenzied train of events took place in the name of the presumption against prior restraints created by the First Amendment. Due regard for the extraordinarily important and difficult questions involved in these litigations should have led the Court to shun such a precipitate timetable. In order to decide the merits of these cases properly, some or all of the following questions should have been faced:

1. Whether the Attorney General is authorized to bring these suits in the name of the United States. . . .

2. Whether the First Amendment permits the federal courts to enjoin publication of stories which would present a serious threat to national security. . . .

3. Whether the threat to publish highly secret documents is of itself a sufficient implication of national security to justify an injunction on the theory that regardless of the contents of the documents harm enough results simply from the demonstration of such a breach of secrecy.

4. Whether the unauthorized disclosure of any of these particular documents would seriously impair the national security.

5. What weight should be given to the opinion of high officers in the Executive Branch of the Government with respect to questions 3 and 4.

6. Whether the newspapers are entitled to retain and use the documents notwithstanding the seemingly uncontested facts that the documents, or the originals of which they are duplicates, were purloined from the Government's possession and that the newspapers received them with knowledge that they had been feloniously acquired. . . .

7. Whether the threatened harm to the national security or the Government's possessory interest in the documents justifies the issuance of an injunction against publication in light of—

a. The strong First Amendment policy against prior restraints on publication;

b. The doctrine against enjoining conduct in violation of criminal statutes; and

c. The extent to which the materials at issue have apparently already been otherwise disseminated.

These are difficult questions of fact, of law, and of judgment: the potential consequences of erroneous decision are enormous. The time which has been available to us, to the lower courts, and to the parties has been wholly inadequate for giving these cases the kind of consideration they deserve. It is a reflection on the stability of the judicial process that these great issues—as important as any that have arisen during my time on the Court—should have been decided under the pressures engendered by the torrent of publicity that has attended these litigations from their inception.

Forced as I am to reach the merits of these cases, I dissent from the opinion and judgments of the Court. . . .

It is plain to me that the scope of the judicial function in passing upon the activities of the Executive Branch of the Government in the field of foreign affairs is very narrowly restricted. This view is, I think, dictated by the concept of separation of powers upon which our constitutional system rests.

In a speech on the floor of the House of Representatives, Chief Justice John MARSHALL, then a member of that body, stated:

> "The President is the sole organ of the nation in its external relations, and its sole representative with foreign nations." 10 Annals of Cong. 613.

From that time, shortly after the founding of the Nation, to this, there has been no substantial challenge to this description of the scope of executive power. . . . I agree that, in performance of its duty to protect the values of the First Amendment against political pressures, the judiciary must review the initial Executive determination to the point of satisfying itself that the subject matter of the dispute does lie within the proper compass of the President's foreign relations power. Constitutional considerations forbid "a complete abandonment of judicial control." Moreover the judiciary may properly insist that the determination that disclosure of the subject matter would irreparably impair the national security be made by the head of the Executive Department concerned—here the Secretary of State or the Secretary of Defense—after actual personal consideration by that officer. This safeguard is required in the analogous area of executive claims of privilege for secrets of state. . . .

But in my judgment the judiciary may not properly go beyond these two inquiries and redetermine for itself the probable impact of disclosure on the national security.

Justice BLACKMUN dissenting.

The country would be none the worse off were the cases tried quickly, to be sure, but in the customary and properly deliberative manner. The most recent of the material, it is said, dates no later than 1968, already about three years ago, and the Times itself took three months to formulate its plan of procedure and, thus, deprived its public for that period.

The First Amendment, after all, is only one part of an entire Constitution. Article II of the great document vests in the Executive Branch primary power over the conduct of foreign affairs and places in that branch the responsibility for the Nation's safety. Each provision of the Constitution is important, and I cannot subscribe to a doctrine of unlimited absolutism for the First Amendment at the cost of downgrading other provisions. First Amendment absolutism has never commanded a majority of this Court. . . .

What is needed here is a weighing, upon properly developed standards, of the broad right of the press to print and of the very narrow right of the Government to prevent.

B. APPOINTMENT AND REMOVAL POWERS

Article II, Section 2 gives the president the power "to nominate, and by and with the advice and consent of the Senate, shall appoint ambassadors, other public ministers and consuls, judges of the supreme Court, and all other Officers of the United States, whose Appointments are not herein otherwise provided for, and which shall be established by Law." He also has the power to make "recess appointments" when the Senate is not in session, and those appointees may hold office through the next session even without Senate confirmation. However, Article II also provides that "Congress may by Law vest the Appointment of such *inferior Officers,* as they may think proper, in the President alone, in the Courts of Law, or in the Heads of Departments" (emphasis added). Thus while the president has the power to nominate and, with the consent of the Senate, appoint high government officials, Congress has the power to condition, and even deny the president, the appointment power over "inferior" government officials.

In theory, the nomination of government officials is the "sole act of the President," as Chief Justice Marshall observed in *Marbury v. Madison* (1803) (see page 45). Appointment of high-ranking officials—members of the cabinet and the Supreme Court—is generally a matter of personal presidential prerogative, although in extraordinary circumstances the Senate may deny confirmation for broad political reasons. The Constitutional Convention, however, envisioned some senatorial participation in the nomination and appointment process. And since the 1840s the tradition of "senatorial courtesy" has guaranteed a high de-

CONSTITUTIONAL HISTORY
Supreme Court Nominations Rejected, Postponed, or Withdrawn due to Senate Opposition[a]

Nominee	Year Nominated	Nominated by	Actions[b]
William Paterson[c]	1793	Washington	Withdrawn (for technical reasons)
John Rutledge[d]	1795	Washington	Rejected
Alexander Wolcott	1811	Madison	Rejected
John J. Crittenden	1828	J. Q. Adams	Postponed, 1829
Roger B. Taney[e]	1835	Jackson	Postponed
John C. Spencer	1844	Tyler	Rejected
Reuben H. Walworth	1844	Tyler	Withdrawn
Edward King	1844	Tyler	Postponed
Edward King[f]	1844	Tyler	Withdrawn, 1845
John M. Read	1845	Tyler	No action
George W. Woodward	1845	Polk	Rejected, 1846
Edward A. Bradford	1852	Fillmore	No action
George E. Badger	1853	Fillmore	Postponed
William C. Micou	1853	Fillmore	No action
Jeremiah S. Black	1861	Buchanan	Rejected
Henry Stanbery	1866	Johnson	No action
Ebenezer R. Hoar	1869	Grant	Rejected, 1870
George H. Williams[d]	1873	Grant	Withdrawn, 1874
Caleb Cushing[d]	1874	Grant	Withdrawn
Stanley Matthews[c]	1881	Hayes	No action
William B. Hornblower	1893	Cleveland	Rejected, 1894
Wheeler H. Peckham	1894	Cleveland	Rejected
John J. Parker	1930	Hoover	Rejected
Abe Fortas[g]	1968	Johnson	Withdrawn
Homer Thornberry	1968	Johnson	No action
Clement F. Haynsworth, Jr.	1969	Nixon	Rejected
G. Harrold Carswell	1970	Nixon	Rejected
Robert H. Bork	1987	Reagan	Rejected
Douglas H. Ginsburg	1987	Reagan	Withdrawn

[a] Article II of the Constitution provides the president shall nominate Supreme Court justices and lower court judges "with the advice and consent to the Senate." These are the nominees to the Supreme Court that the Senate has rejected or forced to be withdrawn from consideration.

[b] A year is given if different from the year of nomination.

[c] Reappointed and confirmed.

[d] Nominated for chief justice.

[e] Taney was reappointed and confirmed as chief justice.

[f] Second appointment.

[g] Associated justice nominated for chief justice.

gree of Senate participation in the nomination process, depending on the political strength or weakness of the president and whether the Senate is controlled by a loyal or opposition party. According to this tradition, the White House pays deference to a senator's preferences in filling vacancies in that senator's home state for offices, such as U.S. marshals, attorneys, and district judges.[1] Moreover, the Civil Service Act of 1883 restricts the president's prerogative over appointments within the executive branch to those among the highest grades of the civil service.

By contrast with the appointment power, the Constitution is silent about the removal power. It only expressly provides that the president, federal judges, and all civil officials are subject to "[i]mpeachment for, and Conviction of, Treason, Bribery, or other high Crimes and Misdemeanors." As a result, there are competing views of the power to remove government officials for other than impeachable offenses. Presidents have long contended that they enjoy the sole power of removal. Yet, because appointees are subject to Senate confirmation, it is sometimes claimed that the Senate shares in the removal power. Furthermore, because Congress creates offices, arguably it may place conditions on appointees' tenure and removal.

The Constitutional Convention left the issue of the removal power to be debated in 1789 in connection with the creation of the departments of foreign affairs, war, and the treasury. In the House of Representatives, James Madison initially argued that the secretaries of these departments should be "removable by the President." The "executive power" is vested in the president, who is obligated to "faithfully execute the Laws," Madison reasoned, and the removal power would render the department heads more accountable to the president. But he subsequently drew a distinction between the secretaries of foreign affairs and war, and the comptroller of the treasury. The latter was not "purely of an Executive nature," Madison pointed out, suggesting that "there may be strong reasons why an officer of this kind should not hold his office at the pleasure of the Executive branch of the Government." The House nevertheless passed a bill creating all three departments without specifying the president's power of removal. The Senate, however, distinguished between "executive departments" in giving the president the power to remove the secretaries of foreign affairs and war, while denying him that power over the head of the treasury. But when the House and Senate bills had to be reconciled, the Senate split evenly and Vice-President Adams cast the deciding vote giving the removal power to the president over all three departments.[2]

Despite presidential claims to the sole power of removal, Congress in the nineteenth century specified conditions for removing a number of government officials and even subjected the removal of some to "the advice and consent of the Senate." In the few cases dealing with the removal power that came before it, the Supreme Court indicated that presidential power could be limited when Congress clearly specified the conditions for removing certain inferior appointees from office.[3]

An expansive view of the president's removal power was, nonetheless, embraced by Chief Justice William Howard Taft in *Myers v. United States* (1926) (see page 288) over the sharp dissents of Justices Brandeis, Holmes, and McReynolds. But less than a decade later *Humphrey's Executor v. United States* (1935) (see page 302) unanimously held that a member of the Federal Trade Commission (FTC) could not be removed simply for policy reasons. Writing for the Court, Justice Sutherland drew a distinction between "purely executive" officials—such as the postmaster in *Myers*—which the president may remove at his discretion, and those like a FTC commissioner who have "quasi-judicial and quasi-legislative" duties, who are removable only for reasons specified by Congress.

The distinction between purely executive and quasi-judicial and quasi-legislative officials, as Justice Sutherland concedes, is inexact and invites controversy. *Humphrey's Executor* also remained sharply criticized, especially during the Reagan presidency, for limiting the powers of the president.[4]

The Court reassessed the removal powers of Congress and president in two major rulings in the 1980s. In *Bowsher v. Synar* (1986) (see page 306), the Court relied on *Humphrey's Executor* in striking down a portion of the Balanced Budget and Emergency Deficit Control Act because it empowered the comptroller general, who may be removed by a joint resolution of Congress, to make across-the-board reductions in federal spending if yearly maximums set for federal deficits were not met. Then in *Morrison v. Olson* (1988) (see page 318) Chief Justice Rehnquist reconsidered and rejected *Humphrey's Executor*'s reasoning, when upholding the appointment of independent counsel to investigate the misconduct of executive branch officials under the Ethics in Government Act. Compare the majority's view of the separation of powers with that of Justice Scalia in his dissenting opinion in *Morrison*. Justice Scalia again stood alone in dissenting from *Mistretta v. United States*, 109 S.Ct. 647 (1989). There, the Court upheld the Sentencing Reform Act of 1984, which created the U.S. Sentencing Commission and authorized it to promulgate binding guidelines for a range of determinate sentences for all categories of federal crime. In *Mistretta*, the majority held that Congress had not violated the principle of separation of powers by conferring on the president the power to appoint and to remove "for cause" members of the commission, including federal judges; nor did Congress run afoul of the nondelegation doctrine (discussed in the next section) by broadly delegating to the commission its power to make law.

NOTES

1. For further discussion of the role of Congress in the appointment of Supreme Court justices, see Henry J. Abraham, *Justices and Presidents*, 3rd ed. (New York: Oxford University Press, 1991); in the appointment of lower court judges, see David M. O'Brien, *Judicial Roulette* (New York: The Twentieth Century Fund, 1988); and in the appointment of executive branch officials, see G. Calvin McKenzie, *The Politics of Presidential Appointments* (New York: Free Press, 1981).

2. See Louis Fisher, "Congress and the Removal Powers," 10 *Congress & the Presidency* 63 (1983).

3. See *Parsons v. United States*, 167 U.S. 324 (1897) (removal of a U.S. attorney); *Shurtleff v. United States*, 189 U.S. 311 (1903) (customs official); and *Wallace v. United States*, 257 U.S. 541 (1922) (dismissal of officer for Quartermaster Corps.).

4. See Antonia Scalia's article, prepared before his appointment to the Supreme Court, "Historical Anomalies in Administrative Law," 1985 *Yearbook of the Supreme Court Historical Society*, 103.

SELECTED BIBLIOGRAPHY

Abraham, Henry. *Justices and Presidents*, 3rd ed. New York: Oxford University Press, 1991.

McKenzie, G. Galvin. *The Politics of Presidential Appointments*. New York: Free Press, 1981.

O'Brien, David. *Judicial Roulette: Report of the Twentieth Century Fund Task Force on Judicial Appointments*. New York: The Twentieth Century Fund, 1988.

Myers v. United States

272 U.S. 52, 47 S.Ct. 21 (1926)

A series of confrontations between the president and Congress over the removal power began with Andrew Jackson's "spoils system" and removal of more officials than all preceding presidents. Congress eventually passed the Tenure of Office Act in

1867, providing that every appointee confirmed by the Senate was entitled to hold office until a successor was appointed by the president with the advice and consent of the Senate. During the post–Civil War period Congress also passed legislation permitting the removal of officials only with senatorial approval. Among these laws was an 1876 statute requiring senatorial advice and consent for the removal of all first-, second-, and third-class postmasters. Presidential opposition to such restrictions persisted and Congress eventually repealed the Tenure of Office Act in 1887, but others including the 1876 statute governing the removal of postmasters remained enforced.

In 1920, President Woodrow Wilson was embattled with Congress over a section of the budget and accounting bill that provided that the comptroller general could be removed only by impeachment or a concurrent resolution of Congress. He contended that Congress could not in this way limit presidential power. Amid the struggle Wilson directed the postmaster general to remove, in violation of the 1876 law, Frank S. Myers, a postmaster in Portland, Oregon. Myers sued to recover his lost salary in the U.S. Court of Claims, which ruled against him. Louis Myers, the administrator of his estate, then appealed to the Supreme Court and challenged the constitutionality of the president's actions. The six-to-three ruling was announced in an opinion by Chief Justice (and former President) William Howard Taft, upholding a broad interpretation of the president's removal powers and drawing sharp dissents from both the most conservative justice, James McReynolds, and the Court's most liberal justices, Louis Brandeis and Oliver Holmes.

Chief Justice TAFT delivers the opinion of the Court.

This case presents the question whether under the Constitution the President has the exclusive power of removing executive officers of the United States whom he has appointed by and with the advice and consent of the Senate. . . .

The debates in the Constitutional Convention indicated an intention to create a strong executive, and after a controversial discussion the executive power of the government was vested in one person and many of his important functions were specified so as to avoid the humiliating weakness of the Congress during the Revolution and under the Articles of Confederation.

Mr. Madison and his associates in the discussion in the House dwelt at length upon the necessity there was for construing article 2 to give the President the sole power of removal in his responsibility for the conduct of the executive branch, and enforced this by emphasizing his duty expressly declared in the third section of the article to "take care that the laws be faithfully executed." Madison, 1 Annals of Congress, 496, 497.

The vesting of the executive power in the President was essentially a grant of the power to execute the laws. But the President alone and unaided could not execute the laws. He must execute them by the assistance of subordinates. This view has since been repeatedly affirmed by this court. As he is charged specifically to take care that they be faithfully executed, the reasonable implication, even in the absence of express words, was that as part of his executive power he should select those who were to act for him under his direction in the execution of the laws. The further implication must be, in the absence of any express limitation respecting removals, that as his selection of administrative officers is essential to the execution of the laws by him, so must be his power of removing those for whom he cannot continue to be responsible. Fisher Ames, 1 Annals of Congress, 474. It was urged that the natural meaning of the term "executive power" granted the President included the appointment and removal of executive subordinates. If such appointments and removals were not an exercise of the executive power, what were they? They certainly were not the exercise of legislative or judicial power in government as usually understood. . . .

The power to prevent the removal of an officer who has served under the President is different from the authority to consent to or reject his appointment. When a nomination is made, it may be presumed that the Senate is, or may become, as well advised as to the fitness of the nominee as the President, but in the nature of things the defects in ability or intelligence or loyalty in the administration of the laws of one who has served as an officer under the President are facts as to which the President, or his trusted subordinates, must be better informed than the Senate, and the power to remove him may therefore be regarded as confined for very sound and practical reasons, to the governmental authority which has administrative control. The power of removal is incident to the power of appointment, not to the power of advising and consenting to appointment, and when the grant of the executive power is enforced by the express mandate to take care that the laws be faithfully executed, it emphasizes the necessity for including within the executive power as conferred the exclusive power of removal. . . .

The view of Mr. Madison and his associates was that not only did the grant of executive power to the President in the first section of article 2 carry with it the power of removal, but the express recognition of the power of appointment in the second section enforced this view on the well-approved principle of constitutional and statutory construction that the power of removal of executive officers was incident to the power of appointment. It was agreed by the opponents of the bill, with only one or two exceptions, that as a constitutional principle the power of appointment carried with it the power of removal. Roger Sherman, 1 Annals of Congress, 491. This principle as a rule of constitutional and statutory construction, then generally conceded, has been recognized ever since. . . . The reason for the principle is that those in charge of and responsible for administering functions of government, who select their executive subordinates, need in meeting their responsibility to have the power to remove those whom they appoint.

Under section 2 of article 2, however, the power of appointment by the executive is restricted in its exercise by the provision that the Senate, a part of the legislative branch of the government, may check the action of the executive by rejecting the officers he selects. Does this make the Senate part of the removing power? And this, after the whole discussion in the House is read attentively, is the real point which was considered and decided in the negative by the vote already given.

The history of the clause by which the Senate was given a check upon the President's power of appointment makes it clear that it was not prompted by any desire to limit removals. As already pointed out, the important purpose of those who brought about the restriction was to lodge in the Senate, where the small states had equal representation with the larger states, power to prevent the President from making too many appointments from the larger states. . . .

It is reasonable to suppose also that had it been intended to give to Congress power to regulate or control removals in the manner suggested, it would have been included among the specifically enumerated legislative powers in article 1, or in the specified limitations on the executive power in article 2. The difference between the grant of legislative power under article 1 to Congress which is limited to powers therein enumerated, and the more general grant of the executive power to the President under article 2 is significant. The fact that the executive power is given in general terms strengthened by specific terms where emphasis is appropriate, and limited by direct expressions where limitation is needed, and that no express limit is placed on the power of removal by the executive is a convincing indication that none was intended. . . .

It is argued that the denial of the legislative power to regulate removals in some way involves the denial of power to prescribe qualifications for office, or reasonable classification for promotion, and yet that has been often exercised. We see no conflict between the latter power and that of appointment and removal, provided of course that the qualifications do not so limit selection and so trench upon executive choice as to be in effect legislative designation. As Mr. Madison said in the First Congress:

"The powers relative to offices are partly legislative and partly executive. The Legislature creates the office, defines the powers, limits its duration, and annexes a compensation. This done, the legislative power ceases. They ought to have nothing to do with designating the man to fill the office. That I conceive to be of an executive nature. Although it be qualified in the Constitution, I would not extend or strain that qualification beyond the limits precisely fixed for it. We ought always to consider the Constitution with an eye to the principles upon which it was founded. In this point of view, we shall readily conclude that if the Legislature determines the powers, the honors, and emoluments of an office, we should be insecure if they were to designate the officer also. The nature of things restrains and confines the legislative and executive authorities in this respect; and hence it is that the Constitution stipulates for the independence of each branch of the government." 1 Annals of Congress, 581, 582.

Made responsible under the Constitution for the effective enforcement of the law, the President needs as an indispensable aid to meet it the disciplinary influence upon those who act under him of a reserve power of removal. But it is contended that executive officers appointed by the President with the consent of the Senate are bound by the statutory law, and are not his servants to do his will, and that his obligation to care for the faithful execution of the laws does not authorize him to treat them as such. The degree of guidance in the discharge of their duties that the President may exercise over executive officers varies with the character of their service as prescribed in the law under which they act. The highest and most important duties which his subordinates perform are those in which they act for him. In such cases they are exercising not their own but his discretion. This field is a very large one. It is sometimes described as political. . . .

The duties of the heads of departments and bureaus in which the discretion of the President is exercised and which we have described are the most important in the whole field of executive action of the government. There is nothing in the Constitution which permits a distinction between the removal of the head of a department or a bureau, when he discharges a political duty of the President or exercises his discretion, and the removal of executive officers engaged in the discharge of their other normal duties. The imperative reasons requiring an unrestricted power to remove the most important of his subordinates in their most important duties must therefore control the interpretation of the Constitution as to all appointed by him.

But this is not to say that there are not strong reasons why the President should have a like power to remove his appointees charged with other duties than those above described. The ordinary duties of officers prescribed by statute come under the general administrative control of the President by virtue of the general grant to him of the executive power, and he may properly supervise and guide their construction of the statutes under which they act in order to secure that unitary and uniform execution of the laws which article 2 of the Constitution evidently contemplated in vesting general executive power in the President alone. Laws are often passed with specific provision for the adoption of regulations by a department or bureau head to make the law workable and effective. The ability and judgment manifested by the official thus empowered, as well as his energy and stimulation of his subordinates, are subjects which the President must consider and supervise in his administrative control. Finding such officers to be negligent and inefficient, the President should have the power to remove them. Of course there may be duties so peculiarly and specifically committed to the discretion of a particular officer as to raise a question whether the President may overrule or revise the officer's interpretation of his statutory duty in a particular instance. Then there may be duties of a quasi judicial character imposed on executive officers and members of executive tribunals whose decisions after hearing affect interests of individuals, the discharge of which the President cannot in a particular case properly influence or control. But even in such a case he may consider the decision after its rendition as a reason for removing the officer, on the ground that the discretion regularly entrusted to that officer by statute has not been on the whole intelligently or wisely exercised. Otherwise he does not discharge his own constitutional duty of seeing that the laws be faithfully executed.

We have devoted much space to this discussion and decision of the question of the presidential power of removal in the First Congress, not because a congressional conclusion on a constitutional issue is conclusive, but first because of our agreement with the reasons upon which it was avowedly based, second because this was the decision of the First Congress on a question of primary importance in the organization of the government made within two years after the Constitutional Convention and within a much shorter time after its ratification, and third because that Congress numbered among its leaders those who had been members of the convention. It must necessarily constitute a precedent upon which many future laws supplying the machinery of the new government would be based and, if erroneous, would be likely to evoke dissent and departure in future Congresses. It would come at once before the executive branch of the government for compliance and might well be brought before the judicial branch for a test of its validity. As we shall see, it was soon accepted as a final decision of the question by all branches of the government.

It was, of course, to be expected that the decision would be received by lawyers and jurists with something of the same division of opinion as that manifested in Congress, and doubts were often expressed as to its correctness. But the acquiescence which was promptly accorded it after a few years was universally recognized. . . .

We come now to consider an argument, advanced and strongly pressed on behalf of the complainant, that this case concerns only the removal of a postmaster, that a postmaster is an inferior officer, and that such an office was not included within the legislative decision of 1789, which related only to superior officers to be appointed by the President by and with the advice and consent of the Senate. This, it is said, is the distinction which Chief Justice MARSHALL had in mind in Marbury v. Madison in the language already discussed in respect to the President's power of removal of a District of Columbia justice of the peace appointed and confirmed for a term of years. We find nothing in *Marbury v. Madison* to indicate any such distinction. It cannot be certainly affirmed whether the conclusion there stated was based on a dissent from the legislative decision of 1789, or on the fact that the office was created under the special power of Congress exclusively to legislate for the District of Columbia, or on the fact that the office was a judicial one, or on the circumstance that it was an inferior office. In view of the doubt as to what was really the basis of the remarks relied on and their obiter dictum character, they can certainly not be used to give weight to the argument that the 1789 decision only related to superior officers. . . .

Our conclusion on the merits, sustained by the arguments before stated, is that article 2 grants to the President the executive power of the government—i.e., the general administrative control of those executing the laws, including the power of appointment and removal of executive officers—a conclusion confirmed by his obligation to take care that the laws be faithfully executed; that article 2 excludes the exercise of legislative power by Congress to provide for appointments and removals, except only as granted therein to Congress in the matter of inferior offices; that Congress is only given power to provide for appointments and removals of inferior officers after it has vested, and on condition that it does vest, their appointment in other authority than the President with the Senate's consent; that the provisions of the second section of article 2, which blend action by the legislative branch, or by part of it, in the work of the executive, are limitations to be strictly construed, and not to be extended by implication; that the President's power of removal is further established as an incident to his specifically enumerated function of appointment by and with the advice of the Senate, but that such incident does not by implication extend to removals the Senate's power of checking appointments; and, finally, that to hold otherwise would make it impossible for the President, in case of political or other difference with the Senate or Congress, to take care that the laws be faithfully executed.

We come now to a period in the history of the government when both houses of Congress attempted to reverse this constitutional construction, and to subject the power of removing executive officers appointed by the President and confirmed by the Senate to the control of the Senate, indeed finally to the assumed power in Congress to place the removal of such officers anywhere in the government.

This reversal grew out of the serious political difference between the two houses of Congress and President Johnson. There was a two-thirds majority of the Republican party, in control of each house of Congress, which resented what it feared would be Mr. Johnson's obstructive course in the enforcement of the reconstruction measures in respect to the states whose people had lately been at war against the national government. This led the two houses to enact legislation to curtail the then acknowledged powers of the President.

[T]he chief legislation in support of the reconstruction policy of Congress was the Tenure of Office Act of March 2, 1867, 14 Stat. 430, c. 154, providing that all officers appointed by and with the consent of the Senate should hold their offices until their successors should have in like manner been appointed and qualified; that certain heads of departments, including the Secretary of War, should hold their offices during the term of the President by whom appointed and one month thereafter, subject to removal by consent of the Senate. The Tenure of Office Act was vetoed, but it was passed over the veto. . . . [Objections to Congress's limiting the removal power of the President, from Grant to Coolidge, were then discussed by the Chief Justice.]

In spite of the foregoing presidential declarations, it is contended that, since the passage of the Tenure of Office Act, there has been general acquiescence by the executive in the power of Congress to forbid the President alone to remove executive officers, an acquiescence which has changed any formerly accepted constitutional construction to the contrary. Instances are cited of the signed approval by President Grant and other Presidents of legislation in derogation of such construction. We think these are all to be explained, not by acquiescence therein, but by reason of the otherwise valuable effect of the legislation approved. Such is doubtless the explanation of the executive approval of the act of 1876, which we are considering, for it was an appropriation act on which the section here in question was imposed as a rider. . . .

The fact seems to be that all departments of the government have constantly had in mind, since the passage of the Tenure of Office Act, that the question of power of removal by the President of officers appointed by him with the Senate's consent has not been settled adversely to the legislative action of 1789, but, in spite of congressional action, has remained open until the conflict should be subjected to judicial investigation and decision.

The action of this court cannot be said to constitute assent to a departure from the legislative decision of 1789, when the Parsons and Shurtleff Cases, one decided in 1897, and the other in 1903, are considered, for they certainly leave the question open. *Wallace v. United States,* 257 U. S. 541 [1922]. Those cases indicate no tendency to depart from the view of the First Congress. This court has since the Tenure of Office Act manifested an earnest desire to avoid a final settlement of the question until it should be inevitably presented, as it is here.

An argument ab inconvenienti has been made against our conclusion in favor of the executive power of removal by the President, without the consent of the Senate, that it will open the door to a reintroduction of the spoils system. The evil of the spoils system aimed at in the Civil Service Law and its amendments is in respect to inferior offices. It has never been attempted to extend that law beyond them. . . .

For the reasons given, we must therefore hold that the provision of the law of 1876 by which the unrestricted power of removal of first-class postmasters is denied to the President is in violation of the Constitution and invalid. This leads to an affirmance of the judgment of the Court of Claims.

Justice McREYNOLDS dissenting.

May the President oust at will all postmasters appointed with the Senate's consent for definite terms under an act which inhibits removal without consent of that body? May he approve a statute which creates an inferior office and prescribes restrictions on removal, appoint an incumbent, and then remove without regard to the restrictions? Has he power to appoint to an inferior office for a definite term under an act which prohibits removal except as therein specified, and then arbitrarily dismiss the incumbent and deprive him of the emoluments? I think there is no such power. Certainly it is not given by any plain words of the Constitution; and the argument advanced to establish it seems to me forced and unsubstantial.

A certain repugnance must attend the suggestion that the President may ignore any provision of an act of Congress under which he has proceeded. He should promote and not subvert orderly government. The serious evils which followed the practice of dismissing civil officers as caprice or interest dictated, long permitted under congressional enactments, are known to all. It brought the public service to a low estate and caused insistent demand for reform. "Indeed, it is utterly impossible not to feel, that, if this unlimited power of removal does exist, it may be made, in the hands of a bold and designing man, of high ambition and feeble principles, an instrument of the worst oppression and most vindictive vengeance." Story on the Constitution. . . .

Constitutional provisions should be interpreted with the expectation that Congress will discharge its duties no less faithfully than the executive will attend to his. The Legislature is charged with the duty of making laws for orderly administration obligatory upon all. It possesses supreme power over national affairs and may wreck as well as speed them. It holds the purse; every branch of the government functions under statutes which embody its will; it may impeach and expel all civil officers. The duty is upon it "to make all laws which shall be necessary and proper for carrying into execution" all powers of the federal government. We have no such thing as three totally distinct and independent departments; the others must look to the legislative for direction and support. "In republican government the legislative authority necessarily predominates." The Federalist, XLVI, XVII. Perhaps the chief duty of the President is to carry into effect the will of Congress through such instrumentalities as it has chosen to provide. . . .

I find no suggestion of the theory that "the executive power" of article 2, § 1, includes all possible federal authority executive in nature unless definitely excluded by some constitutional provision, prior to the well-known House debate of 1789, when Mr. Madison seems to have given it support. A resolution looking to the establishment of an executive department—Department of Foreign Affairs (afterwards State)—provided for a secretary, "who shall be appointed by the President by and with the advice and consent of the Senate and to be removable by the President." Discussion arose upon a motion to strike out, "to be removable by the President." The distinction between superior and inferior officers was clearly recognized; also that the proposed officer was superior and must be appointed by the President with the Senate's consent. The bill prescribed no definite term—the incumbent would serve until death, resignation or removal. In the circumstances most of the speakers recognize the rule that where there is no constitutional or legislative restriction power to remove is incidental to that of appointment. Accordingly, they thought the President could remove the proposed officer; but many supposed he must do so with consent of the Senate. They maintained that the power to appoint is joint. . . .

In any rational search for answer to the questions arising upon this record, it is important not to forget—

That this is a government of limited powers, definitely enumerated and granted by a written Constitution.

That the Constitution must be interpreted by attributing to its words the meaning which they bore at the time of its adoption, and in view of commonly-accepted canons of construction, its history, early and long-continued practices under it, and relevant opinions of this court.

That the Constitution endows Congress with plenary powers

"to establish post offices and post roads."

That, exercising this power during the years from 1789 to 1836, Congress provided for postmasters and vested the power to appoint and remove all of them at pleasure in the Postmaster General.

That the Constitution contains no words which specifically grant to the President power to remove duly appointed officers. And it is definitely settled that he cannot remove those whom he has not appointed—certainly they can be removed only as Congress may permit.

That postmasters are inferior officers within the meaning of article 2, § 2, of the Constitution.

That from its first session to the last one Congress has often asserted its right to restrict the President's power to remove inferior officers, although appointed by him with consent of the Senate.

That many Presidents have approved statutes limiting the power of the executive to remove, and that from the beginning such limitations have been respected in practice.

That this court, as early as 1803, in an opinion never overruled and rendered in a case where it was necessary to decide the question, positively declared that the President had no power to remove at will an inferior officer appointed with consent of the Senate to serve for a definite term fixed by an act of Congress.

That the power of Congress to restrict removals by the President was recognized by this court as late as 1903, in *Shurtleff v. United States* [189 U.S. 311 (1903)].

That the proceedings in the Constitutional Convention of 1787, the political history of the times, contemporaneous opinion, common canons of construction, the action of Congress from the beginning and opinions of this court, all oppose the theory that by vesting "the executive power" in the President the Constitution gave him an illimitable right to remove inferior officers.

That this court has emphatically disapproved the same theory concerning "the judicial power" vested in the courts by words substantially the same as those which vest "the executive power" in the President. "The executive power shall be vested in a President of the United States of America." "The judicial power of the United States, shall be vested in one Supreme Court, and in such inferior courts as the Congress may from time to time ordain and establish."

That to declare the President vested with indefinite and illimitable executive powers would extend the field of his possible action far beyond the limits observed by his predecessors, and would enlarge the powers of Congress to a degree incapable of fair appraisement.

Considering all these things, it is impossible for me to accept the view that the President may dismiss, as caprice may suggest, any inferior officer whom he has appointed with consent of the Senate, notwithstanding a positive inhibition by Congress. In the last analysis, that view has no substantial support, unless it be the polemic opinions expressed by Mr. Madison (and eight others) during the debate of 1789, when he was discussing questions relating to a "superior officer" to be appointed for an indefinite term. Notwithstanding his justly exalted reputation as one of the creators and early expounder of the Constitution, sentiments expressed under such circumstances ought not now to outweigh the conclusion which Congress affirmed by deliberate action while he was leader in the House and has consistently maintained down to the present year, the opinion of this court solemnly announced through the great CHIEF JUSTICE more than a century ago, and the canons of construction approved over and over again.

Judgment should go for the appellant.

Justice BRANDEIS dissenting.

May the President, having acted under the statute in so far as it creates the office and authorizes the appointment, ignore, while the Senate is in session, the provision which prescribes the condition under which a removal may take place?

It is this narrow question, and this only, which we are required to decide. We need not consider what power the President, being Commander-in-Chief, has over officers in the Army and the Navy. We need not determine whether the President, acting alone, may remove high political officers. We need not even determine whether, acting alone, he may remove inferior civil officers when the Senate is not in session. . . .

Over removal from inferior civil offices, Congress has, from the foundation of our government, exercised continuously some measure of control by legislation. The instances of such laws are many. Some of the statutes were directory in character. Usually, they were mandatory. Some of them, comprehensive in scope, have endured for generations. During the first 40 years of our government, there was no occasion to curb removals. . . .

In the later period, which began after the spoils system had prevailed for a generation, the control of Congress over inferior offices was exerted to prevent removals. The removal clause here in question was first introduced by the Currency Act of February 25, 1863, c. 58, § 1, 12 Stat. 665, which was approved by President Lincoln. That statute provided for the appointment of the Comptroller, and that he "shall hold his office for the term of five years unless sooner removed by the President, by and with the advice and consent of the Senate." In 1867 this provision was inserted in the Tenure of Office Act of March 2, 1867, c. 154, §§ 1, 3, 6, 14 Stat. 430, 431, which applied, in substance, to all presidential offices. It was passed over President Johnson's veto. . . .

The practice of Congress to control the exercise of the executive power of removal from inferior offices is evidenced by many statutes which restrict it in many ways besides the removal clause here in question. Each of these restrictive statutes became law with the approval of the President. Every President who has held office since 1861, except President Garfield, approved one or more of such statutes. Some of these statutes, prescribing a fixed term, provide that removal shall be made only for one of several specified causes. Some provide a fixed term, subject generally to removal for cause. Some provide for removal only after hearing. Some provide a fixed term, subject to removal for reasons to be communicated by the President to the Senate. Some impose the restriction in still other ways. . . .

The historical data submitted present a legislative practice, established by concurrent affirmative action of Congress and the President, to make consent of the Senate a condition of removal from statutory inferior, civil, executive offices to which the appointment is made for a fixed term by the President with such consent. They show that the practice has existed, without interruption, continuously for the last 58 years; that throughout this period, it has governed a great majority of all such offices; that the legislation applying the removal clause specifically to the office of postmaster was enacted more than half a century ago; and that recently the practice has, with the President's approval, been extended to several newly created offices. The data show further that the insertion of the removal clause in acts creating inferior civil offices with fixed tenures is part of the broader legislative practice, which has prevailed since the formation of our government, to restrict or regulate in many ways both removal from and nomination to such offices. A persistent legislative practice which involves a delimitation of the respective powers of Congress and the President, and which has been so established and maintained, should be deemed tantamount to judicial construction, in the absence of any decision by any court to the contrary. . . .

The persuasive effect of this legislative practice is strengthened by the fact that no instance has been found, even in the earlier period of our history, of concurrent affirmative action of Congress and the President which is inconsistent with the legislative practice of the last 58 years to impose the removal clause. Nor has any instance been found of action by Congress which involves recognition in any other way of the alleged uncontrollable executive power to remove an inferior civil officer. The action taken by Congress in 1789 after the great debate does not present such an instance. The vote then taken did not involve a decision that the President had uncontrollable power. It did not involve a decision of the question whether Congress could confer upon the

Senate the right, and impose upon it the duty, to participate in removals. It involved merely the decision that the Senate does not, in the absence of legislative grant thereof, have the right to share in the removal of an officer appointed with its consent, and that the President has, in the absence of restrictive legislation, the constitutional power of removal without such consent. Moreover, as Chief Justice MARSHALL recognized, the debate and the decision related to a high political office, not to inferior ones.

It is true that several Presidents have asserted that the Constitution conferred a power of removal uncontrollable by Congress. But of the many statutes enacted since the foundation of our government which in express terms controlled the power of removal, either by the clause here in question or otherwise, only two were met with a veto: The Tenure of Office Act of 1867, which related to high political officers among others, and the Budget Act of 1921 (Comp. St. § 400½ et. seq.), which denied to the President any participation in the removal of the Comptroller and Assistant Comptroller. One was passed over the President's veto; the other was approved by the succeeding President. It is true also that several Presidents have and others at times insisted that for the exercise of their power they were not accountable to the Senate. But even these Presidents have at other times complied with requests that the ground of removal of inferior officers be stated. Many of the Presidents have furnished the desired information without questioning the right to request it. And neither the Senate nor the House has at any time receded from the claim that Congress has power both to control by legislation removal from inferior offices and to require the President to report to it the reasons for removals made there from. . . .

The separation of the powers of government did not make each branch completely autonomous. It left each in some measure, dependent upon the others, as it left to each power to exercise, in some respects, functions in their nature executive, legislative and judicial. Obviously the President cannot secure full execution of the laws, if Congress denies to him adequate means of doing so. Full execution may be defeated because Congress declines to create offices indispensable for that purpose; or because Congress, having created the office, declines to make the indispensable appropriation; or because Congress, having both created the office and made the appropriation, prevents, by restrictions which it imposes, the appointment of officials who in quality and character are indispensable to the efficient execution of the law. If, in any such way, adequate means are denied to the President, the fault will lie with Congress. The President performs his full constitutional duty, if, with the means and instruments provided by Congress and within the limitations prescribed by it; he uses his best endeavors to secure the faithful execution of the laws enacted.

The doctrine of the separation of powers was adopted by the

convention of 1787 not to promote efficiency but to preclude the exercise of arbitrary power. The purpose was not to avoid friction, but, by means of the inevitable friction incident to the distribution of the governmental powers among three departments, to save the people from autocracy.

Justice HOLMES dissenting.

The arguments drawn from the executive power of the President, and from his duty to appoint officers of the United States (when Congress does not vest the appointment elsewhere), to take care that the laws be faithfully executed, and to commission all officers of the United States, seem to me spiders' webs inadequate to control the dominant facts.

We have to deal with an office that owes its existence to Congress and that Congress may abolish to-morrow. Its duration and the pay attached to it while it lasts depend on Congress alone. Congress alone confers on the President the power to appoint to it and at any time may transfer the power to other hands. With such power over its own creation, I have no more trouble in believing that Congress has power to prescribe a term of life for it free from any interference than I have in accepting the undoubted power of Congress to decree its end. I have equally little trouble in accepting its power to prolong the tenure of an incumbent until Congress or the Senate shall have assented to his removal. The duty of the President to see that the laws be executed is a duty that does not go beyond the laws or require him to achieve more than Congress sees fit to leave within his power.

Humphrey's Executor v. United States
295 U.S. 602, 55 S.Ct. 869 (1935)

William E. Humphrey was a conservative nominated by President Herbert Hoover and confirmed by the Senate as a commissioner of the FTC in 1931. According to the FTC Act, a commissioner could be removed by the president only for "inefficiency, neglect of duty, or malfeasance in office." However, in 1933 President Franklin D. Roosevelt asked Humphrey to resign, because the FTC had jurisdiction over many New Deal programs. When he refused, the president dismissed him on policy grounds, rather than those specified in the FTC Act. Shortly thereafter Humphrey died, but the executor of his estate challenged the dismissal and sought to recover his salary in the court of claims and eventually in the Supreme Court. The justices unanimously agreed that Humphrey had been improperly removed from office and with Justice George Sutherland's opinion for the Court that limited the earlier ruling in *Meyers v. United States* (1926) (see page 288).

Justice SUTHERLAND delivers the opinion of the Court.

The question first to be considered is whether, by the provisions of section 1 of the Federal Trade Commission Act, . . . the President's power is limited to removal for the specific causes enumerated therein. . . .

The commission is to be nonpartisan; and it must, from the very nature of its duties, act with entire impartiality. It is charged with the enforcement of no policy except the policy of the law. Its duties are neither political nor executive, but predominantly quasi judicial and quasi legislative. Like the Interstate Commerce Commission, its members are called upon to exercise the trained judgment of a body of experts "appointed by law and informed by experience.". . .

The legislative reports in both houses of Congress clearly reflect the view that a fixed term was necessary to the effective and fair administration of the law. . . .

The debates in both houses demonstrate that the prevailing view was that the Commission was not to be "subject to anybody in the government but . . . only to the people of the United States"; free from "political domination or control" or the "probability or possibility of such a thing"; to be "separate and apart from any existing department of the government—not subject to the orders of the President.". . .

Thus, the language of the act, the legislative reports, and the general purposes of the legislation as reflected by the debates, all combine to demonstrate the congressional intent to create a body of experts who shall gain experience by length of service; a body which shall be independent of executive authority; *except in its selection,* and free to exercise its judgment without the leave or hindrance of any, other official or any department of the government. To the accomplishment of these purposes, it is clear that Congress was of opinion that length and certainty of tenure would vitally contribute. And to hold that, nevertheless, the members of the commission continue in office at the mere will of the President, might be to thwart, in large measure, the very ends which Congress sought to realize by definitely fixing the term of office.

We conclude that the intent of the act is to limit the executive power of removal to the causes enumerated, the existence of none of which is claimed here; and we pass to the second question.

Second: To support its contention that the removal provision of section 1, as we have just construed it, is an unconstitutional interference with the executive power of the President, the government's chief reliance is *Myers v. United States,* 272 U.S. 52 [1926]. That case has been so recently decided, and the prevailing and dissenting opinions so fully review the general subject of the power of executive removal, that further discussion would add little of value to the wealth of material there collected. These opinions examine at length the historical, legislative, and judicial data bearing upon the question, beginning with what is called "the decision of 1789" in the first Congress and coming down almost to the day when the opinions were delivered. They occupy 243 pages of the volume in which they are printed. Nevertheless, the narrow point actually decided was only that the President had power to remove a postmaster of the first class, without the advice and consent of the Senate as required by act of Congress. In the course of the opinion of the court, expressions occur which tend to sustain the government's contention, but these are beyond the point involved and, therefore, do not come within the rule of *stare decisis.* In so far as they are out of harmony with the views here set forth, these expressions are disapproved. . . .

The office of a postmaster is so essentially unlike the office now involved that the decision in the *Myers* Case cannot be accepted as controlling our decision here. A postmaster is an executive officer restricted to the performance of executive functions. He is charged with no duty at all related to either the legislative or judicial power. The actual decision in the *Myers* Case finds support in the theory that such an officer is merely one of the units in the executive department and, hence, inherently subject to the exclusive and illimitable power of removal by the Chief Executive, whose subordinate and aid he is. Putting aside *dicta,* which may be followed if sufficiently persuasive but which are not controlling, the necessary reach of the decision goes far enough to include all purely executive officers. It goes no farther;—much less does it include an officer who occupies no place in the executive department and who exercises no part of the executive power vested by the Constitution in the President.

The Federal Trade Commission is an administrative body created by Congress to carry into effect legislative policies embodied in the statute in accordance with the legislative standard therein prescribed, and to perform other specified duties as a legislative or as a judicial aid. Such a body cannot in any proper sense be characterized as an arm or an eye of the executive. Its duties are performed without executive leave and, in the contemplation of the statute, must be free from executive control. In administering the provisions of the statute in respect of "unfair methods of competition," that is to say, in filling in and administering he details embodied by that general standard, the commission acts in part quasi legislatively and in part quasi judicially. In making investigations and reports thereon for the information of Congress under section 6, in aid of the legislative power, it acts as a legislative agency. Under section 7, which authorizes the commission to act as a master in chancery under rules prescribed by the court, it acts as an agency of the judiciary. To the extent that it exercises any executive function, as distinguished from executive power in the constitutional sense, it does so in the discharge and effectuation of its quasi legislative or quasi judicial powers, or as an agency of the legislative or judicial departments of the government.

If Congress is without authority to prescribe causes for removal of members of the trade commission and limit executive power of removal accordingly, that power at once becomes practically all-inclusive in respect of civil officers with the exception of the judiciary provided for by the Constitution. The Solicitor General, at the bar, apparently recognizing this to be true, with commendable candor, agreed that his view in respect of the removability of members of the Federal Trade Commission necessitated a like view in respect of the Interstate Commerce Commission and the Court of Claims. We are thus confronted with the serious question whether not only the members of these quasi legislative and quasi judicial bodies, but the judges of the legislative Court of Claims exercising judicial power . . . continue in office only at the pleasure of the President. . . .

We think it plain under the Constitution that illimitable power of removal is not possessed by the President in respect of officers of the character of those just named. The authority of Congress, in creating quasi legislative or quasi judicial agencies, to require them to act in discharge of their duties independently of executive control cannot well be doubted; and that authority includes, as an appropriate incident, power to fix the period during which they shall continue, and to forbid their removal except for cause in the meantime. For it is quite evident that one who holds his office only during the pleasure of another cannot be depended upon to maintain an attitude of independence against the latter's will.

The fundamental necessity of maintaining each of the three general departments of government entirely free from the control or coercive influence, direct or indirect, of either of the others, has often been stressed and is hardly open to serious question. So much is implied in the very fact of the separation of the powers of these departments by the Constitution; and in the rule which recognizes their essential coequality. The sound application of a principle that makes one master in his own house precludes him from imposing his control in the house of another who is master there.

The result of what we now have said is this: Whether the power of the President to remove an officer shall prevail over the authority of Congress to condition the power by fixing a definite term and precluding a removal except for cause will depend upon the character of the office; the *Myers* decision, affirming the power of the President alone to make the removal, is confined to purely executive officers; and as to officers of the kind here under consideration, we hold that no removal can be made during the prescribed term for which the officer is appointed, except for one or more of the causes named in the applicable statute.

To the extent that, between the decision in the *Myers* Case, which sustains the unrestrictable power of the President to remove purely executive officers, and our present decision that such power does not extend to an office such as that here involved, there shall remain a field of doubt, we leave such cases as may fall within it for future consideration and determination as they may arise.

Justice McREYNOLDS concurred in a separate opinion.

Bowsher v. Synar
478 U.S. 714, 106 S.Ct. 3181 (1986)

Faced with mounting federal budget deficits, in 1985 Congress enacted the Balanced Budget and Emergency Deficit Control Act—known also as the Gramm-Rudman-Hollings Act. It sets annual ceilings for deficits and, if these are exceeded, requires across-the-board reductions in federal spending. To achieve the reductions, the act requires the Office of Management and the Budget of the executive branch and the Congressional Budget Office to submit deficit estimates and possible budget reductions to the comptroller general, who makes his own recommendations for budget reduction to the president, who then must order the spending reductions. Opposition to the bill in Congress focused on whether the principle of separation of powers was violated by delegating the power to recommend budget reductions to a member of the executive branch, the comptroller general, who is removable by a joint resolution of Congress. As a result, a "fallback" provision was included in the event that a federal court struck down the delegation to the comptroller general.

Immediately after President Reagan signed the bill into law, Congressman Michael Synar and eleven others opposed to the law filed suit in the Court of Appeals for the District of Columbia Circuit challenging the constitutionality of the Act. A three-judge panel held, in an opinion joined by then-Judge Antonia Scalia, that the empowerment of the comptroller general was unconstitutional. An appeal was promptly made to the Supreme Court which expedited consideration of the case. Note that only a bare majority of the Court joined Chief Justice Warren Burger's opinion; Justice John Stevens, joined by Justice Thurgood Marshall, concurred in the judgment but not in reasoning of the majority; and dissenting Justices Byron White and Harry Blackmun criticize the majority's "formalistic view of separation of powers."

Chief Justice BURGER delivers the opinion of the Court.

The question presented by these appeals is whether the assignment by Congress to the Comptroller General of the United States of certain functions under the Balanced Budget and Emergency Deficit Control Act of 1985 violates the doctrine of separation of powers.

On December 12, 1985, the President signed into law the Balanced Budget and Emergency Deficit Control Act of 1985, Pub.L. 99–177, 99 Stat. 1038, 2 U.S.C.A. § 901 *et seq.* (Supp. 1986), popularly known as the "Gramm-Rudman-Hollings Act." The purpose of the Act is to eliminate the federal budget deficit. To that end, the Act sets a "maximum deficit amount" for federal spending for each of fiscal years 1986 through 1991. The size of that maximum deficit amount progressively reduces to zero in fiscal year 1991. If in any fiscal year the federal budget deficit exceeds the maximum deficit amount by more than a specified sum, the Act requires across-the-board cuts in federal spending to reach the targeted deficit level, with half of the cuts made to defense programs and the other half made to non-defense programs. The Act exempts certain priority programs from these cuts. § 255.

These "automatic" reductions are accomplished through a rather complicated procedure, spelled out in § 251, the so-called "reporting provisions" of the Act. Each year, the Directors of the Office of Management and Budget (OMB) and the Congressional Budget Office (CBO) independently estimate the amount of the federal budget deficit for the upcoming fiscal year. If that deficit exceeds the maximum targeted deficit amount for that fiscal year by more than a specified amount, the Directors of OMB and CBO independently calculate, on a program-by-program basis, the budget reductions necessary to ensure that the deficit does not exceed the maximum deficit amount. The Act then requires the Directors to report jointly their deficit estimates and budget reduction calculations to the Comptroller General.

The Comptroller General, after reviewing the Directors' reports, then reports his conclusions to the President. § 251(b). The President in turn must issue a "sequestration" order mandating the spending reductions specified by the Comptroller General. § 252. There follows a period during which Congress may by legislation reduce spending to obviate, in whole or in part, the need for the sequestration order. If such reductions are not enacted, the sequestration order becomes effective and the spending reductions included in that order are made. . . .

Within hours of the President's signing of the Act, Congressman Synar, who had voted against the Act, filed a complaint seeking declaratory relief that the Act was unconstitutional. Eleven other Members later joined Congressman Synar's suit. A virtually identical lawsuit was also filed by the National Treasury Employees Union. The Union alleged that its members had been injured as a result of the Act's automatic spending reduction provisions, which have suspended certain cost-of-living benefit increases to the Union's members.

A three-judge District Court, appointed pursuant to 2 U.S.C.A. § 922(a)(5) (Supp. 1986), invalidated the reporting provisions. *Synar v. United States,* 626 F.Supp. 1374 (DC 1986) (SCALIA, JOHNSON, GASCH, JJ.). . . .

Although the District Court concluded that the Act survived a delegation doctrine challenge, it held that the role of the Comptroller General in the deficit reduction process violated the constitutionally imposed separation of powers. The court first explained that the Comptroller General exercises executive functions under the Act. However, the Comptroller General, while appointed by the President with the advice and consent of the Senate, is removable not by the President but only by a joint resolution of Congress or by impeachment. The District Court reasoned that this arrangement could not be sustained under this Court's decisions in *Myers v. United States,* 272 U.S. 52 (1926), and *Humphrey's Executor v. United States,* 295 U.S. 602 (1935). Under the separation of powers established by the Framers of the Constitution, the court concluded, Congress may not retain the power of removal over an officer performing executive functions. . . .

Appeals were taken directly to this Court pursuant to § 274(b) of the Act. We noted probable jurisdiction and expedited consideration of the appeals. We affirm. . . .

We noted recently that "[t]he Constitution sought to divide the delegated powers of the new Federal Government into three defined categories, Legislative, Executive, and Judicial," *INS v. Chadha,* 462 U.S. 919 (1983). The declared purpose of separating and dividing the powers of government, of course, was to "diffus[e] power the better to secure liberty." *Youngstown Sheet & Tube Co. v. Sawyer,* 343 U.S. 579 (JACKSON, J., concurring). Justice JACKSON's words echo the famous warning of Montesquieu, quoted by James Madison in The Federalist No. 47, that "there can be no liberty where the legislative and executive powers are united in the same person, or body of magistrates'. . . ." The Federalist No. 47.

Even a cursory examination of the Constitution reveals the influence of Montesquieu's thesis that checks and balances were the foundation of a structure of government that would protect liberty. The Framers provided a vigorous legislative branch and a separate and wholly independent executive branch, with each branch responsible ultimately to the people. The Framers also provided for a judicial branch equally independent with "[t]he judicial Power . . . extend[ing] to all Cases, in Law and Equity, arising under this Constitution, and the Laws of the United States." Art. III, § 2.

Other, more subtle, examples of separated powers are evident as well. Unlike parliamentary systems such as that of Great Britain, no person who is an officer of the United States may serve as a Member of the Congress. Art. I, § 6. Moreover, unlike parliamentary systems, the President, under Article II, is responsible not to the Congress but to the people, subject only to impeachment proceedings which are exercised by the two Houses as representatives of the people. Art. II, § 4. And even in the impeachment of a President the presiding officer of the ultimate tribunal is not a member of the legislative branch, but the Chief Justice of the United States. Art. I, § 3.

That this system of division and separation of powers produces conflicts, confusion, and discordance at times is inherent, but it was deliberately so structured to assure full, vigorous and open debate on the great issues affecting the people and to provide avenues for the operation of checks on the exercise of governmental power.

The Constitution does not contemplate an active role for Congress in the supervision of officers charged with the execution of the laws it enacts. The President appoints "Officers of the United States" with the "Advice and Consent of the Senate. . . ." Article II, § 2. Once the appointment has been made and confirmed, however, the Constitution explicitly provides for removal of Officers of the United States by Congress only upon impeachment by the House of Representatives and conviction by the Senate. An impeachment by the House and trial by the Senate can rest only on "Treason, Bribery or other high Crimes and Misdemeanors." Article II, § 4. A direct congressional role in the removal of officers charged with the execution of the laws beyond this limited one is inconsistent with separation of powers. . . .

This Court first directly addressed this issue in *Myers v. United States.* At issue in *Myers* was a statute providing that certain postmasters could be removed only "by and with the advice and consent of the Senate." The President removed one such postmaster without Senate approval, and a lawsuit ensued. Chief Justice TAFT, writing for the Court, declared the statute unconstitutional on the ground that for Congress to "draw to itself, or to either branch of it, the power to remove or the right to participate in the exercise of that power . . . would be . . . to infringe the constitutional principle of the separation of governmental powers.". . .

A decade later, in *Humphrey's Executor v. United States* (1935), relied upon heavily by appellants, a Federal Trade Commissioner who had been removed by the President sought back pay. *Humphrey's Executor* involved an issue not presented either in the *Myers* case or in this case—i.e., the power of Congress to limit the President's powers of removal of a Federal Trade Commissioner. . . . The relevant statute permitted removal "by the President," but only "for inefficiency, neglect of duty, or malfeasance in office." Justice SUTHERLAND, speaking for the Court, upheld the statute, holding that "illimitable power of removal is not possessed by the President [with respect to Federal Trade Commissioners]." The Court distinguished *Myers*, reaffirming its holding that congressional participation in the removal of executive officers is unconstitutional. The Court reached a similar result in *Wiener v. United States*, 357 U.S. 349 (1958), concluding that, under *Humphrey's Executor,* the President did not have unrestrained removal authority over a member of the War Crimes Commission.

In light of these precedents, we conclude that Congress cannot reserve for itself the power of removal of an officer charged with the execution of the laws except by impeachment. To permit the execution of the laws to be vested in an officer answerable only to Congress would, in practical terms, reserve in Congress control over the execution of the laws. As the District Court observed, "Once an officer is appointed, it is only the authority that can remove him, and not the authority that appointed him, that he must fear and, in the performance of his functions, obey." The structure of the Constitution does not permit Congress to execute the laws; it follows that Congress cannot grant to an officer under its control what it does not possess. . . .

The dangers of congressional usurpation of Executive Branch functions have long been recognized. "[T]he debates of the Constitutional Convention, and the Federalist Papers, are replete with expressions of fear that the Legislative Branch of the National Government will aggrandize itself at the expense of the other two branches." *Buckley v. Valeo*, 424 U.S. 1 (1976). Indeed, we also have observed only recently that "[t]he hydraulic pressure inherent within each of the separate Branches to exceed the outer limits of its power, even to accomplish desirable objectives, must be resisted." With these principles in mind, we turn to consideration of whether the Comptroller General is controlled by Congress. . . .

The critical factor lies in the provisions of the statute defining the Comptroller General's office relating to removability. Although the Comptroller General is nominated by the President from a list of three individuals recommended by the Speaker of the House of Representatives and the President pro tempore of the Senate, see 31 U.S.C. § 703(a)(2), and confirmed by the Senate, he is removable only at the initiative of Congress. He may be removed not only by impeachment but also by Joint Resolution of Congress "at any time" resting on any one of the following bases:

"(i) permanent disability;
"(ii) inefficiency;
"(iii) neglect of duty;
"(iv) malfeasance; or
"(v) a felony or conduct involving moral turpitude."
31 U.S.C. § 703(e)(1).

This provision was included, as one Congressman explained in urging passage of the Act, because Congress "felt that [the Comptroller General] should be brought under the sole control of Congress, so that Congress at the moment when it found he was inefficient and was not carrying on the duties of his office as he should and as the Congress expected, could remove him without the long, tedious process of a trial by impeachment." 61 Cong.Rec. 1081 (1921). . . .

It is clear that Congress has consistently viewed the Comptroller General as an officer of the Legislative Branch. The Reorganization Acts of 1945 and 1949, for example, both stated that the Comptroller General and the GAO are "a part of the legislative branch of the Government." 59 Stat. 616; 63 Stat. 205. Similarly, in the Accounting and Auditing Act of 1950, Congress required the Comptroller General to conduct audits "as an agent of the Congress." 64 Stat. 835. . . .

Against this background, we see no escape from the conclusion that, because Congress had retained removal authority over the Comptroller General, he may not be entrusted with executive powers. The remaining question is whether the Comptroller General has been assigned such powers in the Balanced Budget and Emergency Deficit Control Act of 1985. . . .

The primary responsibility of the Comptroller General under the instant Act is the preparation of a "report." This report must contain detailed estimates of projected federal revenues and expenditures. The report must also specify the reductions, if any, necessary to reduce the deficit to the target for the appropriate fiscal year. The reductions must be set forth on a program-by-program basis. . . .

The executive nature of the Comptroller General's functions under the Act is revealed in § 252(a)(3) which gives the Comptroller General the ultimate authority to determine the budget cuts to be made. Indeed, the Comptroller General commands the

President himself to carry out, without the slightest variation (with exceptions not relevant to the constitutional issues presented), the directive of the Comptroller General as to the budget reductions:

"The [Presidential] order *must provide* for reductions in the manner specified in section 251(a)(3), *must incorporate* the provisions of the [Comptroller General's] report submitted under section 251(b), and *must be consistent with such report in all respects.* The President *may not modify or recalculate any of the estimates, determinations, specifications, bases, amounts, or percentages* set forth in the report submitted under section 251(b) in determining the reductions to be specified in the order with respect to programs, projects, and activities, or with respect to budget activities, within an account. . . ." § 252(a)(3) (emphasis added).

See also § 251(d)(3)(A).

Congress of course initially determined the content of the Balanced Budget and Emergency Deficit Control Act; and undoubtedly the content of the Act determines the nature of the executive duty. However, as *Chadha* makes clear, once Congress makes its choice in enacting legislation, its participation ends. Congress can thereafter control the execution of its enactment only indirectly—by passing new legislation. *Chadha.* By placing the responsibility for execution of the Balanced Budget and Emergency Deficit Control Act in the hands of an officer who is subject to removal only by itself, Congress in effect has retained control over the execution of the Act and has intruded into the executive function. The Constitution does not permit such intrusion. . . .

No one can doubt that Congress and the President are confronted with fiscal and economic problems of unprecedented magnitude, but "the fact that a given law or procedure is efficient, convenient, and useful in facilitating functions of government, standing alone, will not save it if it is contrary to the Constitution. Convenience and efficiency are not the primary objectives—or the hallmarks—of democratic government. . . ." *Chadha.* . . .

We conclude the District Court correctly held that the powers vested in the Comptroller General under § 251 violate the command of the Constitution that the Congress play no direct role in the execution of the laws. Accordingly, the judgment and order of the District Court are affirmed.

Justice STEVENS, with whom Justice MARSHALL joins, concurring.

When this Court is asked to invalidate a statutory provision that has been approved by both Houses of the Congress and signed by the President, particularly an Act of Congress that confronts a deeply vexing national problem, it should only do so for the most compelling constitutional reasons. I agree with the Court that the "Gramm-Rudman-Hollings" Act contains a constitutional infirmity so severe that the flawed provision may not stand. I disagree with the Court, however, on the reasons why the Constitution prohibits the Comptroller General from exercising the powers assigned to him by § 251(b) and § 251(c)(2) of the Act. It is not the dormant, carefully circumscribed congressional removal power that represents the primary constitutional evil. Nor do I agree with the conclusion of both the majority and the dissent that the analysis depends on a labeling of the functions assigned to the Comptroller General as "executive powers." Rather, I am convinced that the Comptroller General must be characterized as an agent of Congress because of his longstanding statutory responsibilities; that the powers assigned to him under the Gramm-Rudman-Hollings Act require him to make policy that will bind the Nation; and that, when Congress, or a component or an agent of Congress, seeks to make policy that will bind the Nation, it must follow the procedures mandated by Article I of the Constitution—through passage by both Houses and presentment to the President. In short, Congress may not exercise its fundamental power to formulate national policy by delegating that power to one of its two Houses, to a legislative committee, or to an individual agent of the Congress such as the Speaker of the House of Representatives, the Sergeant at Arms of the Senate, or the Director of the Congressional Budget Office. *INS v. Chadha* (1983). That principle, I believe, is applicable to the Comptroller General.

Justice WHITE dissenting.

The Court, acting in the name of separation of powers, takes upon itself to strike down the Gramm-Rudman-Hollings Act, one of the most novel and far-reaching legislative responses to a national crisis since the New Deal. The basis of the Court's action is a solitary provision of another statute that was passed over sixty years ago and has lain dormant since that time. I cannot concur in the Court's action. Like the Court, I will not purport to speak to the wisdom of the policies incorporated in the legislation the Court invalidates; that is a matter for the Congress and the Executive, *both* of which expressed their assent to the statute barely half a year ago. I will, however, address the wisdom of the Court's willingness to interpose its distressingly formalistic view of separation of powers as a bar to the attainment of governmental objectives through the means chosen by the Congress and the President in the legislative process established by the Constitution. . . .

Before examining the merits of the Court's argument, I wish

to emphasize what it is that the Court quite pointedly and correctly does *not* hold: namely, that "executive" powers of the sort granted the Comptroller by the Act may only be exercised by officers removable at will by the President. The Court's apparent unwillingness to accept this argument, which has been tendered in this Court by the Solicitor General, is fully consistent with the Court's longstanding recognition that it is within the power of Congress under the "Necessary and Proper" Clause, Art. I, § 8, to vest authority that falls within the Court's definition of executive power in officers who are not subject to removal at will by the President and are therefore not under the President's direct control. See, *e.g., Humphrey's Executor v. United States* (1935); *Wiener v. United States* (1958). In an earlier day, in which simpler notions of the role of government in society prevailed, it was perhaps plausible to insist that all "executive" officers be subject to an unqualified presidential removal power, see *Myers v. United States* (1926); but with the advent and triumph of the administrative state and the accompanying multiplication of the tasks undertaken by the Federal Government, the Court has been virtually compelled to recognize that Congress may reasonably deem it "necessary and proper" to vest some among the broad new array of governmental functions in officers who are free from the partisanship that may be expected of agents wholly dependent upon the President. . . .

If, as the Court seems to agree, the assignment of "executive" powers under Gramm-Rudman to an officer not removable at will by the President would not in itself represent a violation of the constitutional scheme of separated powers, the question remains whether, as the Court concludes, the fact that the officer to whom Congress has delegated the authority to implement the Act is removable by a joint resolution of Congress should require invalidation of the Act. The Court's decision, as I have stated above, is based on a syllogism: the Act vests the Comptroller with "executive power"; such power may not be exercised by Congress or its agents; the Comptroller is an agent of Congress because he is removable by Congress; therefore the Act is invalid. I have no quarrel with the proposition that the powers exercised by the Comptroller under the Act may be characterized as "executive" in that they involve the interpretation and carrying out of the Act's mandate. I can also accept the general proposition that although Congress has considerable authority in designating the officers who are to execute legislation, the constitutional scheme of separated powers does prevent Congress from reserving an executive role for itself or for its "agents." *Buckley v. Valeo,* (WHITE, J., concurring in part and dissenting in part). I cannot accept, however, that the exercise of authority by an officer removable for cause by a joint resolution of Congress is analogous to the impermissible execution of the law by Congress itself, nor would I hold that the congressional role in the removal process renders the Comptroller an "agent" of the Congress, incapable of receiving "executive" power. . . .

The deficiencies in the Court's reasoning are apparent. First, the Court baldly mischaracterizes the removal provision when it suggests that it allows Congress to remove the Comptroller for "executing the laws in any fashion found to be unsatisfactory"; in fact, Congress may remove the Comptroller only for one or more of five specified reasons, which "although not so narrow as to deny Congress any leeway, circumscribe Congress' power to some extent by providing a basis for judicial review of congressional removal." *Ameron, Inc. v. United States Army Corps of Engineers,* 787 F.2d 875 (CA3 1986) (BECKER, J., concurring in part). Second, and more to the point, the Court overlooks or deliberately ignores the decisive difference between the congressional removal provision and the legislative veto struck down in *Chadha*: under the Budget and Accounting Act, Congress may remove the Comptroller only through a joint resolution, which by definition must be passed by both Houses and signed by the President. See *United States v. California,* 332 U.S. 19 (1947). In other words, a removal of the Comptroller under the statute *satisfies the requirements of bicameralism and presentment laid down in Chadha.* The majority's citation of *Chadha* for the proposition that Congress may only control the acts of officers of the United States "by passing new legislation," in no sense casts doubt on the legitimacy of the removal provision, for that provision allows Congress to effect removal only through action that constitutes legislation as defined in *Chadha.* . . .

The statute does not permit anyone to remove the Comptroller at will; removal is permitted only for specified cause, with the existence of cause to be determined by Congress following a hearing. Any removal under the statute would presumably be subject to post-termination judicial review to ensure that a hearing had in fact been held and that the finding of cause for removal was not arbitrary. See *Ameron, Inc. v. United States Army Corps of Engineers* (BECKER, J., concurring in part). These procedural and substantive limitations on the removal power militate strongly against the characterization of the Comptroller as a mere agent of Congress by virtue of the removal authority. Indeed, similarly qualified grants of removal power are generally deemed to protect the officers to whom they apply and to establish their independence from the domination of the possessor of the removal power. See *Humphrey's Executor v. United States.* Removal authority limited in such a manner is more properly viewed as motivating adherence to a substantive standard established by law than as inducing subservience to the particular institution that enforces that standard. That the agent enforcing the standard is Congress may be of some significance to the Comptroller, but Congress' substantively limited removal power will undoubtedly be less of a spur to subservience than Congress' unquestionable and unqualified power to enact legislation reducing the Comptroller's salary, cutting the funds available to his department, reducing his personnel, limiting or expanding his duties, or even abolishing his position altogether.

More importantly, the substantial role played by the President in the process of removal through joint resolution reduces to utter insignificance the possibility that the threat of removal will induce subservience to the Congress. As I have pointed out above, a joint resolution must be presented to the President and is ineffective if it is vetoed by him, unless the veto is overridden by the constitutionally prescribed two-thirds majority of both Houses of Congress. The requirement of presidential approval obviates the possibility that the Comptroller will perceive himself as so completely at the mercy of Congress that he will function as its tool. If the Comptroller's conduct in office is not so unsatisfactory to the President as to convince the latter that removal is required under the statutory standard, Congress will have no independent power to coerce the Comptroller unless it can muster a two-thirds majority in both Houses—a feat of bipartisanship more difficult than that required to impeach and convict. The incremental *in terrorem* effect of the possibility of congressional removal in the face of a presidential veto is therefore exceedingly unlikely to have any discernible impact on the extent of congressional influence over the Comptroller.

The practical result of the removal provision is not to render the Comptroller unduly dependent upon or subservient to Congress, but to render him one of the most independent officers in the entire federal establishment. Those who have studied the office agree that the procedural and substantive limits on the power of Congress and the President to remove the Comptroller make dislodging him against his will practically impossible. As one scholar put it nearly fifty years ago, "Under the statute the Comptroller General, once confirmed, is safe so long as he avoids a public exhibition of personal immorality, dishonesty, or failing mentality." H. Mansfield, The Comptroller General 75–76 (1939). The passage of time has done little to cast doubt on this view: of the six Comptrollers who have served since 1921, none has been threatened with, much less subjected to, removal. Recent students of the office concur that "[b]arring resignation, death, physical or mental incapacity, or extremely bad behavior, the Comptroller General is assured his tenure if he wants it, and not a day more." F. Mosher, The GAO 242 (1979). The threat of "here-and-now subservience," obviously remote indeed.

Realistic consideration of the nature of the Comptroller General's relation to Congress thus reveals that the threat to separation of powers conjured up by the majority is wholly chimerical. The power over removal retained by the Congress is not a power that is exercised outside the legislative process as established by the Constitution, nor does it appear likely that it is a power that adds significantly to the influence Congress may exert over executive officers through other, undoubtedly constitutional exercises of legislative power and through the constitutionally guaranteed impeachment power. Indeed, the removal power is so constrained by its own substantive limits and by the requirement of presidential approval "that, as a practical matter, Congress has not exercised, and probably will never exercise, such control over the Comptroller General that his non-legislative powers will threaten the goal of dispersion of power, and hence the goal of individual liberty, that separation of powers serves." *Ameron, Inc. v. United States Army Corps of Engineers* (BECKER, J., concurring in part).

The majority's contrary conclusion rests on the rigid dogma that, outside of the impeachment process, any "direct congressional role in the removal of officers charged with the execution of the laws . . . is inconsistent with separation of powers." Reliance on such an unyielding principle to strike down a statute posing no real danger of aggrandizement of congressional power is extremely misguided and insensitive to our constitutional role. . . .

I dissent.

Justice BLACKMUN dissenting.

The Court may be correct when it says that Congress cannot constitutionally exercise removal authority over an official vested with the budget-reduction powers that § 251 of the Balanced Budget and Emergency Deficit Control Act of 1985 gives to the Comptroller General. This, however, is not because "[t]he removal powers over the Comptroller General's office dictate that he will be subservient to Congress." I agree with Justice WHITE that any such claim is unrealistic. Furthermore, I think it is clear under *Humphrey's Executor v. United States* (1935), that "executive" powers of the kind delegated to the Comptroller General under the Deficit Control Act need not be exercised by an officer who serves at the President's pleasure; Congress certainly could prescribe the standards and procedures for removing the Comptroller General. But it seems to me that an attempt by Congress to participate *directly* in the removal of an executive officer—other than through the constitutionally prescribed procedure of impeachment— might well violate the principle of separation of powers by assuming for Congress part of the President's constitutional responsibility to carry out the laws.

In my view, however, that important and difficult question need not be decided in this case, because no matter how it is resolved the plaintiffs, now appellees, are not entitled to the relief they have requested. Appellees have not sought invalidation of the 1921 provision that authorizes Congress to remove the Comptroller General by joint resolution; indeed, it is far from clear they would have standing to request such a judgment. The only relief sought in this case is nullification of the automatic budget-reduction provisions of the Deficit Control Act, and that relief should not be awarded even if the Court is correct that those provisions are constitutionally incompatible with Congress' authority to remove the Comptroller General by joint resolution. Any incompatibility, I feel, should be cured by refusing to allow congressional removal—if it ever is attempted—and not by striking down the central provisions of the Deficit Control Act. However wise or foolish it may be, that statute unquestionably ranks among the most important federal enactments of the past several decades. I cannot see the sense of invalidating legislation of this magnitude in order to preserve a cumbersome, 65-year-old removal power that has never been exercised and appears to have been all but forgotten until this litigation. . . .

I do not claim that the 1921 removal provision is a piece of statutory deadwood utterly without contemporary significance. But it comes close. Rarely if ever invoked even for symbolic purposes, the removal provision certainly pales in importance beside the legislative scheme the Court strikes down today—an extraordinarily far-reaching response to a deficit problem of unprecedented proportions. Because I believe that the constitutional defect found by the Court cannot justify the remedy it has imposed, I respectfully dissent.

Morrison v. Olson

108 S.Ct. 2597 (1988)

In the wake of the "Watergate crisis" (see "Unraveling the Watergate Affair," page 368) Congress passed the Ethics in Government Act in 1978. It provides for independent counsel to investigate presidential subordinates if warranted after a preliminary review by the attorney general. The attorney general must request the appointment of counsel from a "Special Division" of the U.S. Court of Appeals for the District of Columbia. Once appointed, counsel may be removed by the attorney general only for reasons specified in the act.

Independent counsels initially provoked controversy with the appointment of a special prosecutor assigned to investigate President Nixon's involvement in the Watergate cover-up. In 1973, Nixon ordered the dismissal of Archibald Cox, the Watergate special prosecutor. After the attorney general and his assistant resigned rather than remove Cox, Acting Attorney General Robert H. Bork discharged him. A lower federal court, in *Nader v. Bork*, 366 F.Supp. 104 (D.D.C., 1973), later held that the dismissal was illegal.

The constitutionality of independent counsel was controversial again in 1987, when four separate counsels were investigating the Iran-Contra affair and allegations of wrongdoing by Attorney General Edwin Meese III and other former presidential aides. This case, however, arose from independent counsel Alexia Morrison's 1986 investigation of allegations that former Assistant Attorney General Theodore Olson lied before a congressional subcommittee in 1983 concerning the withholding of Environmental Protection Agency documents from Congress. Olson challenged the constitutionality of Morrison's appointment in the U.S. Court of Appeals for the District of Columbia. A three-judge panel split two to one when finding the appointment of independent counsel to violate principles of separation of powers. Morrison, then, appealed to the Supreme Court, which expedited briefing and oral arguments in the spring of 1988. President Ronald Reagan's last appointee to the Court did not participate in the decision. With the exception of Justice Antonin Scalia, who issued a sharp dissenting opinion, the rest of the Court joined in Chief Justice William Rehnquist's opinion upholding the constitutionality of the appointment special prosecutors. Three months after the Court's ruling, Morrison concluded her two-year investigation, deciding that there was not enough evidence to seek an indictment of Olson.

Chief Justice REHNQUIST delivers the opinion of the Court.

This case presents us with a challenge to the independent counsel provisions of the Ethics in Government Act of 1978. We hold today that these provisions of the Act do not violate the Appointments Clause of the Constitution, Art. II, § 2, cl. 2, or the limitations of Article III, nor do they impermissibly interfere with the President's authority under Article II in violation of the constitutional principle of separation of powers. . . .

The Appointments Clause of Article II reads as follows:

"[The President] shall nominate, and by and with the Advice and Consent of the Senate, shall appoint Ambassadors, other public Ministers and Consuls, Judges of the Supreme Court, and all other Officers of the United States, whose Appointments are not herein otherwise provided for, and which shall be established by Law: but the Congress may by Law vest the Appointment of such inferior Officers, as they think proper, in the

President alone, in the Courts of Law, or in the Heads of Departments."

The parties do not dispute that "[t]he Constitution for purposes of appointment . . . divides all its officers into two classes." *United States v. Germaine*, 99 U.S. (9 Otto) 508 (1879). As we stated in *Buckley v. Valeo*, 424 U.S. 1 (1976), "[p]rincipal officers are selected by the President with the advice and consent of the Senate. Inferior officers Congress may allow to be appointed by the President alone, by the heads of departments, or by the Judiciary." The initial question is, accordingly, whether appellant is an "inferior" or a "principal" officer. If she is the latter, as the Court of Appeals concluded, then the Act is in violation of the Appointments Clause.

The line between "inferior" and "principal" officers is one that is far from clear, and the Framers provided little guidance into where it should be drawn. . . . We need not attempt here to decide exactly where the line falls between the two types of officers, because in our view appellant clearly falls on the "inferior officer" side of that line. Several factors lead to this conclusion.

First, appellant is subject to removal by a higher Executive Branch official. Although appellant may not be "subordinate" to the Attorney General (and the President) insofar as she possesses a degree of independent discretion to exercise the powers delegated to her under the Act, the fact that she can be removed by the Attorney General indicates that she is to some degree "inferior" in rank and authority. Second, appellant is empowered by the Act to perform only certain, limited duties. An independent counsel's role is restricted primarily to investigation and, if appropriate, prosecution for certain federal crimes. Admittedly, the Act delegates to appellant "full power and independent authority to exercise all investigative and prosecutorial functions and powers of the Department of Justice," but this grant of authority does not include any authority to formulate policy for the Government or the Executive Branch, nor does it give appellant any administrative duties outside of those necessary to operate her office. The Act specifically provides that in policy matters appellant is to comply to the extent possible with the policies of the Department. . . .

Third, appellant's office is limited in jurisdiction. Not only is the Act itself restricted in applicability to certain federal officials suspected of certain serious federal crimes, but an independent counsel can only act within the scope of the jurisdiction that has been granted by the Special Division pursuant to a request by the Attorney General. Finally, appellant's office is limited in tenure. . . . In our view, these factors relating to the "ideas of tenure, duration . . . and duties" of the independent counsel, *Germaine,* are sufficient to establish that appellant is an "inferior" officer in the constitutional sense. . . .

This does not, however, end our inquiry under the Appointments Clause. Appellees argue that even if appellant is an "inferior" officer, the Clause does not empower Congress to place the power to appoint such an officer outside the Executive Branch. They contend that the Clause does not contemplate congressional authorization of "interbranch appointments," in which an officer of one branch is appointed by officers of another branch. The relevant language of the Appointments Clause is worth repeating. It reads: ". . . but the Congress may by Law vest the Appointment of such inferior Officers, as they think proper, in the President alone, in the courts of Law, or in the Heads of Departments." On its face, the language of this "excepting clause," admits of no limitation on interbranch appointments. Indeed, the inclusion of "as they think proper" seems clearly to give Congress significant discretion to determine whether it is "proper" to vest the appointment of, for example, executive officials in the "courts of Law.". . .

We also note that the history of the clause provides no support for appellees' position. Throughout most of the process of drafting the Constitution, the Convention concentrated on the problem of who should have the authority to appoint judges. [T]here was little or no debate on the question of whether the Clause empowers Congress to provide for interbranch appointments, and there is nothing to suggest that the Framers intended to prevent Congress from having that power.

We do not mean to say that Congress' power to provide for interbranch appointments of "inferior officers" is unlimited. In addition to separation of powers concerns, which would arise if such provisions for appointment had the potential to impair the constitutional functions assigned to one of the branches, [*Ex parte*] *Siebold* [100 U.S. 371 (1880)] itself suggested that Congress' decision to vest the appointment power in the courts would be improper if there was some "incongruity" between the functions normally performed by the courts and the performance of their duty to appoint. . . . In this case, however, we do not think it impermissible for Congress to vest the power to appoint independent counsels in a specially created federal court. . . . Congress of course was concerned when it created the office of independent counsel with the conflicts of interest that could arise in situations when the Executive Branch is called upon to investigate its own high-ranking officers. If it were to remove the appointing authority from the Executive Branch, the most logical place to put it was in the Judicial Branch. In the light of the Act's provision making the judges of the Special Division ineligible to participate in any matters relating to an independent counsel they have appointed, we do not think that appointment of the independent counsels by the court runs afoul of the constitutional limitation on "incongruous" interbranch appointments.

Appellees next contend that the powers vested in the Special

Division by the Act conflict with Article III of the Constitution.

Most importantly, the Act vests in the Special Division the power to choose who will serve as independent counsel and the power to define his or her jurisdiction.

Clearly, once it is accepted that the Appointments Clause gives Congress the power to vest the appointment of officials such as the independent counsel in the "courts of Law," there can be no Article III objection to the Special Division's exercise of that power, as the power itself derives from the Appointments Clause, a source of authority for judicial action that is independent of Article III. . . .

The Act also vests in the Special Division various powers and duties in relation to the independent counsel that, because they do not involve appointing the counsel or defining her jurisdiction, cannot be said to derive from the Division's Appointments Clause authority. These duties include granting extensions for the Attorney General's preliminary investigation; receiving the report of the Attorney General at the conclusion of his preliminary investigation . . . referring matters to the counsel upon request, receiving reports from the counsel regarding expenses incurred . . . receiving a report from the Attorney General following the removal of an independent counsel; granting attorney's fees upon request to individuals who were investigated but not indicted by an independent counsel; receiving a final report from the counsel, § 594(h)(1)(B); deciding whether to release the counsel's final report to Congress or the public and determining whether any protective orders should be issued, § 594(h)(2); and terminating an independent counsel when his task is completed, § 596(b)(2).

Leaving aside for the moment the Division's power to terminate an independent counsel, we do not think that Article III absolutely prevents Congress from vesting these other miscellaneous powers in the Special Division pursuant to the Act. As we observed above, one purpose of the broad prohibition upon the courts' exercise of "executive or administrative duties of a nonjudicial nature," *Buckley* is to maintain the separation between the judiciary and the other branches of the Federal Government by ensuring that judges do not encroach upon executive or legislative authority or undertake tasks that are more properly accomplished by those branches. In this case, the miscellaneous powers described above do not impermissibly trespass upon the authority of the Executive Branch. Some of these allegedly "supervisory" powers conferred on the court are passive: the Division merely "receives" reports from the counsel or the Attorney General, it is not entitled to act on them or to specifically approve or disapprove of their contents. Other provisions of the Act do require the court to exercise some judgment and discretion, but the powers granted by these provisions are themselves essentially ministerial. The Act simply does not give the Division the power to "supervise" the independent counsel in the exercise of her investigative or prosecutorial authority. And, the functions that the Special Division is empowered to perform are not inherently "Executive"; indeed, they are directly analogous to functions that federal judges perform in other contexts, such as deciding whether to allow disclosure of matters occurring before a grand jury, see Fed. Rule Crim.Proc. 6(e), deciding to extend a grand jury investigation, Rule 6(g), or awarding attorney's fees. . . .

We are more doubtful about the Special Division's power to terminate the office of the independent counsel pursuant to § 596(b)(2). As appellees suggest, the power to terminate, especially when exercised by the Division on its own motion, is "administrative" to the extent that it requires the Special Division to monitor the progress of proceedings of the independent counsel and come to a decision as to whether the counsel's job is "completed." It also is not a power that could be considered typically "judicial," as it has few analogues among the court's more traditional powers. Nonetheless, we do not, as did the Court of Appeals, view this provision as a significant judicial encroachment upon executive power or upon the prosecutorial discretion of the independent counsel. . . .

Nor do we believe, as appellees contend, that the Special Division's exercise of the various powers specifically granted to it under the Act poses any threat to the "impartial and independent federal adjudication of claims within the judicial power of the United States." We reach this conclusion for two reasons. First, the Act as it currently stands gives the Special Division itself no power to review any of the actions of the independent counsel or any of the actions of the Attorney General with regard to the counsel. Accordingly, there is no risk of partisan or biased adjudication of claims regarding the independent counsel by that court. Second, the Act prevents members of the Special Division from participating in "*any* judicial proceeding concerning a matter which involves such independent counsel while such independent counsel is serving in that office or which involves the exercise of such independent counsel's official duties, regardless of whether such independent counsel is still serving in that office." (emphasis added); see also § 596(a)(3) (preventing members of the Special Division from participating in review of the Attorney General's decision to remove an independent counsel). We think both the special court and its judges are sufficiently isolated by these statutory provisions from the review of the activities of the independent counsel so as to avoid any taint of the independence of the judiciary such as would render the Act invalid under Article III. . . .

We now turn to consider whether the Act is invalid under the constitutional principle of separation of powers. Two related issues must be addressed: The first is whether the provision of the Act restricting the Attorney General's power to remove the independent counsel to only those instances in which he can show "good cause," taken by itself, impermissibly interferes with the President's exercise of his constitutionally appointed functions. The second is whether, taken as a whole, the Act violates the separation of powers by reducing the President's ability to control the prosecutorial powers wielded by the independent counsel.

Unlike both *Bowsher [v. Synar*, 478 U.S. 714 (1986)] and *Myers*, this case does not involve an attempt by Congress itself to gain a role in the removal of executive officials other than its established powers of impeachment and conviction. The Act instead puts the removal power squarely in the hands of the Executive Branch; an independent counsel may be removed from office, "only by the personal action of the Attorney General, and only for good cause." There is no requirement of congressional approval of the Attorney General's removal decision, though the decision is subject to judicial review. In our view, the removal provisions of the Act make this case more analogous to *Humphrey's Executor v. United States*, 295 U.S. 602 (1935), and *Wiener v. United States*, 357 U.S. (1958), than to *Myers* or *Bowsher*. . . .

Appellees contend that *Humphrey's Executor* and *Wiener* are distinguishable from this case because they did not involve officials who performed a "core executive function." They argue that our decision in *Humphrey's Executor* rests on a distinction between "purely executive" officials and officials who exercise "quasi-legislative" and "quasi-judicial" powers. In their view, when a "purely executive" official is involved, the governing precedent is *Myers*, not *Humphrey's Executor*. And, under *Myers*, the President must have absolute discretion to discharge "purely" executive officials at will.

We undoubtedly did rely on the terms "quasi-legislative" and "quasi-judicial" to distinguish the officials involved in *Humphrey's Executor* and *Wiener* from those in *Myers*, but our present considered view is that the determination of whether the Constitution allows Congress to impose a "good cause"-type restriction on the President's power to remove an official cannot be made to turn on whether or not that official is classified as "purely executive." The analysis contained in our removal cases is designed not to define rigid categories of those officials who may or may not be removed at will by the President, but to ensure that Congress does not interfere with the President's exercise of the "executive power" and his constitutionally appointed duty to "take care that the laws be faithfully executed" under Article II. *Myers* was undoubtedly correct in its holding, and in its broader suggestion that there are some "purely executive" officials who must be removable by the President at will if he is to be able to accomplish his constitutional role. . . . But as the Court noted in *Wiener*,

> "The assumption was short-lived that the *Myers* case recognized the President's inherent constitutional power to remove officials

no matter what the relation of the executive to the discharge of their duties and no matter what restrictions Congress may have imposed regarding the nature of their tenure.". . .

At the other end of the spectrum from *Myers*, the characterization of the agencies in *Humphrey's Executor* and *Wiener* as "quasi-legislative" or "quasi-judicial" in large part reflected our judgment that it was not essential to the President's proper execution of his Article II powers that these agencies be headed up by individuals who were removable at will. We do not mean to suggest that an analysis of the functions served by the officials at issue is irrelevant. But the real question is whether the removal restrictions are of such a nature that they impeded the President's ability to perform his constitutional duty, and the functions of the officials in question must be analyzed in that light.

Considering for the moment the "good cause" removal provision in isolation from the other parts of the Act at issue in this case, we cannot say that the imposition of a "good cause" standard for removal by itself unduly trammels on executive authority. There is no real dispute that the functions performed by the independent counsel are "executive" in the sense that they are law enforcement functions that typically have been undertaken by officials within the Executive Branch. As we noted above, however, the independent counsel is an inferior officer under the Appointments Clause, with limited jurisdiction and tenure and lacking policymaking or significant administrative authority. Although the counsel exercises no small amount of discretion and judgment in deciding how to carry out her duties under the Act, we simply do not see how the President's need to control the exercise of that discretion is so central to the functioning of the Executive Branch as to require as a matter of constitutional law that the counsel be terminable at will by the President.

Nor do we think that the "good cause" removal provision at issue here impermissibly burdens the President's power to control or supervise the independent counsel, as an executive official, in the execution of her duties under the Act. This is not a case in which the power to remove an executive official has been completely stripped from the President, thus providing no means for the President to ensure the "faithful execution" of the laws. Rather, because the independent counsel may be terminated for "good cause," the Executive, through the Attorney General, retains ample authority to assure that the counsel is competently performing her statutory responsibilities in a manner that comports with the provisions of the Act. Although we need not decide in this case exactly what is encompassed within the term "good cause" under the Act, the legislative history of the removal provision also makes clear that the Attorney General may remove an independent counsel for "misconduct." See H.R.Conf.Rep. No. 100–452, p. 37 (1987). Here, as with the provision of the Act conferring the appointment authority of the independent counsel on the special court, the congressional determination to limit the removal power of the Attorney General was essential, in the view of Congress, to establish the necessary independence of the office. We do not think that this limitation as it presently stands sufficiently deprives the President of control over the independent counsel to interfere impermissibly with his constitutional obligation to ensure the faithful execution of the laws.

The final question to be addressed is whether the Act, taken as a whole, violates the principle of separation of powers by unduly interfering with the role of the Executive Branch. . . .

We observe first that this case does not involve an attempt by Congress to increase its own powers at the expense of the Executive Branch. Unlike some of our previous cases, most recently *Bowsher v. Synar*, this case simply does not pose a "dange[r] of congressional usurpation of Executive Branch functions." Indeed, with the exception of the power of impeachment—which applies to all officers of the United States—Congress retained for itself no powers of control or supervision over an independent counsel. The Act does empower certain members of Congress to request the Attorney General to apply for the appointment of an independent counsel, but the Attorney General has no duty to comply with the request, although he must respond within a certain time limit. § 529(g). Other than that, Congress' role under the Act is limited to receiving reports or other information and oversight of the independent counsel's activities, § 595(a), functions that we have recognized generally as being incidental to the legislative function of Congress. . . .

Similarly, we do not think that the Act works any *judicial* usurpation of properly executive functions. As should be apparent from our discussion of the Appointments Clause above, the power to appoint inferior officers such as independent counsels is not in itself an "executive" function in the constitutional sense, at least when Congress has exercised its power to vest the appointment of an inferior office in the "courts of Law.". . .

Finally, we do not think that the Act "impermissibly undermine[s]" the powers of the Executive Branch or "disrupts the proper balance between the coordinate branches [by] prevent[ing] the Executive Branch from accomplishing its constitutionally assigned functions," *Nixon v. Administrator of General Services*, [433 U.S. 425 (1977)]. It is undeniable that the Act reduces the amount of control or supervision that the Attorney General and, through him, the President exercises over the investigation and prosecution of a certain class of alleged criminal activity. The Attorney General is not allowed to appoint the individual of his choice; he does not determine the counsel's jurisdiction; and his power to remove a counsel is limited. Nonetheless, the Act does give the Attorney General several means of supervising or controlling the prosecutorial powers that may be wielded by an independent counsel. Most importantly, the Attorney General retains the power to remove the counsel for "good cause," a power that we have already concluded provides the Executive with substantial ability to ensure that the laws are "faithfully executed" by an independent counsel. . . .

In sum, we conclude today that it does not violate the Appointments Clause for Congress to vest the appointment of independent counsels in the Special Division; that the powers exercised by the Special Division under the Act do not violate Article III; and that the Act does not violate the separation of powers principle by impermissibly interfering with the functions of the Executive Branch. The decision of the Court of Appeals is therefore

Reversed.

Justice KENNEDY did not participate in the consideration or decision of this case.

Justice SCALIA dissenting.

The principle of separation of powers is expressed in our Constitution in the first section of each of the first three Articles. Article I, § 1 provides that "[a]ll legislative Powers herein granted shall be vested in a Congress of the United States, which shall consist of a Senate and House of Representatives." Article III, § 1 provides that "[t]he judicial Power of the United States, shall be vested in one supreme Court, and in such inferior Courts as the Congress may from time to time ordain and establish." And the provision at issue here, Art. II, § 1, cl. 1 provides that "[t]he executive Power shall be vested in a President of the United States of America."

But just as the mere words of a Bill of Rights are not self-effectuating, the framers recognized "[t]he insufficiency of a mere parchment delineation of the boundaries" to achieve the separation of powers. Federalist No. 73, (Hamilton). "[T]he great security," wrote Madison, "against a gradual concentration of the several powers in the same department consists in giving to those who administer each department the necessary constitutional means and personal motives to resist encroachments of the others. The provision for defense must in this, as in all other cases, be made commensurate to the danger of attack." Federalist No. 51. Madison continued:

> "But it is not possible to give to each department an equal power of self-defense. In republican government, the legislative authority necessarily predominates. The remedy for this inconveniency is to divide the legislature into different branches;

and to render them, by different modes of election and different principles of action, as little connected with each other as the nature of their common functions and their common dependence on the society will admit. . . . As the weight of the legislative authority requires that it should be thus divided, the weakness of the executive may require, on the other hand, that it should be fortified."

The major "fortification" provided, of course, was the veto power. But in addition to providing fortification, the founders conspicuously and very consciously declined to sap the executive's strength in the same way they had weakened the legislature: by dividing the executive power. . . .

That is what this suit is about. Power. The allocation of power among Congress, the President and the courts in such fashion as to preserve the equilibrium the Constitution sought to establish—so that "a gradual concentration of the several powers in the same department," Federalist No. 51 (J. Madison), can effectively be resisted. Frequently an issue of this sort will come before the Court clad, so to speak, in sheep's clothing: the potential of the asserted principle to effect important change in the equilibrium of power is not immediately evident, and must be discerned by a careful and perceptive analysis. But this wolf comes as a wolf. . . .

[B]y the application of this statute in the present case, Congress has effectively compelled a criminal investigation of a high-level appointee of the President in connection with his actions arising out of a bitter power dispute between the President and the Legislative Branch. Mr. Olson may or may not be guilty of a crime; we do not know. But we do know that the investigation of him has been commenced, not necessarily because the President or his authorized subordinates believe it is in the interest of the United States, in the sense that it warrants the diversion of resources from other efforts, and is worth the cost in money and in possible damage to other governmental interests; and not even, leaving aside those normally considered factors, because the President or his authorized subordinates necessarily believe that an investigation is likely to unearth a violation worth prosecuting; but only because the Attorney General cannot affirm, as Congress demands, that there are *no reasonable grounds to believe* that further investigation is warranted. The decisions regarding the scope of that further investigation, its duration, and, finally, whether or not prosecution should ensue, are likewise beyond the control of the President and his subordinates. . . .

The Court devotes most of its attention to such relatively technical details as the Appointments Clause and the removal power, addressing briefly and only at the end of its opinion the separation of powers. As my prologue suggests, I think that has it backwards.

Our opinions are full of the recognition that it is the principle of separation of powers, and the inseparable corollary that each department's "defense must . . . be made commensurate to the danger of attack," Federalist No. 51 (J. Madison), which gives comprehensible content to the appointments clause, and determines the appropriate scope of the removal power. Thus, while I will subsequently discuss why our appointments and removal jurisprudence does not support today's holding, I begin with a consideration of the fountainhead of that jurisprudence, the separation and equilibration of powers. . . .

To repeat, Art. II, § 1, cl. 1 of the Constitution provides:

> "The executive Power shall be vested in a President of the United States."

As I described at the outset of this opinion, this does not mean *some of* the executive power, but *all of* the executive power. It seems to me, therefore, that the decision of the Court of Appeals invalidating the present statute must be upheld on fundamental separation-of-powers principles if the following two questions are answered affirmatively: (1) Is the conduct of a criminal prosecution (and of an investigation to decide whether to prosecute) the exercise of purely executive power? (2) Does the statute deprive the President of the United States of exclusive control over the exercise of that power? Surprising to say, the Court appears to concede an affirmative answer to both questions, but seeks to avoid the inevitable conclusion that since the statute vests some purely executive power in a person who is not the President of the United States it is void.

The Court concedes that "[t]here is no real dispute that the functions performed by the independent counsel are 'executive'," though it qualifies that concession by adding "in the sense that they are 'law enforcement' functions that typically have been undertaken by officials within the Executive Branch." The qualifier adds nothing but atmosphere. In what *other* sense can one identify "the executive Power" that is supposed to be vested in the President (unless it includes everything the Executive Branch is given to do) *except* by reference to what has always and everywhere—if conducted by Government at all—been conducted never by the legislature, never by the courts, and always by the executive. There is no possible doubt that the independent counsel's functions fit this description. She is vested with the "full power and independent authority to exercise all *investigative and prosecutorial* functions and powers of the Department of Justice [and] the Attorney General." 28 U.S.C. § 594(a) (emphasis added). Governmental investigation and prosecution of crimes is a quintessentially executive function. . . .

As for the second question, whether the statute before us deprives the President of exclusive control over that quintessentially executive activity: The Court does not, and could not possibly, assert that it does not. That is indeed the whole object of the statute. Instead, the Court points out that the President, through his Attorney General, has at least *some* control. That concession is alone enough to invalidate the statute, but I cannot refrain from pointing out that the Court greatly exaggerates the extent of that "some" presidential control. "Most importan[t]" among these controls, the Court asserts, is the Attorney General's "power to remove the counsel for 'good cause.' " This is somewhat like referring to shackles as an effective means of locomotion. As we recognized in *Humphrey's Executor v. United States* (1935)—indeed, what *Humphrey's Executor* was all about—limiting removal power to "good cause" is an impediment to, not an effective grant of, presidential control. We said that limitation was necessary with respect to members of the Federal Trade Commission, which we found to be "an agency of the legislative and judicial departments," and "wholly disconnected from the executive department" because "it is quite evident that one who holds his office only during the pleasure of another, cannot be depended upon to maintain an attitude of independence against the latter's will." What we in *Humphrey's Executor* found to be a means of eliminating presidential control, the Court today considers the "most importan[t]" means of assuring presidential control. Congress, of course, operated under no such illusion when it enacted this statute, describing the "good cause" limitation as "protecting the independent counsel's ability to act independently of the President's direct control" since it permits removal only for "misconduct." H.R.Conf. Rep. 100–452, p. 37 (1987).

Moving on to the presumably "less important" controls that the President retains, the Court notes that no independent counsel may be appointed without a specific request from the Attorney General. As I have discussed above, the condition that renders such a request mandatory (inability to find "no reasonable grounds to believe" that further investigation is warranted) is so insubstantial that the Attorney General's discretion is severely confined. And once the referral is made, it is for the Special Division to determine the scope and duration of the investigation. And in any event, the limited power over referral is irrelevant to the question whether, *once appointed,* the independent counsel exercises executive power free from the President's control. Finally, the Court points out that the Act directs the independent counsel to abide by general Justice Department policy, except when not "possible." The exception alone shows this to be an empty promise. Even without that, however, one would be hard put to come up with many investigative or prosecutorial "policies" (other than those imposed by the Constitution or by Congress through law) that are absolute. Almost all investigative and prosecutorial decisions—including the ultimate decision whether, after a technical violation of the law has been found, prosecution is warranted—involve the balancing of innumerable legal and practical considerations. In sum, the balancing of various legal, practical and political considerations, none of which is absolute, is the very essence of prosecutorial discretion. To take this away is to remove the core of the prosecutorial function, and not merely "some" presidential control.

As I have said, however, it is ultimately irrelevant *how much* the statute reduces presidential control. The case is over when the Court acknowledges, as it must, that "[i]t is undeniable that the Act reduces the amount of control or supervision that the Attorney General and, through him, the President exercises over the investigation and prosecution of a certain class of alleged criminal activity." It effects a revolution in our constitutional jurisprudence for the Court, once it has determined that (1) purely executive functions are at issue here, and (2) those functions have been given to a person whose actions are not fully within the supervision and control of the President, nonetheless to proceed further to sit in judgment of whether "the President's need to control the exercise of [the independent counsel's] discretion is *so central* to the functioning of the Executive Branch" as to require complete control (emphasis added), whether the conferral of his powers upon someone else "*sufficiently* deprives the President of control over the independent counsel to interfere impermissibly with [his] constitutional obligation to ensure the faithful execution of the laws" (emphasis added), and whether "the Act give[s] the Executive Branch *sufficient* control over the independent counsel to ensure that the President is able to perform his constitutionally assigned duties" (emphasis added). It is not for us to determine, and we have never presumed to determine, how much of the purely executive powers of government must be within the full control of the President. The Constitution prescribes that they *all* are. . . .

The Court has, nonetheless, replaced the clear constitutional prescription that the executive power belongs to the President with a "balancing test." What are the standards to determine how the balance is to be struck, that is, how much removal of presidential power is too much? Many countries of the world get along with an Executive that is much weaker than ours—in fact, entirely dependent upon the continued support of the legislature. Once we depart from the text of the Constitution, just where short of that do we stop? The most amazing feature of the Court's opinion is that it does not even purport to give an answer. It simply *announces*, with no analysis, that the ability to control the decision whether to investigate and prosecute the President's closest advisors, and indeed the President himself, is not "so central to the functioning of the Executive Branch" as to be constitutionally required to be within the President's control. Apparently

that is so because we say it is so. Evidently, the governing standard
is to be what might be called the unfettered wisdom of a majority
of this Court, revealed to an obedient people on a case-by-case
basis. This is not only not the government of laws that the Constitution established; it is not a government of laws at all.

In my view, moreover, even as an ad hoc, standardless judgment
the Court's conclusion must be wrong. Before this statute was
passed, the President, in taking action disagreeable to the Congress, or an executive officer giving advice to the President or
testifying before Congress concerning one of those many matters
on which the two branches are from time to time at odds, could
be assured that his acts and motives would be adjudged—insofar
as the decision whether to conduct a criminal investigation and
to prosecute is concerned—in the Executive Branch, that is, in
a forum attuned to the interests and the policies of the Presidency.
That was one of the natural advantages the Constitution gave
to the Presidency, just as it gave Members of Congress (and their
staffs) the advantage of not being prosecutable for anything said
or done in their legislative capacities. See U.S. Const., Art. I,
§ 6, cl. 1; *Gravel v. United States,* 408 U.S. 606 (1972). It is the
very object of this legislation to eliminate that assurance of a
sympathetic forum. Unless it can honestly be said that there are
"no reasonable grounds to believe" that further investigation is
warranted, further investigation must ensue; and the conduct
of the investigation, and determination of whether to prosecute,
will be given to a person neither selected by nor subject to the
control of the President—who will in turn assemble a staff by
finding out, presumably, who is willing to put aside whatever
else they are doing, for an indeterminate period of time, in order
to investigate and prosecute the President or a particular named
individual in his administration. The prospect is frightening (as
I will discuss at some greater length at the conclusion of this
opinion) even outside the context of a bitter, interbranch political
dispute. Perhaps the boldness of the President himself will not
be affected—though I am not even sure of that. (How much
easier it is for Congress, instead of accepting the political damage
attendant to the commencement of impeachment proceedings
against the President on trivial grounds—or, for that matter, how
easy it is for one of the President's political foes outside of Congress—simply to trigger a debilitating criminal investigation of
the Chief Executive under this law.) But as for the President's
high-level assistants, who typically have no political base of support, it is as, utterly unrealistic to think that they will not be
intimidated by this prospect, and that their advice to him and
their advocacy of his interests before a hostile Congress will not
be affected, as it would be to think that the Members of Congress
and their staffs would be unaffected by replacing the Speech or
Debate Clause with a similar provision. It deeply wounds the

President, by substantially reducing the President's ability to protect himself and his staff. That is the whole object of the law, of course, and I cannot imagine why the Court believes it does not succeed.

Besides weakening the Presidency by reducing the zeal of his staff, it must also be obvious that the institution of the independent counsel enfeebles him more directly in his constant confrontations with Congress, by eroding his public support. Nothing is so politically effective as the ability to charge that one's opponent and his associates are not merely wrong-headed, naive, ineffective, but, in all probability, "crooks." And nothing so effectively gives an appearance of validity to such charges as a Justice Department investigation and, even better, prosecution. The present statute provides ample means for that sort of attack. . . .

As I indicated earlier, the basic separation-of-powers principles I have discussed are what give life and content to our jurisprudence concerning the President's power to appoint and remove officers. The same result of unconstitutionality is therefore plainly indicated by our caselaw in these areas. . . .

Because appellant (who all parties and the Court agree is an officer of the United States) was not appointed by the President with the advice and consent of the Senate, but rather by the Special Division of the United States Court of Appeals, her appointment is constitutional only if (1) she is an "inferior" officer within the meaning of the above clause, and (2) Congress may vest her appointment in a court of law.

As to the first of these inquiries, the Court does not attempt to "decide exactly" what establishes the line between principal and "inferior" officers, but is confident that, whatever the line may be, appellant "clearly falls on the 'inferior officer' side" of it. The Court gives three reasons: *First,* she "is subject to removal by a higher Executive branch official," namely the Attorney General. *Second,* she is "empowered by the Act to perform only certain, limited duties." *Third,* her office is "limited in jurisdiction" and "limited in tenure." . . .

The first of these lends no support to the view that appellant is an inferior officer. Appellant is removable only for "good cause" or physical or mental incapacity. By contrast, most (if not all) *principal* officers in the Executive Branch may be removed by the President *at will.* I fail to see how the fact that appellant is more difficult to remove than most principal officers helps to establish that she is an inferior officer. . . .

The second reason offered by the Court—that appellant performs only certain, limited duties—may be relevant to whether she is an inferior officer, but it mischaracterizes the extent of her powers. . . .

The final set of reasons given by the Court for why the independent counsel clearly is an inferior officer emphasizes the limited nature of her jurisdiction and tenure. Taking the latter first, I find nothing unusually limited about the independent counsel's tenure. To the contrary, unlike most high-ranking Executive Branch officials, she continues to serve until she (or the Special Division) decides that her work is substantially completed. . . . This particular independent prosecutor has already served more than two years, which is at least as long as many cabinet officials. As to the scope of her jurisdiction, there can be no doubt that is small (though far from unimportant). But within it she exercises more than the full power of the Attorney General. . . .

More fundamentally, however, it is not clear from the Court's opinion why the factors it discusses—even if applied correctly to the facts of this case—are determinative of the question of inferior officer status. The apparent source of these factors is a statement in *United States v. Germaine*, 99 U.S. (9 Otto) 508 (1879) (discussing *United States v. Hartwell*, 6 Wall. 385 (1868)), that "the term [officer] embraces the ideas of tenure, duration, emolument and duties." Besides the fact that this was dictum, it was dictum in a case where the distinguishing characteristics of inferior officers versus superior officers were in no way relevant, but rather only the distinguishing characteristics of an "officer of the United States" (to which the criminal statute at issue applied) as opposed to a mere *employee*. Rather than erect a theory of who is an inferior officer on the foundation of such an irrelevancy, I think it preferable to look to the text of the Constitution and the division of power that it establishes. These demonstrate, I think, that the independent counsel is not an inferior officer because she is not *subordinate* to any officer in the Executive Branch (indeed, not even to the President). Dictionaries in use at the time of the Constitutional Convention gave the word "inferiour" two meanings which it still bears today: (1) "[l]ower in place, . . . station, . . . rank of life, . . . value or excellency," and (2) "[s]ubordinate." S. Johnson, Dictionary of the English Language (6th ed. 1785). In a document dealing with the structure (the constitution) of a government, one would naturally expect the word to bear the latter meaning—indeed, in such a context it would be unpardonably careless to use the word *unless* a relationship of subordination was intended. If what was meant was merely "lower in station or rank," one would use instead a term such as "lesser officers." At the only other point in the Constitution at which the word "inferior" appears, it plainly connotes a relationship of subordination. Article III vests the judicial Power of the United States in "one supreme Court, and in such *inferior* Courts as the Congress may from time to time ordain and establish." U.S. Const., Art. III, § 1 (emphasis added). In Federalist No. 81, Hamilton pauses to describe the "inferior" courts authorized by Art. III as inferior in the sense that they are "subordinate" to the Supreme Court. . . .

That "inferior" means "subordinate" is also consistent with what little we know about the evolution of the Appointments Clause. . . .

To be sure, it is not a *sufficient* condition for "inferior" officer status that one be subordinate to a principal officer. Even an officer who is subordinate to a department head can be a principal officer. . . .

The independent counsel is not even subordinate to the President. The Court essentially admits as much, noting that "appellant may not be 'subordinate' to the Attorney General (and the President) insofar as she possesses a degree of independent discretion to exercise the powers delegated to her under the Act." In fact, there is no doubt about it. As noted earlier, the Act specifically grants her the "*full* power and *independent* authority to exercise *all* investigative and prosecutorial functions of the Department of Justice" and makes her removable only for "good cause," a limitation specifically intended to ensure that she be *independent* of, not *subordinate* to, the President and the Attorney General. See H.R.Conf.Rep. No. 100–452, 37 (1987).

Because appellant is not subordinate to another officer, she is not an "inferior" officer and her appointment other than by the President with the advice and consent of the Senate is unconstitutional. . . .

There is of course no provision in the Constitution stating who may remove executive officers, except the provisions for removal by impeachment. Before the present decision it was established, however, (1) that the President's power to remove principal officers who exercise purely executive powers could not be restricted, see *Myers v. United States,* 272 U.S. 52 (1926), and (2) that his power to remove inferior officers who exercise purely executive powers, and whose appointment Congress had removed from the usual procedure of presidential appointment with Senate consent, could be restricted, at least where the appointment had been made by an officer of the Executive Branch. . . .

The Court could have resolved the removal power issue in this case by simply relying upon its erroneous conclusion that the independent counsel was an inferior officer, and then extending our holding that the removal of inferior officers appointed by the Executive can be restricted, to a new holding that even the removal of inferior officers appointed by the courts can be restricted. That would in my view be a considerable and unjustified extension, giving the Executive full discretion in *neither* the selection *nor* the removal of a purely executive officer. The course the Court has chosen, however, is even worse.

Since our 1935 decision in *Humphrey's Executor v. United States* —which was considered by many at the time the product of an activist, anti-New Deal court bent on reducing the power of President Franklin Roosevelt—it has been established that the line of permissible restriction upon removal of principal officers lies at the point at which the powers exercised by those officers are no longer purely executive. Thus, removal restrictions have been generally regarded as lawful for so-called "independent regulatory agencies," such as the Federal Trade Commission, the Interstate Commerce Commission, and the Consumer Products Safety Commission, which engage substantially in what has been called the "quasi-legislative activity" of rulemaking, and for members of Article I courts, such as the Court of Military Appeals who engage in the "quasi-judicial" function of adjudication. It has often been observed, correctly in my view, that the line between "purely executive" functions and "quasi-legislative" or "quasi-judicial" functions is not a clear one or even a rational one. . . . But at least it permitted the identification of certain officers, and certain agencies, whose functions were entirely within the control of the President. Congress had to be aware of that restriction in its legislation. Today, however, *Humphrey's Executor* is swept into the dustbin of repudiated constitutional principles. "[O]ur present considered view," the Court says, "is that the determination of whether the Constitution allows Congress to impose a 'good cause'-type restriction on the President's power to remove an official cannot be made to turn on whether or not that official is classified as 'purely executive.' " What *Humphrey's Executor* (and presumably *Myers*) really means, we are now told, is not that there are any "rigid categories of those officials who may or may not be removed at will by the President," but simply that Congress cannot "interefere with the President's exercise of the 'executive power' and his constitutionally appointed duty to 'take care that the laws be faithfully executed.' ". . .

One can hardly grieve for the shoddy treatment given today to *Humphrey's Executor,* which, after all, accorded the same indignity (with much less justification) to Chief Justice TAFT's opinion 10 years earlier in *Myers v. United States, supra*—gutting, in six quick pages devoid of textual or historical precedent for the novel principle it set forth, a carefully researched and reasoned 70-page opinion. It is in fact comforting to witness the reality that he who lives by the *ipse dixit* dies by the *ipse dixit.* But one must grieve for the Constitution. *Humphrey's Executor* at least had the decency formally to observe the constitutional principle that the President had to be the repository of *all* executive power which, as *Myers* carefully explained, necessarily means that he must be able to discharge those who do not perform executive functions according to his liking. As we noted in *Bowsher,* once an officer is appointed " 'it is only the authority that can remove him, and not the authority that appointed him, that he must fear and, in the performance of his functions, obey.' " By contrast, "our present considered view" is simply that *any* Executive officer's removal can be restricted, so long as the President remains "able to accomplish his constitutional role." There are now no lines. If the removal of a prosecutor, the virtual embodiment of the power to "take care that the laws be faithfully executed," can be restricted, what officer's removal cannot? This is an open invitation for Congress to experiment. What about a special Assistant Secretary of State, with responsibility for one very narrow area of foreign policy, who would not only have to be confirmed by the Senate but could also be removed only pursuant to certain carefully designed restrictions? Could this possibly render the President "[un]able to accomplish his constitutional role"? Or a special Assistant Secretary of Defense for Procurement? The possibilities are endless, and the Court does not understand what the separation of powers, what "[a]mbition . . . counteract[ing] ambition," Federalist No. 51 (Madison), is all about, if it does not expect Congress to try them. As far as I can discern from the Court's opinion, it is now open season upon the President's removal power for all executive officers, with not even the superficially principled restriction of *Humphrey's Executor* as cover. The Court essentially says to the President "Trust us. We will make sure that you are able to accomplish your constitutional role." I think the Constitution gives the President—and the people—more protection than that.

The purpose of the separation and equilibration of powers in general, and of the unitary Executive in particular, was not merely to assure effective government but to preserve individual freedom. Those who hold or have held offices covered by the Ethics in Government Act are entitled to that protection as much as the rest of us, and I conclude my discussion by considering the effect of the Act upon the fairness of the process they receive.

Only someone who has worked in the field of law enforcement can fully appreciate the vast power and the immense discretion that are placed in the hands of a prosecutor with respect to the objects of his investigation. . . .

Under our system of government, the primary check against prosecutorial abuse is a political one. The prosecutors who exercise this awesome discretion are selected and can be removed by a President, whom the people have trusted enough to elect. Moreover, when crimes are not investigated and prosecuted fairly, nonselectively with a reasonable sense of proportion, the President pays the cost in political damage to his administration. . . .

That is the system of justice the rest of us are entitled to, but what of that select class consisting of present or former high-level executive-branch officials? If an allegation is made against them of any violation of any federal criminal law (except Class B or C misdemeanors or infractions) the Attorney General must give it his attention. That in itself is not objectionable. But if, after a 90-day investigation without the benefit of normal investigatory tools, the Attorney General is unable to say that there are "no reasonable grounds to believe" that further investigation

is warranted, a process is set in motion that is *not* in the full
control of persons "dependent on the people," and whose flaws
cannot be blamed on the President. An independent counsel is
selected, and the scope of her authority prescribed, by a panel
of judges. What if they are politically partisan, as judges have
been known to be, and select a prosecutor antagonistic to the
administration, or even to the particular individual who has been
selected for this special treatment? There is no remedy for that,
not even a political one. Judges, after all, have life tenure, and
appointing a sure-fire enthusiastic prosecutor could hardly be
considered an impeachable offense. So if there is anything wrong
with the selection, there is effectively no one to blame. The independent counsel thus selected proceeds to assemble a staff. As I
observed earlier, in the nature of things this has to be done by
finding lawyers who are willing to lay aside their current careers
for an indeterminate amount of time, to take on a job that has
no prospect of permanence and little prospect for promotion.
One thing is certain, however: it involves investigating and perhaps prosecuting a particular individual. Can one imagine a less
equitable manner of fulfilling the Executive responsibility to investigate and prosecute? What would be the reaction if, in an area
not covered by this statute, the Justice Department posted a public
notice inviting applicants to assist in an investigation and possible
prosecution of a certain prominent person? Does this not invite
what Justice JACKSON described as "picking the man and then
searching the law books, or putting investigators to work, to pin
some offense on him"? To be sure, the investigation must relate
to the area of criminal offense specified by the life-tenured judges.
But that has often been (and nothing prevents it from being)
very broad—and should the independent counsel or her staff
come up with something beyond that scope, nothing prevents
her from asking the judges to expand her authority or, if that
does not work, referring it to the Attorney General, whereupon
the whole process would recommence and, if there was "reasonable basis to believe" that further investigation was warranted,
that new offense would be referred to the Special Tribunal, which
would in all likelihood assign it to the same independent counsel.
It seems to me not conducive to fairness. But even if it were
entirely evident that unfairness was in fact the result—the judges
hostile to the administration, the independent counsel an old
foe of the President, the staff refugees from the recently defeated
administration—*there would be no one accountable to the public to
whom the blame could be assigned.*

I do not mean to suggest that anything of this sort (other than
the inevitable self-selection of the prosecutory staff) occurred in
the present case. I know and have the highest regard for the
judges on the Special Division, and the independent counsel her-
self is a woman of accomplishment, impartiality and integrity.

But the fairness of a process must be adjudged on the basis of what it permits to happen, not what it produced in a particular case. It is true, of course, that a similar list of horribles could be attributed to an ordinary Justice Department prosecution—a vindictive prosecutor an antagonistic staff, etc. But the difference is the difference that the Founders envisioned when they established a single Chief Executive accountable to the people, the blame can be assigned to someone who can be punished. . . .

The notion that every violation of law should be prosecuted, including—indeed, *especially*—every violation by those in high places, is an attractive one, and it would be risky to argue in an election campaign that that is not an absolutely overriding value. *Fiat justitia, ruat coelum.* Let justice be done, though the heavens may fall. The reality is, however, that it is not an absolutely overriding value, and it was with the hope that we would be able to acknowledge and apply such realities that the Constitution spared us, by life tenure, the necessity of election campaigns. I cannot imagine that there are not many thoughtful men and women in Congress who realize that the benefits of this legislation are far outweighed by its harmful effect upon our system of government, and even upon the nature of justice received by those men and women who agree to serve in the Executive Branch. But it is difficult to vote not to enact, and even more difficult to vote to repeal, a statute called, appropriately enough, the Ethics in Government Act. If Congress is controlled by the party other than the one to which the President belongs, it has little incentive to repeal it; if it is controlled by the same party, it dare not. By its short-sighted action today, I fear the Court has permanently encumbered the Republic with an institution that will do it great harm.

Worse than what it has done, however, is the manner in which it has done it. A government of laws means a government of rules. Today's decision on the basic issue of fragmentation of executive power is ungoverned by rule, and hence ungoverned by law. It extends into the very heart of our most significant constitutional function the "totality of the circumstances" mode of analysis that this Court has in recent years become fond of. Taking all things into account, we conclude that the power taken away from the President here is not really *too* much. The next time executive power is assigned to someone other than the President we may conclude, taking all things into account, that it *is* too much. That opinion, like this one, will not be confined by any rule. We will describe, as we have today (though I hope more accurately) the effects of the provision in question, and will authoritatively announce: "The President's need to control the exercise of the [subject officer's] discretion *is* so central to the functioning of the Executive Branch as to require complete control." This is not analysis; it is ad hoc judgment. And it fails to explain why it is not true that—as the text of the Constitution seems to require, as the Founders seemed to expect, and as our past cases have uniformly assumed—all purely executive power must be under the control of the President.

The ad hoc approach to constitutional adjudication has real attraction, even apart from its work-saving potential. It is guaranteed to produce a result, in every case, that will make a majority of the Court happy with the law. The law is, by definition, precisely what the majority thinks, taking all things into account, it *ought* to be. I prefer to rely upon the judgment of the wise men who constructed our system, and of the people who approved it, and of two centuries of history that have shown it to be sound. Like it or not, that judgment says, quite plainly, that "[t]he executive Power shall be vested in a President of the United States."

C. LEGISLATIVE POWERS IN THE ADMINISTRATIVE STATE

The president's role in initiating and formulating legislation as well as in overseeing and controlling its implementation has expanded enormously as a result of Congress's delegation of its powers to the executive branch and the growth of the institutional presidency. As noted earlier, the president's State of the Union address has become an occasion for the presentation of his legislative and budget recommendations to Congress. Although Congress is given the power of the purse (in Article I, Section 9), since the Budget and Accounting Act of 1921 the president has assumed responsibility for submitting budget estimates to Congress, which then may increase or decrease specific items in the "executive budget." More recently, the Office of Management and Budget was given the major responsibility for preparing budget estimates for the White House.[1]

To safeguard against congressional usurpation of presidential power, the Constitutional Convention guaranteed the president a role in the passage of legislation. Article I, Section 7 requires the president's approval or disapproval of "every order, resolution, or vote to which the concurrance of the State and the House of Representatives may be necessary." The president may veto legislation, although not particular items in a bill, by returning a bill unsigned to the house in which it originated, along with his objections. If within ten days of receiving a bill the president neither signs nor vetoes it, the bill becomes law without his signature. But if Congress goes out of session within that period, then the president may exercise what is called a "pocket veto" by simply not returning the bill. The president's veto power over legislation is qualified, however, because it may be overridden by a two-thirds vote of both houses. Congress may also pass "concurrent resolutions," which do not require approval of the president to become law.

Broad delegations of congressional lawmaking power to the executive branch are almost invariably upheld by the Court. This is so despite the fact that the Constitution delegates the lawmaking power to Congress and the age-old Latin maxim— or nondelegation doctrine—that "delegated power may not be [re]delegated."

In *Wayman v. Southard*, 23 U.S. 1 (1825), the Marshall Court initially sanctioned delegated powers as necessary "to fill in the details" and to implement the general provisions of legislation. Subsequently, the Court upheld virtually every delegation of lawmaking power to administrative agencies so long as Congress laid "down by legislative act an intelligible principle to which the person or body authorized to take action is directed to conform."[2] As a result, Congress delegates to administrative agencies extensive powers under exceeding broad standards, such as legislation authorizing the Interstate Commerce Commission (ICC) to fix "just and reasonable" rates, and the Federal Communications Commission (FCC) to grant radio licenses when in the "public convenience, interest or necessity."

With the exception of a brief period during the New Deal, the Court has refused to enforce the nondelegation doctrine. In two 1935 cases the Court did strike down major pieces of New Deal legislation aimed at easing the Depression for impermissibly delegating power. The "hot oil case," *Panama Refining Company v. Ryan*, 293 U.S. 388 (1935), invalidated part of the National Industry Recovery Act of 1933 for giving the president authority to exclude from interstate commerce oil produced in excess of state regulations. The other is known as "the sick chicken case," *Schechter Poultry Corporation v. United States* (1935) (see page 343). The following year the Court also struck down the Guffey Coal Act, in *Carter v. Carter Coal Co.*, 298 U.S. 238 (1936), as an impermissible delegation of power to set up a regulatory code for the coal industry.

Since 1937 the Court has not found any other legislation to run afoul of the nondelegation doctrine. Most commentators thus view the nondelegation doctrine as "moribund," in the words of Justice Thurgood Marshall in *FPC v. New England Power Co.*, 415 U.S. 345 (1974). However, Chief Justice Rehnquist in several cases, notably in his concurring opinion in *Industrial Union Department, AFL-CIO v. American Petroleum Institute* (1980) (see page 351), argues that the doctrine ought to be revived.[3]

The president and the executive branch also exercise significant power when interpreting and enforcing legislation under

the obligation to "take Care that the Laws be faithfully executed."
But controversies arise when the president and his subordinates
refuse to enforce laws deemed in conflict with their legal policy
goals or detrimental to the nation. While some courts have ruled
that the "take care" clause poses a duty to enforce the laws,
even those with which the president disagrees,[4] the judiciary
tends to defer to the executive branch in recognizing that traditional principles of prosecutorial discretion allow agencies to
decide when and how to enforce laws. *Heckler v. Chaney*, 470
U.S. 821 (1985), for example, refused to scrutinize the Food
and Drug Administration's failure to regulate drugs used by
some states in carrying out capital punishment.

A related controversy involves whether, given the obligation
to faithfully execute the laws, the president may impound funds
for specific programs that Congress has appropriated. Richard
M. Nixon, among other presidents, claimed an inherent power
to refuse to spend funds or otherwise carry out laws as authorized
by Congress. The Court has not yet resolved this constitutional
issue. But in *Train v. City of New York*, 420 U.S. 35 (1975), it
held as a statutory matter that the president could not withhold
funds provided by Congress for the enforcement of the Federal
Water Pollution Control Act.[5]

Jagdish Rai Chadha with his wife and one of their three daughters.
Terrence McCarthy/New York Times Pictures.

Congress nevertheless retains significant powers of overseeing its delegations to the executive branch, through its appropriation and oversight hearings in particular. When delegating broad power to executive agencies, Congress also frequently required agencies to report their decisions to Congress and authorized one or both Houses to overturn, within a specified period of time, agency decisions by passing a "legislative veto." But in a far-reaching 1983 ruling, in *Immigration and Naturalization Service v. Chadha* (1983) (see page 355), the Court ruled that "legislative vetoes" violate the principle of separation of powers.

NOTES

1. See Louis Fisher, *Presidential Spending Power* (Princeton, NJ: Princeton University Press, 1975).
2. *J.W. Hampton, Jr. & Co. v. United States*, 276 U.S. 394 (1928).
3. For a defense of the Court's enforcement of the nondelegation doctrine, see Theodore Lowi, *The End of Liberalism*, 2nd ed. (New York: W. W. Norton, 1977).
4. See *Nader v. Saxbe*, 497 F.2d 676 (D.C.Cir., 1974).
5. For further discussion, see Note, "Presidential Impoundment: Constitutional Theories and Political Realities," 61 *Georgetown Law Journal* 1295 (1973).

SELECTED BIBLIOGRAPHY

Barber, Sotirios. *The Constitution and the Delegation of Congressional Power.* Chicago: University of Chicago Press, 1975.
Craig, Barbara. *Chadha.* New York: Oxford University Press, 1988.
Fisher, Louis. *Presidential Spending Power.* Princeton, NJ: Princeton University Press, 1975.

Schechter Poultry Corporation v. United States
295 U.S. 495, 55 S.Ct. 837 (1935)

In 1933 Congress passed the National Industrial Recovery Act, under its power to regulate interstate commerce and as part of President Franklin D. Roosevelt's New Deal Program, to help stimulate the economy and reduce unemployment. Under the act, the National Recovery Administration was authorized to set fair codes for business competition, including standards for wages, hours, and working conditions.

The Schechter brothers operated slaughterhouses in New York City, which received live chickens from outside the state, slaughtered them, and then sold them to local stores. They were convicted in a federal district court of violating a number of standards set by the National Recovery Administration. After an appellate court affirmed, they appealed to the Supreme Court.

The Court granted the Schechters' petition for *certiorari* and ruled in their favor on two grounds. First, the Court found that the Schechters were engaged in intrastate commerce that had only an indirect effect on interstate commerce and, therefore, their business was outside the scope of Congress's regulatory power over interstate commerce. Second, in the excerpt here, Chief Justice Charles Hughes found a portion of the National Industrial Recovery Act authorizing the establishment of a Live Poultry Code to be an unconstitutional delegation of power to the executive branch.

Chief Justice HUGHES delivers the opinion of the Court.

The Question of the Delegation of Legislative Power.—We recently had occasion to review the pertinent decisions and the general principles which govern the determination of this question. *Panama Refining Company v. Ryan,* 293 U.S. 388 [1935]. The Constitution provides that "All legislative powers herein granted shall be vested in a Congress of the United States, which shall consist of a Senate and House of Representatives." Article 1, § 1. And the Congress is authorized "To make all Laws which shall be necessary and proper for carrying into Execution" its general powers. Article 1, § 8, par. 18. The Congress is not permitted to abdicate or to transfer to others the essential legislative functions with which it is thus vested. We have repeatedly recognized the necessity of adapting legislation to complex conditions involving a host of details with which the national Legislature cannot deal directly. We pointed out in the *Panama Refining Company* Case that the Constitution has never been regarded as denying to Congress the necessary resources of flexibility and practicality, which will enable it to perform its function in laying down policies and establishing standards, while leaving to selected instrumentalities the making of subordinate rules within prescribed limits and the determination of facts to which the policy as declared by the Legislature is to apply. But we said that the constant recognition of the necessity and validity of such provisions, and the wide range of administrative authority which has been developed by means of them, cannot be allowed to obscure the limitations of the authority to delegate, if our constitutional system is to be maintained. . . .

Accordingly, we look to the statute to see whether Congress has overstepped these limitations—whether Congress in authorizing "codes of fair competition" has itself established the standards of legal obligation, thus performing its essential legislative function, or, by the failure to enact such standards, has attempted to transfer that function to others.

The aspect in which the question is now presented is distinct from that which was before us in the case of the Panama Refining Company. There the subject of the statutory prohibition was defined. National Industrial Recovery Act, § 9 (c), 15 USCA § 709 (c). That subject was the transportation in interstate and foreign commerce of petroleum and petroleum products which are produced or withdrawn from storage in excess of the amount permitted by state authority. The question was with respect to the range of discretion given to the President in prohibiting that transportation. As to the "codes of fair competition," under section 3 of the act, the question is more fundamental. It is whether there is any adequate definition of the subject to which the codes are to be addressed.

What is meant by "fair competition" as the term is used in the act? Does it refer to a category established in the law, and is the authority to make codes limited accordingly? Or is it used as a convenient designation for whatever set of laws the formulators of a code for a particular trade or industry may propose and the President may approve (subject to certain restrictions), or the President may himself prescribe, as being wise and beneficient provisions for the government of the trade or industry in order to accomplish the broad purposes of rehabilitation, correction, and expansion which are stated in the first section of title 1? [That section . . . is as follows:

"Section 1. A national emergency productive of widespread unemployment and disorganization of industry, which burdens interstate and foreign commerce, affects the public welfare, and undermines the standards of living of the American people, is hereby declared to exist. It is hereby declared to be the policy of Congress to remove obstructions to the free flow of interstate and foreign commerce which tend to diminish the amount thereof; and to provide for the general welfare by promoting the organization of industry for the purpose of cooperative action among trade groups, to induce and maintain united action of labor and management under adequate governmental sanctions and supervision, to eliminate unfair competitive practices, to promote the fullest possible utilization of the present productive capacity of industries, to avoid undue restriction of production (except as may be temporarily required), to increase the consumption of industrial and agricultural products by increasing purchasing power, to reduce and relieve unemployment, to improve standards of labor, and otherwise to rehabilitate industry and to conserve natural resources."]

The act does not define "fair competition." "Unfair competition," as known to the common law, is a limited concept. Primarily, and strictly, it relates to the palming off of one's goods as those of a rival trader. . . .

In recent years, its scope has been extended. It has been held to apply to misappropriation as well as misrepresentation, to the selling of another's goods as one's own—to misappropriation of what equitably belongs to a competitor. Unfairness in competition has been predicated of acts which lie outside the ordinary course of business and are tainted by fraud or coercion or conduct otherwise prohibited by law. But it is evident that in its widest range, "unfair competition," as it has been understood in the law, does not reach the objectives of the codes which are authorized by the National Industrial Recovery Act. The codes may, indeed, cover conduct which existing law condemns, but they are not limited to conduct of that sort. The government does not contend that the act contemplates such a limitation. It would be opposed both to the declared purposes of the act and to its administrative construction.

The Federal Trade Commission Act (section 5 [15 USCA § 45]) introduced the expression "unfair methods of competition," which were declared to be unlawful. That was an expression new in the law. Debate apparently convinced the sponsors of the legislation that the words "unfair competition," in the light of their meaning at common law, were too narrow. We have said that the substituted phrase has a broader meaning, that it does not admit of precise definition; its scope being left to judicial determination as controversies arise. . . .

What are "unfair methods of competition" are thus to be determined in particular instances, upon evidence, in the light of particular competitive conditions and of what is found to be a specific and substantial public interest. To make this possible, Congress set up a special procedure. A commission, a quasi judicial body, was created. Provision was made for formal complaint, for notice and hearing, for appropriate findings of fact supported by adequate evidence, and for judicial review to give assurance that the action of the commission is taken within its statutory authority. . . .

In providing for codes, the National Industrial Recovery Act dispenses with this administrative procedure and with any administrative procedure of an analogous character. But the difference between the code plan of the Recovery Act and the scheme of the Federal Trade Commission Act lies not only in procedure but in subject-matter. We cannot regard the "fair competition" of the codes as antithetical to the "unfair methods of competition" of the Federal Trade Commission Act. The "fair competition" of the codes has a much broader range and a new significance. The Recovery Act provides that it shall not be construed to impair the powers of the Federal Trade Commission, but, when a code is approved, its provisions are to be the "standards of fair competition" for the trade or industry concerned, and any violation of such standards in any transaction in or affecting interstate or foreign commerce is to be deemed "an unfair method of competition" within the meaning of the Federal Trade Commission Act. Section 3 (b) of the act, 15 USCA § 703 (b).

For a statement of the authorized objectives and content of the "codes of fair competition," we are referred repeatedly to the "Declaration of Policy" in section 1 of title 1 of the Recovery Act (15 USCA § 701). Thus the approval of a code by the President is conditioned on his finding that it "will tend to effectuate the policy of this title." Section 3 (a) of the act, 15 USCA § 703 (a). The President is authorized to impose such conditions "for the protection of consumers, competitors, employees, and others, and in furtherance of the public interest, and may provide such exceptions to and exemptions from the provisions of such code, as the President in his discretion deems necessary to effectuate the policy herein declared." The "policy herein declared" is manifestly that set forth in section 1. That declaration embraces a broad range of objectives. Among them we find the elimination of "unfair competitive practices." But, even if this clause were to be taken to relate to practices which fall under the ban of existing law, either common law or statute, it is still only one of the authorized aims described in section 1. . . .

Under section 3, whatever "may tend to effectuate" these general purposes may be included in the "codes of fair competition." We think the conclusion is inescapable that the authority sought to be conferred by section 3 was not merely to deal with "unfair competitive practices" which offend against existing law, and could be the subject of judicial condemnation without further legislation, or to create administrative machinery for the application of established principles of law to particular instances of violation. Rather, the purpose is clearly disclosed to authorize new and controlling prohibitions through codes of laws which would embrace what the formulators would propose, and what the President would approve or prescribe, as wise and beneficent measures for the government of trades and industries in order to bring about their rehabilitation, correction, and development, according to the general declaration of policy in section 1. Codes of laws of this sort are styled "codes of fair competition."

We find no real controversy upon this point, and we must determine the validity of the code in question in this aspect. . . .

The question, then, turns upon the authority which section 3 of the Recovery Act vests in the President to approve or prescribe. If the codes have standing as penal statutes, this must be due to the effect of the executive action. But Congress cannot delegate legislative power to the President to exercise an unfettered discretion to make whatever laws he thinks may be needed or advisable for the rehabilitation and expansion of trade or industry. See *Panama Refining Company v. Ryan,* supra, and cases there reviewed.

Accordingly we turn to the Recovery Act to ascertain what limits have been set to the exercise of the President's discretion: First, the President, as a condition of approval, is required to find that the trade or industrial associations or groups which propose a code "impose no inequitable restrictions on admission to membership" and are "truly representative." That condition, however, relates only to the status of the initiators of the new laws and not to the permissible scope of such laws. Second, the President is required to find that the code is not "designed to promote monopolies or to eliminate or oppress small enterprises and will not operate to discriminate against them." And to this is added a proviso that the code "shall not permit monopolies or monopolistic practices." But these restrictions leave virtually untouched the field of policy envisaged by section 1, and, in that wide field of legislative possibilities, and proponents of a code, refraining from monopolistic designs, may roam at will, and the President may approve or disapprove their proposals as he may see fit. That is the precise effect of the further finding that the President is to make—that the code "will tend to effectuate the policy of this title." While this is called a finding, it is really but a statement of an opinion as to the general effect upon the promotion of trade or industry of a scheme of laws. These are the only findings which Congress has made essential in order to put into operation a legislative code having the aims described in the "Declaration of Policy."

Nor is the breadth of the President's discretion left to the necessary implications of this limited requirement as to his findings. As already noted, the President in approving a code may impose his own conditions, adding to or taking from what is proposed, as "in his discretion" he thinks necessary "to effectuate the policy" declared by the act. Of course, he has no less liberty when he prescribes a code on his own motion or on complaint, and he is free to prescribe one if a code has not been approved. The act provides for the creation by the President of administrative agencies to assist him, but the action or reports of such agencies, or of his other assistants—their recommendations and findings in relation to the making of codes—have no sanction beyond the will of the President, who may accept, modify, or reject them as he pleases. Such recommendations or findings in no way limit the authority which section 3 undertakes to vest in the President with no other conditions than those there specified. And this authority relates to a host of different trades and industries, thus extending the President's discretion to all the varieties of laws which he may deem to be beneficial in dealing with the vast array of commercial and industrial activities throughout the country.

Such a sweeping delegation of legislative power finds no support in the decisions upon which the government especially relies. By the Interstate Commerce Act (49 USCA § 1 et seq.), Congress has itself provided a code of laws regulating the activities of the common carriers subject to the act, in order to assure the performance of their services upon just and reasonable terms, with adequate facilities and without unjust discrimination. Congress from time to time has elaborated its requirements, as needs have been disclosed. To facilitate the application of the standards prescribed by the act, Congress has provided an expert body. That administrative agency, in dealing with particular cases, is required to act upon notice and hearing, and its orders must be supported by findings of fact which in turn are sustained by evidence. . . .

To summarize and conclude upon this point: Section 3 of the Recovery Act (15 USCA § 703) is without precedent. It supplies no standards for any trade, industry, or activity. It does not undertake to prescribe rules of conduct to be applied to particular states of fact determined by appropriate administrative procedure. Instead of prescribing rules of conduct, it authorizes the making of codes to prescribe them. For that legislative undertaking, section 3 sets up no standards, aside from the statement of the general aims of rehabilitation, correction, and expansion described in section 1. In view of the scope of that broad declaration and of the nature of the few restrictions that are imposed, the discretion of the President in approving or prescribing codes, and thus enacting laws for the government of trade and industry throughout the country, is virtually unfettered. We think that the code-making authority thus conferred is an unconstitutional delegation of legislative power.

Justice CARDOZO concurring.

The delegated power of legislation which has found expression in this code is not canalized within banks that keep it from overflowing. It is unconfined and vagrant, if I may borrow my own words in an earlier opinion. *Panama Refining Co. v. Ryan.* . . .

This court has held that delegation may be unlawful, though the act to be performed is definite and single, if the necessity, time, and occasion of performance have been left in the end to the discretion of the delegate. *Panama Refining Co. v. Ryan,* supra. I thought that ruling went too far. I pointed out in an opinion that there had been "no grant to the Executive of any roving commission to inquire into evils and then, upon discovering them, do anything he pleases." Choice, though within limits, had been given him "as to the occasion, but none whatever as to the means." Here, in the case before us, is an attempted delegation not confined to any single act nor to any class or group of acts identified or described by reference to a standard. Here in effect is a roving commission to inquire into evils and upon discovery correct them.

I have said that there is no standard, definite or even approximate, to which legislation must conform. Let me make my meaning more precise. If codes of fair competition are codes eliminating "unfair" methods of competition ascertained upon inquiry to prevail in one industry or another, there is no unlawful delegation of legislative functions when the President is directed to inquire into such practices and denounce them when discovered. . . .

But there is another conception of codes of fair competition, their significance and function, which leads to very different consequences, though it is one that is struggling now for recognition and acceptance. By this other conception a cede is not to be restricted to the elimination of business practices that would be characterized by general acceptation as oppressive or unfair. It is to include whatever ordinances may be desirable or helpful for the well-being or prosperity of the industry affected. In that view, the function of its adoption is not merely negative, but positive; the planning of improvements as well as the extirpation of abuses. What is fair, as thus conceived, is not something to be contrasted with what is unfair or fraudulent or tricky. The extension becomes as wide as the field of industrial regulation. If that conception shall prevail, anything that Congress may do within the limits of the commerce clause for the betterment of business may be done by the President upon the recommendation of a trade association by calling it a code. This is delegation running riot. No such plenitude of power is susceptible of transfer. The statute, however, aims at nothing less, as one can learn both from its terms and from the administrative practice under it. Nothing less is aimed at by the code now submitted to our scrutiny.

The code does not confine itself to the suppression of methods of competition that would be classified as unfair according to accepted business standards or accepted norms of ethics. It sets up a comprehensive body of rules to promote the welfare of the industry, if not the welfare of the nation, without reference to standards, ethical or commercial, that could be known or predicted in advance of its adoption. . . .

I am authorized to state that Justice STONE joins in this opinion.

Industrial Union Department,
AFL-CIO v. American Petroleum Institute
448 U.S. 607, 100 S.Ct. 2844 (1980)

In the Occupational Safety and Health Act, Congress delegated the power to regulate carcinogenic and toxic substances by authorizing the Occupational Safety and Health Administration (OSHA) to set standards that "most adequately assure, to the extent feasible, on the basis of the best available evidence, that no employee will suffer impairment of health or functional capacity."

After years of study, the OSHA issued a temporary emergency standard for occupational exposure to benzene at 1 part per million (ppm). The American Petroleum Institute and a coalition of other benzene producers and users immediately challenged the standard. After the United States Court of Appeals for the Fifth Circuit struck OSHA's standard down, the Industrial Union Department of the AFL-CIO appealed to the Supreme Court.

The Supreme Court divided five to four in striking down OSHA's benzene standard. Moreover, only three justices in the majority joined the opinion by Justice John Paul Stevens announcing the Court's decision. Justice Marshall wrote a dissenting opinion for the four dissenters who would have upheld OSHA's standard. The crucial fifth vote for the Court's decision was cast by Justice Rehnquist, who issued a concurring opinion (reprinted here) that invokes the nondelegation doctrine, rather than the reasons set forth by Justice Stevens, for overturning the benzene standard.

Justice REHNQUIST concurring.

The statutory provision at the center of the present controversy, § 6(b)(5) of the Occupational Safety and Health Act of 1970, states, in relevant part, that the Secretary of Labor

". . . in promulgating standards dealing with toxic materials or harmful physical agents . . . shall set the standard which most adequately assures, *to the extent feasible,* on the basis of the best available evidence, that no employee will suffer material impairment of health or functional capacity even if such employee has regular exposure to the hazard dealt with by such standard for the period of his working life." 84 Stat. 1594, 29 U.S.C. § 655(b)(5) (emphasis added).

According to the Secretary, who is one of the petitioners herein, § 6(b)(5) imposes upon him an absolute duty, in regulating harmful substances like benzene for which no safe level is known, to set the standard for permissible exposure at the lowest level that "can be achieved at bearable cost with available technology." Brief for Federal Parties 57. While the Secretary does not attempt to refine the concept of "bearable cost," he apparently believes that a proposed standard is economically feasible so long as its impact "will not be such as to threaten the financial welfare of the affected firms or the general economy.". . .

Respondents reply, and the lower court agreed, that § 6(b)(5) must be read in light of another provision in the same Act, § 3(8), which defines an "occupational health and safety standard" as

". . . a standard which requires conditions, or the adoption or use of one or more practices, means, methods, operations, or processes, reasonably necessary or appropriate to provide safe or healthful employment and places of employment." 84 Stat. 1591, 29 U.S.C. § 652(8).

According to respondents, § 6(b)(5), as tempered by § 3(8), requires the Secretary to demonstrate that any particular health standard is justifiable on the basis of a rough balancing of costs and benefits.

In considering these alternative interpretations, my colleagues manifest a good deal of uncertainty, and ultimately divide over whether the Secretary produced sufficient evidence that the proposed standard for benzene will result in any appreciable benefits at all. This uncertainty, I would suggest, is eminently justified, since I believe that this litigation presents the Court with what has to be one of the most difficult issues that could confront a decisionmaker: whether the statistical possibility of future deaths should ever be disregarded in light of the economic costs of preventing those deaths. I would also suggest that the widely varying positions advanced in the briefs of the parties and in the opinions of Justice STEVENS, the CHIEF JUSTICE, Justice POWELL, and Justice MARSHALL demonstrate, perhaps better than any other fact, that Congress, the governmental body best suited and most obligated to make the choice confronting us in this litigation, has improperly delegated that choice to the Secretary of Labor and, derivatively, to this Court.

In his Second Treatise of Civil Government, published in 1690, John Locke wrote that "[t]he power of the legislative, being derived from the people by a positive voluntary grant and institution, can be no other than what that positive grant conveyed, which being only to make laws, and not to make legislators, the legislative can have no power to transfer their authority of making laws and place it in other hands." Two hundred years later, this Court expressly recognized the existence of and the necessity for limits on Congress' ability to delegate its authority to representatives of the Executive Branch: "That Congress cannot delegate legislative power to the president is a principle universally recognized as vital to the integrity and maintenance of the system of government ordained by the Constitution." *Field v. Clark,* 143 U.S. 649 [1892]. . . .

During the third and fourth decades of this century, this Court within a relatively short period of time struck down several Acts of Congress on the grounds that they exceeded the authority of Congress under the Commerce Clause or under the nondelegation principle of separation of powers, and at the same time struck down state statutes because they violated "substantive" due process or interfered with interstate commerce. See generally R. Jackson, The Struggle for Judicial Supremacy 48–123 (1949). When many of these decisions were later overruled, the principle that Congress could not simply transfer its legislative authority to the Executive fell under a cloud. Yet in my opinion decisions such as *Panama Refining Co. v. Ryan,* 293 U.S. 388 (1935), suffer from none of the excesses of judicial policymaking that plagued some of the other decisions of that era. The many later decisions that have upheld congressional delegations of authority to the Executive Branch have done so largely on the theory that Congress may wish to exercise its authority in a particular field, but because the field is sufficiently technical, the ground to be covered sufficiently large, and the Members of Congress themselves not necessarily expert in the area in which they choose to legislate, the most that may be asked under the separation-of-powers doctrine is that Congress lay down the general policy and standards that animate the law, leaving the agency to refine those standards, "fill in the blanks," or apply the standards to particular cases. These decisions, to my mind, simply illustrate the principle stated more than 50 years ago by Chief Justice TAFT that delegations of legislative authority must be judged "according to common sense and the inherent necessities of the governmental co-ordination."

Viewing the legislation at issue here in light of these principles, I believe that it fails to pass muster. Read literally, the relevant portion of § 6(b)(5) is completely precatory, admonishing the Secretary to adopt the most protective standard if he can, but excusing him from that duty if he cannot. In the case of a hazardous substance for which a "safe" level is either unknown or impractical, the language of § 6(b)(5) gives the Secretary absolutely no indication where on the continuum of relative safety he should draw his line. Especially in light of the importance of the interests at stake, I have no doubt that the provision at issue, standing alone, would violate the doctrine against uncanalized delegations of legislative power. For me the remaining question, then, is whether additional standards are ascertainable from the legislative history or statutory context of § 6(b)(5) or, if not, whether such a standard-less delegation was justifiable in light of the "inherent necessities" of the situation. . . .

As formulated and enforced by this Court, the nondelegation doctrine serves three important functions. First, and most abstractly, it ensures to the extent consistent with orderly governmental administration that important choices of social policy are made by Congress, the branch of our Government most responsive to the popular will. . . . Second, the doctrine guarantees that, to the extent Congress finds it necessary to delegate authority, it provides the recipient of that authority with an "intelligible principle" to guide the exercise of the delegated discretion. . . . Third, and derivative of the second, the doctrine ensures that courts charged with reviewing the exercise of delegated legislative discretion will be able to test that exercise against ascertainable standards. . . .

I believe the legislation at issue here fails on all three counts. The decision whether the law of diminishing returns should have any place in the regulation of toxic substances is quintessentially one of legislative policy. For Congress to pass that decision on to the Secretary in the manner it did violates, in my mind, John Locke's caveat—reflected in the cases cited earlier in this opinion—that legislatures are to make laws, not legislators. Nor, as I think the prior discussion amply demonstrates, do the provisions at issue or their legislative history provide the Secretary with any guidance that might lead him to his somewhat tentative conclusion that he must eliminate exposure to benzene as far as technologically and economically possible. Finally, I would suggest that the standard of "feasibility" renders meaningful judicial review impossible. . . .

If we are ever to reshoulder the burden of ensuring that Congress itself make the critical policy decisions, these are surely the cases in which to do it. It is difficult to imagine a more obvious example of Congress simply avoiding a choice which was both fundamental for purposes of the statute and yet politically so divisive that the necessary decision or compromise was difficult, if not impossible, to hammer out in the legislative forge. Far from detracting from the substantive authority of Congress, a declaration that the first sentence of § 6(b)(5) of the Occupational Safety and Health Act constitutes an invalid delegation to the Secretary of Labor would preserve the authority of Congress. If Congress wishes to legislate in an area which it has not previously sought to enter, it will in today's political world undoubtedly run into opposition no matter how the legislation is formulated. But that is the very essence of legislative authority under our system. It is the hard choices, and not the filling in of the blanks, which must be made by the elected representatives of the people. When fundamental policy decisions underlying important legislation about to be enacted are to be made, the buck stops with Congress and the President insofar as he exercises his constitutional role in the legislative process.

Immigration and Naturalization Service v. Chadha
462 U.S. 919, 103 S.Ct. 2764 (1983)

Jagdish Rai Chadha was admitted into the United States on a nonimmigrant student visa in 1966. Following the expiration of the visa in 1972, the district director of the Immigration and Naturalization Service (INS) ordered Chadha to show why he should not be deported. At a hearing in 1974, Chadha agreed that he was deportable but requested time to apply for a suspension of deportation. Upon his application, the deportation order was suspended, pending a hearing by the INS.

Under the Immigration and Naturalization Act, any suspension of deportation orders must be reported by the attorney general to Congress, which then may veto the orders under Section 244(c)2 of the INS Act. The House of Representatives subsequently passed a resolution opposing the granting of permanent residence to Chadha and five other aliens.

On the basis of the House's veto of the INS's suspension of Chadha's deportation, an immigration judge reopened deportation hearings. Chadha unsuccessfully challenged the proceedings on the ground that Section 244(c)2 was unconstitutional. After the Board of Immigration Appeals affirmed the judge's order reinstating deportation, Chadha appealed to the Court of Appeals for the Ninth Circuit. That court held the House's "legislative veto" overturning the INS's suspension order to violate the principle of separation of powers. The Supreme Court granted a petition for *certiorari* and ruled seven to two that legislative vetoes are unconstitutional.

Chief Justice BURGER delivers the opinion of the Court.

We granted *certiorari* . . . [to consider] a challenge to the constitutionality of the provision in § 244(c)(2) of the Immigration and Nationality Act, 8 U.S.C. § 1254(c)(2), authorizing one House of Congress, by resolution, to invalidate the decision of the Executive Branch, pursuant to authority delegated by Congress to the Attorney General of the United States, to allow a particular deportable alien to remain in the United States. . . .

We begin, of course, with the presumption that the challenged statute is valid. Its wisdom is not the concern of the courts; if a challenged action does not violate the Constitution, it must be sustained:

> "Once the meaning of an enactment is discerned and its constitutionality determined, the judicial process comes to an end. We do not sit as a committee of review, nor are we vested with the power of veto." *Tennessee Valley Authority v. Hill*, 437 U.S. 153 (1978).

By the same token, the fact that a given law or procedure is efficient, convenient, and useful in facilitating functions of government, standing alone, will not save it if it is contrary to the Constitution. Convenience and efficiency are not the primary objectives—or the hallmarks—of democratic government and our inquiry is sharpened rather than blunted by the fact that Congressional veto provisions are appearing with increasing frequency in statutes which delegate authority to executive and independent agencies:

> "Since 1932, when the first veto provision was enacted into law, 295 congressional veto-type procedures have been inserted in 196 different statutes as follows: from 1932 to 1939, five statutes were affected; from 1940–49, nineteen statutes; between 1950–59, thirty-four statutes; and from 1960–69, forty-nine. From the year 1970 through 1975, at least one hundred sixty-three such provisions were included in eighty-nine laws." Abourezk, The Congressional Veto: A Contemporary Response to Executive Encroachment on Legislative Prerogatives, 52 Ind.L.Rev. 323, 324 (1977). . . .

Justice WHITE undertakes to make a case for the proposition that the one-House veto is a useful "political invention" and we need not challenge that assertion. We can even concede this utilitarian argument although the long range political wisdom of this "invention" is arguable. But policy arguments supporting even useful "political inventions" are subject to the demands of the Constitution which defines powers and, with respect to this subject, sets out just how those powers are to be exercised.

Explicit and unambiguous provisions of the Constitution prescribe and define the respective functions of the Congress and of the Executive in the legislative process. Since the precise terms of those familiar provisions are critical to the resolution of this case, we set them out verbatim. Art. I provides:

> "All legislative Powers herein granted shall be vested in a Congress of the United States, which shall consist of a Senate *and* a House of Representatives." Art. I, § 1. (Emphasis added).
>
> "Every Bill which shall have passed the House of Representatives *and* the Senate, *shall*, before it becomes a Law, be presented to the President of the United States; . . ." Art. I, § 7, cl. 2. (Emphasis added).

"*Every* Order, Resolution, or Vote to which the Concurrence of the Senate and House of Representatives may be necessary (except on a question of Adjournment) *shall be* presented to the President of the United States; and before the Same shall take Effect, *shall be* approved by him, or being disapproved by him, *shall be* repassed by two thirds of the Senate and House of Representatives, according to the Rules and Limitations prescribed in the Case of a Bill." Art. I, § 7, cl. 3. (Emphasis added).

These provisions of Art. I are integral parts of the constitutional design for the separation of powers. We have recently noted that "[t]he principle of separation of powers was not simply an abstract generalization in the minds of the Framers: it was woven into the documents that they drafted in Philadelphia in the summer of 1787." *Buckley v. Valeo,* [424 U.S. 1 (1976)]. Just as we relied on the textual provision of Art. II, § 2, cl. 2, to vindicate the principle of separation of powers in *Buckley,* we find that the purposes underlying the Presentment Clauses, Art. I, § 7, cls. 2, 3, and the bicameral requirement of Art. I, § 1 and § 7, cl. 2, guide our resolution of the important question presented in this case. The very structure of the articles delegating and separating powers under Arts. I, II, and III exemplify the concept of separation of powers and we now turn to Art. I. . . .

The President's role in the lawmaking process also reflects the Framers' careful efforts to check whatever propensity a particular Congress might have to enact oppressive, improvident, or ill-considered measures. The President's veto role in the legislative process was described later during public debate on ratification:

"It establishes a salutary check upon the legislative body, calculated to guard the community against the effects of faction, precipitancy, or of any impulse unfriendly to the public good which may happen to influence a majority of that body. . . . The primary inducement to conferring the power in question upon the Executive is to enable him to defend himself; the secondary one is to increase the chances in favor of the community against the passing of bad laws through haste, inadvertence, or design." The Federalist No. 73 (A. Hamilton). . . .

The bicameral requirement of Art. I, §§ 1, 7 was of scarcely less concern to the Framers than was the Presidential veto and indeed the two concepts are interdependent. By providing that no law could take effect without the concurrence of the prescribed majority of the Members of both Houses, the Framers reemphasized their belief, already remarked upon in connection with the Presentment Clauses, that legislation should not be enacted unless it has been carefully and fully considered by the Nation's elected officials. . . .

Hamilton argued that a Congress comprised of a single House

was antithetical to the very purposes of the Constitution. Were the Nation to adopt a Constitution providing for only one legislative organ, he warned:

> "we shall finally accumulate, in a single body, all the most important prerogatives of sovereignty, and thus entail upon our posterity one of the most execrable forms of government that human infatuation ever contrived. Thus we should create in reality that very tyranny which the adversaries of the new Constitution either are, or affect to be, solicitous to avert." The Federalist No. 22. . . .

We see therefore that the Framers were acutely conscious that the bicameral requirement and the Presentment Clauses would serve essential constitutional functions. The President's participation in the legislative process was to protect the Executive Branch from Congress and to protect the whole people from improvident laws. The division of the Congress into two distinctive bodies assures that the legislative power would be exercised only after opportunity for full study and debate in separate settings. The President's unilateral veto power, in turn, was limited by the power of two thirds of both Houses of Congress to overrule a veto thereby precluding final arbitrary action of one person. It emerges clearly that the prescription for legislative action in Art. I, §§ 1, 7 represents the Framers' decision that the legislative power of the Federal government be exercised in accord with a single, finely wrought and exhaustively considered, procedure.

The Constitution sought to divide the delegated powers of the new federal government into three defined categories, legislative, executive and judicial, to assure, as nearly as possible, that each Branch of government would confine itself to its assigned responsibility. The hydraulic pressure inherent within each of the separate Branches to exceed the outer limits of its power, even to accomplish desirable objectives, must be resisted.

Although not "hermetically" sealed from one another the powers delegated to the three Branches are functionally identifiable. When any Branch acts, it is presumptively exercising the power the Constitution has delegated to it. When the Executive acts, it presumptively acts in an executive or administrative capacity as defined in Art. II. And when, as here, one House of Congress purports to act, it is presumptively acting within its assigned sphere.

Beginning with this presumption, we must nevertheless establish that the challenged action under § 244(c)(2) is of the kind to which the procedural requirements of Art. I, § 7 apply. Not every action taken by either House is subject to the bicameralism and presentment requirements of Art. I. Whether actions taken by either House are, in law and fact, an exercise of legislative power depends not on their form but upon "whether they contain matter which is properly to be regarded as legislative in its character and effect.". . .

Examination of the action taken here by one House pursuant to § 244(c)(2) reveals that it was essentially legislative in purpose and effect. In purporting to exercise power defined in Art. I, § 8, cl. 4 to "establish an uniform Rule of Naturalization," the House took action that had the purpose and effect of altering the legal rights, duties and relations of persons, including the Attorney General, Executive Branch officials and Chadha, all outside the legislative branch. Section 244(c)(2) purports to authorize one House of Congress to require the Attorney General to deport an individual alien whose deportation otherwise would be cancelled under § 244. The one-House veto operated in this case to overrule the Attorney General and mandate Chadha's deportation; absent the House action, Chadha would remain in the United States. Congress has *acted* and its action has altered Chadha's status.

The legislative character of the one-House veto in this case is confirmed by the character of the Congressional action it supplants. Neither the House of Representatives nor the Senate contends that, absent the veto provision in § 244(c)(2), either of them, or both of them acting together, could effectively require the Attorney General to deport an alien once the Attorney General, in the exercise of legislatively delegated authority, had determined the alien should remain in the United States. Without the challenged provision in § 244(c)(2), this could have been achieved, if at all, only by legislation requiring deportation. Similarly, a veto by one House of Congress under § 244(c)(2) cannot be justified as an attempt at amending the standards set out in § 244(a)(1), or as a repeal of § 244 as applied to Chadha. Amendment and repeal of statutes, no less than enactment, must conform with Art. I.

The nature of the decision implemented by the one-House veto in this case further manifests its legislative character. After long experience with the clumsy, time consuming private bill procedure, Congress made a deliberate choice to delegate to the Executive Branch, and specifically to the Attorney General, the authority to allow deportable aliens to remain in this country in certain specified circumstances. It is not disputed that this choice to delegate authority is precisely the kind of decision that can be implemented only in accordance with the procedures set out in Art. I. Disagreement with the Attorney General's decision on Chadha's deportation—that is, Congress' decision to deport Chadha—no less than Congress' original choice to delegate to the Attorney General the authority to make that decision, involves determinations of policy that Congress can implement in only one way; bicameral passage followed by presentment to the President. Congress must abide by its delegation of authority until that delegation is legislatively altered or revoked.

Finally, we see that when the Framers intended to authorize either House of Congress to act alone and outside of its prescribed bicameral legislative role, they narrowly and precisely defined the procedure for such action. There are but four provisions in the Constitution, explicit and unambiguous, by which one House may act alone with the unreviewable force of law, not subject to the President's veto:

(a) The House of Representatives alone was given the power to initiate impeachments. Art. I, § 2, cl. 6;

(b) The Senate alone was given the power to conduct trials following impeachment on charges initiated by the House and to convict following trial. Art. I, § 3, cl. 5;

(c) The Senate alone was given final unreviewable power to approve or to disapprove presidential appointments. Art. II, § 2, cl. 2;

(d) The Senate alone was given unreviewable power to ratify treaties negotiated by the President. Art. II, § 2, cl. 2.

Clearly, when the Draftsmen sought to confer special powers on one House, independent of the other House, or of the President, they did so in explicit, unambiguous terms. These carefully defined exceptions from presentment and bicameralism underscore the difference between the legislative functions of Congress and other unilateral but important and binding one-House acts provided for in the Constitution. These exceptions are narrow, explicit, and separately justified; none of them authorize the action challenged here. On the contrary, they provide further support for the conclusion that Congressional authority is not to be implied and for the conclusion that the veto provided for in § 244(c)(2) is not authorized by the constitutional design of the powers of the Legislative Branch.

Since it is clear that the action by the House under § 244(c)(2) was not within any of the express constitutional exceptions authorizing one House to act alone, and equally clear that it was an exercise of legislative power, that action was subject to the standards prescribed in Article I. The bicameral requirement, the Presentment Clauses, the President's veto, and Congress' power to override a veto were intended to erect enduring checks on each Branch and to protect the people from the improvident exercise of power by mandating certain prescribed steps. To preserve those checks, and maintain the separation of powers, the carefully defined limits on the power of each Branch must not be eroded. To accomplish what has been attempted by one House of Congress in this case requires action in conformity with the express procedures of the Constitution's prescription for legislative action: passage by a majority of both Houses and presentment to the President.

The veto authorized by § 244(c)(2) doubtless has been in many respects a convenient shortcut; the "sharing" with the Executive by Congress of its authority over aliens in this manner is, on its face, an appealing compromise. In purely practical terms, it is obviously easier for action to be taken by one House without submission to the President; but it is crystal clear from the records of the Convention, contemporaneous writings and debates, that the Framers ranked other values higher than efficiency. The records of the Convention and debates in the States preceding ratification underscore the common desire to define and limit the exercise of the newly created federal powers affecting the states and the people. There is unmistakable expression of a determination that legislation by the national Congress by a step-by-step, deliberate and deliberative process.

The choices we discern as having been made in the Constitutional Convention impose burdens on governmental processes that often seem clumsy, inefficient, even unworkable, but those hard choices were consciously made by men who had lived under a form of government that permitted arbitrary governmental acts to go unchecked. There is no support in the Constitution or decisions of this Court for the proposition that the cumbersomeness and delays often encountered in complying with explicit Constitutional standards may be avoided, either by the Congress or by the President. See *Youngstown Sheet & Tube Co. v. Sawyer,* 343 U.S. 579 (1952). With all the obvious flaws of delay, untidiness, and potential for abuse, we have not yet found a better way to preserve freedom than by making the exercise of power subject to the carefully crafted restraints spelled out in the Constitution.

We hold that the Congressional veto provision in § 244(c)(2) is severable from the Act and that it is unconstitutional. Accordingly, the judgment of the Court of Appeals is

Affirmed.

Justice POWELL concurring.

The Court's decision, based on the Presentment Clauses, Art. I, § 7, cls. 2 and 3, apparently will invalidate every use of the legislative veto. The breadth of this holding gives one pause. Congress has included the veto in literally hundreds of statutes, dating back to the 1930s. Congress clearly views this procedure as essential to controlling the delegation of power to administrative agencies. One reasonably may disagree with Congress' assessment of the veto's utility, but the respect due its judgment as a coordinate branch of Government cautions that our holding should be no more extensive than necessary to decide this case. In my view, the case may be decided on a narrower ground. When Congress finds that a particular person does not satisfy the statutory criteria for permanent residence in this country it has assumed a judicial function in violation of the principle of separation of powers. Accordingly, I concur only in the judgment. . . .

On its face, the House's action appears clearly adjudicatory. The House did not enact a general rule; rather it made its own determination that six specific persons did not comply with certain statutory criteria. It thus undertook the type of decision that traditionally has been left to other branches. Even if the House did not make a *de novo* determination, but simply reviewed the Immigration and Naturalization Service's findings, it still assumed a function ordinarily entrusted to the federal courts. . . .

Where, as here, Congress has exercised a power "that cannot possibly be regarded as merely in aid of the legislative function of Congress," *Buckley v. Valeo,* 424 U.S., [1 (1976)]. The decisions of this Court have held that Congress impermissibly assumed a function that the Constitution entrusted to another branch. In my view, when Congress undertook to apply its rules to Chadha, it exceeded the scope of its constitutionally prescribed authority. I would not reach the broader question whether legislative vetoes are invalid under the Presentment Clauses.

Justice WHITE dissenting.

Today the Court not only invalidates § 244(c)(2) of the Immigration and Nationality Act, but also sounds the death knell for nearly 200 other statutory provisions in which Congress has reserved a "legislative veto." For this reason, the Court's decision is of surpassing importance. And it is for this reason that the Court would have been well-advised to decide the case, if possible, on the narrower grounds of separation of powers, leaving for full consideration the constitutionality of other congressional review statutes operating on such varied matters as war powers and agency rulemaking, some of which concern the independent regulatory agencies.

The prominence of the legislative veto mechanism in our contemporary political system and its importance to Congress can hardly be overstated. It has become a central means by which Congress secures the accountability of executive and independent agencies. Without the legislative veto, Congress is faced with a Hobson's choice: either to refrain from delegating the necessary authority, leaving itself with a hopeless task of writing laws with the requisite specificity to cover endless special circumstances across the entire policy landscape, or in the alternative, to abdicate its lawmaking function to the executive branch and independent agencies. To choose the former leaves major national problems unresolved; to opt for the latter risks unaccountable policymaking by those not elected to fill that role. Accordingly, over the past five decades, the legislative veto has been placed in nearly 200 statutes. The device is known in every field of governmental concern: reorganization, budgets, foreign affairs, war powers, and regulation of trade, safety, energy, the environment and the economy. . . .

[T]he legislative veto is more than "efficient, convenient, and useful." It is an important if not indispensable political invention that allows the President and Congress to resolve major constitutional and policy differences, assures the accountability of independent regulatory agencies, and preserves Congress' control over lawmaking. Perhaps there are other means of accommodation and accountability, but the increasing reliance of Congress upon the legislative veto suggests that the alternatives to which Congress must now turn are not entirely satisfactory.

The history of the legislative veto also makes clear that it has not been a sword with which Congress has struck out to aggrandize itself at the expense of the other branches—the concerns of Madison and Hamilton. Rather, the veto has been a means of defense, a reservation of ultimate authority necessary if Congress is to fulfill its designated role under Article I as the nation's lawmaker. While the President has often objected to particular legislative vetoes, generally those left in the hands of congressional committees, the Executive has more often agreed to legislative review as the price for a broad delegation of authority. To be sure, the President may have preferred unrestricted power, but that could be precisely why Congress thought it essential to retain a check on the exercise of delegated authority.

For all these reasons, the apparent sweep of the Court's decision today is regretable. The Court's Article I analysis appears to invalidate all legislative vetoes irrespective of form or subject. Because the legislative veto is commonly found as a check upon rulemaking by administrative agencies and upon broad-based policy decisions of the Executive Branch, it is particularly unfortunate that the Court reaches its decision in a case involving the exercise of a veto over deportation decisions regarding particular individuals. Courts should always be wary of striking statutes as unconstitutional; to strike an entire class of statutes based on consideration of a somewhat atypical and more-readily indictable exemplar of the class is irresponsible. . . .

If the legislative veto were as plainly unconstitutional as the Court strives to suggest, its broad ruling today would be more comprehensible. But, the constitutionality of the legislative veto is anything but clearcut. The issue divides scholars, courts, attorneys general, and the two other branches of the National Government. If the veto devices so flagrantly disregarded the requirements of Article I as the Court today suggests, I find it incomprehensible that Congress, whose members are bound by oath to uphold the Constitution, would have placed these mechanisms in nearly 200 separate laws over a period of 50 years.

The reality of the situation is that the constitutional question posed today is one of immense difficulty over which the executive and legislative branches—as well as scholars and judges—have understandably disagreed. That disagreement stems from the silence of the Constitution on the precise question: The Constitution does not directly authorize or prohibit the legislative veto. Thus, our task should be to determine whether the legislative veto is consistent with the purposes of Art. I and the principles of Separation of Powers which are reflected in that Article and throughout the Constitution. We should not find the lack of a specific constitutional authorization for the legislative veto surprising, and I would not infer disapproval of the mechanism from its absence. From the summer of 1787 to the present the government of the United States has become an endeavor far beyond the contemplation of the Framers. Only within the last half century has the complexity and size of the Federal Government's responsibilities grown so greatly that the Congress must rely on the legislative veto as the most effective if not the only means to insure their role as the nation's lawmakers. But the wisdom of the Framers was to anticipate that the nation would grow and new problems of governance would require different solutions. Accordingly, our Federal Government was intentionally chartered with the flexibility to respond to contemporary needs without losing sight of fundamental democratic principles. This was the spirit in which Justice JACKSON penned his influential concurrence in the *Steel Seizure Case:*

> "The actual art of governing under our Constitution does not and cannot conform to judicial definitions of the power of any of its branches based on isolated clauses or even single Articles torn from context. While the Constitution diffuses power the better to secure liberty, it also contemplates that practice will integrate the dispersed powers into a workable government." *Youngstown Sheet & Tube Co. v. Sawyer,* 343 U.S. 579 (1952).

This is the perspective from which we should approach the novel constitutional questions presented by the legislative veto. In my view, neither Article I of the Constitution nor the doctrine of separation of powers is violated by this mechanism by which our elected representatives preserve their voice in the governance of the nation.

The Court holds that the disapproval of a suspension of deportation by the resolution of one House of Congress is an exercise of legislative power without compliance with the prerequisites for lawmaking set forth in Art. I of the Constitution. Specifically, the Court maintains that the provisions of § 244(c)(2) are inconsistent with the requirement of bicameral approval, implicit in Art. I, § 1, and the requirement that all bills and resolutions that require the concurrence of both Houses be presented to the President, Art. I, § 7, cl. 2 and 3.

It does not, however, answer the constitutional question before us. The power to exercise a legislative veto is not the power to write new law without bicameral approval or presidential consideration. The veto must be authorized by statute and may only negative what an Executive department or independent agency has proposed. On its face, the legislative veto no more allows one House of Congress to make law than does the presidential veto confer such power upon the President. Accordingly, the Court properly recognizes that it "must establish that the challenged action under § 244(c)(2) is of the kind to which the procedural requirements of Art. I, § 7 apply" and admits that "not every action taken by either House is subject to the bicameralism and presentation requirements of Art. I.". . .

It is long-settled that Congress may "exercise its best judgment in the selection of measures, to carry into execution the constitutional powers of the government," and "avail itself of experience, to exercise its reason, and to accommodate its legislation to circumstances." *McCulloch v. Maryland,* 4 Wheat. 316 (1819) . . .

The Court heeded this counsel in approving the modern administrative state. The Court's holding today that all legislative-type action must be enacted through the lawmaking process ignores that legislative authority is routinely delegated to the Executive branch, to the independent regulatory agencies, and to private individuals and groups. . . .

This Court's decisions sanctioning such delegations make clear that Article I does not require all action with the effect of legislation to be passed as a law.

Theoretically, agencies and officials were asked only to "fill up the details," and the rule was that "Congress cannot delegate any part of its legislative power except under a limitation of a prescribed standard.". . .

In practice, however, restrictions on the scope of the power that could be delegated diminished and all but disappeared. In only two instances did the Court find an unconstitutional delegation. *Panama Refining Co. v. Ryan,* 293 U.S. 388 (1935); *Schechter Poultry Corp. v. United States,* 295 U.S. 495 [1935].

The wisdom and the constitutionality of these broad delegations are matters that still have not been put to rest. But for present purposes, these cases establish that by virtue of congressional delegation, legislative power can be exercised by independent agencies and Executive departments without the passage of new legislation. . . .

If Congress may delegate lawmaking power to independent and executive agencies, it is most difficult to understand Article I as forbidding Congress from also reserving a check on legislative power for itself. Absent the veto, the agencies receiving delegations of legislative or quasi-legislative power may issue regulations having the force of law without bicameral approval and without the

President's signature. It is thus not apparent why the reservation of a veto over the exercise of that legislative power must be subject to a more exacting test. In both cases, it is enough that the initial statutory authorizations comply with the Article I requirements. . . .

Nor does § 244 infringe on the judicial power, as Justice POW-ELL would hold. Section 244 makes clear that Congress has reserved its own judgment as part of the statutory process. Congressional action does not substitute for judicial review of the Attorney General's decisions. The Act provides for judicial review of the refusal of the Attorney General to suspend a deportation and to transmit a recommendation to Congress. But the courts have not been given the authority to review whether an alien should be given permanent status; review is limited to whether the Attorney General has properly applied the statutory standards for essentially denying the alien a recommendation that his deportable status be changed by the Congress. Moreover, there is no constitutional obligation to provide any judicial review whatever for a failure to suspend deportation. "The power of Congress, therefore, to expel, like the power to exclude aliens, or any specified class of aliens, from the country, may be exercised entirely through executive officers; or Congress may call in the aid of the judiciary to ascertain any contested facts on which an alien's right to be in the country has been made by Congress to depend." *Fong Yue Ting v. United States,* 149 U.S. 698 (1893). . . .

I do not suggest that all legislative vetoes are necessarily consistent with separation of powers principles. A legislative check on an inherently executive function, for example that of initiating prosecutions, poses an entirely different question. But the legislative veto device here—and in many other settings—is far from an instance of legislative tyranny over the Executive. It is a necessary check on the unavoidably expanding power of the agencies, both executive and independent, as they engage in exercising authority delegated by Congress.

I regret that I am in disagreement with my colleagues on the fundamental questions that this case presents. But even more I regret the destructive scope of the Court's holding. It reflects a profoundly different conception of the Constitution than that held by the Courts which sanctioned the modern administrative state. Today's decision strikes down in one fell swoop provisions in more laws enacted by Congress than the Court has cumulatively invalidated in its history. I fear it will now be more difficult "to insure that the fundamental policy decisions in our society will be made not by an appointed official but by the body immediately responsible to the people," *Arizona v. California,* 373 U.S. 546 . . . (1963) (HARLAN, J., dissenting). I must dissent.

Justice REHNQUIST dissented in a separate opinion.

D. ACCOUNTABILITY AND IMMUNITIES

The president is politically accountable through the electoral process when running for reelection and in trying to win passage of his programs by Congress. Both Houses also have the power to hold hearings and investigate actions by the president and the executive branch. But the president may not be removed from office (under Article II, Section 4) except "by Impeachment for, and Conviction of, Treason, Bribery, or other High Crimes and Misdemeanors." (The Twenty-fifth Amendment, however, provides an additional procedure for removing a president who because of disability is unable to discharge the powers and duties of his office.)

Congressional investigations of actions of the executive branch may lead to confrontations, when presidents withhold information, or claim an inherent power to withhold information as a matter of "executive privilege" in the interests of preserving the confidentiality of White House communications and national security.[1] Since George Washington, presidents have asserted the power to deny Congress sensitive information, dealing with treaty negotiations, for instance, military operations and executive branch investigations. But they have done so with greater frequency and over a broader range of matters since World War II. Most of the disputes arising between the president and

Richard Nixon after his resignation. *Wide World Photos*

Congress have thus far been resolved by negotiations. The Court, however, recognizes limits to congressional investigatory powers (see Chapter 5) and specifically that Congress "cannot inquire into matters which are within the exclusive province of one of the other branches of Government."[2]

CONSTITUTIONAL HISTORY
Unraveling the Watergate Affair

June 17, 1972—Five men are arrested in the Democratic National Committee's headquarters in the Watergate Hotel in Washington, D.C. One, James W. McCord, Jr., is the security director of the Committee to Re-Elect the President. Two others, E. Howard Hunt, Jr., and Gordon Liddy, who have White House and Nixon campaign ties, are linked to the burglars.

September 15—A federal grand jury indicts Hunt, Liddy, and the Watergate burglars; however, despite evidence of a wider conspiracy, the Justice Department closes its investigation.

January 8, 1973—The Watergate burglary trial begins. Five defendants plead guilty; Liddy and Hunt are convicted after trial.

March 19—In a letter to Judge John J. Sirica, McCord says that the defendants were pressured to plead guilty, that perjury was committed, and that others were involved.

April 30—The White House announces the resignations of Attorney General Richard Kleindienst and presidential aides John Ehrichman and H. R. Haldeman, and the firing of presidential counselor John Dean.

June 25—John Dean begins testifying before the Senate Watergate Committee, revealing that the Watergate break-in was part of a White House program of political espionage and that President Nixon was part of an attempt to cover up the Watergate affair.

July 16—Alexander P. Butterfield, a former White House aide, discloses that there is a tape recorder in the Oval Office used to record presidential conversations.

July 26—After the president refuses to release the White House tapes, the committee obtains subpoenas for several of the taped conversations.

October 20—The Saturday Night Massacre. The special Watergate prosecutor, Archibald Cox, is fired by Acting Attorney General Robert H. Bork, after Attorney General Elliot Richardson and Deputy Attorney General William Ruckelshaus refuse to dismiss Cox and resign instead.

November 5—President Nixon appoints a new special prosecutor, Leon Jaworski, who continues to request that the president turn over tapes of his conversations bearing on Watergate.

March 1, 1974—Seven former presidential aides are indicted for the Watergate cover-up and President Nixon is named as an unindicted coconspirator.

May 9—The House Judiciary Committee begins impeachment proceedings.

July 24—The Supreme Court rules, in *United States v. Nixon,* that the president must turn over the subpoenaed White House tapes to the special prosecutor.

July 27—The House Judiciary Committee approves an article of impeachment, charging the president with obstruction of justice. Later two additional articles are approved.

August 5—The president releases transcripts of three conversations with H. R. Halderman made six days after the break-in. They reveal that he ordered a halt to the Federal Bureau of Investigation's (FBI) probe of the Watergate break-in and cover-up to prevent discovery that his reelection campaign committee was involved.

August 8—Amid growing public outcry calling for his removal from office, President Nixon announces he will resign.

August 9—President Nixon resigns and Vice-President Gerald R. Ford is sworn in as President.

September 8—President Ford pardons former President Nixon.

The Court expressly acknowledged the constitutional status of a president's claim of "executive privilege" in *United States v. Nixon* (1974) (see page 373). But this case involved the assertion by President Richard M. Nixon of an absolute and unreviewable claim of "executive privilege" within the context of a criminal investigation, and not a congressional hearing, by a special prosecutor assigned to the administration's involvement with a break-in of the headquarters of the Democratic National Committee in the Watergate hotel and its subsequent attempts to cover-up the Watergate affair.[3]

A number of other constitutional issues bearing on presidential accountability and immunity arose due to the Watergate affair. For one, questions persisted about whether the chief executive may be subject to them and what happens if he resists. In *Mississippi v. Johnson,* 4 Wall. 162 (1875), the Court declined to issue an injunction against the president on the grounds that if he balked, it would be "without power to enforce its process." But the *Nixon* Court upheld the subpoenas against the president, and he complied with its ruling.

Another question, avoided by the Court in *Nixon,* involves whether the president may be subject to criminal indictment while in office.[4] Article I, Section 3 makes clear that on leaving office the president may be indicted and subject to criminal and civil prosecutions for actions taken while in office. After resigning,

Nixon avoided further criminal prosecution because his successor, Gerald R. Ford, granted him "a full, free and absolute pardon . . . for all offenses against the United States which he . . . committed or may have committed or taken part in during" his presidency.

Although Nixon evaded criminal prosecutions after leaving office, he faced several civil suits that raised the related issue of whether the president enjoys immunity from civil liability. Initially, a suit was brought by Morton Halperin, a former National Security Council employee. He sued Nixon, Henry Kissinger, and several presidential aides for maintaining wiretaps on his home telephone, even after he left government service. In *Halperin v. Kissinger*, 606 F.2d 1192 (1979), the Court of Appeals for the District of Columbia Circuit ruled that Nixon enjoyed a qualified immunity but, along with his former aides, was subject to the suit. That ruling was left undisturbed when the Supreme Court split four to four when reviewing its appeal in *Kissinger v. Halperin*, 452 U.S. 713 (1981).

In two companion cases against Nixon and former senior advisers, the Court upheld absolute immunity for the president, but concluded that senior aides enjoy only qualified immunity in civil liability suits. In *Nixon v. Fitzgerald*, 457 U.S. 731 (1982), newly appointed Justice Sandra Day O'Connor cast the crucial vote in deciding that the president "is entitled to absolute immunity from damages liability predicated on his official acts." A former Pentagon employee, A. Ernest Fitzgerald, sought damages from Nixon and several White House aides after he was fired for publicly criticizing military cost overruns. The justices split five to four in sustaining Nixon's claim of absolute immunity as "a functionally mandated incident of the President's unique office, rooted in the constitutional tradition of the separation of powers and supported by our history." Yet in *Harlow v. Fitzgerald*, 457 U.S. 800 (1982), the companion case brought by Fitzgerald against several White House aides involved in his firing, the Court ruled that senior presidential advisers forfeit immunity if they know or should have known that their actions violate individuals' constitutional rights.

The impeachment proceedings against Nixon posed other important constitutional questions. Under Article I, the House of Representatives has "the sole power of impeachment," which it exercises by passing, by majority vote, "articles of impeachment." The Senate is given "the sole power to try all impeachments." Basically, the House functions as a prosecutor and the Senate sits as a court in passing judgment on impeachment. Article II, section 4, further specifies that the president and other government officials may be "removed from Office on Impeachment for, and Conviction of, Treason, Bribery, or other high Crimes and Misdemeanors." Besides Nixon, impeachment proceedings have been brought against fourteen federal judges—six of whom have been convicted—and two other members of the executive branch, President Andrew Johnson in 1868 and the secretary of war in 1876.

A major question in Nixon's impeachment involved the meaning of "high crimes and misdemeanors"; specifically, whether the president could be impeached for other than indictable criminal offenses? Nixon's attorneys advanced the view that impeachment requires not only "a criminal offense, but one of a very serious nature, committed in one's governmental capacity." At the other extreme, Gerald Ford, as congressman, urged in the House of Representatives during his 1970 drive to impeach Justice William O. Douglas that "an impeachable offense is whatever a majority of the House of Representatives considers it to be at a given moment in history; conviction results from whatever offense or offenses two-thirds of the other body considers to be sufficiently serious to require removal of the accused from office."[5] The staff and a majority of the House Judiciary Committee ultimately took a position midway between these two extreme views. They concluded that the violation of criminal laws was not necessary for impeachment, if the offenses were nevertheless serious. In their view, "[t]o confine impeachable conduct to indictable offenses may well be to set a standard so restrictive as not to reach conduct that might adversely affect the system of government. Some of the most grievous offenses against our constitutional form of government may not entail violations of the criminal law."[6]

In voting three articles of impeachment against President Nixon, the majority of the House Judiciary Committee adopted the latter position, charging the president with (1) obstruction of justice during the Watergate cover-up; (2) abuse of presidential power by misusing the FBI, CIA, and other governmental agencies; and (3) contempt of Congress in refusing to obey the committee's subpoenas for White House materials (see page 381).

The unconditional pardon granted Nixon by President Gerald Ford was controversial and elicited wide public disapproval. Article II, section 2, gives the president the "power to grant reprieves and pardons for offenses against the United States, except in cases of impeachment." Although the constitutional convention rejected a proposal that would have limited the pardon power to cover only individuals indicted and convicted of criminal offenses, some lawyers challenged the constitutionality of Ford's pardon on the ground that Nixon had not been criminally indicted (although he was named as an unindicted coconspirator in the Watergate cover-up). A federal district judge, in *Murphy v. Ford*, 390 F.Supp. 1372 (1975), however, upheld Ford's pardon. In doing so, the judge found support in the very broad language of a Supreme Court's opinion, in *Ex parte Garland*, 4 Wall. (71 U.S.) 333 (1867), that the president's pardoning power "extends to every offense known to the law, and may be exercised at any time after its commission, either before legal proceedings are taken, or during their pendency, or after conviction and judgment [and] cannot be fettered by legislative restrictions."

One additional constitutional question arising in the aftermath of Watergate and bearing on presidential accountability and immunities was settled in *Nixon v. Administrator of General Services*, 433 U.S. 425 (1977). Presidential papers have historically been the property of the president but, because of the circumstances of Nixon's resignation and ongoing criminal investigations of his administration, Congress passed the Presidential Recordings and Materials Preservation Act of 1974. It authorized the General Services Administration to hold and screen Nixon's presidential materials, returning purely private papers to him and making the rest available to the public. Nixon attacked the constitutionality of the act for violating separation of powers, executive privilege, and his constitutionally protected privacy rights. Over the vigorous dissents of Chief Justice Burger and Justice Rehnquist, the Court rejected his claims and upheld the legislation.

NOTES

1. For an examination of the history of claims to executive privilege, see Raoul Berger, *Executive Privilege* (Cambridge, MA: Harvard University Press, 1974). For criticisms of his rejection of the constitutional basis for claims to executive privilege, see Ralph K. Winter, Jr., "The Seedlings for the Forest," 83 *Yale Law Journal* 1730 (1974).

2. *Barenblatt v. United States*, 360 U.S. 109 (1959) (see page 425).

3. For a further discussion of some of the constitutional issues arising out of the Watergate affair, see Philip B. Kurland, *Watergate and the Constitution* (Chicago: University of Chicago Press, 1978).

4. See Raoul Berger, *Impeachment: The Constitutional Problems* (Cambridge, MA: Harvard University Press, 1973); and Raoul Berger, "The President, Congress, and the Courts—Must Impeachment Precede Indictment?" 83 *Yale Law Journal* 1111 (1974).

5. Gerald Ford, *Congressional Record*, 91st Cong., 2d sess., Apr. 15, 1970, 11912–11913.

6. Quoted and discussed in Congressional Quarterly, *1970 CQ Almanac* (Washington, DC: Congressional Quarterly, 1970), 1025.

SELECTED BIBLIOGRAPHY

Ball, Howard. *"We Have A Duty": The Supreme Court and the Watergate Tapes Litigation.* New York: Greenwood, 1990.

Berger, Raoul. *Impeachment: The Constitutional Problems.* Cambridge, MA: Harvard University Press, 1973.

_____. *Executive Privilege.* Cambridge, MA: Harvard University Press, 1974.

Kurland, Philip. *Watergate and the Constitution.* Chicago: University of Chicago Press, 1978.

Labovitz, John. *Presidential Impeachment.* New Haven, CT: Yale University Press, 1978.

United States v. Nixon
418 U.S. 683, 94 S.Ct. 3090 (1974)

On the night of June 17, 1972, five men broke into the headquarters of the National Democratic Party in the Watergate complex in Washington, D.C. "The plumbers," as they were called, were caught by some off-duty policemen, while planting bugging devices so they could monitor the Democratic party's campaign plans for the fall presidential election. On the next day it was learned that one of them worked for President Nixon's reelection committee.

Nixon and his associates managed to cover up involvement in the break-in and won reelection. But congressional committees continued to search for links between the break-in and the White House. At the same time, Judge John Sirica presided over the trial of the five burglars and pressed for full disclosure of White House involvement. In spring 1973, the Senate Select Committee on Presidential Activities of 1972 began its investigations. Nixon's former counsel John Dean, became the star witness, revealing much of the president's involvement in the cover-up. A surprise witness, former White House aide Alexander Butterfield, then disclosed that Nixon had tape-recorded conversations in the Oval Office. The possibility of evidence in the tapes showing Nixon's direct involvement deepened the Watergate crisis.

The Senate committee and a special prosecutor, Archibald Cox, appointed to investigate illegal activities of the White House, immediately sought a small number of the tapes. Nixon refused to relinquish them, claiming executive privilege to withhold information that might damage national security interests.

The special prosecutor subpoenaed Nixon's attorneys to turn over the tapes. When Nixon again refused, Judge Sirica ordered their release but Nixon would still not comply. Cox appealed to the Court of Appeals for the District of Columbia Circuit, whose judges urged that a compromise be found. When none could be reached, the court ruled that Nixon had to surrender the tapes.

After the appellate court's ruling, Nixon announced that he would release summaries of the relevant conversations. But Cox found the deal unacceptable. Nixon then ordered the "Saturday Night Massacre." Chief of Staff Alexander Haig told Attorney General Elliot Richardson to fire the special prosecutor. Instead, Richardson resigned, as did the deputy attorney general. Finally, Solicitor General Robert H. Bork became the acting attorney general and fired Cox. But this unleashed a wave of public anger and within four days Nixon told Judge Sirica that nine tapes would be forthcoming.

The release of the nine tapes only served to intensify the controversy, when it was discovered that an eighteen-and-a-half minute segment of the first conversation after the break-in had been erased. That and other revelations prodded the House of Representatives to create a committee to investigate the possibility of impeachment. And by February 1974, the House directed its Judiciary Committee to begin hearings on impeachment.

Nixon continued to refuse to give additional tapes to the Judiciary Committee and Leon Jaworski, who had replaced Cox as special prosecutor. Then on March 1, 1974, the federal grand jury investigating Watergate indicted top White House aides. It also secretly named Nixon as an unindicted coconspirator and asked that the information against him be turned over to the House Judiciary Committee.

The Judiciary Committee subpoenaed all documents and tapes related to Watergate, but Nixon remained adamant about his right to decide what to release. Jaworski countered by asking Sirica to enforce a subpoena for sixty-four tapes. When Nixon would still not yield, Jaworski appealed directly to the Supreme Court.

On May 31, 1974, the Court announced that it would grant the appeal on an expedited basis. On July 8, during oral arguments Jaworski argued that the basic issue was who is to be the arbitrator of what the Constitution says? Nixon's claim of executive privilege in withholding the tapes, he insisted, placed the president above the law. Jaworski conceded that the Constitution might provide "for such a thing as executive privilege." But what he denied was that Nixon, or any president, could claim an absolute, unreviewable privilege. If he had that power, the president, not the Court, would be the supreme interpreter of the Constitution.

After Jaworski argued for an hour, Nixon's attorney, James St. Clair, asked that the case be dismissed. He argued that there was a "fusion" between the criminal prosecution of presidential aides, on the one hand, and the impeachment proceedings against Nixon, on the other. Information used at the trial of the Watergate conspirators would be turned over to Congress for use against the president. That, he claimed, violated the principle of separation of powers. The dispute, he unsuccessfully urged, "is essentially a political dispute. It is a dispute that this Court ought not to be drawn into."

When the justices later discussed the case in private conference, all agreed that the Court had jurisdiction, that the case did not raise a political question, and that the case should be decided as soon as possible. All agreed, furthermore, that Nixon's claim of executive privilege could not withstand scrutiny. That portion of the Court's opinion dealing with the claim of executive privilege is excerpted here.

Chief Justice BURGER delivers the opinion of the Court.

[W]e turn to the claim that the subpoena should be quashed because it demands "confidential conversations between a President and his close advisors that it would be inconsistent with the public interest to produce." The first contention is a broad claim that the separation of powers doctrine precludes judicial review of a President's claim of privilege. The second contention is that if he does not prevail on the claim of absolute privilege, the court should hold as a matter of constitutional law that the privilege prevails over the subpoena *duces tecum.*

In the performance of assigned constitutional duties each branch of the Government must initially interpret the Constitution, and the interpretation of its powers by any branch is due great respect from the others. The President's counsel, as we have noted, reads the Constitution as providing an absolute privilege of confidentiality for all Presidential communications. Many decisions of this Court, however, have unequivocally reaffirmed the holding of *Marbury v. Madison,* [1 Cr. 137 (1803)], that "[i]t is emphatically the province and duty of the judicial department to say what the law is."

Our system of government "requires that federal courts on occasion interpret the Constitution in a manner at variance with the construction given the document by another branch." *Powell v. McCormack,* [395 U.S. 486 (1969)]. And in *Baker v. Carr,* [369 U.S. 186 (1962)], the Court stated:

"[D]eciding whether a matter has in any measure been committed by the Constitution to another branch of government, or whether the action of that branch exceeds whatever authority has been committed, is itself a delicate exercise in constitutional interpretation, and is a responsibility of this Court as ultimate interpreter of the Constitution."

Notwithstanding the deference each branch must accord the others, the "judicial Power of the United States" vested in the federal courts by Art. III, § 1, of the Constitution can no more be shared with the Executive Branch than the Chief Executive, for example, can share with the Judiciary the veto power, or the Congress share with the Judiciary the power to override a Presidential veto. Any other conclusion would be contrary to the basic concept of separation of powers and the checks and balances that flow from the scheme of a tripartite government. We therefore reaffirm that it is the province and duty of this Court "to say what the law is" with respect to the claim of privilege presented in this case. *Marbury v. Madison.* . . .

In support of his claim of absolute privilege, the President's counsel urges two grounds, one of which is common to all governments and one of which is peculiar to our system of separation of powers. The first ground is the valid need for protection of communications between high Government officials and those who advise and assist them in the performance of their manifold duties: the importance of this confidentiality is too plain to require further discussion. Human experience teaches that those who expect public dissemination of their remarks may well temper candor with a concern for appearances and for their own interests to the detriment of the decisionmaking process. Whatever the nature of the privilege of confidentiality of Presidential communications in the exercise of Art. II powers, the privilege can be said to derive from the supremacy of each branch within its own assigned area of constitutional duties. Certain powers and privileges flow from the nature of enumerated powers; the protection of the confidentiality of Presidential communications has similar constitutional underpinnings.

The second ground asserted by the President's counsel in support of the claim of absolute privilege rests on the doctrine of separation of powers. Here it is argued that the independence of the Executive Branch within its own sphere, *Humphrey's Executor v. United States,* 295 U.S. 602 (1935); *Kilbourn v. Thompson,* 103 U.S. 168 (1881), insulates a President from a judicial subpoena in an ongoing criminal prosecution, and thereby protects confidential Presidential communications.

However, neither the doctrine of separation of powers, nor the need for confidentiality of high-level communications, without more, can sustain an absolute, unqualified Presidential privilege of immunity from judicial process under all circumstances. The President's need for complete candor and objectivity from advisers calls for great deference from the courts. However, when the privilege depends solely on the broad, undifferentiated claim of public interest in the confidentiality of such conversations, a confrontation with other values arises. Absent a claim of need to protect military, diplomatic, or sensitive national security secrets, we find it difficult to accept the argument that even the very important interest in confidentiality of Presidential communications is significantly diminished by production of such material for *in camera* inspection with all the protection that a district court will be obliged to provide.

The impediment that an absolute, unqualified privilege would place in the way of the primary constitutional duty of the Judicial Branch to do justice in criminal prosecutions would plainly conflict with the function of the courts under Art. III. In designing the structure of our Government and dividing and allocating the sovereign power among three co-equal branches, the Framers of the Constitution sought to provide a comprehensive system, but the separate powers were not intended to operate with absolute independence. . . .

To read the Art. II powers of the President as providing an absolute privilege as against a subpoena essential to enforcement of criminal statutes on no more than a generalized claim of the public interest in confidentiality of non-military and nondiplomatic discussions would upset the constitutional balance of "a workable government" and gravely impair the role of the courts under Art. III.

Since we conclude that the legitimate needs of the judicial process may outweigh Presidential privilege, it is necessary to resolve those competing interests in a manner that preserves the essential functions of each branch. The right and indeed the duty to resolve that question does not free the Judiciary from according high respect to the representations made on behalf of the President. *United States v. Burr,* [4 Cr. (8 U.S.) 470 (1807)].

The expectation of a President to the confidentiality of his conversations and correspondence, like the claim of confidentiality of judicial deliberations, for example, has all the values to which we accord deference for the privacy of all citizens and, added to those values, is the necessity for protection of the public interest in candid, objective, and even blunt or harsh opinions in Presidential decisionmaking. A President and those who assist him must be free to explore alternatives in the process of shaping policies and making decisions and to do so in a way many would be unwilling to express except privately. These are the considerations justifying a presumptive privilege for Presidential communications. The privilege is fundamental to the operation of Government and inextricably rooted in the separation of powers under the Constitution. In *Nixon v. Sirica,* 159 U.S. App. D.C. 58 (1973), the Court of Appeals held that such Presidential communications are "presumptively privileged" and this position is accepted by both parties in the present litigation. We agree with Chief Justice MARSHALL's observation, therefore, that "[i]n no case of this kind would a court be required to proceed against the president as against an ordinary individual." *United States v. Burr.* . . .

But this presumptive privilege must be considered in light of our historic commitment to the rule of law. This is nowhere more profoundly manifest than in our view that "the twofold aim [of criminal justice] is that guilt shall not escape or innocence suffer." *Berger v. United States* [295 U.S. 78 (1935)]. We have elected to employ an adversary system of criminal justice in which the parties contest all issues before a court of law. The need to develop all relevant facts in the adversary system is both fundamental and comprehensive. The ends of criminal justice would be defeated if judgments were to be founded on a partial or speculative presentation of the facts. The very integrity of the judicial system and public confidence in the system depend on full disclosure of all the facts, within the framework of the rules of evidence. To ensure that justice is done, it is imperative to the function of courts that compulsory process be available for the production of evidence needed either by the prosecution or by the defense.

Only recently the Court restated the ancient proposition of law, albeit in the context of a grand jury inquiry rather than a trial.

> "that 'the public . . . has a right to every man's evidence,' except for those persons protected by a constitutional, common-law, or statutory privilege. . . ."

The privileges referred to by the Court are designed to protect weighty and legitimate competing interests. Thus, the Fifth Amendment to the Constitution provides that no man "shall be compelled in any criminal case to be a witness against himself." And, generally, an attorney or a priest may not be required to disclose what has been revealed in professional confidence. These and other interests are recognized in law by privileges against forced disclosure, established in the Constitution, by statute, or at common law. Whatever their origins, these exceptions to the demand for every man's evidence are not lightly created nor expansively construed, for they are in derogation of the search for truth.

In this case the President challenges a subpoena served on him as a third party requiring the production of materials for use in a criminal prosecution on the claim that he has a privilege against disclosure of confidential communications. He does not place his claim of privilege on the ground they are military or diplomatic secrets. As to these areas of Art. II duties the courts have traditionally shown the utmost deference to presidential responsibilities. No case of the Court, however, has extended this high degree of deference to a President's generalized interest in confidentiality. Nowhere in the Constitution, as we have noted earlier, is there any explicit reference to a privilege of confidentiality, yet to the extent this interest relates to the effective discharge of a President's powers, it is constitutionally based. . . .

In this case we must weigh the importance of the general privilege of confidentiality of presidential communications in performance of his responsibilities against the inroads of such a privilege on the fair administration of criminal justice. The interest in preserving confidentiality is weighty indeed and entitled to great respect. However we cannot conclude that advisers will be moved to temper the candor of their remarks by the infrequent occasions of disclosure because of the possibility that such conversations will be called for in the context of a criminal prosecution.

On the other hand, the allowance of the privilege to withhold evidence that is demonstrably relevant in a criminal trial could cut deeply into the guarantee of the process of law and gravely impair the basic function of the courts. A President's acknowledged need for confidentiality in the communications of his office is general in nature, whereas the constitutional need for production of relevant evidence in a criminal proceeding is specific and central to the fair adjudication of a particular criminal case in the administration of justice. Without access to specific facts a criminal prosecution may be totally frustrated. The President's broad interest in confidentiality of communications will not be violated by disclosure of a limited number of conversations preliminarily shown to have some bearing on the pending criminal cases.

We conclude that when the ground for asserting privilege as to subpoenaed materials sought for use in a criminal trial is based only on the generalized interest in confidentiality, it cannot prevail over the fundamental demands of due process of law in the fair administration of criminal justice. The generalized assertion of privilege must yield to the demonstrated, specific need for evidence in a pending criminal trial. We have earlier determined that the District Court did not err in authorizing the issuance of the subpoena. If a president concludes that compliance with a subpoena would be injurious to the public interest he may properly, as was done here, invoke a claim of privilege on the return of the subpoena. Upon receiving a claim of privilege from the Chief Executive, it became the further duty of the District Court to treat the subpoenaed material as presumptively privileged and to require the Special Prosecutor to demonstrate that the presidential material was "essential to the justice of the [pending criminal] case." *United States v. Burr.* Here the District Court treated the material as presumptively privileged, proceeded to find that the Special Prosecutor had made a sufficient showing to rebut the presumption and ordered an *in camera* examination of the subpoenaed material. On the basis of our examination of the record we are unable to conclude that the District Court erred in ordering the inspection. Accordingly we affirm the order of the District Court that subpoenaed materials be transmitted to that court. We now turn to the important question of the District Court's responsibilities in conducting the *in camera* examination of presidential materials or communications delivered under the compulsion of the subpoena *duces tecum.*

It is elementary that *in camera* inspection of evidence is always a procedure calling for scrupulous protection against any release or publication of material not found by the court, at that stage, probably admissible in evidence and relevant to the issues of the trial for which it is sought. That being true of an ordinary situation, it is obvious that the District Court has a very heavy responsibility to see to it that Presidential conversations, which are either not relevant or not admissible, are accorded that high degree of respect due the President of the United States. Chief Justice MARSHALL, sitting as a trial judge in the *Burr* case was extraordinarily careful to point out that

> "[i]n no case of this kind would a court be required to proceed against the president as against an ordinary individual." . . .

MARSHALL's statement cannot be read to mean in any sense that a President is above the law, but relates to the singularly unique role under Art. II of a President's communications and activities related to the performance of duties under that Article. Moreover, a Presidents communications and activities encompass a vastly wider range of sensitive material than would be true of any "ordinary individual." It is therefore necessary in the public interest to afford Presidential confidentiality the greatest protection consistent with the fair administration of justice. The need for confidentiality even as to idle conversations with associates in which casual reference might be made concerning political leaders within the country or foreign statesmen is too obvious to call for further treatment. We have no doubt that the District Judge will at all times accord to Presidential records that high degree of deference suggested in *United States v. Burr, supra* and will discharge his responsibility to see to it that until released to the Special Prosecutor no *in camera* material is revealed to anyone. This burden applies with even great force to excised material; once the decision is made to excise, the material is restored to its privileged status and should be returned under seal to its lawful custodian.

Since this matter came before the Court during the pendency

of a criminal prosecution, and on representations that time is of the essence, the mandate shall issue forthwith.

Affirmed.

Justice REHNQUIST did not participate in the consideration or decision of these cases.

Articles of Impeachment against President Richard M. Nixon Recommended by the House Judiciary Committee

Resolved, That Richard M. Nixon, President of the United States, is impeached for high crimes and misdemeanors, and that the following articles of impeachment be exhibited to the Senate:

Articles of impeachment exhibited by the House of Representatives of the United States of America in the name of itself and of all of the people of the United States of America, against Richard M. Nixon, President of the United States of America, in maintenance and support of its impeachment against him for high crimes and misdemeanors.

ARTICLE I

In his conduct of the office of President of the United States, Richard M. Nixon, in violation of his constitutional oath faithfully to execute the office of President of the United States and, to the best of his ability, preserve, protect, and defend the Constitution of the United States, and in violation of his constitutional duty to take care that the laws be faithfully executed, has prevented, obstructed, and impeded the administration of justice, in that:

On June 17, 1972, and prior thereto, agents of the Committee for the Re-election of the President committed unlawful entry of the headquarters of the Democratic National Committee in Washington, District of Columbia, for the purpose of securing political intelligence. Subsequent thereto, Richard M. Nixon, using the powers of his high office, engaged, personally and through his subordinates and agents, in a course of conduct or plan designed to delay, impede, and obstruct the investigation of such unlawful entry; to cover up, conceal and protect those responsible; and to conceal the existence and scope of other unlawful covert activities.

The means used to implement this course of conduct or plan included one or more of the following:

1. Making or causing to be made false or misleading statements

to lawfully authorized investigative officers and employees of the United States;

2. Withholding relevant and material evidence or information from lawfully authorized investigative officers and employees of the United States;

3. Approving, condoning, acquiescing in, and counseling witnesses with respect to the giving of false or misleading statements to lawfully authorized investigative officers and employees of the United States and false or misleading testimony in duly instituted judicial and congressional proceedings;

4. Interfering or endeavoring to interfere with the conduct of investigations by the Department of Justice of the United States, the Federal Bureau of Investigation, the Office of Watergate Special Prosecution Force, and Congressional committees;

5. Approving, condoning, and acquiescing in, the surreptitious payment of substantial sums of money for the purpose of obtaining the silence or influencing the testimony of witnesses, potential witnesses or individuals who participated in such illegal entry and other illegal activities;

6. Endeavoring to misuse the Central Intelligence Agency, an agency of the United States;

7. Disseminating information received from officers of the Department of Justice of the United States to subjects of investigations conducted by lawfully authorized investigative officers and employees of the United States, for the purpose of aiding and assisting such subjects in their attempts to avoid criminal liability;

8. Making false or misleading public statements for the purpose of deceiving the people of the United States into believing that a thorough and complete investigation had been conducted with respect to allegations of misconduct on the part of personnel of the executive branch of the United States and personnel of the Committee for the Re-election of the President, and that there was no involvement of such personnel in such misconduct; or

9. Endeavoring to cause prospective defendants, and individuals duly tried and convicted, to expect favored treatment and consideration in return for their silence or false testimony, or rewarding individuals for their silence or false testimony.

In all of this, Richard M. Nixon has acted in a manner contrary to his trust as President and subversive of constitutional government, to the great prejudice of the cause of law and justice and to the manifest injury of the people of the United States.

Wherefore Richard M. Nixon, by such conduct, warrants impeachment and trial, and removal from office.

ARTICLE II

Using the powers of the office of president of the United States, Richard M. Nixon, in violation of his constitutional oath faithfully to execute the office of president of the United States and, to the best of his ability, preserve, protect and defend the Constitution of the United States, and in disregard of his constitutional duty to take care that the laws be faithfully executed, has repeatedly engaged in conduct violating the constitutional rights of citizens, impairing the due and proper administration of justice and the conduct of lawful inquiries, or contravening the laws governing agencies of the executive branch and the purposes of these agencies.

This conduct has included one or more of the following:

1. He has, acting personally and through his subordinates and agents, endeavored to obtain from the Internal Revenue Service, in violation of the constitutional rights of citizens, confidential information contained in income tax returns for purposes not authorized by law and to cause, in violation of the constitutional rights of citizens, income tax audits or other income tax investigations to be initiated or conducted in a discriminatory manner.

2. He misused the Federal Bureau of Investigation, the Secret Service and other executive personnel in violation or disregard of the constitutional rights of citizens by directing or authorizing such agencies or personnel to conduct or continue electronic surveillance or other investigations for purposes unrelated to national security, the enforcement of laws or any other lawful function of his office; and he did direct the concealment of certain records made by the Federal Bureau of Investigation of electronic surveillance.

3. He has, acting personally and through his subordinates and agents, in violation or disregard of the constitutional rights of citizens, authorized and permitted to be maintained a secret investigative unit within the office of the president, financed in part with money derived from campaign contributions to him, which unlawfully utilized the resources of the Central Intelligence Agency, engaged in covert and unlawful activities and attempted to prejudice the constitutional right of an accused to a fair trial.

4. He has failed to take care that the laws were faithfully executed by failing to act when he knew or had reason to know that his close subordinates endeavored to impede and frustrate lawful inquiries by duly constituted executive, judicial and legislative entities concerning the unlawful entry into the headquarters of the Democratic National Committee and the cover-up thereof, and concerning other unlawful activities including those relating to the confirmation of Richard Kleindienst as attorney general of the United States, the electronic surveillance of private citizens, the break-in into the office of Dr. Lewis Fielding and the campaign financing practices of the Committee to Re-elect the President.

5. In disregard of the rule of law, he knowingly misused the executive power by interfering with agencies of the executive branch, including the Federal Bureau of Investigation, the Criminal Division and the Office of Watergate Special Prosecution

Force, of the Department of Justice and the Central Intelligence Agency, in violation of his duty to take care that the laws be faithfully executed.

In all of this, Richard M. Nixon has acted in a manner contrary to his trust as president and subversive of constitutional government, to the great prejudice of the cause of law and justice and to the manifest injury of the people of the United States.

Wherefore Richard M. Nixon, by such conduct, warrants impeachment and trial and removal from office.

ARTICLE III

In his conduct of the office of president of the United States, Richard M. Nixon, contrary to his oath faithfully to execute the office of president of the United States and, to the best of his ability, preserve, protect and defend the Constitution of the United States, and in violation of his constitutional duty to take care that the laws be faithfully executed, has failed without lawful cause or excuse to produce papers and things as directed by duly authorized subpoenas issued by the Committee on the Judiciary of the House of Representatives on April 11, 1974; May 15, 1974; May 30, 1974, and June 24, 1974, and willfully disobeyed such subpoenas.

The subpoenaed papers and things were deemed necessary by the committee in order to resolve by direct evidence fundamental, factual questions relating to presidential direction, knowledge or approval of actions demonstrated by other evidence to be substantial grounds for impeachment of the president.

In refusing to produce these papers and things Richard M. Nixon substituting his judgment as to what materials were necessary for the inquiry, interposed the powers of the presidency against the lawful subpoenas of the House of Representatives, thereby assuming to himself functions and judgments necessary to the exercise of the sole power of impeachment vested by the Constitution in the House of Representatives.

In all of this, Richard M. Nixon has acted in a manner contrary to his trust as president and subversive of constitutional government, to the great prejudice of the cause of law and justice and to the manifest injury of the people of the United States.

Wherefore, Richard M. Nixon by such conduct, warrants impeachment and trial and removal from office.

5

CONGRESS: MEMBERSHIP, IMMUNITIES, AND INVESTIGATORY POWERS

RTICLE I OF the Constitution provides that all legislative powers "shall be vested in a Congress of the United States." In contrast with the general powers delegated to the president, the powers given Congress are enumerated in considerable detail. Section 8 of the Article lists seventeen specific powers, including the power to regulate commerce, to coin money, to raise and support armies, and to declare war. Congress also has the residual power of passing laws "necessary and proper" to executing its authority. In addition, various constitutional amendments—notably, the Thirteenth, Fourteenth, and Fifteenth Amendments—further expand the powers of Congress.

The authority to make laws does not exhaust congressional powers, however. Congress has the implied power of investigating subjects on which it might legislate and regulate. Both houses assume a judicial function during impeachment proceedings, and the Senate has an executive role in ratifying treaties and consenting to the president's nomination of high government officials (see Chapter 4). If presidential and vice-presidential candidates fail to win a majority vote in the electoral college, the Twelfth Amendment gives both houses an electoral role in choosing the president and vice-president. Finally, Article V gives Congress the power to propose constitutional amendments, subject to ratification by three-quarters of the states.

This chapter examines controversies that have arisen over the structure, membership, and immunities of Congress, as well as Congress's investigatory and contempt powers. Chapter 6 turns to the constitutional politics of the legislative, taxing, and spending powers of Congress.

A. MEMBERSHIP AND IMMUNITIES

The structure of Congress is bicameral: the Senate represents the states and the House represents the people, based on each state's population. This registers a major compromise forged during the Constitutional Convention over the interests of densely and sparsely populated states in achieving representative government.

Each state is guaranteed two representatives in the Senate; hence, with the addition of new states, Alaska (1959) and Hawaii (1959), the size of the Senate has grown from 26 (two senators from each of the thirteen original states) to 100. To ensure that the Senate represents the interests of state governments, the Constitution originally provided for election of senators by state legislatures. But the Seventeenth Amendment (ratified in 1913) made direct popular vote the basis for senatorial election.

Because representation in the House turns on population, a number of controversies have arisen over its composition. The Framers initially provided for sixty-five representatives, based on an estimate of the population (or one representative for every 30,000 people in each state). They also provided for a census within three years after the first Congress, and every ten years thereafter, for determining the apportionment of representatives. But in establishing the basis for representation, the Framers were forced into another compromise due to conflicting interests of Northern and Southern states. As a result, all "free persons" and indentured servants, plus "three-fifths of all other persons [slaves]," were to be counted. With the ratification of the Thirteenth Amendment in 1865, slavery was abolished and blacks were given equal weight in the apportionment of representation. The Fourteenth Amendment (1868) formally specifies that apportionment "among the several states [be] according to their respective numbers, counting the whole number of persons in each State, excluding Indians not taxed."

The basis for apportioning representatives in the House was not further specified and was left for the states and Congress to determine. State legislatures may establish "the times, places and manner of holding elections," but Congress may also "make or alter such regulations." Throughout the nineteenth century, after each census Congress passed apportionment statutes increasing the number of representatives to 435 by 1911. Congress then froze the size of the House and created a mechanism for the reapportionment of representatives after each census in 1929.

Once the size of the House was frozen, controversies emerged over the malapportionment of districts and gerrymandering—the practice of the majority party in state legislatures to redraw district lines to ensure the election of party faithful. Beginning in 1842, Congress required the states to provide "contiguous, equal districts." But this requirement was omitted in the 1929 apportionment statute. And *Wood v. Broom,* 287 U.S. 1 (1932), held that Congress intentionally repealed the requirement for equal voting districts in each state.

The Court in the 1940s and 1950s took the position that malapportionment of districts was a "political question" for Congress to deal with. In Colegrove v. Green, 328 U.S. 549 (1946), for example, district lines in Illinois had not been redrawn since 1901. As a result, the voting strength of Chicago residents was significantly diluted in favor of rural districts. Such reapportionment controversies, in the words of Justice Frankfurter, constituted a "political thicket" the Court should not enter.

In *Baker v. Carr* (1962) (see page 131), however, a majority of the Warren Court held that the "political question" doctrine was no longer an obstacle to cases challenging the malapportionment of state legislative districts. Two years later, in *Wesberry v. Sanders* (1964) (see page 681), Justice Black declared that the principle of equal congressional districts was constitutionally mandated. In his view, "the command of Art. 1, Sec. 2, that Representatives be chosen by the People of the several States' means that as nearly as is practicable one man's vote in a congressional election is to be worth as much as another's." Still, dissenting Justices Harlan and Stewart contended that the Framers of the Constitution "would [not] have subscribed to the principle of 'one person, one vote,'" and that the Court had no authority "to step into every situation where the political branch may be thought to have fallen short."

Qualifications for membership in Congress are specified as well in Article I. Representatives must be at least twenty-five years old, must have been U.S. citizens for seven years, and must reside in the state from which they are elected. Besides the residency requirement, senators must be thirty years of age and must have been citizens for nine years. Members in both houses are also disqualified from simultaneously holding positions in the executive branch, although they may assume temporary diplomatic assignments.[1]

Each house is authorized to judge "the elections, returns and qualifications of its members." But questions have arisen over whether duly elected members may be denied their seats for reasons other than age, citizenship, and residency. Both houses have occasionally had additional requirements for membership. During the Civil War, for instance, the Test Oath Act of 1862 required members to pledge that they would not participate in rebellion. However, *Powell v. McCormack* (1969) (see page 390) held that members could not be excluded for reasons other than those specified in Article I. Subsequently, *Roudebush v. Hartke*, 405 U.S. 15 (1972), held that congressional authority over its membership did not prevent Indiana from recounting the ballots cast in a closely contested 1970 election for one of that state's U.S. senators.

Membership in Congress carries certain privileges and immunities. Members "shall in all cases, except treason, felony and breach of the peace, be privileged from arrest during their attendance at the session of their respective houses, and in going to and returning from the same; and for any speech or debate in either house, they shall not be questioned in any other place." These privileges and immunities are rooted in the struggles between the English Parliament and the Crown that resulted in certain parliamentary privileges. They are designed to prevent harassment of representatives by the executive branch.

The speech or debate clause means that representatives may not be held legally accountable for statements made in their official capacity. *Kilbourn v. Thompson*, 103 U.S. 168 (1881), initially interpreted this protection to include "words spoken in debate" and anything "generally done in a session of the House by one of its members in relation to the business before it." However, in *Gravel v. United States* (1972) (see page 397) the Court drew a line between the "legislative business" of representatives and their broader "political activities." On the one hand, Senator Mike Gravel's reading of portions of the "Pentagon Papers," a classified history of America's involvement in Vietnam, into the public record during a Senate committee session was protected by the speech or debate clause. On the other hand, arrangements he made to have the papers published by a commercial publisher were deemed "not part and parcel of the legislative process."

The scope of "legislative business" covered by the speech or debate clause is broad, as demonstrated by *Eastland v. United States Servicemen's Fund* (1975) (see page 404). There the Court upheld a Senate subcommittee's investigation, which threatened an organization's First Amendment freedoms of speech, press, and right of association, by expansively reading the speech or debate clause to be a shield against judicial scrutiny and interference with legislative work.

The Court defers to Congress on matters "within the sphere of legitimate legislative activity," but continues to draw a sharp line between representatives' "legislative business" and "political activities." In *Hutchinson v. Proxmire* (1979) (see page 407) the Court decided that Senator William Proxmire was immune from libel suits for statements made on the Senate floor and read into the congressional record, but not for those in press releases, newsletters, and telephone calls to executive agencies.

In defining the scope of protected "legislative activities," the Court confronts particular difficulties in cases arising from criminal prosecutions of members of Congress. *United States v. Johnson,* 383 U.S. 169 (1966), unanimously found that a representative, who made a speech on the floor of the House in exchange for money, was protected against having his speeches introduced at trial for the purpose of showing his part in a conspiracy to defraud the government. This ruling forbidding the use of "legislative acts or the motivation for legislative acts" in prosecutions was narrowed in *United States v. Brewster,* 408 U.S. 501 (1972). There the Court held that newsletters mailed to constituents and speeches delivered outside of Congress could be used as evidence in prosecutions for bribery and conspiracy. Bribery and a representative's "promise to deliver a speech, a vote, or to solicit other votes is not 'speech or debate.'" Still, criminal prosecution of such activities remains difficult. For, as the Court reaffirmed in *United States v. Helstoski,* 442 U.S. 477 (1979), the speech or debate clause precludes both the use of "legislative acts" as evidence and judicial inquiry into representatives' "motivations" during criminal trials.[2]

Finally, the Court has had to grapple with whether legislative aides and others involved in the work of Congress enjoy the same immunities as elected representatives under the speech or debate clause. Recall that *Gravel* "treated as one" the senator and his aides in construing the protection afforded by the speech or debate clause. But an earlier case, *Drombrowski v. Eastland,* 387 U.S. 82 (1967), ruled that counsel for a Senate committee, although not the senator chairing the committee, could be sued for conspiring to violate the rights of a group of political activists. And despite the implications of *Gravel,* the Court maintains that legislative immunity "is less absolute, although applicable, when applied to officers or employees of a legislative body, rather than to legislators themselves." Thus in *Doe v. McMillan,* 412 U.S. 306 (1973), members of a congressional committee and their immediate staffs could not be sued for issuing a report containing libelous statements about schoolchildren in the District of Columbia. Whereas, other legislative personnel—including the Government Printing Office—are not likewise protected. In the Court's words, legislative personnel "who participate in distributions of actionable material beyond the reasonable bounds of the legislative task, enjoy no Speech or Debate immunity."

NOTES

1. Members of Congress often hold commissions in the Armed Forces Reserves, however. In *Schlesinger v. Reservists Committee to Stop the War,* 418 U.S. 208 (1974), the Court avoided deciding whether such commissions are incompatible with congressional membership by denying the plaintiffs standing to raise the issue.

2. In *Tenney v. Brandhove,* 341 U.S. 367 (1951), legislative immunity was extended to members of state legislatures. However, *United States v. Gillock,* 445 U.S. 360 (1980), held that the speech or debate clause did not protect state legislators from federal prosecution.

SELECTED BIBLIOGRAPHY

Balinski, Michel, and Young, H. Peyton. *Fair Representation: Meeting the Ideal of One Man, One Vote.* New Haven, CT: Yale University Press, 1982.

Gershman, Bennett. "Abscam, the Judiciary, and the Ethics of Entrapment." 91 *Yale Law Journal* 1565 (1982).

Note, "Evidentiary Implications of the Speech or Debate Clause." 88 *Yale Law Journal* 1280 (1979).

Note, "The Power of a House of Congress to Judge the Qualifications of Its Members." 81 *Harvard Law Review* 673 (1968).

Powell v. McCormack

395 U.S. 486, 89 S.Ct. 1944 (1969)

Adam Clayton Powell was an influential and controversial black congressman from Harlem, New York, elected initially in 1942 to Congress. In November 1966, he won reelection, amid allegations of improper use of government funds and misusing his position as chair of the House Education and Labor Committee. But in January 1967 he was denied his seat by a vote of the House of Representatives to exclude him. Powell then ran in a special election to fill his seat and again won reelection. He also filed a lawsuit against Speaker of the House John

McCormack and several congressional officers, seeking an injunction ordering the House to seat him. Powell contended that the House could exclude him for no other reason than failing to meet the requirements of age, citizenship, and residency set-forth in Article I. A year earlier, in *Bond v. Floyd*, 385 U.S. 116 (1966), the Supreme Court had held that the Georgia legislature violated Julian Bond's First Amendment rights by refusing to seat him due to his public opposition to the draft and the Vietnam War. Still a federal district court dismissed Powell's complaint, ruling that it had no jurisdiction over the dispute. After a court of appeals affirmed that decision, Powell appealed to the Supreme Court. It reversed, holding that federal courts have jurisdiction over suits filed by congressmen against the sergeant at arms (who is an officer, but not an elected member of the House) and no jurisdiction over suits brought by members against the speaker (who is also an elected member of the House), that the issue presented was not a "political question," and that Powell had been unconstitutionally excluded from Congress. Only Justice Potter Stewart dissented.

Chief Justice WARREN delivers the opinion of the Court.

Respondents assert that the Speech or Debate Clause of the Constitution, Art. I, § 6, is an absolute bar to petitioners action. . . .

The Speech or Debate Clause, adopted by the Constitutional Convention without debate or opposition, finds its roots in the conflict between Parliament and the Crown culminating in the Glorious Revolution of 1688 and the English Bill of Rights of 1689. Drawing upon this history, we concluded in *United States v. Johnson*, [383 U.S. 169 (1966)], that the purpose of this clause was "to prevent intimidation [of legislators] by the executive and accountability before a possibly hostile judiciary." Although the clause sprang from a fear of seditious libel actions instituted by the Crown to punish unfavorable speeches made in Parliament, we have held that it would be a "narrow view" to confine the protection of the Speech or Debate Clause to words spoken in debate. Committee reports, resolutions, and the act of voting are equally covered, as are "things generally done in a session of the House by one of its members in relation to the business before it." . . .

Our cases make it clear that the legislative immunity created by the Speech or Debate Clause performs an important function in representative government. It insures that legislators are free to represent the interests of their constituents without fear that they will be later called to task in the courts for that representation. Thus, in *Tenney v. Brandhove*, [341 U.S. 367 (1951)], the Court quoted the writings of James Wilson as illuminating the reason for legislative immunity: "In order to enable and encourage a representative of the publick to discharge his publick trust with firmness and success, it is indispensably necessary, that he should enjoy the fullest liberty of speech, and that he should be protected from the resentment of every one, however powerful, to whom the exercise of that liberty may occasion offense."

Legislative immunity does not, of course, bar all judicial review of legislative acts. That issue was settled by implication as early as 1803, see *Marbury v. Madison,* 1 Cranch (5 U.S.) 137 [1803], and expressly in *Kilbourn v. Thompson* [103 U.S. 168 (1881)], the first of this Court's cases interpreting the reach of the Speech or Debate Clause. Challenged in *Kilbourn* was the constitutionality of a House Resolution ordering the arrest and imprisonment of a recalcitrant witness who had refused to respond to a subpoena issued by a House investigating committee. While holding that the Speech or Debate Clause barred Kilbourn's action for false imprisonment brought against several members of the House, the Court nevertheless reached the merits of Kilbourn's attack and decided that, since the House had no power to punish for contempt, Kilbourn's imprisonment pursuant to the resolution was unconstitutional. It therefore allowed Kilbourn to bring his false imprisonment action against Thompson, the House's Sergeant at Arms, who had executed the warrant for Kilbourn's arrest.

The Court first articulated in *Kilbourn* and followed in *Dombrowski v. Eastland* [387 U.S. 82 (1967)], the doctrine that, although an action against a Congressman may be barred by the Speech or Debate Clause, legislative employees who participated in the unconstitutional activity are responsible for their acts. Despite the fact that petitioners brought this suit against several House employees—the Sergeant at Arms, the Doorkeeper and the Clerk—as well as several Congressmen, respondents argue that *Kilbourn* and *Dombrowski* are distinguishable. Conceding that in *Kilbourn* the presence of the Sergeant at Arms and in *Dombrowski* the presence of a congressional subcommittee counsel as defendants in the litigation allowed judicial review of the challenged congressional action, respondents urge that both cases concerned an affirmative act performed by the employee outside the House having a direct effect upon a private citizen. Here, they continue, the relief sought relates to actions taken by House agents solely within the House. Alternatively, respondents insist that Kilbourn and Dombrowski prayed for damages while petitioner Powell asks that the Sergeant at Arms disburse funds, an assertedly greater interference with the legislative process. We reject the proffered distinctions. . . .

Freedom of legislative activity and the purposes of the Speech or Debate Clause are fully protected if legislators are relieved of the burden of defending themselves. In *Kilbourn* and *Dombrowski* we thus dismissed the action against members of Congress but did not regard the Speech or Debate Clause as a bar to reviewing the merits of the challenged congressional action since congressional employees were also sued. Similarly, though this action may be dismissed against the Congressmen petitioners are entitled to maintain their action against House employees and to judicial review of the propriety of the decision to exclude petitioner Powell. . . .

EXCLUSION OR EXPULSION.

The resolution excluding petitioner Powell was adopted by a vote in excess of two-thirds of the 434 Members of Congress— 307 to 116. Article I, § 5, grants the House authority to expel a member "with the Concurrence of two thirds." Respondents assert that the House may expel a member for any reason whatsoever and that, since a two-thirds vote was obtained, the procedure by which Powell was denied his seat in the 90th Congress should be regarded as an expulsion, not in exclusion. . . .

Although respondents repeatedly urge this Court not to speculate as to the reasons for Powell's exclusion, their attempt to equate exclusion with expulsion would require a similar speculation that the House would have voted to expel Powell had it been faced with that question. Powell had not been seated at the time House Resolution No. 278 was debated and passed. After a motion to bring the Select Committee's proposed resolution to an immediate vote had been defeated, an amendment was offered which mandated Powell's exclusion. Mr. Celler, chairman of the Select Committee, then posed a parliamentary inquiry to determine whether a two-thirds vote was necessary to pass the resolution if so amended "in the sense that it might amount to an expulsion." 113 Cong.Rec. 5020. The Speaker replied that "action by a majority vote would be in accordance with the rules." Had the amendment been regarded as an attempt to expel Powell, a two-thirds vote would have been constitutionally required. The Speaker ruled that the House was voting to exclude Powell, and we will not speculate what the result might have been if Powell had been seated and expulsion proceedings subsequently instituted. . . .

[Under] Art. I, § 5, we necessarily must determine the meaning of the phrase to "be the Judge of the Qualifications of its own Members." Petitioners argue that the records of the debates during the Constitutional Convention; available commentary from the post-Convention, pre-ratification period; and early congressional applications of Art. 1, § 5, support their construction of the section. Respondents insist, however, that a careful examination of the pre-Convention practices of the English Parliament and American colonial assemblies demonstrates that by 1787, a legislature's power to judge the qualifications of its members was generally understood to encompass exclusion or expulsion on the ground that an individual's character or past conduct rendered him unfit to serve. When the Constitution and the debates over its adoption are thus viewed in historical perspective, argue respondents, it becomes clear that the "qualifications" expressly set forth in the Constitution were not meant to limit the long-recognized legislative power to exclude or expel at will, but merely to establish "standing incapacities," which could be altered only by a constitutional amendment. Our examination of the relevant historical materials leads us to the conclusion that petitioners are correct and that the Constitution leaves the House without authority to *exclude* any person, duly elected by his constituents, who meets all the requirements for membership expressly prescribed in the Constitution. . . .

Relying heavily on Charles Warren's analysis of the Convention debates, petitioners argue that the proceedings manifest the Framers' unequivocal intention to deny either branch of Congress the authority to add to or otherwise vary the membership qualifications expressly set forth in the Constitution. We do not completely agree, for the debates are subject to other interpretations. However, we have concluded that the records of the debates, viewed in the context of the bitter struggle for the right to freely choose representatives which had recently concluded in England and in light of the distinction the Framers made between the power to expel and the power to exclude, indicate that petitioners' ultimate conclusion is correct.

The Convention opened in late May 1787. By the end of July, the delegates adopted, with a minimum of debate, age requirements for membership in both the Senate and the House. The Convention then appointed a Committee of Detail to draft a constitution incorporating these and other resolutions adopted during the preceding months. Two days after the Committee was appointed, George Mason of Virginia, moved that the Committee consider a clause " 'requiring certain qualifications of landed property & citizenship' " and disqualifying from membership in Congress persons who had unsettled accounts or who were indebted to the United States. 2 Farrand 121. A vigorous debate ensued. Charles Pinckney and General Charles C. Pinckney both of South Carolina, moved to extend these incapacities to both the judicial and executive branches of the new government. But John Dickinson, of Delaware, opposed the inclusion of any statement of qualifications in the Constitution. He argued that it would be "impossible to make a compleat one, and a partial one would by implication tie up the hands of the Legislature from supplying the omissions." Dickinson's argument was rejected; and, after eliminating the disqualification of debtors and the limitation to "landed" property, the Convention adopted Mason's proposal to instruct the Committee of Detail to draft a property qualification. . . .

The Committee reported in early August, proposing no change in the age requirement; however, it did recommend adding citizenship and residency requirements for membership. After first debating what the precise requirements should be, on August 8, 1787, the delegates unanimously adopted the three qualifications embodied in Art. I, § 2. . . .

On August 10, the Convention considered the Committee of Detail's proposal that the "Legislature of the United States shall have authority to establish such uniform qualifications of the members of each House, with regard to property, as to the said Legislature shall seem expedient." The debate on this proposal discloses much about the views of the Framers on the issue of qualifications. For example, James Madison urged its rejection, stating that the proposal would vest

> "an improper & dangerous power in the Legislature. The qualifications of electors and elected were fundamental articles in a Republican Govt. and ought to be fixed by the Constitution. If the Legislature could regulate those of either, it can by degrees subvert the Constitution. A Republic may be converted into an aristocracy or oligarchy as well by limiting the number capable of being elected, as the number authorised to elect. . . . It was a power also, which might be made subservient to the views of one faction agst. another. Qualifications founded on artificial distinctions may be devised, by the stronger in order to keep out partizans of [a weaker] faction."

Significantly, Madison's argument was not aimed at the imposition of a property qualification as such, but rather at the delegation to the Congress of the discretionary power to establish any qualifications. . . .

The debates at the state conventions also demonstrate the Framers' understanding that the qualifications for members of Congress had been fixed in the Constitution. Before the New York convention, for example, Hamilton emphasized: "[T]he true principle of a republic is, that the people should choose whom they please to govern them. Representation is imperfect in proportion as the current of popular favor is checked. This great source of free government, popular election, should be perfectly pure, and the most unbounded liberty allowed." 2 Debates on the Federal Constitution 257 (J. Elliot ed. 1876) (hereinafter cited as Elliot's Debates). In Virginia, where the Federalists faced powerful opposition by advocates of popular democracy, Wilson Carey Nicholas, a future member of both the House and Senate and later Governor of the State, met the arguments that the new Constitution violated democratic principles with the following interpretation of Art. I, § 2, cl. 2, as it respects the qualifications of the elected: "It has ever been considered a great security to liberty, that very few should be excluded from the right of being chosen to the legislature. This Constitution has amply attended to this idea. We find no qualifications required except those of age and residence, which create a certainty of their judgment being matured, and of being attached to their state." In short, both the intention of the Framers, to the extent it can be determined, and an examination of the basic principles of our democratic system persuade us that the Constitution does not vest in the Congress a discretionary power to deny membership by a majority vote. . . .

Therefore, we hold that, since Adam Clayton Powell, Jr., was duly elected by the voters of the 18th Congressional District of New York and was not ineligible to serve under any provision of the Constitution, the House was without power to exclude him from its membership. . . .

Justice DOUGLAS concurring.

While I join the opinion of the Court, I add a few words. As the Court says, the important constitutional question is whether the Congress has the power to deviate from or alter the qualifications for membership as a Representative contained in Art. I, § 2, cl. 2, of the Constitution. Up to now the understanding has been quite clear to the effect that such authority does not exist. To be House shall be the Judge of the Elections, Returns and Qualifications of its own Members. . . ." Contests may arise over whether an elected official meets the "qualifications" of the Constitution, in which event the House is the sole judge. But the House is not the sole judge when "qualifications" are added which are not specified in the Constitution. . . .

At the root . . . is the basic integrity of the electoral process. Today we proclaim the constitutional principle of "one man, one vote." When that principle is followed and the electors choose a person who is repulsive to the Establishment in Congress, by what constitutional authority can that group of electors be disenfranchised?

Justice STEWART dissenting.

I believe that events which have taken place since certiorari was granted in this case on November 18, 1968, have rendered it moot, and that the Court should therefore refrain from deciding the novel, difficult, and delicate constitutional questions which the case presented at its inception.

The essential purpose of this lawsuit by Congressman Powell and members of his constituency was to regain the seat from which he was barred by the 90th Congress. That purpose, however, became impossible of attainment on January 3, 1969, when the 90th Congress passed into history and the 91st Congress came into being. On that date, the petitioners' prayer for a judicial decree restraining enforcement of House Resolution No. 278 and commanding the respondents to admit Congressman Powell to membership in the 90th Congress became incontestably moot.

The petitioners assert that actions of the House of Representatives of the 91st Congress have prolonged the controversy raised by Powell's exclusion and preserved the need for a judicial declaration in this case. I believe, to the contrary, that the conduct of the present House of Representatives confirms the mootness of the petitioners' suit against the 90th Congress. Had Powell been excluded from the 91st Congress, he might argue that there was a "continuing controversy" concerning the exclusion attacked in this case. And such an argument might be sound even though the present House of Representatives is a distinct legislative body rather than a continuation of its predecessor, and though any grievance caused by conduct of the 91st Congress is not redressable in this action. But on January 3, 1969, the House of Representatives of the 91st Congress admitted Congressman Powell to membership, and he now sits as the Representative of the 18th Congressional District of New York. With the 90th Congress terminated and Powell now a member of the 91st, it cannot seriously be contended that there remains a judicial controversy between these parties over the power of the House of Representatives to exclude Powell and the power of a court to order him reseated.

Gravel v. United States
408 U.S. 606, 92 S.Ct. 2614 (1972)

In the morning of June 29, 1971, the Supreme Court ruled, in *New York Times Co. v. United States,* 403 U.S. 713 (1971) (see page 273), that the Nixon administration could not enjoin the publication of a stolen, top secret history of America's involvement in the Vietnam War, known as the "Pentagon Papers." That evening, to give the "Pentagon Papers" wider circulation, Alaska's Senator Mike Gravel convened his Subcommittee on Public Buildings and Grounds. He read summaries of the papers and later entered all forty-seven volumes of the study into public record as an exhibit. In addition, he arranged to have (without profit for himself) the papers published by a private commercial publisher, the Beacon Press. Subsequently, a federal grand jury investigating the release of the "Pentagon Papers" subpoenaed

Gravel's aide, Leonard Rodberg. Gravel and Rodberg moved to quash the subpoena based on the privileges afforded by the speech or debate clause. A court of appeals issued an order barring the grand jury's inquiry into Gravel's and Rodberg's motives and actions in entering the "Pentagon Papers" into public record and arranging for their publication by a private publisher. But it held that the publisher was not exempt from the grand jury's inquiry. Both Gravel and the government appealed to the Supreme Court. Gravel claimed that his arrangements to have the papers privately published were protected by the speech or debate clause, while the government maintained that they and the activities of Gravel's aide were not shielded from the grand jury's investigation.

Justice BLACKMAN delivers the opinion of the Court by Justice WHITE.

Because the claim is that a Member's aide shares the Member's constitutional privilege, we consider first whether and to what extent Senator Gravel himself is exempt from process or inquiry by a grand jury investigating the commission of a crime. Our frame of reference is Art. I, § 6, cl. 1, of the Constitution. The last sentence of the Clause provides Members of Congress with two distinct privileges. Except in cases of "Treason, Felony and Breach of the Peace," the Clause shields Members from arrest while attending or traveling to and from a session of their House. History reveals, and prior cases so hold, that this part of the Clause exempts Members from arrest in civil cases only. Nor does freedom from arrest confer immunity on a Member from service of process as a defendant in civil matters . . . or as a witness in a criminal case. It is, therefore, sufficiently plain that the constitutional freedom from arrest does not exempt Members of Congress from the operation of the ordinary criminal laws, even though imprisonment may prevent or interfere with the performance of their duties as Members. Indeed, implicit in the narrow scope of the privilege of freedom from arrest is, as Jefferson noted, the judgment that legislators ought not to stand above the law they create but ought generally to be bound by it as are ordinary persons.

In recognition, no doubt, of the force of this part of § 6, Senator Gravel disvows any assertion of general immunity from the criminal law. But he points out that the last portion of § 6 affords Members of Congress another vital privilege—they may not be questioned in any other place for any speech or debate in either House. The claim is not that while one part of § 6 generally permits prosecutions for treason, felony, and breach of the peace, another part nevertheless broadly forbids them. Rather, his insistence is that the Speech or Debate Clause at the very least protects him from criminal or civil liability and from questioning elsewhere than in the Senate, with respect to the events occurring at the subcommittee hearing at which the Pentagon Papers were introduced into the public record. To us this claim is incontrovertible. The Speech or Debate Clause was designed to assure a co-equal branch of the government wide freedom of speech, debate, and deliberation without intimidation or threats from the Executive Branch. It thus protects Members against prosecutions that directly impinge upon or threaten the legislative process. We have no doubt that Senator Gravel may not be made to answer—either in terms of questions or in terms of defending himself from prosecution—for the events that occurred at the subcommittee meeting. Our decision is made easier by the fact that the United States appears to have abandoned whatever position it took to the contrary in the lower courts.

Even so, the United States strongly urges that because the Speech or Debate Clause confers a privilege only upon "Senators and Representatives," Rodberg himself has no valid claim to constitutional immunity from grand jury inquiry. In our view, both courts below correctly rejected this position. We agree with the Court of Appeals that for the purpose of construing the privilege a Member and his aide are to be "treated as one." . . . Both courts recognized what the Senate of the United States urgently presses here: that it is literally impossible, in view of the complexities of the modern legislative process, with Congress almost constantly in session and matters of legislative concern constantly proliferating, for Members of Congress to perform their legislative tasks without the help of aides and assistants; that the day-to-day work of such aides is so critical to the Members' performance that they must be treated as the latter's alter egos; and that if they are not so recognized, the central role of the Speech or Debate Clause—to prevent intimidation of legislators by the Executive and accountability before a possibly hostile judiciary will inevitably be diminished and frustrated.

It is true that the Clause itself mentions only "Senators and Representatives," but prior cases have plainly not taken a literalistic approach in applying the privilege. The Clause also speaks only of "Speech or Debate," but the Court's consistent approach has been that to confine the protection of the Speech or Debate Clause to words spoken in debate would be an unacceptably narrow view. Committee reports, resolutions, and the act of voting are equally covered. . . . Rather than giving the clause a cramped construction, the Court has sought to implement its fundamental purpose of freeing the legislator from executive and judicial oversight that realistically threatens to control his conduct as a legislator. We have little doubt that we are neither exceeding our judicial powers nor mistakenly construing the Constitution by holding that the Speech or Debate Clause applies not only to a Member but also to his aides insofar as the conduct of the latter would be a protected legislative act if performed by the Member himself. . . .

The United States fears the abuses that history reveals have occurred when legislators are invested with the power to relieve others from the operation of otherwise valid civil and criminal laws. But these abuses, it seems to us, are for the most part obviated if the privilege applicable to the aide is viewed, as it must be, as the privilege of the Senator, and invocable only by the Senator or by the aide on the Senator's behalf, and if in all events the privilege available to the aide is confined to those services that would be immune legislative conduct if performed by the Senator himself. This view places beyond the Speech or Debate Clause a variety of services characteristically performed by aides for Members of Congress, even though within the scope of their employment. It likewise provides no protection for criminal conduct threatening the security of the person or property of others, whether performed at the direction of the Senator in preparation for or in execution of a legislative act or done without his knowledge or direction. Neither does it immunize Senator or aide from testifying at trials or grand jury proceedings involving third-party crimes where the questions do not require testimony about or impugn a legislative act. Thus our refusal to distinguish between Senator and aide in applying the Speech or Debate Clause does not mean that Rodberg is for all purposes exempt from grand jury questioning.

We are convinced also that the Court of Appeals correctly determined that Senator Gravel's alleged arrangement with Beacon Press to publish the Pentagon Papers was not protected speech or debate within the meaning of Art. I, § 6, cl. 1, of the Constitution. . . . Legislative acts are not all-encompassing. The heart of the Clause is speech or debate in either House. Insofar as the Clause is construed to reach other matters, they must be an integral part of the deliberative and communicative processes by which Members participate in committee and House proceedings with respect to the consideration and passage or rejection of proposed legislation or with respect to other matters which the Constitution places within the jurisdiction of either House. As the Court of Appeals put it, the courts have extended the privilege to matters beyond pure speech or debate in either House, but "only when necessary to prevent indirect impairment of such deliberations.". . .

Here, private publication by Senator Gravel through the cooperation of Beacon Press was in no way essential to the deliberations of the Senate; nor does questioning as to private publication threaten the integrity or independence of the Senate by impermissibly exposing its deliberations to executive influence. The Senator had conducted his hearings; the record and any report that was forthcoming were available both to his committee and the Senate. Insofar as we are advised, neither Congress nor the full committee ordered or authorized the publication. We cannot but conclude that the Senator's arrangements with Beacon Press were not part and parcel of the legislative process. . . .

Clause recognizes speech, voting, and other legislative acts as exempt from liability that might otherwise attach, it does not privilege either Senator or aide to violate an otherwise valid criminal law in preparing for or implementing legislative acts. If republication of these classified papers would be a crime under an Act of Congress, it would not be entitled to immunity under the Speech or Debate Clause. It also appears that the grand jury was pursuing this very subject in the normal course of a valid investigation. The Speech or Debate Clause does not in our view extend immunity to Rodberg, as a Senator's aide, from testifying before the grand jury about the arrangement between Senator Gravel and Beacon Press or about his own participation, if any, in the alleged transaction, so long as legislative acts of the Senator are not impugned.

Similar considerations lead us to disagree with the Court of Appeals insofar as it fashioned, tentatively at least, a nonconstitutional testimonial privilege protecting Rodberg from any questioning by the grand jury concerning the matter of republication of the Pentagon Papers. This privilege, thought to be similar to that protecting executive officials from liability for libel was considered advisable "[t]o the extent that a congressman has responsibility to inform his constituents. . . ." But we cannot carry a judicially fashioned privilege so far as to immunize criminal conduct proscribed by an Act of Congress or to frustrate the grand jury's inquiry into whether publication of these classified documents violated a federal criminal statute. The so-called executive privilege has never been applied to shield executive officers from prosecution for crime, the Court of Appeals was quite sure that third parties were neither immune from liability nor from testifying about the republication matter, and we perceive no basis for conferring a testimonial privilege on Rodberg as the Court of Appeals seemed to do. . . .

Because the Speech or Debate Clause privilege applies both to Senator and aide, it appears to us that [the lower court's] order, alone, would afford ample protection for the privilege if it forbade questioning any witness, including Rodberg: (1) concerning the Senator's conduct, or the conduct of his aides, at the June 29, 1971, meeting of the subcommittee; (2) concerning the motives and purposes behind the Senator's conduct, or that of his aides, at that meeting; (3) concerning communications between the Senator and his aides during the term of their employment and related to said meeting or any other legislative act of the Senator; (4) except as it proves relevant to investigating possible third-party crime, concerning any act, in itself not criminal, performed by the Senator, or by his aides in the course of their employment, in preparation for the subcommittee hearing. We leave the final form of such an order to the Court of Appeals in the first instance, or, if that court prefers, to the District Court.

The judgment of the Court of Appeals is vacated and the cases are remanded to that court for further proceedings consistent with this opinion.

So ordered.

Justice DOUGLAS, dissenting.

I would construe the Speech or Debate Clause to insulate Senator Gravel and his aides from inquiry concerning the Pentagon Papers, and Beacon Press from inquiry concerning publication of them, for that publication was but another way of informing the public as to what had gone on in the privacy of the Executive Branch concerning the conception and pursuit of the so-called "war" in Vietnam. Alternatively, I would hold that Beacon Press is protected by the First Amendment from prosecution or investigations for publishing or undertaking to publish the Pentagon Papers.

Justice BRENNAN, with whom Justice DOUGLAS, and Justice MARSHALL, join, dissenting.

In holding that Senator Gravel's alleged arrangement with Beacon Press to publish the Pentagon Papers is not shielded from extra-senatorial inquiry by the Speech or Debate Clause, the Court adopts what for me is a far too narrow view of the legislative function. The Court seems to assume that words spoken in debate or written in congressional reports are protected by the Clause, so that if Senator Gravel had recited part of the Pentagon Papers on the Senate floor or copied them into a Senate report, those acts could not be questioned "in any other Place." Yet because he sought a wider audience, to publicize information deemed relevant to matters pending before his own committee, the Senator suddenly loses his immunity and is exposed to grand jury investigation and possible prosecution for the republication. The explanation for this anomalous result is the Court's belief that "Speech or Debate" encompasses only acts necessary to the internal deliberations of Congress concerning proposed legislation. "Here," according to the Court, "private publication by Senator Gravel through the cooperation of Beacon Press was in no way essential to the deliberations of the Senate." Therefore, "the Senator's arrangements with Beacon Press were not part and parcel of the legislative process."

Thus, the Court excludes from the sphere of protected legislative activity a function that I had supposed lay at the heart of our democratic system. I speak, of course, of the legislator's duty to inform the public about matters affecting the administration of government. That this "informing function" falls into the class of things "generally done in a session of the House by one of its members in relation to the business before it." . . .

Unlike the Court, . . . I think that the activities of Congressmen in communicating with the public are legislative acts protected by the Speech or Debate Clause. I agree with the Court that not every task performed by a legislator is privileged; intervention before Executive departments is one that is not. But the informing function carries a far more persuasive claim to the protections of the Clause. It has been recognized by this Court as something "generally done" by Congressmen, the Congress itself has established special concessions designed to lower the cost of such communication, and, most important, the function furthers several well-recognized goals of representative government. To say in the face of these facts that the informing function is not privileged merely because it is not necessary to the internal deliberations of Congress is to give the Speech or Debate Clause an artificial and narrow reading unsupported by reason. . . .

Justice STEWART dissenting in part.

The Court today holds that the Speech or Debate Clause does not protect a Congressman from being forced to testify before a grand jury about sources of information used in preparation for legislative acts. This critical question was not embraced in the petitions for certiorari. It was not dealt with in the written briefs. It was addressed only tangentially during the oral arguments. Yet it is a question with profound implications for the effective functioning of the legislative process. I cannot join in the Court's summary resolution of so vitally important a constitutional issue. . . .

Under the Court's ruling, a Congressman may be subpoenaed by a vindictive Executive to testify about informants who have not committed crimes and who have no knowledge of crime. Such compulsion can occur, because the judiciary has traditionally imposed virtually no limitations on the grand jury's broad investigatory powers; grand jury investigations are not limited in scope to specific criminal acts, and standards of materiality and relevance are greatly relaxed. But even if the Executive had reason to believe that a Member of Congress had knowledge of a specific probable violation of law, it is by no means clear to me that the Executive's interest in the administration of justice must *always* override the public interest in having an informed Congress. Why should we not, given the tension between two competing interests, *each* of constitutional dimensions, balance the claims of the Speech or Debate Clause against the claims of the grand jury in the particularized contexts of specific cases? And why are not the Houses of Congress the proper institutions in most situations to impose sanctions upon a Representative or Senator who withholds information about crime acquired in the course of his legislative duties?

Eastland v. United States Servicemen's Fund
421 U.S. 491, 95 S.Ct. 1813 (1975)

The United States Servicemen's Fund was a nonprofit organization that, among other activities, ran coffeehouses near military bases and distributed "underground newspapers" critical of the Vietnam War. Senator James Eastland, as chair of the Senate Subcommittee on Internal Security, undertook an investigation of the organization and subpoenaed a bank for the release of the fund's financial records. The fund sought in federal district court to stop enforcement of the subpoenea on the grounds that its bank records contained privileged information about its membership, protected by the First Amendment freedoms of speech, press, and right of association. But the district court ruled that the fund failed to show irreparable damage from the disclosure of its bank records and that congressional interests in conducting its investigation prevailed. An appellate court, however, reversed on concluding that the purpose of the subpoena was to discover the identities of the fund's donors and that constituted a substantial interference with the organization's First Amendment rights. Senator Eastland and other members of the subcommittee appealed to the Supreme Court, and the justices (voting eight to one) reversed the appellate court.

Chief Justice BURGER delivers the opinion of the Court.

The question to be resolved is whether the actions of the petitioners fall within the "sphere of legitimate legislative activity." If they do, the petitioners "shall not be questioned in any other Place" about those activities since the prohibitions of the Speech or Debate Clause are absolute. . . .

Without exception, our cases have read the Speech or Debate Clause broadly to effectuate its purposes. . . . The purpose of the Clause is to insure that the legislative function the Constitution allocates to Congress may be performed independently. . . .

The applicability of the Clause to private civil actions is supported by the absoluteness of the terms "shall not be questioned," and the sweep of the terms "in any other Place." In reading the Clause broadly we have said that legislators acting within the sphere of legitimate legislative activity "should be protected not only from the consequences of litigation's results but also from the burden of defending themselves." *Dombrowski v. Eastland*, 387 U.S. [82 (1967)]. Just as a criminal prosecution infringes upon the independence which the Clause is designed to preserve, a private civil action, whether for an injunction or damages, creates a distraction and forces Members to divert their time, energy, and attention from their legislative tasks to defend the litigation. Private civil actions also may be used to delay and disrupt the legislative function. Moreover, whether a criminal action is instituted by the Executive Branch, or a civil action is brought by private parties, judicial power is still brought to bear on Members of Congress and legislative independence is imperiled. We reaffirm that once it is determined that Members are acting within the "legitimate legislative sphere" the Speech or Debate Clause is an absolute bar to interference. *Doe v. McMillan*, 412 U.S. [306 (1973)]. . . .

The power to investigate and to do so through compulsory process plainly falls within that definition. This Court has often noted that the power to investigate is inherent in the power to make laws because "[a] legislative body cannot legislate wisely or effectively in the absence of information respecting the conditions which the legislation is intended to affect or change." Issuance of subpoenas such as the one in question here has long been held to be a legitimate use by Congress of its power to investigate. . . .

The particular investigation at issue here is related to and in furtherance of a legitimate task of Congress. . . . On this record the pleadings show that the actions of the Members and the Chief Counsel fall within the "sphere of legitimate legislative activity." The Subcommittee was acting under an unambiguous resolution from the Senate authorizing it to make a complete study of the "administration, operation, and enforcement of the Internal Security Act of 1950. . . ." S.Res. 341, 91st Cong., 2d Sess. (1970). That grant of authority is sufficient to show that the investigation upon which the Subcommittee had embarked concerned a subject on which "legislation could be had." . . .

We conclude that the Speech or Debate Clause provides complete immunity for the Members for issuance of this subpoena. We draw no distinction between the Members and the Chief Counsel. In *Gravel* [*v. United States*, 408 U.S. 606 (1979)], we made it clear that "the day-to-day work of such aides is so critical to the Members' performance that they must be treated as [the Members'] alter egos. . . ." Here the complaint alleges that the

"Subcommittee members and staff caused the . . . subpoena to be issued . . . under the authority of Senate Resolution 366. . . ." The complaint thus does not distinguish between the activities of the Members and those of the Chief Counsel. Contrast, *Dombrowski v. Eastland.* Since the Members are immune because the issuance of the subpoena is "essential to legislating," their aides share that immunity. . . .

Respondents also contend that the subpoena cannot be protected by the speech or debate immunity because the "sole purpose" of the investigation is to force "public disclosure of beliefs, opinions, expressions and associations of private citizens which may be unorthodox or unpopular." Respondents view the scope of the privilege too narrowly. Our cases make clear that in determining the legitimacy of a congressional act we do not look to the motives alleged to have prompted it. . . . Nor is the legitimacy of a congressional inquiry to be defined by what it produces. The very nature of the investigative function—like any research—is that it takes the searchers up some "blind alleys" and into nonproductive enterprises. To be a valid legislative inquiry there need be no predictable end result.

Finally, respondents argue that the purpose of the subpoena was to "harass, chill, punish and deter" them in the exercise of their First Amendment rights and thus that the subpoena cannot be protected by the Clause. Their theory seems to be that once it is alleged that First Amendment rights may be infringed by congressional action the Judiciary may intervene to protect those rights; the Court of Appeals seems to have subscribed to that theory. That approach, however, ignores the absolute nature of the speech or debate protection and our cases which have broadly construed that protection. . . .

Reversed and remanded.

Justice MARSHALL, with whom Justice BRENNAN and Justice STEWART join, concurring.

I write today only to emphasize that the Speech or Debate Clause does not entirely immunize a congressional subpoena from challenge by a party not in a position to assert his constitutional rights by refusing to comply with it. . . .

I do not read the Court to suggest, however, nor could I agree, that the constitutionality of a congressional subpoena is always shielded from more searching judicial inquiry. For, as the very cases on which the Court relies demonstrate, the protection of the Speech or Debate Clause is personal. It extends to Members and their counsel acting in a legislative capacity; it does not preclude judicial review of their decisions in an appropriate case, whether they take the form of legislation or a subpoena. . . .

The Speech or Debate Clause cannot be used to avoid meaningful review of constitutional objections to a subpoena simply because the subpoena is served on a third party. Our prior cases arising under the Speech or Debate Clause indicate only that a Member of Congress or his aide may not be called upon to defend a subpoena against constitutional objection, and not that the objection will not be heard at all. . . .

This case does not present the questions of what would be the proper procedure, and who might be the proper parties defendant, in an effort to get before a court a constitutional challenge to a subpoena *duces tecum* issued to a third party. As respondent's counsel conceded at oral argument, this case is at an end if the Senate petitioners are upheld in their claim of immunity, as they must be.

Justice DOUGLAS dissenting.

I would affirm the judgment below. . . .

Under our federal regime that delegates, by the Constitution and Acts of Congress, awesome powers to individuals, those powers may not be used to deprive people of their First Amendment or other constitutional rights. It is my view that no official, no matter how high or majestic his or her office, who is within the reach of judicial process, may invoke immunity for his actions for which wrongdoers normally suffer. There may be few occasions when, on the merits, it would be appropriate to invoke such a remedy. But no regime of law that can rightfully claim that name may make trustees of these vast powers immune from actions brought by people who have been wronged by official action. See *Watkins v. United States*, 354 U.S. 178 [(1957)].

Hutchinson v. Proxmire
443 U.S. 111, 99 S.Ct. 2675 (1979)

In March 1975, Senator William Proxmire initiated the "Golden Fleece of the Month" award to publicize wasteful government spending. The second award went to several government agencies for funding research on animal aggression by Dr. Ronald Hutchinson. Proxmire announced the award on a floor of the Senate in a speech (printed in part in the opinion below) and in press releases and newsletters to constituents. His legislative assistant also discussed the award and Hutchinson's study with the sponsoring agencies. Funding for the study was eventually withdrawn. And Hutchinson filed a suit in federal district court, contending that erroneous statements made by Proxmire and his aide defamed him and resulted in a loss of income. The district judge ruled that Proxmire's statements on the Senate floor and in press releases were covered by the Speech or Debate clause, but not those made in newsletters and television interviews. However, the court also held that Hutchinson was a "public figure" and could collect damages only if Proxmire's statements were made with "actual malice"—with the knowing or reckless disregard of their truth or falsity. Because the judge found no evidence of actual malice, Hutchinson was not awarded damages. After an appellate court affirmed that ruling, Hutchinson appealed to the Supreme Court, which granted his petition for *certiorari* and affirmed the lower court's ruling.

Chief Justice BURGER delivers the opinion of the Court.

Ronald Hutchinson, a research behavioral scientist, sued respondents, William Proxmire, a United States Senator, and his legislative assistant, Morton Schwartz, for defamation arising out of Proxmire's giving what he called his "Golden Fleece" award. The "award" went to federal agencies that had sponsored Hutchinson's research. Hutchinson alleged that in making the award and publicizing it nationwide, respondents had libeled him, damaging him in his professional and academic standing, and had interfered with his contractual relations. The District Court granted summary judgment for respondents and the Court of Appeals affirmed. . . .

We reverse and remand to the Court of Appeals for further proceedings consistent with this opinion.

Respondent Proxmire is a United States Senator from Wisconsin. In March 1975, he initiated the "Golden Fleece of the Month Award" to publicize what he perceived to be the most egregious examples of wasteful governmental spending. The second such award, in April 1975, went to the National Science Foundation, the National Aeronautics and Space Administration, and the Office of Naval Research, for spending almost half a million dollars during the preceding seven years to fund Hutchinson's research. . . .

The bulk of Hutchinson's research was devoted to the study of emotional behavior. In particular, he sought an objective measure of aggression, concentrating upon the behavior patterns of certain animals, such as the clenching of jaws when they were exposed to various aggravating stressful stimuli. The National Aeronautics and Space Agency and the Navy were interested in the potential of this research for resolving problems associated with confining humans in close quarters for extended periods of time in space and undersea exploration. . . .

In the speech Proxmire described the federal grants for Hutchinson's research, concluding with the following comment:

> "The funding of this nonsense makes me almost angry enough to scream and kick or even clench my jaw. It seems to me it is outrageous.
>
> "Dr. Hutchinson's studies should make the taxpayers as well as his monkeys grind their teeth. In fact, the good doctor has made a fortune from his monkeys and in the process made a monkey out of the American taxpayer.
>
> "It is time for the Federal Government to get out of this 'monkey business.' In view of the transparent worthlessness of Hutchinson's study of jaw-grinding and biting by angry or hard-drinking monkeys, it is time we put a stop to the bite Hutchinson and the bureaucrats who fund him have been taking of the taxpayer." 121 Cong.Rec. 10803 (1975).

In May 1975, Proxmire referred to his Golden Fleece Awards in a newsletter sent to about 100,000 people whose names were on a mailing list that included constituents in Wisconsin as well as persons in other states. The newsletter repeated the essence of the speech and the press release. Later in 1975, Proxmire appeared on a television interview program where he referred to Hutchinson's research, though he did not mention Hutchinson by name.

The Speech or Debate Clause has been directly passed on by this Court relatively few times in 190 years. . . . Literal reading of the Clause would, of course, confine its protection narrowly to a "Speech or Debate *in* either House." But the Court has given the Clause a practical rather than a strictly literal reading which would limit the protection to utterances made within the four walls of either Chamber. Thus, we have held that committee hearings are protected, even if held outside the Chambers; committee reports are also protected. . . .

Nearly a century ago, in *Kilbourn v. Thompson*, 103 U.S. 168 (1881), this Court held that the Clause extended "to things generally done *in a session* of the House by one of its members *in relation to the business before it.*" . . .

Whatever imprecision there may be in the term "legislative activities," it is clear that nothing in history or in the explicit language of the Clause suggests any intention to create an absolute privilege from liability or suit for defamatory statements made outside the Chamber. . . .

In *Gravel v. United States*, 408 U.S. 606 (1972) we recognized that the doctrine denying immunity for republication had been accepted in the United States. . . .

We reaffirmed that principle in *Doe v. McMillan*, 412 U.S. 306, (1973):

"A Member of Congress may not with impunity publish a libel from the speaker's stand in his home district, and clearly the Speech or Debate Clause would not protect such an act even though the libel was read from an official committee report. The reason is that republishing a libel under such circumstances is not an essential part of the legislative process and is not part of that deliberative process 'by which Members participate in committee and House proceedings.'" . . .

We reach a similar conclusion here. A speech by Proxmire in the Senate would be wholly immune and would be available to other Members of Congress and the public in the Congressional Record. But neither the newsletters nor the press release was "essential to the deliberations of the Senate" and neither was part of the deliberative process. . . .

Voting and preparing committee reports are the individual and collective expressions of opinion within the legislative process. As such, they are protected by the Speech or Debate Clause. Newsletters and press releases, by contrast, are primarily means of informing those outside the legislative forum; they represent the views and will of a single Member. It does not disparage either their value or their importance to hold that they are not entitled to the protection of the Speech or Debate Clause.

Justice STEWART concurred and dissented in part.

Justice BRENNAN, dissenting.

I disagree with the Court's conclusion that Senator Proxmire's newsletters and press releases fall outside the protection of the speech or debate immunity. In my view, public criticism by legislators of unnecessary governmental expenditures, whatever its form, is a legislative act shielded by the Speech or Debate Clause.

B. INVESTIGATORY AND CONTEMPT POWERS

A congressional power to investigate is not expressly granted, but instead an implied power incident to lawmaking. Congress, as the Court recognized, "cannot legislate wisely or effectively in the absence of information respecting the conditions which the legislation is intended to affect or change."[1]

The power was asserted by the House in its first major investigation in 1792. Following an Indian defeat of an expedition led by Major General St. Clair, a House committee requested President George Washington to release all papers and records related to the incident. The president's cabinet considered the request and decided to turn over the materials, but also agreed that

the Executive ought to communicate such papers as the public good would permit, and ought to refuse those, the disclosure of which would injure the public . . . [In addition, the Cabinet concluded,] that neither the committee nor House had a right to call on the Head of a Department, who and whose papers were under the President alone; but that the committee should instruct their chairman to move the House to address the President.[2]

Although the materials in the St. Clair episode were given to Congress, the basis was set for presidential claims of "executive privilege" when withholding documents and for confrontations between the executive branch and Congress over its investigatory power.

Congress's investigatory power is backed by the power to find individuals, who disrupt its proceedings or refuse to testify before its committees, in contempt and to have them arrested and imprisoned.[3] Unlike the investigative and contempt powers of the English Parliament, however, congressional exercise of these powers remains subject to judicial review. In *Anderson v. Dunn*, 6 Wheat. (19 U.S.) 204 (1821), the Marshall Court expressed concerns about the procedural safeguards afforded individuals charged with contempt, when holding that they could not be imprisoned beyond the session of the House finding them in contempt. As a result of these concerns and the irregularity of contempt proceedings, Congress passed legislation in 1857 requiring individuals summoned by either House to appear as witnesses. If they refused to appear or to answer "pertinent questions," a committee could direct the sergeant at arms to hold them until they testified. Alternatively, the committee could punish them by finding them in contempt and directing a United States attorney to seek their indictment by a federal grand jury, and thereupon prosecute them in a federal district court.[4]

Initially, the Court took a narrow view of congressional investigatory and contempt powers in *Kilbourn v. Thompson*, 103 U.S. 168 (1881). Hallet Kilbourn refused to answer certain questions and to deliver to a House committee private papers bearing on a real estate deal. He was found in contempt and imprisoned for forty-five days. On appeal, the Court concluded that the House was overzealous in its inquiry and intruded into a matter already pending in the courts. In doing so, the Court announced three principles limiting congressional investigations: (1) they may not intrude in areas reserved for the executive branch or the courts, (2) they are limited to matters on which Congress may legitimately legislate, and (3) the House resolutions authorizing such investigations must indicate the congressional intent in legislating on the subject under investigation.

The Court later qualified *Kilbourn* and adopted a broader view of Congress's powers in a case arising from an investigation of Attorney General Harry M. Daugherty and other Department of Justice officials in connection with the Teapot Dome scandal, which involved graft and corruption in the administration of President Warren G. Harding. Mally S. Daugherty, the brother of the attorney general, refused to appear before and to bring records subpoenaed by a Senate committee. In *McGrain v. Daugherty,* 273 U.S. 135 (1927), the Court unanimously affirmed Congress's power to compel a private individual to testify. Although noting that Congress has no "general power to inquire into private matters," the Court ruled that it may investigate legitimate subjects of potential legislation, or which have a "proper legislative purpose," and require testimony pertinent to that inquiry.[5]

After affirming Congress's broad investigatory powers, the Court then confronted claims that individuals' civil liberties were being denied by congressional inquiries. This was especially so during the early Cold War years in the 1940s and 1950s, when fear of communism was at its peak. At that time the House Un-American Activities Committee (HUAC) (finally abolished in 1974) and the Senate Permanent Investigations Subcommittee, chaired by Senator Joseph R. McCarthy, subpoenaed hundreds of individuals in and out of government to testify about alleged Communist activities of their own and their acquaintances. In response to challenges to these investigations, the Court ruled that witnesses may refuse to answer vague or irrelevant questions and that the committees' inquiries may not go beyond its authorizing resolutions.[6] In addition, the Warren Court, in 1955, reversed the convictions of individuals who had refused to testify about their alleged membership in the Communist party on the grounds that that would violate their Fifth Amendment privilege against self-incrimination.[7]

The problem for witnesses claiming the Fifth Amendment when refusing to testify before the HUAC was that they could not "take the Fifth" selectively. If they took it for one, they took it for all questions. Those who did were then open to any form of questioning which might imply, if not prove, their support of Communist activities. As a result, many witnesses were often branded, in the words of Senator McCarthy, "Fifth Amendment Communists." They could forego their Fifth Amendment rights by testifying in exchange for a congressional grant of immunity (which guaranteed that their testimony would not be used against them in criminal trial).[8] Still, whether they claimed the Fifth Amendment in refusing to testify or waived that right and testified, they frequently suffered damage to their reputations and lost their jobs due to the adverse publicity.

The First Amendment provides another possible defense against congressional inquiries. Claims that the HUAC abridged witnesses' freedoms of speech and association and aimed simply at punishing them for their political views, nonetheless, had little success until *Watkins v. United States* (1957) (see page 415). There Chief Justice Warren acknowledged the relevancy of the First Amendment, warning that "there is no congressional power to expose for the sake of exposure." But in reversing Watkins's conviction for contempt for refusing to answer certain questions, Warren ultimately rested the Court's decision on the due process clause of the Fifth Amendment.

Two years later, a First Amendment challenge to the House's investigation of the Communist party was squarely faced and rejected. In *Barenblatt v. United States* (1959) (see page 425), the Court divided five to four in finding that First Amendment interests were overridden by those of Congress in ensuring society's self-preservation. This ruling provoked a sharp dissent from Justice Black in one of his most-notable opinions.

The Court remained divided five to four in finding congressional interests in investigations to outweigh First Amendment claims until Justices Frankfurter and Whittaker retired in 1962.[9] They were replaced by Democratic President John F. Kennedy's appointees, Justices Byron White and Arthur Goldberg, and the latter cast the pivotal vote in *Gibson v. Florida Legislative Investigation Committee* (1963) (see page 434), upholding the First Amendment in a case involving state rather than congressional investigations. Since *Gibson* the Court has continued to acknowledge First Amendment limitations on the scope of legislative investigations.[10]

The Court has not yet squarely dealt with a claim of executive privilege in withholding government documents from a congressional investigatory committee. However, in *Barenblatt* the Court noted that Congress "cannot inquire into matters which are within the exclusive province of one of the other branches of Government." Arguably, this would include materials bearing on a treaty being negotiated, for example, or confidential White House communications, and "sensitive" investigatory files. There have been a number of clashes between Congress and the executive branch over the withholding of information from congressional committees, but thus far compromises have been achieved before litigation has reached the Court.[11]

NOTES

1. *McGrain v. Daugherty,* 273 U.S. 135 (1927).

2. Thomas Jefferson, *The Writings of Thomas Jefferson,* Vol. 1 (Washington, DC: Memorial Edition, 1903), 303–305.

3. *Groppi v. Leslie,* 404 U.S. 496 (1972), upheld the use of contempt powers against those disrupting legislative proceedings.

4. This procedure for contempt proceedings was upheld in *In re Chapman,* 166 U.S. 661 (1897). In 1978, Congress also provided that, if a witness refuses to comply with a Senate subpoena, the Senate may request a court order requiring immediate compliance, subject to its imposing the penalty of civil contempt for a witnesses' continued refusal to testify.

5. See also *Sinclair v. United States,* 279 U.S. 263 (1929). Note, however, that under *Eastland v. United States Servicemens' Fund* (1975) (see page 404), the Court does not require a "predictable end result" of a "valid legislative inquiry" and that congressional investigations may lead up "blind alleys."

6. *United States v. Rumely,* 345 U.S. 41 (1953); *Deutch v. United States,* 367 U.S. 456 (1961); and *Gojack v. United States,* 384 U.S. 702 (1966).

7. See *Quinn v. United States,* 349 U.S. 155 (1955); and *Emspak v. United States,* 349 U.S. 190 (1955).

8. *Ullmann v. United States,* 350 U.S. 422 (1956), upheld the Immunity Act of 1954, providing congressional committees to grant immunity for witnesses who waived their Fifth Amendment rights and testified. See also *Kastigar v. United States,* 406 U.S. 441 (1972).

9. See *Wilkinson v. United States,* 365 U.S. 399 (1961); and *Braden v. United States,* 365 U.S. 431 (1961).

10. See, for example, *DeGregory v. Attorney General of New Hampshire,* 383 U.S. 825 (1966). But see again the Burger Court's ruling in *Eastland v. United States Servicemen's Fund* (1975) (see page 404) on how congressional committees are shielded by the speech or debate clause.

11. For further discussion, see Joseph W. Bishop, Jr., "The Executive's Right of Privacy: An Unresolved Constitutional Question," 66 *Yale Law Journal* 477 (1957); Rex E. Lee, "Executive Privilege, Congressional Subpoena Power, and Judicial Review: Three Branches, Three Powers, and Some Relationships," 1978 *Brigham Young Law Review* 231 (1978); John F. Murphy, "Knowledge is Power: Foreign Policy and Information Exchange among Congress, the Executive Branch, and the Public," 49 *Tulane Law Review* 505 (1975); and Harold C. Relyea, ed., *The Presidency and Information Policy* (Boulder, CO: Westview, 1981).

SELECTED BIBLIOGRAPHY

Beck, Carl. *Contempt of Congress.* New Orleans, LA: Hauser Press, 1959.
Goodman, Walter. *The Committee: The Extraordinary Career of the House Committee on Un-American Activities.* New York: Farrar, Straus & Giroux, 1968.

Hamilton, James. *The Power to Probe: A Study of Congressional Investigations.* New York: Random House, 1976.

McGeary, M. Nelson. *The Development of Congressional Investigative Power.* New York: Columbia University Press, 1940.

Pritchett, C. Herman. *Congress versus the Supreme Court: 1957–1960.* Minneapolis: University of Minnesota Press, 1961.

Watkins v. United States
354 U.S. 178, 77 S.Ct. 1173 (1957)

John Watkins was one of 129 people found in contempt of Congress for refusing to answer questions about the Communist party and other "subversive organizations," when appearing before the House Un-American Activities Committee between 1950 and 1965. In 1954, as a labor organizer for the United Automobile Workers, he was summoned and appeared before the subcommittee. Although testifying about his activities and those of others he believed to still be members of the Communist party, Watkins declined to answer questions about the activities of those who were no longer members. Because these questions did not bear on his activities, he could not invoke his Fifth Amendment privilege against self-incrimination when refusing to testify. Instead, Watkins contended that these questions were irrelevant and not pertinent to the committee's investigation. The House voted him in contempt and Watkins was convicted in a federal district court. After a court of appeals upheld his conviction, Watkins appealed to the Supreme Court.

Chief Justice WARREN delivers the opinion of the Court.

This is a review by certiorari of a conviction under 2 U.S.C. § 192, for "contempt of Congress." The misdemeanor is alleged to have been committed during a hearing before a congressional investigating committee. It is not the case of a truculent or contumacious witness who refuses to answer all questions or who, by boisterous or discourteous conduct, disturbs the decorum of the committee room. Petitioner was prosecuted for refusing to make certain disclosures which he asserted to be beyond the authority of the committee to demand. The controversy thus rests upon fundamental principles of the power of the Congress and the limitations upon that power. We approach the questions presented with conscious awareness of the far-reaching ramifications that can follow from a decision of this nature. . . .

We start with several basic premises on which there is general agreement. The power of the Congress to conduct investigations is inherent in the legislative process. That power is broad. It encompasses inquiries concerning the administration of existing laws as well as proposed or possibly needed statutes. It includes surveys of defects in our social, economic or political system for the purpose of enabling the Congress to remedy them. It comprehends probes into departments of the Federal Government to expose corruption, inefficiency or waste. But, broad as is this power of inquiry, it is not unlimited. There is no general authority to expose the private affairs of individuals without justification in terms of the functions of the Congress. This was freely conceded by the Solicitor General in his argument of this case. Nor is the Congress a law enforcement or trial agency. These are functions of the executive and judicial departments of government. No inquiry is an end in itself; it must be related to, and in furtherance of, a legitimate task of the Congress. Investigations conducted solely for the personal aggrandizement of the investigators or to "punish" those investigated are indefensible.

It is unquestionably the duty of all citizens to cooperate with the Congress in its efforts to obtain the facts needed for intelligent legislative action. It is their unremitting obligation to respond to subpoenas, to respect the dignity of the Congress and its committees and to testify fully with respect to matters within the province of proper investigation. This, of course, assumes that the constitutional rights of witnesses will be respected by the Congress as they are in a court of justice. The Bill of Rights is applicable to investigations as to all forms of governmental action. Witnesses cannot be compelled to give evidence against themselves. They cannot be subjected to unreasonable search and seizure. Nor can the First Amendment freedoms of speech, press, religion, or political belief and association be abridged. . . .

The history of contempt of the legislature in this country is notably different from that of England. In the early days of the United States, there lingered the direct knowledge of the evil effects of absolute power. Most of the instances of use of compulsory process by the first Congresses concerned matters affecting the qualification or integrity of their members or came about in inquiries dealing with suspected corruption or mismanagement of government officials. Unlike the English practice, from the very outset the use of contempt power by the legislature was deemed subject to judicial review. . . .

There was very little use of the power of compulsory process in early years to enable the Congress to obtain facts pertinent to the enactment of new statutes or the administration of existing laws. The first occasion for such an investigation arose in 1827 when the House of Representatives was considering a revision of the tariff laws. In the Senate, there was no use of a fact-finding investigation in aid of legislation until 1859. In the Legislative Reorganization Act, the Committee on Un-American Activities was the only standing committee of the House of Representatives that was given the power to compel disclosures. . . .

It is not surprising, from the fact that the Houses of Congress so sparingly employed the power to conduct investigations, that there have been few cases requiring judicial review of the power. The Nation was almost one hundred years old before the first case reached this Court to challenge the use of compulsory process as a legislative device, rather than in inquiries concerning the elections or privileges of Congressmen. In *Kilbourn v. Thompson,* 103 U.S. 168 [1881], decided in 1881, an investigation had been authorized by the House of Representatives to learn the circumstances surrounding the bankruptcy of Jay Cooke & Company, in which the United States had deposited funds. The committee became particularly interested in a private real estate pool that was a part of the financial structure. The Court found that the subject matter of the inquiry was "in its nature clearly judicial and therefore one in respect to which no valid legislation could be enacted." The House had thereby exceeded the limits of its own authority.

Subsequent to the decision in Kilbourn, until recent times, there were very few cases dealing with the investigative power. The matter came to the fore again when the Senate undertook to study the corruption in the handling of oil leases in the 1920's. In *McGrain v. Daugherty,* 273 U.S. 135 [1927], and *Sinclair v. United States,* 279 U.S. 263 [1929], the Court applied the precepts of Kilbourn to uphold the authority of the Congress to conduct the challenged investigations. The Court recognized the danger to effective and honest conduct of the Government if the legislature's power to probe corruption in the executive branch were unduly hampered.

In the decade following World War II, there appeared a new kind of congressional inquiry unknown in prior periods of American history. Principally this was the result of the various investigations into the threat of subversion of the United States Government, but other subjects of congressional interest also contributed to the changed scene. This new phase of legislative inquiry involved a broad-scale intrusion into the lives and affairs of private citizens. It brought before the courts novel questions of the appropriate limits of congressional inquiry. Prior cases, like *Kilbourn, McGrain* and *Sinclair,* had defined the scope of investigative power in terms of the inherent limitations of the sources of that power. In the more recent cases, the emphasis shifted to problems of accommodating the interest of the Government with the rights and privileges of individuals. The central theme was the application of the Bill of Rights as a restraint upon the assertion of governmental power in this form.

It was during this period that the Fifth Amendment privilege against self-incrimination was frequently invoked and recognized as a legal limit upon the authority of a committee to require that witness answer its questions. Some early doubts as to the applicability of that privilege before a legislative committee never matured. When the matter reached this Court, the Government did not challenge in any way that the Fifth Amendment protection was available to the witness, and such a challenge could not have prevailed. It confined its argument to the character of the answers sought and to the adequacy of the claim of privilege. . . .

A far more difficult task evolved from the claim by witnesses that the committees' interrogations were infringements upon the freedoms of the First Amendment. Clearly, an investigation is subject to the command that the Congress shall make no law abridging freedom of speech or press or assembly. While it is true that there is no statute to be reviewed, and that an investigation is not a law, nevertheless an investigation is part of lawmaking. It is justified solely as an adjunct to the legislative process. The First Amendment may be invoked against infringement of the protected freedoms by law or by lawmaking.

Abuses of the investigative process may imperceptibly lead to abridgment of protected freedoms. The mere summoning of a witness and compelling him to testify, against his will, about his beliefs, expressions or associations is a measure of governmental interference. And when those forced revelations concern matters that are unorthodox, unpopular, or even hateful to the general public, the reaction in the life of the witness may be disastrous. This effect is even more harsh when it is past beliefs, expressions or associations that are disclosed and judged by current standards rather than those contemporary with the matters exposed. Nor does the witness alone suffer the consequences. Those who are identified by witnesses and thereby placed in the same glare of publicity are equally subject to public stigma, scorn and obloquy. Beyond that, there is the more subtle and immeasurable effect upon those who tend to adhere to the most orthodox and uncontroversial views and associations in order to avoid a similar fate at some future time. That this impact is partly the result of nongovernmental activity by private persons cannot relieve the investigators of their responsibility for initiating the reaction.

The Court recognized the restraints of the Bill of Rights upon congressional investigations in *United States v. Rumely,* 345 U.S. 41 [1953]. The magnitude and complexity of the problem of applying the First Amendment to that case led the Court to construe narrowly the resolution describing the committee's authority. It was concluded that, when First Amendment rights are threatened, the delegation of power to the committee must be clearly revealed in its charter. . . .

We have no doubt that there is no congressional power to

expose for the sake of exposure. The public is, of course, entitled to be informed concerning the workings of its government. That cannot be inflated into a general power to expose where the predominant result can only be an invasion of the private rights of individuals. But a solution to our problem is not to be found in testing the motives of committee members for this purpose. Such is not our function. Their motives alone would not vitiate an investigation which had been instituted by a House of Congress if that assembly's legislative purpose is being served. . . .

It would be difficult to imagine a less explicit authorizing resolution. Who can define the meaning of "un-American"? What is that single, solitary "principle of the form of government as guaranteed by our Constitution"? There is no need to dwell upon the language, however. At one time, perhaps, the resolution might have been read narrowly to confine the Committee to the subject of propaganda. The events that have transpired in the fifteen years before the interrogation of petitioner make such a construction impossible at this date. . . .

Combining the language of the resolution with the construction it has been given, it is evident that the preliminary control of the Committee exercised by the House of Representatives is slight or non-existent. No one could reasonably deduce from the charter the kind of investigation that the Committee was directed to make. As a result, we are asked to engage in a process of retroactive rationalization. Looking backward from the events that transpired, we are asked to uphold the Committee's actions unless it appears that they were clearly not authorized by the charter. As a corollary to this inverse approach, the Government urges that we must view the matter hospitably to the power of the Congress—that if there is any legislative purpose which might have been furthered by the kind of disclosure sought, the witness must be punished for withholding it. No doubt every reasonable indulgence of legality must be accorded to the actions of a coordinate branch of our Government. But such deference cannot yield to an unnecessary and unreasonable dissipation of precious constitutional freedoms.

The Government contends that the public interest at the core of the investigations of the Un-American Activities Committee is the need by the Congress to be informed of efforts to overthrow the Government by force and violence so that adequate legislative safeguards can be erected. From this core, however, the Committee can radiate outward infinitely to any topic thought to be related in some way to armed insurrection. The outer reaches of this domain are known only by the content of "unAmerican activities." Remoteness of subject can be aggravated by a probe for a depth of detail even farther removed from any basis of legislative action. A third dimension is added when the investigators turn their attention to the past to collect minutiae on remote topics, on the hypothesis that the past may reflect upon the present.

The consequences that flow from this situation are manifold. In the first place, a reviewing court is unable to make the kind of judgment made by the Court in *United States v. Rumely,* supra. The Committee is allowed, in essence, to define its own authority, to choose the direction and focus of its activities. In deciding what to do with the power that has been conferred upon them, members of the Committee may act pursuant to motives that seem to them to be the highest. Their decisions, nevertheless, can lead to ruthless exposure of private lives in order to gather data that is neither desired by the Congress nor useful to it. Yet it is impossible in this circumstance, with constitutional freedoms in jeopardy, to declare that the Committee has ranged beyond the area committed to it by its parent assembly because the boundaries are so nebulous.

More important and more fundamental than that, however, it insulates the House that has authorized the investigation from the witnesses who are subjected to the sanctions of compulsory process. There is a wide gulf between the responsibility for the use of investigative power and the actual exercise of that power. This is an especially vital consideration in assuring respect for constitutional liberties. Protected freedoms should not be placed in danger in the absence of a clear determination by the House or the Senate that a particular inquiry is justified by a specific legislative need.

It is, of course, not the function of this Court to prescribe rigid rules for the Congress to follow in drafting resolutions establishing investigating committees. That is a matter peculiarly within the realm of the legislature, and its decisions will be accepted by the courts up to the point where their own duty to enforce the constitutionally protected rights of individuals is affected. An excessively broad charter, like that of the House Un-American Activities Committee, places the courts in an untenable position if they are to strike a balance between the public need for a particular interrogation and the right of citizens to carry on their affairs free from unnecessary governmental interference. It is impossible in such a situation to ascertain whether any legislative purpose justifies the disclosures sought and, if so, the importance of that information to the Congress in furtherance of its legislative function. The reason no court can make this critical judgment is that the House of Representatives itself has never made it. Only the legislative assembly initiating an investigation can assay the relative necessity of specific disclosures.

Absence of the qualitative consideration of petitioner's questioning by the House of Representatives aggravates a serious problem, revealed in this case, in the relationship of congressional investigating committees and the witnesses who appear before them. Plainly these committees are restricted to the missions delegated to them, i.e., to acquire certain data to be used by the House or the Senate in coping with a problem that falls within its legislative sphere. No witness can be compelled to make disclosures on matters outside that area. This is a jurisdictional concept of pertinency drawn from the nature of a congressional committee's source of authority. It is not wholly different from nor unrelated to the element of pertinency embodied in the criminal statute under which petitioner was prosecuted. When the definition of jurisdictional pertinency is as uncertain and wavering as in the case of the Un-American Activities Committee, it becomes extremely difficult for the Committee to limit its inquiries to statutory pertinency.

Since World War II, the Congress has practically abandoned its original practice of utilizing the coercive sanction of contempt proceedings at the bar of the House. The sanction there imposed is imprisonment by the House until the recalcitrant witness agrees to testify or disclose the matters sought, provided that the incarceration does not extend beyond adjournment. The Congress has instead invoked the aid of the federal judicial system in protecting itself against contumacious conduct. It has become customary to refer these matters to the United States Attorneys for prosecution under criminal law.

The appropriate statute is found in 2 U.S.C. § 192. It provides:

> "Every person who having been summoned as a witness by the authority of either House of Congress to give testimony or to produce papers upon any matter under inquiry before either House, or any joint committee established by a joint or concurrent resolution of the two Houses of Congress, or any committee of either House of Congress, willfully makes default, or who, having appeared, refuses to answer any question pertinent to the question under inquiry, shall be deemed guilty of a misdemeanor, punishable by a fine of not more than $1,000 nor less than $100 and imprisonment in a common jail for not less than one month nor more than twelve months."

In fulfillment of their obligation under this statute, the courts must accord to the defendants every right which is guaranteed to defendants in all other criminal cases. Among these is the right to have available, through a sufficiently precise statute, information revealing the standard of criminality before the commission of the alleged offense. Applied to persons prosecuted under § 192, this raises a special problem in that the statute defines the crime as refusal to answer "any question pertinent to the question under inquiry." Part of the standard of criminality, therefore, is the pertinency of the questions propounded to the witness.

The problem attains proportion when viewed from the standpoint of the witness who appears before a congressional committee. He must decide at the time the questions are propounded whether or not to answer. . . . An erroneous determination on his part, even if made in the utmost good faith, does not exculpate him if the court should later rule that the questions were pertinent to the question under inquiry.

It is obvious that a person compelled to make this choice is entitled to have knowledge of the subject to which the interrogation is deemed pertinent. That knowledge must be available with the same degree of explicitness and clarity that the Due Process Clause requires in the expression of any element of a criminal offense. The "vice of vagueness" must be avoided here as in all other crimes. There are several sources that can outline the "question under inquiry" in such a way that the rules against vagueness are satisfied. The authorizing resolution, the remarks of the chairman or members of the committee, or even the nature of the proceedings themselves, might sometimes make the topic clear. This case demonstrates, however, that these sources often leave the matter in grave doubt.

Fundamental fairness demands that no witness be compelled to [determine whether a question is pertinent to a legitimate legislative purpose] . . . with so little guidance. Unless the subject matter has been made to appear with undisputable clarity, it is the duty of the investigative body, upon objection of the witness on grounds of pertinency, to state for the record the subject under inquiry at that time and the manner in which the propounded questions are pertinent thereto. To be meaningful, the explanation must describe what the topic under inquiry is and the connective reasoning whereby the precise questions asked relate to it.

The statement of the Committee Chairman in this case, in response to petitioner's protest, was woefully inadequate to convey sufficient information as to the pertinency of the questions to the subject under inquiry. Petitioner was thus not accorded a fair opportunity to determine whether he was within his rights in refusing to answer, and his conviction is necessarily invalid under the Due Process Clause of the Fifth Amendment.

We are mindful of the complexities of modern government and the ample scope that must be left to the Congress as the sole constitutional depository of legislative power. Equally mindful are we of the indispensable function, in the exercise of that power, of congressional investigations. The conclusions we have reached in this case will not prevent the Congress, through its committees, from obtaining any information it needs for the proper fulfillment of its role in our scheme of government. The legislature is free to determine the kinds of data that should be collected. It is only those investigations that are conducted by use of compulsory process that give rise to a need to protect the rights of individuals against illegal encroachment. That protection can be readily achieved through procedures which prevent the separation of power from responsibility and which provide the constitutional requisites of fairness for witnesses. A measure of added care on the part of the House and the Senate in authorizing the use of compulsory process and by their committees in exercising that power would suffice. That is a small price to pay if it serves to uphold the principles of limited, constitutional government without constricting the power of the Congress to inform itself.

Justice BURTON and Justice WHITTAKER did not participate in the consideration or decision of this case.

Justice FRANKFURTER concurring.

I deem it important to state what I understand to be the Court's holding. Agreeing with its holding, I join its opinion. By thus making the federal judiciary the affirmative agency for enforcing the authority that underlies the congressional power to punish for contempt, Congress necessarily brings into play the specific provisions of the Constitution relating to the prosecution of offenses and those implied restrictions under which courts function.

To turn to the immediate problem before us, the scope of inquiry that a committee is authorized to pursue must be defined with sufficiently unambiguous clarity to safeguard a witness from the hazards of vagueness in the enforcement of the criminal process against which the Due Process Clause protects. The questions must be put with relevance and definiteness sufficient to enable the witness to know whether his refusal to answer may lead to conviction for criminal contempt and to enable both the trial and the appellate courts readily to determine whether the particular circumstances justify a finding of guilt. . . . The circumstances of this case were wanting in these essentials.

Justice CLARK dissenting.

As I see it the chief fault in the majority opinion is its mischievous curbing of the informing function of the Congress. . . .

[T]he Court reverses the judgment because: (1) The subject matter of the inquiry was not "made to appear with undisputable clarity" either through its "charter" or by the Chairman at the time of the hearing and, therefore, Watkins was deprived of a clear understanding of "the manner in which the propounded questions [were] pertinent thereto"; and (2) the present committee system of inquiry of the House, as practiced by the Un-American Activities Committee, does not provide adequate safeguards for the protection of the constitutional right of free speech. I subscribe to neither conclusion. . . .

I think the Committee here was acting entirely within its scope and that the purpose of its inquiry was set out with "undisputable clarity." In the first place, the authorizing language of the Reorganization Act must be read as a whole, not dissected. It authorized investigation into subversive activity, its extent, character, objects, and diffusion. While the language might have been more explicit than using such words as "un-American," or phrases like "principle of the form of government," still these are fairly well understood terms. We must construe them to give them meaning if we can. Our cases indicate that rather than finding fault with the use of words or phrases, we are bound to presume that the action of the legislative body in granting authority to the Committee was with a legitimate object "if [the action] is *capable* of being so construed." . . . . Before we can deny the authority "it must be obvious that" the Committee has "exceeded the bounds of legislative power." *Tenney v. Brandhove,* 341 U.S. 367 [1951]. The fact that the Committee has often been attacked has caused close scrutiny of its acts by the House as a whole and the House has repeatedly given the Committee its approval. "Power" and "responsibility" have not been separated. But the record in this case does not stop here. It shows that at the hearings involving Watkins, the Chairman made statements explaining the functions of the Committee. And, furthermore, Watkins' action at the hearing clearly reveals that he was well acquainted with the purpose of the hearing. It was to investigate Communist infiltration into his union. This certainly falls within the grant of authority from the Reorganization Act and the House has had ample opportunity to limit the investigative scope of the Committee if it feels that the Committee has exceeded its legitimate bounds. I do not see how any First Amendment rights were endangered here. There is nothing in the First Amendment that provides the guarantees Watkins claims. That Amendment was designed to prevent attempts by law to curtail freedom of speech. It forbids Congress from making any law "abridging the freedom of speech, or of the press." It guarantees Watkins' right to join any organization and make any speech that does not have an intent to incite to crime. . . . But Watkins was asked whether he knew named individuals and whether they were Communists. He refused to answer on the ground that his rights were being abridged. What he was actually seeking to do was to protect his former associates, not himself, from embarrassment. He had already admitted his own involvement. He sought to vindicate the rights, if any, of his associates. . . .

As already indicated, even if Watkins associates were on the stand they could not decline to disclose their Communist connections on First Amendment grounds. While there may be no restraint by the Government of one's beliefs, the right of free belief has never been extended to include the withholding of knowledge of past events or transactions. There is no general privilege of silence. The First Amendment does not make speech or silence permissible to a person in such measure as he chooses. Watkins has here exercised his own choice as to when he talks, what questions he answers, and when he remains silent. A witness is not given such a choice by the Amendment. Remote and indirect disadvantages such as "public stigma, scorn and obloquy" may be related to the First Amendment, but they are not enough to block investigation.

Barenblatt v. United States
360 U.S. 109, 79 S.Ct. 1081 (1959)

The ruling in *Watkins v. United States* (1957) (see page 415) touched off a firestorm of protest in Congress. Conservative Republicans and Southern Democrats charged that the Warren Court "[i]ntruded on Congress's right of investigation by reversing certain citations for contempt of Congress" and "[e]ndangered the national security by rulings in subversive activities cases." In particular, Indiana's Senator William Jenner introduced a bill that would withdraw the Supreme Court's jurisdiction over, among things, "any committee or sub-committee of the United States Congress or any action or proceedings against a witness charged with contempt of Congress." While the Jenner and other bills were being debated in Congress, the justices granted review of the case brought by Lloyd Barenblatt, a college professor, convicted for refusing to answer certain questions asked by a subcommittee of the House Un-American Activities Committee. Justice Harlan's opinion for a bare majority of the Court, in affirming Barenblatt's conviction, further discusses the facts of the case. Notably, on the same day this decision was announced, in *Uphaus v. Wyman*, 364 U.S. 388 (1959), the Court also ruled that a director of a summer camp could be forced to supply the names of all guests at the camp during a two-year period to the New Hampshire attorney general, who was investigating for the state legislature whether there were any "subversive persons" in the state. The rulings in *Barenblatt* and *Uphaus* helped diffuse the controversy over the Court, and Jenner's and similar Court-curbing legislation was defeated in Congress.

Justice HARLAN delivers the opinion of the Court.

Once more the Court is required to resolve the conflicting constitutional claims of congressional power and of an individual's right to resist its exercise. The congressional power in question concerns the internal process of Congress in moving within its legislative domain; it involves the utilization of its committees to secure "testimony needed to enable it efficiently to exercise a legislative function belonging to it under the Constitution." . . . Broad as it is, the power is not, however, without limitations. Since Congress may only investigate into those areas in which it may potentially legislate or appropriate, it cannot inquire into matters which are within the exclusive province of one of the other branches of the Government. Lacking the judicial power given to the Judiciary, it cannot inquire into matters that are exclusively the concern of the Judiciary. Neither can it supplant the Executive in what exclusively belongs to the Executive. And the Congress, in common with all branches of the Government, must exercise its powers subject to the limitations placed by the Constitution on governmental action, more particularly in the context of this case the relevant limitations of the Bill of Rights.

The congressional power of inquiry, its range and scope, and an individual's duty in relation to it, must be viewed in proper perspective. The power and the right of resistance to it are to be judged in the concrete, not on the basis of abstractions. In the present case congressional efforts to learn the extent of a nation-wide, indeed worldwide, problem have brought one of its investigating committees into the field of education. Of course, broadly viewed, inquiries cannot be made into the teaching that is pursued in any of our educational institutions. When academic teaching-freedom and its corollary learning-freedom, so essential to the well-being of the Nation, are claimed, this Court will always be on the alert against intrusion by Congress into this constitutionally protected domain. But this does not mean that the Congress is precluded from interrogating a witness merely because he is a teacher. An educational institution is not a constitutional sanctuary from inquiry into matters that may otherwise be within the constitutional legislative domain merely for the reason that inquiry is made of someone within its walls. . . .

We here review petitioner's conviction . . . for contempt of Congress, arising from his refusal to answer certain questions put to him by a Subcommittee of the House Committee on Un-American Activities during the course of an inquiry concerning alleged Communist infiltration into the field of education. . . .

Pursuant to a subpoena, and accompanied by counsel, petitioner on June 28, 1954, appeared as a witness before this congressional Subcommittee. After answering a few preliminary questions and testifying that he had been a graduate student and teaching fellow at the University of Michigan from 1947 to 1950 and an instructor in psychology at Vassar College from 1950 to shortly before his appearance before the Subcommittee, petitioner objected generally to the right of the Subcommittee to inquire into his "political" and "religious" beliefs or any "other personal and private affairs" or "associational activities," upon grounds set forth in a previously prepared memorandum which he was allowed to file with the Subcommittee. Thereafter petitioner specifically declined to answer each of the following five questions:

"Are you now a member of the Communist Party? [Count One.]

"Have you ever been a member of the Communist Party? [Count Two.]

"Now, you have stated that you knew Francis Crowley. Did you know Francis Crowley as a member of the Communist Party? [Count Three.]

"Were you ever a member of the Haldane Club of the Communist Party while at the University of Michigan? [Count Four.]

"Were you a member while a student of the University of Michigan Council of Arts, Sciences, and Professions?" [Count Five.]

In each instance the grounds of refusal were those set forth in the prepared statement. Petitioner expressly disclaimed reliance upon "the Fifth Amendment." . . .

Petitioner's various contentions resolve themselves into three propositions: First, the compelling of testimony by the Subcommittee was neither legislatively authorized nor constitutionally permissible because of the vagueness of Rule XI of the House of Representatives, Eighty-third Congress, the charter of authority of the parent Committee. Second, petitioner was not adequately apprised of the pertinency of the Subcommittee's questions to the subject matter of the inquiry. Third, the questions petitioner refused to answer infringed rights protected by the First Amendment.

SUBCOMMITTEE'S AUTHORITY TO COMPEL TESTIMONY.

At the outset it should be noted that Rule XI authorized this Subcommittee to compel testimony within the framework of the investigative authority conferred on the Un-American Activities Committee. Petitioner contends that *Watkins v. United States,* [354 U.S. 178 (1957)], nevertheless held the grant of this power in all circumstances ineffective because of the vagueness of Rule XI in delineating the Committee jurisdiction to which its exercise was to be appurtenant. . . .

The *Watkins* case cannot properly be read as standing for such a proposition. A principal contention in *Watkins* was that the refusals to answer were justified because the requirement of 2 U.S.C. § 192, that the questions asked be "pertinent to the question under inquiry" had not been satisfied. . . . This Court reversed the conviction solely on that ground, holding that Watkins had not been adequately apprised of the subject matter of the Subcommittee's investigation or the pertinency thereto of the questions he refused to answer. In so deciding the Court drew upon Rule XI only as one of the facets in the total *mise en scène* in its search for the "question under inquiry" in that particular investigation. That the vagueness of Rule XI was not alone determinative is also shown by the Court's further statement that aside from the Rule "the remarks of the chairman or members of the committee, or even the nature of the proceedings themselves, might sometimes make the topic [under inquiry] clear." In short, while *Watkins* was critical of Rule XI, it did not involve the broad and inflexible holding petitioner now attributes to it.

Petitioner also contends, independently of *Watkins,* that the vagueness of Rule XI deprived the Subcommittee of the right to compel testimony in this investigation into Communist activity. We cannot agree with this contention which in its furthest reach would mean that the House Un-American Activities Committee under its existing authority has no right to compel testimony in any circumstances. Granting the vagueness of the Rule, we may not read it in isolation from its long history in the House of Representatives. Just as legislation is often given meaning by the gloss of legislative reports, administrative interpretation, and long usage, so the proper meaning of an authorization to a congressional committee is not to be derived alone from its abstract terms unrelated to the definite content furnished them by the course of congressional actions. The Rule comes to us with a "persuasive gloss of legislative history" which shows beyond doubt that in pursuance of its legislative concerns in the domain of "national security" the House has clothed the Un-American Activities Committee with pervasive authority to investigate Communist activities in this country. . . .

PERTINENCY CLAIM.

Undeniably a conviction for contempt under 2 U.S.C. § 192 cannot stand unless the questions asked are pertinent to the subject matter of the investigation. *Watkins v. United States.* But the factors which led us to rest decision on this ground in Watkins were very different from those involved here.

In Watkins the petitioner had made specific objection to the Subcommittee's questions on the ground of pertinency; the question under inquiry had not been disclosed in any illuminating manner; and the questions asked the petitioner were not only amorphous on their face, but in some instances clearly foreign to the alleged subject matter of the investigation—"Communism in labor.". . .

In contrast, petitioner in the case before us raised no objections on the ground of pertinency at the time any of the questions were put to him. . . .

We need not, however, rest decision on petitioner's failure to object on this score, for here "pertinency" was made to appear "with undisputable clarity." First of all, it goes without saying that the scope of the Committee's authority was for the House, not a witness, to determine, subject to the ultimate reviewing responsibility of this Court. What we deal with here is whether petitioner was sufficiently apprised of "the topic under inquiry" thus authorized "and the connective reasoning whereby the precise questions asked relate[d] to it." In light of his prepared memorandum of constitutional objections there can be no doubt that this petitioner was well aware of the Subcommittee's authority and purpose to question him as it did. In addition the other sources of this information which we recognized in *Watkins* . . . leave no room for a "pertinency" objection on this record. The subject matter of the inquiry had been identified at the commencement of the investigation as Communist infiltration into the field of education. Just prior to petitioner's appearance before the Subcommittee, the scope of the day's hearings had been announced as "in the main communism in education and the experiences and background in the party by Francis X. T. Crowley. It will deal with activities in Michigan, Boston, and in some small degree, New York." Petitioner had heard the Subcommittee interrogate the witness Crowley along the same lines as he, petitioner, was evidently to be questioned, and had listened to Crowley's testimony identifying him as a former member of an alleged Communist student organization at the University of Michigan while they both were in attendance there. Further, petitioner had stood mute in the face of the Chairman's statement as to why he had been called as a witness by the Subcommittee. And, lastly, unlike *Watkins,* petitioner refused to answer questions as to his own Communist Party affiliations, whose pertinency of course was clear beyond doubt. . . .

CONSTITUTIONAL CONTENTIONS.

The precise constitutional issue confronting us is whether the Subcommittee's inquiry into petitioner's past or present membership in the Communist Party transgressed the provisions of the First Amendment, which of course reach and limit congressional investigations. . . . Undeniably, the First Amendment in some circumstances protects an individual from being compelled to disclose his associational relationships. However, the protections of the First Amendment, unlike a proper claim of the privilege against self-incrimination under the Fifth Amendment, do not afford a witness the right to resist inquiry in all circumstances. Where First Amendment rights are asserted to bar governmental interrogation resolution of the issue always involves a balancing by the courts of the competing private and public interests at stake in the particular circumstances shown. These principles were recognized in the *Watkins* case, where, in speaking of the First Amendment in relation to congressional inquiries, we said, "It is manifest that despite the adverse effects which follow upon compelled disclosure of private matters, not all such inquiries are barred. The critical element is the existence of, and the weight to be ascribed to, the interest of the Congress in demanding disclosures from an unwilling witness." . . .

That Congress has wide power to legislate in the field of Communist activity in this Country, and to conduct appropriate investigations in aid thereof, is hardly debatable. The existence of such power has never been questioned by this Court, and it is sufficient to say, without particularization, that Congress has enacted or considered in this field a wide range of legislative measures, not a few of which have stemmed from recommendations of the very Committee whose actions have been drawn in question here. In the last analysis this power rests on the right of self-preservation, "the ultimate value of any society." . . .

On these premises, this Court in its constitutional adjudications has consistently refused to view the Communist Party as an ordinary political party, and has upheld federal legislation aimed at the Communist problem which in a different context would certainly have raised constitutional issues of the gravest character. . . . To suggest that because the Communist Party may also sponsor peaceable political reforms the constitutional issues before us should now be judged as if that Party were just an ordinary political party from the standpoint of national security, is to ask this Court to blind itself to world affairs which have determined the whole course of our national policy since the close of World War II. . . . An investigation of advocacy of or preparation for overthrow certainly embraces the right to identify a witness as a member of the Communist Party, and to inquire into the various manifestations of the Party's tenets. The strict requirements of a prosecution under the Smith Act are not the measure of the permissible scope of a congressional investigation into "overthrow," for of necessity the investigatory process must proceed step by step. Nor can it fairly be concluded that this investigation was directed at controlling what is being taught at our universities rather than at overthrow. The statement of the Subcommittee Chairman at the opening of the investigation evinces no such intention, and so far as this record reveals nothing thereafter transpired which would justify our holding that the thrust of the investigation later changed. The record discloses considerable testimony concerning the foreign domination and revolutionary purposes and efforts of the Communist Party. That there was also testimony on the abstract philosophical level does not detract from the dominant theme of this investigation—Communist infiltration furthering the alleged ultimate purpose of overthrow. And certainly the conclusion would not be justified that the questioning of petitioner would have exceeded permissible bounds had he not shut off the Subcommittee at the threshold.

Nor can we accept the further contention that this investigation should not be deemed to have been in furtherance of a legislative purpose because the true objective of the Committee and of the Congress was purely "exposure." So long as Congress acts in pursuance of its constitutional power, the Judiciary lacks authority to intervene on the basis of the motives which spurred the exercise of that power. "It is, of course, true," as was said in *McCray v. United States* [195 U.S. 27 (1904)], "that if there be no authority in the judiciary to restrain a lawful exercise of power by another department of the government, where a wrong motive or purpose has impelled to the exertion of the power, that abuses of a power conferred may be temporarily effectual. The remedy for this however, lies, not in the abuse by the judicial authority of its functions, but in the people, upon whom, after all, under our institutions, reliance must be placed for the correction of abuses committed in the exercise of a lawful power." These principles of course apply as well to committee investigations into the need for legislation as to the enactments which such investigations may produce. . . .

We conclude that the balance between the individual and the governmental interests here at stake must be struck in favor of the latter, and that therefore the provisions of the First Amendment have not been offended.

We hold that petitioner's conviction for contempt of Congress discloses no infirmity, and that the judgment of the Court of Appeals must be affirmed.

Affirmed.

Justice BLACK, with whom The CHIEF JUSTICE and Justice DOUGLAS join, dissenting.

The First Amendment says in no equivocal language that Congress shall pass no law abridging freedom of speech, press, assembly or petition. The activities of this Committee, authorized by Congress, do precisely that, through exposure, obloquy and public scorn. See *Watkins v. United States.* The Court does not really deny this fact but relies on a combination of three reasons for permitting the infringement: (A) The notion that despite the First Amendment's command Congress can abridge speech and association if this Court decides that the governmental interest in abridging speech is greater than an individual's interest in exercising that freedom, (B) the Government's right to "preserve itself," (C) the fact that the Committee is only after Communists or suspected Communists in this investigation. . . .

To apply the Court's balancing test under such circumstances is to read the First Amendment to say "Congress shall pass no law abridging freedom of speech, press, assembly and petition, unless Congress and the Supreme Court reach the joint conclusion that on balance the interest of the Government in stifling these freedoms is greater than the interest of the people in having them exercised." This is closely akin to the notion that neither the First Amendment nor any other provision of the Bill of Rights should be enforced unless the Court believes it is *reasonable* to do so. Not only does this violate the genius of our *written* Constitution, but it runs expressly counter to the injunction to Court and Congress made by Madison when he introduced the Bill of Rights. "If they [the first ten amendments] are incorporated into the Constitution, independent tribunals of justice will consider themselves in a peculiar manner the guardians of those rights: they will be an impenetrable bulwark against *every* assumption of power in the Legislative or Executive; they will be naturally led to resist *every* encroachment upon rights expressly stipulated for in the Constitution by the declaration of rights." Unless we return to this view of our judicial function, unless we once again accept the notion that the Bill of Rights means what it says and that this Court must enforce that meaning, I am of the opinion that our great charter of liberty will be more honored in the breach than in the observance.

But even assuming what I cannot assume, that some balancing is proper in this case, I feel that the Court after stating the test ignores it completely. At most it balances the right of the Government to preserve itself, against Barenblatt's right to refrain from revealing Communist affiliations. Such a balance, however, mistakes the factors to be weighed. In the first place, it completely leaves out the real interest in Barenblatt's silence, the interest of the people as a whole in being able to join organizations, advocate causes and make political "mistakes" without later being subjected to governmental penalties for having dared to think for themselves. It is this right, the right to err politically, which keeps us strong as a Nation. For no number of laws against communism can have as much effect as the personal conviction which comes from having heard its arguments and rejected them, or from having once accepted its tenets and later recognized their worthlessness. Instead, the obloquy which results from investigations such as this not only stifles "mistakes" but prevents all but the most courageous from hazarding any views which might at some later time become disfavored. This result, whose importance cannot be overestimated, is doubly crucial when it affects the universities, on which we must largely rely for the experimentation and development of new ideas essential to our country's welfare. It is these interests of society, rather than Barenblatt's own right to silence, which I think the Court should put on the balance against the demands of the Government, if any balancing process is to be tolerated. Instead they are not mentioned, while on the other side the demands of the Government are vastly overstated and called "self preservation." . . .

Moreover, I cannot agree with the Court's motion that First Amendment freedoms must be abridged in order to "preserve" our country. That notion rests on the unarticulated premise that this Nation's security hangs upon its power to punish people because of what they think, speak or write about, or because of those with whom they associate for political purposes. The Government, in its brief, virtually admits this position when it speaks of the "communication of unlawful ideas." I challenge this premise, and deny that ideas can be proscribed under our Constitution. . . .

Our Constitution assumes that the common sense of the people and their attachment to our country will enable them, after free discussion, to withstand ideas that are wrong. . . .

Finally, I think Barenblatt's conviction violates the Constitution because the chief aim, purpose and practice of the House Un-American Activities Committee, as disclosed by its many reports, is to try witnesses and punish them because they are or have been Communists or because they refuse to admit or deny Communist affiliations. The punishment imposed is generally punishment by humiliation and public shame. There is nothing strange or novel about this kind of punishment. It is in fact one of the oldest forms of governmental punishment known to mankind; branding, the pillory, ostracism and subjection to public hatred being but a few examples of it. . . .

I cannot agree that this is a legislative function. Such publicity is clearly punishment, and the Constitution allows only one way in which people can be convicted and punished. As we said in *United States v. Lovett* [328 U.S. 303 (1946)], "Those who wrote our Constitution well knew the danger inherent in special legislative acts which take away the life, liberty, or property of particular named persons, because the legislature thinks them guilty of conduct which deserves punishment. *They intended to "safeguard the people of this country from punishment without trial by duly constituted courts.*" . . .

Ultimately all the questions in this case really boil down to one—whether we as a people will try fearfully and futilely to preserve democracy by adopting totalitarian methods, or whether in accordance with our traditions and our Constitution we will have the confidence and courage to be free.

I would reverse this conviction.

Gibson v. Florida Legislative Investigation Committee

372 U.S. 539, 83 S.Ct. 889 (1963)

Following the watershed ruling in *Brown v. Board of Education of Topeka, Kansas,* 347 U.S. 483 (1954) (see Vol. 2, Ch. 12), the National Association for the Advancement of Colored People (NAACP) spearheaded further litigation to force Southern states to begin school desegregation. As a result, the NAACP was subject to great hostility, as state officials sought in a variety of ways to thwart its activities. In Alabama, officials endeavored to stop the NAACP's efforts by requiring it to register and produce a list of its members. The NAACP complied, except for producing its membership list on the ground that violated its First Amendment freedom of association. After being found in contempt and fined $100,000 for refusing to turn over its membership lists, the NAACP appealed to the Supreme Court. In *National Association for the Advancement of Colored People v. Alabama,* 357 U.S. 449 (1958) (see Vol. 2, Ch. 5), the Court upheld the organization's claims that disclosure of its membership lists would abridge its First Amendment right of lawful association. In 1958, the Florida Supreme Court likewise ruled that the NAACP could not be compelled to release its membership lists to a state legislative committee. But it also held that the "custodian" of its records could be compelled to bring them to the hearings and to refer to them in answering questions. The next year, the Florida legislature established a Legislative Investigation Committee to investigate "subversive organizations"—such as the Communist party— and their infiltration of the NAACP. Theodore Gibson, the president of the Miami branch of the NAACP, was subpoenaed to appear and to bring the membership lists of his branch for reference to hearings of the committee. Gibson agreed to answer questions about members but refused to bring the records to the committee's hearings. He contended that that request infringed on members' freedom of association. After a state court found him in contempt, and the Florida Supreme Court affirmed, Gibson appealed to the Supreme Court and a bare majority reversed the decision of the state supreme court.

Justice GOLDBERG delivers the opinion of the Court.

We are here called upon once again to resolve a conflict between individual rights of free speech and association and governmental interest in conducting legislative investigations. Prior decisions illumine the contending principles.

This Court has repeatedly held that rights of association are within the ambit of the constitutional protections afforded by the First and Fourteenth Amendments. . . . The respondent Committee does not contend otherwise, nor could it, for, as was said in *N.A.A.C.P. v. Alabama,* "It is beyond debate that freedom to engage in association for the advancement of beliefs and ideas is an inseparable aspect of the 'liberty' assured by the Due Process Clause of the Fourteenth Amendment, which embraces freedom of speech." And it is equally clear that the guarantee encompasses protection of privacy of association in organizations such as that of which the petitioner is president; indeed, in both the Bates and Alabama cases, supra, this Court held N.A.A.C.P. membership lists of the very type here in question to be beyond the States' power of discovery in the circumstances there presented.

The First and Fourteenth Amendment rights of free speech and free association are fundamental and highly prized, and "need breathing space to survive." *N.A.A.C.P. v. Button,* 371 U.S. 415 [1963]. "Freedoms such as these are protected not only against heavy-handed frontal attack, but also from being stifled by more subtle governmental interference." *Bates v. Little Rock* [361 U.S. 516 (1960)]. And, as declared in *N.A.A.C.P. v. Alabama,* "It is hardly a novel perception that compelled disclosure of affiliation with groups engaged in advocacy may constitute [an] . . . effective . . . restraint on freedom of association. . . . This Court has recognized the vital relationship between freedom to associate and privacy in one's associations. . . . Inviolability of privacy in group association may in many circumstances be indispensable to preservation of freedom of association, particularly where a group espouses dissident beliefs." So it is here.

At the same time, however, this Court's prior holdings demonstrate that there can be no question that the State has power adequately to inform itself—through legislative investigation, if it so desires—in order to act and protect its legitimate and vital interests. . . .

Significantly, the parties are in substantial agreement as to the proper test to be applied to reconcile the competing claims of government and individual and to determine the propriety of the Committee's demands. As declared by the respondent Committee in its brief to this Court, "Basically, this case hinges entirely on the question of whether the evidence before the Committee [was] . . . sufficient to show probable cause or nexus between the N.A.A.C.P. Miami Branch, and Communist activities." We understand this to mean—regardless of the label applied, be it "nexus," "foundation," or whatever—that it is an essential prerequisite to the validity of an investigation which intrudes into the area of constitutionally protected rights of speech, press, association and petition that the State convincingly show a substantial relation between the information sought and a subject of overriding and compelling state interest. Absent such a relation between the N.A.A.C.P. and conduct in which the State may have a compelling regulatory concern, the Committee has not "demonstrated so cogent an interest in obtaining and making public" the membership information sought to be obtained as to "justify the substantial abridgment of associational freedom which such disclosures will effect." . . .

Applying these principles to the facts of this case, the respondent Committee contends that the prior decisions of this Court . . . compel a result here upholding the legislative right of inquiry. In *Barenblatt* [*v. United States*, 360 U.S. 109 (1959)], *Wilkinson* [v. United States, 365 U.S. 431 (1961)], and *Braden* [v. United States, 365 U.S. 431 (1961)], however, it was a refusal to answer a question or questions concerning the witness' *own* past or present membership *in the Communist Party* which supported his conviction. It is apparent that the necessary preponderating governmental interest and, in fact, the very result in those cases were founded on the holding that the Communist Party is not an ordinary or legitimate political party, as known in this country, and that, because of its particular nature, membership therein is *itself* a permissible subject of regulation and legislative scrutiny. Assuming the correctness of the premises on which those cases were decided, no further demonstration of compelling governmental interest was deemed necessary, since the direct object of the challenged questions there was discovery of membership in the Communist Party, a matter held pertinent to a proper subject then under inquiry.

Here, however, it is not alleged Communists who are the witnesses before the Committee and it is not discovery of their membership in that party which is the object of the challenged inquiries. Rather, it is the N.A.A.C.P. itself which is the subject of the investigation, and it is its local president, the petitioner, who was called before the Committee and held in contempt because he refused to divulge the contents of its membership records. There is no suggestion that the Miami branch of the N.A.A.C.P. or the national organization with which it is affiliated was, or is, itself a subversive organization. Nor is there any indication that the activities or policies of the N.A.A.C.P. were either Communist dominated or influenced. In fact, this very record indicates that the association was and is against communism and has voluntarily taken steps to keep Communists from being members. Each year since 1950, the N.A.A.C.P. has adopted resolutions barring Communists from membership in the organization. Moreover, the petitioner testified that all prospective officers of the local organization are thoroughly investigated for Communist or subversive connections and, though subversive activities constitute grounds for termination of association membership, no such expulsions from the branch occurred during the five years preceding the investigation.

Thus, unlike the situation in *Barenblatt, Wilkinson* and *Braden,* supra, the Committee was not here seeking from the petitioner or the records of which he was custodian any information as to whether he, himself, or even other persons were members of the Communist Party, Communist front or affiliated organizations, or other allegedly subversive groups; instead, the entire thrust of the demands on the petitioner was that he disclose whether other persons were members of the N.A.A.C.P., itself a concededly legitimate and nonsubversive organization. Compelling such an organization, engaged in the exercise of First and Fourteenth Amendment rights, to disclose its membership presents, under our cases, a question wholly different from compelling the Communist Party to disclose its own membership. Moreover, even to say, as in *Barenblatt* . . . that it is permissible to inquire into the subject of Communist infiltration of educational or other organizations does not mean that it is permissible to demand or require from such other groups disclosure of their membership by inquiry into their records when such disclosure will seriously inhibit or impair the exercise of constitutional rights and has not itself been demonstrated to bear a crucial relation to a proper governmental interest or to be essential to fulfillment of a proper governmental purpose. The prior holdings that governmental interest in controlling subversion and the particular character of the Communist Party and its objectives outweigh the right of individual Communists to conceal party membership or affiliations by no means require the wholly different conclusion that other groups—concededly legitimate—automatically forfeit their rights to privacy of association simply because the general subject matter of the legislative inquiry is Communist subversion or infiltration. The fact that governmental interest was deemed compelling in *Barenblatt, Wilkinson,* and *Braden* and held to support the inquiries there made into membership in the Communist Party does not resolve the issues here, where the challenged questions go to membership in an admittedly lawful organization.

In the absence of directly determinative authority, we turn, then, to consideration of the facts now before us. Obviously, if the respondent were still seeking discovery of the entire membership list, we could readily dispose of this case on the authority of *Bates v. Little Rock,* and *N.A.A.C.P. v. Alabama,* supra; a like result would follow if it were merely attempting to do piecemeal what could not be done in a single step. Though there are indications that the respondent Committee intended to inquire broadly into the N.A.A.C.P. membership records, there is no need to base our decision today upon a prediction as to the course which the Committee might have pursued if initially unopposed by the petitioner. Instead, we rest our result on the fact that the record in this case is insufficient to show a substantial connection between the Miami branch of the N.A.A.C.P. and Communist *activities* which the respondent Committee itself concedes is an essential prerequisite to demonstrating the immediate, substantial, and subordinating state interest necessary to sustain its right of inquiry into the membership lists of the association.

Basically, the evidence relied upon by the respondent to demonstrate the necessary foundation consists of the testimony of R. J. Strickland, an investigator for the Committee and its predecessors, and Arlington Sands, a former association official.

Strickland identified by name some 14 persons whom he said either were or had been Communists or members of Communist "front" or "affiliated" organizations. His description of their connection with the association was simply that "each of them has been a member of and/or participated in the meetings and other affairs of the N.A.A.C.P. in Dade County, Florida." In addition, one of the group was identified as having made, at an unspecified time, a contribution of unspecified amount to the local organization.

We do not know from this ambiguous testimony how many of the 14 were supposed to have been N.A.A.C.P. members. For all that appears, and there is no indicated reason to entertain a contrary belief, each or all of the named persons may have attended no more than one or two wholly public meetings of the N.A.A.C.P., and such attendance, like their membership, to the extent it existed, in the association, may have been wholly peripheral and begun and ended many years prior even to commencement of the present investigation in 1956. In addition, it is not clear whether the asserted Communist affiliations and the association with the N.A.A.C.P., however slight, coincided in time. . . .

This summary of the evidence discloses the utter failure to demonstrate the existence of any substantial relationship between the N.A.A.C.P. and subversive or Communist activities. In essence, there is here merely indirect, less than unequivocal, and mostly hearsay testimony that in years past some 14 people who were asserted to be, or to have been, Communists or members of Communist front or "affiliated organizations" attended occasional meetings of the Miami branch of the N.A.A.C.P. "and/or" were members of that branch, which had a total membership of about 1,000. . . .

Of course, a legislative investigation—as any investigation—must proceed "step by step," *Barenblatt v. United States,* supra, but step by step or in totality, an adequate foundation for inquiry must be laid before proceeding in such a manner as will substantially intrude upon and severely curtail or inhibit constitutionally protected activities or seriously interfere with similarly protected associational rights. No such foundation has been laid here. The respondent Committee has failed to demonstrate the compelling and subordinating governmental interest essential to support direct inquiry into the membership records of the N.A.A.C.P.

Nothing we say here impairs or denies the existence of the underlying legislative right to investigate or legislate with respect to subversive activities by Communists or anyone else; our decision today deals only with the manner in which such power may be exercised and we hold simply that groups which themselves are neither engaged in subversive or other illegal or improper activities nor demonstrated to have any substantial connections with such activities are to be protected in their rights of free and private association. . . .

To permit legislative inquiry to proceed on less than an adequate foundation would be to sanction unjustified and unwarranted intrusions into the very heart of the constitutional privilege to be secure in associations in legitimate organizations engaged in the exercise of First and Fourteenth Amendment rights; to impose a lesser standard than we here do would be inconsistent with the maintenance of those essential conditions basic to the preservation of our democracy.

The judgment below must be and is reversed.

Reversed.

Justice BLACK concurring.

I concur in the Court's opinion and judgment reversing the judgment of the Supreme Court of Florida although, for substantially the same reasons stated by Justice DOUGLAS in his concurring opinion, I would prefer to reach our decision by a different approach. . . .

In my view the constitutional right of association includes the privilege of any person to associate with Communists or anti-Communists, Socialists or anti-Socialists, or, for that matter with people of all kinds of beliefs, popular or unpopular. I have expressed these views in many other cases and I adhere to them now. Since, as I believe, the National Association for the Advancement of Colored People and its members have a constitutional right to choose their own associates, I cannot understand by what constitutional authority Florida can compel answers to questions which abridge that right. Accordingly, I would reverse here on the ground that there has been a direct abridgment of the right of association of the National Association for the Advancement of Colored People and its members. But, since the Court assumes for purposes of this case that there was no direct abridgment of First Amendment freedoms, I concur in the Court's opinion, which is based on constitutional principles laid down in *Schneider v. Irvington*, 308 U.S. 147 (1939), and later cases of this Court following Schneider.

Justice DOUGLAS concurring.

In my view, government is not only powerless to legislate with respect to membership in a lawful organization; it is also precluded from probing the intimacies of spiritual and intellectual relationships in the myriad of such societies and groups that exist in this country, regardless of the legislative purpose sought to be served. . . .

There is no other course consistent with the Free Society envisioned by the First Amendment. For the views a citizen entertains, the beliefs he harbors, the utterances he makes, the ideology he embraces and the people he associates with are no concern of government. That article of faith marks indeed the main difference between the Free Society which we espouse and the dictatorships both on the Left and on the Right. . . .

In sum, the State and the Federal Governments, by force of the First Amendment, are barred from investigating any person's faith or ideology by summoning him or by summoning officers or members of his society, church, or club.

Government can intervene only when belief, thought, or expression moves into the realm of action that is inimical to society. That was Jefferson's view. In his Bill for Establishing Religious Freedom he spoke primarily of religious liberty but in terms applicable to freedom of the mind in all of its aspects. It was his view that in the Free Society men's ideas and beliefs, their speech and advocacy are no proper concern of government. Only when they become brigaded with action can government move against them.

Justice HARLAN, with whom Justice CLARK, Justice STEWART, and Justice WHITE join, dissenting.

This Court rests reversal on its finding that the Committee did not have sufficient justification for including the Miami Branch of the N.A.A.C.P. within the ambit of its investigation—that, in the language of our cases (*Uphaus v. Wyman*, 360 U.S. 72 [1959]), an adequate "nexus" was lacking between the N.A.A.C.P. and the subject matter of the Committee's inquiry.

The Court's reasoning is difficult to grasp. I read its opinion as basically proceeding on the premise that the governmental interest in investigating Communist infiltration into admittedly nonsubversive organizations, as distinguished from investigating organizations themselves suspected of subversive activities, is not sufficient to overcome the countervailing right to freedom of association. On this basis "nexus" is seemingly found lacking because it was never claimed that the N.A.A.C.P. Miami Branch had itself engaged in subversive activity, and because none of the Committee's evidence relating to any of the 52 alleged Communist Party members was sufficient to attribute such activity to the local branch or to show that it was dominated, influenced, or used "by Communists."

But, until today, I had never supposed that any of our decisions relating to state or federal power to investigate in the field of Communist subversion could possibly be taken as suggesting any difference in the degree of governmental investigatory interest as between Communist infiltration *of* organizations and Communist activity *by* organizations. . . .

Given the unsoundness of the basic premise underlying the Court's holding as to the absence of "nexus," this decision surely falls of its own weight. For unless "nexus" requires an investigating agency to prove in advance the very things it is trying to find out, I do not understand how it can be said that the information preliminarily developed by the Committee's investigator was not sufficient to satisfy, under any reasonable test, the requirement of "nexus."

Apart from this, the issue of "nexus" is surely laid at rest by the N.A.A.C.P.'s own "Anti-Communism" resolution, first adopted in 1950, which petitioner had voluntarily furnished the Committee before the curtain came down on his examination:

"Anti-Communism

"Whereas, certain branches of the National Association for the Advancement of Colored People are being rocked by internal conflicts between groups who follow the Communist line and those who do not, which threaten to destroy the confidence of the public in the Association and which will inevitably result in its eventual disruption; and

"Whereas, it is apparent from numerous attacks by Communists in their official organs 'The Daily Worker' and 'Political Affairs' upon officials of the Association that there is a well-organized, nationwide conspiracy by Communists either to capture or split and wreck the NAACP; therefore be it

"Resolved, that this Forty-First Convention of the National Association for the Advancement of Colored People go on record as unequivocally condemning attacks by Communists and their fellow-travelers upon the Association and its officials, and in order to safeguard the good-name of the Association, promote and develop unity, eliminate internal ideological friction, increase the membership and build the necessary power effectively to wage the fight for civil rights, herewith, call upon, direct and instruct the National Board of Directors to appoint a committee to investigate and study the ideological composition and trends of the membership and leadership of the local units with a view to determining causes of the aforementioned conflicts, confusion and loss of membership; be it further

"Resolved, that this Convention go on record as directing and instructing the Board of Directors to take the necessary action to eradicate such *infiltration,* and if necessary to suspend and reorganize, or lift the charter and expel any unit, which, in the judgment of the Board of Directors, upon a basis of the findings of the aforementioned investigation and study of local units comes under Communist or other political control and combination." (Emphasis added.)

It hardly meets the point at issue to suggest, as the Court does that the resolution only serves to show that the Miami Branch was in fact free of any Communist influences—unless self-investigation is deemed constitutionally to block official inquiry.

I also find it difficult to see how this case really presents any serious question as to interference with freedom of association. Given the willingness of the petitioner to testify from recollection as to individual memberships in the local branch of the N.A.A.C.P., the germaneness of the membership records to the subject matter of the Committee's investigation, and the limited purpose for which their use was sought—as an aid to refreshing the witness' recollection, involving their divulgence only to the petitioner himself . . . —this case of course bears no resemblance whatever to *N.A.A.C.P. v. Alabama,* or *Bates v. Little Rock.* In both of those cases the State had sought general divulgence of local N.A.A.C.P. membership lists without any showing of a justifying state interest. In effect what we are asked to hold here is that the petitioner had a constitutional right to give only partial or inaccurate testimony, and that indeed seems to me the true effect of the Court's holding today.

Justice WHITE dissenting.

In my view, the opinion of the Court represents a serious limitation upon the Court's previous cases dealing with this subject matter and upon the right of the legislature to investigate the Communist Party and its activities. Although one of the classic and recurring activities of the Communist Party is the infiltration and subversion of other organizations, either openly or in a clandestine manner, the Court holds that even where a legislature has evidence that a legitimate organization is under assault and even though that organization is itself sounding open and public alarm, an investigating committee is nevertheless forbidden to compel the organization or its members to reveal the fact, or not, of membership in that organization of named Communists assigned to the infiltrating task.

6

CONGRESS: LEGISLATIVE, TAXING, AND SPENDING POWERS

T HE LEGISLATIVE POWERS of Congress, as noted in the last
chapter, are expressly *enumerated*. Article 1 lists 17 specific
powers, including the power to regulate commerce, to lay and
collect taxes, and to "provide for the common Defense and general welfare of the United States." In addition, Congress was
given an important residual power of enacting all laws "necessary
and proper" to the execution of its authority and other delegated
powers.

Basically, Congress may enact four types of law: those that
(1) provide substantive or procedural rules of general application
governing, for example, interstate commerce; (2) govern the
collection of revenues for the national government; (3) appropriate revenues for expenditure by the government; and (4) confer
benefits on or adjust claims of individuals against the government. Although extensive, this power is not unlimited. Congress
may not, for example, pass *ex post facto* laws (criminal statutes
that have retroactive application). Nor may it deny or infringe
on guarantees of the Bill of Rights.

The detailed enumeration of Congress's legislative powers registers the Framers' aim of correcting the defects of the Articles
of Confederation by creating a national government with vastly
greater, although nonetheless limited, powers. As James Madison explains in *The Federalist*, No. 42, under the Articles of Con-

federation a central problem was that the Continential Congress could not effectively regulate commerce among the states or with foreign nations. For this reason, among seventeen areas over which legislative power is granted in Article I, the commerce clause empowers Congress "to regulate commerce with foreign nations, and among the several states, and with Indian tribes."

In specifically enumerating legislative powers, the Constitutional Convention rejected Alexander Hamilton's proposal that Congress have the "power to pass all laws which they shall judge necessary to the common defense and general welfare of the Union."[1] However, the convention agreed to add the necessary and proper clause, recognizing an *implied* power of Congress "[t]o make all Laws which shall be necessary and proper for carrying into Execution the foregoing Powers, and all other Powers vested by this Constitution in the Government of the United States, or in any Department or Officer thereof."

Besides enumerated and implied powers, Congress possesses *inherent* powers that flow from the concept of sovereignty. For example, the Constitution does not specifically confer on Congress the power to govern territories acquired by acquisition or through treaties. Yet as Chief Justice Marshall observed, "The right to govern, may be the inevitable consequence of the right to acquire territory. Whichever may be the source, whence the power is derived, the possession of it is unquestioned."[2] In *United States v. Kagama*, 118 U.S. 375 (1886), the Court more emphatically acknowledged the inherent powers of Congress:

[T]his power of Congress to organize territorial governments and make laws for their inhabitants, arises not so much from the clause in the Constitution in regard to disposing or making rules and regulations concerning the Territory and other property of the United States, as from the ownership of the country in which the Territories are, and the right of exclusive sovereignty which must exist in the National Government and can be found nowhere else.

In addition to enumerated, implied and inherent powers, constitutional amendments are a source of expanding congressional powers. In particular, the "Reconstruction Amendments" (the Thirteenth, Fourteenth, and Fifteenth Amendments) contain provisions expanding Congress's enforcement powers; they generated major controversy over the passage of the Voting Rights Act, forbidding racial discrimination in voting, see *South Carolina v. Katzenbach* (1966) (see page 662).

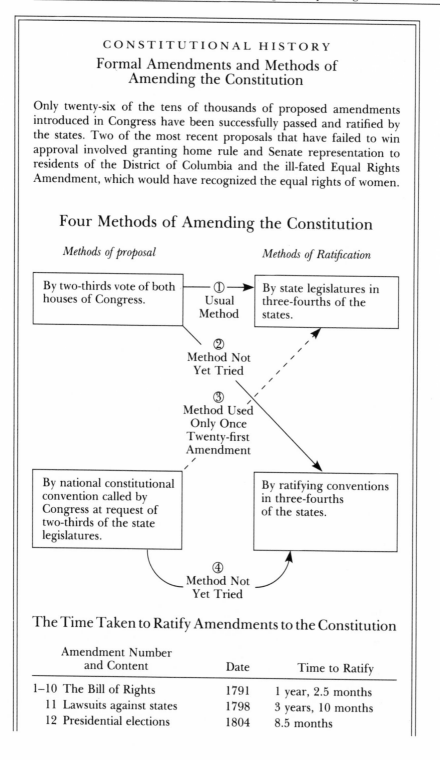

CONSTITUTIONAL HISTORY

Formal Amendments and Methods of Amending the Constitution

Only twenty-six of the tens of thousands of proposed amendments introduced in Congress have been successfully passed and ratified by the states. Two of the most recent proposals that have failed to win approval involved granting home rule and Senate representation to residents of the District of Columbia and the ill-fated Equal Rights Amendment, which would have recognized the equal rights of women.

Four Methods of Amending the Constitution

Methods of proposal　　　　　　　　　*Methods of Ratification*

| By two-thirds vote of both houses of Congress. | ① Usual Method | By state legislatures in three-fourths of the states. |

② Method Not Yet Tried

③ Method Used Only Once Twenty-first Amendment

| By national constitutional convention called by Congress at request of two-thirds of the state legislatures. | | By ratifying conventions in three-fourths of the states. |

④ Method Not Yet Tried

The Time Taken to Ratify Amendments to the Constitution

Amendment Number and Content	Date	Time to Ratify
1–10 The Bill of Rights	1791	1 year, 2.5 months
11 Lawsuits against states	1798	3 years, 10 months
12 Presidential elections	1804	8.5 months

Amendment Number and Content	Date	Time to Ratify
13 Abolition of slavery	1865	10.5 months
14 Equal civil rights	1868	2 years, 1.5 months
15 Voting rights for freemen (black men)	1870	1 year, 1 month
16 Federal income tax	1913	3 years, 7.5 months
17 Senatorial elections	1913	1 year and 0.5 months
18 Prohibition	1919	1 year, 1.5 months
19 Women's suffrage	1920	1 year, 2.5 months
20 Terms of office	1933	11 months
21 Repeal of prohibition	1933	9.5 months
22 Limit on president's terms	1951	3 years, 11.5 months
23 Voting rights for the District of Columbia	1961	9 months
24 Abolition of poll taxes	1964	1 year, 5.5 months
25 Presidential succession	1965	1 year, 6.5 months
26 Eighteen year old's suffrage	1971	4 months

While the Constitutional Convention aimed at ensuring extensive legislative powers for Congress, it also sought to preserve for the states those powers not delegated to the national government. But during the ratification period Anti-Federalists charged that Congress was given too much power, especially with "the sweeping" necessary and proper clause. As the Centinel cautioned in the fall of 1787, "Whatever law congress may deem necessary and proper for carrying into execution any of the powers vested in them, may be enacted; and by virtue of this clause, they may controul and abrogate any and every of the laws of the state governments, on the allegation that they interfere with the execution of their powers."[3] Likewise, when opposing New York's ratification of the Constitution, leading Anti-Federalist Brutus warned that under the necessary and proper clause Congress "may so exercise this power as entirely to annihilate all the state governments, and reduce this country to one single government."[4]

Because of the Anti-Federalists' opposition and dire predictions, the first Congress added the Tenth Amendment. It underscores that "powers not delegated to the United States by the Constitution . . . are reserved to the States respectively, or to the people." However, the Tenth Amendment by no means resolved the essential tension between congressional and state powers (see Chapter 7).

Constitutional controversies continue to arise from the debate initially sparked by the Federalists and Anti-Federalists over the scope of Congress's legislative powers and competing claims of "states' rights" and federalism. In this chapter the development of Congress's expansive legislative powers is examined, and in Chapter 7 their limitations and the scope of states's regulatory powers over commerce is considered.

NOTES

1. A. Hamilton, in *Records of the Federal Convention*, Vol. 3, ed. Max Farrand (New Haven, CT: Yale University Press, 1911), 617, 627.
2. *American Insurance Co. v. Canter*, 26 U.S. (1 Pet.) 516 (1828).
3. The Centinel, in *The Complete Anti-Federalist*, Vol. 2, ed. Herbert J. Storing, (Chicago: University of Chicago Press, 1981), 168–169.
4. Brutus, in *The Complete Anti-Federalist*, Vol. 2, ed. Herbert J. Storing (Chicago: University of Chicago Press, 1981), 366.

SELECTED BIBLIOGRAPHY

Benson, Paul. *The Supreme Court and the Commerce Clause, 1937–1970.* New York: Dunnellen, 1971.
Frankfurter, Felix. *The Commerce Clause under Marshall, Taney and Waite.* Chapel Hill: University of North Carolina Press, 1971.
Gunther, Gerald, ed. *John Marshall's Defense of McCulloch v. Maryland.* Stanford, CA: Stanford University Press, 1969.

A. THE CLASSIC VIEW OF CONGRESS'S LEGISLATIVE POWERS

The scope of Congress's legislative powers, and, indeed, the power of the national government, became the focus of an enduring struggle almost immediately after ratification of the Constitution. In December 1790, Secretary of the Treasury Alexander Hamilton proposed that Congress charter a national bank. The ensuing debate over its constitutionality pitted Hamilton and the Federalists against Madison and Jefferson over not just the allocation of governmental power but fundamental principles of constitutional interpretation and politics.

Hamilton contended that a national bank was needed and would strengthen the national government by aiding in tax collection, administering public finances, and in securing loans to the government. And he persuasively argued that Congress had the broad constitutional authority to establish such a corporation:

Now it appears to the Secretary of the Treasury, that this *general principle is inherent in the very definition of Government* and *essential* to every step of the progress to be made by that of the United States; namely— that every power vested in a Government is in its nature *sovereign,* and includes by *force* of the *term,* a right to employ all the *means* requisite, and fairly *applicable* to the attainment of the *ends* of such power; and which are not precluded by restrictions & exceptions specified in the constitution; or not immoral, or not contrary to the essential ends of political activity. . . .

It is not denied, that there are *implied,* as well as *express* powers, and that the former are as effectually delegated as the latter. . . .

Then it follows, that as a power of erecting a corporation may as well be *implied* as any other thing; it may as well be employed as an *instrument* or *mean* of carrying into execution any of the specified powers, as any other instrument or mean whatever. The only question must be, in this as in every other case, whether the mean to be employed, or in this instance the corporation to be erected, has a natural relation to any of the acknowledged objects or lawful ends of the government. Thus a corporation may not be erected by congress, for superintending the police of the city of Philadelphia because they are not authorized to *regulate* the *police* of that city; but one may be erected in relation to the collection of taxes, or to the trade with foreign countries, or the trade between the States, or with the Indian Tribes, because it is the province of the federal government to regulate those objects & because it is incident to a general *sovereign* or *legislative power* to *regulate* a thing, to employ all the means which relate to its regulation to the *best & greatest advantage.* . . .

[T]he doctrine which is contended for . . . does not affirm that the National government is sovereign in all respects, but that it is sovereign to a certain extent: that is, to the extent of the objects of its specified powers.

It leaves therefore a criterion of what is constitutional, and of what is not so. This criterion is the *end* to which the measure relates as a *mean.* If the end be clearly comprehended within any of the specified powers, & if the measure have an obvious relation to that end, and is not forbidden by any particular provision of the constitution—it may be safely deemed to come within the compass of the national authority.[1]

The Senate, half of whose members had been delegates to the Constitutional Convention, unanimously endorsed Hamilton's proposal.

By contrast, in the House of Representatives, Madison maintained that creation of the bank was beyond the scope of Congress's delegated powers:

Mark the reasoning on which the validity of the bill depends. To borrow money is made the end, and the accumulation of capitals implied as the means. The accumulation of money is then the end, and the Bank implied as the means. The Bank is then the end, and a charter of incorporation . . . implied as the means.

If implications, thus remote and thus multiplied, can be linked together, a chain may be formed that will reach every object of legislation, every object within the whole compass of political economy. . . .

[T]he proposed Bank could not be called necessary to the Government; at most could be but convenient. Its uses to the Government could be supplied by keeping the taxes a little in advance; by loans from individuals; by other Banks, over which the Government would have equal command; nay greater, as it might grant or refuse to these the privilege (a free and irrevocable gift to the proposed Bank) of using their notes in the Federal Revenue.[2]

Jefferson, serving as Secretary of State, expressed similar opposition. In a memorandum to President Washington, he explained:

I consider the foundation of the Constitution as laid on this ground: That "all powers not delegated to the United States, by the Constitution, nor prohibited by it to the States, are reserved to the States or to the people." To take a single step beyond the boundaries thus specially drawn around the powers of Congress is to take possession of a boundless field of power, no longer susceptible of any definition.

The incorporation of a bank, and the powers assumed by this bill, have not, in my opinion, been delegated to the United States by the Constitution. . . .

It has been urged that a bank will give great facility or convenience in the collection of taxes. Suppose this were true; yet the Constitution allows only the means which are *"necessary,"* not those which are merely "convenient" for effecting the enumerated powers. If such a latitude of construction be allowed to this phrase as to give any non-enumerated power, it will go to every one, for there is not one which ingenuity may not torture into a *convenience* in some instance *or other,* to *some one* of so long a list of enumerated powers. It would swallow up all the delegated powers, and reduce the whole to one power, as before observed. Therefore it was that the Constitution restrained them to the *necessary* means, that is to say, to those means without which the grant of power would be nugatory.[3]

Despite these arguments, by a vote of thirty-nine to twenty the House adopted a bill chartering the bank. On February 25, 1791, Washington signed the act incorporating, and granting a twenty-year charter to, the first Bank of the United States.

When the bank's charter expired in 1811, its renewal was defeated in Congress by just one vote. Jeffersonian-Republicans and private business and banking interests led the opposition.

Notably, though, President Madison and Jefferson now supported the bank and deemed its constitutionality settled. Four years later Congress established the second Bank of the United States with another twenty-year charter. This time, economic hardships brought about by the War of 1812 and the national government's reliance on state banks for loans, rather than the constitutionality of the bank, was the overriding consideration in Congress.

Opposition to a national bank, however, remained strong in the states and eventually led to the landmark decision in *McCulloch v. Maryland* (1819) (see page 453). Chief Justice Marshall, an ardent Federalist, upheld the constitutionality of the bank with a broad reading of congressional powers reminiscent of Hamilton's arguments decades earlier. In his classic formulation: "Let the end be legitimate, let it be within the scope of the constitution, and all means which are appropriate, which are plainly adapted to that end, which are not prohibited, but consistent with the letter and spirit of the constitution, are constitutional."

Although Madison and Jefferson agreed with *McCulloch*'s holding, they continued to bristle at the expansive interpretation of

Chief Justice John Marshall. *Supreme Court Historical Society.*

the power of Congress and the national government advanced by the Marshall Court. In Jefferson's words, "The judiciary of the United States is the subtle core of sappers and miners constantly working underground to undermine the foundations of our confederated fabric. They are construing our Constitution from a coordination of general [i.e., national] and special [i.e., state] government to a general and supreme one alone. This will lay all things at their feet."[4]

Opposition persisted and support for the bank gradually diminished by 1832, when Congress passed another bill extending the bank's charter. President Andrew Jackson vetoed the bill and again challenged the Marshall Court's interpretation of and authority over the Constitution, see "Jackson's Veto Message of 1832," (see page 60).

The Marshall Court nonetheless successfully established the basis for a broad interpretation of Congress's plenary power. Moreover, Marshall's analysis in *McCulloch* rests on the Constitution's structure or allocation of governmental authority, rather than primarily on its granting congressional authority to make all necessary and proper laws.[5] And that analysis was subsequently incorporated into the necessary and proper clause in justifying expansive legislation. In the *Legal Tender Cases*, 110 U.S. 421 (1884), for example, the national government's use of legal tender to repay private debts was upheld as a "necessary and proper" exercise of its power to create a national currency, based on its express authority to coin money.[6] Later, in *Katzenbach v. Morgan*, 384 U.S. 641 (1966), the Court again reaffirmed Congress's plenary power under the necessary and proper clause when upholding the Voting Rights Act of 1965, which forbids racial discrimination in voting.

Five years after *McCulloch*, Marshall further advanced his vision of national governmental power by broadly construing the commerce clause in *Gibbons v. Ogden* (1824) (see page 465). Congress itself did not even assert its authority over commerce among the states until the late nineteenth century. Yet *Gibbons* affirmed broad congressional authority in striking down state regulations for infringing on the power, even if unexercised, of Congress. Marshall did so by (1) defining "commerce" as all "intercourse" that (2) "affects more states than one," and holding that Congress's power over commerce is (3) complete and (4) does not stop at state boundaries.

Gibbons was immediately heralded for securing the freedom of interstate transportation. As a result, tax and other barriers erected among the states were eliminated, the basis for a national "common market" was laid, and economic growth in the country promoted. In addition, Marshall's definition of *commerce* as intercourse among the states would later serve as a basis for upholding federal regulation under the commerce clause over an expanding range of activities, including, for example, the sale of lottery tickets,[7] "white slave trade,"[8] oil pipes running across state lines,[9] and radio waves.[10]

Through a broad interpretation of the plenary powers of Congress in *McCulloch* and *Gibbons*, the Marshall Court advanced the interests of the national government over those of the states and buttressed its own power of judicial review.

NOTES

1. A. Hamilton, "Opinion on the Constitutionality of an Act to Establish a Bank," in *The Papers of Alexander Hamilton*, Vol. 8, ed. Harold C. Syrett (New York: Columbia University Press, 1961–1979), 97.

2. J. Madison, in *The Debates and Proceedings in the Congress of the United States*, Vol. 2 (Washington, DC: Gales and Seaton, 1834), 1944–1954.

3. T. Jefferson, "Opinion on the Constitutionality of the Bill for Establishing a National Bank," in *The Papers of Thomas Jefferson*, Vol. 19, ed. Julian Boyd (Princeton, NJ: Princeton University Press, 1974), 275.

4. Quoted and further discussed in Dumas Malone, *Jefferson The President* (Boston: Little, Brown, 1970), 146–153.

5. See Charles Black, *Structure and Relationship in Constitutional Law* (Baton Rouge: Louisiana State University, 1969).

6. The Court upheld as well the Interstate Commerce Act of 1887 as a necessary and proper exercise of congressional authority, *Interstate Commerce Commission v. Brimson*, 154 U.S. 447 (1894). For other decisions relying on the necessary and proper clause, see *Lichter v. United States*, 334 U.S. 743 (1948); *Adams v. Maryland*, 347 U.S. 179 (1954); and *United States v. Oregon*, 366 U.S. 643 (1961).

7. *Champion v. Ames*, 188 U.S. 321 (1907).

8. *Caminetti v. United States*, 242 U.S. 470 (1917).

9. *The Pipe Line Cases*, 234 U.S. 548 (1914).

10. *Federal Radio Commission v. Nelson Brothers*, 289 U.S. 266 (1933).

SELECTED BIBLIOGRAPHY

Corwin, Edward S. *The Commerce Power Versus State Rights*. Princeton, NJ: Princeton University Press, 1936.

Frankfurter, Felix. *The Commerce Clause under Marshall, Taney and Waite*. Chapel Hill: University of North Carolina, 1937.

McCulloch v. Maryland
4 Wheat. (17 U.S.) 316 (1819)

Two years after Congress chartered the Second Bank of the United States, Maryland passed a law imposing an annual tax of $15,000 on all banks operating in the state that were not chartered by the state legislature. James McCulloch, the cashier for the Maryland branch of the Bank of the United States, refused to pay the tax assessed against the bank. As a result, Maryland successfully sued McCulloch, who then appealed to the Supreme Court.

Chief Justice MARSHALL delivers the opinion of the Court.

In the case now to be determined, the defendant, a sovereign state, denies the obligation of a law enacted by the legislature of the Union, and the plaintiff, on his part, contests the validity of an act which has been passed by the legislature of that state. The constitution of our country, in its most interesting and vital parts, is to be considered; the conflicting powers of the government of the Union and of its members, as marked in that constitution, are to be discussed; and an opinion given, which may essentially influence the great operations of the government. No tribunal can approach such a question without a deep sense of its importance, and of the awful responsibility involved in its decision. But it must be decided peacefully, or remain a source of hostile legislation, perhaps of hostility of a still more serious nature; and if it is to be so decided, by this tribunal alone can the decision be made. On the Supreme Court of the United States has the constitution of our country devolved this important duty.

The first question made in the cause is, has Congress power to incorporate a bank?

It has been truly said that this can scarcely be considered as an open question, entirely unprejudiced by the former proceedings of the nation respecting it. The principle now contested was introduced at a very early period of our history, has been recognized by many successive legislatures, and has been acted upon by the judicial department, in cases of peculiar delicacy, as a law of undoubted obligation.

It will not be denied that a bold and daring usurpation might be resisted, after an acquiescence still longer and more complete than this. But it is conceived that a doubtful question, one on which human reason may pause, and the human judgment be suspended, in the decision of which the great principles of liberty are not concerned, but the respective powers of those who are equally the representatives of the people, are to be adjusted; if not put at rest by the practice of the government, ought to receive a considerable impression from that practice. An exposition of the constitution, deliberately established by legislative acts, on the faith of which an immense property has been advanced, ought not to be lightly disregarded.

The power now contested was exercised by the first Congress elected under the present constitution. The bill for incorporating the bank of the United States did not steal upon an unsuspecting legislature, and pass unobserved. Its principle was completely understood, and was opposed with equal zeal and ability. After being resisted, first in the fair and open field of debate, and afterwards in the executive cabinet, with as much persevering talent as any measure has ever experienced, and being supported by arguments which convinced minds as pure and as intelligent as this country can boast, it became a law. The original act was permitted to expire; but a short experience of the embarrassments to which the refusal to revive it exposed the government, convinced those who were most prejudiced against the measure of its necessity and induced the passage of the present law. It would require no ordinary share of intrepidity to assert that a measure adopted under these circumstances was a bold and plain usurpation, to which the constitution gave no countenance.

These observations belong to the cause; but they are not made under the impression that, were the question entirely new, the law would be found irreconcilable with the constitution.

In discussing this question, the counsel for the state of Maryland have deemed it of some importance, in the construction of the constitution, to consider that instrument not as emanating from the people, but as the act of sovereign and independent states. The powers of the general government, it has been said, are delegated by the states, who alone are truly sovereign; and must be exercised in subordination to the states, who alone possess supreme dominion.

It would be difficult to sustain this proposition. The convention which framed the constitution was indeed elected by the state legislatures. But the instrument, when it came from their hands, was a mere proposal, without obligation, or pretensions to it. It was reported to the then existing Congress of the United States, with a request that it might "be submitted to a convention of delegates, chosen in each state by the people thereof, under the recommendation of its legislature, for their assent and ratification." This mode of proceeding was adopted; and by the convention, by Congress, and by the state legislatures, the instrument was submitted to the people. They acted upon it in the only manner in which they can act safely, effectively, and wisely, on such a subject, by assembling in convention. It is true, they assembled in their several states—and where else should they have assembled? No political dreamer was ever wild enough to think of breaking down the lines which separate the states, and of compounding the American people into one common mass. Of consequence, when they act, they act in their states. But the measures they adopt do not, on that account, cease to be the measures of the people themselves, or become the measures of the state governments.

From these conventions the constitution derives its whole authority. The government proceeds directly from the people; is "ordained and established" in the name of the people; and is declared to be ordained, "in order to form a more perfect union, establish justice, insure domestic tranquillity, and secure the blessings of liberty to themselves and to their posterity." The assent of the states, in their sovereign capacity, is implied in calling a convention, and thus submitting that instrument to the people. But the people were at perfect liberty to accept or reject it; and their act was final. It required not the affirmance, and could not be negatived, by the state governments. The constitution, when thus adopted, was of complete obligation, and bound the state sovereignties. . . .

The government of the Union, then (whatever may be the influence of this fact on the case), is, emphatically, and truly, a government of the people. In form and in substance it emanates from them. Its powers are granted by them, and are to be exercised directly on them, and for their benefit.

This government is acknowledged by all to be one of enumerated powers. The principle, that it can exercise only the powers granted to it, would seem too apparent to have required to be enforced by all those arguments which its enlightened friends, while it was depending before the people, found it necessary to urge, That principle is now universally admitted. But the question respecting the extent of the powers actually granted, is perpetually arising, and will probably continue to arise, as long as our system shall exist.

In discussing these questions, the conflicting powers of the general and state governments must be brought into view, and the supremacy of their respective laws, when they are in opposition, must be settled.

If any one proposition could command the universal assent of mankind, we might expect it would be this—that the government of the Union, though limited in its powers, is supreme within its sphere of action. This would seem to result necessarily from its nature. It is the government of all; its powers are delegated by all; it represents all, and acts for all. Though any one state may be willing to control its operations, no state is willing to allow others to control them. The nation, on those subjects on which it can act, must necessarily bind its component parts. But this question is not left to mere reason; the people have, in express terms, decided it by saying, "this constitution, and the laws of the United States, which shall be made in pursuance thereof," "shall be the supreme law of the land," and by requiring that the members of the state legislatures, and the officers of the executive and judicial departments of the states shall take the oath of fidelity to it. . . .

Among the enumerated powers, we do not find that of establishing a bank or creating a corporation. But there is no phrase in the instrument which, like the articles of confederation, excludes incidental or implied powers; and which requires that everything granted shall be expressly and minutely described. Even the 10th amendment, which was framed for the purpose of quieting the excessive jealousies which had been excited, omits the word "expressly," and declares only that the powers "not delegated to the United States, nor prohibited to the states, are reserved to the states or to the people"; thus leaving the question, whether the particular power which may become the subject of contest has been delegated to the one government, or prohibited to the other, to depend on a fair construction of the whole instrument. The men who drew and adopted this amendment had experienced the embarrassments resulting from the insertion of this word in the articles of confederation, and probably omitted it to avoid those embarrassments. A constitution, to contain an accurate detail of all the subdivisions of which its great powers will admit, and of all the means by which they may be carried into execution, would partake of a prolixity of a legal code, and could scarcely be embraced by the human mind. It would probably never be understood by the public. Its nature, therefore, requires, that only its great outline should be marked, its important objects designated, and the minor ingredients which compose those objects be deduced from the nature of the objects themselves. That this idea was entertained by the framers of the American constitution, is not only to be inferred from the nature of the instrument, but from the language. Why else were some of the limitations, found in the ninth section of the 1st article, introduced? It is also, in some degree warranted by their having omitted to use are restrictive term which might prevent its receiving a fair and just interpretation. In considering this question, then, we must never forget that it is a constitution we are expounding.

Although, among the enumerated powers of government, we do not find the word "bank" or "incorporation," we find the great power to lay and collect taxes; to borrow money; to regulate commerce; to declare and conduct war; and to raise and support armies and navies. The sword and the purse, all the enternal relations, and no inconsiderable portion of the industry of the nation, are entrusted to its government. It can never be pretended that these vast powers draw after them others of inferior importance, merely because they are inferior. Such an idea can never be advanced. But it may with great reason be contended, that a government, entrusted with such ample powers, on the do execution of which the happiness and prosperity of the nation so vitally depends, must also be entrusted with ample means for the execution. The power being given, it is the interest of the nation to facilitate its execution. It can never be their interest, as cannot be presumed to have been their intention, to clog and embarrass its execution in withholding the most appropriate means. Throughout this vast republic, from the St. Croix to the Gulf of Mexico, from the Atlantic to the Pacific, revenue is to be collected and expended, armies are to be marched and supported. The exigencies of the nation may require that the treasure raised in the north should be transported to the south, that raised in the east conveyed to the west, or that this order should be reversed. Is that construction of the constitution to be preferred which would render these operations difficult, hazardous, and expensive? Can we adopt that construction (unless the words imperiously require it) which would impute to the framers of that instrument, when granting these powers for the public good, the intention of impeding their exercise by withholding a choice of means? . . .

On what foundation does this argument rest? On this alone: The power of creating a corporation, is one appertaining to sovereignty, and is not expressly conferred on Congress. This is true. But all legislative powers appertain to sovereignty. The original power of giving the law on any subject whatever, is a sovereign power; and if the government of the Union is restrained from creating a corporation, as a means for performing its functions, on the single reason that the creation of a corporation is an act of sovereignty; if the sufficiency of this reason be acknowledged, there would be some difficulty in sustaining the authority of Congress to pass other laws for the accomplishment of the same objects. . . .

But the constitution of the United States has not left the right of Congress to employ the necessary means for the execution of the powers conferred on the government to general reasoning. To its enumeration of powers is added that of making "all laws which shall be necessary and proper, for carrying into execution the foregoing powers, and all other powers vested by this constitution, in the government of the United States, or in any department thereof."

The counsel for the State of Maryland have urged various arguments, to prove that this clause, though in terms a grant of power, is not so in effect; but is really restrictive of the general right, which might otherwise be implied, of selecting means for executing the enumerated powers. . . .

[T]he argument on which most reliance is placed, is drawn from the peculiar language of this clause. Congress is not empowered by it to make all laws, which may have relation to the powers conferred on the government; but such only as may be "necessary and proper" for carrying them into execution. The word "necessary" is considered as controlling the whole sentence, and as limiting the right to pass laws for the execution of the granted powers, to such as are indispensable, and without which the power would be nugatory. That it excludes the choice of means, and leaves to Congress, in each case, that only which is most direct and simple.

Is it true that this is the sense in which the word "necessary" is always used? Does it always import an absolute physical necessity, so strong that one thing, to which another may be termed necessary, cannot exist without that other? We think it does not. If reference be had to its use, in the common affairs of the world, or in approved authors, we find that it frequently imports no more than that one thing is convenient, or useful, or essential to another. To employ the means necessary to an end, is generally understood as employing any means calculated to produce the end, and not as being confined to those single means, without which the end would be entirely unattainable. Such is the character of human language, that no word conveys to the mind, in all situations, one single definite idea; and nothing is more common than to use words in a figurative sense. Almost all compositions contain words, which, taken in their rigorous sense, would convey a meaning different from that which is obviously intended. It is essential to just construction, that many words which import something excessive should be understood in a more mitigated sense—in that sense which common usage justifies. The word "necessary" is of this description. It has not a fixed character peculiar to itself. It admits of all degrees of comparison; and is often connected with other words, which increase or diminish the impression the mind receives of the urgency it imports. A thing may be necessary, very necessary, absolutely or indispensably necessary. To no mind would the same idea be conveyed by these several phrases. This comment on the word is well illustrated by the passage cited at the bar, from the 10th section of the 1st article of the constitution. It is, we think, impossible to compare the sentence which prohibits a state from laying "imposts or duties on imports or exports, except what may be absolutely necessary for executing its inspection laws," with that which authorizes Congress "to make all laws which shall be necessary and proper for carrying into execution" the powers of the general government, without feeling a conviction that the convention understood itself to change materially the meaning of the word "necessary," by prefixing the word "absolutely." This word, then, like others, is used in various senses; and, in its construction, the subject, the context, the intention of the person using them, are all to be taken into view.

Let this be done in the case under consideration. The subject is the execution of those great powers on which the welfare of a nation essentially depends. It must have been the intention of those who gave these powers, to insure, as far as human prudence could insure, their beneficial execution. This could not be done by confiding the choice of means to such narrow limits as not to leave it in the power of Congress to adopt any which might be appropriate, and which were conducive to the end. This provision is made in a constitution intended to endure for ages to come, and, consequently, to be adapted to the various crises of human affairs. To have prescribed the means by which government should, in all future time, execute its powers, would have been to change, entirely, the character of the instrument, and give it the properties of a legal code. It would have been an unwise attempt to provide, by immutable rules, for exigencies which, if foreseen at all, must have been seen dimly, and which can be best provided for as they occur. To have declared that the best means shall not be used, but those alone without which the power given would be nugatory, would have been to deprive the legislature of the capacity to avail itself of experience, to exercise its reason, and to accommodate its legislation to circumstances. If we apply this principle of construction to any of the powers of the government, we shall find it so pernicious in its operation that we shall be compelled to discard it. . . .

So, with respect to the whole penal code of the United States: whence arises the power to punish in cases not prescribed by the constitution? All admit that the government may, legitimately, punish any violation of its laws; and yet, this is not among the enumerated powers of Congress. The right to enforce the observance of law, by punishing its infraction, might be denied with more plausibility because it is expressly given in some cases. Congress is empowered "to provide for the punishment of counterfeiting the securities and current coin of the United States," and "to define and punish piracies and felonies committed on the high seas, and offenses against the law of nations." The several powers of Congress may exist, in a very imperfect state, to be sure, but they may exist and be carried into execution, although no punishment should be inflicted in cases where the right to punish is not expressly given.

Take, for example, the power "to establish post-offices and post-roads." This power is executed by the single act of making the establishment. But, from this has been inferred the power and duty of carrying the mail along the post-road, from one post-office to another. And, from this implied power, has again been inferred the right to punish those who steal letters from the post-office, or rob the mail. It may be said, with some plausibility, that the right to carry the mail, and to punish those who rob it, is not indispensably necessary to the establishment of a post-office and post-road. This right is indeed essential to the beneficial exercise of the power, but not indispensably necessary to its existence. So, of the punishment of the crimes of stealing or falsifying a record or process of a court of the United States, or of perjury in such court. To punish these offenses is certainly conducive to the due administration of justice. But courts may exist, and may decide the causes brought before them, though such crimes escape punishment.

The baneful influence of this narrow construction on all the operations of the government, and the absolute impracticability of maintaining it without rendering the government incompetent to its great objects, might be illustrated by numerous examples drawn from the constitution, and from our laws. . . .

In ascertaining the sense in which the word "necessary" is used in this clause of the constitution, we may derive some aid from that with which it is associated. Congress shall have power "to make all laws which shall be necessary and proper to carry into execution" the powers of the government. If the word "necessary" was used in that strict and rigorous sense for which the counsel for the state of Maryland contend, it would be an extraordinary departure from the usual course of the human mind, as exhibited in composition, to add a word, the only possible effect of which is to qualify that strict and rigorous meaning; to present to the mind the idea of some choice of means of legislation not straightened and compressed within the narrow limits for which gentlemen contend.

But the argument which most conclusively demonstrates the error of the construction contended for by the counsel for the state of Maryland, is founded on the intention of the convention, as manifested in the whole clause. To waste time and argument in proving that without it Congress might carry its powers into execution, would be not much less idle than to hold a lighted taper to the sun. As little can it be required to prove, that in the absence of this clause, Congress would have some choice of means. That it might employ those which, in its judgment, would most advantageously effect the object to be accomplished. That any means adapted to the end, any means which tended directly to the execution of the constitutional powers of the government, were in themselves constitutional. This clause, as construed by the state of Maryland, would abridge, and almost annihilate this useful and necessary right of the legislature to select its means. That this could not be intended, is, we should think, had it not been already controverted, too apparent for controversy. We think so for the following reasons:

1st. The clause is placed among the powers of Congress, not among the limitations on those powers.

2d. Its terms purport to enlarge, not to diminish the powers vested in the government. It purports to be an additional power, not a restriction on those already granted. No reason has been, or can be assigned for thus concealing an intention to narrow the discretion of the national legislature under words which purport to enlarge it. . . .

The result of the most careful and attentive consideration bestowed upon this clause is, that if it does not enlarge, it cannot be construed to restrain the powers of Congress, or to impair the right of the legislature to exercise its best judgment in the selection of measures to carry into execution the constitutional powers of the government. If no other motive for its insertion can be suggested, a sufficient one is found in the desire to remove all doubts respecting the right to legislate on that vast mass of incidental powers which must be involved in the constitution, if that instrument be not a splendid bauble.

We admit, as all must admit, that the powers of the government are limited, and that its limits are not to be transcended. But we think the sound construction of the constitution must allow to the national legislature that discretion, with respect to the means by which the powers it confers are to be carried into execution, which will enable that body to perform the high duties assigned to it, in the manner most beneficial to the people. Let the end be legitimate, let it be within the scope of the constitution, and all means which are appropriate, which are plainly adapted to that end, which are not prohibited, but consist with the letter and spirit of the constitution, are constitutional. . . .

If a corporation may be employed indiscriminately with other means to carry into execution the powers of the government, no particular reason can be assigned for excluding the use of a bank, if required for its fiscal operations. To use one, must be within the discretion of Congress, if it be an appropriate mode of executing the powers of government. That it is a convenient, a useful, and essential instrument in the prosecution of its fiscal operations, is not now a subject of controversy. All those who have been concerned in the administration of our finances, have concurred in representing the importance and necessity; and so strongly have they been felt, that statesmen of the first class, whose previous opinions against it had been confirmed by every circumstance which can fix the human judgment, have yielded those opinions to the exigencies of the nation. Under the confederation, Congress, justifying the measure by its necessity, transcended perhaps its powers to obtain the advantage of a bank; and our own legislation attests the universal conviction of the utility of this measure. The time has passed away when it can be necessary to enter into any discussion in order to prove the importance of this instrument, as a means to effect the legitimate objects of the government.

But, were its necessity less apparent, none can deny its being an appropriate measure; and if it is, the degree of its necessity, as has been very justly observed, is to be discussed in another place. Should Congress, in the execution of its powers, adopt measures which are prohibited by the constitution; or should Congress, under the pretext of executing its powers, pass laws for the accomplishment of objects not entrusted to the government, it would become the painful duty of this tribunal, should a case requiring such a decision come before it, to say that such an act was not the law of the land. But where the law is not prohibited, and is really calculated to effect any of the objects entrusted to the government, to undertake here to inquire into the degree of its necessity, would be to pass the line which circumscribes the judicial department, and to tread on legislative ground. This court disclaims all pretensions to such a power. . . .

It being the opinion of the court that the act incorporating the bank is constitutional, and that the power of establishing a branch in the state of Maryland might be properly exercised by the bank itself, we proceed to inquire:

2. Whether the state of Maryland may, without violating the constitution, tax that branch?

That the power of taxation is one of vital importance; that it is retained by the states; that it is not abridged by the grant of a similar power to the government of the Union; that it is to be concurrently exercised by the two governments: are truths which have never been denied. But, such is the paramount character of the constitution that its capacity to withdraw any subject from the action of even this power, is admitted. The states are expressly forbidden to lay any duties on imports or exports, except what may be absolutely necessary for executing their inspection laws. If the obligation of this prohibition must be conceded—if it may restrain a state from the exercise of its taxing power on imports and exports—the same paramount character would seem to restrain, as it certainly may restrain, a state from such other exercise of this power, as is in its nature incompatible with, and repugnant to, the constitutional laws of the Union. A law, absolutely repugnant to another, as entirely repeals that other as if express terms of repeal were used.

On this ground the counsel for the bank place its claim to be exempted from the power of a state to tax its operations. There is no express provision for the case, but the claim has been sustained on a principle which so entirely pervades the constitution, is so intermixed with the materials which compose it, so interwoven with its web, so blended with its texture, as to be incapable of being separated from it without rendering it into shreds.

This great principle is, that the constitution and the laws made in pursuance thereof are supreme; that they control the constitution and laws of the respective states, and cannot be controlled by them. From this, which may be almost termed an axiom, other propositions are deduced as corollaries, on the truth or error of which, and on their application to this case, the cause has been supposed to depend. These are, 1st. that a power to create implies a power to preserve. 2d. That a power to destroy, if wielded by a different hand, is hostile to, and incompatible with these powers to create and to preserve. 3d. That where this repugnancy exists, that authority which is supreme must control, not yield to that over which it is supreme. . . .

That the power of taxing it by the states may be exercised so as to destroy it, is too obvious to be denied. But taxation is said to be an absolute power, which acknowledges no other limits than those expressly prescribed in the constitution, and like sovereign power of every other description, is trusted to the discretion of those who use it. But the very terms of this argument admit that the sovereignty of the state, in the article of taxation itself, is subordinate to, and may be controlled by the constitution of the United States. How far it has been controlled by that instrument must be a question of construction. In making this construction, no principle not declared can be admissible, which would defeat the legitimate operations of a supreme government. It is of the very essence of supremacy to remove all obstacles to its action within its own sphere, and so to modify every power vested in subordinate governments as to exempt its own operations from their own influence. This effect need not be stated in terms. It is so involved in the declaration of supremacy, so necessarily implied in it, that the expression of it could not make it more certain. We must, therefore, keep it in view while construing the constitution.

The argument on the part of the state of Maryland is, not that the states may directly resist a law of Congress, but that they may exercise their acknowledged powers upon it, and that the constitution leaves them this right in the confidence that they will not abuse it.

Before we proceed to examine this argument, and to subject it to the test of the constitution, we must be permitted to bestow a few considerations on the nature and extent of this original right of taxation, which is acknowledged to remain with the states. It is admitted that the power of taxing the people and their property is essential to the very existence of government, and may be legitimately exercised on the objects to which it is applicable, to the utmost extent to which the government may choose to carry it. The only security against the abuse of this power is found in the structure of the government itself. In imposing a tax the legislature acts upon its constituents. This is in general a sufficient security against erroneous and oppressive taxation.

The people of a state, therefore, give to their government a right of taxing themselves and their property, and as the exigencies of government cannot be limited, they prescribe no limits to the exercise of this right, resting confidently on the interest of the legislator, and on the influence of the constituents over their representative, to guard them against its abuse. But the means employed by the government of the Union have no such security, nor is the right of a state to tax them sustained by the same theory. Those means are not given by the people of a particular state, not given by the constituents of the legislature, which claim the right to tax them, but by the people of all the states. They are given by all for the benefit of all—and upon theory, should be subjected to that government only which belongs to all. . . .

We find, then, on just theory, a total failure of this original right to tax the means employed by the government of the Union, for the execution of its powers. The right never existed, and the question whether it has been surrendered, cannot arise.

But, waiving this theory for the present, let us resume the inquiry, whether this power can be exercised by the respective states, consistently with a fair construction of the constitution.

That the power to tax involves the power to destroy; that the power to destroy may defeat and render useless the power to create; that there is a plain repugnance, in conferring on one government a power to control the constitutional measures of another, which other, with respect to those very measures, is declared to be supreme over that which exerts the control, are propositions not to be denied. But all inconsistencies are to be reconciled by the magic of the word confidence. Taxation, it is said, does not necessarily and unavoidably destroy. To carry it to the excess of destruction would be an abuse, to presume which, would banish that confidence which is essential to all government.

But is this a case of confidence? Would the people of any one state trust those of another with a power to control the most insignificant operations of their state government? We know they would not. Why, then, should we suppose that the people of any one state should be willing to trust those of another with a power to control the operations of a government to which they have confided the most important and most valuable interests? In the legislature of the Union alone, are all represented. The legislature of the Union alone, therefore, can be trusted by the people with the power of controlling measures which concern all, in the confidence that it will not be abused. This, then, is not a case of confidence, and we must consider it as it really is.

If we apply the principle for which the state of Maryland contends, to the constitution generally, we shall find it capable of changing totally the character of that instrument. We shall find it capable of arresting all the measures of the government, and of prostrating it at the foot of the states. The American people have declared their constitution, and the laws made in pursuance thereof, to be supreme; but this principle would transfer the supremacy, in fact, to the states. . . .

It has also been insisted, that, as the power of taxation in the general and state governments is acknowledged to be concurrent, every argument which would sustain the right of the general government to tax banks chartered by the states, will equally sustain the right of the states to tax banks chartered by the general government.

But the two cases are not on the same reason. The people of all the states have created the general government, and have conferred upon it the general power of taxation. The people of all the states, and the states themselves, are represented in Congress, and, by their representatives, exercise this power. When they tax the chartered institutions of the states, they tax their constituents; and these taxes must be uniform. But, when a state taxes the operations of the government of the United States, it acts upon institutions created, not by their own constituents, but by people over whom they claim no control. It acts upon the measures of a government created by others as well as themselves, for the benefit of others in common with themselves. The difference is that which always exists, and always must exist, between the action of the whole on a part, and the action of a part on the whole—between the laws of a government declared to be supreme, and those of a government which, when in opposition to those laws, is not supreme.

But if the full application of this argument could be admitted, it might bring into question the right of Congress to tax the state banks, and could not prove the right of the states to tax the Bank of the United States. . . .

We are unanimously of opinion that the law passed by the legislature of Maryland, imposing a tax on the Bank of the United States, is unconstitutional and void.

Gibbons v. Ogden
9 Wheat. (22 U.S.) 1 (1824)

Robert Livingston and Robert Fulton were granted by the New York legislature a monopoly on the operation of steamboats in the state's waters. They in turn licensed Aaron Ogden to exclusively operate a ferry between New York City and various ports in New Jersey. Subsequently, on the basis of his license, Ogden sought in New York courts an injunction against Gibbons, who ran a competing ferry between New York City and Elizabethtown Point, New Jersey. Gibbons countered that his boats were licensed under an 1793 act of Congress for vessels "employed in the coasting trade and fishiers." But when enjoining Gibbons from operating his ferries, the New York courts upheld Ogden's claims on the grounds that the 1793 act covered only coasting vessels and Congress had not passed legislation specifically regulating steamboats. Gibbons then appealed to the Supreme Court, which held that the monopoly granted by New York interfered with Congress's power to regulate interstate commerce.

Chief Justice MARSHALL delivers the opinion of the Court.

The appellant contends that this decree is erroneous, because the laws which purport to give the exclusive privilege it sustains, are repugnant to . . . that clause in the constitution which authorizes Congress to regulate commerce. . . .

[The Constitution] contains an enumeration of powers expressly granted by the people to their government. It has been said that these powers ought to be construed strictly. But why ought they to be so construed? Is there one sentence in the constitution which gives countenance to this rule? In the last of the enumerated powers, that which grants, expressly, the means of carrying all others into execution, Congress is authorized "to make all laws which shall be necessary and proper" for the purpose. But this limitation on the means which may be used, is not extended to the powers which are conferred; nor is there one sentence in the constitution which has been pointed out by the gentlemen of the bar, or which we have been able to discern, that prescribes this rule. We do not, therefore, think ourselves justified in adopting it. What do gentlemen mean by a strict construction? If they contend only against that enlarged construction which would extend words beyond their natural and obvious import, we might question the application of the term, but should not controvert the principle. If they contend for that narrow construction which, in support of some theory not to be found in the constitution, would deny to the government those powers which the words of the grant, as usually understood, import, and which are consistent with the general views and objects of the instrument; for that narrow construction, which would cripple the government and render it unequal to the objects for which it is declared to be instituted, and to which the powers given, as fairly understood, render it competent; then we cannot perceive the propriety of this strict construction, nor adopt it as the rule by which the constitution is to be expounded. As men, whose intentions require no concealment, generally employ the words which most directly and aptly express the ideas they intend to convey, the enlightened patriots who framed our constitution, and the people who adopted it, must be understood to have employed words in their natural sense, and to have intended what they have said. . . . We know of no rule for construing the extent of such powers, other than is given by the language of the instrument which confers them, taken in connection with the purposes for which they were conferred.

The words are: "Congress shall have power to regulate commerce with foreign nations, and among the several states, and with the Indian tribes."

The subject to be regulated is commerce; and our constitution being, as was aptly said at the bar, one of enumeration, and not of definition, to ascertain the extent of the power it becomes necessary to settle the meaning of the word. The counsel for the appellee would limit it to traffic, to buying and selling, or the interchange of commodities, and do not admit that it comprehends navigation. This would restrict a general term, applicable to many objects, to one of its significations. Commerce, undoubtedly, is traffic, but it is something more; it is intercourse. It describes the commercial intercourse between nations, and parts of nations, in all its branches, and is regulated by prescribing rules for carrying on that intercourse. The mind can scarcely conceive a system for regulating commerce between nations, which shall exclude all laws concerning navigation, which shall be silent on the admission of the vessels of the one nation into the ports of the other, and be confined to prescribing rules for the conduct of individuals, in the actual employment of buying and selling, or of barter. . . .

All America understands, and has uniformly understood, the word "commerce" to comprehend navigation. It was so understood, and must have been so understood, when the constitution was framed. The power over commerce, including navigation, was one of the primary objects for which the people of America adopted their government, and must have been contemplated in forming it. The convention must have used the word in that sense; because all have understood it in that sense, and the attempt to restrict it comes too late. . . .

The word used in the constitution, then, comprehends, and has been always understood to comprehend, navigation within its meaning; and a power to regulate navigation is as expressly granted as if that term had been added to the word "commerce."

To what commerce does this power extend? The constitution informs us, to commerce "with foreign nations, and among the several states, and with the Indian tribes."

It has, we believe, been universally admitted that these words comprehend every species of commercial intercourse between the United States and foreign nations. No sort of trade can be carried on between this country and any other, to which this power does not extend. It has been truly said, that commerce, as the word is used in the constitution, is a unit, every part of which is indicated by the term.

If this be the admitted meaning of the word, in its application to foreign nations, it must carry the same meaning throughout the sentence, and remain a unit, unless there be some plain intelligible cause which alters it.

The subject to which the power is next applied, is to commerce "among the several states." The word "among" means intermingled with. A thing which is among others, is intermingled with them. Commerce among the states cannot stop at the external boundary line of each state, but may be introduced into the interior.

It is not intended to say that these words comprehend that commerce which is completely internal, which is carried on between man and man in a state, or between different parts of the same state, and which does not extend to or affect other states. Such a power would be inconvenient, and is certainly unnecessary.

Comprehensive as the word "among" is, it may very properly be restricted to that commerce which concerns more states than one. The phrase is not one which would probably have been selected to indicate the completely interior traffic of a state, because it is not an apt phrase for that purpose; and the enumeration of the particular classes of commerce to which the power was to be extended, would not have been made had the intention been to extend the power to every description. The enumeration presupposes something not enumerated; and that something, if we regard the language or the subject of the sentence, must be the exclusively internal commerce of a state. The genius and character of the whole government seem to be, that its action is to be applied to all the external concerns of the nation, and to those internal concerns which affect the states generally; but not to those which are completely within a particular state, which do not affect other states, and with which it is not necessary to interfere, for the purpose of executing some of the general powers of the government. The completely internal commerce of a state, then, may be considered as reserved for the state itself.

But, in regulating commerce with foreign nations, the power of Congress does not stop at the jurisdictional lines of the several states. It would be a very useless power if it could not pass those lines. The commerce of the United States with foreign nations, is that of the whole United States. Every district has a right to participate in it. The deep streams which penetrate our country in every direction, pass through the interior of almost every state in the Union, and furnish the means of exercising this right. If Congress has the power to regulate it, that power must be exercised whenever the subject exists. If it exists within the states, if a foreign voyage may commence or terminate at a port within a state, then the power of Congress may be exercised within a state.

This principle is, if possible, still more clear, when applied to commerce "among the several states." They either join each other, in which case they are separated by a mathematical line, or they are remote from each other, in which case other states lie between them. What is commerce "among" them; and how is it to be conducted? Can a trading expedition between two adjoining states commence and terminate outside of each? And if the trading intercourse be between two states remote from each other, must it not commence in one, terminate in the other, and probably pass through a third? Commerce among the states must, of necessity, be commerce with the states. In the regulation of trade with the Indian tribes, the action of the law, especially when the constitution was made, was chiefly within a state. The power of Congress, then, whatever it may be, must be exercised within the territorial jurisdiction of the several states. The sense of the nation, on this subject, is unequivocally manifested by the provisions made in the laws for transporting goods, by land, between Baltimore and Providence, between New York and Philadelphia, and between Philadelphia and Baltimore.

We are now arrived at the inquiry, What is this power?

It is the power to regulate; that is, to prescribe the rule by which commerce is to be governed. This power, like all others vested in Congress, is complete in itself, may be exercised to its utmost extent, and acknowledges no limitations, other than are prescribed in the constitution. These are expressed in plain terms, and do not affect the questions which arise in this case, or which have been discussed at the bar. If, as has always been understood, the sovereignty of Congress, though limited to specified objects, is plenary as to those objects, the power over commerce with foreign nations, and among the several States, is vested in Congress as absolutely as it would be in a single government, having in its constitution the same restrictions on the exercise of the power as are found in the constitution of the United States. The wisdom and the discretion of Congress, their identity with the people, and the influence which their constituents possess at election, are, in this, as in many other instances, as that, for example, of declaring war, the sole restraints on which they have relied, to secure them from its abuse. They are the restraints on which the people must often rely solely, in all representative governments.

The power of Congress, then, comprehends navigation within the limits of every state in the Union; so far as that navigation may be, in any manner, connected with "commerce with foreign nations, or among the several states, or with the Indian tribes." It may, of consequence, pass the jurisdictional line of New York, and act upon the very waters to which the prohibition now under consideration applies.

But it has been urged with great earnestness, that although the power of Congress to regulate commerce with foreign nations, and among the several states, be co-extensive with the subject itself, and have no other limits than are prescribed in the constitution, yet the states may severally exercise the same power within their respective jurisdictions. In support of this argument, it is said that they possessed it as an inseparable attribute of sovereignty, before the formation of the constitution, and still retain it, except so far as they have surrendered it by that instrument; that this principle results from the nature of the government, and is secured by the tenth amendment; that an affirmative grant of power is not exclusive, unless in its own nature it be such that the continued exercise of it by the former possessor is inconsistent with the grant, and that this is not of that description.

The appellant, conceding these postulates, except the last, contends that full power to regulate a particular subject, implies the whole power, and leaves no residuum; that a grant of the whole is incompatible with the existence of a right in another to any part of it. . . .

The grant of the power to lay and collect taxes is, like the power to regulate commerce, made in general terms, and has never been understood to interfere with the exercise of the same power by the states; and hence has been drawn an argument which has been applied to the question under consideration. But the two grants are not, it is conceived, similar in their terms or their nature. Although many of the powers formerly exercised by the states, are transferred to the government of the Union, yet the state governments remain, and constitute a most important part of our system. The power of taxation is indispensable to their existence, and is a power which, in its own nature, is capable of residing in, and being exercised by, different authorities at the same time. . . .

Congress is authorized to lay and collect taxes, etc., to pay the debts, and provide for the common defense and general welfare of the United States. This does not interfere with the power of the states to tax for the support of their own governments; nor is the exercise of that power by the states an exercise of any portion of the power that is granted to the United States. . . . There is no analogy, then, between the power of taxation and the power of regulating commerce. . . .

The sole question is, can a state regulate commerce with foreign nations and among the state, while Congress is regulating it? . . .

[I]nspection laws are said to be regulations of commerce, and are certainly recognized in the constitution, as being passed in the exercise of a power remaining with the states.

That inspection laws may have a remote and considerable influence on commerce, will not be denied; but that a power to regulate commerce is the source from which the right to pass them is derived, cannot be admitted. The objects of inspection laws is to improve the quality of articles produced by the labor of the country; to fit them for exportation; or, it may be, for domestic use. They act upon the subject before it becomes an article of foreign commerce, or of commerce among the states, and prepared it for that purpose. They form a portion of that immense mass of legislation which embraces everything within the territory of a state not surrendered to the general government; all which can be most advantageously exercised by the states themselves. Inspection laws, quarantine laws, health laws of every description, as well as laws for regulating the internal commerce of a state, and those which respect turnpike-roads, ferries, etc., are component parts of this mass.

No direct general power over these objects is granted to Congress; and, consequently, they remain subject to state legislation. If the legislative power of the Union can reach them, it must be for national purposes; it must be where the power is expressly given for a special purpose, or is clearly incidental to some power which is expressly given. It is obvious, that the government of the Union, in the exercise of its express powers, that, for example, of regulating commerce with foreign nations and among the states, may use means that may also be employed by a state, in the exercise of its acknowledged power; that, for example, of regulating commerce within the state. If Congress license vessels to sail from one port to another, in the same state, the act is supposed to be, necessarily, incidental to the power expressly granted to Congress, and implies no claim of a direct power to regulate the purely internal commerce of a state, or to act directly on its system of police. So, if a state, in passing laws on subjects acknowledged to be within its control, and with a view to those subjects, shall adopt a measure of the same character with one which Congress may adopt, it does not derive its authority from the particular power which has been granted, but from some other, which remains with the state, and may be executed by the same means. All experience shows that the same measures, or measures scarcely distinguishable from each other, may flow from distinct powers; but this does not prove that the powers themselves are identical. Although the means used in their execution may sometimes approach each other so nearly as to be confounded, there are other situations in which they are sufficiently distinct to establish their individuality.

In our complex system, presenting the rare and difficult scheme of one general government, whose action extends over the whole, but which possesses only certain enumerated powers, and of numerous state governments, which retain and exercise all powers not delegated to the Union, contests respecting power must arise. Were it even otherwise, the measures taken by the respective governments to execute their acknowledged powers, would often be of the same description, and might, sometimes, interfere. This, however, does not prove that the one is exercising, or has a right to exercise, the powers of the other. . . .

[The Act of 1793, licensing steamboats] demonstrates the opinion of Congress, that steamboats may be enrolled and licensed, in common with vessels using sails. They are, of course, entitled to the same privileges, and can no more be restrained from navigating waters, and entering ports which are free to such vessels, than if they were wafted on their voyage by the winds, instead of being propelled by the agency of fire. The one element may be as legitimately used as the other, for every commercial purpose authorized by the laws of the Union; and the act of a state inhibiting the use of either to any vessel having a license under the act of Congress, comes, we think, in direct collision with that act. . . .

Powerful and ingenious minds, taking, as postulates, that the powers expressly granted to the government of the Union are to be contracted, by construction, into the narrowest possible compass, and that the original powers of the States are retained, if any possible construction will retain them, may, by a course of well digested, but refined and metaphysical reasoning, founded on these premises, explain away the constitution of our country, and leave it a magnificent structure indeed, to look at, but totally unfit for use. They may so entangle and perplex the understanding, as to obscure principles which were before thought quite plain, and induce doubts where, if the mind were to pursue its own course, none would be perceived. In such a case, it is peculiarly necessary to recur to safe and fundamental principles to sustain those principles, and, when sustained, to make them the tests of the arguments to be examined.

Justice JOHNSON concurring in part.

The judgment entered by the court in this cause has my entire approbation: but having adopted my conclusions on views of the subject materially different from those of my brethren, I feel it incumbent on me to exhibit those views. . . .

In attempts to construe the constitution, I have never found much benefit resulting from the inquiry, whether the whole, or any part of it, is to be construed strictly, or literally. The simple, classical, precise, yet comprehensive language in which it is couched, leaves, at most, but very little latitude for construction; and when its intent and meaning is discovered, nothing remains but to execute the will of those who made it, in the best manner to effect the purposes intended. The great and paramount purpose, was to unite this mass of wealth and power, for the protection of the humblest individual; his rights, civil and political, his interests and prosperity, are the sole end; the rest are nothing but the means. But the principal of those means, one so essential as to approach nearer the characteristics of an end, was the independence and harmony of the states, that they may the better subserve the purposes of cherishing and protecting the respective families of this great republic.

The strong sympathies, rather than the feeble government, which bound the states together during a common war, dissolved on the return of peace; and the very principles which gave rise to the war of the revolution, began to threaten the confederacy with anarchy and ruin. The states had resisted a tax imposed by the parent state, and now reluctantly submitted to, or altogether rejected, the moderate demands of the confederation. Everyone recollects the painful and threatening discussions which arose on the subject of the five per cent duty. Some states rejected it altogether; others insisted on collecting it themselves; scarcely any acquiesced without reservations, which deprived it altogether of the character of a national measure; and, at length, some repealed the laws by which they had signified their acquiescence.

For a century the states had submitted, with murmurs, to the commercial restrictions imposed by the parent state; and now, finding themselves in the unlimited possession of those powers over their own commerce, which they had so long been deprived of, and so earnestly coveted, that selfish principle which, well controlled, is so salutary, and which, unrestricted, is so unjust and tyrannical, guided by inexperience and jealousy, began to show itself in iniquitous laws and impolitic measures, from which grew up a conflict of commercial regulations, destructive to the harmony of the states, and fatal to their commercial interests abroad.

This was the immediate cause that led to the forming of a convention. . . .

The history of the times will, therefore, sustain the opinion that the grant of power over commerce, if intended to be commensurate with the evils existing, and the purpose of remedying those evils, could be only commensurate with the power of the states over the subject. And this opinion is supported by a very remarkable evidence of the general understanding of the whole American people when the grant was made.

There was not a state in the Union in which there did not, at that time, exist a variety of commercial regulations, concerning which it is too much to suppose that the whole ground covered by those regulations was immediately assumed by actual legislation, under the authority of the Union. But where was the existing statute on this subject, that a state attempted to execute? or by what state was it ever thought necessary to repeal those statutes? By common consent, those laws dropped lifeless from their statute-books, for want of the sustaining power, that had been relinquished to Congress. . . .

The "power to regulate commerce," here meant to be granted,

was that power to regulate commerce which previously existed in the states. But what was that power? The states were, unquestionably, supreme, and each possessed that power over commerce which is acknowledged to reside in every sovereign state. . . .

The power of a sovereign state over commerce, therefore, amounts to nothing more than a power to limit and restrain it at pleasure. And since the power to prescribe the limits to its freedom necessarily implies the power to determine what shall remain unrestrained, it follows that the power must be exclusive; it can reside but in one potentate; and hence, the grant of this power carries with it the whole subject, leaving nothing for the state to act upon. . . .

It is impossible, with the views which I entertained of the principle on which the commercial privileges of the people of the United States, among themselves, rests, to concur in the view which this court takes of the effect of the coasting license in this cause. I do not regard it as the foundation of the right set up in behalf of the appellant. If there was any one object riding over every other in the adoption of the constitution, it was to keep the commercial intercourse among the states free from all invidious and partial restraints. And I cannot overcome the conviction, that if the licensing act was repealed to-morrow, the rights of the appellant to a reversal of the decision complained of, would be as strong as it is under this license. One-half the doubts in life arise from the defects of language, and if this instrument had been called an exemption instead of a license, it would have given a better idea of its character. Licensing acts, in fact, in legislation, are universally restraining acts; as, for example, acts licensing, gaming houses, retailers of spirituous liquors, etc. The act, in this instance, is distinctly of that character, and forms part of an extensive system, the object of which is to encourage American shipping, and place them on an equal footing with the shipping of other nations. . . . I consider the license, therefore, as nothing more than what it purports to be, according to the 1st section of this act, conferring on the licensed vessel certain privileges in that trade, not conferred on other vessels; but the abstract right of commercial intercourse, stripped of those privileges, is common to all.

Yet there is one view in which the license may be allowed considerable influence in sustaining the decision of this court.

It has been contended that the grants of power to the United States over any subject, do not, necessarily, paralyze the arm of the states, or deprive them of the capacity to act on the same subject. That this can be the effect only of prohibitory provisions in their own constitutions, or in that of the general government. The vis vitae of power is still existing in the states, if not extinguished by the constitution of the United States. That, although as to all those grants of power which may be called aboriginal, with relation to the government, brought into existence by the constitution, they, of course, are out of the reach of state power; yet, as to all concessions of powers which previously existed in the states, it was otherwise. The practice of our government certainly has been, on many subjects, to occupy so much only of the field opened to them as they think the public interests require. . . . But the license furnishes a full answer to this objection; for, although one grant of power over commerce should not be deemed a total relinquishment of power over the subject, but amounting only to a power to assume, still the power of the states must be at an end, so far as the United States have, by their legislative act, taken the subject under their immediate superintendence. So far as relates to the commerce coastwise, the act under which this license is granted contains a full expression of Congress on this subject. Vessels, from five tons upwards, carrying on the coasting trade, are made the subjects of regulation by that act. And this license proves that this vessel has complied with that act, and been regularly ingrafted into one class of the commercial marine of the country. . . .

It would be in vain to deny the possibility of a clashing and collision between the measures of the two governments. The line cannot be drawn with sufficient distinctness between the municipal powers of the one and the commercial powers of the other. In some points they meet and blend so as scarcely to admit of separation. Hitherto the only remedy has been applied which the case admits of—that of a frank and candid co-operation for the general good. Witness the laws of Congress requiring its officers to respect the inspection laws of the states, and to aid in enforcing their health laws; that which surrenders to the states the superintendence of pilotage, and the many laws passed to permit a tonnage duty to be levied for the use of their ports. Other instances could be cited, abundantly to prove that collision must be sought to be produced; and when it does arise, the question must be decided how far the powers of Congress are adequate to put it down. Wherever the powers of the respective governments are frankly exercised, with a distinct view to the ends of such powers, they may act upon the same object, or use the same means, and yet the powers be kept perfectly distinct. A resort to the same means, therefore, is no argument to prove the identity of their respective powers.

B. FROM LEGAL FORMALISM TO THE NEW DEAL CRISIS

Chief Justice Marshall's unitary conception of commerce and standard for determining Congress's power over commerce— whether commerce "extend[s] to or affect[s] other States"—was nationalist. Indeed, following *Gibbons* he struck down a Maryland law requiring importers to pay a license fee on the grounds that states could not tax items imported through foreign commerce so long as they remained in their "original package."[1]

Gibbons also implied, however, a distinction between Congress's power over *interstate* commerce and that of the states over *intrastate* commerce. Although holding that Congress's power over commerce "among the several states" is complete and "cannot stop at the external boundary line of each State, but may be introduced into the interior," Chief Justice Marshall also observed, "It is not intended to say that these words comprehend that commerce which is completely internal, which is carried on between man and man in a State, or between different parts of the same State, and which does not extend to or affect other States. Such a power would be inconvenient, and is certainly unnecessary." And he added, "Comprehensive as the word 'among' is, it may very properly be restricted to that commerce which concerns more States than one." Hence, "the completely internal commerce of a State," Marshall noted, "may be considered as reserved for the State itself."

From Marshall's *dicta* in *Gibbons* the Court under Chief Justice Roger Taney, who was more sympathetic to claims of states' rights, developed the interstate-intrastate distinction. In *The License Cases,* 5 How. (46 U.S.) 504 (1847), Taney suggested two separate, mutually exclusive commerce powers in noting the existence of "internal or domestic commerce, which belongs to the States, and over which congress can exercise no control." Two years later, Justice John McLean further elaborated this view: "All commercial action within the limits of a State, and which does not extend to any other State or foreign country, is exclusively under state regulation."[2]

With the introduction into constitutional law of the interstate-intrastate commerce distinction, the touchstone for determining the powers of Congress and the states became whether commerce crossed a state line. Not until after the Civil War, however, did Congress actually assert its power over commerce. And in the absence of congressional statutes the Court employed the interstate-intrastate distinction to uphold state regulations. In *Paul v. Virginia,* 8 Wall. (75 U.S.) 168 (1869), for instance, state regulation of interstate insurance companies was upheld on the grounds that "issuing a policy of insurance is not a transaction of commerce" and insurance contracts "are not articles of commerce."

By the late nineteenth century the interstate-intrastate distinction was applied in a formalistic way. This development reflected political changes in the country and in the Court. A new era in government regulation was inaugurated with the passage of the Interstate Commerce Act of 1887 and the Sherman Antitrust

Act of 1890. The Interstate Commerce Act created the first regulatory commission in the United States, the ICC, and authorized it to investigate and regulate the operation of interstate railroads. The Sherman Antitrust Act made it illegal for interstate businesses to form trusts, combinations, or monopolies and authorized the executive branch to prosecute business that formed monopolies and entered into conspiracies to restrain trade and fix prices. This expansion of congressional power responded to pressures brought by the Industrial Revolution and a successful national economy. It also registered a new conception of the role of the national government in promoting freedom that had evolved since the Reconstruction era. At the same time, industries, railroad companies, and corporations, opposing regulation by the national government, contended that only states could regulate their activities; yet, states could not regulate those businesses that operated in more than one state. Coincidentally, the Court's composition also changed with the addition of justices who had been corporate lawyers and sympathized with private business interests. In 1888, Melville Fuller, a successful commercial attorney, was appointed chief justice and joined on the bench conservative Justices Stephen Field and Samuel Miller. He was then followed by others opposed to social change and embracing laissez-faire capitalism, notably, Justices David Brewer (in 1890), Edward White (in 1894), and Rufus Peckham (in 1896).[3]

Between 1887 and 1937 the Court relied on the interstate-intrastate dichotomy in upholding state regulations and striking down congressional legislation as unauthorized under the commerce clause. In doing so the Court invented some additional rules for further defining the boundaries between state and federal power. One of the most important of these was that between the activities of *production,* or *manufacturing* (over which states enjoyed virtually exclusive authority), and those of *distribution,* or *commercial transportation* (which Congress might regulate). This *production/distribution* rule enabled the Court, on the one hand, to uphold state regulation or taxation of commercial interests that sought exemption by claiming their activities were subject only to congressional regulation and, on the other hand, strike down federal regulations and thereby limit the reach of congressional power over commerce.

For example, in *Kidd v. Pearson,* 128 U.S. 1 (1888), the Court upheld Iowa's ban on the manufacture of liquor as applied to a distillery in the state that exported its entire product to other states. In rejecting the distillery's claim that manufacturing a product sold exclusively out of state constituted interstate commerce, the Court observed, "No distinction is more popular to the common mind, or more clearly expressed in economic and political literature, than that between manufacturing and commerce. Manufacturing is transformation—the fashioning of raw materials into a change of form for use. The functions of commerce are different. The buying and selling and the transportation incident thereto constitute commerce."

United States v. E. C. Knight Company (1895) (see page 482) illustrates the Court's use of the production/distribution rule to defeat the congressional power under the commerce clause. In that case, over the forceful dissent of Justice Harlan, the Fuller Court ruled that the Sherman Antitrust regulation of monopolies did not apply to the country's largest sugar refining company because it viewed the company's production of sugar as a local activity distinctly separate from the industry's sugar distribution.

The Court later applied the production/distribution rule in defining the scope of congressional and state regulatory powers over mining;[4] fishing, farming, and oil production;[5] and hydroelectric power.[6] The most extreme use of the rule came in *Hammer v. Dagenhart* (1918) (see page 488), when a bare majority of the Court struck down the Federal Child Labor Act of 1916. A year earlier, in *Wilson v. New*, 243 U.S. 332 (1917), the justices divided five to four in upholding employment regulations for railroad workers. However, in *Hammer* the majority found that Congress impermissibly barred shipment in interstate commerce of goods produced in factories that employed children under fourteen or allowed children between the ages of fourteen and sixteen to work more than eight hours a day or more than six days a week. In his opinion for the majority, Justice Day narrowly read federal power over commerce to be limited to regulating the *means* of transportation. And he distinguished earlier cases upholding congressional regulation of lottery tickets, prostitution, and impure food[7] on the grounds that these goods are harmful per se, whereas goods produced by child labor are harmless. Justice Holmes, writing for the dissenters, rejected the majority's formalistic reasoning and blasted it for reading its own "moral conceptions" into constitutional law.

Hammer was extraordinary in challenging congressional authority and was eventually overruled in *United States v. Darby* (1941) (see page 504). Still, even when a majority of the Court could be mustered to uphold progressive legislation it relied on other formal rules and tests derived from the distinction between interstate and intrastate commerce. In particular, the Court rationalized federal regulation on an "effect on commerce" rule, that is, whether an activity within a state has an obvious effect or impact on interstate commerce so as to justify the exercise of federal power. But applying this rule required the Court to invent various tests for gauging the impact of local activities on interstate commerce.

One test used to implement the effects rule was whether local activities were in the *stream of commerce*. This was the basis for the Court's rejecting the claim of Chicago stockyard firms, made when challenging federal prosecutions for conspiring to restrain trade, that the purchase and sale of cattle in Chicago stockyards was not commerce among the states. As Justice Holmes observed in *Swift & Company v. United States,* 196 U.S. 375 (1905):

Commerce among the states is not a technical legal conception, but a practical one, drawn from the course of business. When cattle are sent for sale from a place in one State, with the expectation that they will end their transit, after purchase, in another, and when in effect they do so, with only the interruption necessary to find a purchaser at the stock yards, and when this is a typical, constantly recurring course, the current thus existing is a current of commerce among the States, and the purchase of the cattle is a part and incident of such commerce.

The stream of commerce test was subsequently employed in sustaining federal regulation of stockyards[8] and grain and cotton exchanges.[9]

Another test centered on whether intrastate commerce was so physically *intermingled* or *intertwined* with interstate commerce as to make it impractical to distinguish federal and state regulatory powers. In *Southern Railway Co. v. United States,* 222 U.S. 20 (1911), the Court upheld federal regulations applied to a company carrying on its interstate railroad three cars not equipped with safety couplers, as required under the Safety Appliance Act, even though these cars were used solely in intrastate transportation. In Justice Van Devanter's words, "This is so, not because Congress possesses any power to regulate intrastate commerce as such, but because its power to regulate interstate commerce is plenary and consequently may be exerted to secure the safety of the persons and property transported therein and of those who are employed in such transportation, no matter what may be the source of the dangers which threaten it."

The *Shreveport doctrine* was yet another test used to justify the exercise of federal power over intrastate commerce. *The Shreveport Rate Case,* 234 U.S. 342 (1914), affirmed an order of the ICC requiring Texas intrastate rates from Dallas and Houston to be equalized with the interstate rates for travel from Shreveport, Louisiana, to Texas. This was because the interstate rates set by the ICC for transportation from Shreveport to Texas were higher than those for intrastate travel set by the Texas Railroad Commission. And as a result Shreveport was economically disadvantaged in competing for trade in Texas. In sustaining federal power here, Justice Hughes explained, "Wherever the interstate and intrastate transactions of carriers are so related that the government of the one involves the control of the other, it is Congress, and not the State, that is entitled to prescribe the final and dominant rule, for otherwise Congress would be denied the exercise of its constitutional authority and the State, and not the Nation, would be supreme within the national field."

Finally, the Court employed a distinction between *direct* and *indirect* effects on commerce. Note that in *E. C. Knight*, Chief Justice Fuller held that the government cannot forbid the merger of sugar companies under the Sherman Antitrust Act based on the possibility that "trade or commerce might be indirectly affected." But as with the other tests, the problem remained how the categories of direct and indirect effects were to be defined in practice. And the Court's rigid definition of them when striking down important pieces of President Franklin D. Roosevelt's program for economic recovery during the Depression precipitated the crisis over the New Deal.

In *Schechter Poultry Corporation v. United States*, 295 U.S. 495 (1935) (see page 343), Chief Justice Hughes struck down the National Recovery Act as an unconstitutional delegation of power. In addition, he found that the Schechter Corporation in Brooklyn, New York, was neither engaged in interstate commerce nor part of the stream of commerce. Nor did Schechter's purchase and transportation of chickens from elsewhere in New York and Pennsylvania to its slaughterhouse, where they were sold to local retailers, have a direct effect on interstate commerce. Although Hughes did not try to further define direct and indirect effects, he observed that it was "clear in principle" and "a fundamental one, essential to the maintenance of our constitutional system. Otherwise," he added, "there would be virtually no limit to the federal power and for all practical purposes we should have a completely centralized government."

One year later in *Carter v. Carter Coal Company*, 298 U.S. 238 (1936), the Court split sharply over striking down another piece of New Deal legislation, the Bituminous Coal Conservation Act, under which codes for employment practices were established for the coal industry. This time Justice Sutherland, writing for the majority, endeavored to precisely demark the difference between direct and indirect effects on commerce:

The word "direct" implies that the activity or condition invoked or blamed shall operate proximately—not mediately, remotely, or collaterally—to produce the effect. It connotes the absence of an efficient intervening agency or condition. And the extent of the effect bears no logical relation to its character. The distinction between a direct and an indirect effect turns, not upon the magnitude of either the cause or the effect, but merely upon the manner in which the effect has been brought about. If the production by one man of a single ton of coal intended for interstate sale and shipment . . . affects interstate commerce indirectly, the effect does not become direct by multiplying the tonnage, or increasing the number of men employed, or adding to the expense or complexities of the business, or by all combined.

In applying the distinction here, Sutherland further observed:

Much stress is put upon the evils which come from the struggle between employers and employees over the matter of wages, working conditions, the right of collective bargaining, etc., and the resulting strikes, curtailment and irregularity of production and effect on prices; and it is insisted that interstate commerce is *greatly* affected thereby. But . . . the conclusive answer is that the evils are all local evils over which the federal government has no legislative control. The relation of employer and employee is a local relation. . . . And the controversies and evils, which it is the object of the act to regulate and minimize, are local controversies and evils affecting local work undertaken to accomplish that local result. Such effect as they may have upon commerce, however extensive it may be, is secondary and indirect. An increase in the greatness of the effect adds to it importance. It does not alter its character.

This rigid use of the direct and indirect effects test provoked a sharp dissent from Justice Cardozo who, along with Justices Brandeis and Stone, maintained that Congress's commerce power was "as broad as the need that evokes it."

The Court's striking down important New Deal legislation in *Schechter* and *Carter Coal Company* resulted in a major confrontation between it and the country. President Roosevelt, after winning a landslide reelection in 1936, was embittered by the invalidation of his programs. And he responded by proposing judicial reforms that would expand the size of the Court to fifteen. His "Court-packing plan" called for the appointment of a new member of the Court for every justice over seventy years of age. That would have enabled him to secure a majority on the Court sympathetic to his programs (see "President Roosevelt's Radio Broadcast, March 9, 1937," on page 63).

NOTES

1. *Brown v. Maryland*, 25 U.S. (12 Wheat.) 419 (1827).
2. *The Passenger Cases*, 7 How. 283 (1849).
3. For further discussion, see Benjamin R. Twiss, *Lawyers and the Constitution: How Laissez Faire Came to the Supreme Court* (1942); and William F. Swindler, *Court and Constitution in the 20th Century: The Old Legality, 1889–1932* (Indianapolis: Bobbs-Merrill, 1969).
4. *United Mine Workers v. Coronado Coal Company*, 259 U.S. 344 (1922).
5. *Champlin Refining Company v. Corporation Commission*, 286 U.S. 210 (1932).

6. *Utah Power and Light v. Pfost*, 286 U.S. 165 (1932).

7. See the discussion and cases cited in section A of this chapter.

8. *Stafford v. Wallace*, 258 U.S. 495 (1922).

9. *Chicago Board of Trade v. Olsen*, 262 U.S. 543 (1923); and *Allenberg Cotton Company, Inc. v. Pittman*, 419 U.S. 20 (1974).

SELECTED BIBLIOGRAPHY

Corwin, Edward S. *Liberty against Government*. Baton Rouge: Louisiana State University Press, 1948.

Horowitz, Morton. *The Transformation of American Law, 1780–1860*. Cambridge: Harvard University Press, 1977.

McCloskey, Robert. *American Conservativism: In the Age of Enterprise 1865–1910*. Cambridge: Harvard University Press, 1951.

United States v. E. C. Knight Company
156 U.S. 1, 15 S.Ct. 249 (1895)

The Sherman Antitrust Act of 1890 made it illegal for businesses to contract, combine, or conspire to create a trust or monopoly for the purpose of restraining free trade and monopolizing interstate or foreign commerce. The American Sugar Refining Company, which already controlled a majority of the sugar-refining companies in the United States, subsequently purchased stock in and arranged to control four other companies, including E. C. Knight. The American Sugar Refining Company would thereby control over 98 percent of the country's sugar-refining business. The Department of Justice sought a court order forbidding the stock sale and other arrangements made by E. C. Knight, the American Sugar Refining Company, and three other Philadelphia firms. It contended that the companies had conspired and entered into combinations in restraint of trade in violation of the Sherman Antitrust Act. But lower federal courts denied relief, holding that the companies were engaged in manufacturing, not interstate commerce, and hence not subject to the antitrust regulations. The government thereupon appealed to the Supreme Court.

Chief Justice FULLER delivers the opinion of the court.

By the purchase of the stock of the four Philadelphia refineries with shares of its own stock the American Sugar Refining Company acquired nearly complete control of the manufacture of refined sugar within the United States. The bill charged that the contracts under which these purchases were made constituted combinations in restraint of trade, and that in entering into them the defendants combined and conspired to restrain the trade and commerce in refined sugar among the several states and with foreign nations, contrary to the act of congress of July 2, 1890.

The relief sought was the cancellation of the agreements under which the stock was transferred, the redelivery of the stock to the parties respectively, and an injunction against the further performance of the agreements and further violations of the act. . . .

The fundamental question is whether, conceding that the existence of a monopoly in manufacture is established by the evidence, that monopoly can be directly suppressed under the act of congress in the mode attempted by this bill.

It cannot be denied that the power of a state to protect the lives, health, and property of its citizens, and to preserve good order and the public morals, "the power to govern men and things within the limits of its dominion," is a power originally and always belonging to the states, not surrendered by them to the general government, nor directly restrained by the constitution of the United States, and essentially exclusive. The relief of the citizens of each state from the burden of monopoly and the evils resulting from the restraint of trade among such citizens was left with the states to deal with, and this court has recognized their possession of that power even to the extent of holding that an employment or business carried on by private individuals, when it becomes a matter of such public interest and importance as to create a common charge or burden upon the citizen, in other words, when it becomes a practical monopoly, to which the citizen is compelled to resort, and by means of which a tribute can be exacted from the community,—is subject to regulation by state legislative power. On the other hand, the power of congress to regulate commerce among the several states is also exclusive. The constitution does not provide that interstate commerce shall be free, but, by the grant of this exclusive power to regulate it, it was left free, except as congress might impose restraints. Therefore it has been determined that the failure of congress to exercise this exclusive power in any case is an expression of its will that the subject shall be free from restrictions or impositions upon it by the several states, and if a law passed by a state in the exercise of its acknowledged powers comes into conflict with that will, the congress and the state cannot occupy the position of equal opposing sovereignties, because the constitution declares its supremacy, and that of the laws passed in pursuance thereof; and that which is not supreme must yield to that which is supreme. "Commerce undoubtedly is traffic," said Chief Justice MARSHALL, "but it is something more; it is intercourse. It describes the commercial intercourse between nations and parts of nations in all its branches, and is regulated by prescribing rules for carrying on that intercourse." That which belongs to commerce is within the jurisdiction of the United States, but that which does not belong to commerce is within the jurisdiction of the police power of the state. . . .

The argument is that the power to control the manufacture of refined sugar is a monopoly over a necessary of life, to the enjoyment of which by a large part of the population of the United States interstate commerce is indispensable, and that, therefore, the general government, in the exercise of the power to regulate commerce, may repress such monopoly directly, and set aside the instruments which have created it. But this argument cannot be confined to necessaries of life merely, and must include all articles of general consumption. Doubtless the power to control the manufacture of a given thing involves, in a certain sense, the control of its disposition, but this is a secondary, and not the primary, sense; and, although the exercise of that power may result in bringing the operation of commerce into play, it does not control it, and affects it only incidentally and indirectly. Commerce succeeds to manufacture, and is not a part of it. The power to regulate commerce is the power to prescribe the rule by which commerce shall be governed, and is a power independent of the power to suppress monopoly. But it may operate in repression of monopoly whenever that comes within the rules by which commerce is governed, or whenever the transaction is itself a monopoly of commerce.

It is vital that the independence of the commercial power and of the police power, and the delimitation between them, however sometimes perplexing, should always be recognized and observed, for, while the one furnishes the strongest bond of union, the other is essential to the preservation of the autonomy of the states as required by our dual form of government; and acknowledged evils, however grave and urgent they may appear to be, had better be borne, than the risk be run, in the effort to suppress them, of more serious consequences by resort to expedients of even doubtful constitutionality.

It will be perceived how far-reaching the proposition is that the power of dealing with a monopoly directly may be exercised by the general government whenever interstate or international commerce may be ultimately affected. The regulation of commerce applies to the subjects of commerce, and not to matters of internal police. Contracts to buy, sell, or exchange goods to be transported among the several states, the transportation and its instrumentalities, and articles bought, sold, or exchanged for the purposes of such transit among the states, or put in the way of transit, may be regulated; but this is because they form part of interstate trade or commerce. The fact that an article is manufactured for export to another state does not of itself make it an article of interstate commerce, and the intent of the manufacturer does not determine the time when the article or product passes from the control of the state and belongs to commerce. . . .

Contracts, combinations, or conspiracies to control domestic enterprise in manufacture, agriculture, mining, production in all its forms, or to raise or lower prices or wages, might unquestionably tend to restrain external as well as domestic trade, but the restraint would be an indirect result, however inevitable, and whatever its extent, and such result would not necessarily determine the object of the contract, combination, or conspiracy. . . .

Slight reflection will show that, if the national power extends to all contracts and combinations in manufacture, agriculture, mining, and other productive industries, whose ultimate result may affect external commerce, comparatively little of business corporations and affairs would be left for state control.

It was in the light of well-settled principles that the act of July 2, 1890, was framed. Congress did not attempt thereby to assert the power to deal with monopoly directly as such; or to limit and restrict the rights of corporations created by the states or the citizens of the states in the acquisition, control, or disposition of property; or to regulate or prescribe the price or prices at which such property or the products thereof should be sold; or to make criminal the acts of persons in the acquisition and control of property which the states of their residence or creation sanctioned or permitted. Aside from the provisions applicable where congress might exercise municipal power, what the law struck at was combinations, contracts, and conspiracies to monopolize trade and commerce among the several states or with foreign nations; but the contracts and acts of the defendants related exclusively to the acquisition of the Philadelphia refineries and the business of sugar refining in Pennsylvania, and bore no direct relation to commerce between the states or with foreign nations. The object was manifestly private gain in the manufacture of the commodity, but not through the control of interstate or foreign commerce. It is true that the bill alleged that the products of these refineries were sold and distributed among the several states, and that all the companies were engaged in trade or commerce with the several states and with foreign nations; but this was no more than to say that trade and commerce served manufacture to fulfill its function. Sugar was refined for sale, and sales were probably made at Philadelphia for consumption, and undoubtedly for resale by the first purchasers throughout Pennsylvania and other states, and refined sugar was also forwarded by the companies to other states for sale. Nevertheless it does not follow that an attempt to monopolize, or the actual monopoly of, the manufacture was an attempt, whether executory or consummated, to monopolize commerce, even though, in order to dispose of the product, the instrumentality of commerce was necessarily invoked. There was nothing in the proofs to indicate any intention to put a restraint upon trade or commerce, and the fact, as we have seen, that trade or commerce might be indirectly affected, was not enough to entitle complainants to a decree.

Justice HARLAN dissenting.

The court holds it to be vital in our system of government to recognize and give effect to both the commercial power of the nation and the police powers of the states, to the end that the Union be strengthened, and the autonomy of the states preserved. In this view I entirely concur. Undoubtedly, the preservation of the just authority of the states is an object of deep concern to every lover of his country. . . . But it is equally true that the preservation of the just authority of the general government is essential as well to the safety of the states as to the attainment of the important ends for which that government was ordained by the people of the United States; and the destruction of that authority would be fatal to the peace and well-being of the American people. . . .

It would seem to be indisputable that no combination of corporations or individuals can, of right, impose unlawful restraints upon interstate trade, whether upon transportation or upon such interstate intercourse and traffic as precede transportation, any more than it can, of right, impose unreasonable restraints upon the completely internal traffic of a state. The supposition cannot be indulged that this general proposition will be disputed. If it be true that a combination of corporations or individuals may, so far as the power of congress is concerned, subject interstate trade, in any of its stages, to unlawful restraints, the conclusion is inevitable that the constitution has failed to accomplish one primary object of the Union, which was to place commerce among the states under the control of the common government of all the people, and thereby relieve or protect it against burdens or restrictions imposed, by whatever authority, for the benefit of particular localities or special interests. . . .

The power of congress covers and protects the absolute freedom of such intercourse and trade among the states as may or must succeed manufacture and precede transportation from the place of purchase. This would seem to be conceded, for the court in the present case expressly declare that "contracts to buy, sell, or exchange goods to be transported among the several states, the transportation and its instrumentalities, and articles bought, sold, or exchanged for the purpose of such transit among the states, or put in the way of transit, may be regulated, but this is because they form part of interstate trade or commerce." Here is a direct

admission—one which the settled doctrines of this court justify—
that contracts to buy, and the purchasing of goods to be transported from one state to another, and transportation, with its
instrumentalities, are all parts of interstate trade or commerce.
Each part of such trade is then under the protection of
congress. . . .

In my judgment, the citizens of the several states composing
the Union are entitled of right to buy goods in the state where
they are manufactured, or in any other state, without being confronted by an illegal combination whose business extends throughout the whole country, which, by the law everywhere, is an enemy
to the public interests, and which prevents such buying, except
at prices arbitrarily fixed by it. I insist that the free course of
trade among the states cannot coexist with such combinations.
When I speak of trade I mean the buying and selling of articles
of every kind that are recognized articles of interstate commerce.
Whatever improperly obstructs the free course of interstate intercourse and trade, as involved in the buying and selling of articles
to be carried from one state to another, may be reached by congress
under its authority to regulate commerce among the states. The
exercise of that authority so as to make trade among the states
in all recognized articles of commerce absolutely free from unreasonable or illegal restrictions imposed by combinations is justified
by an express grant of power to congress, and would redound
to the welfare of the whole country. I am unable to perceive
that any such result would imperil the autonomy of the states,
especially as that result cannot be attained through the action
of any one state. . . .

To the general government has been committed the control
of commercial intercourse among the states, to the end that it
may be free at all times from any restraints except such as congress
may impose or permit for the benefit of the whole country. The
common government of all the people is the only one that can
adequately deal with a matter which directly and injuriously affects
the entire commerce of the country, which concerns equally all
the people of the Union, and which, it must be confessed, cannot
be adequately controlled by any one state. Its authority should
not be so weakened by construction that it cannot reach and
eradicate evils that, beyond all question, tend to defeat an object
which that government is entitled, by the constitution, to accomplish. "Powerful and ingenious minds," this court has said, "taking,
as postulates, that the powers expressly granted to the government
of the Union are to be contracted by construction into the narrowest possible compass, and that the original powers of the states
are retained, if any possible construction will retain them, may,
by a course of well-digested but refined and metaphysical reasoning, founded on these premises, explain away the constitution
of our country, and leave it, a magnificent structure, indeed, to

look at, but totally unfit for use. They may so entangle and perplex the understanding as to obscure principles which were before thought quite plain, and induce doubts where, if the mind were to pursue its own course, none would be perceived." *Gibbons v. Ogden,* 9 Wheat. 1 [1824].

Hammer v. Dagenhart
247 U.S. 251, 38 S.Ct. 529 (1918)

The Federal Child Labor Act of 1916 forbade the shipment in interstate commerce of goods produced in factories employing children under the age of fourteen or allowing children between ages fourteen and sixteen to work more than eight hours a day, at night, or for more than six days a week. Roland Dagenhart, the father of two minor sons who worked in a cotton mill in North Carolina, sought in federal district court an injunction against W. C. Hammer, a United States attorney, from enforcing the act. The district judge granted the injunction on the ground that the legislation was unconstitutional. The government, then, appealed to the Supreme Court, which granted review and by a five-to-four vote struck down the Federal Child Labor Act.

Justice DAY delivers the opinion of the Court.

[T]he power [to regulate commerce] is one way to control the means by which commerce is carried on, which is directly the contrary of the assumed right to forbid commerce from moving and thus destroying it as to particular commodities. But it is insisted that adjudged cases in this court establish the doctrine that the power to regulate given to Congress incidentally includes the authority to prohibit the movement of ordinary commodities and therefore that the subject is not open for discussion. The cases demonstrate the contrary. They rest upon the character of the particular subjects dealt with and the fact that the scope of governmental authority, state or national, possessed over them is such that the authority to prohibit is as to them but the exertion of the power to regulate.

The first of these cases is *Champion v. Ames,* 188 U.S. 321 [1903], the so-called Lottery Case, in which it was held that Congress might pass a law having the effect to keep the channels of commerce free from use in the transportation of tickets used in the promotion of lottery schemes. In *Hipolite Egg Co. v. United States,* 220 U. S. 45 [1911]. This court sustained the power of Congress to pass the Pure Food and Drug Act, which prohibited the introduction into the states by means of interstate commerce of impure foods and drugs. In *Hoke v. United States,* 227 U. S. 308 [1913], this court sustained the constitutionality of the so-called "White Slave Traffic Act," whereby the transportation of a woman in interstate commerce for the purpose of prostitution was forbidden. . . .

In each of these instances the use of interstate transportation was necessary to the accomplishment of harmful results. In other words, although the power over interstate transportation was to regulate, that could only be accomplished by prohibiting the use of the facilities of interstate commerce to effect the evil intended.

This element is wanting in the present case. The thing intended to be accomplished by this statute is the denial of the facilities of interstate commerce to those manufacturers in the states who employ children within the prohibited ages. The act in its effect does not regulate transportation among the states, but aims to standardize the ages at which children may be employed in mining and manufacturing within the states. The goods shipped are of themselves harmless. The act permits them to be freely shipped after thirty days from the time of their removal from the factory. When offered for shipment, and before transportation begins, the labor of their production is over, and the mere fact that they were intended for interstate commerce transportation does not make their production subject to federal control under the commerce power. . . . The making of goods and the mining of coal are not commerce, nor does the fact that these things are to be afterwards shipped, or used in interstate commerce, make their production a part thereof. . . .

Over interstate transportation, or its incidents, the regulatory power of Congress is ample, but the production of articles, intended for interstate commerce, is a matter of local regulation.

If it were otherwise, all manufacture intended for interstate shipment would be brought under federal control to the practical exclusion of the authority of the states, a result certainly not contemplated by the framers of the Constitution when they vested in Congress the authority to regulate commerce among the States. . . .

It is further contended that the authority of Congress may be exerted to control interstate commerce in the shipment of child-made goods because of the effect of the circulation of such goods in other states where the evil of this class of labor has been recognized by local legislation, and the right to thus employ child labor has been more rigorously restrained than in the state of production. In other words, that the unfair competition, thus engendered, may be controlled by closing the channels of interstate commerce to manufacturers in those states where the local laws do not meet what Congress deems to be the more just standard of other states.

There is no power vested in Congress to require the states to exercise their police power so as to prevent possible unfair competition. Many causes may co-operate to give one state, by reason of local laws or conditions, an economic advantage over others. The commerce clause was not intended to give to Congress a general authority to equalize such conditions. In some of the states laws have been passed fixing minimum wages for women, in others the local law regulates the hours of labor of women in various employments. Business done in such states may be at an economic disadvantage when compared with states which have no such regulations; surely, this fact does not give Congress the power to deny transportation in interstate commerce to those who carry on business where the hours of labor and the rate of compensation for women have not been fixed by a standard in use in other states and approved by Congress.

The grant of power to Congress over the subject of interstate commerce was to enable it to regulate such commerce, and not to give it authority to control the states in their exercise of the police power over local trade and manufacture.

The grant of authority over a purely federal matter was not intended to destroy the local power always existing and carefully reserved to the states in the Tenth Amendment to the Constitution. . . .

In interpreting the Constitution it must never be forgotten that the nation is made up of states to which are entrusted the powers of local government. And to them and to the people the powers not expressly delegated to the national government are reserved. . . . The power of the states to regulate their purely internal affairs by such laws as seem wise to the local authority is inherent and has never been surrendered to the general government. . . . To sustain this statute would not be in our judgment a recognition of the lawful exertion of congressional authority over interstate commerce, but would sanction an invasion by the federal power of the control of a matter purely local in its character, and over which no authority has been delegated to Congress in conferring the power to regulate commerce among the states. . . .

For these reasons we hold that this law exceeds the constitutional authority of Congress. It follows that the decree of the District Court must be Affirmed.

Justice HOLMES dissenting.

[I]f an act is within the powers specifically conferred upon Congress, it seems to me that it is not made any less constitutional because of the indirect effects that it may have, however obvious it may be that it will have those effects, and that we are not at liberty upon such grounds to hold it void.

The first step in my argument is to make plain what no one is likely to dispute—that the statute in question is within the power expressly given to Congress if considered only as to its immediate effects and that if invalid it is so only upon some collateral ground. The statute confines itself to prohibiting the carriage of certain goods in interstate or foreign commerce. Congress is given power to regulate such commerce in unqualified terms. It would not be argued today that the power to regulate does not include the power to prohibit. Regulation means the prohibition of something, and when interstate commerce is the matter to be regulated I cannot doubt that the regulation may prohibit any part of such commerce that Congress sees fit to forbid. At all events it is established by the Lottery Case and others that have followed it that a law is not beyond the regulative power of Congress merely because it prohibits certain transportation out and out. *Champion v. Ames*, 188 U. S. 321 [1903]. So I repeat that this statute in its immediate operation is clearly within the Congress's constitutional power.

The question then is narrowed to whether the exercise of its otherwise constitutional power by Congress can be pronounced unconstitutional because of its possible reaction upon the conduct of the States in a matter upon which I have admitted that they are free from direct control. I should have thought that that matter had been disposed of so fully as to leave no room for doubt. I should have thought that the most conspicuous decisions of this Court had made it clear that the power to regulate commerce and other constitutional powers could not be cut down or qualified by the fact that it might interfere with the carrying out of the domestic policy of any State.

The manufacture of oleomargarine is as much a matter of State regulation as the manufacture of cotton cloth. Congress levied a tax upon the compound when colored so as to resemble butter that was so great as obviously to prohibit the manufacture and sale. In a very elaborate discussion the present Chief Justice excluded any inquiry into the purpose of an act which apart from that purpose was within the power of Congress. . . . Fifty years ago a tax on state banks, the obvious purpose and actual effect of which was to drive them, or at least their circulation, out of existence, was sustained, although the result was one that Congress had no constitutional power to require. The Court made short work of the argument as to the purpose of the Act. "The Judicial cannot prescribe to the Legislative Departments of the Government limitations upon the exercise of its acknowledged powers." *Veazie Bank v. Fenno*, 8 Wall. [75 U.S.] 533 [1869]. . . .

The notion that prohibition is any less prohibition when applied to things now thought evil I do not understand. But if there is any matter upon which civilized countries have agreed—far more unanimously than they have with regard to intoxicants and some other matters over which this country is now emotionally aroused—it is the evil of premature and excessive child labor. I should have thought that if we were to introduce our own moral conceptions where in my opinion they do not belong, this was preeminently a case for upholding the exercise of all its powers by the United States.

But I had thought that the propriety of the exercise of a power admitted to exist in some cases was for the consideration of Congress alone and that this Court always had disavowed the right to intrude its judgment upon questions of policy or morals. It is not for this Court to pronounce when prohibition is necessary to regulation if it ever may be necessary—to say that it is permissible as against strong drink but not as against the product of ruined lives.

The Act does not meddle with anything belonging to the States. They may regulate their internal affairs and their domestic commerce as they like. But when they seek to send their products across the State line they are no longer within their rights. If there were no Constitution and no Congress their power to cross the line would depend upon their neighbors. Under the Constitution such commerce belongs not to the States but to Congress to regulate. It may carry out its views of public policy whatever indirect effect they may have upon the activities of the States. Instead of being encountered by a prohibitive tariff at her boundaries the State encounters the public policy of the United States which it is for Congress to express. The public policy of the United States is shaped with a view to the benefit of the nation as a whole. . . . The national welfare as understood by Congress may require a different attitude within its sphere from that of some self-seeking State. It seems to me entirely constitutional for Congress to enforce its understanding by all the means at its command.

Justice MCKENNA, Justice BRANDEIS, and Justice CLARKE concur in this opinion.

C. FROM THE NEW DEAL CRISIS TO THE ADMINISTRATIVE STATE

A ground swell of opposition to the Court was emerging in the country by February 5, 1937, when President Roosevelt sent his "Court-packing plan" to Congress. Besides *Schechter* and *Carter Coal*, the Court had struck down provisions of the National Industrial Recovery Act in *Panama Refining Co. v. Ryan*, 293 U.S. 388

(1935); a railroad retirement program in *Railroad Retirement Board v. Alton R.R. Co.*, 295 U.S. 330 (1935); and a scheme for farm subsides under the Agricultural Adjustment Act in *United States v. Butler*, 297 U.S. 1 (1936).[1] In addition, a New York minimum wage law for women was overturned by a five-to-four vote in *Morehead v. New York ex rel. Tipaldo*, 298 U.S. 587 (1936).[2] The only significant New Deal legislation sustained (five to four) was that dealing with eliminating the gold standard and devaluation of the dollar.[3] The constitutionality of crucial New Deal programs was thus in doubt and for the Court to still rule on, including the National Labor Relations Act (or Wagner Act), the Social Security Act, and the Public Utility Holding Company Act.

While the Senate Judiciary Committee considered FDR's proposal for expanding the Court in the spring of 1937, Senator Burton Wheeler, an opponent of the plan at the suggestion of Justice Brandeis, asked Chief Justice Hughes if he would send a letter to the committee indicating what the justices thought about their workload and whether more justices were needed. On March 21, Hughes responded with a skillfully crafted letter implying that all the justices opposed the plan. (Hughes in fact talked only with Van Devanter and Brandeis; Cardozo and Stone later strongly disapproved of his actions and would have refused to sign the letter.) Immediately, Wheeler proclaimed that the Court was "unanimous with reference to the letter of the Chief Justice" and used the letter to mobilize opposition.

More dramatically on March 29, the Court voted five to four to uphold Washington state's minimum wage law in *West Coast Hotel Company v. Parrish*, 300 U.S. 379 (1937) (see Vol. 2, Ch. 3). Then, two weeks later in *National Labor Relations Board v. Jones & Laughlin Steel Corporation* (1937) (see page 497) the justices in a five-to-four decision upheld a vital part of the New Deal program, the National Labor Relations Act. Both cases signified a "switch in time that saved nine," because the Court had been split five to four when striking down progressive state and federal legislation. Justices Sutherland, McReynolds, Butler, and Van Devanter—the "Four Horsemen"—voted together as a laissez-faire protectionist bloc, while Stone and Cardozo followed Brandeis in supporting progressive economic legislation. Hughes and Roberts were the swing votes, the latter, less-tractable justice casting the pivotal vote striking down FDR's programs. But Roberts was persuaded by Hughes in December to change his mind, and when these rulings came down they dealt a death blow to FDR's Court-packing plan.

Chief Justice Hughes's opinion in *Jones & Laughlin,* upholding the National Labor Relation Board's (NLRB) jurisdiction over any person engaging in unfair labor practices "affecting commerce," reaffirmed Congress's plenary power under the commerce clause, at once returning to the themes expounded in *Gibbons* and laying the basis for the contemporary exercise of congressional power. And underscoring the Court's renewed deference to Congress on the day *Jones & Laughlin* came down, the justices approved enforcement of the Wagner Act against a trailer manufacturer and a small clothing company.[4] Almost invariably since *Jones & Laughlin*,[5] the Court has approved extending the coverage of the act over a wide range of businesses and labor relations.[6]

Congress responded to the Court's changed position and passed the Fair Labor Standards Act of 1938, one of the last major pieces of New Deal legislation. The act makes it unlawful to ship in interstate commerce goods produced in violation of employment standards set by the law for all employees "engaged in commerce or in the production of goods for commerce." The justices unanimously upheld the act in *United States v. Darby Lumber Company* (1941) (see page 504) and expressly overruled its earlier decision in *Hammer v. Dagenhart.*

The following year in *Wickard v. Filburn* (1942) (see page 508), the Court again demonstrated that it would affirm extensive congressional power and in the process discarded the direct and indirect effects rule. In this case, marketing penalties under the Agricultural Adjustment Act of 1938 were upheld against a farmer who grew only twenty-three acres of wheat for consumption on his farm alone.

These rulings typify the modern Court's approach to congressional power under the commerce clause. Congressional regulation of navigable waters and hydroelectric power,[7] for example, and extensive enforcement of the Sherman Antitrust Act were thus sanctioned.[8] With few exceptions in the aftermath of the New Deal crisis the Court legitimated a steady expansion of the reach of congressional power (see Chapter 7).

One consequence of the Court's legitimizing expansive congressional control over commerce has been to enlarge Congress's power to make federal criminal law.[9] Under the commerce clause, for instance, Congress passed the Consumer Credit Protection Act of 1968, the Omnibus Crime Control and Safe Streets Act of 1968, and the Federal Travel Act of 1970, all of which impose criminal penalties for various activities bearing some connection to interstate transportation.[10] *Perez v. United States*, 402 U.S. 146 (1971), is indicative of how deferential the Court became after its 1937 turnaround. There Justice Douglas for the majority upheld Congress's prohibition of "loan sharking"—that is, organized crime's extraction of payments for loans—under the Consumer Credit Protection Act on the grounds that congressional hearings had established a connection between local loan sharks and interstate commerce. Only dissenting Justice Stewart protested that

> the Framers of the Constitution never intended that the National Government might define as a crime and prosecute such wholly local activity through the enactment of federal criminal laws. . . . [I]t is not enough to say that some loan sharking is a national problem, for all crime is a national problem. It is not enough to say that some loan sharking has interstate characteristics, for any crime may have an interstate setting.

Another significant use of Congress's commerce power was in passing civil rights legislation. On the authority of the commerce clause, Congress enacted the Civil Rights Act of 1964, banning racial discrimination in public accommodations and, in Title VII of the act, discrimination in employment, as well as created the Equal Employment Opportunity Commission. So too, Title VIII of the Civil Rights Act of 1968 prohibits discrimination on the basis of race, color, religion, or national origin in the sale or rental of housing. When constitutional challenges were initially made to the Civil Rights Act, the Court rebuffed them in *Heart of Atlanta Motel, Inc. v. United States* (1964) (see page 512) and *Katzenbach v. McClung* (1964) (see page 512).[11] See also *South Carolina v. Katzenbach,* (1966) upholding Congress's power to enact the Voting Rights Act of 1965 (see page 662).

NOTES

1. The Court also struck down the Farm Mortgage Act and the Municipal Bankruptcy Act in, respectively, *Louisville Joint Stock Land Bank v. Radford,* 295 U.S. 555 (1935); and *Ashton v. Cameron County District,* 298 U.S. 513 (1936).

2. By five-to-four votes, however, the Court sustained a New York laws on unemployment compensation and setting minimum prices for milk, in *Associated Industries v. Department of Labor,* 299 U.S. 587 (1936); and *Nebbia v. New York,* 291 U.S. 502 (1934). And in *Home Building & Loan Co. v. Blaisdell* (1934) (see Vol. 2, Ch. 3), a bare majority upheld the Minnesota Mortgage Moratorium law.

3. See *The Gold Clause Cases,* 294 U.S. 240 (1935). The Court also upheld federal legislation prohibiting the shipment in interstate commerce of convict-made goods into states that prohibited such goods. See *Whitfield v. Ohio,* 297 U.S. 431 (1936); and *Kentucky Whip and Collar Co. v. Illinois Central Railroad Co.,* 299 U.S. 334 (1937).

4. *National Labor Relations Board v. Freuhauf Trailer Co.,* 301 U.S. 49 (1937); and *National Labor Relations Board v. Friedman-Harry Marks Clothing Company,* 301 U.S. 58 (1937).

5. In *McCulloch v. Sociedad Nacional de Marineros de Honduras,* 372 U.S. 10 (1963), the Court denied the NLRB's jurisdiction over foreign seamen and, in *NLRB v. Catholic Bishop of Chicago,* 440 U.S. 490 (1979), over lay faculty in Catholic high schools.

6. See *Associated Press v. NLRB,* 301 U.S. 103 (1937); *Consolidated Edison Co. v. NLRB,* 305 U.S. 197 (1938); *Santa Cruz Fruit Packing Co. v. NLRB,* 303 U.S. 453 (1938); *NLRB v. Fainblatt,* 306 U.S. 601 (1939); *Polish Alliance v. Labor Board,* 322 U.S. 643 (1944); *Guss v. Utah Labor Board,* 353 U.S. 1 (1957); and *NLRB v. Reliance Fuel Oil Corporation,* 371 U.S. 224 (1963).

7. See *United States v. Appalachian Electric Power Co.,* 311 U.S. 377 (1940), upholding the Federal Water Power Act of 1920; *Arizona v. California,* 283 U.S. 423 (1931), upholding the Boulder Canyon Project Act of 1928; and *Tennessee Electric Power Company v. T.V.A.,* 306 U.S. 118 (1939), denying utility companies standing to challenge the constitutionality of the Tennessee Valley Authority.

8. See *United States v. South-Eastern Underwriters Association,* 322 U.S. 533 (1944), upholding application of antitrust laws to insurance companies; and *Goldfarb v. Virginia State Bar,* 421 U.S. 773 (1975), holding a bar association's imposition of minimum fees for legal services constituted price fixing. In *Flood v. Kuhn,* 407 U.S. 258 (1972), however, the Court upheld an exemption for organized baseball from the Sherman Act, when denying a challenge to the "reserve clause," under which a club that first signs a player obtains an exclusive right to his services.

9. Prior to 1937 the Court upheld congressional power to ban interstate transportation of stolen cars, in *Brooks v. United States,* 267 U.S. 432 (1925); and to enact the Federal Kidnapping Act, in *Gooch v. United States,* 297 U.S. 124 (1936).

10. While the Court has not seriously questioned the constitutionality of such legislation, it on occasion has reversed convictions under these statutes. *United States v. Bass,* 404 U.S. 336 (1971), for example, overturned a conviction under the Omnibus Crime Control and Safe Streets Act because there was no showing that firearms were used in interstate commerce, whereas, *Scarbough v. United States,* 431 U.S. 563 (1977), affirmed a conviction based on the government's showing that firearms had moved at least once in commerce.

11. In addition, in *Daniel v. Paul,* 395 U.S. 298 (1969), the Court upheld enforcement of provisions of the Civil Rights against a "private club" in Arkansas, which racially discriminated in selling its "memberships" for twenty-five cents on the grounds that the club served interstate travelers and served food that had moved in interstate commerce.

SELECTED BIBLIOGRAPHY

Baker, Leonard. *Back to Back: The Duel between FDR and the Supreme Court.* New York: Macmillan, 1967.

Pritchett, C. Herman. *The Roosevelt Court: A Study in Judicial Politics and Values.* New York: Macmillan, 1947.
White, Morton. *Social Thought in America: The Revolt against Formalism.* New York: Viking, 1949.

National Labor Relations Board v. Jones & Laughlin Steel Corporation

301 U.S. 1, 57 S.Ct. 615 (1937)

After the Court struck down the National Industrial Recovery Act in *Schechter Poultry Corporation v. United States,* 295 U.S. 495 (1935) (see page 343), Congress passed the National Labor Relations Act, or so-called Wagner Act. With that act Congress, again, sought to protect the right of workers to organize and to encourage collective bargaining, created the new NLRB and authorized it to prevent unfair labor practices on the rationale that they might lead to strikes that would affect the flow of commerce. An affiliate of the Amalgamated Association of Iron & Tin Workers of America charged before the NLRB that Jones & Laughlin, one of the largest steel producers in the country, discouraged employees from joining the union and fired ten employees for their union activities. Following a hearing, the NLRB ordered Jones & Laughlin to reinstate the ten employees. The corporation refused to do so, contending that the Wagner Act was unconstitutional because it governed labor relations, not commerce. The NLRB, as provided in the act, petitioned a federal court of appeals to enforce its order, but that court declined. Whereupon, the NLRB appealed to the Supreme Court. Although the Court had unanimously struck down the National Industrial Recovery Act two years earlier in *Schechter,* Chief Justice Hughes managed to mass a bare majority in this case for upholding Congress's power to enact the National Labor Relations Act.

Chief Justice HUGHES delivers the opinion of the Court.

In a proceeding under the National Labor Relations Act of 1935 the National Labor Relations Board found that the respondent, Jones & Laughlin Steel Corporation, had violated the act by engaging in unfair labor practices affecting commerce. . . . The unfair labor practices charged were that the corporation was discriminating against members of the union with regard to hire and tenure of employment, and was coercing and intimidating its employees in order to interfere with their self-organization. . . .

Jones & Laughlin . . . is engaged in the business of manufacturing iron and steel in plants situated in Pittsburgh and nearby Aliquippa, Pa. It manufactures and distributes a widely diversified line of steel and pig iron, being the fourth largest producer of steel in the United States. With its subsidiaries—nineteen in number—it is a completely integrated enterprise, owning and operating ore, coal and limestone properties, lake and river transportation facilities and terminal railroads located at its manufacturing plants. It owns or controls mines in Michigan and Minnesota. It operates four ore steamships on the Great Lakes, used in the transportation of ore to its factories. It owns coal mines in Pennsylvania. It operates towboats and steam barges used in carrying coal to its factories. It owns limestone properties in various places in Pennsylvania and West Virginia. It owns the Monongahela connecting railroad which connects the plants of the Pittsburgh works and forms an interconnection with the Pennsylvania, New York Central and Baltimore & Ohio Railroad systems. It owns the Aliquippa & Southern Railroad Company, which connects the Aliquippa works with the Pittsburgh & Lake Erie, part of the New York Central system. Much of its product is shipped to its warehouses in Chicago, Detroit, Cincinnati and Memphis,—to the last two places by means of its own barges and transportation equipment. In Long Island City, New York, and in New Orleans it operates structural steel fabricating shops in connection with the warehousing of semifinished materials sent from its works. Through one of its wholly-owned subsidiaries it owns, leases, and operates stores, warehouses, and yards for the distribution of equipment and supplies for drilling and operating oil and gas mills and for pipe lines, refineries and pumping stations. It has sales offices in twenty cities in the United States and a wholly-owned subsidiary which is devoted exclusively to distributing its product in Canada. Approximately 75 per cent of its product is shipped out of Pennsylvania.

Summarizing these operations, the Labor Board concluded that the works in Pittsburgh and Aliquippa "might be likened to the heart of a self-contained, highly integrated body. They draw in the raw materials from Michigan, Minnesota, West Virginia, Pennsylvania in part through arteries and by means controlled by the respondent; they transform the materials and then pump them out to all parts of the nation through the vast mechanism which the respondent has elaborated."

To carry on the activities of the entire steel industry, 33,000 men mine ore, 44,000 men mine coal, 4,000 men quarry limestone, 16,000 men manufacture coke, 343,000 men manufacture steel, and 83,000 men transport its product. Respondent has about

10,000 employees in its Aliquippa plant, which is located in a community of about 30,000 persons.

Respondent points to evidence that the Aliquippa plant, in which the discharged men were employed, contains complete facilities for the production of finished and semifinished iron and steel products from raw materials. . . . [T]he iron ore which is procured from mines in Minnesota and Michigan and transported to respondent's plant is stored in stock piles for future use, the amount of ore in storage varying with the season but usually being enough to maintain operations from nine to ten months. . . .

Practically all the factual evidence in the case . . . supports the findings of the Board that respondent discharged these men "because of their union activity and for the purpose of discouraging membership in the union." We turn to the questions of law which respondent urges in contesting the validity and application of the act.

First. The Scope of the Act.—The act is challenged in its entirety as an attempt to regulate all industry, thus invading the reserved powers of the States over their local concerns. It is asserted that the references in the act to interstate and foreign commerce are colorable at best; that the act is not a true regulation of such commerce or of matters which directly affect it, but on the contrary has the fundamental object of placing under the compulsory supervision of the federal government all industrial labor relations within the nation.

The critical words of [the Act] prescribing the limits of the Board's authority in dealing with the labor practices, are "affecting commerce." The act specifically defines . . . 'affecting commerce' [as] in commerce, or burdening or obstructing commerce or the free flow of commerce, or having led or tending to lead to a labor dispute burdening or obstructing commerce or the free flow of commerce."

This definition is one of exclusion as well as inclusion. The grant of authority to the Board does not purport to extend to the relationship between all industrial employees and employers. Its terms do not impose collective bargaining upon all industry regardless of effects upon interstate or foreign commerce. It purports to reach only what may be deemed to burden or obstruct that commerce and, thus qualified, it must be construed as contemplating the exercise of control within constitutional bounds. It is a familiar principle that acts which directly burden or obstruct interstate or foreign commerce, or its free flow, are within the reach of the congressional power. Acts having that effect are not rendered immune because they grow out of labor disputes. . . .

It is the effect upon commerce, not the source of the injury which is the criterion. Whether or not particular action does affect commerce in such a close and intimate fashion as to be subject to federal control, and hence to lie within the authority conferred upon the Board, is left by the statute to be determined as individual cases arise. We are thus to inquire whether in the instant case the constitutional boundary has been passed.

Second. The Unfair Labor Practices in Question. . . . . [I]n its present application, the statute goes no further than to safeguard the right of employees to self-organization and to select representatives of their own choosing for collective bargaining or other mutual protection without restraint or coercion by their employer.

That is a fundamental right. Employees have as clear a right to organize and select their representatives for lawful purposes as the respondent has to organize in business and select its own officers and agents. Discrimination and coercion to prevent the free exercise of the right of employees to self-organization and representation is a proper subject for condemnation by competent legislative authority. Long ago we stated the reason for labor organizations. We said that they were organized out of the necessities of the situation; that a single employee was helpless in dealing with an employer; that he was dependent ordinarily on his daily wage for the maintenance of himself and family; that, if the employer refused to pay him the wages that he thought fair, he was nevertheless unable to leave the employ and resist arbitrary and unfair treatment; that union was essential to give laborers opportunity to deal on an equality with their employer. . . .

Third. The Application of the Act to Employees Engaged in Production.—The Principle Involved. Respondent says that, whatever may be said of employees engaged in interstate commerce, the industrial relations and activities in the manufacturing department of respondent's enterprise are not subject to federal regulation. The argument rests upon the proposition that manufacturing in itself is not commerce. . . .

The government distinguishes these cases. The various parts of respondent's enterprise are described as interdependent and as thus involving "a great movement of iron ore, coal and limestone along well-defined paths to the steel mills, thence through them, and thence in the form of steel products into the consuming centers of the country—a definite and well-understood course of business." It is urged that these activities constitute a "stream" or "flow" of commerce, of which the Aliquippa manufacturing plant is the focal point, and that industrial strife at that point would cripple the entire movement. . . .

We do not find it necessary to determine whether these features of defendant's business dispose of the asserted analogy to the "stream of commerce" cases. The instances in which that metaphor has been used are but particular, and not exclusive, illustrations of the protective power which the government invokes in support of the present act. The congressional authority to protect interstate commerce from burdens and obstructions is not limited to transactions which can be deemed to be an essential part of a "flow" of interstate or foreign commerce. Burdens and obstructions may be due to injurious action springing from other sources. . . . Although activities may be intrastate in character when separately considered, if they have such a close and substantial relation to interstate commerce that their control is essential or appropriate to protect that commerce from burdens and obstructions, Congress cannot be denied the power to exercise that control. *Schechter Corporation v. United States.* Undoubtedly the scope of this power must be considered in the light of our dual system of government and may not be extended so as to embrace effects upon interstate commerce so indirect and remote that to embrace them, in view of our complex society, would effectually obliterate the distinction between what is national and what is local and create a completely centralized government. . . . The question is necessarily one of degree. . . .

That intrastate activities, by reason of close and intimate relation to interstate commerce, may fall within federal control is demonstrated in the case of carriers who are engaged in both interstate and intrastate transportation. There federal control has been found essential to secure the freedom of interstate traffic from interference or unjust discrimination and to promote the efficiency of the interstate service. *The Shreveport Case (Houston, E. & W. T. R. Co. v. United States)*, 234 U.S. 342 [1914]. . . .

The close and intimate effect which brings the subject within the reach of federal power may be due to activities in relation to productive industry although the industry when separately viewed is local. . . .

It is thus apparent that the fact that the employees here concerned were engaged in production is not determinative. The question remains as to the effect upon interstate commerce of the labor practice involved. In the *Schechter Case,* we found that the effect there was so remote as to be beyond the federal power. To find "immediacy or directness" there was to find it "almost everywhere," a result inconsistent with the maintenance of our federal system. In the *Carter Case [Carter v. Carter Coal Co.,* 298 U.S. 238 (1936)], the Court was of the opinion that the provisions of the statute relating to production were invalid upon several grounds,—that there was improper delegation of legislative power, and that the requirements not only went beyond any sustainable measure of protection of interstate commerce but were also inconsistent with due process. These cases are not controlling here.

Fourth. Effects of the Unfair Labor Practice in Respondent's Enterprise. Giving full weight to respondent's contention with respect to a break in the complete continuity of the "stream of commerce" by reason of respondent's manufacturing operations, the fact remains that the stoppage of those operations by industrial strife would have a most serious effect upon interstate commerce. In view of respondent's far-flung activities, it is idle to say that the effect would be indirect or remote. It is obvious that it would be immediate and might be catastrophic. We are asked to shut our eyes to the plainest facts of our national life and to deal with the question of direct and indirect effects in an intellectual vacuum. Because there may be but indirect and remote effects upon interstate commerce in connection with a host of local enterprises throughout the country, it does not follow that other industrial activities do not have such a close and intimate relation to interstate commerce as to make the presence of industrial strife a matter of the most urgent national concern. When industries organize themselves on a national scale, making their relation to interstate commerce the dominant factor in their activities, how can it be maintained that their industrial labor relations constitute a forbidden field into which Congress may not enter when it is necessary to protect interstate commerce from the paralyzing consequences of industrial war. We have often said that interstate commerce itself is a practical conception. It is equally true that interferences with that commerce must be appraised by a judgment that does not ignore actual experience.

Experience has abundantly demonstrated that the recognition of the right of employees to self-organization and to have representatives of their own choosing for the purpose of collective bargaining is often an essential condition of industrial peace. Refusal to confer and negotiate has been one of the most prolific causes of strife. This is such an outstanding fact is the history of labor disturbances that it is a proper subject of judicial notice and requires no citation of instances. . . .

The steel industry is one of the great basic industries of the United States, with ramifying activities affecting interstate commerce at every point. The Government aptly refers to the steel strike of 1919–1920 with its far-reaching consequences. The fact that there appears to have been no major disturbance in that industry in the more recent period did not dispose of the possibilities of future and like dangers to interstate commerce which Congress was entitled to foresee and to exercise its protective power to forestall. It is not necessary again to detail the facts as to respondent's enterprise. Instead of being beyond the pale, we think that it presents in a most striking way the close and intimate relation which a manufacturing industry may have to interstate commerce and we have no doubt that Congress had constitutional authority to safeguard the right of respondent's employees to self-organization and freedom in the choice of representatives for collective bargaining.

Justice MCREYNOLDS dissenting.

Justice VAN DEVANTER, Justice SUTHERLAND, Justice BUTLER and I are unable to agree with this decisions just announced. . . .

Considering the far-reaching import of these decisions, the departure from what we understand has been consistently ruled here, and the extraordinary power confirmed to a Board of three, the obligation to present our views becomes plain.

The Court as we think departs from well-established principles followed in *Schechter Poultry Corporation v. United States,* and *Carter v. Carter Coal Co.* . . .

It puts into the hands of a Board power of control over purely local industry beyond anything heretofore deemed permissible. . . .

We are told that Congress may protect the "stream of commerce" and that one who buys raw material without the state, manufactures it therein, and ships the output to another state is in that stream. Therefore it is said he may be prevented from doing anything which may interfere with its flow.

This, too, goes beyond the constitutional limitations heretofore enforced. If a man raises cattle and regularly delivers them to a carrier for interstate shipment, may Congress prescribe the conditions under which he may employ or discharge helpers on the ranch? The products of a mine pass daily into interstate commerce; many things are brought to it from other states. Are the owners and the miners within the power of Congress in respect of the latter's tenure and discharge? May a mill owner be prohibited from closing his factory or discontinuing his business because so to do would stop the flow of products to and from his plant in interstate commerce? . . .

If the ruling of the Court just announced is adhered to, these questions suggest some of the problems certain to arise. . . .

That Congress has power by appropriate means, not prohibited by the Constitution, to prevent direct and material interference with the conduct of interstate commerce is settled doctrine. But the interference struck at must be direct and material, not some mere possibility contingent on wholly uncertain events; and there must be no impairment of rights guaranteed. A state by taxation on property may indirectly but seriously affect the cost of transportation; it may not lay a direct tax upon the receipts from interstate transportation. The first is an indirect effect, the other direct. . . .

The things inhibited by the Labor Act relate to the management of a manufacturing plant—something distinct from commerce and subject to the authority of the state. And this may not be abridged because of some vague possibility of distant interference with commerce. . . .

It seems clear to us that Congress has transcended the powers granted.

United States v. Darby Lumber Company
312 U.S. 100, 61 S.Ct. 451 (1941)

Fred Darby, the owner of a Georgia lumber business, was indicted for violating provisions of the Fair Labor Standards Act of 1938. That act prohibits in interstate commerce the shipping and producing of goods for commerce by companies whose employees are paid less than the minimum wage (set, at the time, at twenty cents per hour by the act) or who work more than forty hours a week with overtime pay, and requires companies to keep records on their employees' wages and hours. In federal district court, a judge quashed the indictment on finding the act unconstitutional because, relying on *Hammer v. Dagenhart*, 247 U.S. 251 (1918) (see page 488) and other rulings of the Supreme Court, Congress had no authority to control the conditions of production and manufacturing under the commerce clause. The Department of Justice appealed that ruling to the Supreme Court, which after granting and hearing the case reversed the lower court and overturned *Hammer v. Dagenhart*.

Justice STONE delivers the opinion of the Court.

The Fair Labor Standards Act set up a comprehensive legislative scheme for preventing the shipment in interstate commerce of certain products and commodities produced in the United States under labor conditions as respects wages and hours which fail to conform to standards set up by the Act. Its purpose . . . is to exclude from interstate commerce goods produced for the commerce and to prevent their production for interstate commerce, under conditions detrimental to the maintenance of the minimum standards of living necessary for health and general well-being; and to prevent the use of interstate commerce as the means of competition in the distribution of goods so produced, and as the means of spreading and perpetuating such substandard labor conditions among the workers of the several states. . . .

[We] confine our decision to the validity and construction of the statute. . . .

While manufacture is not of itself interstate commerce the shipment of manufactured goods interstate is such commerce and the prohibition of such shipment by Congress is indubitably a regulation of the commerce. The power to regulate commerce is the power "to prescribe the rule by which commerce is to be governed." *Gibbons v. Ogden.* It extends not only to those regulations which aid, foster and protect the commerce, but embraces those which prohibit it. It is conceded that the power of Congress to prohibit transportation in interstate commerce includes noxious articles, stolen articles, kidnapped persons, and articles such as intoxicating liquor or convict made goods, traffic in which is forbidden or restricted by the laws of the state of destination. . . .

But it is said that the present prohibition falls within the scope of none of these categories; that while the prohibition is nominally a regulation of the commerce its motive or purpose is regulation of wages and hours of persons engaged in manufacture, the control of which has been reserved to the states and upon which Georgia and some of the states of destination have placed no restriction; that the effect of the present statute is not to exclude the prescribed articles from interstate commerce in aid of state regulation as in *Kentucky Whip & Collar Co. v. Illinois Central R. Co.,* [299 U.S. 334 (1937)] but instead, under the guise of a regulation of interstate commerce, it undertakes to regulate wages and hours within the state contrary to the policy of the state which has elected to leave them unregulated.

The power of Congress over interstate commerce "is complete in itself, may be exercised to its utmost extent, and acknowledges no limitations, other than are prescribed by the constitution." *Gibbons v. Ogden.* That power can neither be enlarged nor diminished by the exercise or non-exercise of state power. Congress, following its own conception of public policy concerning the restrictions which may appropriately be imposed on interstate commerce, is free to exclude from the commerce articles whose use in the states for which they are destined it may conceive to be injurious to the public health, morals or welfare, even though the state has not sought to regulate their use. . . .

Such regulation is not a forbidden invasion of state power merely because either its motive or its consequence is to restrict the use of articles of commerce within the states of destination and is not prohibited unless by other Constitutional provisions. It is no objection to the assertion of the power to regulate interstate commerce that its exercise is attended by the same incidents which attend the exercise of the police power of the states. . . .

The motive and purpose of the present regulation is plainly to make effective the Congressional conception of public policy that interstate commerce should not be made the instrument of competition in the distribution of goods produced under substandard labor conditions, which competition is injurious to the commerce and to the states from and to which the commerce flows.

The motive and purpose of a regulation of interstate commerce are matters for the legislative judgment upon the exercise of which the Constitution places no restriction and over which the courts are given no control. . . .

Whatever their motive and purpose, regulations of commerce which do not infringe some constitutional prohibition are within the plenary power conferred on Congress by the Commerce Clause. Subject only to that limitation, presently to be considered, we conclude that the prohibition of the shipment interstate of goods produced under the forbidden substandard labor conditions is within the constitutional authority of Congress.

In the more than a century which has elapsed since the decision of *Gibbons v. Ogden,* these principles of constitutional interpretation have been so long and repeatedly recognized by this Court as applicable to the Commerce Clause, that there would be little occasion for repeating them now were it not for the decision of this Court twenty-two years ago in *Hammer v. Dagenhart.* . . .

Hammer v. Dagenhart has not been followed. The distinction on which the decision was rested that Congressional power to prohibit interstate commerce is limited to articles which in themselves have some harmful or deleterious property—a distinction which was novel when made and unsupported by any provision of the Constitution—has long since been abandoned.

The conclusion is inescapable that *Hammer v. Dagenhart,* was a departure from the principles which have prevailed in the interpretation of the commerce clause both before and since the decision and that such vitality, as a precedent, as it then had has long since been exhausted. It should be and now is overruled.

Validity of the wage and hour requirements. Section 15(a)(2) and §§ 6 and 7 require employers to conform to the wage and hour provisions with respect to all employees engaged in the production of goods for interstate commerce. As appellee's employees are not alleged to be "engaged in interstate commerce" the validity of the prohibition turns on the question whether the employment, under other than the prescribed labor standards, of employees engaged in the production of goods for interstate commerce is so related to the commerce and so affects it as to be within the reach of the power of Congress to regulate it. . . .

[W]e think the acts alleged in the indictment are within the sweep of the statute. The obvious purpose of the Act was not only to prevent the interstate transportation of the proscribed product, but to stop the initial step toward transportation, production with the purpose of so transporting it. Congress was not unaware that most manufacturing businesses shipping their product in interstate commerce make it in their shops without reference to its ultimate destination and then after manufacture select some of it for shipment interstate and some intrastate according to the daily demands of their business, and that it would be practically impossible; without disrupting manufacturing businesses, to re-strict the prohibited kind of production to the particular pieces of lumber, cloth, furniture or the like which later move in interstate rather than intrastate commerce. . . .

There remains the question whether such restriction on the production of goods for commerce is a permissible exercise of commerce power. The power of Congress over interstate com-merce is not confined to the regulation of commerce among the states. It extends to those activities intrastate which so affect inter-state commerce or the exercise of the power of Congress over it as to make regulation of them appropriate means to the attainment of a legitimate end, the exercise of the granted power of Congress to regulate interstate commerce. . . .

Congress, having by the present Act adopted the policy of excluding from interstate commerce all goods produced for the commerce which do not conform to the specified labor standards, it may choose the means reasonably adapted to the attainment of the permitted end, even though they involve control of intra-state activities. Such legislation has often been sustained with re-spect to powers, other than the commerce power granted to the national government, when the means chosen, although not them-selves within the granted power, were nevertheless deemed appro-priate aids to the accomplishment of some purpose within an admitted power of the national government. . . . A familiar like exercise of power is the regulation of intrastate transactions which are so commingled with or related to interstate commerce that all must be regulated if the interstate commerce is to be effectively controlled. . . .

Similarly Congress may require inspection and preventive treat-ment of all cattle in a disease infected area in order to prevent shipment in interstate commerce of some of the cattle without the treatment. It may prohibit the removal, at destination, of labels required by the Pure Food & Drugs Act, 21 U.S.C.A. § 1 et seq., to be affixed to articles transported in interstate commerce.

We think also that § 15(a)(2), now under consideration, is sus-tainable independently of § 15(a)(1), which prohibits shipment or transportation of the proscribed goods. As we have said the evils aimed at by the Act are the spread of substandard labor conditions through the use of the facilities of interstate commerce for competition by the goods so produced with those produced under the prescribed or better labor conditions; and the conse-quent dislocation of the commerce itself caused by the impairment or destruction of local businesses by competition made effective through interstate commerce. The Act is thus directed at the suppression of a method or kind of competition in interstate commerce which it has in effect condemned as "unfair," as the Clayton Act, 38 Stat. 730, has condemned other "unfair methods of competition" made effective through interstate commerce. . . .

The means adopted by § 15(a) (2) for the protection of interstate commerce by the suppression of the production of the condemned goods for interstate commerce is so related to the commerce and so affects it as to be within the reach of the commerce power. . . .

Our conclusion is unaffected by the Tenth Amendment which provides: "The powers not delegated to the United States by the Constitution, nor prohibited by it to the States, are reserved to the States respectively, or to the people." The amendment states but a truism that all is retained which has not been surrendered. There is nothing in the history of its adoption to suggest that it was more than declaratory of the relationship between the national and state governments as it had been established by the Constitution before the amendment or that its purpose was other than to allay fears that the new national government might seek to exercise powers not granted, and that the states might not be able to exercise fully their reserved powers. . . .

Validity of the requirement of records of wages and hours. § 15(a) (5) and § 11(c). These requirements are incidental to those for the prescribed wages and hours, and hence validity of the former turns on validity of the latter. Since, as we have held, Congress may require production for interstate commerce to conform to those conditions, it may require the employer, as a means of enforcing the valid law, to keep a record showing whether he has in fact complied with it. The requirement for records even of the intrastate transaction is an appropriate means to the legitimate end.

Wickard v. Filburn

317 U.S. 111, 63 S.Ct. 82 (1941)

Under the Agricultural Adjustment Act of 1938, as amended in 1941, Secretary of Agriculture Claude Wickard was directed to set national acreage allotments for wheat to stabilize agricultural production. This required apportioning the allotments among the states and establishing quotas for individual farmers, who were subject to penalties for growing more wheat than their assigned quota. The act also provided that if more than one-third of the farmers subject to the regulations objected by referendum to the proposed national allotments, then the act would be suspended. Filburn owned a small dairy farm in Ohio and was allotted a little over eleven acres for wheat. But he planted twenty-three acres, intending to use the excess crops to feed his livestock, and harvested 239 bushels more than his allotted 222 bushels under the program. As a result, he was fined $117.11, based on a penalty of $0.49 for each bushel produced in excess of his quota. Filburn refused to pay and filed a complaint in federal district court, asking for an injunction against enforcement of the penalty and for a declaratory judgment that the legislation as applied to him violated the commerce clause and the Fifth Amendment. A three-judge court issued an injunction on the grounds that the secretary of agriculture had made misleading speeches in support of the adoption of the quotas by referendum. The government then appealed to the Supreme Court, which reversed the lower court's holding and addressed (in the excerpt here) the constitutional challenge to Congress's commerce power.

Justice JACKSON delivers the opinion of the Court.

It is urged that under the Commerce Clause of the Constitution, Article I, § 8, clause 3, Congress does not possess the power it has in this instance sought to exercise. The question would merit little consideration since our decision in *United States v. Darby* [1941], sustaining the federal power to regulate production of goods for commerce except for the fact that this Act extends federal regulation to production not intended in any part for commerce but wholly for consumption on the farm. The Act includes a definition of "market" and its derivatives so that as related to wheat in addition to its conventional meaning it also means to dispose of "by feeding (in any form) to poultry or livestock which, or the products of which, are sold, bartered, or exchanged, or to be so disposed of." Hence, marketing quotas not only embrace all that may be sold without penalty but also what may be consumed on the premises. . . .

Appellee says that this is a regulation of production and consumption of wheat. Such activities are, he urges, beyond the reach of Congressional power under the Commerce Clause, since they are local in character, and their effects upon interstate commerce are at most "indirect." In answer the Government argues that the statute regulates neither production nor consumption, but only marketing; and, in the alternative, that if the Act does go beyond the regulation of marketing it is sustainable as a "necessary and proper" implementation of the power of Congress over interstate commerce.

The Government's concern lest the Act be held to be a regulation of production or consumption rather than of marketing is attributable to a few dicta and decisions of this Court which might be understood to lay it down that activities such as "production," "manufacturing," and "mining" are strictly "local" and, except in special circumstances which are not present here, cannot be regulated under the commerce power because their effects upon interstate commerce are, as matter of law, only "indirect." Even today, when this power has been held to have great latitutde, there is no decision of this Court that such activities may be regulated where no part of the product is intended for interstate commerce or intermingled with the subjects thereof. We believe that a review of the course of decision under the Commerce Clause will make plain, however, that questions of the power of Congress are not to be decided by reference to any formula which would give controlling force to nomenclature such as "production" and "indirect" and foreclose consideration of the actual effects of the activity in question upon interstate commerce.

At the beginning Chief Justice MARSHALL described the federal commerce power with a breadth never yet exceeded. *Gibbons v. Ogden* [1824]. He made emphatic the embracing and penetrating nature of this power by warning that effective restraints on its exercise must proceed from political rather than from judicial processes. . . .

For nearly a century, however, decisions of this Court under the Commerce Clause dealt rarely with questions of what Congress might do in the exercise of its granted power under the Clause and almost entirely with the permissibility of state activity which it was claimed discriminated against or burdened interstate commerce. During this period there was perhaps little occasion for the affirmative exercise of the commerce power, and the influence of the Clause on American life and law was a negative one, resulting almost wholly from its operation as a restraint upon the powers of the states. . . .

It was not until 1887 with the enactment of the Interstate Commerce Act that the interstate commerce power began to exert positive influence in American law and life. This first important federal resort to the commerce power was followed in 1890 by the Sherman Anti-Trust Act and, thereafter, mainly after 1903, by many others. These statutes ushered in new phases of adjudication, which required the Court to approach the interpretation of the Commerce Clause in the light of an actual exercise by Congress of its power thereunder.

When it first dealt with this new legislation, the Court adhered to its earlier pronouncements, and allowed but little scope to the power of Congress. *United States v. E. C. Knight Co.* [1895]. These earlier pronouncements also played an important part in several of the five cases in which this Court later held that Acts of Congress under the Commerce Clause were in excess of its power. . . .

The Court's recognition of the relevance of the economic effects in the application of the Commerce Clause exemplified by this statement has made the mechanical application of legal formulas no longer feasible. Once an economic measure of the reach of the power granted to Congress in the Commerce Clause is accepted, questions of federal power cannot be decided simply by finding the activity in question to be "production" nor can consideration of its economic effects be foreclosed by calling them "indirect.". . .

Whether the subject of the regulation in question was "production," "consumption," or "marketing" is, therefore, not material for purposes of deciding the question of federal power before us. That an activity is of local character may help in a doubtful case to determine whether Congress intended to reach it. . . .

The parties have stipulated a summary of the economics of the wheat industry. Commerce among the states in wheat is large and important. Although wheat is raised in every state but one, production in most states is not equal to consumption. Sixteen states on average have had a surplus of wheat above their own requirements for feed, seed, and food. Thirty-two states and the District of Columbia, where production has been below consumption, have looked to these surplus-producing states for their supply as well as for wheat for export and carryover.

The wheat industry has been a problem industry for some years. Largely as a result of increased foreign production and import restrictions, annual exports of wheat and flour from the United States during the ten-year period ending in 1940 averaged less than 10 per cent of total production, while during the 1920's they averaged more than 25 per cent. The decline in the export trade has left a large surplus in production which in connection with an abnormally large supply of wheat and other grains in recent years caused congestion in a number of markets; tied up railroad cars; and caused elevators in some instances to turn away grains, and railroads to institute embargoes to prevent further congestion. . . .

The maintenance by government regulation of a price for wheat undoubtedly can be accomplished as effectively by sustaining or increasing the demand as by limiting the supply. The effect of the statute before us is to restrict the amount which may be produced for market and the extent as well to which one may forestall resort to the market by producing to meet his own needs. That appellee's own contribution to the demand for wheat may be trivial by itself is not enough to remove him from the scope of federal regulation where, as here, his contribution, taken together with that of many others similarly situated, is far from trivial. . . .

One of the primary purposes of the Act in question was to increase the market price of wheat and to that end to limit the volume thereof that could affect the market. It can hardly be denied that a factor of such volume and variability as home-consumed wheat would have a substantial influence on price and market conditions. This may arise because being in marketable condition such wheat overhangs the market and if induced by rising prices tends to flow into the market and check price increases. But if we assume that it is never marketed, it supplies a need of the man who grew it which would otherwise be reflected by purchases in the open market. Home-grown wheat in this sense competes with wheat in commerce. The stimulation of commerce is a use of the regulatory function quite as definitely as prohibitions or restrictions thereon. This record leaves us in no doubt that Congress may properly have considered that wheat consumed on the farm where grown if wholly outside the scheme of regulation would have a substantial effect in defeating and obstructing its purpose to stimulate trade therein at increased prices.

It is said, however, that this Act, forcing some farmers into the market to buy what they could provide for themselves, is an unfair promotion of the markets and prices of specializing wheat growers. It is of the essence of regulation that it lays a restraining hand on the self-interest of the regulated and that advantages from the regulation commonly fall to others. The conflicts of economic interest between the regulated and those who advantage by it are wisely left under our system to resolution by the Congress under its more flexible and responsible legislative process. Such conflicts rarely lend themselves to judicial determination. And with the wisdom, workability, or fairness, of the plan of regulation we have nothing to do.

Heart of Atlanta Motel, Inc. v. United States
379 U.S. 241, 85 S.Ct. 348 (1964)

Katzenbach v. McClung
379 U.S. 294, 85 S.Ct. 377 (1964)

Through litigation, sit-ins, and marches the civil rights movement sought to end racial discrimination in public schools and public accommodations. The Warren Court responded in cases such as *Peterson v. Greenville,* 373 U.S. 244 (1963), ruling that a restaurant that discriminated against blacks ran afoul of the Fourteenth Amendment's "equal protection of the law" because a city ordinance required the separation of races. However, the Court was limited by the "state action" doctrine, announced in *The Civil Rights Cases,* 109 U.S. 3 (1883) (see Vol. 2, Ch. 12), holding that the Fourteenth Amendment does not prohibit discrimination in privately owned public accommodations like hotels and restaurants, unless private discrimination is "sanctioned in some way by the state" or "done under state authority." In addition, litigation was costly and had limited effectiveness.

With the Civil Rights Act of 1964, or so-called Public Accommodations Act, Congress responded by forbidding racial discrimination or segregation in hotels, motels, restaurants and catering establishments of all kinds, as well as bars, barber shops, gasoline stations, entertainment, and other facilities on the premises of the establishments covered by the act—excluded were "private clubs," boarding houses with five or less rooms for rent, and other facilities closed to the public. In passing the act, Congress relied on its authority under the commerce clause and its enforcement power in Section 5 of the Fourteenth Amendment. When the Department of Justice sought to enforce the act, constitutional challenges were immediately raised.

In the *Heart of Atlanta Hotel* case, the owners of a downtown Atlanta hotel refused to rent any of their 216 rooms to blacks and unsuccessfully sought a declaratory judgment from a three-judge district court that the legislation was unconstitutional. The hotel advertised in national magazines and on billboards, and about 75 percent of its guests were from out of state. The Heart of Atlanta Hotel appealed the district court's injunction against its refusal to comply with the act to the Supreme Court.

In the other case, the owner of Ollie's Barbecue, a local restaurant in Birmingham, Alabama, successfully fought enforcement of the act in federal district court. In this instance, the lower court found the act's provision barring racial discrimination in any restaurant that "serves or offers to serve interstate travelers, or a substantial portion of the food which it serves . . . has moved in commerce" to apply, since about half of the food served in the restaurant had "moved" in commerce. However, the court concluded that the restaurant, which began operation in 1925, would lose substantial business if it were forced to serve blacks. Attorney General Nicholas Katzenbach appealed that decision to the Supreme Court.

Justice Tom Clark's opinion for the majority in both cases upholds the constitutionality of the Civil Rights Act solely on Congress's authority under the commerce clause, whereas Justices Douglas and Goldberg would have relied on the Fourteenth Amendment as well. Justice Black's concurring opinion raises issues about whether there are any limits on congressional power to regulate commerce.

Justice CLARK delivers the opinion of the Court [in *Heart of Atlanta Motel, Inc. v. United States*].

Congress first evidenced its interest in civil rights legislation in the Civil Rights or Enforcement Act of April 9, 1866. There followed four Acts with a fifth, the Civil Rights Act of March 1, 1875, culminating the series. In 1883 this Court struck down the public accommodations sections of the 1875 Act in the Civil Rights Cases. No major legislation in this field had been enacted by Congress for 82 years when the Civil Rights Act of 1957 became law. It was followed by the Civil Rights Act of 1960. Three years later, on June 19, 1963, the late President Kennedy called for civil rights legislation in a message to Congress to which he attached a proposed bill. Its stated purpose was

> "to promote the general welfare by eliminating discrimination based on race, color, religion, or national origin in . . . public accommodations through the exercise by Congress of the powers conferred upon it . . . to enforce the provisions of the fourteenth and fifteenth amendments, to regulate commerce among the several States, and to make laws necessary and proper to execute the powers conferred upon it by the Constitution."

Bills were introduced in each House of the Congress, embodying the President's suggestion. . . .

After extended hearings each of these bills was favorably reported to its respective house. . . . Although each bill originally incorporated extensive findings of fact these were eliminated from the bills as they were reported. . . . Our only frame of reference as to the legislative history of the Act is, therefore, the hearings, reports and debates on the respective bills in each house.

The Act as finally adopted was most comprehensive, undertaking to prevent through peaceful and voluntary settlement discrimination in voting, as well as in places of accommodation and public facilities, federally secured programs and in employment. Since Title II is the only portion under attack here, we confine our consideration to those public accommodation provisions.

TITLE II OF THE ACT.

This Title is divided into seven sections beginning with § 201(a) which provides that:

> "All persons shall be entitled to the full and equal enjoyment of the goods, services, facilities, privileges, advantages, and accommodations of any place of public accommodation, as defined in this section, without discrimination or segregation on the ground of race, color, religion, or national origin."

There are listed in § 201(b) four classes of business establishments, each of which "serves the public" and "is a place of public accommodation" within the meaning of § 201(a) "if its operations affect commerce, or if discrimination or segregation by it is supported by State action." The covered establishments are . . .

any inn, hotel, motel, or other establishment which provides lodging to transient guests, other than an establishment located within a building which contains not more than five rooms for rent or hire and which is actually occupied by the proprietor of such establishment as his residence. . . .

Section 201(c) defines the phrase "affect commerce" as applied to the above establishments. It first declares that "any inn, hotel, motel, or other establishment which provides lodging to transient guests" affects commerce *per se.* . . .

THE CIVIL RIGHTS CASES, 109 U.S. 3, 3 S.CT. 18 (1883), AND THEIR APPLICATION.

In light of our ground for decision, it might be well at the outset to discuss the Civil Rights Cases, supra, which declared provisions of the Civil Rights Act of 1875 unconstitutional. 18 Stat. 335, 336. We think that decision inapposite, and without precedential value in determining the constitutionality of the present Act. Unlike Title II of the present legislation, the 1875 Act broadly proscribed discrimination in "inns, public conveyances on land or water, theaters, and other places of public amusement," without limiting the categories of affected businesses to those impinging upon interstate commerce. In contrast, the applicability of Title II is carefully limited to enterprises having a direct and substantial relation to the interstate flow of goods and people, except where state action is involved. Further, the fact that certain kinds of businesses may not in 1875 have been sufficiently involved in interstate commerce to warrant bringing them within the ambit of the commerce power is not necessarily dispositive of the same question today. Our populace had not reached its present mobility, nor were facilities, goods and services circulating as readily in interstate commerce as they are today. Although the principles which we apply today are those first formulated by Chief Justice MARSHALL in *Gibbons v. Ogden,* the conditions of transportation and commerce have changed dramatically, and we must apply those principles to the present state of commerce. The sheer increase in volume of interstate traffic alone would give discriminatory practices which inhibit travel a far larger impact upon the Nation's commerce than such practices had on the economy of another day. Finally, there is language in the Civil Rights Cases which indicates that the Court did not fully consider whether the 1875 Act could be sustained as an exercise of the commerce power. . . .

THE BASIS OF CONGRESSIONAL ACTION.

While the Act as adopted carried no congressional findings the record of its passage through each house is replete with evidence of the burdens that discrimination by race or color places upon interstate commerce. . . .

This testimony included the fact that our people have become increasingly mobile with millions of people of all races traveling from State to State; that Negroes in particular have been the subject of discrimination in transient accommodations, having to travel great distances to secure the same; that often they have been unable to obtain accommodations and have had to call upon friends to put them up overnight, and that these conditions had become so acute as to require the listing of available lodging for Negroes in a special guidebook which was itself "dramatic testimony to the difficulties" Negroes encounter in travel. . . . These exclusionary practices were found to be nationwide, the Under Secretary of Commerce testifying that there is "no question that this discrimination in the North still exists to a large degree" and in the West and Midwest as well. . . . This testimony indicated a qualitative as well as quantitative effect on interstate travel by Negroes. The former was the obvious impairment of the Negro traveler's pleasure and convenience that resulted when he continually was uncertain of finding lodging. As for the latter, there was evidence that this uncertainty stemming from racial discrimination had the effect of discouraging travel on the part of a substantial portion of the Negro community. This was the conclusion not only of the Under Secretary of Commerce but also of the Administrator of the Federal Aviation Agency who wrote the Chairman of the Senate Commerce Committee that it was his "belief that air commerce is adversely affected by the denial to a substantial segment of the traveling public of adequate and desegregated public accommodations." We shall not burden this opinion with further details since the voluminous testimony presents overwhelming evidence that discrimination by hotels and motels impedes interstate travel.

THE POWER OF CONGRESS OVER INTERSTATE TRAVEL.

The same interest in protecting interstate commerce which led Congress to deal with segregation in interstate carriers and the white-slave traffic has prompted it to extend the exercise of its power to gambling, *Lottery Case (Champion v. Ames)*, [188 U.S. 321] (1903); to criminal enterprises, *Brooks v. United States*, [267 U.S. 432] (1925); to deceptive practices in the sale of products, *Federal Trade Comm. v. Mandel Bros., Inc.*, [359 U.S. 385] (1959); to fraudulent security transactions, *Securities & Exchange Comm. v. Ralston Purina Co.*, [346 U.S. 119] (1953); to misbranding of drugs, *Weeks v. United States*, [232 U.S. 383] (1914); to wages and hours, *United States v. Darby*, [321 U.S. 100] (1941); to members of labor unions, *National Labor Relations Board v. Jones & Laughlin Steel Corp.*, [310 U.S. 1] (1937); to crop control, *Wickard v. Filburn* (1942); to discrimination against shippers, *United States v. Baltimore & Ohio R. Co.*, [317 U.S. 111] (1948); to the protection of small business from injurious price cutting, *Moore v. Mead's Fine Bread*

Co., [333 U.S. 169] (1954); to resale price maintenance, *Hudson Distributors, Inc. v. Eli Lilly & Co.*, [348 U.S. 115] (1964); *Schwegmann Bros. v. Calvert Distillers Corp.*, [377 U.S. 386] (1951); to professional football, *Radovich v. National Football League*, [352 U.S. 445] (1957); and to racial discrimination by owners and managers of terminal restaurants, *Boynton v. Com. of Virginia*, [362 U.S. 454] (1960).

That Congress was legislating against moral wrongs in many of these areas rendered its enactments no less valid. In framing Title II of this Act Congress was also dealing with what it considered a moral problem. But that fact does not detract from the overwhelming evidence of the disruptive effect that racial discrimination has had on commercial intercourse. It was this burden which empowered Congress to enact appropriate legislation, and, given this basis for the exercise of its power, Congress was not restricted by the fact that the particular obstruction to interstate commerce with which it was dealing was also deemed a moral and social wrong.

It is said that the operation of the motel here is of a purely local character. But, assuming this to be true, "[i]f it is interstate commerce that feels the pinch, it does not matter how local the operation which applies the squeeze." *United States v. Women's Sportswear Mfg. Ass'n*, 336 U.S. 460 (1949). . . . Thus the power of Congress to promote interstate commerce also includes the power to regulate the local incidents thereof, including local activities in both the States of origin and destination, which might have a substantial and harmful effect upon that commerce. One need only examine the evidence which we have discussed above to see that Congress may—as it has—prohibit racial discrimination by motels serving travelers, however "local" their operations may appear.

Nor does the Act deprive appellant of liberty or property under the Fifth Amendment. The commerce power invoked here by the Congress is a specific and plenary one authorized by the Constitution itself. The only questions are: (1) whether Congress had a rational basis for finding that racial discrimination by motels affected commerce, and (2) if it had such a basis, whether the means it selected to eliminate that evil are reasonable and appropriate. If they are, appellant has no "right" to select its guests as it sees fit, free from governmental regulation. . . .

We . . . conclude that the action of the Congress in the adoption of the Act as applied here to a motel which concededly serves interstate travelers is within the power granted it by the Commerce Clause of the Constitution, as interpreted by this Court for 140 years. It may be argued that Congress could have pursued other methods to eliminate the obstructions it found in interstate commerce caused by racial discrimination. But this is a matter of policy that rests entirely with the Congress not with the courts.

How obstructions in commerce may be removed—what means are to be employed—is within the sound and exclusive discretion of the Congress. It is subject only to one caveat—that the means chosen by it must be reasonably adapted to the end permitted by the Constitution. We cannot say that its choice here was not so adapted. The Constitution requires no more.

Justice CLARK delivers the opinion of the Court [in *Katzenbach v. McClung*].

Ollie's Barbecue is a family-owned restaurant in Birmingham, Alabama, specializing in barbecued meats and homemade pies, with a seating capacity of 220 customers. It is located on a state highway 11 blocks from an interstate one and a somewhat greater distance from railroad and bus stations. The restaurant caters to a family and white-collar trade with a take-out service for Negroes. It employs 36 persons, two-thirds of whom are Negroes.

In the 12 months preceding the passage of the Act, the restaurant purchased locally approximately $150,000 worth of food, $69,683 or 46% of which was meat that it bought from a local supplier who had procured it from outside the State. The District Court expressly found that a substantial portion of the food served in the restaurant had moved in interstate commerce. The restaurant has refused to serve Negroes in its dining accommodations since its original opening in 1927, and since July 2, 1964, it has been operating in violation of the Act. The court below concluded that if it were required to serve Negroes it would lose a substantial amount of business. . . .

The basic holding in *Heart of Atlanta Motel,* answers many of the contentions made by the appellees. There we outlined the overall purpose and operational plan of Title II and found it a valid exercise of the power to regulate interstate commerce insofar as it requires hotels and motels to serve transients without regard to their race or color. In this case we consider its application to restaurants which serve food a substantial portion of which has moved in commerce. . . . Sections 201(b) (2) and (c) place any "restaurant . . . principally engaged in selling food for consumption on the premises" under the Act "if . . . it serves or offers to serve interstate travelers or a substantial portion of the food which it serves . . . has moved in commerce."

Ollie's Barbecue admits that it is covered by these provisions of the Act. . . .

As we noted in *Heart of Atlanta Motel* both Houses of Congress conducted prolonged hearings on the Act. And, as we said there, while no formal findings were made, which of course are not necessary, it is well that we make mention of the testimony at these hearings the better to understand the problem before Congress and determine whether the Act is a reasonable and appropriate means toward its solution. The record is replete with testimony of the burdens placed on interstate commerce by racial discrimination in restaurants. . . .

Moreover there was an impressive array of testimony that discrimination in restaurants had a direct and highly restrictive effect upon interstate travel by Negroes. This resulted, it was said, because discriminatory practices prevent Negroes from buying prepared food served on the premises while on a trip, except in isolated and unkempt restaurants and under most unsatisfactory and often unpleasant conditions. This obviously discourages travel and obstructs interstate commerce for one can hardly travel without eating. Likewise, it was said, that discrimination deterred professional, as well as skilled, people from moving into areas where such practices occurred and thereby caused industry to be reluctant to establish there. . . .

We believe that this testimony afforded ample basis for the conclusion that established restaurants in such areas sold less interstate goods because of the discrimination, that interstate travel was obstructed directly by it, that business in general suffered and that many new businesses refrained from establishing there as a result of it. Hence the District Court was in error in concluding that there was no connection between discrimination and the movement of interstate commerce. The court's conclusion that such a connection is outside "common experience" flies in the face of stubborn fact. . . .

The appellees contend that Congress has arbitrarily created a conclusive presumption that all restaurants meeting the criteria set out in the Act "affect commerce." Stated another way, they object to the omission of a provision for a case-by-case determination—judicial or administrative—that racial discrimination in a particular restaurant affects commerce.

But Congress' action in framing this Act was not unprecedented. In *United States v. Darby* (1941), this Court held constitutional the Fair Labor Standards Act of 1938. . . .

Here, as there, Congress has determined for itself that refusals of service to Negroes have imposed burdens both upon the interstate flow of food and upon the movement of products generally. Of course, the mere fact that Congress has said when particular activity shall be deemed to affect commerce does not preclude further examination by this Court. But where we find that the legislators, in light of the facts and testimony before them, have a rational basis for finding a chosen regulatory scheme necessary to the protection of commerce, our investigation is at an end. The only remaining question—one answered in the affirmative by the court below—is whether the particular restaurant either serves or offers to serve interstate travelers or serves food a substantial portion of which has moved in interstate commerce. . . .

Confronted as we are with the facts laid before Congress, we must conclude that it had a rational basis for finding that racial discrimination in restaurants had a direct and adverse effect on the free flow of interstate commerce. Insofar as the sections of the Act here relevant are concerned, §§ 201(b) (2) and (c), Congress prohibited discrimination only in those establishments having a close tie to interstate commerce, i.e., those, like the McClungs', serving food that has come from out of the State. We think in so doing that Congress acted well within its power to protect and foster commerce in extending the coverage of Title II only to those restaurants offering to serve interstate travelers or serving food, a substantial portion of which has moved in interstate commerce.

The absence of direct evidence connecting discriminatory restaurant service with the flow of interstate food, factor on which the appellees place much reliance, is not, given the evidence as to the effect of such practices on other aspects of commerce, a crucial matter.

The power of Congress in this field is broad and sweeping; where it keeps within its sphere and violates no express constitutional limitation it has been the rule of this Court, going back almost to the founding days of the Republic, not to interfere. The Civil Rights Act of 1964, as here applied, we find to be plainly appropriate in the resolution of what the Congress found to be a national commercial problem of the first magnitude. We find it in no violation of any express limitations of the Constitution and we therefore declare it valid.

The judgment is therefore reversed.

Justice BLACK, Justice DOUGLAS and Justice GOLDBERG concurred in separate opinions.

Justice BLACK concurring.

It requires no novel or strained interpretation of the Commerce Clause to sustain Title II as applied [here]. . . . At least since *Gibbons v. Ogden*, decided in 1824 in an opinion by Chief Justice John MARSHALL, it has been uniformly accepted that the power of Congress to regulate commerce among the States is plenary, "complete in itself, may be exercised to its utmost extent, and acknowledges no limitations, other than are prescribed in the constitution." Nor is "Commerce" as used in the Commerce Clause to be limited to a narrow, technical concept. It includes not only, as Congress has enumerated in the Act, "travel, trade, traffic, commerce, transportation, or communication," but also all other unitary transactions and activities that take place in more States than one. That some parts or segments of such unitary transactions may take place only in one State cannot, of course, take from Congress its plenary power to regulate them in the national interest. The facilities and instrumentalities used to carry on this commerce, such as railroads, truck lines, ships, rivers, and even highways are also subject to congressional regulation, so far as is necessary to keep interstate traffic upon fair and equal terms. . . .

Furthermore, it has long been held that the Necessary and Proper Clause, Art. I, § 8, cl. 18, adds to the commerce power of Congress the power to regulate local instrumentalities operating within a single State if their activities burden the flow of commerce among the States. . . .

The Heart of Atlanta Motel is a large 216-room establishment strategically located in relation to Atlanta and interstate travelers. It advertises extensively by signs along interstate highways and in various advertising media. As a result of these circumstances approximately 75% of the motel guests are transient interstate travelers. It is thus an important facility for use by interstate travelers who travel on highways, since travelers in their own cars must find lodging places to make their journeys comfortably and safely. . . .

The foregoing facts are more than enough, in my judgment, to show that Congress acting within its discretion and judgment has power under the Commerce Clause and the Necessary and Proper Clause to bar racial discrimination in the Heart of Atlanta Motel.

Justice DOUGLAS concurring.

Though I join the Court's opinions, I am somewhat reluctant here . . . to rest solely on the Commerce Clause. My reluctance is not due to any conviction that Congress lacks power to regulate commerce in the interests of human rights. It is rather my belief that the right of people to be free of state action that discriminates against them because of race, like the "right of persons to move freely from State to State" (*Edwards v. People of State of California*) [314 U.S. 160 (1941)], "occupies a more protected position in our constitutional system than does the movement of cattle, fruit, steel and coal across state lines.". . .

Hence I would prefer to rest on the assertion of legislative power contained in § 5 of the Fourteenth Amendment which states: "The Congress shall have power to enforce, by appropriate legislation, the provisions of this article"—a power which the Court concedes was exercised at least in part in this Act.

A decision based on the Fourteenth Amendment would have a more settling effect, making unnecessary litigation over whether a particular restaurant or inn is within the commerce definitions of the Act or whether a particular customer is an interstate traveler. Under my construction, the Act would apply to all customers in all the enumerated places of public accommodation. And that construction would put an end to all obstructionist strategies and finally close one door on a bitter chapter in American history. . . .

Thus while I agree with the Court that Congress in fashioning the present Act used the Commerce Clause to regulate racial segregation, it also used (and properly so) some of its power under § 5 of the Fourteenth Amendment.

D. TAXING AND SPENDING POWERS

Congress has broad (but not unlimited) powers to tax and spend under Sections 8 and 9 of Article 1. The first clause of Section 8 provides that "[t]he Congress shall have power to lay and collect taxes, duties, imposts and excises, to pay the debts and provide for the common defense and general welfare of the United States." Since *McCulloch v. Mayland* (1819) (see page 453), congressional power to tax has been construed to be plenary and to reach virtually "every subject."[1] Article 1, Section 9, though, limits Congress's power in providing that "[n]o capitation, or other direct tax shall be laid, unless in proportion to the census or enumeration herein before directed to be taken." This prohibition of "direct" taxation was interpreted as barring only capitation and land taxes in *Hylton v. United States*, 3 U.S. (3 Dall.) 171 (1796), which upheld a federal tax on carriages.

A major controversy, however, erupted over Congress's levying federal income taxes. Congress resorted to taxing incomes to raise revenues during the Civil War and the Court initially rebuffed the argument that income taxes were unconstitutional direct taxes in *Springer v. United States*, 102 U.S. 586 (1881). Charles Pollock, a major stockholder in the Farmers' Loan and Trust Company, challenged the constitutionality of congressional legislation in 1894 that imposed a tax of 2 percent on income in excess of $4,000. He sought to enjoin his bank from paying the tax on the grounds that it amounted to direct taxation and a denial of property rights under the due process clause.

Federal income tax was a piece of progressive legislation and attacked by Pollock's attorney, Joseph H. Choate, as "communistic in its purposes and tendencies, and is defended here upon principles as communistic, socialistic—what should I call them— populistic as ever have been addressed to any political assembly in the world"[2] Justice Howell E. Jackson was ill with tuberculous and absent from the bench when the Fuller Court heard *Pollock v. Farmer's Loan and Trust Co.,* 157 U.S. 428 (1895). Six of the eight justices who heard the case accepted Choate's argument that an income tax levied on land violated Article I, Section 9. But the eight justices were equally divided over whether income from personal property was a direct tax.

Because of the importance of the controversy, Choate asked that the Court rehear the case. And six weeks later, in *Pollock v. Farmer's Loan and Trust Co.,* 158 U.S. 601 (1895), a bare majority struck down as unconstitutional the entire system of federal income tax. Giving vent to the Court's defense of property rights and laissez-faire capitalism (see Vol. 2, Ch. 3), Chief Justice Fuller announced, "Taxes on real estate being indisputable direct taxes, taxes on the rents or income of real estate are equally direct taxes. . . . [And] taxes on personal property, or on the income from personal property, are likewise direct taxes."

The four dissenters in *Pollock* protested the majority's turning its back on a century of precedents upholding Congress's plenary power in an attempt to block the forces of change brought by the current of progressive politics. In Justice John Harlan's words,

The practical effect of the decision today is to give certain kinds of property a position of favoritism and advantage inconsistent with the fundamental principles of our social organization, and to invest them with power and influence that may be perilous to that portion of the American people upon whom rests the larger part of the burden of the government, and who ought not to be subjected to the dominion of aggregated wealth any more than the property of the country should be at the mercy of the lawless.

As a result of *Pollock* and the Court's defense of interests in private property under the guise of a "liberty of contract" (see Vol. 2, Ch. 3) between 1887 and 1937, the Court was criticized by progressives for becoming the instrument of the rich and of corporate America. A movement to overturn the Court's ruling finally led to the passage and ratification in 1913 of the Sixteenth Amendment, which provides that, "Congress shall have power to lay and collect taxes on incomes, from whatever source derived, without apportionment among the several States, and without regard to any census or enumeration."

The Court's defense of laissez-faire capitalism and stand against progressive legislation ultimately concluded with the "constitutional crisis" of 1937 and the Court's reversal of its interpretation of Congress's power under the commerce clause and abandonment of the doctrine of a "liberty of contract" (see section C, this chapter, and Vol. 2, Ch. 3). In the 1920s and 1930s, though, the Court carried its defense of laissez-faire capitalism over to its construction of Congress's taxing power and thereby sharply limited that power. This was so in spite of the fact that since 1789 Congress had passed protective tariffs and laws taxing activities for purposes other than primarily raising revenues. In *J. W. Hampton, Jr., & Co. v. United States*, 276 U.S. 294 (1928), the Court affirmed the constitutionality of such uses of taxation, observing that "the existence of other motives in the selection of the subjects of taxes can not invalidate Congressional action." Indeed, in *McCray v. United States*, 194 U.S. 27 (1904), a congressional tax on oleomargarine that was colored to look like butter was upheld with the Court disclaiming any power to scrutinize "the motives or purposes of Congress when enacting legislation."[3]

In the Court's confrontation with progressive legislation and the New Deal, Congress's power to tax for purposes other than raising revenues was nevertheless sharply limited. In response to the Court's striking down the Child Labor Act of 1916 in *Hammer v. Dagenhart* (1918) (see page 488), Congress passed the Federal Child Labor Tax Act of 1919, imposing a 10 percent tax on the annual profits of businesses using child labor in violation of the law's standards for employing child labor. When this law was attacked in *Bailey v. Drexel Furniture Co.*, 259 U.S. 20 (1920), the Taft Court struck it down for imposing a regulatory penalty on the use of child labor instead of being a tax per se.[4]

Along with the Court's "switch in time that saved nine" in *National Labor Relations Board v. Jones & Laughlin Steel Corporation* (1937) (see page 497) and *West Coast Hotel v. Parrish*, 300 U.S. 379 (1937) (see Vol. 2, Ch. 3), a bare majority of the Court affirmed a major piece of New Deal legislation, the Social Security Act of 1935, in *Steward Machine Co. v. Davis* (1937) (see page 526). Notice that as in *NLRB* and *West Coast Hotel*, the Four Horsemen—Justices Butler, McReynolds, Sutherland, and Van Devanter—dissented from the revolution in constitutional politics that these rulings signified.

The Court, though, persisted for a time in imposing its notion of "dual federalism," which it initially developed as a limitation on congressional power over commerce (see Chapter 7). *United States v. Kahriger* (1953) (see page 531) illustrates how the doctrine of "dual federalism" remained infused in the Court's interpretation of the use of Congress's taxing power to regulate certain activities. *Kahriger*'s sustaining of Congress's power to tax the earnings of gamblers and to require them to register was eventually overturned as an infringement of individual's Fifth Amendment privilege against self-incrimination in *Marchetti v. United States*, 390 U.S. 39 (1968) (see Vol. 2, Ch. 8).

Since the constitutional revolution forged in 1937, the Court has generally upheld Congress's broad powers to tax and spend when rejecting arguments, like those advanced by the four dissenters in *Steward Machine Co.*, that the Tenth Amendment's reserved powers for the states limits Congress. In *Brown v. Public Agencies Opposed to Social Security Entrapment,* 477 U.S. 41 (1986), for example, the Burger Court unanimously upheld Congress's amending the Social Security Act to deny the right of states to withdraw participating by state and local employees from the social security system.

Since 1937 the Court has also consistently affirmed Congress's broad power to spend for the purpose of promoting the general welfare. *Buckley v. Valeo,* 424 U.S. 1 (1976) (see page 720), for instance, upheld the major provisions of the Federal Election Campaign Act of 1971 and when doing so turned aside the argument that public financing of presidential elections was contrary to the "general welfare." The general welfare clause, observed the Court, is "a general grant of power, the scope of which is quite expansive [and] for Congress to decide which expenditures will promote the general welfare."

In *South Dakota v. Dole* (1987) (see page 536), Chief Justice Rehnquist sustained Congress's authorizing the secretary of transportation to withhold federal highway funds from states that failed to enact laws setting the minimum drinking age at twenty-one. Notably, dissenting Justices Brennan and O'Connor contended that Congress's spending power was limited by the Twentieth-first Amendment, which repealed the Eighteenth Amendment's prohibition on the manufacturing and sale of liquor and reserved the power of regulating liquor to the states.

Finally, it bears noting that the taxing power is a concurrent power, exercised by Congress and the states. Article I, Section 10, though, prohibits the states from laying "any imposts or duties on imports or exports, except what may be absolutely necessary for executing its inspection laws." The major limitation on states' powers of taxation is, nonetheless, Congress's power over interstate commerce. Basically, states may not adopt taxes that discriminate against interstate commerce or that have "the practical effect" of unduly favoring states and localities. In *Davis v. Michigan Department of Treasury,* 109 S.Ct. 1500 (1989), for example, the Rehnquist Court, with only Justice Stevens dissenting, ruled that states may not tax federal pensions if they exempt from taxation the pensions of retired state and local employees. In *Wardair Canada, Inc. v. Florida Department of Revenue,* 477 U.S. 1 (1986), Justice Brennan summarized the tests used by the Court in determining the constitutionality of state tax affecting interests in interstate commerce: "When a state tax is challenged as violative of the dormant interstate Commerce Clause, we have asked four questions: is the tax applied to an activity with a substantial nexus with the taxing State; is the tax fairly apportioned; does the tax discriminate against interstate commerce; is the tax fairly related to the services provided by the State."

NOTES

1. *License Tax Cases*, 5 Wall. 462 (1867). See also *Brushaber v. Union Pacific Rail Road*, 240 U.S. 1 (1916).

2. Quoted in Alpheus T. Mason and William Beany, *The Supreme Court in a Free Society* (Englewood Cliffs, NJ: Prentice Hall, 1959), 131.

3. See also *Head Money Cases*, 112 U.S. 580 (1884); *United States v. Doremus*, 249 U.S. 86 (1919); and *Sunshine Anthracite Coal Co. v. Adkins*, 310 U.S. 381 (1940).

4. See also *United States v. Constantine*, 296 U.S. 287 (1935).

SELECTED BIBLIOGRAPHY

Morgan, Donald. *Congress and the Constitution*. Cambridge: Harvard University Press, 1966.

Schmidhauser, John, and Berg, Larry. *The Supreme Court and Congress: Conflict and Interaction, 1945–1968*. New York: Free Press, 1972.

Shapiro, Martin. *Who Guards the Guardians?* Athens: University of Georgia, 1988.

Sunstein, Cass. *After the Rights Revolution: Reconceiving the Regulatory State*. Cambridge: Harvard University Press, 1990.

Steward Machine Co. v. Davis
301 U.S. 548, 57 S.Ct. 883 (1937)

As part of the New Deal, Congress passed the Social Security Act of 1935, requiring employers of eight or more employees to pay a federal excise tax on a percentage of their employees' wages. Under the program, the funds were collected as general revenue and deposited in the United States Treasury. Employers who contributed to state unemployment funds could credit such payments against the federal tax, but state unemployment compensation funds had to meet federal standards and to be deposited with the U.S. Treasury.

Steward Machine Company paid $46.14 to the federal government under the law, but then promptly sued Harwell Davis, an Internal Revenue Service official, for a refund on the grounds that the Social Security Act was unconstitutional. A federal district court dismissed the complaint. After that decision was upheld by a court of appeals, Steward Machine Company appealed to the Supreme Court, which affirmed the ruling of the appellate court by a five-to-four vote.

Justice CARDOZO delivers the opinion of the Court.

The validity of the tax imposed by the Social Security Act (42 U.S.C.A. §§ 301–1305) on employers of eight or more is here to be determined. . . .

The assault on the statute proceeds on an extended front. Its assailants take the ground that the tax is not an excise; that it is not uniform throughout the United States as excises are required to be; that its exceptions are so many and arbitrary as to violate the Fifth Amendment; that its purpose was not revenue, but an unlawful invasion of the reserved powers of the states; and that the states in submitting to it have yielded to coercion and have abandoned governmental functions which they are not permitted to surrender.

The objections will be considered seriatim with such further explanation as may be necessary to make their meaning clear.

First: The tax, which is described in the statute as an excise, is laid with uniformity throughout the United States as a duty, an impost, or an excise upon the relation of employment. . . .

The subject-matter of taxation open to the power of the Congress is as comprehensive as that open to the power of the states, though the method of apportionment may at times be different. "The Congress shall have Power to lay and collect Taxes, Duties, Imposts and Excises." Article 1, § 8. If the tax is a direct one, it shall be apportioned according to the census or enumeration. If it is a duty, impost, or excise, it shall be uniform throughout the United States. Together, these classes include every form of tax appropriate to sovereignty. . . . Whether the tax is to be classified as an "excise" is in truth not of critical importance. If not that, it is an "impost." A capitation or other "direct" tax it certainly is not. "Although there have been, from time to time, intimations that there might be some tax which was not a direct tax, nor included under the words 'duties, imposts, and excises,' such a tax, for more than 100 years of national existence, has as yet remained undiscovered, notwithstanding the stress of particular circumstances has invited thorough investigation into sources of revenue." There is no departure from that thought in later cases, but rather a new emphasis of it. . . .

The tax being an excise, its imposition must conform to the canon of uniformity. There has been no departure from this requirement. According to the settled doctrine, the uniformity exacted is geographical, not intrinsic. . . .

Second: The excise is not invalid under the provisions of the Fifth Amendment by force of its exemptions.

The statute does not apply, as we have seen, to employers of less than eight. It does not apply to agricultural labor, or domestic service in a private home or to some other classes of less importance. Petitioner contends that the effect of these restrictions is an arbitrary discrimination vitiating the tax.

The Fifth Amendment unlike the Fourteenth has no equal protection clause. . . .

The classifications and exemptions directed by the statute now in controversy have support in considerations of policy and practical convenience that cannot be condemned as arbitrary. . . .

Third: The excise is not void as involving the coercion of the states in contravention of the Tenth Amendment or of restrictions implicit in our federal form of government.

The proceeds of the excise when collected are paid into the Treasury at Washington, and thereafter are subject to appropriation like public moneys generally. No presumption can be indulged that they will be misapplied or wasted. Even if they were collected in the hope or expectation that some other and collateral good would be furthered as an incident, that without more would not make the act invalid. This indeed is hardly questioned. The case for the petitioner is built on the contention that here an ulterior aim is wrought into the very structure of the act, and what is even more important that the aim is not only ulterior, but essentially unlawful. In particular, the 90 per cent credit is relied upon as supporting that conclusion. But before the statute succumbs to an assault upon these lines, two propositions must be made out by the assailant. There must be a showing in the first place that separated from the credit the revenue provisions are incapable of standing by themselves. There must be a showing in the second place that the tax and the credit in combination are weapons of coercion, destroying or impairing the autonomy of the states. The truth of each proposition being essential to the success of the assault, we pass for convenience to a consideration of the second, without pausing to inquire whether there has been a demonstration of the first.

To draw the line intelligently between duress and inducement, there is need to remind ourselves of facts as to the problem of unemployment that are now matters of common knowledge. . . . The relevant statistics are gathered in the brief of counsel for the government. Of the many available figures a few only will be mentioned. During the years 1929 to 1936, when the country was passing through a cyclical depression, the number of the unemployed mounted to unprecedented heights. Often the average was more than 10 million; at times a peak was attained of 16 million or more. Disaster to the breadwinner meant disaster to dependents. Accordingly the roll of the unemployed, itself formidable enough, was only a partial roll of the destitute or needy. The fact developed quickly that the states were unable to give the requisite relief. The problem had become national in area and dimensions. There was need of help from the nation if the people were not to starve. It is too late today for the argument to be heard with tolerance that in a crisis so extreme the use of the moneys of the nation to relieve the unemployed and their dependents is a use for any purpose narrower than the promotion of the general welfare. . . .

The Social Security Act is an attempt to find a method by which all these public agencies may work together to a common end. Every dollar of the new taxes will continue in all likelihood to be used and needed by the nation as long as states are unwilling, whether through timidity or for other motives, to do what can be done at home. At least the inference is permissible that Congress so believed, though retaining undiminished freedom to spend the money as it pleased. On the other hand, fulfillment of the home duty will be lightened and encouraged by crediting the taxpayer upon his account with the Treasury of the nation to the extent that his contributions under the laws of the locality have simplified or diminished the problem of relief . . .

Who then is coerced through the operation of this statute? Not the taxpayer. He pays in fulfillment of the mandate of the local legislature. Not the state. Even now she does not offer a suggestion that in passing the unemployment law she was affected by duress. For all that appears, she is satisfied with her choice, and would be sorely disappointed if it were now to be annulled. The difficulty with the petitioner's contention is that it confuses motive with coercion "Every tax is in some measure regulatory. To some extent it interposes an economic impediment to the activity taxed as compared with others not taxed." *Sonzinskh v. United States* [300 U.S. 506 (1937)]. In like manner every rebate from a tax when conditioned upon conduct is in some measure a temptation. But to hold that motive or temptation is equivalent to coercion is to plunge the law in endless difficulties. . . .

In ruling as we do, we leave many questions open. We do not say that a tax is valid, when imposed by act of Congress, if it is laid upon the condition that a state may escape its operation through the adoption of a statute unrelated in subject-matter to activities fairly within the scope of national policy and power. No such question is before us. . . .

The judgment is affirmed.

Justice McREYNOLDS dissenting.

That portion of the Social Security legislation here under consideration, I think, exceeds the power granted to Congress. It unduly interferes with the orderly government of the state by her own people and otherwise offends the Federal Constitution. . . .

Forever, so far as we can see, the states are expected to function under federal direction concerning an internal matter. By the sanction of this adventure, the door is open for progressive inauguration of others of like kind under which it can hardly be expected that the states will retain genuine independence of action. And without independent states a Federal Union as contemplated by the Constitution becomes impossible. . . .

Ordinarily, I must think, a denial that the challenged action of Congress and what has been done under it amount to coercion and impair freedom of government by the people of the state would be regarded as contrary to practical experience. Unquestionably our federate plan of government confronts an enlarged peril.

Justice SUTHERLAND, with whom Justice VAN DEVANTER joins, dissenting.

With most of what is said in the opinion just handed down, I concur. I agree that the pay roll tax levied is an excise within the power of Congress; that the devotion of not more than 90 per cent of it to the credit of employers in states which require the payment of a similar tax under so-called unemployment-tax laws is not an unconstitutional use of the proceeds of the federal tax; that the provision making the adoption by the state of an unemployment law of a specified character a condition precedent to the credit of the tax does not render the law invalid. I agree that the states are not coerced by the federal legislation into adopting unemployment legislation. The provisions of the federal law may operate to induce the state to pass an employment law if it regards such action to be in its interest. But that is not coercion. If the act stopped here, I should accept the conclusion of the court that the legislation is not unconstitutional.

But the question with which I have difficulty is whether the administrative provisions of the act invade the governmental administrative powers of the several states reserved by the Tenth Amendment. A state may enter into contracts; but a state cannot, by contract or statute, surrender the execution, or a share in the execution, of any of its governmental powers either to a sister state or to the federal government, any more than the federal government can surrender the control of any of its governmental powers to a foreign nation. The power to tax is vital and fundamental, and, in the highest degree, governmental in character. Without it, the state could not exist. Fundamental also, and no less important, is the governmental power to expend the moneys realized from taxation, and exclusively to administer the laws in respect of the character of the tax and the methods of laying and collecting it and expending the proceeds. . . .

The precise question, therefore, which we are required to answer by an application of these principles is whether the congressional act contemplates a surrender by the state to the federal government, in whole or in part, of any state governmental power to administer its own unemployment law or the state pay roll-tax funds which it has collected for the purposes of that law. An affirmative answer to this question, I think, must be made.

I do not, of course, doubt the power of the state to select and utilize a depository for the safe-keeping of its funds; but it is quite another thing to agree with the selected depository that the funds shall be withdrawn for certain stipulated purposes, and for no other. Nor do I doubt the authority of the federal government and a state government to co-operate to a common end, provided each of them is authorized to reach it. But such co-operation must be effectuated by an exercise of the powers which they severally possess, and not by an exercise, through invasion or surrender, by one of them of the governmental power of the other. . . .

If we are to survive as the United States, the balance between the powers of the nation and those of the states must be maintained. There is grave danger in permitting it to dip in either direction, danger—if there were no other—in the precedent thereby set for further departures from the equipoise. The threat implicit in the present encroachment upon the administrative functions of the states is that greater encroachments, and encroachments upon other functions, will follow.

For the foregoing reasons, I think the judgment below should be reversed.

Justice BUTLER dissented.

United States v. Kahriger
345 U.S. 22, 73 S.Ct. 510 (1953)

Mr. Kahriger was indicted for failing to register as a gambler and to pay an occupation tax on his earnings as a gambler as required by Congress under the Gamblers' Occupational Tax Act of 1951. At a hearing in a federal district court, Kahriger moved to dismiss the charge on the grounds that the law was unconstitutional in infringing on the states' police powers under the Tenth Amendment and his Fifth Amendment right against self-incrimination. The district court granted Kahriger's motion and the government appealed to the Supreme Court. Five justices joined in Justice Stanley Reed's opinion upholding Congress's power over the claim of state police powers, while Justices Felix Frankfurter and William Douglas (who often disagreed) dissented together and contended that Congress was intruding on the powers of the states. Justice Douglas also joined the dissenting opinion of his usual ally, Justice Hugo Black, who maintained that the requirement that gamblers register with the government violated their Fifth Amendment right against self-incrimination.

Justice REED delivers the opinion of the Court.

The issue raised by this appeal is the constitutionality of the occupational tax provisions of the Revenue Act of 1951, which levy a tax on persons engaged in the business of accepting wagers, and require such persons to register with the Collector of Internal Revenue. The unconstitutionality of the tax is asserted on two grounds. First, it is said that Congress, under the pretense of exercising its power to tax has attempted to penalize illegal intrastate gambling through the regulatory features of the Act, 26 U.S.C. (Supp. V) § 3291, 26 U.S.C.A. § 3291, and has thus infringed the police power which is reserved to the states. Secondly, it is urged that the registration provisions of the tax violate the privilege against self-incrimination and are arbitrary and vague, contrary to the guarantees of the Fifth Amendment. . . .

The substance of respondent's position with respect to the Tenth Amendment is that Congress has chosen to tax a specified business which is not within its power to regulate. The precedents are many upholding taxes similar to this wagering tax as a proper exercise of the federal taxing power. . . .

Appellee would have us say that because there is legislative history indicating a congressional motive to suppress wagering, this tax is not a proper exercise of such taxing power. In *The License Cases* [*Thurlow v. Massachusetts*, 5 How. 504 (1847)], it was admitted that the federal license "discouraged" the activities. The intent to curtail and hinder, as well as tax, was also manifest in the following cases, and in each of them the tax was upheld: *Veazie Bank v. Fenno*, 8 Wall. 533 [1869] (tax on paper money issued by state banks); *McCray v. United States*, 195 U.S. 27 [1904] (tax on colored oleomargarine); *United States v. Doremus*, 249 U.S. 86 [1919] and *Nigro v. United States*, 276 U.S. 332 [1928] (tax on narcotics); *Sonzinsky v. United States*, 300 U.S. 506 [1937] (tax on firearms); *United States v. Sanchez*, 340 U.S. 42 [1950] (tax on marihuana).

It is conceded that a federal excise tax does not cease to be valid merely because it discourages or deters the activities taxed. Nor is the tax invalid because the revenue obtained its negligible. Appellee, however, argues that the sole purpose of the statute is to penalize only illegal gambling in the states through the guise of a tax measure. As with the above excise taxes which we have held to be valid, the instant tax has a regulatory effect. But regardless of its regulatory effect, the wagering tax produces revenue. As such it surpasses both the narcotics and firearms taxes which we have found valid.

It is axiomatic that the power of Congress to tax is extensive and sometimes falls with crushing effect on businesses deemed unessential or inimical to the public welfare, or where, as in dealings with narcotics, the collection of the tax also is difficult. As is well known, the constitutional restraints on taxing are few. . . .

Where federal legislation has rested on other congressional powers, such as the Necessary and Proper Clause or the Commerce Clause, this Court has generally sustained the statutes, despite their effect on matters ordinarily considered state concern. When federal power to regulate is found, its exercise is a matter for Congress. Where Congress has employed the taxing clause a greater variation in the decisions has resulted. The division in this Court has been more acute. Without any specific differentiation between the power to tax and other federal powers, the indirect results from the exercise of the power to tax have raised more doubts. . . . It is hard to understand why the power to tax should raise more doubts because of indirect effects than other federal powers. . . .

Unless there are provisions, extraneous to any tax need, courts are without authority to limit the exercise of the taxing power. All the provisions of this excise are adapted to the collection of a valid tax.

Nor do we find the registration requirements of the wagering tax offensive. All that is required is the filing of names, addresses, and places of business. This is quite general in tax returns. Such data are directly and intimately related to the collection of the tax and are "obviously supportable as in aid of a revenue purpose." *Sonzinsky v. United States*, [1937]. The registration provisions make the tax simpler to collect.

Appellee's second assertion is that the wagering tax is unconstitutional because it is a denial of the privilege against self-incrimination as guaranteed by the Fifth Amendment.

Since appellee failed to register for the wagering tax, it is difficult to see how he can now claim the privilege even assuming that the disclosure of violations of law is called for. In *United States v. Sullivan*, 274 U.S. 259 [1927], defendant was convicted of refusing to file an income tax return. . . .

Assuming that respondent can raise the self-incrimination issue, that privilege has relation only to past acts, not to future acts that may or may not be committed. If respondent wishes to take wagers subject to excise taxes, he must pay an occupational tax and register. Under the registration provisions of the wagering tax, appellee is not compelled to confess to acts already committed, he is merely informed by the statute that in order to engage in the business of wagering in the future he must fulfill certain conditions.

Justice JACKSON concurring.

I concur in the judgment and opinion of the Court, but with such doubt that if the minority agreed upon an opinion which did not impair legitimate use of the taxing power I probably would join it. But we deal here with important and contrasting values in our scheme of government, and it is important that neither be allowed to destroy the other.

On the one hand, the Fifth Amendment provides that no person "shall be compelled in any criminal case to be a witness against himself." This has been broadly construed to confer immunity not only "in any criminal case" but in any federal inquiry where the information might be useful later to convict of a federal crime. Extension of the immunity doctrines to the federal power to inquire as to income derived from violation of state penal laws would create a large number of immunities from reporting which would vary from state to state. Moreover, the immunity can be claimed without being established, otherwise one would be required to prove guilt to avoid admitting it. Sweeping and undiscriminating application of the immunity doctrines to taxation would almost give the taxpayer an option to refuse to report, as it now gives witnesses a virtual option to refuse to testify. The Fifth Amendment should not be construed to impair the taxing power conferred by the original Constitution, and especially by the Sixteenth Amendment, further than is absolutely required. . . .

But here is a purported tax law which requires no reports and lays no tax except on specified gamblers whose calling in most states is illegal. It requires this group to step forward and identify themselves, not because they like others have income, but because of its source. This is difficult to regard as a rational or good-faith revenue measure, despite the deference that is due Congress. On the contrary, it seems to be a plan to tax out of existence the professional gambler whom it has been found impossible to prosecute out of existence. . . . It will be a sad day for the revenues if the good will of the people toward their taxing system is frittered away in efforts to accomplish by taxation moral reforms that cannot be accomplished by direct legislation. But the evil that can come from this statute will probably soon make itself manifest to Congress. The evil of a judicial decision impairing the legitimate taxing power by extreme constitutional interpretations might not be transient. Even though this statute approaches the fair limits of constitutionality, I join the decision of the Court.

Justice FRANKFURTER dissenting.

The Court's opinion manifests a natural difficulty in reaching its conclusion. Constitutional issues are likely to arise whenever Congress draws on the taxing power not to raise revenue but to regulate conduct. This is so, of course, because of the distribution of legislative power as between the Congress and the State Legislatures in the regulation of conduct. . . .

[W]hen oblique use is made of the taxing power as to matters which substantively are not within the powers delegated to Congress, the Court cannot shut its eyes to what is obviously, because designedly, an attempt to control conduct which the Constitution left to the responsibility of the States, merely because Congress wrapped the legislation in the verbal cellophane of a revenue measure. . . .

Justice DOUGLAS, while not joining in the entire opinion, agrees with the views expressed herein that this tax is an attempt by the Congress to control conduct which the Constitution has left to the responsibility of the States.

Justice BLACK, with whom Justice DOUGLAS joins, dissenting.

The Fifth Amendment declares that no person "shall be compelled in any criminal case to be a witness against himself." The Court nevertheless here sustains an Act which requires a man to register and confess that he is engaged in the business of gambling. I think this confession can provide a basis to convict him of a federal crime for having gambled before registration without paying a federal tax. Whether or not the Act has this effect, I am sure that it creates a squeezing device contrived to put a man in federal prison if he refuses to confess himself into a state prison as a violator of state gambling laws. The coercion of confessions is a common but justly criticized practice of many countries that do not have or live up to a Bill of Rights. But we have a Bill of Rights that condemns coerced confessions, however refined or legalistic may be the technique of extortion. I would hold that this Act violates the Fifth Amendment.

South Dakota v. Dole

107 S.Ct. 2793 (1987)

In response to wide spread concern over the numbers of minors involved in automobile accidents while under the influence of alcohol and at the insistence of the administration of President Ronald Reagan, Congress amended the Surface Transportation Assistance Act in 1984 to encourage states to raise the minimum drinking age to twenty-one. The secretary of transportation was authorized to withhold part of state's federal highway funds for 1987 and 1988 if, by October 1986, the state did not raise its minimum drinking age.

In South Dakota individuals nineteen years old or older could purchase beer with a 3.2 percent alcohol content, and the state refused to change its law because the state legislature deemed Congress's action an intrusion on the powers of the states under the Tenth and Twentieth-first Amendments. As a result, the state was expected to lose $4 million in federal highway funds in 1987 and double that in 1988. The state, therefore, sued Elizabeth Dole, the secretary of transportation. The suit was dismissed by a federal district court and the state appealed the affirmance of that decision by a federal appellate court to the Supreme Court. Although considered a strong supporter of the powers of the states, Chief Justice William Rehnquist delivered the Court's opinion upholding Congress's spending power, whereas dissenting Justices William Brennan and Sandra O'Connor agreed that Congress here had run afoul of the Twentieth-first Amendment.

Chief Justice REHNQUIST delivers the opinion of the Court.

Here, Congress has acted indirectly under its spending power to encourage uniformity in the States' drinking ages. As we explain below, we find this legislative effort within constitutional bounds even if Congress may not regulate drinking ages directly.

The Constitution empowers Congress to "lay and collect Taxes, Duties, Imposts, and Excises, to pay the Debts and provide for the common Defence and general Welfare of the United States." Art. I, § 8, cl. 1. Incident to this power, Congress may attach conditions on the receipt of federal funds, and has repeatedly employed the power "to further broad policy objectives by conditioning receipt of federal moneys upon compliance by the recipient with federal statutory and administrative directives." *Fullilove v. Klutznick*, 448 U.S. 448 [1980]. The breadth of this power was made clear in *United States v. Butler*, 297 U.S. 1 (1936), where the Court, resolving a longstanding debate over the scope of the Spending Clause, determined that "the power of Congress to authorize expenditure of public moneys for public purposes is not limited by the direct grants of legislative power found in the Constitution." Thus, objectives not thought to be within Article I's "enumerated legislative fields," may nevertheless be attained through the use of the spending power and the conditional grant of federal funds.

The spending power is of course not unlimited, but is instead subject to several general restrictions articulated in our cases. The first of these limitations is derived from the language of the Constitution itself: the exercise of the spending power must be in pursuit of "the general welfare." Second, we have required that if Congress desires to condition the States' receipt of federal funds, it "must do so unambiguously, . . . enabl[ing] the States to exercise their choice knowingly, cognizant of the consequences of their participation." Third, our cases have suggested (without significant elaboration) that conditions on federal grants might be illegitimate if they are unrelated "to the federal interest in particular national projects or programs." Finally, we have noted that other constitutional provisions may provide an independent bar to the conditional grant of federal funds. . . .

South Dakota does not seriously claim that § 158 is inconsistent with any of the first three restrictions mentioned above. We can readily conclude that the provision is designed to serve the general welfare, especially in light of the fact that "the concept of welfare or the opposite is shaped by Congress. . . ." *Helvering v. Davis* [301 U.S. 619 (1937)]. Congress found that the differing drinking ages in the States created particular incentives for young persons to combine their desire to drink with their ability to drive, and that this interstate problem required a national solution. The means it chose to address this dangerous situation were reasonably calculated to advance the general welfare. . . .

The remaining question about the validity of § 158—and the basic point of disagreement between the parties—is whether the Twenty-first Amendment constitutes an "independent constitutional bar" to the conditional grant of federal funds. Petitioner, relying on its view that the Twenty-first Amendment prohibits *direct* regulation of drinking ages by Congress, asserts that "Congress may not use the spending power to regulate that which it is prohibited from regulating directly under the Twenty-first Amendment." Brief for Petitioner 52–53. But our cases show that this "independent constitutional bar" limitation on the spending power is not of the kind petitioner suggests. *United States v. Butler* [297 U.S. 1 (1936)], for example, established that the constitutional limitations on Congress when exercising its spending power are less exacting than those on its authority to regulate directly.

We have also held that a perceived Tenth Amendment limitation on congressional regulation of state affairs did not concomitantly limit the range of conditions legitimately placed on federal grants.

Our decisions have recognized that in some circumstances the financial inducement offered by Congress might be so coercive as to pass the point at which "pressure turns into compulsion." *Steward Machine Co. v. Davis* [301 U.S. 548 (1937)]. Here, however, Congress has directed only that a State desiring to establish a minimum drinking age lower than 21 lose a relatively small percentage of certain federal highway funds. Petitioner contends that the coercive nature of the program is evident from the degree of success it has achieved. We cannot conclude however, that a conditional grant of federal money of this sort is unconstitutional simply by reason of its success in achieving the congressional objective. . . .

Accordingly, the judgment of the Court of Appeals is Affirmed.

Justice BRENNAN dissenting.

I agree with Justice O'CONNOR that regulation of the minimum age of purchasers of liquor falls squarely within the ambit of those powers reserved to the State by the Twenty-first Amendment. Since States possess this constitutional power, Congress can not condition a federal grant in a manner that abridges this right. The Amendment, itself, strikes the proper balance between federal and state authority. I therefore dissent.

Justice O'CONNOR dissenting.

The Court today upholds the National Minimum Drinking Age Amendment, 23 U.S.C. § 158 (1982 ed., Supp. III), as a valid exercise of the Spending Power conferred by Article I, § 8. But § 158 is not a condition on spending reasonably related to the expenditure of federal funds and cannot be justified on that ground. Rather, it is an attempt to regulate the sale of liquor, an attempt that lies outside Congress' power to regulate commerce because it falls within the ambit of § 2 of the Twenty-first Amendment. . . .

When Congress appropriates money to build a highway, it is entitled to insist that the highway be a safe one. But it is not entitled to insist as a condition of the use of highway funds that the State impose or change regulations in other areas of the State's social and economic life because of an attenuated or tangential relationship to highway use or safety. Indeed, if the rule were otherwise, the Congress could effectively regulate almost any area of a State's social, political, or economic life on the theory that use of the interstate transportation system is somehow enhanced. . . .

If the Spending Power is to be limited only by Congress' notion of the general welfare, the reality, given the vast financial resources of the Federal Government, is that the Spending Clause gives "power to the Congress to tear down the barriers, to invade the states' jurisdiction, and to become a parliament of the whole people, subject to no restrictions save such as are self-imposed." *United States v. Butler*. This, of course, as *Butler* held, was not the Framers' plan and it is not the meaning of the Spending Clause.

Our later cases are consistent with the notion that, under the Spending Power, the Congress may only condition grants in ways that can fairly be said to be related to the expenditure of federal funds. For example, in *Fullilove v. Klutznick*, 448 U.S. 448 (1980), the Court upheld a condition on federal grants that 10% of the money be "set aside" for contracts with minority business enterprises. But the Court found that the condition could be justified as a valid regulation under the Commerce Power and § 5 of the Fourteenth Amendment. . . .

As discussed above, a condition that a State will raise its drinking age to 21 cannot fairly be said to be reasonably related to the expenditure of funds for highway construction. The only possible connection, highway safety, has nothing to do with how the funds Congress has appropriated are expended. Rather than a condition determining how federal highway money shall be expended, it is a regulation determining who shall be able to drink liquor. As such it is not justified by the Spending Power.

7

THE STATES AND AMERICAN FEDERALISM

FEDERALISM IS A distinctive feature and integral part of American constitutional politics and the administration of public affairs. Yet, in denoting the separation of state and national powers, federalism conceals complex and ambiguous connections. This is because there occurred a fundamental conceptual change in the understanding of federalism during the founding period. The Constitutional Convention rejected the eighteenth-century notion of federalism as a confederation or league of equal and independent sovereign states. But there still remained wide-ranging disagreement over the exact relationship of the national government to the states. In creating a new form of federalism, the Constitution thus laid the basis for ongoing debates and political struggles over the roles and responsibilities of national and state governments in providing social services.

During the founding period, the meaning of federalism was less clear and more controversial than today. The terms of constitutional politics were fluid and ambiguous. States were spoken of as sovereign, free, and independent, yet coordinate, coequal, and coextensive with the national government. As one delegate opposing Maryland's ratification of the Constitution, Luther Martin, complained, "the language of the States being *sovereign* and *independent* was once familiar and understood" but now "strange and obscure."[1]

Referring to the states as both independent and coordinate

projected the appealing imagery of a union of two gravitational centers of authority: nation and state. This "compound government of the United States," James Madison explained, "is without a model, and to be explained by itself, not by similitude or analogies."[2] Still, it seems fair to say the meaning of federalism was not fully grasped by its supporters or opponents; without any such model, each side was continuing to proffer its own definition during a process of political give and take.

Supporters of the Constitution shrewdly co-opted the label "Federalist" and worked an irreversible change in the meaning of *federalism*. In the eighteenth century, *federalism* denoted a "confederal system," a league of formally equal and independent sovereign states, much like the European Common Market today. And the Constitutional Convention in 1787 was called for the purpose of remedying the defects of (con)federalism in the nation's first constitution. The Articles of Confederation specified (in Article II) that "[e]ach State retains its sovereignty, freedom and independence, and every power, jurisdiction and right, which is not by this confederation expressly delegated to the United States, in Congress assembled."

What had been associated with federalism—namely, states' sovereignty—was denied during the Constitutional Convention. Even before the convention, Madison among others sought a middle ground between the existing (con)federation of states and their complete consolidation into a single republic. Yet states' sovereignty was even excluded from this middle ground. "[A] due supremacy of national authority," along with room for "the local authorities wherever they can be subordinately useful," is what Madison wanted. In any event, a national veto *"in all cases whatsoever* on the legislative acts of the States [was] the least possible encroachment on the State jurisdictions."[3]

During the convention, compromises forced acceptance of a "mixed form" of government, combining national and federal elements. As Madison analyzed the proposed constitution in *Federalist,* No. 39, "In its foundation it is federal, not national; in the sources from which the ordinary powers of the government are drawn, it is partly federal and partly national; in the operation of these powers, it is national, not federal; in the extent of them, again, it is federal, not national; and, finally in the authoritative mode of introducing amendments, it is neither wholly federal nor wholly national." This account implicitly denies the sovereignty, although not the existence or status, of the states. Nor could it have been otherwise. By definition *sovereignty* is indivisible and absolute. Supporters and opponents of the second constitution agreed it was "a solecism in politics for two coordinate sovereignties to exist together."[4]

The drafters and defenders of the Constitution did not claim sovereignty for the proposed federal government, any more than did most of those in opposition, the Anti-Federalists, claim absolute sovereignty for the states. Sovereignty was considered to reside in the nation, in the people of the several states.

The method of ratifying the Constitution called for by the convention (in Article VII) is revealing in this regard. Under the Articles of Confederation, amendments were to be ratified by *all* state legislatures. Instead of having the Constitution submitted to state legislatures, however, the convention recommended that Congress send the document to the states for ratification, by special conventions of the people, and that at least *nine* states give their approval. Congress and the thirteen states agreed, thereby amending the Articles of Confederation and affirming the principle of popular sovereignty.

Ratification by special state conventions was politically strategic. It also signified that the Constitution was not a mere treaty "among the Governments and Independent States," but the expression of "the supreme authority of the people themselves."[5] This was in keeping with the widely held view, expressed in the Declaration of Independence, that "the good people of these colonies" acted, in some respects, as one people. And popular, not state, sovereignty is boldly proclaimed in the opening line of the Constitution's Preamble, "We the People . . . form a more Perfect Union."

The significance of such explicit repudiation of states' sovereignty was not lost on some Anti-Federalists. During Virginia's ratifying convention, Patrick Henry thundered, "what right had they to say, *We, the People?* . . . [W]ho authorized them to speak the language of, *We, the People,* instead of *We, the States?* States are the characteristics, and the soul of a confederation. If the States are not the agents of this compact, it must be one great consolidated National Government of the people of all the States."[6] But Henry's position was on the losing side of history. The pretense of state sovereignty had undermined the Articles of Confederation and discredited the traditional understanding of federalism. The Constitution remedied that defect, Federalists and most Anti-Federalists agreed, much as Abraham Lincoln later claimed the existence of the states depended on a union older than the states themselves.[7]

Most Anti-Federalists were as committed to the union as to the states. Far from inflexible in their understanding of federalism, they reluctantly accepted a constitution that by earlier standards hardly embodied principles of federalism. They considered themselves the "true" Federalists in defending the states because states, smaller in size and more accountable to the people, were deemed essential to preserving individual liberty.

The Federal Farmer, for one, referred to those insisting on "Distinct republics" connected under a "federal head" as "pretended federalists." Traditional federalism could not "answer the purposes of government," any more than complete consolidation would prove practical. Like other "true federalists" and those "honest federalists" among the Constitution's supporters, he embraced a "partial consolidation" of the states "united under an efficient federal head."[8]

The deep division between the Federalists and Anti-Federalists was over republicanism and preservation of individual liberty. The debate no longer revolved around "whether the proposed union deprived states of the full sovereignty befitting members of a federal system, but whether the proposed union threatened to deprive them of their independence."[9] Differences turned on questions of degree: how far and in what form the federal government's power would extend. Federal power was limited, but "limitations were not to be imposed by considerations of state sovereignty."[10] Such considerations were ruled out by the way in which *federalism* was redefined as a separation of governmental power within a union of states sharing in a larger national political structure and process.

The meaning of America's new federalism was by no means settled with ratification of the Constitution or the Bill of Rights in 1791. That and other important questions of constitutional politics remained unresolved. As John Mercer anticipated toward the end of the Constitutional Convention, "It is a great mistake to suppose that the paper we are to propose will govern the United States. It is the men whom it will bring into the government and interest in maintaining it that is to govern them. The paper will only mark out the mode and the form. Men are the substance and must do the business."[11] The "true and safe construction" of the Constitution, Madison likewise allowed, would emerge with the "uniform sanction of successive legislative bodies; through a period of years and under the varied ascendency of parties."[12]

The idea of states' sovereignty continued to inspire imaginations. Differences within the Court provoked the first crisis over federalism in 1793. In *Chisholm v. Georgia,* 2 Dall. 419 (1793), Justice James Wilson, a former delegate to the Constitutional Convention and Pennsylvania's ratifying convention, held that citizens of one state could sue another state in federal courts. "As to the purposes of the union," he emphatically stated, "Georgia is not a sovereign state." That provoked an angry dissent from Justice James Iredell, a Southerner who had attended North Carolina's ratifying convention. His dissent invited the adoption of the Eleventh Amendment, overturning *Chisholm* and guaranteeing sovereign immunity for states from lawsuits brought by citizens of other states.

Five years later, a major reassertion of state sovereignty came from none other than James Madison and Thomas Jefferson, during their heated confrontation with the Federalists. In 1798, they issued the Virginia and Kentucky Resolutions (see Chapter 1) in response to the Alien and Sedition Acts, which aimed at silencing Jeffersonian-Republicans. Besides contending the acts ran afoul of the First Amendment, Madison and Jefferson claimed the states had the power to judge the constitutionality of federal law. Jefferson went so far as to assert that states could nullify federal laws they deemed unconstitutional. The "sovereign and independent" states, in his words, "have the unquestionable right to judge . . . and, that a nullification [by] those sovereignties, of all unauthorized acts done under color of that instrument is the rightful remedy."[13]

The Virginia and Kentucky Resolutions were extreme in both claiming state nullification as an attribute of state sovereignty, and returning to the older view of federalism. That view of federalism, to be sure, periodically resurfaced in various parts of the country. But Madison's and Jefferson's invocation of states' sovereignty failed to command support among the states. Moreover, it neither accurately reflected their understanding of the Constitution, nor accorded with their practices once each became president. The language of the Virginia and Kentucky Resolutions was that of protest marshaled in a moment of personal and political confrontation.[14]

Although no longer prevailing, the doctrine of states' sovereignty survived into the 1800s. Its revival came in the South, where it *gradually* evolved along with the political career of South Carolina's John C. Calhoun. Elected to Congress in 1810 as a fierce nationalist, Calhoun emerged in the 1820s as an advocate of states' sovereignty and an apologist for slavery. In futile efforts to preserve the South's way of life, he advanced the ideas of state nullification of federal law and of a "concurrent majority," by which either the North or South could veto the will of the national majority as registered in congressional legislation. Calhoun's theory of state sovereignty survived his death in 1850 as a rationale for the Confederacy.

It took three decades for these ideas to culminate in the Civil War. In 1832, no state followed South Carolina in nullifying a federal tariff based on then Vice-President Calhoun's theory of state sovereignty. President Andrew Jackson rebuffed the state's action as inconsistent with the union, and the state backed down. No state, again, joined South Carolina's 1851 call to secede in protest of the Compromise of 1850, admitting California into the Union as a "free state."

Southern states continued to look for accommodation and vindication of their interests in the Supreme Court under Chief Justice Roger B. Taney. He did not disappoint them. But his decision in *Dred Scott v. Sandford*, 60 U.S. 393 (1857) (see Vol. 2, Ch. 12) spelled disaster for the Court and the country. Taney sustained the power of southern states by striking down Congress's Missouri Compromise, excluding slavery from the territories. As far as the Constitution and the federal government were concerned, he proclaimed, blacks possessed "no rights." His decision triggered resistence in northern states, which in turn underscored for Southerners that their interests could not be preserved within the union. Immediately following Lincoln's inauguration in 1861, ten slave-holding states sided with South Carolina in forming the Confederate States of America.

The Civil War was as much over constitutional principle as economics, slavery, and differences in northern and southern ways of life. Secessionists frankly denied what earlier Anti-Federalists, even if reluctantly, conceded; namely, state sovereignty has no place within the framework of the Constitution. Alas, the nation's sovereignty had to be redeemed on the battlefield.

Defenders of states' sovereignty were defeated but not laid to rest by the war. During the Reconstruction period, the Supreme Court sought to accommodate both by developing a non sequitur, the doctrine of "dual federalism." "The Constitution," as the Supreme Court observed in *Texas v. White*, 7 Wall. (74 U.S.) 700 (1869), "look[ed] to an indestructable Union composed of indestructable States." Justice Samuel Miller pushed further in *The Slaughterhouse Cases*, 16 Wall. 36 (1873) (see Vol. 2, Ch. 3), advancing the idea of dual citizenship in sharply limiting the Fourteenth Amendment's application to the states. In *The Civil Rights Cases*, 109 U.S. 3 (1883) (see Vol. 2, Ch. 12) the last major piece of Reconstruction legislation, the Civil Rights Act of 1875, was overturned. The Supreme Court, then, effectively returned control of race relations to the states by upholding the doctrine of separate but equal in *Plessy v. Ferguson*, 163 U.S. 537 (1896) (see Vol. 2, Ch. 12), which upheld an 1890 Louisiana law requiring "equal but separate accommodations for the white and colored races" in all state passenger railway cars.

When the doctrine of separate but equal was finally abandoned in *Brown v. Board of Education*, 347 U.S. 483 (1954) (see Vol. 2, Ch. 12), the Warren Court's landmark school desegregation decision provoked massive resistance, violent protests, and widespread noncompliance. Controversy over states' sovereignty was rekindled, and the discredited idea of state nullification, or inter-position, revived.[15] But in *Bush v. Orleans School Board*, 364 U.S. 500 (1960), in response to states' resistence to desegregation, the Court underscored that "[t]he conclusion is clear that [state] interposition is not a *constitutional* doctrine."

While the vices and virtues of the national political process for safeguarding the interests of the states continue to be debated,[16] it bears pointing out that the Constitution recognizes few "attributes of state sovereignty," and even fewer present insurmountable barriers to the exercise of federal power. Article I guarantees the people of each state representation in the House and the representation of the states in the Senate. Article IV provides that no new state shall be created from territory in an existing state or group of states without the states' consent. Article V guarantees equal state representation in the Senate. The Tenth Amendment suggests other attributes, such as the power to tax and legislate, but only to the extent that they are not superceded or preempted by Congress. And the Eleventh Amendment protects states from being sued in federal courts by citizens of other states or foreign countries.

That the Constitution omits any affirmative mention of states' sovereignty does not appear fatal for its defenders, because the Constitution limits federal powers to those specifically enumerated and does so against the background of existing state governments. In other words, the enumeration of federal powers presupposed the states, whose powers are not conferred by the Constitution. Still, the absence of any constitutional affirmation of states' sovereignty carries great weight in light of the disassociation of federalism from states' sovereignty, and indeed the rejection of the latter, during the adoption and ratification of the Constitution.

In addition, the Constitution expressly grants plenary powers to the federal government and sharply limits states powers. The states are prohibited, in Article I, from conducting independent foreign and monetary policies, imposing export duties, impairing the obligations of contract, granting titles of nobility, and passing bills of attainder or *ex post facto* laws. Under Article III, they have no sovereign immunity from suits by other states or the United States.[17] Article IV further constrains them in several ways, including limiting their powers to determine state citizenship and to control their geographical boundaries. Most notably, Article IV puts into the hands of the federal government, not the states, the responsibility for guaranteeing that each state has a "Republican Form of Government." Finally, the supremacy clause in Article VI not only declares the supremacy of federal over state laws, but forces state courts in certain cases to apply federal law. Support for states' sovereignty thus cannot be constitutionally grounded in geographical territory or in terms of exclusive authority over its people, due to the coexistence and supremacy of the federal government.

In creating a new form of federalism, the Constitution presumed the existence, not the sovereignty, of the states. Indisputably, the states have a crucial role and responsibility in the administration of social services. Congress and the federal government depend heavily on them in sharing the burdens of governing. Individuals find continued protection for civil liberties and civil rights in the states and state constitutional law. And as Justice Louis Brandeis pointed out, dissenting in *New State Ice Co. v. Liebmann*, 285 U.S. 262 (1932): "It is one of the happy incidents of the federal system that a single courageous state may, if its citizens choose, serve as a laboratory; and try novel social and economic experiments without risk to the rest of the country."

This chapter examines the constitutional politics of federalism and continuing controversies over the powers of the states and intergovernmental relations. Issues involving state powers to regulate commerce and other subjects not preempted by Congress are taken up (see also Chapter 6). Then the focus is on the contemporary debate within the Rehnquist Court over the Tenth Amendment, which recognizes the "reserved" powers of the states. Finally, judicial federalism, the independence and interrelation of federal and state courts, as well as changes in the role of state supreme courts in interpreting federal and state constitutions are discussed.

NOTES

1. Quoted in James Madison, *Notes of Debates in the Federal Convention of 1787* (Athens: Ohio University Press, 1966), 217.

2. Quoted and further discussed in Rufas S. Davis, *The Federal Principle* (Berkeley: University of California Press, 1978), 118.

3. James Madison to George Washington, April 16, 1787, reprinted in Philip Kurland and Ralph Lerner, eds., *The Founders' Constitution*, Vol. 1 (Chicago: University of Chicago, 1987), 250.

4. Quoted and discussed in Herbert J. Storing, *What the Anti-Federalists Were For* (Chicago: University of Chicago, 1981), 12.

5. James Madison, in *The Records of the Federal Convention of 1787*, Vol. 1, ed. Max Farrand (New Haven, CT: Yale University Press, 1974), 122–123.

6. Patrick Henry, in *The Complete Anti-Federalist*, Vol. 5, ed. Herbert J. Storing (Chicago: University of Chicago, 1981), 211.

7. See Abraham Lincoln, "Message to Congress, Special Session," July 4, 1861, in *A Compilation of the Messages and Papers of the Presidents,* 20 vols., ed. J. D. Richardson (New York: Bureau of National Literature, 1917).

8. Federal Farmer, in *The Founders' Constitution,* Vol. 1, ed. Kurland and Lerner, 258–259, 273.

9. Kurland and Lerner, *The Founders' Constitution,* Vol. 1, ed. Kurland and Lerner, 243.

10. William Murphy, *The Triumph of Nationalism* (Chicago: Quadrangle, 1967), 410. See also S. Huntington, "The Founding Fathers and the Division of Powers," in *Area and Power,* ed. Authur Maas (Glencoe, IL: Free Press, 1959), 150.

11. Quoted in Madison, *Notes of Debates in the Federal Convention of 1787,* 455–456.

12. Quoted and further discussed in Robert Morgan, *James Madison on the Constitution and the Bill of Rights* (Westport, CT: Greenwood, 1988), 196.

13. See "Virginia Resolutions of 1798," and "Kentucky Resolutions of 1798 and 1799," in *The Debates in the Several State Conventions on the Adoption of the Federal Constitution,* Vol. 4, ed., Jonathan Elliot (New York: Burt Franklin Reprints, 1974), Ch. 1, 528–529, 540–544.

14. See Dumas Malone, *Jefferson and the Ordeal of Liberty* (Boston: Little, Brown, 1962), 395; and Robert Morgan, *James Madison on the Constitution* (Westport, CT: Greenwood Press, 1988).

15. See C. Herman Pritchett, *Constitutional Law of the Federal System* (Englewood Cliffs, NJ: Prentice Hall, 1984), 64–65; and David M. O'Brien, *Storm Center: The Supreme Court in American Politics* (New York: W. W. Norton, 1986), 287–306.

16. See and compare Choper, *Judicial Review and the National Political Process* (Chicago: University of Chicago, 1980) with M. Derthick, "Preserving Federalism," *The Brookings Review* (Winter/Spring, 1986): 32.

17. See *Monaco v. Mississippi,* 292 U.S. 313 (1934).

SELECTED BIBLIOGRAPHY

Barber, Sotirios. "National League of Cities v. Usery: New Meaning for the Tenth Amendment." In *The Supreme Court Review,* edited by Philip Kurland. Chicago: University of Chicago, 1977.

Berger, Raoul. *Federalism: The Founders' Design.* Norman: University of Oklahoma, 1987.

Choper, Jesse. *Judicial Review and the National Political Process* (Chicago: University of Chicago, 1980.

Derthick, Martha. "Preserving Federalism: Congress, the States, and the Supreme Court." *The Brookings Review* 32 (Winter/Spring, 1986).

Nagel, Robert. "Federalism as a Fundamental Value: National League of Cities in Perspective." In *The Supreme Court Review,* edited by Philip

Kurland, Gerhard Casper, and Dennis Hutchinson. Chicago: University of Chicago, 1982.

Wechsler, Herbert. "The Political Safeguards of Federalism: The Role of the States in the Composition and Selection of the National Government." 54 *Columbia Law Review* 543 (Apr. 1954).

A. STATES' POWER OVER COMMERCE AND REGULATION

Congress's ineffective regulation of commerce, as Madison explained in *The Federalist,* No. 42, was a central problem with the Articles of Confederation. For that reason, Article I of the Constitution specifically empowers Congress "to regulate commerce with foreign nations, and among the several states, and with Indian tribes."

Congress remained reluctant to assert its authority over commerce until the late nineteenth century. But in *Gibbons v. Ogden,* 9 Wheat. 1 (1824) (see page 465), Chief Justice John Marshall set forth an enduring principle of constitutional law. Congress's power is plenary and does not stop at state lines, while defining *commerce* as all "intercourse" that "affects more states than one." His standard for determining the scope of congressional power was nationalist and immediately heralded for securing the freedom of interstate transportation. As a result, tax and other barriers erected among the states were eliminated, the basis for a national "common market" was laid, and economic growth in the country was promoted.

In *Gibbons,* though, Marshall also implied a distinction between Congress's power over *interstate* commerce and that of the states over *intrastate* commerce. "[T]he completely internal commerce of a State," he noted, "may be considered as reserved for the State itself." Under Marshall's successor, Chief Justice Taney, the Court proved much more sympathetic to state power over commerce. In *Mayor of City of New York v. Miln,* 11 Pet. (36 U.S.) 102 (1837), for example, the Taney Court upheld a New York law, aimed at discouraging the immigration of indigents. The law required shipmasters entering New York's port from another state or country to report on its passengers and, if demanded by the mayor, to pay bonds for foreign passengers who later went on welfare rolls. When holding that the law was an exercise of state police powers, akin to inspection laws and "not a regulation of commerce," Justice Philip Barbour explained, "We think it as competent and as necessary for a State to provide precautionary measures against the moral pestilence of paupers, vagabonds, and possibly convicts, as it is to guard against the physical pestilence which may arise from unsound and infectious articles imported, or from a ship, the crew of which may be laboring under an infectious disease." But dissenting Justice Joseph Story, who was a leading intellectual influence as a Harvard law school professor and Chief Justice Marshall's closest ally on the Court, countered that the law was an unconstitutional restraint on interstate commerce and falling "directly within the principles established in the case of *Gibbons v. Ogden.*"

The Taney Court's interpretation in *Miln* was extreme and no longer controlling. In *Edwards v. California,* 314 U.S. 160 (1941), the Court unanimously struck down California's law, making it a misdemeanor knowingly to bring into the state an indigent. A majority agreed that California's law was "an unconstitutional barrier to interstate commerce," while four other justices deemed the law to violate a fundamental right to interstate travel. The Court further repudiated *Miln* in *Shapiro v. Thompson,* 394 U.S. 618 (1969) (see Vol. 2, Ch. 12), when holding that

Chief Justice Roger B. Taney. A photograph (the subject's name is misspelled on the mat) taken in the 1850s. *National Portrait Gallery, Smithsonian Institution.*

states may not impose one-year residency requirements as a condition for receiving public assistance.

Of far more lasting significance than *Miln* is *Cooley v. The Board of Wardens of the Port of Philadelphia* (1852) (see page 559), in which the Taney Court held that in some areas the regulation of commerce is a shared power of national and state governments. And for the first time the Court grappled with the issue of what standard should be employed in drawing the line differentiating the areas of permissible state regulation from those exclusively subject to Congress's power under the commerce clause.

The commerce clause is, of course, not self-interpreting. And there have been four rival interpretative theories of the relationship between the national government and the states in regulating commerce. In *Gibbons*, Marshall rejected Ogden's argument that there is a *concurrent power* over commerce, akin to the taxing power that both national and state governments may exercise. On this theory, no area of commerce would be exclusively reserved for Congress. Under the supremacy clause of Article VI, federal regulation would displace that of the states but states could regulate in the absence of federal regulation. Marshall, though, rejected this theory and the analogy drawn between the powers to tax and to regulate commerce.

Justice William Johnson's concurring opinion in *Gibbons* advanced what has been called the *dormant power* theory. On this interpretation, the commerce clause would bar state regulation of commerce regardless of whether Congress had exercised its powers over commerce. Marshall took no position on this theory in *Gibbons*, but a majority embraced it in *The Passenger Cases*, 7 How. 283 (1849), holding that state taxing power is limited over interstate commerce by the "affirmative grants of power to the general government."[1] However, writing for the Court in *Cooley*, Justice Benjamin Curtis rejected this theory.

Curtis also rejected a third interpretation, that of *mutual exclusiveness*. In *Gibbons*, Marshall appeared to accept this view when rejecting the concurrent powers theory and noting that states could regulate internal commerce with inspection and health laws, for example, as well as "everything within the territory of a State, not surrendered to [the] general government."

In *Cooley*, Curtis proposed a fourth theory, that of *selective exclusiveness*. According to this theory, Congress's power is complete and exclusive in some areas, while in others the states are free to regulate commerce. As to the standard for distinguishing the subjects of national versus state regulation, Curtis proposed, "Whatever subjects of this power are in their nature national, or admit only of one uniform system, or plan of regulation, may justly be said to be of such a nature as to require exclusive legislation by Congress."

As a result of the Court's writing the theory of selective exclusiveness into the constitutional law of the commerce clause, it inevitably had to define the categories subject to state regulation and those exclusively reserved for Congress. Central to the Court's subsequent interpretation and line drawing has been whether or not states regulate commerce in the absence of federal legislation.

In those areas where Congress has not yet legislated, the Court basically applies the standard set down in *Cooley*. State regulation is valid if the activity is basically local and the Court determines there is no need for a uniform national standard. In *Bob-Lo Excursion Co. v. Michigan*, 333 U.S. 28 (1948), for example, Michigan's civil rights act was upheld as applied against an amusement park running an excursion steamer to an island on the Canadian side of the Detroit river. Bob-Lo Excursion Company refused to transport blacks and contended that the state law was inapplicable because it was engaged in foreign commerce and hence subject only to congressional legislation. The Court rejected that claim, observing, "It is difficult to imagine what national interest or police, whether of securing uniformity in regulating commerce, affecting relations with foreign nations or otherwise, could reasonably be found to be adversely affected by applying Michigan's statute to those facts or to outweigh her interest in doing so."

When determining whether an activity subject to state regulation is "essentially local," the Court considers the burden placed on interstate commerce by a state regulation. *South Carolina Highway Department v. Barnwell Brothers*, 303 U.S. 177 (1938), upheld a state law forbidding on state highways trucks and trailers wider than ninety inches and weighing more than 20,000 pounds, despite its being stricter than the laws of surrounding states. However, *Southern Pacific Co. v. Arizona* (1945) (see page 565), overturned a regulation of the length of trains as an undue burden on interstate commerce, touching a subject requiring a national standard. See also *Bibb v. Navajo Freight Lines, Inc.* (1959) (see page 569).

A related controversy involves whether state regulation aims to discriminate against businesses in other states so as to erect commercial or other barriers. In such controversies, the Court must decide whether a state regulation is too burdensome and what kinds and levels of burdens are acceptable. *Maine v. Taylor* (1986) (see page 572) is instructive on the Court's analysis of this kind of controversy.

THE DEVELOPMENT OF LAW

Other Rulings on State Regulation of Commerce in the Absence of Federal Legislation

Case	Ruling
Dean Milk Company v. City of Madison, 340 U.S. 349 (1956)	Invalidated an ordinance prohibiting the sale of milk in the city of Madison, Wisconsin, unless it was bottled at an approved plant, for erecting an economic barrier against the sale of milk produced in Illinois.
Head v. New Mexico Board of Examiners, 374 U.S. 424 (1963)	Upheld a state law forbidding the advertising of the price of eyeglasses and rejected the claim of an out-of-state optometrist that the law burdened interstate commerce.
Colorado Anti-Discrimination Commission, v. Continental Airlines, 372 U.S. 714 (1963)	Upheld a state antidiscrimination law as applied to Continental Airlines, an interstate carrier, as posing no undue burden.
Great Atlantic & Pacific Tea Co. v. Cottrell, 424 U.S. 366 (1976)	Held that Mississippi may not bar sales of milk produced in Louisiana that met its health standards simply because Louisiana refused to sign a reciprocity agreement.
Hunt v. Washington State Apple Advertising Commission, 432 U.S. 333 (1977)	Struck down North Carolina's labeling requirements for apples as an undue burden on and discrimination against Washington state apple growers.
City of Philadelphia v. New Jersey, 437 U.S. 617 (1978)	Struck down New Jersey's ban on the disposal of out-of-state garbage as an undue burden on interstate commerce.
Exxon Corporation v. Governor of Maryland, 437 U.S. 117 (1978)	Upheld a state prohibition against producers and refiners of petroleum products from operating service stations in the state.
Hughes v. Oklahoma, 441 U.S. 322 (1979)	Struck down a law forbidding the shipping of minnows for out-of-state sales.

Case	Ruling
Raymond Motor Transportation v. Rice and Kassell v. Consolidated Freightways Corporation, 450 U.S. 662 (1981)	Invalidated Wisconsin's and Iowa's bans on the operation on state highways of sixty-five–foot double trucks as burdens on interstate commerce.
Minnesota v. Clover Leaf Creamery Co., 449 U.S. 459 (1981)	Upheld a conservation law "banning the retail sale of milk in plastic nonreturnable, nonrefillable containers, but permitting such sale in other nonreturnable, nonrefillable containers, such as paperboard milk cartons" as an "incidential burden imposed on commerce."
New England Power Co. v. New Hampshire, 455 U.S. 331 (1982)	States may not forbid companies from selling power to other states even though produced by utilities in the state.
Sporhase v. Nebraska, 458 U.S. 941 (1982)	Upheld a Nebraska law requiring permits for the shipment and sale of ground water insofar as permits were issued on findings that the shipment and sale was (1) reasonable, (2) not contrary to the conservation of water, and (3) not detrimental to the public welfare, but held that the state could not require a reciprocity agreement with the state to which the water was shipped and sold.
Hartigan v. General Electric Company and Don't Waste Washington Legal Defense Foundation v. Washington, 461 U.S. 913 (1983)	Let stand lower court rulings that states may not bar out-of-state nuclear waste from being transported and stored within their borders.
White v. Massachusetts Council, 460 U.S. 204 (1983)	Upheld a restriction on public works contracts to companies agreeing to use Boston workers in at least half of their jobs.
South-Central Timber Development, Inc. v. Wunnicke, 467 U.S. 82 (1984)	Congress authorized Alaska to require that timber harvested on federal land in the state be processed within the state prior to export, but failed to similarly regulate timber on state land. Alaska's requirement that timber har-

Case	Ruling
	vested on state land be processed within the state, nevertheless, has an undue burden on interstate commerce in affecting out-of-state processing markets.
Brown-Forman Distillers Corp v. New York Liquor Authority, 476 U.S. 573 (1986)	Held that states may not force an out-of-state merchant to seek regulatory approval in one state before conducting business in another.
Goldberg v. Sweet, 109 S.Ct. 528 (1988)	A 5 percent state tax on all telephone calls, including interstate calls, does not violate the commerce clause.
Healy v. Beer Institute, Inc., 109 S.Ct. 2491 (1989)	Struck down as an undue burden on commerce Connecticut's statute requiring out-of-state shippers of beer to affirm that their prices for products sold in state are not higher than the prices of those products sold out of state.
Cotton Petroleum v. New Mexico, 109 S.Ct. 1069 (1989)	States are not specifically preempted by Congress from taxing oil and gas taken from Indian reservations.

When Congress has enacted legislation regulating interstate commerce, challenges to state regulation require the Court to decide whether Congress has completely occupied the field and whether states may still enact nonconflicting legislation. Since *McCulloch v. Maryland,* 4 Wheat. 316 (1819) (see page 453), the Court has maintained that federal legislation preempts conflicting state regulation under the supremacy clause of Article VI.[2]

Cooley's holding that some subjects are inherently local far from solved the problem of determining which subjects are "national" and which are exclusively "local." In the early nineteenth century, the Court attempted to resolve this problem in several ways. In *Brown v. Maryland,* 25 U.S. 419 (1827), the Marshall Court ruled that states could not tax items of interstate commerce as long as they remained in their "original package."[3] And in *Wilson v. Black Bird Creek Marsh Co.,* 27 U.S. 245 (1829), the Marshall Court suggested that the purpose of legislation may be important, when ruling that a state's authorization for a dam on a stream deep enough to be used by boats in interstate commerce did not violate the commerce clause.

Rather than attempting to define activities that are inherently local or determine the purpose of state legislation, the Court now generally employs the *doctrine of federal preemption*—that Congress has preempted state regulation in an area by its own legislation. Sometimes a federal statute expressly preempts state regulation. In *Shaw v. Delta Air Lines*, 463 U.S. 85 (1983), the Court held that the federal Employment Retirement Income Security Act (ERISA) preempted "all State laws insofar as they . . . relate to any employee benefit plan." In other circumstances, though, Congress may not explicitly state that it is preempting state regulation and the Court must analyze the costs and benefits of state regulation under the federal preemption doctrine. The doctrine has been applied in a large number of areas. In *Pennsylvania v. Nelson* (1956) (see page 575), Chief Justice Warren outlined the basic considerations in applying the doctrine. Other important rulings limiting state regulatory powers are *Missouri v. Holland*, 252 U.S. 416 (1920) (see page 210); *Steward Machine Co. v. Davis*, 301 U.S. 548 (1937) (see page 526); and *South Dakota v. Dole*, 107 S.Ct. 2793 (1987) (see page 536).

THE DEVELOPMENT OF LAW

Other Rulings on State Regulatory Powers in Alleged Conflict with Federal Legislation

Case	Ruling
Allen-Bradley Local v. Wisconsin Employment Relations Board, 315 U.S. 740 (1942)	Federal legislation did not preempt states from punishing offense conduct related to "traditionally local matters as public safety and order and the use of streets and highways."
Hill v. Florida, 325 U.S. 528 (1945)	State law requiring licenses for labor union agents conflicted with the National Labor Relations Act.
International Union v. O'Brien, 339 U.S. 454 (1950)	State laws interfering with the right to strike are preempted by federal legislation.
Garner v. Teamster Union, 346 U.S. 485 (1953)	States forbidden from barring peaceful picketing.
Weber v. Annhauser-Busch, 348 U.S. 468 (1955), and *Teamsters Union v. Oliver*, 358 U.S. 283 (1957)	State antitrust laws preempted as applied to enjoining labor strikes and collective bargaining agreements.

Case	Ruling
Farmers Educational & Cooperative Union v. WDAY, 360 U.S. 525 (1958)	The Federal Communications Act, requiring broadcasters to carry some political speeches without censoring them, occupied the field and thus immunized broadcasters from liability under state libel laws.
Huron Portland Cement Co. v. Detroit, 362 U.S. 440 (1960)	Upheld the conviction of a ship operating in interstate commerce and whose boiler met federal standards, for violating Detroit's smoke-abatement ordinance.
City of Burbank v. Lockheed Air Terminal, 411 U.S. 624 (1973)	Struck down local noise abatement ordinance as being preempted by federal airline regulations.
Jackson Transit Authority v. Amalgamated Transit Union, 457 U.S. 15 (1982)	Held that the urban Mass Transportation Act of 1964 did not preempt states from their traditional control over labor relations involving local governments and unions.
Pacific Gas & Electric Co. v. State Energy Commission, 461 U.S. 190 (1983)	Held the Atomic Energy Act does not preempt states from some regulation of nuclear power plants; states may forbid the building of plants until the federal government has approved of the methods of nuclear waste disposal.
Silkwood v. Kerr-McGee Corporation, 464 U.S. 283 (1984)	Held that state laws for awarding punitive damages for injuries resulting from escaped plutonium at a nuclear power plant are not preempted; held that state safety, but not economic, regulations are preempted.
Metropolitan Life Insurance Co. v. Ward, 470 U.S. 869 (1985)	Upheld state regulation of insurance contracts as not constituting interstate commerce.
Nantahala Power & Light Co. v. Thornburg, 476 U.S. 953 (1986)	States may not differ from the Federal Energy Regulatory Commission's standards in setting intrastate retail rates.
Mississippi Power & Light Co. v. Mississippi ex rel. Moore, 108 S.Ct. 2428 (1988)	Federal Energy Regulatory Commission preempted state rate-making authority.

Case	Ruling
Felder v. Casey, 109 S.Ct. 2302 (1988)	Section 1983 of the United States Code, providing for federal civil rights suits, preempts Wisconsin's notice-of-claim statute (which had barred lawsuits against any state governmental agency or officer unless a written notice of the injury suffered was submitted within 120 days of the injury).
California v. Federal Energy Regulatory Commission, 110 S.Ct. 2024 (1990)	Held that California's regulations setting standards for minimum stream flows on a river, in which federally licensed hydroelectric power plant was located, were preempted by the Federal Power Act.
Perpich v. Department of Defense, 110 S.Ct. 2418 (1990)	The Court held that, over the objections of a state governor, the federal government may order state National Guard troops to take part in peacetime training abroad, and reaffirmed federal preemption based on the recognition of "the supremacy of the federal government in the area of military affairs."

NOTES

1. See also *The License Cases*, 5 How. 504 (1847).
2. See also *Havenstein v. Lynham*, 100 U.S. 483 (1880).
3. See also *Leisy v. Hardin*, 135 U.S. 100 (1890). *Brown v. Maryland*, however was limited in *Michigan Tire Co. v. Wages*, 423 U.S. 276 (1976).

SELECTED BIBLIOGRAPHY

Corwin, Edward S. *The Commerce Clause versus States Rights*. Princeton, NJ: Princeton University Press, 1936.
Frankfurter, Felix. *The Commerce Clause*. Introduction by Wallace Mendelson. Chicago, IL: Quadrangle, 1964.

Cooley v. The Board of Wardens of the Port of Philadelphia

12 How. (53 U.S.) 229 (1851)

In 1803, Pennsylvania passed a law requiring, with certain exceptions, ships entering or leaving Philadelphia's harbor to employ a pilot from the city to navigate and provided that shipowners who failed to comply were required to pay one-half of the pilotage fees into a pilot's pension fund. When two of Aaron Cooley's ships did not use local pilots, the Board of Wardens of the Port of Philadelphia sued in a court of common pleas, which found in their favor. The Pennsylvania Supreme Court affirmed and Cooley appealed to the Supreme Court, arguing that the law was an unconstitutional tax on commerce and not a pilot regulation, since Congress had passed in 1789 a law permitting the states to regulate pilots.

Justice CURTIS delivers the opinion of the court.

That the power to regulate commerce includes the regulation of navigation, we consider settled. And when we look to the nature of the service performed by pilots, to the relations which that service and its compensations bear to navigation between the several States, and between the ports of the United States, and foreign countries, we are brought to the conclusion, that the regulation of the qualifications of pilots, of the modes and times of offering and rendering their services, of the responsibilities which shall rest upon them, of the powers they shall possess, of the compensation they may demand, and of the penalties by which their rights and duties may be enforced, do constitute regulations of navigation, and consequently of commerce, within the just meaning of this clause of the Constitution. . . .

It becomes necessary, therefore, to consider whether this law of Pennsylvania, being a regulation of commerce, is valid.

The Act of Congress of the 7th of August, 1789, sec. 4, is as follows:

"That all pilots in the bays, inlets, rivers, harbors, and ports of the United States, shall continue to be regulated in conformity with the existing laws of the States, respectively, wherein such pilots may be, or with such laws as the States may respectively hereafter enact for the purpose, until further legislative provision shall be made by Congress."

If the law of Pennsylvania, now in question, had been in existence at the date of this Act of Congress, we might hold it to have been adopted by Congress, and thus made a law of the United States, and so valid. Because this Act does, in effect, give the force of an Act of Congress, to the then existing state laws on this subject, so long as they should continue unrepealed by the State which enacted them.

But the law on which these actions are founded was not enacted till 1803. What effect, then, can be attributed to so much of the Act of 1789 as declares that pilots shall continue to be regulated in conformity "with such laws as the States may respectively hereafter enact for the purpose, until further legislative provision shall be made by Congress?"

If the States were devested of the power to legislate on this subject by the grant of the commercial power to Congress, it is plain this Act could not confer upon them power thus to legislate. If the Constitution excluded the States from making any law regulating commerce, certainly Congress cannot regrant, or in any manner reconvey to the States that power. And yet this Act of 1789 gives its sanction only to laws enacted by the States. This necessarily implies a constitutional power to legislate; for only a rule created by the sovereign power of a state acting in its legislative capacity, can be deemed a law, enacted by a state; and if the State has so limited its sovereign power that it no longer extends to a particular subject, manifestly it cannot, in any proper sense, be said to enact laws thereon. Entertaining these views we are brought directly and unavoidably to the consideration of the question, whether the grant of the commercial power to Congress, did per se deprive the States of all power to regulate pilots. This question has never been decided by this court, nor, in our judgment, has any case depending upon all the considerations which must govern this one, come before this court. The grant of commercial power to Congress does not contain any terms which expressly exclude the States from exercising an authority over its subject matter. If they are excluded it must be because the nature of the power, thus granted to Congress, requires that a similar authority should not exist in the States. If it were conceded on the one side, that the nature of this power, like that to legislate for the District of Columbia, is absolutely and totally repugnant to the existence of similar power in the States, probably no one would deny that the grant of the power to Congress, as effectually and perfectly excludes the States from all future legislation on the subject, as if express words had been used to exclude them. And on the other hand, if it were admitted that the existence of this power in Congress, like the power of taxation, is compatible with the existence of a similar power in the States, then it would be in conformity with the contemporary exposition of the Constitution (Federalist, No. 32), and with the judicial construction, given from time to time by this court, after the most deliberate consideration, to hold that the mere grant

of such a power to Congress, did not imply a prohibition on
the States to exercise the same power; that it is not the mere
existence of such a power, but its exercise by Congress, which
may be incompatible with the exercise of the same power by
the States, and that the States may legislate in the absence of
congressional regulations. . . .

The diversities of opinion, therefore, which have existed on
this subject, have arisen from the different views taken of the
nature of this power. But when the nature of a power like this
is spoken of, when it is said that the nature of the power requires
that it should be exercised exclusively by Congress, it must be
intended to refer to the subjects of that power, and to say they
are of such a nature as to require exclusive legislation by Congress.
Now, the power to regulate commerce, embraces a vast field,
containing not only many, but exceedingly various subjects, quite
unlike in their nature; some imperatively demanding a single
uniform rule, operating equally on the commerce of the United
States in every port; and some like the subject now in question,
as imperatively demanding that diversity, which alone can meet
the local necessities of navigation.

Either absolutely to affirm, or deny, that the nature of this
power requires exclusive legislation by Congress, is to lose sight
of the nature of the subjects of this power, and to assert concerning
all of them, what is really applicable but to a part. Whatever
subjects of this power are in their nature national, or admit only
of one uniform system, or plan of regulation, may justly be said
to be of such a nature as to require exclusive legislation by Congress. That this cannot be affirmed of laws for the regulation of
pilots and pilotage is plain. The Act of 1789 contains a clear
and authoritative declaration by the first Congress, that the nature
of this subject is such, that until Congress should find it necessary
to exert its power, it should be left to the legislation of the States;
that it is local and not national; that it is likely to be the best
provided for, not by one system, or plan of regulations, but by
as many as the legislative discretion of the several States should
deem applicable to the local peculiarities of the ports within their
limits.

Viewed in this light, so much of this Act of 1789 as declares
that pilots shall continue to be regulated "by such laws as the
States may respectively hereafter enact for that purpose," instead
of being held to be inoperative, as an attempt to confer on the
States a power to legislate, of which the Constitution had deprived
them, is allowed an appropriate and important signification. It
manifests the understanding of Congress, at the outset of the
government, that the nature of this subject is not such as to
require its exclusive legislation. The practice of the States, and
of the national government, has been in conformity with this
declaration, from the origin of the national government to this

time; and the nature of the subject, when examined, is such as to leave no doubt of the superior fitness and propriety, not to say the absolute necessity, of different systems of regulation, drawn from local knowledge and experience, and conformed to local wants. How, then, can we say, that by the mere grant of power to regulate commerce, the States are deprived of all the power to legislate on this subject, because from the nature of the power the legislation of Congress must be exclusive. This would be to affirm that the nature of the power is, in any case, something different from the nature of the subject to which, in such case, the power extends, and that the nature of the power necessarily demands, in all cases, exclusive legislation by Congress, while the nature of one of the subjects of that power, not only does not require such exclusive legislation, but may be best provided for by many different systems enacted by the States, in conformity with the circumstances of the ports within their limits. In construing an instrument designed for the formation of a government, and in determining the extent of one of its important grants of power to legislate, we can make no such distinction between the nature of the power and the nature of the subject on which that power was intended practically to operate, nor consider the grant more extensive by affirming of the power, what is not true of its subject now in question.

It is the opinion of a majority of the court that the mere grant to Congress of the power to regulate commerce, did not deprive the States of power to regulate pilots, and that although Congress has legislated on this subject, its legislation manifests an intention, with a single exception, not to regulate this subject, but to leave its regulation to the several States. To these precise questions, which are all we are called on to decide, this opinion must be understood to be confined. It does not extend to the question what other subjects, under the commercial power, are within the exclusive control of Congress, or may be regulated by the States in the absence of all congressional legislation; nor to the general question how far any regulation of a subject by Congress may be deemed to operate as an exclusion of all legislation by the States upon the same subject. We decide the precise questions before us, upon what we deem sound principles, applicable to this particular subject in the state in which the legislation of Congress has left it. We go no farther. . . .

We are of opinion that this state law was enacted by virtue of a power, residing in the State to legislate; that it is not in conflict with any law of Congress; that it does not interfere with any system which Congress has established by making regulations, or by intentionally leaving individuals to their own unrestricted action; that this law is therefore valid, and the judgement of the Supreme Court of Pennsylvania in each case must be affirmed.

Justice McLEAN and Justice WAYNE dissented. Justice DAN-
IEL, although he concurred in the judgment of the court, dissented from its reasoning.

Justice McLEAN dissenting.

It is with regret that I feel myself obliged to dissent from the
opinion ŏf a majority of my brethren in this case.

As expressing my views on the question involved, I will copy
a few sentences from the opinion of Chief Justice MARSHALL
in the opinion in *Gibbons v. Ogden.* "It has been said," says that
illustrious judge, "that the Act of August 7th, 1789, acknowledges
a concurrent power in the States to regulate the conduct of pilots,
and hence is inferred an admission of their concurrent right with
Congress to regulate commerce with foreign nations and amongst
the States. But this inference is not, we think, justified by the
fact. . . .

"The Act unquestionably manifests an intention to leave this
subject entirely to the States, until Congress should think proper
to interpose; but the very enactment of such a law indicates an
opinion that it was necessary; that the existing system would not
be applicable to the new state of things, unless expressly applied
to it by Congress. But this section is confined to pilots within
the bays, inlets, rivers, harbors, and ports of the United States,
which are, of course, in whole or in part, also within the limits
of some particular state. The acknowledged power of a state to
regulate its police, its domestic trade, and to govern its own citizens, may enable it to legislate on this subject, to a considerable
extent; and the adoption of its system by Congress, and the application of it to the whole subject of commerce, does not seem to
the court to imply a right in the States so to apply it of their
own authority. But the adoption of the state system being temporary, being only 'until further legislative provision shall be made
by Congress,' shows conclusively, an opinion that Congress could
control the whole subject, and might adopt the system of the
States or provide one of its own."

Why did Congress pass the Act of 1789, adopting the pilot
laws of the respective States Laws they unquestionably were, having been enacted by the States before the adoption of the Constitution. But were they laws under the Constitution? If they had
been so considered by Congress, they would not have been
adopted by a special Act. There is believed to be no instance in
the legislation of Congress, where a state law has been adopted,
which, before its adoption, applied to federal powers. To suppose
such a case, would be an imputation of ignorance as to federal
powers, least of all chargeable against the men who formed the
Constitution and who best understood it.

Congress adopted the pilot laws of the States, because it was well understood, they could have had no force, as regulations of foreign commerce or of commerce among the States, if not so adopted. By their adoption they were made Acts of Congress, and ever since they have been so considered and enforced.

Each State regulates the commerce within its limits; which is not within the range of federal powers. So far, and no farther could effect have been given to the pilot laws of the States, under the Constitution. But those laws were only adopted "until further legislative provisions shall be made by Congress."

This shows that Congress claimed the whole commercial power on this subject, by adopting the pilot laws of the States, making them Acts of Congress; and also by declaring that the adoption was only until some further legislative provision could be made by Congress.

Justice DANIEL concurring in part.

I agree with the majority in their decision, that the judgments of the Supreme Court of Pennsylvania in these cases should be affirmed, though I cannot go with them in the process or argument by which their conclusion has been reached. . . . The power delegated to Congress by the Constitution relates properly to the terms on which commercial engagements may be prosecuted; the character of the articles which they may embrace; the permission or terms according to which they may be introduced; and do not necessarily nor even naturally extend to the means of precaution and safety adopted within the waters or limits of the States by the authority of the latter for the preservation of vessels and cargoes, and the lives of navigators or passengers. These last subjects are essentially local—they must depend upon local necessities which call them into existence, must differ according to the degrees of that necessity. It is admitted, on all hands, that they cannot be uniform or even general, but must vary so as to meet the purposes to be accomplished. . . . The true question here is, whether the power to enact pilot laws is appropriate and necessary, or rather most appropriate and necessary to the State or the federal governments. It being conceded that this power has been exercised by the States from their very dawn of existence; that it can be practically and beneficially applied by the local authorities only; it being conceded, as it must be, that the power to pass pilot laws, as such, has not been in any express terms delegated to Congress, and does not necessarily conflict with the right to establish commercial regulations, I am forced to conclude that this is an original and inherent power in the States, and not one to be merely tolerated, or held subject to the sanction of the federal government.

Southern Pacific Co. v. Arizona
325 U.S. 761, 65 S.Ct. 1515 (1945).

In 1940, Arizona's state attorney general sued the Southern Pacific Company for operating two interstate trains in violation of the state's Train Limit Law of 1912, prohibiting the operation of trains with more than fourteen passenger or seventy freight cars. Attorneys for the company attacked the constitutionality of the law on grounds that it violated the commerce clause and the due process clause of the Fourteenth Amendment. The trial court found in favor of Southern Pacific Company but the Supreme Court of Arizona reversed. Southern Pacific Company then appealed to the Supreme Court.

Chief Justice STONE delivers the opinion of the Court.

Although the commerce clause conferred on the national government power to regulate commerce, its possession of the power does not exclude all state power of regulation. . . . [I]t has been recognized that, in the absence of conflicting legislation by Congress, there is a residuum of power in the state to make laws governing matters of local concern which nevertheless in some measure affect interstate commerce or even, to some extent, regulate it. . . . Thus the states may regulate matters which, because of their number and diversity, may never be adequately dealt with by Congress. . . . When the regulation of matters of local concern is local in character and effect, and its impact on the national commerce does not seriously interfere with its operation, and the consequent incentive to deal with them nationally is slight, such regulation has been generally held to be within state authority.

But ever since *Gibbons v. Ogden,* the states have not been deemed to have authority to impede substantially the free flow of commerce from state to state, or to regulate those phases of the national commerce which, because of the need of national uniformity, demand that their regulation, if any, be prescribed by a single authority. Whether or not this long recognized distribution of power between the national and the state governments is predicated upon the implications of the commerce clause itself, or upon the presumed intention of Congress, where Congress has not spoken, the result is the same.

In the application of these principles some enactments may be found to be plainly within and others plainly without state power. But between these extremes lies the infinite variety of cases in which regulation of local matters may also operate as a regulation of commerce, in which reconciliation of the conflicting claims of state and national power is to be attained only by some appraisal and accommodation of the competing demands of the state and national interests involved. . . .

For a hundred years it has been accepted constitutional doctrine that the commerce clause, without the aid of Congressional legislation, thus affords some protection from state legislation inimical to the national commerce, and that in such cases, where Congress has not acted, this Court, and not the state legislature, is under the commerce clause the final arbiter of the competing demands of state and national interests. . . .

Congress has undoubted power to redefine the distribution of power over interstate commerce. It may either permit the states to regulate the commerce in a manner which would otherwise not be permissible, or exclude state regulation even of matters of peculiarly local concern which nevertheless affect interstate commerce. . . .

But in general Congress has left it to the courts to formulate the rules thus interpreting the commerce clause in its application, doubtless because it has appreciated the destructive consequences to the commerce of the nation if their protection were withdrawn and has been aware that in their application state laws will not be invalidated without the support of relevant factual material which will "afford a sure basis" for an informed judgment. Meanwhile, Congress has accommodated its legislation, as have the states, to these rules as an established feature of our constitutional system. There has thus been left to the states wide scope for the regulation of matters of local state concern, even though it in some measure affects the commerce, provided it does not materially restrict the free flow of commerce across state lines, or interfere with it in matters with respect to which uniformity of regulation is of predominant national concern.

Hence the matters for ultimate determination here are the nature and extent of the burden which the state regulation of interstate trains, adopted as a safety measure, imposes on interstate commerce, and whether the relative weights of the state and national interests involved are such as to make inapplicable the rule, generally observed, that the free flow of interstate commerce and its freedom from local restraints in matters requiring uniformity of regulation are interests safeguarded by the commerce clause from state interference. . . .

The findings show that the operation of long trains, that is trains of more than fourteen passenger and more than seventy freight cars, is standard practice over the main lines of the railroads of the United States, and that, if the length of trains is to be regulated at all, national uniformity in the regulation adopted, such as only Congress can prescribe, is practically indispensable to the operation of an efficient and economical national railway system. On many railroads passenger trains of more than fourteen cars and freight trains of more than seventy cars are operated, and on some systems freight trains are run ranging from one hundred and twenty-five to one hundred and sixty cars in length. . . .

In Arizona, approximately 93% of the freight traffic and 95% of the passenger traffic is interstate. Because of the Train Limit Law appellant is required to haul over 30% more trains in Arizona than would otherwise have been necessary. The record shows a definite relationship between operating costs and the length of trains, the increase in length resulting in a reduction of operating costs per car. The additional cost of operation of trains complying with the Train Limit Law in Arizona amounts for the two railroads traversing that state to about $1,000,000 a year. The reduction in train lengths also impedes efficient operation. More locomotives and more manpower are required; the necessary conversion and reconversion of train lengths at terminals and the delay caused by breaking up and remaking long trains upon entering and leaving the state in order to comply with the law, delays the traffic and diminishes its volume moved in a given time, especially when traffic is heavy. . . .

The unchallenged findings leave no doubt that the Arizona Train Limit Law imposes a serious burden on the interstate commerce conducted by appellant. It materially impedes the movement of appellant's interstate trains through that state and interposes a substantial obstruction to the national policy proclaimed by Congress, to promote adequate, economical and efficient railway transportation service. Enforcement of the law in Arizona, while train lengths remain unregulated or are regulated by varying standards in other states, must inevitably result in an impairment of uniformity of efficient railroad operation because the railroads are subjected to regulation which is not uniform in its application. . . .

We think, as the trial court found, that the Arizona Train Limit Law, viewed as a safety measure, affords at most slight and dubious advantage, if any, over unregulated train lengths. . . .

Here we conclude that the state does go too far. Its regulation of train lengths, admittedly obstructive to interstate train operation, and having a seriously adverse effect on transportation efficiency and economy, passes beyond what is plainly essential for safety since it does not appear that it will lessen rather than increase the danger of accident. Its attempted regulation of the operation of interstate trains cannot establish nation-wide control such as is essential to the maintenance of an efficient transportation system, which Congress alone can prescribe. The state interest cannot be preserved at the expense of the national interest by an enactment which regulates interstate train lengths without securing such control, which is a matter of national concern. To this the interest of the state here asserted is subordinate.

Appellees especially rely on *South Carolina Highway Dept. v. Barnwell Bros.* [303 U.S. 177 (1938)] as supporting the state's authority to regulate the length of interstate trains. . . .

South Carolina State Highway Dept. v. Barnwell Bros. was concerned with the power of the state to regulate the weight and width of motor cars passing interstate over its highways, a legislative field over which the state has a far more extensive control than over interstate railroads. In that case . . . we were at pains to point out that there are few subjects of state regulation affecting interstate commerce which are so peculiarly of local concern as is the use of the state's highways. Unlike the railroads local highways are built, owned and maintained by the state or its municipal subdivisions. The state is responsible for their safe and economical administration. Regulations affecting the safety of their use must be applied alike to intrastate and interstate traffic. The fact that they affect alike shippers in interstate and intrastate commerce in great numbers, within as well as without the state, is a safeguard against regulatory abuses. Their regulation is akin to quarantine measures, game laws, and like local regulations of rivers, harbors, piers, and docks, with respect to which the state has exceptional scope for the exercise of its regulatory power, and which, Congress not acting, have been sustained even though they materially interfere with interstate commerce. . . .

The contrast between the present regulation and the highway safety regulations, in point of the nature of the subject of regulation and the state's interest in it, illustrate and emphasize the considerations which enter into a determination of the relative weights of state and national interests where state regulation affecting interstate commerce is attempted. Here examination of all the relevant factors makes it plain that the state interest is outweighed by the interest of the nation in an adequate, economical and efficient railway transportation service, which must prevail.

Reversed.

Justice RUTLEDGE concurred.

Justice BLACK dissenting.

[W]hether it is in the interest of society for the length of trains to be governmentally regulated is a matter of public policy. Someone must fix that policy—either the Congress, or the state, or the courts. A century and a half of constitutional history and government admonishes this Court to leave that choice to the elected legislative representatives of the people themselves, where it properly belongs both on democratic principles and the requirements of efficient government.

Justice DOUGLAS, dissenting.

My view has been that the courts should intervene only where the state legislation discriminated against interstate commerce or was out of harmony with laws which Congress had enacted. It seems to me particularly appropriate that that course be followed here. For Congress has given the Interstate Commerce Commission broad powers of regulation over interstate carriers. The Commission is the national agency which has been entrusted with the task of promoting a safe, adequate, efficient, and economical transportation service. It is the expert on this subject. It is in a position to police the field. And if its powers prove inadequate for the task, Congress, which has paramount authority in this field, can implement them. . . .

Whether the question arises under the Commerce Clause or the Fourteenth Amendment, I think the legislation is entitled to a presumption of validity. If a State passed a law prohibiting the hauling of more than one freight car at a time, we would have a situation comparable in effect to a state law requiring all railroads within its borders to operate on narrow gauge tracks. The question is one of degree and calls for a close appraisal of the facts. I am not persuaded that the evidence adduced by the railroads overcomes the presumption of validity to which this trainlimit law is entitled.

Bibb v. Navajo Freight Lines, Inc.
359 U.S. 520, 79 S.Ct. 962 (1959)

Attorneys for Navajo Freight Lines, Inc., a New Mexico corporation, sought in federal district court an injunction against the enforcement of an Illinois law requiring all trucks and trailers to have special mudgards, unlike those required in other states. The court found this an undue burden on interstate commerce. Joseph Bibb, the director of Illinois's Department of Public Safety, appealed to the Supreme Court.

Justice DOUGLAS delivers the opinion of the Court.

We are asked in this case to hold that an Illinois statute requiring the use of a certain type of rear fender mudguard on trucks and trailers operated on the highways of that State conflicts with the Commerce Clause of the Constitution. . . .

The power of the State to regulate the use of its highways is broad and pervasive. We have recognized the peculiarly local nature of this subject of safety, and have upheld state statutes applicable alike to interstate and intrastate commerce, despite the fact that they may have an impact on interstate commerce. The regulation of highways "is akin to quarantine measures, game laws, and like local regulations of rivers, harbors, piers, and docks, with respect to which the state has exceptional scope for the exercise of its regulatory power, and which, Congress not acting, have been sustained even though they materially interfere with interstate commerce." *Southern Pacific Co. v. State of Arizona.* . . .

These safety measures carry a strong presumption of validity when challenged in court. If there are alternative ways of solving a problem, we do not sit to determine which of them is best suited to achieve a valid state objective. Policy decisions are for the state legislature, absent federal entry into the field. Unless we can conclude on the whole record that "the total effect of the law as a safety measure in reducing accidents and casualties is so slight or problematical as not to outweigh the national interest in keeping interstate commerce free from interferences which seriously impede it" (*Southern Pacific Co. v. State of Arizona*), we must uphold the statute.

The District Court found that "since it is impossible for a carrier operating in interstate commerce to determine which of its equipment will be used in a particular area, or on a particular day, or days, carriers operating into or through Illinois . . . will be required to equip all their trailers in accordance with the requirements of the Illinois Splash Guard statute." With two possible exceptions the mudflaps required in those States which have mudguard regulations would not meet the standards required by the Illinois statute. The cost of installing the contour mudguards is $30 or more per vehicle. The District Court found that the initial cost of installing those mudguards on all the trucks owned by the appellees ranged from $4,500 to $45,840. There was also evidence in the record to indicate that the cost of maintenance and replacement of these guards is substantial.

Illinois introduced evidence seeking to establish that contour mudguards had a decided safety factor in that they prevented the throwing of debris into the faces of drivers of passing cars and into the windshields of a following vehicle. But the District Court in its opinion stated that it was "conclusively shown that the contour mud flap possesses no advantages over the conventional or straight mud flap previously required in Illinois and presently required in most of the states" and that "there is rather convincing testimony that use of the contour flap creates hazards previously unknown to those using the highways."

These findings on cost and on safety are not the end of our problem. . . . State control of the width and weight of motor trucks and trailers sustained in *South Carolina State Highway Dept.*

v. Barnwell Bros., [303 U.S. 177 (1935)], involved nice questions of judgment concerning the need of those regulations so far as the issue of safety was concerned. That case also presented the problem whether interstate motor carriers, who were required to replace all equipment or keep out of the State, suffered an unconstitutional restraint on interstate commerce. The matter of safety was said to be one essentially for the legislative judgment; and the burden of redesigning or replacing equipment was said to be a proper price to exact from interstate and intrastate motor carriers alike. . . .

Cost taken into consideration with other factors might be relevant in some cases to the issue of burden on commerce. But it has assumed no such proportions here. If we had here only a question whether the cost of adjusting an interstate operation to these new local safety regulations prescribed by Illinois unduly burdened interstate commerce, we would have to sustain the law under the authority of the *Sproles* [*v. Binford*, 286 U.S. 347 (1937)], *Barnwell*, and *Maurer* [*v. Hamilton*, 309 U.S. 598 (1940)], cases. The same result would obtain if we had to resolve the much discussed issues of safety presented in this case.

This case presents a different issue. The equipment in the *Sproles, Barnwell,* and *Maurer* cases could pass muster in any State, so far as the records in those cases reveal. We were not faced there with the question whether one State could prescribe standards for interstate carriers that would conflict with the standards of another State, making it necessary, say, for an interstate carrier to shift its cargo to differently designed vehicles once another state line was reached. We had a related problem in *Southern Pacific Co. v. State of Arizona,* where the Court invalidated a statute of Arizona prescribing a maximum length of 70 cars for freight trains moving through that State. . . .

An order of the Arkansas Commerce Commission, already mentioned, requires that trailers operating in that State be equipped with straight or conventional mudflaps. Vehicles equipped to meet the standards of the Illinois statute would not comply with Arkansas standards, and vice versa. Thus if a trailer is to be operated in both States, mudguards would have to be interchanged, causing a significant delay in an operation where prompt movement may be of the essence. It was found that from two to four hours of labor are required to install or remove a contour mudguard. Moreover, the contour guard is attached to the trailer by welding and if the trailer is conveying a cargo of explosives (e.g., for the United States Government) it would be exceedingly dangerous to attempt to weld on a contour mudguard without unloading the trailer. . . .

This in summary is the rather massive showing of burden on interstate commerce which appellees made at the hearing. . . .

This is one of those cases—few in number—where local safety

measures that are nondiscriminatory place an unconstitutional burden on interstate commerce. . . . The conflict between the Arkansas regulation and the Illinois regulation also suggests that this regulation of mudguards is not one of those matters "admitting of diversity of treatment, according to the special requirements of local conditions," to use the words of Chief Justice HUGHES in *Sproles v. Binford.* A State which insists on a design out of line with the requirements of almost all the other States may sometimes place a great burden of delay and inconvenience on those interstate motor carriers entering or crossing its territory. Such a new safety device—out of line with the requirements of the other States—may be so compelling that the innovating State need not be the one to give way. But the present showing—balanced against the clear burden on commerce—is far too inconclusive to make this mudguard meet that test.

We deal not with absolutes but with questions of degree. The state legislatures plainly have great leeway in providing safety regulations for all vehicles—interstate as well as local. Our decisions so hold. Yet the heavy burden which the Illinois mudguard law places on the interstate movement of trucks and trailers seems to us to pass the permissible limits even for safety regulations. Affirmed.

Justice HARLAN, with whom Justice STEWART joins, concurring.

The opinion of the Court clearly demonstrates the heavy burden, in terms of cost and interference with "interlining," which the Illinois statute here involved imposes on interstate commerce. In view of the findings of the District Court . . . to the effect that the contour mudflap "possesses no advantages" in terms of safety over the conventional flap permitted in all other States, and indeed creates certain safety hazards, this heavy burden cannot be justified on the theory that the Illinois statute is a necessary, appropriate, or helpful local safety measure. Accordingly, I concur in the judgment of the Court.

Maine v. Taylor

477 U.S. 131, 106 S.Ct. 2440 (1986)

Justice Harry Blackmun discusses the facts of this case, challenging Maine's law prohibiting the importation of live baitfish, in his opinion for the Court.

Justice BLACKMUN delivers the opinion of the Court.

Appellee Robert J. Taylor operates a bait business in Maine. Despite a Maine statute prohibiting the importation of live baitfish, he arranged to have 158,000 live golden shiners delivered to him from outside the State. The shipment was intercepted, and a federal grand jury in the District of Maine indicted Taylor for violating and conspiring to violate the Lacey Act Amendments of 1981, 95 Stat. 1073, 16 U.S.C. §§ 3371–3378. Section 3(a)(2)(A) of those Amendments, 16 U.S.C. § 3372(a)(2)(A), makes it a federal crime "to import, export, transport, sell, receive, acquire, or purchase in interstate or foreign commerce . . . any fish or wildlife taken, possessed, transported, or sold in violation of any law or regulation of any State or in violation of any foreign law."

Taylor moved to dismiss the indictment on the ground that Maine's import ban unconstitutionally burdens interstate commerce and therefore may not form the basis for a federal prosecution under the Lacey Act. . . . Maine intervened to defend the validity of its statute, arguing that the ban legitimately protects the State's fisheries from parasites and non-native species that might be included in shipments of live baitfish. The District Court found the statute constitutional and denied the motion to dismiss. The Court of Appeals for the First Circuit reversed, agreeing with Taylor that the underlying state statute impermissibly restricts interstate trade. . . . Maine appealed. . . .

Maine's statute restricts interstate trade in the most direct manner possible, blocking all inward shipments of live baitfish at the State's border. Still, as both the District Court and the Court of Appeals recognized, this fact alone does not render the law unconstitutional. The limitation imposed by the Commerce Clause on state regulatory power "is by no means absolute," and "the States retain authority under their general police powers to regulate matters of 'legitimate local concern,' even though interstate commerce may be affected.". . .

In determining whether a State has overstepped its role in regulating interstate commerce, this Court has distinguished between state statutes that burden interstate transactions only incidentally, and those that affirmatively discriminate against such transactions. While statutes in the first group violate the Commerce Clause only if the burdens they impose on interstate trade are "clearly excessive in relation to the putative local benefits" statutes in the second group are subject to more demanding scrutiny. The Court explained in *Hughes v. Oklahoma*, 441 U.S. 322 (1979), that once a state law is shown to discriminate against interstate commerce "either on its face or in practical effect," the burden falls on the State to demonstrate both that the statute "serves a legitimate local purpose," and that this purpose could not be served as well by available nondiscriminatory means. . . .

The District Court and the Court of Appeals both reasoned correctly that, since Maine's import ban discriminates on its face against interstate trade, it should be subject to the strict requirements of *Hughes v. Oklahoma*, notwithstanding Maine's argument that those requirements were waived by the Lacey Act Amendments of 1981. It is well established that Congress may authorize the States to engage in regulation that the Commerce Clause would otherwise forbid. But because of the important role the Commerce Clause plays in protecting the free flow of interstate trade, this Court has exempted state statutes from the implied limitations of the Clause only when the congressional direction to do so has been "unmistakably clear.". . .

Maine's ban on the importation of live baitfish thus is constitutional only if it satisfies the requirements ordinarily applied under *Hughes v. Oklahoma* to local regulation that discriminates against interstate trade: the statute must serve a legitimate local purpose, and the purpose must be one that cannot be served as well by available nondiscriminatory means.

The District Court found after an evidentiary hearing that both parts of the *Hughes* test were satisfied, but the Court of Appeals disagreed. We conclude that the Court of Appeals erred in setting aside the findings of the District Court. . . .

Nor do we think that much doubt is cast on the legitimacy of Maine's purposes by what the Court of Appeals took to be signs of protectionist intent. Shielding in-state industries from out-of-state competition is almost never a legitimate local purpose, and state laws that amount to "simple economic protectionism" consequently have been subject to a "virtually *per se* rule of invalidity." . . .

The Commerce Clause significantly limits the ability of States and localities to regulate or otherwise burden the flow of interstate commerce, but it does not elevate free trade above all other values. As long as a State does not needlessly obstruct interstate trade or attempt to "place itself in a position of economic isolation," *Baldwin v. G.A.F. Seelig, Inc.*, 294 U.S. 511 (1935), it retains broad regulatory authority to protect the health and safety of its citizens and the integrity of its natural resources. The evidence in this case amply supports the District Court's findings that Maine's ban on the importation of live baitfish serves legitimate local purposes that could not adequately be served by available nondiscriminatory alternatives. This is not a case of arbitrary discrimination against interstate commerce; the record suggests that Maine has legitimate reasons, "apart from their origin, to treat [out-of-state baitfish] differently," *Philadelphia v. New Jersey*, 437 U.S. [617 (1978)]. The judgment of the Court of Appeals setting aside appellee's conviction is therefore reversed.

Justice STEVENS dissenting.

There is something fishy about this case. Maine is the only State in the Union that blatantly discriminates against out-of-state baitfish by flatly prohibiting their importation. Although golden shiners are already present and thriving in Maine (and, perhaps not coincidentally, the subject of a flourishing domestic industry), Maine excludes golden shiners grown and harvested (and, perhaps not coincidentally sold) in other States. This kind of stark discrimination against out-of-state articles of commerce requires rigorous justification by the discriminating State. . . .

This is not to derogate the State's interest in ecological purity. But the invocation of environmental protection or public health has never been thought to confer some kind of special dispensation from the general principle of nondiscrimination in interstate commerce. . . .

If Maine wishes to rely on its interest in ecological preservation, it must show that interest, and the infeasibility of other alternatives, with far greater specificity. Otherwise, it must further that asserted interest in a manner far less offensive to the notions of comity and cooperation that underlie the Commerce Clause. . . .

Pennsylvania v. Nelson
350 U.S. 497, 76 S.Ct. 477 (1956)

Steve Nelson, a member of the Communist party, was convicted in a state trial court of violating Pennsylvania's Sedition Act, making the advocacy of the overthrow of the government a crime. He was sentenced to twenty years of imprisonment, fined $10,000, and assigned the costs of his prosecution in the sum of $13,000. On appeal, the Pennsylvania State Supreme Court overturned Nelson's conviction after concluding that the state law was superceded by federal legislation, the Smith Act of 1940. The Commonwealth of Pennsylvania appealed that ruling to the Supreme Court of the United States.

Chief Justice WARREN delivers the opinion of the Court.

It should be said at the outset that the decision in this case does not affect the right of States to enforce their sedition laws at times when the Federal Government has not occupied the field and is not protecting the entire country from seditious conduct. The distinction between the two situations was clearly recognized by the court below. Nor does it limit the jurisdiction of the States where the Constitution and Congress have specifically given them concurrent jurisdiction, as was done under the Eighteenth Amendment and the Volstead Act. . . . Neither does it limit the right of the State to protect itself at any time against sabotage or attempted violence of all kinds. Nor does it prevent the State from prosecuting where the same act constitutes both a federal offense and a state offense under the police power. . . .

Where, as in the instant case, Congress has not stated specifically whether a federal statute has occupied a field in which the States are otherwise free to legislate, different criteria have furnished touchstones for decision. Thus,

> "[t]his Court, in considering the validity of state laws in the light of . . . federal laws touching the same subject, has made use of the following expressions: conflicting; contrary to; occupying the field; repugnance; difference; irreconcilability; inconsistency; violation; curtailment; and interference. But none of these expressions provides an infallible constitutional test or an exclusive constitutional yardstick. In the final analysis, there can be no one crystal clear distinctly marked formula." *Hines v. Davidowitz*, 312 U.S. 52 [1941].

In this case, we think that each of several tests of supersession is met.

First, "[t]he scheme of federal regulation [is] so pervasive as to make reasonable the inference that Congress left no room for the States to supplement it." *Rice v. Santa Fe Elevator Corp.* [331 U.S. 218 (1947)]. The Congress determined in 1940 that it was necessary for it to re-enter the field of antisubversive legislation, which had been abandoned by it in 1921. In that year, it enacted the Smith Act which proscribes advocacy of the overthrow of any government—federal, state or local—by force and violence and organization of and knowing membership in a group which so advocates. Conspiracy to commit any of these acts is punishable under the general criminal conspiracy provisions in 18 U.S.C. § 371, 18 U.S. C.A. § 371. The Internal Security Act of 1950 is aimed more directly at Communist organizations. It distinguishes between "Communist-action organizations" and "Communist-front organizations," requiring such organizations to register and to file annual reports with the Attorney General giving complete details as to their officers and funds. Members of Communist-action organizations who have not been registered by their organization must register as individuals. Failure to register in accordance with the requirements of Sections 786–787 is punishable by a fine of not more than $10,000 for an offending organization and by a fine of not more than $10,000 or imprisonment for not more than five years or both for an individual offender— each day of failure to register constituting a separate offense.

And the Act imposes certain sanctions upon both "action" and "front" organizations and their members. The Communist Control Act of 1954 declares "that the Communist Party of the United States, although purportedly a political party, is in fact an instrumentality of a conspiracy to overthrow the Government of the United States" and that "its role as the agency of a hostile foreign power renders its existence a clear present and continuing danger to the security of the United States." It also contains a legislative finding that the Communist Party is a " 'Communist-action' organization" within the meaning of the Internal Security Act of 1950 and provides that "knowing" members of the Communist Party are "subject to all the provisions and penalties" of that Act. It furthermore sets up a new classification of "Communist-infiltrated organizations" and provides for the imposition of sanctions against them.

We examine these Acts only to determine the congressional plan. Looking to all of them in the aggregate, the conclusion is inescapable that Congress has intended to occupy the field of sedition. Taken as a whole, they evince a congressional plan which makes it reasonable to determine that no room has been left for the States to supplement it. Therefore, a state sedition statute is superseded regardless of whether it purports to supplement the federal law. . . .

Second, the federal statutes "touch a field in which the federal interest is so dominant that the federal system [must] be assumed to preclude enforcement of state laws on the same subject." *Rice v. Santa Fe Elevator Corp.* Congress has devised an all-embracing program for resistance to the various forms of totalitarian aggression. Our external defenses have been strengthened, and a plan to protect against internal subversion has been made by it. It has appropriated vast sums, not only for our own protection, but also to strengthen freedom throughout the world. It has charged the Federal Bureau of Investigation and the Central Intelligence Agency with responsibility for intelligence concerning Communist seditious activities against our Government, and has denominated such activities as part of a world conspiracy. It accordingly proscribed sedition against all government in the nation—national, state and local. Congress declared that these steps were taken "to provide for the common defense, to preserve the sovereignty of the United States as an independent nation, and to guarantee to each State a republican form of government. . . ." Congress having thus treated seditious conduct as a matter of vital national concern, it is in no sense a local enforcement problem. . . .

Third, enforcement of state sedition acts presents a serious danger of conflict with the administration of the federal program. Since 1939, in order to avoid a hampering of uniform enforcement of its program by sporadic local prosecutions, the Federal Government has urged local authorities not to intervene in such matters, but to turn over to the federal authorities immediately and unevaluated all information concerning subversive activities. . . .

In his brief, the Solicitor General states that forty-two States plus Alaska and Hawaii have statutes which in some form prohibit advocacy of the violent overthrow of established government. These statutes are entitled anti-sedition statutes, criminal anarchy laws, criminal syndicalist laws, etc. Although all of them are primarily directed against the overthrow of the United States Government, they are in no sense uniform. And our attention has not been called to any case where the prosecution has been successfully directed against an attempt to destroy state or local government. Some of these Acts are studiously drawn and purport to protect fundamental rights by appropriate definitions, standards of proof and orderly procedures in keeping with the avowed congressional purpose "to protect freedom from those who would destroy it, without infringing upon the freedom of all our people." Others are vague and are almost wholly without such safeguards. Some even purport to punish mere membership in subversive organizations which the federal statutes do not punish where federal registration requirements have been fulfilled.

When we were confronted with a like situation in the field of labor-management relations, Justice JACKSON wrote:

> "A multiplicity of tribunals and a diversity of procedures are quite as apt to produce incompatible or conflicting adjudications as are different rules of substantive law."

Should the States be permitted to exercise a concurrent jurisdiction in this area, federal enforcement would encounter not only the difficulties mentioned by Justice JACKSON, but the added conflict engendered by different criteria of substantive offenses.

Since we find that Congress has occupied the field to the exclusion of parallel state legislation, that the dominant interest of the Federal Government precludes state intervention, and that administration of state Acts would conflict with the operation of the federal plan, we are convinced that the decision of the Supreme Court of Pennsylvania is unassailable. . . .

The judgment of the Supreme Court of Pennsylvania is affirmed.

Justice REED, with whom Justice BURTON and Justice MINTON join, dissenting.

Congress has not, in any of its statutes relating to sedition, specifically barred the exercise of state power to punish the same Acts under state law. And, we read the majority opinion to assume for this case that, absent federal legislation, there is no constitutional bar to punishment of sedition against the United States by both a State and the Nation. The majority limits to the federal courts the power to try charges of sedition against the Federal Government.

First, the Court relies upon the pervasiveness of the antisubversive legislation embodied in the Smith Act of 1940. . . .

We cannot agree that the federal criminal sanctions against sedition directed at the United States are of such a pervasive character as to indicate an intention to void state action.

Secondly, the Court states that the federal sedition statutes touch a field "in which the federal interest is so dominant" they must preclude state laws on the same subject. . . .

We look upon the Smith Act as a provision for controlling incitements to overthrow by force and violence the Nation, or any State, or any political subdivision of either. Such an exercise of federal police power carries, we think, no such dominancy over similar state powers as might be attributed to continuing federal regulations concerning foreign affairs or coinage, for example. In the responsibility of national and local governments to protect themselves against sedition, there is no "dominant interest.". . .

Thirdly, the Court finds ground for abrogating Pennsylvania's antisedition statute because, in the Court's view, the State's administration of the Act may hamper the enforcement of the federal law. . . . But . . . fear by courts of possible difficulties does not seem to us in these circumstances a valid reason for ousting a State from exercise of its police power. Those are matters for legislative determination.

Finally, and this one point seems in and of itself decisive, there is an independent reason for reversing the Pennsylvania Supreme Court. The Smith Act appears in Title 18 of the United States Code, 18 U.S.C.A., which Title codifies the federal criminal laws. Section 3231 of that Title provides:

> "Nothing in this title shall be held to take away or impair the jurisdiction of the courts of the several States under the laws thereof."

That declaration springs from the federal character of our Nation. It recognizes the fact that maintenance of order and fairness rests primarily with the States.

B. THE TENTH AMENDMENT AND THE STATES

In response to the Anti-Federalists' concerns about safeguarding individual liberty, the first Congress adopted the Bill of Rights, including the Tenth Amendment, which provides that "[t]he powers not delegated to the United States by the Constitution, nor prohibited by it to the States, are reserved to the States respectively, or to the people." The amendment long stood, as the Court put it *United States v. Darby Lumber Company*, 312 U.S. 100 (1941) (see page 504), as a truism, without independent force in constraining federal powers. It reaffirms the Constitution's structure and limitations of federal powers to those specifically granted. Indeed, during the First Congress's debate over the amendment, Elbridge Gerry, who had been a delegate from Massachusetts to the Constitutional Convention, proposed inserting the word *expressly* so the amendment would read, "the powers not *expressly* delegated by the Constitution, nor prohibited to the States, are reserved to the States respectively, or to the people." Rejection of his proposal and the addition of the last clause—reserving powers "to the people"—underscores that the federal government's powers are delegated and plenary; any others belong to the people of the states.

Since Chief Justice William Rehnquist's appointment to the Court in 1972, however, he has championed the idea of states' sovereignty. In *National League of Cities v. Usery*, 426 U.S. 833 (1976), he persuaded four other justices to hold that the exercise of congressional power over commerce threatened "the separate and independent existence" of the states as "sovereign political entit[ies]." On that basis, he struck down three 1974 amendments to the Fair Labor Standards Act extending minimum-wage and maximum-hours standards to all state, county, and municipal employees.

National League of Cities v. Usery bitterly divided the Court. Just a year before, with only Rehnquist dissenting, the Court upheld federal restrictions on salary increases for state employees.[1] Indeed, not since striking down much of the early New Deal legislation and the constitutional crisis of 1937 had the Court sought to limit Congress's power in this area. And Rehnquist was forced to overturn *Maryland v. Wirtz*, 392 U.S. 183 (1968), upholding similar labor standards for state employees in hospitals, institutions, and schools. In that earlier ruling, Justice John Harlan saw no point in denying congressional power over state employees when it indisputably covered all private-sector employees. Rehnquist conceded that federal regulation of state employees was "within the scope of the Commerce Clause." But he asserted that "there are attributes of sovereignty attaching to every state government which may not be impaired by Congress, not because Congress lacks an affirmative grant of legislative authority to reach the matter, but because the Constitution prohibits it from exercising the authority in that manner."

Chief Justice William H. Rehnquist *Abe Frajndlich/© 1988 SYGMA*

Rehnquist supported his decision with a novel reading of the Tenth Amendment. As interpreted by Rehnquist, the amendment is an "affirmative limitation" on Congress "akin to" others in the Bill of Rights, "running in favor of the States *as States*." Congress may not regulate the "States *qua* States" or deny their "freedom to structure integral operations in areas of traditional governmental functions." Thus despite conceding Congress's power to regulate the working conditions of state employees and finding no express prohibitions to its doing so, Rehnquist held that extending federal labor standards to state employees was "not within the authority granted Congress." In delivering his opinion in *National League of Cities v. Usery*, Rehnquist wrote,

It is one thing to recognize the authority of Congress to enact laws regulating individual businesses necessary subject to the dual sovereignty of the government of the Nation and of the State in which they reside. It is quite another to uphold a similar exercise of congressional authority directed not to private citizens, but to the States as States. We have repeatedly recognized that there are attributes of sovereignty attaching to every state government which may not be impaired by Congress, not because Congress may lack an affirmative grant of legislative authority to reach the matter, but because the Constitution prohibits it from exercising the authority in that manner. . . .

One undoubted attribute of state sovereignty is the State's power to determine the wages which shall be paid to those whom they employ in order to carry out their governmental functions, what hours those persons will work, and what compensation will be provided where these employees may be called upon to work overtime. The question we must resolve in this case, then is whether these determinations are "functions essential to separate and independent existence" . . . so that Congress may not abrogate the States' otherwise plenary authority to make them.

Among the four dissenters in *National League of Cities,* Justice William J. Brennan, Jr., protested that the Constitution neither guarantees state sovereignty nor requires or permits its judicial enforcement and reiterated that "restraints on [Congress's commerce power] must proceed from political rather than judicial processes."

It bears emphasizing, though, that Rehnquist's interpretation of the Tenth Amendment is modest in limiting congressional powers only under the commerce clause. Within a week of *National League of Cities,* he held the Fourteenth Amendment empowers Congress to prohibit state and local employers, no less than those in the private sector, from practicing racial discrimination in violation of the Civil Rights Act of 1964.[2] Moreover, he relied on *South Carolina v. Katzenbach,* 383 U.S. 301 (1966) (see page 662), a decision clearly denying states' sovereignty in upholding the 1965 Voting Rights Act, which authorizes federal examiners to determine voter qualifications and approve state voting laws. Nor does the Tenth Amendment stand as an obstacle to Congress's taxing and spending powers. In *South Dakota v. Dole,* 483 U.S. 203 (1987) (see page 536), Rehnquist upheld the withholding of federal highway funds from states refusing to adopt a minimum drinking age of twenty-one.

National League of Cities did, though, renew debate over federalism. Besides raising states' sovereignty to the level of constitutional law, Rehnquist left unexplained both how "traditional" or "essential" state activities were to be determined and why the Court, not Congress, should define and defend them. Subsequent decisions reformulated Rehnquist's ruling into a three-pronged test for curbing Congress's commerce power based on showing that legislation (1) regulated "States as States," (2) addressed "matters that are indisputably 'attributes of state sovereignty,'" and (3) would force "States' compliance" in ways that "directly impair their ability 'to structure integral operations in areas of traditional function.'"[3] But on this test, a majority of the Court refused to further limit Congress's control over state and local employees.[4]

Finally, Justice Harry Blackmun, who cast the crucial fifth vote in *National League of Cities,* changed his mind about the wisdom of judicial line drawing in defense of interests of the states as states. In *Garcia v. San Antonio Metropolitan Transit Authority* (1985) (see page 584), he joined the four justices who had dissented in *National League of Cities* and expressly overturned that ruling. *Garcia*'s majority reaffirmed that federalism is a political structure in which states' interests are represented, for better or worse, in the national political process. And that is precisely what *Garcia*'s dissenters deny in maintaining that the national political process inadequately safeguards states' "sphere of sovereignty," and that the Court stands as a last defense for states' sovereignty.

State powers have been eroded, *Garcia*'s dissenters point out, due to several factors: "the recent expansion of the commerce power," the "unprecedented growth of federal regulatory activity," the Seventeenth Amendment's substitution of popular election of senators for that of selection by state legislatures as originally provided, and "the expanded influence of national interest groups" in Congress and the national political process. In addition to other developments, the Fourteenth Amendment greatly expanded congressional power, the Sixteenth Amendment gave Congress the power to levy a federal income tax, the Court has expansively read Congress's taxing and spending powers since the New Deal, and (see Vol. 2, Ch. 4) the Court nationalized the Bill of Rights, making those guarantees limit the powers of the states no less than the federal government.

NOTES

1. See *Fry v. United States*, 421 U.S. 524 (1975).
2. *Fitzpatrick v. Bitzer*, 427 U.S. 445, 445 (1976).
3. *Hodel v. Virginia Surface Mining*, 452 U.S. 264, 287–288 (1981). In a footnote, the majority added a fourth requirement and important qualification: "Demonstrating that these three requirements are met does not, however, guarantee that a Tenth Amendment challenge to congressional commerce power action will succeed. There are situations in which the nature of the federal interest advanced may be such that it justifies state submission."
4. See *Hodel v. Virginia Surface Mining*, 452 U.S. 264 (1981); *FERC v. Mississippi*, 456 U.S. 742 (1982); *United Transportation Union v. Long Island Railroad Company*, 455 U.S. 678 (1982); and *EEOC v. Wyoming*, 460 U.S. 222 (1983).

SELECTED BIBLIOGRAPHY

Berns, Walter. "The Meaning of the Tenth Amendment." In *A Nation of States*, edited by Robert Goldwin. New York: Rand McNally, 1974.

Lofgren, Charles A. *Government from Reflection and Choice*. New York: Oxford University Press, 1986.

O'Brien, David M. "Federalism as a Metaphor in the Constitutional Politics of Public Administration." 49 *Public Administration Review* 411 (Sept./Oct. 1989).

Garcia v. San Antonio Metropolitan Transit Authority

469 U.S. 528, 105 S.Ct. 1005 (1985)

In 1974, Congress amended the Fair Labor Standards Act (FLSA) to apply to virtually all state and local government employees and to require state and local governments to comply with minimum-wage and overtime standards. The San Antonio Metropolitan Transit Authority (SAMTA) sought in federal district court a declaratory judgment exempting it from FLSA's provisions on the grounds that the amendment to the law violated the Tenth Amendment. The court entered a summary judgment, without hearing oral arguments, for the transit authority. Joe Garcia, a transit authority employee, appealed that decision to the Supreme Court.

Justice BLACKMUN delivers the opinion of the Court.

We revisit in these cases an issue raised in *National League of Cities v. Usery*, 426 U.S. 833 (1976). In that litigation, this Court, by a sharply divided vote, ruled that the Commerce Clause does not empower Congress to enforce the minimum-wage and overtime provisions of the Fair Labor Standards Act (FLSA) against the States "in areas of traditional governmental functions." Although *National League of Cities* supplied some examples of "traditional governmental functions," it did not offer a general explanation of how a "traditional" function is to be distinguished from a "nontraditional" one. Since then, federal and state courts have struggled with the task, thus imposed, of identifying a traditional function for purposes of state immunity under the Commerce Clause.

In the present cases, a Federal District Court concluded that municipal ownership and operation of a mass-transit system is a traditional governmental function and thus, under *National League of Cities*, is exempt from the obligations imposed by the FLSA. Faced with the identical question, three Federal Courts of Appeals and one state appellate court have reached the opposite conclusion.

Our examination of this "function" standard applied in these and other cases over the last eight years now persuades us that the attempt to draw the boundaries of state regulatory immunity in terms of "traditional governmental function" is not only unworkable but is inconsistent with established principles of federalism and, indeed, with those very federalism principles on which *National League of Cities* purported to rest. That case, accordingly, is overruled. . . .

Appellees have not argued that SAMTA [San Antonio Metropolitan Transit Authority] is immune from regulation under the FLSA on the ground that it is a local transit system engaged in intrastate commercial activity. In a practical sense, SAMTA's operations might well be characterized as "local." Nonetheless, it long has been settled that Congress' authority under the Commerce Clause extends to intrastate economic activities that affect interstate commerce. See, e.g., *Hodel v. Virginia Surface Mining & Recl. Assn.*, 452 U.S. 264 (1981); *Heart of Atlanta Motel, Inc. v. United States*, 379 U.S. 241 (1964); *Wickard v. Filburn*, 317 U.S. 111 (1942); *United States v. Darby*, 312 U.S. 100 (1941). Were SAMTA a privately owned and operated enterprise, it could not credibly argue that Congress exceeded the bounds of its Commerce Clause powers in prescribing minimum wages and overtime rates for SAMTA's employees. Any constitutional exemption from the requirements of the FLSA therefore must rest on SAMTA's status as a governmental entity rather than on the "local" nature of its operations.

The prerequisites for governmental immunity under *National League of Cities* were summarized by this Court in *Hodel*. . . . Under that summary, four conditions must be satisfied before a state activity may be deemed immune from a particular federal regulation under the Commerce Clause. First, it is said that the federal statute at issue must regulate "the 'States as States.' " Second, the statute must "address matters that are indisputably 'attribute[s] of state sovereignty.' " Third, state compliance with the federal obligation must "directly impair [the States'] ability 'to structure integral operations in areas of traditional governmental functions.' " Finally, the relation of state and federal interests must not be such that "the nature of the federal interest . . . justifies state submission.". . .

The controversy in the present cases has focused on the third *Hodel* requirement—that the challenged federal statue trench on "traditional governmental functions." The District Court voiced a common concern: "Despite the abundance of adjectives, identifying which particular state functions are immune remains difficult." 557 F.Supp., at 447. Just how troublesome the task has been is revealed by the results reached in other federal cases. Thus, [lower] courts have held that regulating ambulance services, . . . licensing automobile drivers, . . . operating a municipal airport, . . . performing solid waste disposal, . . . and operating a highway authority, . . . are functions *protected* under *National League of Cities.* At the same time, courts have held that issuance of industrial development bonds, . . . regulation of intrastate natural gas sales, . . . regulation of traffic on public roads, . . . regulation of air transportation, . . . operation of a telephone system, . . . leasing and sale of natural gas, . . . operation of a mental health facility, . . . and provision of in-house domestic services for the aged and handicapped, . . . are *not* entitled to immunity. We find it difficult, if not impossible, to identify an organizing principle that places each of the cases in the first group on one side of a line and each of the cases in the second group on the other side. The constitutional distinction between licensing drivers and regulating traffic, for example, or between operating a highway authority and operating a mental health facility, is elusive at best.

Thus far, this Court itself has made little headway in defining the scope of the governmental functions deemed protected under *National League of Cities.* In that case the Court set forth examples of protected and unprotected functions, . . . but provided no explanation of how those examples were identified. The only other case in which the Court has had occasion to address the problem is [*Transportation Union v.*] *Long Island* [455 U.S. 678 (1982)]. We there observed: "The determination of whether a federal law impairs a state's authority with respect to 'areas of traditional [state] functions' may at times be a difficult one." The accuracy of that statement is demonstrated by this Court's own difficulties in *Long Island* in developing a workable standard for "traditional governmental functions." We relied in large part there on "the *historical reality* that the operation of railroads is not among the functions *traditionally* performed by state and local governments," but we simultaneously disavowed "a static historical view of state functions generally immune from federal regulation" (first emphasis added; second emphasis in original). We held that the inquiry into a particular function's "traditional" nature was merely a means of determining whether the federal statute at issue unduly handicaps "basic state prerogatives" but we did not offer an explanation of what makes one state function a "basic prerogative" and another function not basic. Finally, having disclaimed a rigid reliance on the historical pedigree of state involvement in a particular area, we nonetheless found it appropriate to emphasize the extended historical record of *federal* involvement in the field of rail transportation. . . .

Many constitutional standards involve "undoubte[d] . . . gray areas," *Fry v. United States,* 421 U.S. 542 (1975) (dissenting opinion), and, despite the difficulties that this Court and other courts have encountered so far, it normally might be fair to venture the assumption that case-by-case development would lead to a workable standard for determining whether a particular governmental function should be immune from federal regulation under the Commerce Clause. A further cautionary note is sounded, however, by the Court's experience in the related field of state immunity from federal taxation. In *South Carolina v. United States* [199 U.S. 437] (1905), the Court held for the first time that the state tax immunity recognized in *Collector v. Day* [11 Wall. 113] (1870), extended only to the "ordinary" and "strictly governmental" instrumentalities of state governments and not to instrumentalities "used by the State in the carrying on of an ordinary private business." While the Court applied the distinction outlined in *South Carolina* for the following 40 years, at no time during that period did the Court develop a consistent formulation of the kinds of governmental functions that were entitled to immunity. The Court identified the protected functions at various times as "essential," "usual," "traditional," or "strictly governmental." While "these differences in phraseology . . . must not be too literally contradistinguished" . . . they reflect an inability to specify precisely what aspects of a governmental function made it necessary to the "unimpaired existence" of the States. Indeed, the Court ultimately chose "not, by an attempt to formulate any general test, [to] risk embarrassing the decision of cases [concerning] activities of a different kind which may arise in the future.". . .

If these tax immunity cases had any common thread, it was in the attempt to distinguish between "governmental" and "proprietary" functions. To say that the distinction between "governmental" and "proprietary" proved to be stable, however, would be something of an overstatement. . . . It was this uncertainty and instability that led the Court in *New York v. United States* [326 U.S. 572] (1946), unanimously to conclude that the distinction between "governmental" and "proprietary" functions was "untenable" and must be abandoned. . . .

The distinction the Court discarded as unworkable in the field of tax immunity has proved no more fruitful in the field of regulatory immunity under the Commerce Clause. Neither do any of the alternative standards that might be employed to distinguish between protected and unprotected governmental functions appear manageable. We rejected the possibility of making immunity turn on a purely historical standard of "tradition" in *Long Island*, and properly so. The most obvious defect of a historical approach to state immunity is that it prevents a court from accommodating changes in the historical functions of States, changes that have resulted in a number of once-private functions like education being assumed by the States and their subdivisions. At the same time, the only apparent virtue of a rigorous historical standard, namely, its promise of a reasonably objective measure for state immunity, is illusory. Reliance on history as an organizing principle results in linedrawing of the most arbitrary sort; the genesis of state governmental functions stretches over a historical continuum from before the Revolution to the present, and courts would have to decide by fiat precisely how longstanding a pattern of state involvement had to be for federal regulatory authority to be defeated.

A nonhistorical standard for selecting immune governmental functions is likely to be just as unworkable as is a historical standard. The goal of identifying "uniquely" governmental functions, for example, has been rejected by the Court in the field of governmental tort liability in part because the notion of a "uniquely" governmental function is unmanageable. Another possibility would be to confine immunity to "necessary" governmental services, that is, services that would be provided inadequately or not at all unless the government provided them. . . . The set of services that fits into this category, however, may well be negligible. The fact that an unregulated market produces less of some service than a State deems desirable does not mean that the State itself must provide the service; in most if not all cases, the State can "contract out" by hiring private firms to provide the service or simply by providing subsidies to existing suppliers. It also is open to question how well equipped courts are.

We believe, however, that there is a more fundamental problem at work here, a problem that explains why the Court was never able to provide a basis for the governmental/proprietary distinction in the intergovernmental tax immunity cases and why an attempt to draw similar distinctions with respect to federal regulatory authority under *National League of Cities* is unlikely to succeed regardless of how the distinctions are phrased. The problem is that neither the governmental proprietary distinction nor any other that purports to separate out important governmental functions can be faithful to the role of federalism in a democratic society. The essence of our federal system is that within the realm of authority left open to them under the Constitution, the States must be equally free to engage in any activity that their citizens choose for the common weal, no matter how unorthodox or unnecessary anyone else—including the judiciary—deems state involvement to be. Any rule of state immunity that looks to the "traditional," "integral," or "necessary" nature of governmental functions inevitably invites an unelected federal judiciary to make decisions about which state policies it favors and which ones it dislikes. "The science of government . . . is the science of experiment," *Anderson v. Dunn* [19 U.S. 204] (1821), and the States cannot serve as laboratories for social and economic experiment, see *New State Ice Co. v. Liebmann*, 285 U.S. 262 (1932) (BRANDEIS, J., dissenting), if they must pay an added price when they meet the changing needs of their citizenry by taking up functions that an earlier day and a different society left in private hands. . . .

We therefore now reject, as unsound in principle and unworkable in practice, a rule of state immunity from federal regulation that turns on a judicial appraisal of whether a particular governmental function is "integral" or "traditional." Any such rule leads to inconsistent results at the same time that it disserves principles of democratic self-governance, and it breeds inconsistency precisely because it is divorced from those principles. If there are to be limits on the Federal Government's power to interfere with state functions—as undoubtedly there are—we must look elsewhere to find them. We accordingly return to the underlying issue that confronted this Court in *National League of Cities*—the manner in which the Constitution insulates States from the reach of Congress' power under the Commerce Clause.

The central theme of *National League of Cities* was that the States occupy a special position in our constitutional system and that the scope of Congress' authority under the Commerce Clause must reflect that position. Of course, the Commerce Clause by its specific language does not provide any special limitation on Congress' actions with respect to the States. . . . It is equally true, however, that the text of the Constitution provides the beginning rather than the final answer to every inquiry into questions of federalism, for "[b]ehind the words of the constitutional provisions are postulates which limit and control." *Monaco v. Mississippi*, 292 U.S. 313 (1934). *National League of Cities* reflected the general conviction that the Constitution precludes "the National Government [from] devour[ing] the essentials of state sovereignty." *Maryland v. Wirtz*, 392 U.S. [183 (1968)] (dissenting opinion).

In order to be faithful to the underlying federal premises of the Constitution, courts must look for the "postulates which limit and control."

What has proved problematic is not the perception that the Constitution's federal structure imposes limitations on the Commerce Clause, but rather the nature and content of those limitations. One approach to defining the limits on Congress' authority to regulate the States under the Commerce Clause is to identify certain underlying elements of political sovereignty that are deemed essential to the States' "separate and independent existence." *Lane County v. Oregon* [7 Wall. 71] (1869). This approach obviously underlay the Court's use of the "traditional governmental function" concept in *National League of Cities*. It also has led to the separate requirement that the challenged federal statute "address matters that are indisputably 'attribute[s] of state sovereignty.'" *Hodel*. In *National League of Cities* itself, for example, the Court concluded that decisions by a State concerning the wages and hours of its employees are an "undoubted attribute of state sovereignty." . . . The opinion did not explain what aspects of such decisions made them such an "undoubted attribute," and the Court since then has remarked on the uncertain scope of the concept. See *EEOC v. Wyoming*, [460 U.S. 266 (1983)]. The point of the inquiry, however, has remained to single out particular features of a State's internal governance that are deemed to be intrinsic parts of state sovereignty.

We doubt that courts ultimately can identify principled constitutional limitations on the scope of Congress' Commerce Clause powers over the States merely by relying on *a priori* definitions of state sovereignty. In part, this is because of the elusiveness of objective criteria for "fundamental" elements of state sovereignty, a problem we have witnessed in the search for "traditional governmental functions." There is, however, a more fundamental reason: the sovereignty of the States is limited by the Constitution itself. A variety of sovereign powers, for example, are withdrawn from the States by Article I, § 10, Section 8 of the same Article works an equally sharp contraction of state sovereignty by authorizing Congress to exercise a wide range of legislative powers and (in conjunction with the Supremacy Clause of Article VI) to displace contrary state legislation. By providing for final review of questions of federal law in this Court, Article III curtails the sovereign power of the States' judiciaries to make authoritative determinations of law. See *Martin v. Hunter's Lessee,* 1 Wheat. 304 (1816). Finally, the developed application, through the Fourteenth Amendment, of the greater part of the Bill of Rights to the States limits the sovereign authority that States otherwise would possess to legislate with respect to their citizens and to conduct their own affairs.

The States unquestionably do "retai[n] a significant measure of sovereign authority." They do so, however, only to the extent that the Constitution has not divested them of their original powers and transferred those powers to the Federal Government. In the words of James Madison to the Members of the First Congress: "Interference with the power of the States was no constitutional criterion of the power of Congress. If the power was not given, Congress could not exercise it; if given, they might exercise it, although it should interfere with the laws, or even the Constitution of the States.". . .

As a result, to say that the Constitution assumes the continued role of the States is to say little about the nature of that role. Only recently, this Court recognized that the purpose of the constitutional immunity recognized in *National League of Cities* is not to preserve "a sacred province of state autonomy." *EEOC v. Wyoming.* With rare exceptions, like the guarantee, in Article IV, § 3, of state territorial integrity, the Constitution does not carve out express elements of state sovereignty that Congress may not employ its delegated powers to displace. James Wilson reminded the Pennsylvania ratifying convention in 1787: "It is true, indeed, sir, although it presupposes the existence of state governments, yet this Constitution does not suppose them to be the sole power to be respected." 2 Debates in the Several State Conventions on the Adoption of the Federal Constitution 439 (J. Elliot 2d ed. 1876). The power of the Federal Government is a "power to be respected" as well, and the fact that the States remain sovereign as to all powers not vested in Congress or denied them by the Constitution offers no guidance about where the frontier between state and federal power lies. In short, we have no license to employ freestanding conceptions of state sovereignty when measuring congressional authority under the Commerce Clause.

When we look for the States' "residuary and inviolable sovereignty," The Federalist No. 39 (J. Madison), in the shape of the constitutional scheme rather than in predetermined notions of sovereign power, a different measure of state sovereignty emerges. Apart from the limitation on federal authority inherent in the delegated nature of Congress' Article I powers, the principal means chosen by the Framers to ensure the role of the States in the federal system lies in the structure of the Federal Government itself. It is no novelty to observe that the composition of the Federal Government was designed in large part to protect the States from overreaching by Congress. The Framers thus gave the States a role in the selection both of the Executive and the Legislative Branches of the Federal Government. The States were vested with indirect influence over the House of Representatives and the Presidency by their control of electoral qualifications and their role in presidential elections. U.S. Const., Art. I, § 2, and Art. II, § 1. They were given more direct influence in the Senate, where each State received equal representation and each Senator was to be selected by the legislature of his State. Art. I, § 3. The significance attached to the States' equal representation in the Senate is underscored by the prohibition of any constitutional amendment divesting a State of equal representation without the State's consent. Art. V. . . .

In short, the Framers chose to rely on a federal system in which special restraints on federal power over the States inhered principally in the workings of the National Government itself, rather than in discrete limitations on the objects of federal authority. State sovereign interests, then, are more properly protected by procedural safeguards inherent in the structure of the federal system than by judicially created limitations on federal power.

The effectiveness of the federal political process in preserving the States' interests is apparent even today in the course of federal legislation. On the one hand, the States have been able to direct a substantial proportion of federal revenues into their own treasuries in the form of general and program-specific grants in aid. The federal role in assisting state and local governments is a longstanding one; Congress provided federal land grants to finance state governments from the beginning of the Republic, and direct cash grants were awarded as early as 1887 under the Hatch Act. In the past quarter-century alone, federal grants to States and localities have grown from $7 billion to $96 billion. As a result, federal grants now account for about one-fifth of state and local government expenditures. The States have obtained federal funding for such services as police and fire protection, education, public health and hospitals, parks and recreation, and sanitation. Moreover, at the same time that the States have exercised their influence to obtain federal support, they have been able to exempt themselves from a wide variety of obligations imposed by Congress under the Commerce Clause. For example, the Federal Power Act, the National Labor Relations Act, the Labor-Management Reporting and Disclosure Act, the Occupational Safety and Health Act, the Employee Retirement Insurance Security Act, and the Sherman Act all contain express or implied exemptions for States and their subdivisions. The fact that some federal statutes such as the FLSA extend general obligations to the States cannot obscure the extent to which the political position of the States in the federal system has served to minimize the burdens that the States bear under the Commerce Clause. . . .

[A]gainst this background, we are convinced that the fundamental limitation that the constitutional scheme imposes on the Commerce Clause to protect the "States as States" is one of process rather than one of result. Any substantive restraint on the exercise of Commerce Clause powers must find its justification in the procedural nature of this basic limitation, and it must be tailored to compensate for possible failings in the national political process rather than to dictate a "sacred province of state autonomy.". . . .

Insofar as the present cases are concerned, then, we need go no further than to state that we perceive nothing in the overtime and minimum-wage requirements of the FLSA, as applied to SAMTA, that is destructive of state sovereignty or violative of any constitutional provision. SAMTA faces nothing more than the same minimum-wage and overtime obligations that hundreds of thousands of other employers, public as well as private, have to meet.

This analysis makes clear that Congress' action in affording SAMTA employees the protections of the wage and hour provisions of the FLSA contravened no affirmative limit on Congress' power under the Commerce Clause. The judgment of the District Court therefore must be reversed. . . .

Justice POWELL, with whom the CHIEF JUSTICE, Justice REHNQUIST and Justice O'CONNOR join, dissenting.

The Court today, in its 5–4 decision, overrules *National League of Cities v. Usery* (1976), a case in which we held that Congress lacked authority to impose the requirements of the Fair Labor Standards Act on state and local governments. Because I believe this decision substantially alters the federal system embodied in the Constitution, I dissent.

There are, of course, numerous examples over the history of

this Court in which prior decisions have been reconsidered and overruled. There have been few cases, however, in which the principle of *stare decisis* and the rationale of recent decisions were ignored as abruptly as we now witness. The reasoning of the Court in *National League of Cities,* and the principle applied there, have been reiterated consistently over the past eight years. Since its decision in 1976, *National League of Cities* has been cited and quoted in opinions joined by every member of the present Court. . . .

Whatever effect the Court's decision may have in weakening the application of *stare decisis,* it is likely to be less important than what the Court has done to the Constitution itself. A unique feature of the United States is the *federal* system of government guaranteed by the Constitution and implicit in the very name of our country. Despite some genuflecting in Court's opinion to the concept of federalism, today's decision effectively reduces the Tenth Amendment to meaningless rhetoric when Congress acts pursuant to the Commerce Clause. . . .

Much of the Court's opinion is devoted to arguing that it is difficult to define *a priori* "traditional governmental functions." *National League of Cities* neither engaged in, nor required, such a task. The Court discusses and condemns as standards "traditional governmental function[s]," "purely historical" functions, " 'uniquely' governmental functions," and " 'necessary' governmental services." But nowhere does it mention that *National League of Cities* adopted a familiar type of balancing test for determining whether Commerce Clause enactments transgress constitutional limitations imposed by the federal nature of our system of government. This omission is noteworthy, since the author of today's opinion joined *National League of Cities* and concurred separately to point out that the Court's opinion in that case "adopt[s] a balancing approach [that] does not outlaw federal power in areas . . . where the federal interest is demonstrably greater and where state . . . compliance with imposed federal standards would be essential." (BLACKMUN, J., concurring). . . .

In overruling *National League of Cities,* the Court incorrectly characterizes the mode of analysis established therein and developed in subsequent cases.

Moreover, the statute at issue in this case, the FLSA, is the identical statute that was at issue in *National League of Cities.* Although Justice BLACKMUN's concurrence noted that he was "not untroubled by certain possible implications of the Court's opinion" in *National League of Cities,* it also stated that "the result with respect to the statute under challenge here [the FLSA] is *necessarily correct*" (emphasis added). His opinion for the Court today does not discuss the statute, nor identify any changed circumstances that warrant the conclusion today that *National League of Cities* is *necessarily wrong.*

Today's opinion does not explain how the States' role in the electoral process guarantees that particular exercises of the Commerce Clause power will not infringe on residual State sovereignty. Members of Congress are elected from the various States, but once in office they are members of the federal government. . . .

The Court apparently thinks that the State's success at obtaining federal funds for various projects and exemptions from the obligations of some federal statutes is indicative of the "effectiveness of the federal political process in preserving the States' interests." But such political success is not relevant to the question whether the political *processes* are the proper means of enforcing constitutional limitations. The fact that Congress generally does not transgress constitutional limits on its power to reach State activities does not make judicial review any less necessary to rectify the cases in which it does do so. The States' role in our system of government is a matter of constitutional law, not of legislative grace. "The powers not delegated to the United States by the Constitution, nor prohibited by it to the States, are reserved to the States, respectively, or to the people." U.S. Const., Amend. 10.

More troubling than the logical infirmities in the Court's reasoning is the result of its holding, i.e., that federal political officials, invoking the Commerce Clause, are the sole judges of the limits of their own power. This result is inconsistent with the fundamental principles of our constitutional system. See, e.g., The Federalist No. 78 (Hamilton). At least since *Marbury v. Madison* it has been the settled province of the federal judiciary "to say what the law is" with respect to the constitutionality of acts of Congress. In rejecting the role of the judiciary in protecting the States from federal overreaching, the Court's opinion offers no explanation for ignoring the teaching of the most famous case in our history.

In our federal system, the States have a major role that cannot be preempted by the national government. As contemporaneous writings and the debates at the ratifying conventions make clear, the States' ratification of the Constitution was predicated on this understanding of federalism. Indeed, the Tenth Amendment was adopted specifically to ensure that the important role promised the States by the proponents of the Constitution was realized. . . .

[T]he harm to the States that results from federal overreaching under the Commerce Clause is not simply a matter of dollars and cents. Nor is it a matter of the wisdom or folly of certain policy choices. Rather, by usurping functions traditionally performed by the States, federal overreaching under the Commerce Clause undermines the constitutionally mandated balance of power between the States and the federal government, a balance designed to protect our fundamental liberties.

The emasculation of the powers of the States that can result from the Court's decision is predicated on the Commerce Clause as a power "delegated to the United States" by the Constitution.

The relevant language states: "Congress shall have power . . . to regulate commerce with foreign nations and among the several states and with the Indian tribes." Art. I, § 8. Section eight identifies a score of powers, listing the authority to lay taxes, borrow money on the credit of the United States, pay its debts, and provide for the common defense and the general welfare *before* its brief reference to "Commerce." It is clear from the debates leading up to the adoption of the Constitution that the commerce to be regulated was that which the states themselves lacked the practical capability to regulate. Indeed, the language of the clause itself focuses on activities that only a national government could regulate: commerce with foreign nations and Indian tribes and *"among"* the several states.

To be sure, this Court has construed the Commerce Clause to accommodate unanticipated changes over the past two centuries. As these changes have occurred, the Court has had to decide whether the federal government has exceeded its authority by regulating activities beyond the capability of a single state to regulate or beyond legitimate federal interests that outweighed the authority and interests of the States. In so doing, however, the Court properly has been mindful of the essential role of the States in our federal system.

The opinion for the Court in *National League of Cities* was faithful to history in its understanding of federalism. The Court observed that "our federal system of government imposes definite limits upon the authority of Congress to regulate the activities of States as States by means of the commerce power." The Tenth Amendment was invoked to prevent Congress from exercising its "power in a fashion that impairs the States' integrity or their ability to function effectively in a federal system.". . .

This Court has recognized repeatedly that state sovereignty is a fundamental component of our system of government. More than a century ago, in *Lane County v. Oregon* (1868), the Court stated that the Constitution recognized "the necessary existence of the States, and, within their proper spheres, the independent authority of the States." It concluded, as Madison did, that this authority extended to "nearly the whole charge of interior regulation; to [the States] and to the people all powers not expressly delegated to the national government are reserved." Recently, in *Community Communications Co. v. City of Boulder* [455 U.S. 40] (1982), the Court recognized that the state action exemption from the antitrust laws was based on state sovereignty. Similarly, in *United Transportation Union v. Long Island R. Co.* (1982), although finding the Railway Labor Act applicable to a stateowned railroad, the unanimous Court was careful to say that the States possess constitutionally preserved sovereign powers. . . .

In contrast, the Court today propounds a view of federalism that pays only lip service to the role of the States. Although it

says that the States "unquestionably do 'retai[n] a significant measure of sovereign authority,'" it fails to recognize the broad, yet
specific areas of sovereignty that the Framers intended the States
to retain. Indeed, the Court barely acknowledges that the Tenth
Amendment exists. That Amendment states explicitly that "[t]he
powers not delegated to the United States . . . are reserved to
the States." U.S. Const., Amend. 10. The Court recasts this language to say that the States retain their sovereign powers "only
to the extent that the Constitution has not divested them of their
original powers and transferred those powers to the Federal Government." This rephrasing is not a distinction without a difference;
rather, it reflects the Court's unprecedented view that Congress
is free under the Commerce Clause to assume a State's traditional
sovereign power, and to do so without judicial review of its action.
Indeed, the Court's view of federalism appears to relegate the
States to precisely the trivial role that opponents of the Constitution feared they would occupy.

In *National League of Cities,* we spoke of fire prevention, police
protection, sanitation, and public health as "typical of [the services]
performed by state and local governments in discharging their
dual functions of administering the public law and furnishing
public services." Not only are these activities remote from any
normal concept of interstate commerce, they are also activities
that epitomize the concerns of local, democratic self-government.
In emphasizing the need to protect traditional governmental functions, we identified the kinds of activities engaged in by state
and local governments that affect the everyday lives of citizens.
These are services that people are in a position to understand
and evaluate, and in a democracy, have the right to oversee.
We recognized that "it is functions such as these which governments are created to provide . . ." and that the states and local
governments are better able than the national government to
perform them.

The Court maintains that the standard approved in *National
League of Cities* "disserves principles of democratic self-government." In reaching this conclusion, the Court looks myopically
only to persons elected to positions in the federal government.
It disregards entirely the far more effective role of democratic
self-government at the state and local levels. One must compare
realistically the operation of the state and local governments with
that of the federal government. Federal legislation is drafted primarily by the staffs of the congressional committees. In view of
the hundreds of bills introduced at each session of Congress and
the complexity of many of them, it is virtually impossible for
even the most conscientious legislators to be truly familiar with
many of the statutes enacted. Federal departments and agencies
customarily are authorized to write regulations. Often these are
more important than the text of the statutes. As is true of the

original legislation, these are drafted largely by staff personnel. The administration and enforcement of federal laws and regulations necessarily are largely in the hands of staff and civil service employees. These employees may have little or no knowledge of the States and localities that will be affected by the statutes and regulations for which they are responsible. In any case, they hardly are as accessible and responsive as those who occupy analogous positions in State and local governments. . . .

The question presented in this case is whether the extension of the FLSA to the wages and hours of employees of a city-owned transit system unconstitutionally impinges on fundamental state sovereignty. The Court's sweeping holding does far more than simply answer this question in the negative. In overruling *National League of Cities,* today's opinion apparently authorizes federal control, under the auspices of the Commerce Clause, over the terms and conditions of employment of all state and local employees. Thus, for purposes of federal regulation, the Court rejects the distinction between public and private employers that had been drawn carefully in *National League of Cities.* The Court's action reflects a serious misunderstanding, if not an outright rejection, of the history of our country and the intention of the Framers of the Constitution. . . .

As I view the Court's decision today as rejecting the basic precepts of our federal system and limiting the constitutional role of judicial review, I dissent.

Justice REHNQUIST dissented in a separate opinion.

Justice O'CONNOR, with whom Justice POWELL and Justice REHNQUIST join, dissenting.

The Court today surveys the battle scene of federalism and sounds a retreat. Like Justice POWELL, I would prefer to hold the field and, at the very least, render a little aid to the wounded. I join Justice POWELL's opinion. I also write separately to note my fundamental disagreement with the majority's views of federalism and the duty of this Court. . . .

In my view, federalism cannot be reduced to the weak "essence" distilled by the majority today. There is more to federalism than the nature of the constraints that can be imposed on the States in "the realm of authority left open to them by the Constitution." The central issue of federalism, of course, is whether any realm *is* left open to the States by the Constitution—whether any area remains in which a State may act free of federal interference. . . . The true "essence" of federalism is that the States *as States* have legitimate interests which the National Government is bound to respect even though its laws are supreme. *Younger v. Harris,*

401 U.S. 37 (1971). If federalism so conceived and so carefully cultivated by the Framers of our Constitution is to remain meaningful, this Court cannot abdicate its constitutional responsibility to oversee the Federal Government's compliance with its duty to respect the legitimate interests of the States.

Due to the emergence of an integrated and industrialized national economy, this Court has been required to examine and review a breathtaking expansion of the powers of Congress. In doing so the Court correctly perceived that the Framers of our Constitution intended Congress to have sufficient power to address national problems. But the Framers were not single-minded. The Constitution is animated by an array of intentions. . . . Just as surely as the Framers envisioned a National Government capable of solving national problems, they also envisioned a republic whose vitality was assured by the diffusion of power not only among the branches of the Federal Government, but also between the Federal Government and the States. . . .

We would do well to recall the constitutional basis for federalism and the development of the commerce power which has come to displace it. The text of the Constitution does not define the precise scope of state authority other than to specify, in the Tenth Amendment, that the powers not delegated to the United States by the Constitution are reserved to the States. In the view of the Framers, however, this did not leave state authority weak or defenseless; the powers delegated to the United States, after all, were "few and defined." The Federalist No. 45. The Framers' comments indicate that the sphere of state activity was to be a significant one, as Justice POWELL's opinion clearly demonstrates. The States were to retain authority over those local concerns of greatest relevance and importance to the people. . . .

It is worth recalling the cited passage in *McCulloch v. Maryland* (1819), that lies at the source of the recent expansion of the commerce power. "Let the end be legitimate, let it be within the scope of the constitution," Chief Justice MARSHALL said, "and all means which are appropriate, which are plainly adapted to that end, which are not prohibited, but consist with the letter *and spirit* of the constitution, are constitutional." (emphasis added). The *spirit* of the Tenth Amendment, of course, is that the States will retain their integrity in a system in which the laws of the United States are nevertheless supreme. . . .

It is not enough that the "end be legitimate"; the means to that end chosen by Congress must not contravene the spirit of the Constitution. Thus many of this Court's decisions acknowledge that the means by which national power is exercised must take into account concerns for state autonomy. . . . For example, Congress might rationally conclude that the location a State chooses for its capital may affect interstate commerce, but the Court has suggested that Congress would nevertheless be barred from dictating that location because such an exercise of a delegated power would undermine the state sovereignty inherent in the Tenth Amendment. *Coyle v. Oklahoma,* 221 U.S. 559 (1911). Similarly, Congress in the exercise of its taxing and spending powers can protect federal savings and loan associations, but if it chooses to do so by the means of converting quasi-public state savings and loan associations into federal associations, the Court has held that it contravenes the reserved powers of the States because the conversion is not a reasonably necessary exercise of power to reach the desired end. *Hopkins Federal Savings & Loan Association v. Cleary,* 296 U.S. 315 (1935). The operative language of these cases varies, but the underlying principle is consistent: state autonomy is a relevant factor in assessing the means by which Congress exercises its powers.

This principle requires the Court to enforce affirmative limits on federal regulation of the States to complement the judicially crafted expansion of the interstate commerce power. *National League of Cities v. Usery* represented an attempt to define such limits. The Court today rejects *National League of Cities* and washes its hands of all efforts to protect the States. In the process, the Court opines that unwarranted federal encroachments on state authority are and will remain " 'horrible possibilities that never happen in the real world.' " There is ample reason to believe to the contrary.

The last two decades have seen an unprecedented growth of federal regulatory activity, as the majority itself acknowledges. . . . The political process has not protected against these encroachments on state activities, even though they directly impinge on a State's ability to make and enforce its laws. With the abandonment of *National League of Cities,* all that stands between the remaining essentials of state sovereignty and Congress is the latter's underdeveloped capacity for self-restraint.

The problems of federalism in an integrated national economy are capable of more responsible resolution than holding that the States as States retain no status apart from that which Congress chooses to let them retain. The proper resolution, I suggest, lies in weighing state autonomy as a factor in the balance when interpreting the means by which Congress can exercise its authority on the States as States. It is insufficient, in assessing the validity of congressional regulation of a State pursuant to the commerce power, to ask only whether the same regulation would be valid if enforced against a private party. . . . As far as the Constitution is concerned, a State should not be equated with any private litigant. . . . Instead, the autonomy of a State is an essential component of federalism. If state autonomy is ignored in assessing the means by which Congress regulates matters affecting commerce, then federalism becomes irrelevant simply because the set of activities remaining beyond the reach of such a commerce power "may well be negligible."

It has been difficult for this Court to craft bright lines defining the scope of the state autonomy protected by *National League of Cities*. Such difficulty is to be expected whenever constitutional concerns as important as federalism and the effectiveness of the commerce power come into conflict. Regardless of the difficulty, it is and will remain the duty of this Court to reconcile these concerns in the final instance. That the Court shuns the task today by appealing to the "essence of federalism" can provide scant comfort to those who believe our federal system requires something more than a unitary, centralized government. I would not shirk the duty acknowledged by *National League of Cities* and its progeny, and I share Justice REHNQUIST's belief that this Court will in time again assume its constitutional responsibility.

I respectfully dissent.

C. JUDICIAL FEDERALISM

Judicial power is divided and decentralized in the United States. Along side the federal judiciary, each state has its own independent judicial system. Article III, Section 2 (see Chapter 2) gives the Supreme Court jurisdiction over cases "arising under the Constitution" and controversies between states and citizens of different states. The supremacy clause of Article VI, of course, necessitates that the Court has authority to review decisions of state supreme courts when in conflict with federal law. In addition, the Judiciary Act of 1789 in Section 5 extended federal appellate jurisdiction to the final judgments and decrees "in the highest court of law or equity of a State in which a decision in the suit could be had" in three areas: where a state draws into question the validity of federal law; where a state statute was challenged as "repugnant to the constitution, treaties or laws of the United States" but upheld; and where state courts construing federal law decide against the title, right, privilege, or exemption claimed.

The Court's review of state supreme court decisions has been a source of long-standing controversy in constitutional politics. In *Fairfax's Devisee v. Hunter's Lessee,* 7 Cr. (11 U.S.) 603 (1813), for example, Virginia refused to honor a ruling of the Marshall Court, reversing a decision of that state's supreme court on the rights of British subjects under the Jay Treaty. Virginia maintained that, despite being bound by the Constitution, its interpretations of federal law (not those of federal courts) were controlling. Three years later, Justice Joseph Story reasserted federal judicial power to review state court decisions in *Martin v. Hunter's Lessee* (1816) (see page 603), when rebuffing Virginia's contention by pointing out that the Constitution was established not by the states but the "people of the United States."[1]

Periodically, state courts, legislatures, and government officials have balked at enforcing federal law and asserted the power of state nullification. In one of the Court's first encounters with such a controversy, arising from the Pennsylvania's legislature's refusal to comply with a lower federal court decision, in *United States v. Peters*, 5 Cr. 115 (1809), Chief Justice Marshall dismissed out of hand the state's position: "If the legislatures of the several States may, at will, annul the judgments of the courts of the United States, and destroy the rights acquired under those judgments, the constitution itself becomes a solemn mockery; and the nation is deprived of the means of enforcing its laws by the instrumentality of its own tribunals."

Prior to the Civil War, a number of northern states refused to comply with the Fugitive Slave Law of 1793, requiring the return of escaped slaves. In *Ableman v. Booth,* 21 How. (62 U.S.) 506 (1859), arising from the Wisconsin state supreme court's declaration that the fugitive slave law was unconstitutional, the Taney Court resoundly reasserted federal supremacy. Although a strong defender of state power, Chief Justice Taney declared that "no power is more clearly conferred by the Constitution and laws of the United States, than the power of this court to decide, ultimately and finally, all cases arising under such Constitution and laws."

State nullification or interposition was revived by southern states in opposition to the Warren Court's 1954 landmark ruling on school desegregation. The Alabama legislature, for example, declared,

WHEREAS the states, being the parties to the constitutional compact, it follows of necessity that there can be no tribunal above their authority to decide, in the last resort, whether the compact made by them be violated; and consequently, they must decide themselves, in the last resort, such questions as may be of sufficient magnitude to require their interposition. . . .

The decisions and orders of the Supreme Court of the United States relating to the separation of races in the public schools are, as a matter of right, null, void, and of no effect; and . . . as a matter of right, this State is not bound to abide thereby.

The Court, however, once again rejected that contention in the controversy over Little Rock, Arkansas's opposition to school desegregation in *Cooper v. Aaron* (1958) (see page 609).

State courts may exercise concurrent jurisdiction with federal courts, unless Congress has conferred exclusive jurisdiction on the federal judiciary. Article VI also provides that "the judges in every state shall be bound [by the Supremacy Clause], anything in the Constitution or laws of any state to the contrary notwithstanding."[2]

Although neither federal nor state courts may issue injunctions enjoining each others' proceedings,[3] federal courts may enjoin state officials from enforcing unconstitutional state laws. The injunctive power was first asserted in *Osborn v. Bank of the United States*, 9 Wheat. 738 (1824), though the Marshall Court held that state officials could be enjoined only after a court had declared a state law invalid. *Ex parte Young*, 209 U.S. 123 (1908) further expanded federal injunctive powers, when holding that a state attorney general could be enjoined from enforcing a statute while the statute's validity is being determined in a federal court. In response to that ruling in 1910, Congress enacted legislation forbidding federal judges sitting alone from enjoining the enforcement of state laws and requiring that such injunctions be issued by a panel or three-judge court.

The injunctive power of federal courts was greatly expanded in *Dombrowski v. Pfister* 380 U.S. 82 (1967). There the Warren Court held that where a state law is vague and susceptible to unconstitutional application, federal courts may enjoin its enforcement until a state court has issued a declaratory judgment narrowing its construction. Subsequent rulings, however, have substantially limited *Dombrowski*.[4] The leading case is *Younger v. Harris* (1971) (see page 614).[5]

Another important instrument for federal supervision of state courts is the use of habeas corpus review of the constitutionality for holding a person in prison and the law and procedure under which he was convicted and sentenced. The Court requires that defendants exhaust state remedies before seeking habeas corpus review in federal district courts.[6] But *Fay v. Noia*, 372 U.S. 391 (1963), held that a state prisoner may apply for habeas corpus review even though he failed to comply with state court procedures and lost the opportunity to raise federal questions in the state court.

As a result of the Warren Court's extension of the guarantees of the Bill of Rights to the states (see Vol. 2, Ch. 4), the number of applications for habeas corpus review escalated in the 1970s and 1980s. In response, the Burger and Rehnquist Courts have moved to cutback sharply on the availability of federal habeas corpus review.[7] *Stone v. Powell* (1976) (see page 619) is a leading illustrative case. See also the opinions by Justices O'Connor and Marshall in *Duckworth v. Eagan*, 109 S.Ct. 2875 (1989) (see Vol. 2, Ch. 8).

NOTES

1. See also *Cohens v. Virginia*, 6 Wheat. 264 (1821).
2. *Prigg v. Pennsylvania*, 16 Pet. 539 (1942), held that states could

not be forced to enforce federal penal statutes, but that ruling was subsequently abandoned.

3. Congress limited the powers of the federal courts in 1793 and with a number of later statutes. The Court denied the power of states to enjoin the proceedings of lower federal courts as essential to the independence of the two judicial systems. See *McKim v. Voorhies*, 7 Cr. 279 (1812); and *United States ex rel. Riggs v. Johnson County*, 6 Wall. 166 (1868).

4. See *Steffel v. Thompson*, 415 U.S. 452 (1974); *Kugler v. Helfant*, 421 U.S. 117 (1975); *Rizzo v. Goode*, 423 U.S. 362 (1976); *Justice v. Vail*, 430 U.S. 327 (1977); and *Middlesex County Ethics Committee v. Garden State Bar Association*, 457 U.S. 423 (1982).

5. *Huffman v. Purse, Ltd.*, 420 U.S. 592 (1975), extended *Younger* to civil proceedings.

6. See, for example, *Pitchess v. Davis*, 421 U.S. 482 (1975).

7. See also *Francis v. Henderson*, 425 U.S. 536 (1976); *Estelle v. Williams*, 425 U.S. 501 (1976); *Holmberg v. Parratt*, 431 U.S. 969 (1977); and *Rose v. Lundy*, 455 U.S. 509 (1982).

SELECTED BIBLIOGRAPHY

Fiss, Owen. *The Civil Rights Injunction*. Bloomington: Indiana University Press, 1978.

Glick, Henry. *Supreme Courts in State Politics*. New York: Basic Books, 1971.

Kagen, Robert, Cartwright, Bliss, Friedman, Lawrence, and Wheeler, Stanton. "The Business of State Supreme Courts, 1870–1970." 30 *Stanford Law Review* 121 (1977)

Tarr, G. Allan, and Porter, Mary C. *State Supreme Courts in State and Nation*. New Haven, CT: Yale University Press, 1988.

Martin v. Hunter's Lessee
1 Wheat. (14 U.S.) 304, 14 S.Ct. 97 (1816)

Denny Martin sought to recover a body of land in Virginia he inherited from Lord Fairfax and contended that his rights were secured under the Treaty of Peace with Great Britian in 1783. Virginia's highest appellate court had denied his and other British citizens land rights, but the Supreme Court reversed that decision in *Fairfax's Devisee v. Hunter's Lessee*, 7 Cr. (11 U.S.) 603 (1813). However, on remand of that case the Virginia court refused to abide by the Supreme Court's ruling and held unconstitutional the portion of Section 25 of the Judiciary Act 1789 which extended federal jurisdiction over decisions of state supreme courts. Martin once again appealed to the Supreme Court.

Justice STORY delivers the opinion of the Court.

The third article of the constitution is that which must principally attract our attention. The first section declares, "the judicial power of the United States shall be vested in one Supreme Court, and in such other inferior courts as the Congress may, from time to time, ordain and establish." The second section declares, that "the judicial power shall extend to all cases in law or equity, arising under this constitution, the laws of the United States, and the treaties made, or which shall be made, under their authority; to all cases affecting ambassadors, other public ministers and consuls; to all cases of admiralty and maritime jurisdiction; to controversies to which the United States shall be a party; to controversies between two or more states; between a state and citizens of another state; between citizens of different states; between citizens of the same state, claiming lands under the grants of different states; and between a state or the citizens thereof, and foreign states, citizens, or subjects." It then proceeds to declare, that "in all cases affecting ambassadors, other public ministers and consuls, and those in which a state shall be a party, the Supreme Court shall have original jurisdiction. In all the other cases before mentioned the Supreme Court shall have appellate jurisdiction, both as to law and fact, with such exceptions, and under such regulations, as the Congress shall make.". . .

Let this article be carefully weighed and considered. The language of the article throughout is manifestly designed to be mandatory upon the legislature. Its obligatory force is so imperative that Congress could not, without a violation of its duty, have refused to carry it into operation. The judicial power of the United States shall be vested (not may be vested) in one supreme court, and in such inferior courts as Congress may, from time to time, ordain and establish. . . .

The judicial power must, therefore, be vested in some court, by Congress; and to suppose that it was not an obligation binding on them, but might, at their pleasure, be omitted or declined, is to suppose that, under the sanction of the constitution they might defeat the constitution itself; a construction which would lead to such a result cannot be sound. . . .

If, then, it is the duty of Congress to vest the judicial power of the United States, it is a duty to vest the whole judicial power. The language, if imperative as to one part, is imperative as to all. If it were otherwise, this anomaly would exist, that Congress might successively refuse to vest the jurisdiction in any one class of cases enumerated in the constitution, and thereby defeat the jurisdiction as to all; for the constitution has not singled out any class on which Congress are bound to act in preference to others. . . .

This leads us to the consideration of the great question as to the nature and extent of the appellate jurisdiction of the United States. We have already seen that appellate jurisdiction is given by the constitution to the Supreme Court in all cases, where it has not original jurisdiction; subject, however, to such exceptions and regulations as Congress may prescribe. It is, therefore, capable of embracing every case enumerated in the constitution, which is not exclusively to be decided by way of original jurisdiction. . . .

[B]y the terms of the constitution, the . . . appellate power is not limited by the terms of the third article to any particular courts. The words are, "the judicial power (which includes appellate power) shall extend to all cases," etc., and "in all other cases before mentioned the Supreme Court shall have appellate jurisdiction." It is the case, then, and not the court, that gives the jurisdiction. If the judicial power extends to the case, it will be in vain to search in the letter of the constitution for any qualification as to the tribunal where it depends. . . .

If the constitution meant to limit the appellate jurisdiction to cases pending in the courts of the United States, it would necessarily follow that the jurisdiction of these courts would, in all the cases enumerated in the constitution, be exclusive of state tribunals. How otherwise could the jurisdiction extend to all cases arising under the constitution, laws and treaties of the United States, or to all cases of admiralty and maritime jurisdiction? If some of these cases might be entertained by state tribunals, and no appellate jurisdiction as to them should exist, then the appellate power would not extend to all, but to some, cases. If state tribunals might exercise concurrent jurisdiction over all or some of the other classes of cases in the constitution without control, then the appellate jurisdiction of the United States might, as to such cases, have no real existence, contrary to the manifest intent of the constitution. Under such circumstances, to give effect to the judicial power, it must be construed to be exclusive; and this not only when the casus faederis should arise directly, but when it should arise, incidentally, in cases pending in state courts. This construction would abridge the jurisdiction of such courts far more than has been ever contemplated in any act of Congress. . . .

[I]t is plain that the framers of the constitution did contemplate that cases within the judicial cognizance of the United States not only might but would arise in the state courts, in the exercise of their ordinary jurisdiction. With this view the sixth article declares, that "this constitution, and the laws of the United States which shall be made in pursuance thereof, and all treaties made, or which shall be made, under the authority of the United States, shall be the supreme law of the land and the judges in every state shall be bound thereby, anything in the constitution or laws of any state to the contrary notwithstanding." It is obvious that this obligation is imperative upon the state judges in their official, and not merely in their private, capacities. From the very nature of their judicial duties they would be called upon to pronounce the law applicable to the case in judgment. They were not to decide merely according to the laws or constitution of the state, but according to the constitution, laws and treaties of the United States—"the supreme law of the land."

A moment's consideration will show us the necessity and propriety of this provision in cases where the jurisdiction of the state courts is unquestionable. Suppose a contract for the payment of money is made between citizens of the same state, and performance thereof is sought in the courts of that state; no person can doubt that the jurisdiction completely and exclusively attaches, in the first instance, to such courts. Suppose at the trial the defendant sets up in his defense a tender under a state law, making paper money a good tender, or a state law, impairing the obligation of such contract, which law, if binding, would defeat the suit. The constitution of the United States has declared that no state shall make anything but gold or silver coin a tender in payment of debts, or pass a law impairing the obligation of contracts. If Congress shall not have passed a law providing for the removal of such a suit to the courts of the United States, must not the state court proceed to hear and determine it? Can a mere plea in defense be of itself a bar to further?

It must, therefore, be conceded that the constitution not only contemplated, but meant to provide for cases within the scope of the judicial power of the United States, which might yet depend before state tribunals. It was foreseen that in the exercise of their ordinary jurisdiction, state courts would incidentally take cognizance of cases arising under the constitution, the laws and treaties of the United States. Yet to all these cases the judicial power, by the very terms of the constitution, is to extend. It cannot extend by original jurisdiction if that was already rightfully and exclusively attached in the state courts, which (as has been already shown) may occur; it must, therefore, extend by appellate jurisdiction, or not at all. It would seem to follow that the appellate power of the United States must, in such cases, extend to state tribunals; and if in such cases, there is no reason why it should not equally attach upon all others within the purview of the constitution.

It has been argued that such an appellate jurisdiction over state courts is inconsistent with the genius of our governments, and the spirit of the constitution. That the latter was never designed to act upon state sovereignties, but only upon the people, and that if the power exists, it will materially impair the sovereignty of the states, and the independence of their courts. We cannot yield to the force of this reasoning; it assumes principles which we cannot admit, and draws conclusions to which we do not yield our assent.

It is a mistake that the constitution was not designed to operate upon states, in their corporate capacities. It is crowded with provisions which restrain or annul the sovereignty of the states in some of the highest branches of their prerogatives. The tenth section of the first article contains a long list of disabilities and prohibitions imposed upon the states. Surely, when such essential portions of state sovereignty are taken away, or prohibited to be exercised, it cannot be correctly asserted that the constitution does not act upon the states. The language of the constitution is also imperative upon the states as to the performance of many duties. It is imperative upon the state legislatures to make laws prescribing the time, places, and manner of holding elections for senators and representatives, and for electors of President and Vice-President. And in these, as well as some other cases, Congress have a right to revise, amend, or supersede the laws which may be passed by state legislatures. When, therefore, the states are stripped of some of the highest attributes of sovereignty, and the same are given to the United States; when the legislatures of the states are, in some respects, under the control of Congress, and in every case are, under the constitution, bound by the paramount authority of the United States; it is certainly difficult to support the argument that the appellate power over the decisions of state courts is contrary to the genius of our institutions. The courts of the United States can, without question, revise the proceedings of the executive and legislative authorities of the states, and if they are found to be contrary to the constitution, may declare them to be of no legal validity. Surely the exercise of the same right over judicial tribunals is not a higher or more dangerous act of sovereign power.

Nor can such a right be deemed to impair the independence of state judges. It is assuming the very ground in controversy to assert that they possess an absolute independence of the United States. In respect to the powers granted to the United States, they are not independent; they are expressly bound to obedience by the letter of the constitution; and if they should unintentionally transcend their authority, or misconstrue the constitution, there is no more reason for giving their judgments an absolute and irresistible force than for giving it to the acts of the other co-ordinate departments of state sovereignty.

It is further argued that no great public mischief can result from a construction which shall limit the appellate power of the United States to cases in their own courts; first, because state judges are bound by an oath to support the constitution of the United States, and must be presumed to be men of learning and integrity; and, secondly, because Congress must have an unquestionable right to remove all cases within the scope of the judicial power from the state courts to the courts of the United States, at any time before final judgment, though not after final judgment. As to the first reason—admitting that the judges of the state courts are, and always will be, of as much learning, integrity, and wisdom, as those of the courts of the United States (which we very cheerfully admit), it does not aid the argument. It is manifest that the constitution has proceeded upon a theory of its own, and given or withheld powers according to the judgment of the American people, by whom it was adopted. We can only construe its powers, and cannot inquire into the policy or principles which induced the grant of them. The constitution has presumed (whether rightly or wrongly we do not inquire) that state attachments, state prejudices, state jealousies, and state interests, might sometimes obstruct, or control, or be supposed to obstruct or control, the regular administration of justice. Hence, in controversies between states; between citizens of different states; between citizens claiming grants under different states; between a state and its citizens, or foreigners, and between citizens and foreigners, it enables the parties, under the authority of Congress, to have the controversies heard, tried, and determined before the national tribunals. No other reason than that which has been stated can be assigned, why some, at least, of those cases should not have been left to the cognizance of the state courts. In respect to the other enumerated cases—the cases arising under the constitution, laws, and treaties of the United States, cases affecting ambassadors and other public ministers, and cases of admiralty and maritime jurisdiction—reasons of a higher and more extensive nature, touching the safety, peace, and sovereignty of the nation, might well justify a grant of exclusive jurisdiction.

This is not all. A motive of another kind, perfectly compatible with the most sincere respect for state tribunals, might induce the grant of appellate power over their decisions. That motive is the importance, and even necessity of uniformity of decisions throughout the whole United States, upon all subjects within the purview of the constitution. Judges of equal learning and integrity, in different states, might differently interpret a statute, or a treaty of the United States, or even the constitution itself. If there were no revising authority to control these jarring and discordant judgments, and harmonize them into uniformity, the laws, the treaties, and the constitution of the United States would be different in different states, and might, perhaps, never have precisely the same construction, obligation, or efficacy, in any two states. The public mischiefs that would attend such a state of things would be truly deplorable; and it cannot be believed that they could have escaped the enlightened convention which formed the constitution. What, indeed, might then have been only prophecy, has now become fact; and the appellate jurisdiction must continue to be the only adequate remedy for such evils.

There is an additional consideration, which is entitled to great weight. The constitution of the United States was designed for the common and equal benefit of all the people of the United States. The judicial power was granted for the same benign and salutary purposes. It was not to be exercised exclusively for the benefit of parties who might be plaintiffs, and would elect the national forum, but also for the protection of defendants who might be entitled to try their rights, or assert their privileges, before the same forum. Yet, if the construction contended for be correct, it will follow, that as the plaintiff may always elect the state court, the defendant, may be deprived of all the security which the constitution intended in aid of his rights. Such a state of things can in no respect be considered as giving equal rights. . . .

On the whole, the court are of opinion that the appellate power of the United States does extend to cases pending in the state courts; and that the 25th section of the judiciary act, which authorizes the exercise of this jurisdiction in the specified cases, by a writ of error, is supported by the letter and spirit of the constitution. We find no clause in that instrument which limits this power; and we dare not interpose a limitation where the people have not been disposed to create one.

Justice JOHNSON concurred in a separate opinion.

Cooper v. Aaron
358 U.S. 1, 78 S.Ct. 1401 (1958)

In 1958, Governor Orval Faubus encouraged southern segregationists to oppose the Supreme Court's ruling on school desegregation and violence erupted in Little Rock, Arkansas. The federal National Guard had to be called out to maintain order. The school board in Little Rock pleaded with the Supreme Court to postpone its mandate for the desegregation of public schools. The Court granted the petition and expedited proceedings, hearing oral arguments three days after the petition was filed.

After the justices unanimously voted to deny the school board's request for a delay in desegregating its public schools, Justice Brennan prepared a draft of the opinion that would announce the Court's decision. But in an unusual move all nine justices gathered in their private conference room and reworked portions of the opinion. The Court also took the unusual step of noting in the opinion that three justices—Brennan, Stewart, and Whitaker—were not on the Court when the landmark ruling in *Brown v. Board of Education of Topeka, Kansas* (1954) (see Vol. 2, Ch. 12) was handed down but that they would have joined the unanimous decision if they had been. All nine justices then signed the Court's opinion to emphasize their unanimity and because Justice Frankfurter insisted on adding a concurring opinion. This departure from the typical practice of having one justice sign the opinion was strongly opposed by Douglas and angered Brennan and Chief Justice Warren. But all agreed to depart in this way so that Frankfurter's concurring opinion "would not be accepted as any dilution or interpretation of the views expressed in the Court's joint opinion." Frankfurter insisted on publishing a concurring opinion because many of his former students at Harvard Law School were leading members of the southern bar and because the ex-justice (and former governor of South Carolina) James Byrnes had published an attack on *Brown* and an article written by one of Frankfurter's favorite former law clerks, Alexander Bickel. As a clerk, Bickel had prepared a lengthy research report on segregated schools when the Court first considered *Brown*. Later, when back at Harvard, Bickel revised and published it in the *Harvard Law Review*. Given Byrnes's attack, Frankfurter personally felt the need to lecture southern lawyers on the legitimacy of the Court's ruling in *Brown*.

The CHIEF JUSTICE, Justice BLACK, Justice FRANKFURTER, Justice DOUGLAS, Justice BURTON, Justice CLARK, Justice HARLAN, Justice BRENNAN, and Justice WHITTAKER deliver the opinion of the Court.

As this case reaches us it raises questions of the highest importance to the maintenance of our federal system of government. It necessarily involves a claim by the Governor and Legislature of a State that there is no duty on state officials to obey federal court orders resting on this Court's considered interpretation of the United States Constitution. Specifically it involves actions by the Governor and Legislature of Arkansas upon the premise that they are not bound by our holding in *Brown v. Board of Education* [1954]. That holding was that the Fourteenth Amendment forbids States to use their governmental powers to bar children on racial grounds from attending schools where there is state participation through any arrangement, management, funds or property. We are urged to uphold a suspension of the Little Rock School Board's plan to do away with segregated public schools in Little Rock until state laws and efforts to upset and nullify our holding in

Brown v. Board of Education have been further challenged and tested in the courts. We reject these contentions. . . .

In affirming the judgment of the Court of Appeals which reversed the District Court we have accepted without reservation the position of the School Board, the Superintendent of Schools, and their counsel that they displayed entire good faith in the conduct of these proceedings and in dealing with the unfortunate and distressing sequence of events which has been outlined. We likewise have accepted the findings of the District Court as to the conditions at Central High School during the 1957–1958 school year, and also the findings that the educational progress of all the students, white and colored, of that school has suffered and will continue to suffer if the conditions which prevailed last year are permitted to continue.

The significance of these findings, however, is to be considered in light of the fact, indisputably revealed by the record before us, that the conditions they depict are directly traceable to the actions of legislators and executive officials of the State of Arkansas, taken in their official capacities, which reflect their own determination to resist this Court's decision in the Brown case and which have brought about violent resistance to that decision in Arkansas. In its petition for certiorari filed in this Court, the School Board itself describes the situation in this language: "The legislative, executive, and judicial departments of the state government opposed the desegregation of Little Rock schools by enacting laws, calling out troops, making statements villifying federal law and federal courts, and failing to utilize state law enforcement agencies and judicial processes to maintain public peace."

One may well sympathize with the position of the Board in the face of the frustrating conditions which have confronted it, but, regardless of the Board's good faith, the actions of the other state agencies responsible for those conditions compel us to reject the Board's legal position. Had Central High School been under the direct management of the State itself, it could hardly be suggested that those immediately in charge of the school should be heard to assert their own good faith as a legal excuse for delay in implementing the constitutional rights of these respondents, when vindication of those rights was rendered difficult or impossible by the actions of other state officials. The situation here is in no different posture because the members of the School Board and the Superintendent of Schools are local officials; from the point of view of the Fourteenth Amendment, they stand in this litigation as the agents of the State. . . .

The controlling legal principles are plain. The command of the Fourteenth Amendment is that no "State" shall deny to any person within its jurisdiction the equal protection of the laws. "A State acts by its legislative, its executive, or its judicial authorities. It can act in no other way. The constitutional provision, therefore, must mean that no agency of the State, or of the officers or agents by whom its powers are exerted, shall deny to any person within its jurisdiction the equal protection of the laws. Whoever, by virtue of public position under a State government . . . denies or takes away the equal protection of the laws, violates the constitutional inhibition; and as he acts in the name and for the State, and is clothed with the State's power, his act is that of the State. This must be so, or the constitutional prohibition has no meaning." *Ex parte Virginia,* 100 U.S. 339 [1880]. Thus the prohibitions of the Fourteenth Amendment extend to all action of the State denying equal protection of the laws; whatever the agency of the State taking the action, or whatever the guise in which it is taken. In short, the constitutional rights of children not to be discriminated against in school admission on grounds of race or color declared by this Court in the Brown case can neither be nullified openly and directly by state legislators or state executive or judicial officers, nor nullified indirectly by them through evasive schemes for segregation whether attempted "ingeniously or ingenuously." *Smith v. Texas,* 311 U.S. 128 [1940]. . . .

What has been said, in the light of the facts developed, is enough to dispose of the case. However, we should answer the premise of the actions of the Governor and Legislature that they are not bound by our holding in the Brown case. It is necessary only to recall some basic constitutional propositions which are settled doctrine.

Article VI of the Constitution makes the Constitution the "supreme Law of the Land." In 1803, Chief Justice MARSHALL, speaking for a unanimous Court, referring to the Constitution as "the fundamental and paramount law of the nation," declared in the notable case of *Marbury v. Madison* that "It is emphatically the province and duty of the judicial department to say what the law is." This decision declared the basic principle that the federal judiciary is supreme in the exposition of the law of the Constitution, and that principle has ever since been respected by this Court and the Country as a permanent and indispensable feature of our constitutional system. It follows that the interpretation of the Fourteenth Amendment enunciated by this Court in the Brown case is the supreme law of the land, and Art. VI of the Constitution makes it of binding effect on the States "any Thing in the Constitution or Laws of any State to the Contrary notwithstanding." Every state legislator and executive and judicial officer is solemnly committed by oath taken pursuant to Art. VI, § 3 "to support this Constitution.". . .

No state legislator or executive or judicial officer can war against the Constitution without violating his undertaking to support it. Chief Justice MARSHALL spoke for a unanimous Court in saying that: "If the legislatures of the several states may, at will, annul the judgments of the courts of the United States, and destroy the rights acquired under those judgments, the constitution itself becomes a solemn mockery. . . ." *United States v. Peters,* 5 Cranch 115 [1809].

It is, of course, quite true that the responsibility for public education is primarily the concern of the States, but it is equally true that such responsibilities, like all other state activity, must be exercised consistently with federal constitutional requirements as they apply to state action. The Constitution created a government dedicated to equal justice under law. The Fourteenth Amendment embodied and emphasized that ideal. State support of segregated schools through any arrangement, management, funds, or property cannot be squared with the Amendment's command that no State shall deny to any person within its jurisdiction the equal protection of the laws. The right of a student not to be segregated on racial grounds in schools so maintained is indeed so fundamental and pervasive that it is embraced in the concept of due process of law. *Bolling v. Sharpe,* 347 U.S. 497 [1954]. The basic decision in *Brown* was unanimously reached by this Court only after the case had been briefed and twice argued and the issues had been given the most serious consideration. Since the first Brown opinion three new Justices have come to the Court. They are at one with the Justices still on the Court who participated in that basic decision as to its correctness, and that decision is now unanimously reaffirmed. The principles announced in that decision and the obedience of the States to them, according to the command of the Constitution, are indispensable for the protection of the freedoms guaranteed by our fundamental charter for all of us. Our constitutional ideal of equal justice under law is thus made a living truth.

Justice FRANKFURTER concurring.

While unreservedly participating with my brethren in our joint opinion, I deem it appropriate also to deal individually with the great issue here at stake. . . .

We are now asked to hold that the illegal, forcible interference by the State of Arkansas with the continuance of what the Constitution commands, and the consequences in disorder that it entrained, should be recognized as justification for undoing what the Board of Education had formulated, what the District Court in 1955 had directed to be carried out, and what was in process of obedience. No explanation that may be offered in support of such a request can obscure the inescapable meaning that law should bow to force. To yield to such a claim would be to enthrone official lawlessness and lawlessness if not checked is the precursor of anarchy. . . .

The duty to abstain from resistance to "the supreme Law of the Land," U.S. Const., Art. VI, § 2, as declared by the organ of our Government for ascertaining it, does not require immediate approval of it nor does it deny the right of dissent. Criticism need not be stilled. Active obstruction or defiance is barred. Our kind of society cannot endure if the controlling authority of the Law as derived from the Constitution is not to be the tribunal specially charged with the duty of ascertaining and declaring what is "the supreme Law of the Land."

Younger v. Harris
401 U.S. 37, 91 S.Ct. 746 (1971)

John Harris, Jr., was indicted in state court for violating California's Criminal Syndicalism Act, which forbade the advocacy of criminal syndicalism or teaching of the "necessity or propriety of committing any crime, sabotage, violence or any unlawful method of terrorism as a means of accomplishing" economic and political change. While his prosecution was pending in state court, he promptly filed a complaint in federal district court, asking that it enjoin Evelle Younger, the district attorney of Los Angeles County, from prosecuting him on the grounds that the law unconstitutionally denied him the freedom of speech and press under the First and Fourteenth Amendments. A three-judge federal court held in a declaratory judgment that California's law was void for vagueness and overbreadth in violation of the First and Fourteenth Amendments and, accordingly, issued an injunction restraining Younger from prosecuting Harris in state court. Younger then appealed to the Supreme Court, which reversed the lower federal court's declaratory judgment and injunction.

Justice BLACK delivers the opinion of the Court.

Since the beginning of this country's history Congress has, subject to few exceptions, manifested a desire to permit state courts to try state cases free from interference by federal courts. In 1793 an Act unconditionally provided: "[N]or shall a writ of injunction be granted to stay proceedings in any court of a state. . . ." A comparison of the 1793 Act with 28 U.S.C. § 2283, its present-day successor, graphically illustrates how few and minor have been the exceptions granted from the flat, prohibitory language of the old Act. During all this lapse of years from 1793 to 1970 the statutory exceptions to the 1793 congressional enactment have been only three: (1) "except as expressly authorized by Act of Congress"; (2) "where necessary in aid of its jurisdiction"; and (3) "to protect or effectuate its judgments." In addition, a judicial exception to the long-standing policy evidenced by the statute has been made where a person about to be prosecuted in a state court can show that he will, if the proceeding in the state court is not enjoined, suffer irreparable damages. See *Ex parte Young*, 209 U.S. 123 (1908).

The precise reasons for this long-standing public policy against federal court interference with state court proceedings have never been specifically identified but the primary sources of the policy are plain. One is the basic doctrine of equity jurisprudence that courts of equity should not act, and particularly should not act to restrain a criminal prosecution, when the moving party has an adequate remedy at law and will not suffer irreparable injury if denied equitable relief. The doctrine may originally have grown out of circumstances peculiar to the English judicial system and not applicable in this country, but its fundamental purpose of restraining equity jurisdiction within narrow limits is equally important under our Constitution, in order to prevent erosion of the role of the jury and avoid a duplication of legal proceedings and legal sanctions where a single suit would be adequate to protect the rights asserted. This underlying reason for restraining courts of equity from interfering with criminal prosecutions is reinforced by an even more vital consideration, the notion of "comity," that is, a proper respect for state functions, a recognition of the fact that the entire country is made up of a Union of separate state governments, and a continuance of the belief that the National Government will fare best if the States and their institutions are left free to perform their separate functions in their separate ways. This, perhaps for lack of a better and clearer way to describe it, is referred to by many as "Our Federalism," and one familiar with the profound debates that ushered our Federal Constitution into existence is bound to respect those who remain loyal to the ideals and dreams of "Our Federalism." The concept does not mean blind deference to "States' Rights" any more than it means centralization of control over every important issue in our National Government and its courts. The Framers rejected both these courses. What the concept does represent is a system in which there is sensitivity to the legitimate interests of both State and National Governments, and in which the National Government, anxious though it may be to vindicate and protect federal rights and federal interests, always endeavors to do so in ways that will not unduly interfere with the legitimate activities of the States. It should never be forgotten that this slogan, "Our Federalism," born in the early struggling days of our Union of States, occupies a highly important place in our Nation's history and its future.

This brief discussion should be enough to suggest some of

the reasons why it has been perfectly natural for our cases to repeat time and time again that the normal thing to do when federal courts are asked to enjoin pending proceedings in state courts is not to issue such injunctions. . . .

In [earlier] cases the Court stressed the importance of showing irreparable injury, the traditional prerequisite to obtaining an injunction. In addition, however, the Court also made clear that in view of the fundamental policy against federal interference with state criminal prosecutions, even irreparable injury is insufficient unless it is "both great and immediate." Certain types of injury, in particular, the cost, anxiety, and inconvenience of having to defend against a single criminal prosecution, could not by themselves be considered "irreparable" in the special legal sense of that term. Instead, the threat to the plaintiff's federally protected rights must be one that cannot be eliminated by his defense against a single criminal prosecution. . . .

[I]n *Douglas [v. City of Jeannette*, 319 U.S. 157 (1943)], we made clear, after reaffirming this rule, that:

> "It does not appear from the record that petitioners have been threatened with any injury other than that incidental to every criminal proceeding brought lawfully and in good faith. . . ."

This is where the law stood when the Court decided *Dombrowski v. Pfister*, 380 U.S. 479 (1965), and held that an injunction against the enforcement of certain state criminal statutes could properly issue under the circumstances presented in that case. In *Dombrowski*, unlike many of the earlier cases denying injunctions, the complaint made substantial allegations that:

> "the threats to enforce the statutes against appellants are not made with any expectation of securing valid convictions, but rather are part of a plan to employ arrests, seizures, and threats of prosecution under color of the statutes to harass appellants and discourage them and their supporters from asserting and attempting to vindicate the constitutional rights of Negro citizens of Louisiana.". . .

[T]he Court in *Dombrowski* went on to say:

> "But the allegations in this complaint depict a situation in which defense of the State's criminal prosecution will not assure adequate vindication of constitutional rights. They suggest that a substantial loss of or impairment of freedoms of expression will occur if appellants must await the state court's disposition and ultimate review in this Court of any adverse determination. These allegations, if true, clearly show irreparable injury.". . .

And the Court made clear that even under these circumstances the District Court issuing the injunction would have continuing power to lift it at any time and remit the plaintiffs to the state courts if circumstances warranted. . . .

It is against the background of these principles that we must judge the propriety of an injunction under the circumstances of the present case. Here a proceeding was already pending in the state court, affording Harris an opportunity to raise his constitutional claims. There is no suggestion that this single prosecution against Harris is brought in bad faith or is only one of a series of repeated prosecutions to which he will be subjected. In other words, the injury that Harris faces is solely "that incidental to every criminal proceeding brought lawfully and in good faith," *Douglas*, and therefore under the settled doctrine we have already described he is not entitled to equitable relief "even if such statutes are unconstitutional.". . .

The District Court, however, thought that the *Dombrowski* decision substantially broadened the availability of injunctions against state criminal prosecutions and that under that decision the federal courts may give equitable relief, without regard to any showing of bad faith or harassment, whenever a state statute is found "on its face" to be vague or overly broad, in violation of the First Amendment. We recognize that there are some statements in the *Dombrowski* opinion that would seem to support this argument. But, as we have already seen, such statements were unnecessary to the decision of that case, because the Court found that the plaintiffs had alleged a basis for equitable relief under the long-established standards. In addition, we do not regard the reasons adduced to support this position as sufficient to justify such a substantial departure from the established doctrines regarding the availability of injunctive relief. It is undoubtedly true, as the Court stated in *Dombrowski*, that "[a] criminal prosecution under a statute regulating expression usually involves imponderables and contingencies that themselves may inhibit the full exercise of First Amendment freedoms." But this sort of "chilling effect," as the Court called it, should not by itself justify federal intervention. In the first place, the chilling effect cannot be satisfactorily eliminated by federal injunctive relief. . . .

Moreover, the existence of a "chilling effect," even in the area of First Amendment rights, has never been considered a sufficient basis, in and of itself, for prohibiting state action. Where a statute does not directly abridge free speech, but—while regulating a subject within the State's power—tends to have the incidental effect of inhibiting First Amendment rights, it is well settled that the statute can be upheld if the effect on speech is minor in relation to the need for control of the conduct and the lack of alternative means for doing so. . . .

Beyond all this is another, more basic consideration. Procedures for testing the constitutionality of a statute "on its face" in the manner apparently contemplated by *Dombrowski,* and for then enjoining all action to enforce the statute until the State can obtain court approval for a modified version, are fundamentally at odds with the function of the federal courts in our constitutional plan. The power and duty of the judiciary to declare laws unconstitutional is in the final analysis derived from its responsibility for resolving concrete disputes brought before the courts for decision; a statute apparently governing a dispute cannot be applied by judges, consistently with their obligations under the Supremacy Clause, when such an application of the statute would conflict with the Constitution. *Marbury v. Madison* (1803). But this vital responsibility, broad as it is, does not amount to an unlimited power to survey the statute books and pass judgment on laws before the courts are called upon to enforce them. . . .

For these reasons, fundamental not only to our federal system but also to the basic functions of the Judicial Branch of the National Government under our Constitution, we hold that the *Dombrowski* decision should not be regarded as having upset the settled doctrines that have always confined very narrowly the availability of injunctive relief against state criminal prosecutions.

Justice BRENNAN with whom Justice WHITE and Justice MARSHALL join, concurring.

I agree that the judgment of the District Court should be reversed. Appellee Harris had been indicted for violations of the California Criminal Syndicalism Act before he sued in federal court. He has not alleged that the prosecution was brought in bad faith to harass him. His constitutional contentions may be adequately adjudicated in the state criminal proceeding, and federal intervention at his instance was therefore improper.

Justice STEWART, with whom Justice HARLAN joined, concurred in a separate opinion.

Justice DOUGLAS dissenting.

The fact that we are in a period of history when enormous extrajudicial sanctions are imposed on those who assert their First Amendment rights in unpopular causes emphasizes the wisdom of *Dombrowski v. Pfister*. There we recognized that in times of repression, when interests with powerful spokesmen generate symbolic pogroms against nonconformists, the federal judiciary, charged by Congress with special vigilance for protection of civil rights, has special responsibilities to prevent an erosion of the individual's constitutional rights.

Dombrowski represents an exception to the general rule that federal courts should not interfere with state criminal prosecutions. The exception does not arise merely because prosecutions are threatened to which the First Amendment will be the proffered defense. *Dombrowski* governs statutes which are a blunderbuss by themselves or when used *en masse*—those that have an "overbroad" sweep. "If the rule were otherwise, the contours of regulation would have to be hammered out case by case—and tested only by those hardy enough to risk criminal prosecution to determine the proper scope of regulation." It was in the context of overbroad state statutes that we spoke of the "chilling effect upon the exercise of First Amendment rights" caused by state prosecutions. . . .

The special circumstances when federal intervention in a state criminal proceeding is permissible are not restricted to bad faith on the part of state officials or the threat of multiple prosecutions. They also exist where for any reason the state statute being enforced is unconstitutional on its face.

Stone v. Powell
428 U.S. 465, 96 S.Ct. 3037 (1976)

Lloyd Powell was convicted of murder in state court, in part on the basis of his testimony concerning a revolver found in his possession when he was arrested for violating an ordinance prohibiting vagrancy. The trial judge rejected his claim that the testimony should have been excluded because the ordinance was unconstitutional and that, therefore, the arrest was invalid. A state appellate court agreed, and Powell then applied for *habeas corpus* relief in federal district court. The federal district court concluded that the arresting officer had probable cause to arrest Powell. And even if the vagrancy ordinance were unconstitutional, the deterrent purpose of the Fourth Amendment's exclusionary rule did not require the suppression at trial of statements Powell made to the arresting officer at the time of his arrest. The Court of Appeals for the Ninth Circuit then reversed. And California's prison warden, W. T. Stone, appealed to the Supreme Court.

Justice POWELL delivers the opinion of the Court.

The question presented is whether a federal court should consider, in ruling on a petition for habeas corpus relief filed by a state prisoner, a claim that evidence obtained by an unconstitutional search or seizure was introduced at his trial, when he has previously been afforded an opportunity for full and fair litigation of his claim in the state courts. The issue is of considerable importance to the administration of criminal justice. . . .

Respondents allege violations of Fourth Amendment rights guaranteed them through the Fourteenth Amendment. The question is whether state prisoners—who have been afforded the opportunity for full and fair consideration of their reliance upon the exclusionary rule with respect to seized evidence by the state courts at trial and on direct review—may invoke their claim again on federal habeas corpus review. The answer is to be found by weighing the utility of the exclusionary rule against the costs of extending it to collateral review of Fourth Amendment claims.

The costs of applying the exclusionary rule even at trial and on direct review are well known: the focus of the trial, and the attention of the participants therein, is diverted from the ultimate question of guilt or innocence that should be the central concern in a criminal proceeding. Moreover, the physical evidence sought to be excluded is typically reliable and often the most probative information bearing on the guilt or innocence of the defendant. . . . Application of the rule thus deflects the truthfinding process and often frees the guilty. The disparity in particular cases between the error committed by the police officer and the windfall afforded a guilty defendant by application of the rule is contrary to the idea of proportionality that is essential to the concept of justice. Thus, although the rule is thought to deter unlawful police activity in part through the nurturing of respect for Fourth Amendment values, if applied indiscriminately it may well have the opposite effect of generating disrespect for the law and administration of justice. These long-recognized costs of the rule persist when a criminal conviction is sought to be overturned on collateral review on the ground that a search-and-seizure claim was erroneously rejected by two or more tiers of state courts.

Evidence obtained by police officers in violation of the Fourth Amendment is excluded at trial in the hope that the frequency of future violations will decrease. Despite the absence of supportive empirical evidence, we have assumed that the immediate effect of exclusion will be to discourage law enforcement officials from violating the Fourth Amendment by removing the incentive to disregard it. More importantly, over the long term, this demonstration that our society attaches serious consequences to violation of constitutional rights is thought to encourage those who formulate law enforcement policies, and the officers who implement them, to incorporate Fourth Amendment ideals into their value system.

We adhere to the view that these considerations support the implementation of the exclusionary rule at trial and its enforcement on direct appeal of state court convictions. But the additional contribution, if any, of the consideration of search-and-seizure claims of state prisoners on collateral review is small in relation to the costs. To be sure, each case in which such claim is considered may add marginally to an awareness of the values protected by the Fourth Amendment. There is no reason to believe, however, that the overall educative effect of the exclusionary rule would be appreciably diminished if search-and-seizure claims could not be raised in federal habeas corpus review of state convictions. Nor is there reason to assume that any specific disincentive already created by the risk of exclusion of evidence at trial or the reversal of convictions on direct review would be enhanced if there were the further risk that a conviction obtained in state court and affirmed on direct review might be overturned in collateral proceedings often occurring years after the incarceration of the defendant. The view that the deterrence of Fourth Amendment violations would be furthered rests on the dubious assumption that law enforcement authorities would fear that federal habeas review might reveal flaws in a search or seizure that went undetected at trial and on appeal. Even if one rationally could assume that some additional incremental deterrent effect would be presented in isolated cases, the resulting advance of the legitimate goal of furthering Fourth Amendment rights would be outweighed by the acknowledged costs to other values vital to a rational system of criminal justice.

In sum, we conclude that where the State has provided an opportunity for full and fair litigation of a Fourth Amendment claim, a state prisoner may not be granted federal habeas corpus relief on the ground that evidence obtained in an unconstitutional search or seizure was introduced at his trial. In this context the contribution of the exclusionary rule, if any, to the effectuation of the Fourth Amendment is minimal, and the substantial societal costs of application of the rule persist with special force.

Accordingly, the judgments of the Courts of Appeals are Reversed.

Chief Justice BURGER concurring.

I concur in the Court's opinion. By way of dictum, and somewhat hesitantly, the Court notes that the holding in this case leaves undisturbed the exclusionary rule as applied to criminal trials. For reasons stated in my dissent in *Bivens v. Six Unknown Named Federal Agents*, 403 U.S. 388 (1971), it seems clear to me that the exclusionary rule has been operative long enough to demonstrate its flaws. The time has come to modify its reach, even if it is retained for a small and limited category of cases.

Over the years, the strains imposed by reality, in terms of the costs to society and the bizarre miscarriages of justice that have been experienced because of the exclusion of reliable evidence when the "constable blunders," have led the Court to vacillate as to the rationale for deliberate exclusion of truth from the factfinding process. The rhetoric has varied with the rationale to the point where the rule has become a doctrinaire result in search of validating reasons.

In evaluating the exclusionary rule, it is important to bear in mind exactly what the rule accomplishes. Its function is simple—the exclusion of truth from the factfinding process. . . . The operation of the rule is therefore unlike that of the Fifth Amendment's protection against compelled self-incrimination. A confession produced after intimidating or coercive interrogation is inherently dubious. If a suspect's will has been overborne, a cloud hangs over his custodial admissions; the exclusion of such statements is based essentially on their lack of reliability. This is not the case as to *reliable* evidence—a pistol, a packet of heroin, counterfeit money, or the body of a murder victim—which may be judicially declared to be the result of an "unreasonable" search. The reliability of such evidence is beyond question; its probative value is certain. . . .

To vindicate the continued existence of this judge-made rule, it is incumbent upon those who seek its retention—and surely its *extension*—to demonstrate that it serves its declared deterrent purpose and to show that the results outweigh the rule's heavy costs to rational enforcement of the criminal law. The burden rightly rests upon those who ask society to ignore trustworthy evidence of guilt, at the expense of setting obviously guilty criminals free to ply their trade. . . .

In *Bivens,* I suggested that, despite its grave shortcomings, the rule need not be totally abandoned until some meaningful alternative could be developed to protect innocent persons aggrieved by police misconduct. With the passage of time, it now appears that the continued existence of the rule, as presently implemented, inhibits the development of rational alternatives. The reason is quite simple: incentives for developing new procedures or remedies will remain minimal or nonexistent so long as the exclusionary rule is retained in its present form.

It can no longer be assumed that other branches of government will act while judges cling to this Draconian, discredited device in its present absolutist form. Legislatures are unlikely to create statutory alternatives, or impose direct sanctions on errant police officers or on the public treasury by way of tort actions so long as persons who commit serious crimes continue to reap the enormous and undeserved benefits of the exclusionary rule. And of course, by definition the direct beneficiaries of this rule can be none but persons guilty of crimes. With this extraordinary "remedy" for Fourth Amendment violations, however slight, inadvertent or technical, legislatures might assume that nothing more should be done, even though a grave defect of the exclusionary rule is that it offers no relief whatever to victims of overzealous police work who never appear in court. . . .

And even if legislatures were inclined to experiment with alternative remedies, they have no assurance that the judicially created rule will be abolished or even modified in response to such legislative innovations. The unhappy result, as I see it, is that alternatives will inevitably be stymied by rigid adherence on our part to the exclusionary rule. I venture to predict that overruling this judicially contrived doctrine—or limiting its scope to egregious, bad-faith conduct—would inspire a surge of activity toward providing some kind of statutory remedy for persons injured by police mistakes or misconduct.

Justice BRENNAN, with whom Justice MARSHALL joins, dissenting.

The Court adheres to the holding of *Mapp* [*v. Ohio*, 367 U.S. 643 (1961)] that the Constitution "require[d] exclusion" of the evidence admitted at respondents' trials. However, the Court holds that the Constitution "does not require" that respondents be accorded habeas relief if they were accorded "an opportunity for full and fair litigation of [their] Fourth Amendment claim[s]" in state courts. Yet once the Constitution was interpreted by *Mapp* to require exclusion of certain evidence at trial, the Constitution became irrelevant to the manner in which that constitutional right was to be enforced in the federal courts; *that* inquiry is only a matter of respecting Congress' allocation of federal judicial power between this Court's appellate jurisdiction and a federal district court's habeas jurisdiction. Indeed, by conceding that today's "decision does not mean that the federal [district] court lacks jurisdiction over [respondents'] claim[s]" the Court admits that respondents have sufficiently alleged that they are "in custody in violation of the Constitution" within the meaning of § 2254 and that there is no "constitutional" rationale for today's holding. Rather, the constitutional "interest balancing" approach to this case is untenable, and I can only view the constitutional garb in which the Court dresses its result as a disguise for rejection of the longstanding principle that there are no "second class" constitutional rights for purposes of federal habeas jurisdiction; it is nothing less than an attempt to provide a veneer of respectability for an obvious usurpation of Congress'' Art. III power to delineate the jurisdiction of the federal courts.

[T]he real ground of today's decision—a ground that is particularly troubling in light of its portent for habeas jurisdiction generally—is the Court's novel reinterpretation of the habeas statutes; this would read the statutes as requiring the District Courts routinely to deny habeas relief to prisoners "in custody in violation of the Constitution or laws of the United States" as a matter of judicial "discretion"—a "discretion" judicially manufactured today contrary to the express statutory language—because such claims are "different in kind" from other constitutional violations in that they "do not 'impugn the integrity of the fact-finding process'" and because application of such constitutional strictures "often frees the guilty." Much in the Court's opinion suggests that a construction of the habeas statutes to deny relief for non-"guilt-related" constitutional violations, based on this Court's vague notions of comity and federalism is the actual premise for today's decision, and although the Court attempts to bury its underlying premises in footnotes, those premises mark this case as a harbinger of future eviscerations of the habeas statutes that plainly does violence to congressional power to frame the statutory contours of habeas jurisdiction. For we are told that "[r]esort to habeas corpus, especially for purposes other than to assure that no innocent person suffers an unconstitutional loss of liberty, results in serious intrusions on values important to our system of government," including waste of judicial resources, lack of finality of criminal convictions, friction between the federal and state judiciaries, and incursions on "federalism." We are told that federal determination of Fourth Amendment claims merely involves "an issue that has no bearing on the basic justice of [the defendant's] incarceration," and that "the ultimate question [in the criminal process should invariably be] guilt or innocence." We are told that the "policy arguments" of respondents to the effect that federal courts must be the ultimate arbiters of federal constitutional rights, and that our certiorari jurisdiction is inadequate to perform this task, "stem from a basic mistrust of the state courts as fair and competent forums for the adjudication of federal constitutional rights"; the Court, however, finds itself "unwilling to assume that there now exists a general lack of appropriate sensitivity to constitutional rights in the trial and appellate courts of the several States," and asserts that it is "unpersuaded" by "the argument that federal judges are more expert in applying federal constitutional law" because "there is 'no intrinsic reason why the fact that a man is a federal judge should make him more competent, or conscientious, or learned with respect to the [consideration of Fourth Amendment claims] than his neighbor in the state courthouse." Finally, we are provided a revisionist history of the genesis and growth of federal habeas corpus jurisdiction. If today's decision were only that erroneous state court resolution of Fourth Amendment claims did not render the defendant's resultant confinement "in violation of the Constitution," these pronouncements would have been wholly irrelevant and unnecessary. I am therefore justified in apprehending that the groundwork is being laid today for a drastic withdrawal of federal habeas jurisdiction, if not for all grounds of alleged unconstitutional detention, then at least for claims—for example, of double jeopardy, entrapment, self-incrimination, *Miranda* violations, and use of invalid identification procedures—that this Court later decides are not "guilt-related."

To the extent the Court is actually premising its holding on an interpretation of 28 U.S.C. § 2243 or § 2254, it is overruling the heretofore settled principle that federal habeas relief is available to redress *any* denial of asserted constitutional rights, whether or not denial of the right affected the truth or fairness of the fact-finding process. . . .

Without even paying the slightest deference to principles of *stare decisis* or acknowledging Congress' failure for two decades to alter the habeas statutes in light of our interpretation of congressional intent to render all federal constitutional contentions cognizable on habeas, the Court today rewrites Congress' jurisdictional statutes as heretofore construed and bars access to federal courts by state prisoners with constitutional claims distasteful to a majority of my Brethren. . . .

I would address the Court's concerns for effective utilization of scarce judicial resources, finality principles, federal-state friction, and notions of "federalism" only long enough to note that such concerns carry no more force with respect to non-"guilt-related" constitutional claims than they do with respect to claims that affect the accuracy of the fact-finding process. Congressional conferral of federal habeas jurisdiction for the purpose of entertaining petitions from state prisoners necessarily manifested a conclusion that such concerns could not be controlling, and any argument for discriminating among constitutional rights must therefore depend on the nature of the constitutional right involved.

The Court, focusing on Fourth Amendment rights as it must to justify such discrimination, thus argues that habeas relief for non-"guilt-related" constitutional claims is not mandated because such claims do not affect the "basic justice" of a defendant's detention; this is presumably because the "ultimate goal" of the criminal justice system is "truth and justice." This denigration of constitutional guarantees and *constitutionally mandated procedures,* relegated by the Court to the status of mere utilitarian tools, must appall citizens taught to expect judicial respect and support for their constitutional rights. Even if punishment of the "guilty" were society's highest value—and procedural safeguards denigrated to this end—in a constitution that a majority of the members of this Court would prefer, that is not the ordering of priorities under the Constitution forged by the Framers, and this Court's sworn duty is to uphold that Constitution and not to frame its own. The procedural safeguards mandated in the Framers' Constitution are not admonitions to be tolerated only to the extent they serve functional purposes that ensure that the "guilty" are punished and the "innocent" freed; rather, every guarantee enshrined in the Constitution, our basic charter and the guarantor of our most precious liberties, is by it endowed with an independent vitality and value, and this Court is not free to curtail those constitutional guarantees even to punish the most obviously guilty. . . .

[U]nlike the Court I consider that the exclusionary rule is a constitutional ingredient of the Fourth Amendment, any modification of that rule should at least be accomplished with some modicum of logic and justification not provided today. . . .

The Court does not disturb the holding of *Mapp v. Ohio* that, as a matter of federal constitutional law, illegally obtained evidence must be excluded from the trial of a criminal defendant whose rights were transgressed during the search that resulted in acquisition of the evidence. In light of that constitutional rule it is a matter for Congress, not this Court, to prescribe what federal courts are to review state prisoners' claims of constitutional error committed by state courts. Until this decision, our cases have never departed from the construction of the habeas statutes as embodying a congressional intent that, however substantive constitutional rights are delineated or expanded, those rights may be asserted as a procedural matter under federal habeas jurisdiction. Employing the transparent tactic that today's is a decision construing the Constitution, the Court usurps the authority—vested by the Constitution in the Congress—to reassign federal judicial responsibility for reviewing state prisoners' claims of failure of state courts to redress violations of their Fourth Amendment rights. Our jurisdiction is eminently unsuited for that task, and as a practical matter the only result of today's holding will be that denials by the state courts of claims by state prisoners of violations of their Fourth Amendment rights will go unreviewed by a federal tribunal. I fear that the same treatment ultimately will be accorded state prisoners' claims of violations of other constitutional rights; thus the potential ramifications of this case for federal habeas jurisdiction generally are ominous. The Court, no longer content just to restrict forthrightly the constitutional rights of the citizenry, has embarked on a campaign to water down even such constitutional rights as it purports to acknowledge by the device of foreclosing resort to the federal habeas remedy for their redress.

I would affirm the judgments of the Courts of Appeals.

Justice WHITE dissenting.

For many of the reasons stated by Justice BRENNAN, I cannot agree that the writ of habeas corpus should be any less available to those convicted of state crimes where they allege Fourth Amendment violations than where other constitutional issues are presented to the federal court. . . .

I feel constrained to say, however, that I would join four or more other Justices in substantially limiting the reach of the exclusionary rule as presently administered under the Fourth Amendment in federal and state criminal trials.

Whether I would have joined the Court's opinion in *Mapp v. Ohio*, 367 U.S. 643 (1961), had I then been a Member of the Court, I do not know. But as time went on after coming to this bench, I became convinced that both *Weeks v. United States*, 232 U.S. 383 (1914), and *Mapp v. Ohio* had overshot their mark insofar as they aimed to deter lawless action by law enforcement personnel and that in many of its applications the exclusionary rule was not advancing that aim in the slightest and that in this respect it was a senseless obstacle to arriving at the truth in many criminal trials.

The rule has been much criticized and suggestions have been made that it should be wholly abolished, but I would overrule neither *Weeks v. United States* nor *Mapp v. Ohio*. I am nevertheless of the view that the rule should be substantially modified so as to prevent its application in those many circumstances where the evidence at issue was seized by an officer acting in the good-faith belief that his conduct comported with existing law and having reasonable grounds for this belief. These are recurring situations; and recurringly evidence is excluded without any realistic expectation that its exclusion will contribute in the slightest to the purposes of the rule, even though the trial will be seriously affected or the indictment dismissed. . . .

When law enforcement personnel have acted mistakenly, but in good faith and on reasonable grounds, and yet the evidence they have seized is later excluded, the exclusion can have no deterrent effect. The officers, if they do their duty, will act in similar fashion in similar circumstances in the future; and the only consequence of the rule as presently administered is that unimpeachable and probative evidence is kept from the trier of fact and the truth-finding function of proceedings is substantially impaired or a trial totally aborted. . . .

The exclusionary rule, a judicial construct, seriously shortchanges the public interest as presently applied. I would modify it accordingly.

D. STATE COURTS AND STATE CONSTITUTIONAL LAW

State courts handle the overwhelming volume of all litigation—well over 90 percent of all filings. In the 1980s about 190,000 civil and 40,000 criminal cases were annually filed in federal courts. By comparison, state courts annually faced over 26 million filings. The type of litigation in state courts also tends to diverge from that in federal courts. Apart from criminal cases, the largest portion of state supreme court litigation involves economic issues—whether relating to state regulation of public utilities, zoning, and small businesses or labor relations and workmen's compensation, natural resources, energy, and the environment. Litigation varies from state to state as well, depending on factors such as population size, urbanization, and socioeconomic conditions.[1]

The Supreme Court's nationalization of guarantees of the Bill of Rights (see Vol. 2, Ch. 4) profoundly altered constitutional politics and the federal-state court relationships. With the increasing prominence of the federal judiciary, the role of state courts and state constitutional law tended to be overshadowed, but that is no longer the case.

The important role of state courts in interpreting their own state constitutions is underscored by the fact the Supreme Court intrudes on state court policymaking in only a very narrow class of litigation—the class of cases in which state courts deal with questions of federal legislation and federal constitutional law. Federal questions rarely emerge from the grist of state courts, emphasized Justice Brennan, a former New Jersey state supreme court judge: "If cases were grains of sand, federal question cases would be hard to find on the beach. The final and vital decisions of most controversies upon which depend life, liberty, and property are made by the state courts."[2] If a case does not raise a substantial federal question or is decided on *independent state grounds*—a state constitution or bill of rights—then the Court declines review and respects the principle of comity between federal and state judiciaries.

Federal-state court relations have always been uneasy, but they have evolved rather dramatically in the last thirty years with the changes in the composition and direction of the Supreme Court. In the 1950s and 1960s, when state supreme courts tended to be much more conservative than the Warren Court, relations were often especially acrimonious. The Conference of State Chief Justices in 1958 went so far as to pass a resolution condemning the Warren Court for its erosion of federalism and its tendency "to adopt the role of policymaker without proper judicial restraint."[3] By contrast, in the 1970s and 1980s the direction of the Burger and Rehnquist Courts' policymaking moved in more conservative directions, while some state supreme courts became far more protective of individual rights. Although not outright reversing some of the most controversial and landmark Warren Court rulings, the Burger and Rehnquist Courts refused further extensions and achieved retrenchment in a number of areas. More-liberal state supreme courts accordingly refused to follow the rulings of the Court when interpreting individual rights under state constitutional law. "Why should we always be the tail being wagged by the Federal dog?" asked New Hampshire State Supreme Court Justice Charles Douglas and other state judges. "Liberal state courts have taken the doctrines of federalism and states' rights, heretofore associated with [conservatives] like George Wallace," California's Justice Stanley Mosk has explained, "and adapted them to give citizens more rights under their state constitutions rather than to oppress them."[4]

The resurgence in state constitutional law protecting individual rights has renewed controversy within the Supreme Court over its power to patrol the decisions of state supreme courts, particularly in the area of individual rights. Indeed, since Chief Justice Warren Burger's appointment in 1969 and the Court's move in more conservative directions, state supreme courts in well over 600 cases have vindicated rights broader than or left unprotected by the Supreme Court.

The shift in state constitutional law in the view of Brennan is a sign of "the strength of our federal system."[5] Oregon State Supreme Court Justice Hans Linde, a leading influence on the development of state constitutional law, agreed. He argued that state courts should turn to their state constitutions first because they are "first in time and first in logic:"

It was not unheard of in 1776, long before the drafting of the Federal Constitution, for the revolutionaries of that day to declare in their charters of their new states that [individuals enjoyed certain fundamental rights and liberties]. . . .

Far from being the model for the states, the Federal Bill of Rights was added to the Constitution to meet demands for the same guarantees against the new central government that people had secured against their own local officials. Moreover, the states that adopted new constitutions during the following decades took their bills of rights from the preexisting state constitutions rather than from the federal amendments. . . .

The Federal Bill of Rights did not supercede those of the states. It was not interposed between the citizen and his state. When the Fifth Amendment was invoked against the City of Baltimore in 1833, John Marshall replied that its adoption "could never have occurred to any human being, as a mode of doing that which might be effected by the state itself." Only the Civil War made it clear that it might sometimes be necessary to use federal law as a mode of doing that which a state could but did not effect for itself—the protection of some of its citizens against those in control of its government.

It is the Fourteenth Amendment that has bound the states to observe the guarantees of the Federal Bill of Rights. . . .

We tend to forget how recently the application of the Federal Bill of Rights to the states developed. Throughout the nineteenth century and the first quarter of the twentieth, state courts decided questions on constitutional rights under their own state constitutions. In 1925, it was only a hypothesis that the states were bound by the First Amendment. That was really settled only after 1937. Fifth Amendment guarantees against compulsory self-incrimination and double jeopardy did not bind the states until 1964 and 1969, respectively. I shall not go through the catalogue; most of the decisions binding the states to observe the procedures of the Fourth, Fifth, and Sixth amendments date from the same period. Of course, the states had all these guarantees in their own laws long before the Federal Bill of Rights was applied to the states. State courts had been administering these laws, sometimes generously, more often not, for a century or more without awaiting an interpretation of the United States Supreme Court.

Historically, the states' commitment to individual rights came first. Restraints on the federal government were patterned upon the states' declarations of rights. . . .

Just as rights under state constitutions were first in time, they also are first in the logic of constitutional law. For lawyers, the point is quickly made. Whenever a person asserts a particular right, and a state court recognizes and protects that right under state law, then the state is not depriving the person of whatever federal claim he or she might otherwise assert. There is no federal question.[6]

In contrast to Justice Brennan and others sharing his views, the more conservative members of the Court have sought to bring state courts into line by reversing decisions vindicating broader constitutional rights than they approved. *Michigan v. Long* (1983) (see page 631) is illustrative of the Court's concern. There Justice O'Connor for the majority ruled that state supreme courts must clearly indicate that their rulings rest on adequate and independent state grounds, otherwise the Court will feel free to reverse those rulings with which it disagrees. *People v. P. J. Video, Inc.* (1986) (see page 637) illustrates how state supreme courts may nevertheless refuse to back down from their interpretation of guarantees for individual rights, even after their prior decisions have been reversed by the Supreme Court. Law professor Ronald Collins and political scientist Peter Galie examine the methods of developing state constitutional law in the article that follows (see page 641).

NOTES

1. See for example, Henry Glick and Kenneth Vines, *State Court Systems* (Englewood Cliffs, NJ: Prentice Hall, 1973).

2. William J. Brennan, "Address," 31 *Pennsylvania Bar Association Quarterly* 394 (1960).

3. "Report of the Committee on Federal-State Relationships as Affected by Judicial Decisions," reprinted in *Cong. Record,* 73rd Cong., 2d sess., Appendix, A7784 (Aug. 25, 1958).

4. Quoted in David M. O'Brien, *Storm Center: The Supreme Court in America Politics* (New York: W. W. Norton, 2d. ed., 1990), 358.

5. See William J. Brennan, Jr., "State Constitutions and the Protection of Individual Rights," 90 *Harvard Law Review* 489 (1977).

6. Hans Linde, "First Things First: Rediscovering the States' Bill of Rights," 9 *University of Baltimore Law Review* 379 (1980).

SELECTED BIBLIOGRAPHY

Brennan, William J. Jr. "Guardians of Our Liberties—State Courts No Less Than Federal." In *Views from the Bench: The Judiciary and Constitutional Politics,* edited by Mark Cannon and David M. O'Brien. Chatham, NJ: Chatham House, 1985.

"Developments in the Law: The Interpretation of State Constitutional Rights." 95 *Harvard Law Review* 1324 (1982).

Galie, Peter. "The Other Supreme Courts: Judicial Activism among State Supreme Courts." 33 *Syracuse Law Review* 731 (1982).

O'Connor, Sandra Day. "Trends in the Relationship between the Federal and State Courts." In *Views from the Bench: The Judiciary and Constitutional Politics,* edited by Mark Cannon and David M. O'Brien. (Chatham, NJ: Chatham House, 1985).

Porter, Mary, and Tarr, Allan, eds. *State Supreme Courts: Policymakers in the Federal System.* Westport, CT: Greenwood Press, 1982.

Symposium on the Revolution in State Constitutional Law. 13 *Vermont Law Review* 1 (1988).

Williams, Robert F. "In the Supreme Court's Shadow: Legitimacy of State Rejection of Supreme Court Reasoning and Result." 35 *South Carolina Law* 353 (1984).

Michigan v. Long
463 U.S. 1036, 103 S.Ct. 3469 (1983)

David Long was convicted of possession of marijuana and he appealed. A state appellate court affirmed his conviction but the Michigan Supreme Court reversed on the grounds that police had made an illegal search in violation of "the Fourth Amendment to the United States Constitution *and* Art. 1 § 11 of the

Michigan Constitution" (emphasis added). The state attorney general appealed that ruling to the Supreme Court.

Justice O'CONNOR delivers the opinion of the Court.

In *Terry v. Ohio*, 392 U.S. 1 (1968), we upheld the validity of a protective search for weapons in the absence of probable cause to arrest because it is unreasonable to deny a police officer the right "to neutralize the threat of physical harm," when he possesses an articulable suspicion that an individual is armed and dangerous. We did not, however, expressly address whether such a protective search for weapons could extend to an area beyond the person in the absence of probable cause to arrest. In the present case, respondent David Long was convicted for possession of marihuana found by police in the passenger compartment and trunk of the automobile that he was driving. The police searched the passenger compartment because they had reason to believe that the vehicle contained weapons potentially dangerous to the officers. We hold that the protective search of the passenger compartment was reasonable under the principles articulated in *Terry* and other decisions of this Court. We also examine Long's argument that the decision below rests upon an adequate and independent state ground, and we decide in favor of our jurisdiction. . . .

Before reaching the merits, we must consider Long's argument that we are without jurisdiction to decide this case because the decision below rests on an adequate and independent state ground. The court below referred twice to the State Constitution in its opinion, but otherwise relied exclusively on federal law. Long argues that the Michigan courts have provided greater protection from searches and seizures under the State Constitution than is afforded under the Fourth Amendment, and the references to the State Constitution therefore establish an adequate and independent ground for the decision below.

Although we have announced a number of principles in order to help us determine whether various forms of references to state law constitute adequate and independent state grounds, we openly admit that we have thus far not developed a satisfying and consistent approach for resolving this vexing issue. In some instances, we have taken the strict view that if the ground of decision was at all unclear, we would dismiss the case. . . . In other instances, we have vacated or continued a case in order to obtain clarification about the nature of a state-court decision. . . . In more recent cases, we have ourselves examined state law to determine whether state courts have used federal law to guide their application of state law or to provide the actual basis for the decision that was reached. . . .

This ad hoc method of dealing with cases that involve possible adequate and independent state grounds is antithetical to the doctrinal consistency that is required when sensitive issues of federal-state relations are involved. Moreover, none of the various methods of disposition that we have employed thus far recommends itself as the preferred method that we should apply to the exclusion of others, and we therefore determine that it is appropriate to reexamine our treatment of this jurisdictional issue in order to achieve the consistency that is necessary.

The process of examining state law is unsatisfactory because it requires us to interpret state laws with which we are generally unfamiliar, and which often, as in this case, have not been discussed at length by the parties. Vacation and continuance for clarification have also been unsatisfactory both because of the delay and decrease in efficiency of judicial administration and, more important, because these methods of disposition place significant burdens on state courts to demonstrate the presence or absence of our jurisdiction. . . . Finally, outright dismissal of cases is clearly not a panacea because it cannot be doubted that there is an important need for uniformity in federal law, and that this need goes unsatisfied when we fail to review an opinion that rests primarily upon federal grounds and where the *independence* of an alleged state ground is not apparent from the four corners of the opinion. We have long recognized that dismissal is inappropriate "where there is strong indication . . . that the federal constitution as judicially construed controlled the decision below.". . .

Respect for the independence of state courts, as well as avoidance of rendering advisory opinions, have been the cornerstones of this Court's refusal to decide cases where there is an adequate and independent state ground. It is precisely because of this respect for state courts, and this desire to avoid advisory opinions, that we do not wish to continue to decide issues of state law that go beyond the opinion that we review, or to require state courts to reconsider cases to clarify the grounds of their decisions. Accordingly, when, as in this case, a state court decision fairly appears to rest primarily on federal law, or to be interwoven with the federal law, and when the adequacy and independence of any possible state law ground is not clear from the face of the opinion, we will accept as the most reasonable explanation that the state court decided the case the way it did because it believed that federal law required it to do so. If a state court chooses merely to rely on federal precedents as it would on the precedents of all other jurisdictions, then it need only make clear by a plain statement in its judgment or opinion that the federal cases are being used only for the purpose of guidance, and do not themselves compel the result that the court has reached. In this way, both justice and judicial administration will be greatly improved. If the state court decision indicates clearly and expressly that it is alternatively based on bona fide separate, adequate, and independent grounds, we, of course, will not undertake to review the decision.

This approach obviates in most instances the need to examine state law in order to decide the nature of the state court decision, and will at the same time avoid the danger of our rendering advisory opinions. It also avoids the unsatisfactory and intrusive practice of requiring state courts to clarify their decisions to the satisfaction of this Court. We believe that such an approach will provide state judges with a clearer opportunity to develop state jurisprudence unimpeded by federal interference, and yet will preserve the integrity of federal law. . . .

The principle that we will not review judgments of state courts that rest on adequate and independent state grounds is based, in part, on "the limitations of our own jurisdiction." The jurisdictional concern is that we not "render an advisory opinion, and if the same judgment would be rendered by the state court after we corrected its views of federal laws, our review could amount to nothing more than an advisory opinion." Our requirement of a "plain statement" that a decision rests upon adequate and independent state grounds does not in any way authorize the rendering of advisory opinions. Rather, in determining, as we must, whether we have jurisdiction to review a case that is alleged to rest on adequate and independent state grounds . . . we merely assume that there are no such grounds when it is not clear from the opinion itself that the state court relied upon an adequate and independent state ground and when it fairly appears that the state court rested its decision primarily on federal law.

Our review of the decision below under this framework leaves us unconvinced that it rests upon an independent state ground. Apart from its two citations to the State Constitution, the court below relied *exclusively* on its understanding of *Terry* and other federal cases. Not a single state case was cited to support the state court's holding that the search of the passenger compartment was unconstitutional. Indeed, the court declared that the search in this case was unconstitutional because "[t]he Court of Appeals erroneously applied the principles of *Terry v. Ohio* to the search of the interior of the vehicle in this case." The references to the State Constitution in no way indicate that the decision below rested on grounds in any way *independent* from the state court's interpretation of federal law. Even if we accept that the Michigan Constitution has been interpreted to provide independent protection for certain rights also secured under the Fourth Amendment, it fairly appears in this case that the Michigan Supreme Court rested its decision primarily on federal law.

Rather than dismissing the case, or requiring that the state court reconsider its decision on our behalf solely because of a mere possibility that an adequate and independent ground supports the judgment, we find that we have jurisdiction in the absence of a plain statement that the decision below rested on an adequate and independent state ground. It appears to us that the state court "felt compelled by what it understood to be federal constitutional considerations to construe . . . its own law in the manner it did.". . .

The court below held, and respondent Long contends, that Deputy Howell's entry into the vehicle cannot be justified under the principles set forth in *Terry* because "*Terry* authorized only a limited pat-down search of a *person* suspected of criminal activity" rather than a search of an area. Although *Terry* did involve the protective frisk of a person, we believe that the police action in this case is justified by the principles that we have already established in *Terry* and other cases. . . .

The judgment of the Michigan Supreme Court is reversed, and the case is remanded for further proceedings not inconsistent with this opinion.

It is so ordered.

Justice BLACKMUN concurring in part.

While I am satisfied that the Court has jurisdiction in this particular case, I do not join the Court . . . in fashioning a new presumption of jurisdiction over cases coming here from state courts. Although I agree with the Court that uniformity in federal criminal law is desirable, I see little efficiency and an increased danger of advisory opinions in the Court's new approach.

Justice BRENNAN, with whom Justice MARSHALL joined, dissented.

Justice STEVENS dissenting.

The jurisprudential questions presented in this case are far more important than the question whether the Michigan police officer's search of respondent's car violated the Fourth Amendment. The case raises profoundly significant questions concerning the relationship between two sovereigns—the State of Michigan and the United States of America.

The Supreme Court of the State of Michigan expressly held "that the deputies' search of the vehicle was proscribed by the Fourth Amendment to the United States Constitution and *art. 1, § 11 of the Michigan Constitution*" (emphasis added). The state law ground is clearly adequate to support the judgment, but the question whether it is independent of the Michigan Supreme Court's understanding of federal law is more difficult. Four possible ways of resolving that question present themselves: (1) asking the Michigan Supreme Court directly, (2) attempting to infer from all possible sources of state law what the Michigan Supreme Court meant, (3) presuming that adequate state grounds are independent unless it clearly appears otherwise, or (4) presuming that adequate state grounds are *not* independent unless it clearly appears otherwise. This Court has, on different occasions, employed each of the first three approaches; never until today has it even hinted at the fourth. In order to "achieve the consistency that is necessary," the Court today undertakes a reexamination of all the possibilities. It rejects the first approach as inefficient and unduly burdensome for state courts, and rejects the second approach as an inappropriate expenditure of our resources. Although I find both of those decisions defensible in themselves, I cannot accept the Court's decision to choose the fourth approach over the third—to presume that adequate state grounds are intended to be dependent on federal law unless the record plainly shows otherwise. I must therefore dissent.

If we reject the intermediate approaches, we are left with a choice between two presumptions: one in favor of our taking jurisdiction, and one against it. Historically, the latter presumption has always prevailed. [*Lynch v. New York ex. rel. Pierson,* 293 U.S. 52 (1934).] The rule, as succinctly stated in *Lynch,* was as follows:

> "Where the judgment of the state court rests on two grounds, one involving a federal question and the other not, or if it does not appear upon which of two grounds the judgment was based, and the ground independent of a federal question is sufficient in itself to sustain it, this Court will not take jurisdiction. . . ."

The Court today points out that in several cases we have weakened the traditional presumption by using the other two intermediate approaches identified above. Since those two approaches are now to be rejected, however, I would think that *stare decisis* would call for a return to historical principle. Instead, the Court seems to conclude that because some precedents are to be rejected, we must overrule them all. . . .

I believe that in reviewing the decisions of state courts, the primary role of this Court is to make sure that persons who seek to *vindicate* federal rights have been fairly heard. That belief resonates with statements in many of our prior cases. . . .

Until recently we had virtually no interest in cases of this type. Thirty years ago, this Court reviewed only one. *Nevada v. Stacher,* 358 U.S. 907 (1953). Indeed, that appears to have been the only case during the entire 1953 Term in which a State even sought review of a decision by its own judiciary. Fifteen years ago, we did not review any such cases, although the total number of requests had mounted to three. Some time during the past decade, perhaps about the time of the 5-to-4 decision in *Zacchini v. Scripps-*

Howard Broadcasting Co., 433 U.S. 562 (1977), our priorities shifted. The result is a docket swollen with requests by States to reverse judgments that their courts have rendered in favor of their citizens. I am confident that a future Court will recognize the error of this allocation of resources. When that day comes, I think it likely that the Court will also reconsider the propriety of today's expansion of our jurisdiction.

The Court offers only one reason for asserting authority over cases such as the one presented today: "an important need for uniformity in federal law [that] goes unsatisfied when we fail to review an opinion that rests primarily upon federal grounds and where the independence of an alleged state ground is not apparent from the four corners of the opinion." Of course, the supposed need to "review an opinion" clashes directly with our oft-repeated reminder that "our power is to correct wrong judgments, not to revise opinions." The clash is not merely one of form: the "need for uniformity in federal law" is truly an ungovernable engine. That same need is no less present when it is perfectly clear that a state ground is both independent and adequate. . . .

I respectfully dissent.

People v. P. J. Video, Inc.
68 N.Y. 2d 296, 501 N.E. 2d 556 (N.Y., 1986)

In *New York v. P. J. Video, Inc.,* 475 U.S. 868 (1986), the Supreme Court reversed a ruling of the New York Court of Appeals (the state's highest appellate court), which had held that a state court judge erred when issuing a search warrant for the seizure of allegedly obscene video cassette films. The New York court ruled that for the seizure of books and films, which are subject to First Amendment protection, a "higher" standard of probable cause applies than the usual "fair probability" that evidence of crime will be found on a police search. The Supreme Court reversed and remanded the case back to the New York court for further proceedings not inconsistent with its rejection of a "higher" standard of probable cause for search warrants for allegedly obscene materials. But the New York Court of Appeals responded with the opinion delivered by Judge Simons.

Judge SIMONS.

In our earlier decision in this case we held that the issuing magistrate erred in approving a warrant authorizing the seizure of video cassette films as evidence that defendants were promoting obscenity. . . .

On certiorari review, the Supreme Court judged probable cause by applying the totality of the circumstances/fair probability test of *Illinois v. Gates* [462 U.S. 213 (1983)]. The *Gates* rule originally was adopted to test the reliability of anonymous informants' tips. It overruled the established two-pronged *Aguilar-Spinelli* test (*Aguilar v. Texas*, 378 U.S. 108 [1964]; *Spinelli v. United States*, 393 U.S. 410 [1969]) which required a court to review both the basis of the informant's knowledge and the reliability of his information, to permit a magistrate to now decide whether, given all the circumstances set forth in the police affidavit, there is a *fair probability* that contraband or evidence of a crime will be found in a particular place. In this case, the Supreme Court extended the reach of this "totality of the circumstances/fair probability" standard and applied it, for the first time, to an obscenity case to permit the magistrate to focus generally on the explicit nature of pornographic material without specifically considering the other statutory elements of the crime (*see, New York v. P.J. Video*). Having done so, it remanded the case to us for our further consideration.

State courts are bound by the decisions of the Supreme Court when reviewing Federal statutes or applying the Federal Constitution. Under established principles of federalism, however, the States also have sovereign powers. When their courts interpret State statutes or the State Constitution the decisions of these courts are conclusive if not violative of Federal law. Although State courts may not circumscribe rights guaranteed by the Federal Constitution, they may interpret their own law to supplement or expand them. . . . Thus, notwithstanding that the evidence before the magistrate was sufficient to establish probable cause under the Federal Constitution, we have the power on remand to interpret article I, § 12 of the New York Constitution as requiring more. We turn then to the question whether we should measure probable cause in this case by different standards under the State Constitution.

Courts and commentators have identified many considerations and concerns upon which a State court may rely when determining that its Constitution accords greater protection to individual liberties and rights than the protection guaranteed by the Federal Constitution. . . .

One basis for relying on the State Constitution arises from an interpretive review of its provisions. If the language of the State Constitution differs from that of its Federal counterpart, then the court may conclude that there is a basis for a different interpretation of it. Such an analysis considers whether the textual language of the State Constitution specifically recognizes rights not enumerated in the Federal Constitution; whether language in the State Constitution is sufficiently unique to support a broader interpretation of the individual right under State law; whether the history of the adoption of the text reveals an intention to make the State provision coextensive with, or broader than, the parallel Federal provision; and whether the very structure and purpose of the State Constitution serves to expressly affirm certain rights rather than merely restrain the sovereign power of the State. To contrast, noninterpretive review proceeds from a judicial perception of sound policy, justice and fundamental fairness. . . . A noninterpretive analysis attempts to discover, for example, any preexisting State statutory or common law defining the scope of the individual right in question; the history and traditions of the State in its protection of the individual right; any identification of the right in the State Constitution as being one of peculiar State or local concern; and any distinctive attitudes of the State citizenry toward the definition, scope or protection of the individual right.

Our determination rests on noninterpretive grounds. We rely principally on established Federal and State law because we believe the arguments supporting that body of law are more persuasive than the arguments supporting application of the *Gates* rule in this obscenity case, and are consistent with the admonition of an earlier Supreme Court that constitutional provisions for the security of persons and property are to be liberally construed (*see, Boyd v. United States,* 116 U.S. 616 [1886]). Our decision, however, is also based on principles of federalism and on New York's long tradition of interpreting our State Constitution to protect individual rights. In this case, we consider two fundamental rights, the right of free expression and the right of citizens to be free from unlawful governmental intrusions.

In the past we have frequently applied the State Constitution, in both civil and criminal matters, to define a broader scope of protection than that accorded by the Federal Constitution in cases concerning individual rights and liberties. Our conduct in the area of Fourth Amendment rights has been somewhat more restrained because the history of section 12 supports the presumption that the provision "against unlawful searches and seizures contained in NY Constitution, article I, § 12 conforms with that found in the 4th Amendment, and that this identity of language supports a policy of uniformity between State and Federal courts." . . . Based on this, we have sought to fashion search and seizure rules that promote consistency in the interpretations we have given these parallel clauses. The interest of Federal-State uniformity, however, is simply one consideration to be balanced against other considerations that may argue for a different State rule. When weighed against the ability to protect fundamental constitutional rights, the practical need for uniformity can seldom be a decisive factor. Thus, notwithstanding an interest in conforming our State Constitution's restrictions on searches and seizures to those of the Federal Constitution where desirable, this court has adopted independent standards under the State Constitution when doing so best promotes "predictability and precision in judicial review of search and seizure cases and the protection of the individual rights of our citizens.". . .

In addition, we have sought to provide and maintain "bright line" rules to guide the decisions of law enforcement and judicial personnel who must understand and implement our decisions in their day-to-day operations in the field. To this end, we have rejected the reasoning behind the so-called good-faith exception to the warrant requirement recently articulated by the Supreme Court, refusing, on State constitutional grounds, to apply it. Similarly, although asked to do so, we have not reached out to adopt the *Gates* "totality of the circumstances" test in warrant cases, and we have declined to extend it to review warrantless arrests predicated on hearsay information. . . .

These decisions reflect a concern that the Fourth Amendment rules governing police conduct have been muddied, and judicial supervision of the warrant process diluted, thus heightening the danger that our citizens' rights against unreasonable police intrusions might be violated. We see the Supreme Court's present ruling as a similar dilution of the requirements of judicial supervision in the warrant process and as a departure from prior law on the subject. As we read the court's decision, it condones a probable cause determination by a magistrate based only upon the strength of the showing of probable cause as it relates to one of several necessary elements of the crime involved. While the "totality of the circumstances/fair probability" formulation may satisfy some as an acceptable analytical framework when used to evaluate whether an informant's tip should be credited as *one* element bearing on probable cause, the argument for its validity breaks down where, as here, the standard is applied in a different, nonhearsay, probable cause context. . . .

Several years ago we summarized our past decisions on the subject, restating a rigorous, fact-specific standard of review imposed upon the magistrate determining probable cause. . . . It imposed a specific, nondelegable burden on the magistrate which required that he, not the police, determine probable cause, and it required that his determination be objectively verifiable. . . . This is the standard that should be applied to protect the rights of New York citizens.

Our decision to rely on article I, § 12, rather than on the Supreme Court's Fourth Amendment pronouncement in this case, is motivated also by concerns of federalism and separation of powers. The States exist as sovereign entities independent of the national Government and the Tenth Amendment reserves to them and the people "[t]he powers not delegated to the United States by the Constitution, nor prohibited by it to the States" (U.S. Const.

10th Amend.). Thus, the "structure of state governments and their sphere of operations simply are not the subjects of the Constitution, except insofar as the Constitution shifts power from the states to the national government, or protects the rights of individuals from governmental violations" (Tribe, American Constitutional Law § 5–20, at 300). One of the powers reserved to the States is the power to define what conduct shall be criminal within its borders. . . . Given that our Legislature, consonant with Federal constitutional mandates has determined that an offensive, explicit depiction of sexual conduct, standing alone, is not obscene (*see,* Penal Law § 235.00[1]), neither an issuing magistrate nor a reviewing court can legitimately override that legislative intent and find probable cause that the crime of obscenity has been committed based solely on a showing that sexually oriented material is explicit and offensive. The Supreme Court's decision in this case has, in effect, stated that certain elements of our statutory definition of a crime are not significant. We are not free to similarly ignore or recast the legislative mandate. . . .

The legal reasoning supporting our views, our understanding of principles of federalism, and this State's legal and cultural traditions all lead us to conclude that we should depart from the Federal rule stated in this case. We hold, therefore, that this warrant application did not demonstrate the probable cause required under the provisions of article I, § 12 of the State Constitution and accordingly, on reargument following remand from the United States Supreme Court, we affirm the order of the County Court.

"Models of Post-Incorporation Judicial Review: State Constitutional Individual Rights Decisions"
by Ronald K. L. Collins and Peter J. Galie

[T]he "new federalism" revolution has diminished the Supreme Court's once virtual dominance in the field of rights protection.* But . . . federal decisional law continues to influence much of the thinking of those working with parallel state constitutional guarantees. This is not surprising given present trends in legal education, litigation habits, and the abundance of federal precedents. Yet within the framework of post-incorporation decision-making, there are developing various models of state constitutional judicial review. . . .

---

* Reprinted with the authors' permission from 55 *University of Cincinnati Law Review* 317 (1986) (footnotes omitted).

[I]t is important to be clear about the interpretive options left open to state judges in rendering state constitutional law decisions. It is an article of faith of the "new federalism" that under state constitutions judges can give "more" protection to rights claimants than what has been allowed by the U.S. Supreme Court in interpreting the U.S. Bill of Rights. Judges can also recognize the same degree of protection for either the same or different reasons. They may even find that the state constitution actually affords "less" protection than its federal counterpart. In any case, they still may not interfere with or abridge any federally protected rights or interests. With this understanding of the law, we proceed to the following five models of post-incorporation judicial review. . . .

A. The Equivalence Model

According to this model, U.S. Supreme Court decisions are automatically presumed to establish the contours and character of state constitutional law. In its most extreme form, this model dictates, for example, that a particular state constitutional provision always be interpreted in the same way as the U.S. Supreme Court would interpret a parallel federal provision. . . . This model is typically found in cases where the state constitutional provision is worded similarly or identically to the corresponding federal provision. In its radical form, the equivalence rationale is applied to *differently* worded state and federal provisions.

Adherents of the equivalence model deny that state judges have any independent responsibility to be the caretakers of state law. Practically speaking, for them, state bills or declarations of rights have no functional significance. And in light of *Michigan v. Long*'s presumptive jurisdiction over state decisions, rights-affirming decisions of this kind forfeit the finality of review that would otherwise attach to state court interpretations of state law. As such, state courts cease to be tribunals of final review; instead, they operate as another tier in the federal judicial system. Decision-making responsibility for charting the bounds of state law is delegated to the U.S. Supreme Court. Thus, the role of state judges in "interpreting" state law is to hypothesize how the U.S. Supreme Court might rule on a given question. In practice, under the equivalence model there is little, if any, difference between a state court's interpretations of either the federal or state constitution.

B. The Equivalence Plus Model

Like the pure equivalence model, this model of state judicial review is premised on a certain presumptive deference to U.S. Supreme Court decisions when parallel guarantees are interpreted. The presumption, however, is less rigid. Basically, the equivalence plus model operates in such a way that state and federal standards, as well as the reasons for those standards, will typically be the same. When explicitly using this model, a court announces its general inclination to align state and federal law protections while reserving for itself the power to interpret state law beyond the federal minimums. . . .

The equivalence plus model is a reactive or supplemental one. The underlying premise of this model is rights maximization. It employs state law as a means to this end. Thus, this model would not have been especially relevant during the liberal Warren Court era. During the more conservative Burger Court era, however, the model has assumed a position of some import. . . .

One significant feature of the equivalence plus model is its need to incorporate federal precedents into state law. That is, before a state court moves beyond federal law, it will typically first have to incorporate some federal foundational precedent without which such "expansions" would be impossible. Thus, in *People v. Bigelow*, the New York Court of Appeals *sub silentio* adopted a state law-based exclusionary rule as a necessary prerequisite for rejecting any exception to it, thereby making *Bigelow* significant for two reasons: (1) it recognized an independent state constitutional law exclusionary rule, and (2) it disavowed a "good faith" exception to the rule. . . .

C. The Equivalence Minus Model

The equivalence minus model posits that it is, theoretically speaking, possible to recognize "less" protection under the state constitution than under the U.S. Constitution. This model is foreign to much of what is typically held out as the "new federalism." It is, according to the conventional rights-maximizing view, something of a constitutional heresy. Unlike the obstructionist states' rights brand of nineteenth-century federalism, however, it does not condone the use of state law to interfere with any federally protected right or interest. It merely states that as a matter of state constitutional law, state judges need not accept federal standards. Of course, having once denied a claim based on state law, state judges must accord to a rights claimant any or all rights guaranteed under federal law. . . .

D. The Nonequivalent Text Model

Unlike the models discussed above, this is not primarily a relational model. That is, this model is based not on the relationship of state decisional law to federal decisional law but rather on the differences between federal and state constitutional texts. Strict equivalence is not always possible where the texts of the state and federal guarantees are significantly different or where the U.S. Constitution has no analogue for a right explicitly contained in a state charter. Examples of the former are the right to bear arms provisions found in many state constitutions. Examples of the latter are the "right to a legal remedy" provisions contained in one form or another in the constitutions of some thirty-five states. The nonequivalent text model does not presume that such textual dissimilarities will necessarily produce different or identical results from those found in federal cases.

This model is less concerned with outcomes than it is with questions of independent analysis—questions related to text, structure, and historical intent as well as analytical soundness. By contrast, adherents of the equivalence plus model sometimes turn to textual dissimilarity as a way to "legitimate" what is feared might be seen as an unprincipled departure from federal norms. Sometimes adherents of the equivalence model ignore important textual differences in order to keep state and federal law aligned. Finally, adherents of the equivalence minus model "justify" their deviation from federal law standards on the grounds of textual dissimilarity. For example, the Mississippi Constitution contains no equality of treatment or equal protection guarantees like those found in other state constitutions and in the fourteenth amendment. The absence of such an explicit provision makes it difficult or impossible to employ state law either to match or to exceed federal standards. . . .

Greenberg v. Kimmelman, a 1985 New Jersey Supreme Court opinion, involved a constitutional challenge to a New Jersey law which prohibited state employees and their immediate families from being employed by casinos located within the state. The plaintiff, the wife of a New Jersey judge, contested the law on the theory that it violated her federal and state due process, equal protection, and associational rights in addition to her right to marry. A unanimous court denied all claims. Significantly, after the court concluded its preliminary federal law analysis, it proceeded to the state law side of the ledger and noted: "The analysis of fundamental rights under the New Jersey Constitution differs from the analysis of those rights under the United States Constitution." Thereafter, the court . . . indicated its disapproval of the federal two-tier equal protection standard and its preference for a more flexible "balancing" approach.

Thinking in relational equivalence terms, the court "justified" its departure from federal strictures on the grounds of textual dissimilarity, noting that the pertinent texts from which the respective rights derive are dissimilar. The bedrock of the New Jersey opinion was the following state constitutional provision:

> All persons are by nature free and independent, and have certain natural and inalienable rights, among which are those of enjoying and defending life and liberty, of acquiring, possessing, and protecting property, and of pursuing and obtaining safety and happiness.

Once the court erected the text-based foundational platform for its state constitutional construct, it proceeded to build upon it a state law-based right to employment, marriage, familial association, and privacy. Although the independent protection provided to these rights is "greater" than any protection provided under the U.S. Constitution, the New Jersey court denied the petitioner's claims. . . .

E. The Nonequivalent Analysis Model

In several ways, this model is similar to the various equivalence ones. Like the pure equivalence model, the nonequivalent analysis model may follow federal decisional law even though its adherents do not accord any presumptive force to such decisions. It is similar to the equivalence plus and equivalence minus models to the extent that it allows for the possibility of both "more" and "less" protection, though adherents of the nonequivalent analysis model see no need, apart from analytical dictates, to justify such departures from federal law. This model is also similar to the nonequivalent text model in that it is not relational. Yet unlike the nonequivalent text model, the analysis model does not depend on textual differences as the sole basis for deviations from federal decisional law.

Despite these similarities, the nonequivalent analysis model is different in one significant sense—its *systematic* reliance on state law. As a process-based model, this approach does not operate on an ad hoc basis like the equivalence plus and equivalence minus approaches. Unlike all of the equivalence models, the nonequivalent analysis approach is less concerned with relational constitutionalism than with analytical soundness. That is, it is more concerned with the proper state constitutional premises than it is with measuring state law against federal benchmarks. U.S. Supreme Court decisions may be regarded as instructive or persuasive, and to that extent, they are valued by adherents of the analysis approach in much the same way as a decision of a sister-state supreme court might be respected. Finally, the nonequivalent analysis model bears a certain resemblance to pre-incorporation models of judicial review, though it does not question or challenge the wisdom (as distinguished from the method) of applying certain provisions of the U.S. Bill of Rights to the states.

State v. Koppel is a prime example of the nonequivalent analysis model. Writing for the New Hampshire Supreme Court, Justice David Brock commenced his analysis in a search and seizure case with the following statement:

> We begin, *as we must,* by first making an independent analysis of the protections afforded under the New Hampshire Constitution . . . using decisions of the United States Supreme Court and other jurisdictions only as aids in our analysis. . . . Thereafter, *we need address federal constitutional issues only insofar as federal law would provide greater protection.*

After considering the respective issues concerning the constitutionality of police roadblocks aimed at apprehending drunk drivers, a majority of the New Hampshire court found the practice violative of the state search and seizure guarantee. (This guarantee is worded similarly to the fourth amendment.) Justice Brock then closed his opinion by observing: "Because our holding rests on our interpretation of the New Hampshire Constitution, we need not discuss the scope of the protection provided by the Fourth Amendment to the United States Constitution."

Note that in the *Koppel* variation of the model the federal question is never even addressed. For that reason, the clearly delineated state law basis of the judgment lends finality to the New Hampshire decision. Note also that the approach announced is one applied in all cases. In recent years, this approach has been approved by the high courts of Oregon, Maine, Washington, and New Hampshire. The constitutional logic of this approach, maintains Oregon Supreme Court Justice Hans Linde, derives from the notion that there is no judicially cognizable cause of action available under the fourteenth amendment if state law provides the relief sought. . . .

Perhaps the best example of the ability of the nonequivalent analysis model to survive within the complex web of federal statutory and constitutional law is the Oregon Supreme Court's decision in *Salem College & Academy v. Employment Division*. The question in the case required the state justices to examine the state and federal law governing unemployment compensation taxes affecting religious schools. Salem College & Academy, an interdenominational Christian college and primary school, challenged the imposition of liability for unemployment compensation paid to four of its former employees. Under federal and state law, church supported schools were exempt from unemployment compensation taxes but independent religious schools, like Salem College & Academy, were obligated to pay the same tax.

It was within this context that the state high court analyzed the relationship between the Oregon unemployment compensation law and the Federal Unemployment Tax Act (FUTA). Oregon, like all other states, elected to qualify under the federal program, which provides federal tax credits for employees paying state unemployment taxes. For that reason, the state statutory law was drafted to mirror its federal counterpart. Under both federal and state law, churches, or institutions "principally supported" by a church, were exempt from paying unemployment compensation taxes. After reviewing the petitioner's claims, the state court of appeals declined to decide the state constitutional question. Instead, it "declared the state and federal formula an unconstitutional establishment of religion forbidden by the First Amendment" insofar as the formula discriminates between a religious school that is affiliated with, and one that is independent of, a church or association of churches.

In religion cases, state courts, for instance the Washington Supreme Court, sometimes pass over state constitutional questions. In *Salem College & Academy,* this approach led an intermediate state court to declare a federal law unconstitutional. Taking a more moderate approach, the Oregon Supreme Court limited its decision to a state constitutional evaluation of the state statutory scheme. Writing for a unanimous court Justice Hans Linde prefaced his state constitutional analysis by noting:

> It is, of course, proper to take account of federal requirements (in this case statutory as well as constitutional) in deciding what the state law is . . . but . . . the state cannot violate its own constitution in order to satisfy a federal program that *Congress has not made obligatory* under the Supremacy Clause.

After discussing the pertinent state constitutional provisions and how they were intended to foster religious pluralism, Justice Linde ruled that under state law the Oregon legislature cannot discriminate between religious institutions, regardless of whether they are church supported, in providing tax exemptions. The legislature might exempt all religious schools from state unemployment compensation taxes only at the risk of falling below federal standards. After reviewing the legislative record, however, the state justices concluded that rather than run the "risk of jeopardizing Oregon's compliance with FUTA," the state legislature had not intended to exempt "all religious schools and their employees from unemployment compensation." Because the state constitution allows no distinction to be made among religious schools, and because the Congress apparently requires that such schools be covered by the statute, Salem College & Academy was obligated to provide unemployment benefits.

The complexity and novelty of the *Salem College & Academy* opinion demonstrate the extent to which exponents of the nonequivalent analysis model will go in order to settle the meaning of state law in a manner that does not necessitate a federal constitutional ruling. Had the Oregon Supreme Court followed the state appellate court and grounded its ruling in federal law, the decision would not have been a final one, and the constitutional law of Oregon would have remained undecided on this point. . . .

Any analysis of state constitutional law today must also consider the relationship between the federal courts and state courts. This is so, not only because the U.S. Supreme Court has incorporated most of the provisions of the U.S. Bill of Rights, thereby creating a massive body of law governing individual rights and liberties, but also because the Supreme Court has jurisdiction to review decisions of state courts in order to determine whether they rest on an adequate and independent state ground. Moreover, lower federal courts are empowered to interpret and apply state constitutional provisions.

The post-1970 resurgence of interest in state courts and state constitutional law has not gone unnoticed by the Burger Court. A majority of the Court, as evidenced by its *certiorari* record, has taken a more active interest in monitoring state court decisions affirming rights. This trend has become particularly apparent since 1983 when the Court refashioned the "independent and adequate state grounds" doctrine. In what follows we highlight the major aspects of the Burger Court's concern with state court attempts to vindicate rights and then offer a comparative glimpse at the Warren Court record. We then proceed to discuss the Burger Court's surprisingly tolerant attitude toward federal court reliance on state law as a means of precluding subsequent Supreme Court review.

The Burger Court has an uneven record when it comes to federalism principles and review of state court individual rights decisions. While *Michigan v. Long* clearly evidences a propensity on the part of the Court to review and even reverse state decisions that affirm rights, the same Court has shown a certain willingness either to sustain state court vindications of rights or to reverse state court denials of such claims. The Court's record has, however, been lopsided in favor of state prosecutors when granting summary dispositions in criminal cases. In 1985, Justice John Paul Stevens renewed his complaint that his colleagues should exercise more restraint in this area and thereby grant the state courts "some latitude in the development of their criminal law."

Moreover, *Long* and its progeny demonstrate that the Burger Court has positioned itself so that it has ample power to review individual rights decisions rendered by state courts. The *Long* Court's statement of its presumptive power to review state court decisions reveals the degree to which the Court is prepared to employ the adequate and independent state grounds doctrine as a method to police state court attempts to vindicate rights. In the interest of state court autonomy, the *Long* Court could have announced a rule whereby it would not review a state court judgment upholding a right in the absence of a "plain statement" that state law does *not* provide the relief sought. This rule of review, which would establish a presumption exactly opposite to that of *Long*, would curb rather than expand the Court's jurisdictional powers.

Admittedly, there are instances where state courts for one reason or another decline to base their rulings on state law and thereby invite the possibility of federal review. Still, the Burger Court's redefinition of the adequate and independent state grounds doctrine affords the Court the opportunity, heretofore largely unrealized, of either scrutinizing the "independent" basis of a purported state law decision or testing the "adequacy" of that decision. Importantly, in the latter instance, the Court is in reality positioning itself to inquire into the genuineness of a state law ruling quite apart from its independent characterization. Whether the Burger

Court or its successors will move beyond the "independent" prong of the jurisdictional doctrine to the "adequacy" prong is unclear. For the time being, the Court has signaled its readiness to open its jurisdictional gates to state officials challenging state court affirmations of civil rights and civil liberties claims.

During oral arguments in *Colorado v. Nunez,* Justice William Rehnquist was heard to say: "We can think that they [state judges] are bananas if we want to, but if [their decision rests on an] adequate state ground, it is none of our business." Of course, cases such as *Montana v. Jackson* and *Michigan v. Long* reveal the extent to which the Court has from time-to-time made it its "business" to test the "adequacy" and "independence" of rights-enhancing state court decisions with which it disagrees. Justice Rehnquist's quip notwithstanding, the Court has by its rule in *Long* created an atmosphere where government attorneys (particularly prosecutors) are invited to seek review even where the federal law basis for doing so would otherwise be questionable or doubtful.

In many ways, the present Court is clearly receptive to entertaining claims brought by state prosecutors. If the Court elects to act in a summary fashion in a criminal case, it is quite likely to side with the complaining state official. Overall, the Court is more disposed to grant full review to a petitioning state prosecutor than to a petitioning rights claimant. But while the current jurisdictional law affords wide latitude to review state judgments, the Burger Court cannot always be counted on to invoke its jurisdictional powers. Finally, once *certiorari* has been granted, the overall numerical record shows a slight bias in favor of granting the relief sought by state officials.

8

REPRESENTATIVE GOVERNMENT, VOTING RIGHTS, AND ELECTORAL POLITICS

F AIR AND REPRESENTATIVE government is the bedrock for the constitutional politics of free government. It is the basis for political struggles over governmental accountability, federalism, majority rule versus minority rights, and much else. The idea was not new to the Framers, but the Constitution provided a foundation for an unprecedented experiment in representative government and for later expansion of the franchise.

John Locke, the English philosopher championed "fair and *equal*" representation in his *Second Treatise of Government* (1689), when attacking the rotten boroughs of the British system of representing towns and counties:

[Section] 157. Things of this World are in so constant a Flux, that nothing remains long in the same State. . . . But things not always changing equally, and private interest often keeping up Customs and Priviledges, when the reasons of them are ceased, it often comes to pass, that in Governments, where part of the Legislative consists of *Representatives* chosen by the People, that in tract of time this *Representation* becomes very *unequal* and disproportionate to the reasons it was at first establish'd upon. To what gross absurdities the following of Custom, when Reason has left it, may lead, we may be satisfied when we see the bare Name of a Town, of which there remains not so much as the ruines, where scarce so much Housing as a Sheep-coat; or more inhabitants than a Shepherd is to be found, sends *as many Representatives* to the Assembly of Law-makers, as a whole County numerous in People, and powerful in riches. This Strangers stands amazed at, and every one must confess needs a remedy. . . .

[W]henever the People shall chuse their *Representatives upon* just and undeniable *equal measures* suitable to the original Frame of the Government, it cannot be doubted to be the will and act of the Society, whoever permitted, or caused them so to do.[1]

Denial of representation to the colonies gave rise to the slogan "No taxation without representation." On October 14, 1774, the Continential Congress proclaimed,

[T]he foundation of English liberty, of all free government, is a right in the people to participate in their legislative council: and as the English colonists are not represented, and from their local and other circumstances, cannot properly be represented in the British parliament, they are entitled to a free and exclusive power of legislation in their several provincial legislatures, where their right of representation can alone be preserved, in all cases of taxation and internal policy, subject only to the negative of their sovereign, in such manner as has been heretofore used and accustomed.[2]

Two years later, the failure of King George III to respond to colonial demands for fair and equal representation was cited as one of the justifications for revolution in the Declaration of Independence: "He has dissolved Representative Houses repeatedly, for opposing with manly firmness his invasions in the rights of the people. He has refused for a long time, after such dissolutions, to cause others to be elected, whereby the Legislative Powers, incapable of Annihilation, have returned to the People at large for their exercise."

Following the Declaration of Independence and the Revolutionary War, novel institutions of representative government emerged in the states and in the eventual formulation of the national government. But that was only the beginning. The history of the constitutional politics of the franchise and representative government is one of long-fought struggles to expand voting rights and to make the electoral process more democratic.

CONSTITUTIONAL HISTORY

Thomas Paine on the Right to Vote and Representative Government

The revolutionary pamphleteer, Thomas Paine, in his *Dissertation on the First Principles of Government* (1795), linked the right to vote with representative government in a natural rights argument:

The true and only true basis of representative government is equality of rights. Every man has a right to one vote, and no more in the choice of representatives. The rich have no more right to exclude the poor from the right of voting, or of electing and being elected, than the poor have to exclude the rich; and wherever it is attempted, or proposed, on either side, it is a question of force and not of right. Who is he that would exclude another? That other has a right to exclude him. . . .

Personal rights, of which the right of voting for representatives is one, are a species of property of the most sacred kind: and he that would employ his pecuniary property, or presume upon the influence it gives him, to dispossess or rob another of his property as he would use fire-arms, and merits to have it taken from him.

Inequality of rights is created by a combination in one part of the community to exclude another part from its rights. Whenever it be made an article of a constitution, or a law, that the right of voting, or of electing and being elected, shall appertain exclusively to persons possessing that quantity to exclude those who do not possess the same quantity. It is investing themselves with powers as a self-created part of society, to the exclusion of the rest. . . .

The only ground upon which exclusion from the right of voting is consistent with justice would be to inflict it as a punishment for a certain time upon those who should propose to take away that right from others. The right of voting for representatives is the primary right by which other rights are protected.

To take away this right is to reduce a man to slavery, for slavery consists in being subject to the will of another, and he that has not a vote in the election of representatives is in this case. The proposal therefore to disfranchise any class of men is as criminal as the proposal to take away property.

NOTES

1. John Locke, *Two Treatises of Government,* ed. Peter Laslett (New York: Mentor, 1960), 418–419.
2. "Declaration and Resolves of the First Continental Congress, 1774," reprinted in *The Roots of the Bill of Rights,* Vol. 1, ed. Bernard Schwartz (New York: Chelsea House, 1980), 217.

SELECTED BIBLIOGRAPHY

Goldwin, Robert, and Schambra, William, eds. *How Democratic Is the Constitution?* Washington, DC: American Enterprise Institute, 1980.
Kurland, Philip B. and Lerner, Ralph, eds. *The Founders' Constitution* Vol. 1. Chicago: University of Chicago Press, 1987.
McDonald, Forrest. *Novus Ordo Seclorum: The Intellectual Origins of the Constitution.* Lawrence, KS: University of Kansas, 1985.
Pangle, Thomas. *The Spirit of Modern Republicanism.* Chicago: University of Chicago Press, 1988.
White, Morton. *The Philosophy of the American Revolution.* New York: Oxford University Press, 1978.

A. REPRESENTATIVE GOVERNMENT AND THE FRANCHISE

The Framers agreed that representative government was the only alternative to both the tyranny of being ruled and that of direct democracy; both were deemed politically unacceptable. Still, there was disagreement as to who and what was to be represented as well as to how to achieve representation.

Anti-Federalists, such as the Federal Farmer, argued that "a full and equal representation is that in which the interests, feelings, opinions, and views of the people are collected, in such a manner as they would be were all the people assembled."[1] Anti-Federalists tended to reside in rural and agricultural areas, and wanted assurance of representation of their people. They distrusted the Federalists, those in urban areas along the Atlantic seaboard and associated with commercial and banking interests. As Republicus, the pen name of a Kentucky Anti-Federalist, put it, "the constitution should provide for a fair and equal representation. That is that every member of the union have a freedom of suffrage and that every equal number of people have an equal number of representatives."[2]

By contrast, Federalists tended to take a dim view of those who, in Alexander Hamilton's words, wanted "an actual representation of all classes of the people by persons of each class." The Federalists favored representation by a natural aristocracy— "gentlemen of fortune and ability," as Hamilton put during the Constitutional Convention.[3] So too, John Adams feared that representation might be carried so far as "to confound and destroy all distinctions, and prostrate all ranks to one common level."[4]

To allay the fears of both supporters and opponents of the Constitution, in *The Federalist*, Nos. 10 and 63, James Madison, made the ingenious argument that representative government in a large, "extended republic" would prevent the spread of two kinds of political "diseases": the corruption of representatives who play on their popularity to exploit voters and to dominate the people, and the election of representatives bent on venting popular passions and prejudices by denying individual rights.

[T]he greater number of citizens and extent of territory which may be brought within the compass of republican, than of democratic government; and it is this circumstance principally which renders factious combinations less to be dreaded in the former, than in the latter. The smaller the society, the fewer probably will be the distinct parties and interests composing it; the fewer the distinct parties and interests, the more frequently will a majority be found of the same party; and smaller the number of individuals composing a majority, and the smaller the compass within which they are placed, the more easily will they concert and execute their plans of oppression. Extend the sphere, and you take in a greater variety of parties and interests; you make it less probable that a majority of the whole will have a common motive to invade the rights of other citizens; or if such a common motive exists, it will be more difficult for all who feel it to discover their own strength, and to act in unison with each other. . . .

The influence of actious leaders may kindle a flame within their particular States, but will be unable to spread a general conflagration through the other States: a religious sect, may degenerate into a political faction in a part of the Confederacy; but the variety of sects dispersed over the entire face of it, must secure the national Councils against any danger from that source. . . .

In the extent and proper structure of the Union, therefore, we behold a Republican remedy for the diseases most incident to Republican Government. And accordingly to the degree of pleasure and pride, we feel in being Republicans, ought to be our zeal in cherishing the spirit and supporting the character of Federalists.

In granting the franchise, however, the states followed the British-colonial model. Voting rights were generally limited to "freeholders" (white males who owned land and were at least twenty-one years old) and some states imposed religious qualifications as well. Under the Articles of Confederation, each state was free to determine the qualifications of voters. The Constitution did not change that. At the Constitutional Convention, Gouverneur Morris had proposed that the federal franchise be limited to freeholders. But Benjamin Franklin, among others, took issue with that, observing that "[i]t is of great consequence that we should not depress the virtue & public spirit of our common people; of which they displayed a great deal during the war."[5] In spite of the revolutionary rhetoric, there thus remained great inequalities. Thomas Jefferson, for instance, lamented that Virginia's constitution of 1776 limited voting rights only to the minority of that state's freeholders and disenfranchised the majority of those "who pay and fight."[6]

The Constitution, along with subsequent amendments, deals with voting rights more than any other subject. Remarkably, though, the universe and qualification of voters are not affirmatively defined. Instead, the Constitution and amendments have made the franchise more inclusive by progressively eliminating barriers for exercising voting rights and excluding blacks, women, poor, and the young from the electorate. Representation and voting rights are addressed in two sections of Article 1. Section 2, providing that electors of members of the House of Representatives "have the qualification requisite for electors of the most numerous branch of the state legislature," was a compromise designed to ensure a popular basis for the House without creating a national electorate independent of state electorates. The times, places, and manner clause of Section 4 gives Congress the power to require that representatives be elected from districts, rather than on a statewide basis. As discussed in Chapter 3, the Seventeenth Amendment (ratified in 1913) provides for the popular election of senators. Five other amendments greatly expanded the franchise and made the electoral process more democratic: the Fourteenth, Fifteenth, Nineteenth, Twenty-fourth and Twenty-sixth Amendments.

The Framers wholly failed to foresee the rise of political parties. Yet, after more than a decade of Federalists domination of the presidency and Congress, the fourth presidential election in 1800 brought into office Thomas Jefferson and the Jeffersonian-Republicans. Ever since, state and federal elections have been a contest between candidates of opposing political parties. And one consequence of the emergence of political parties was the expansion of the franchise and electorate. Notably, during Andrew Jackson's presidency (1829–1837) the property qualification was eliminated or replaced with the taxpayer qualification. Still, the electorate remained principally that of white males over twenty-one years old.

The struggle for further extension of suffrage grew from a 1848 convention of women in Seneca Falls, New York. There, Elizabeth Stanton pushed for the convention's adoption of a resolution "that it is the duty of the women of this country to secure to themselves their sacred right to the elective franchise." Stanton was supported by Frederick Douglass, the great black orator and abolistionist. Douglass tied equal rights for women with the abolition of slavery. And from this early beginning of the women's movement through the Civil War, suffrage for women and blacks were linked.

Following the Civil War, two Reconstruction amendments held out the possibility of voting rights for women and blacks. Ratified in 1868, the Fourteenth Amendment's first section guaranteed "the privileges and immunities of citizens of the United States" against abridgement by the states. Section 2 provides that any state denying participation in state or federal elections to "any of the male inhabitants of such State, being twenty-one years of age, and citizens of the United States . . . except for participating in rebellion, or other crime" shall have the number of its representatives and delegates to the Electoral College proportionately reduced.

The narrow victory of General Ulysses S. Grant in the 1868 presidential election, then, convinced the Republican party that to maintain its control of Congress it needed black votes. And so it proposed the Fifteenth Amendment (ratified in 1870), specifically guaranteeing black voting rights by forbidding the abridgement of any citizen's right to vote "on account of race, color, or previous condition of servitude."

Despite continued disenfranchisement, some women held out hope that they might win the right to vote in federal election by claiming it was a guarantee of the Fourteenth Amendment's privileges and immunities clause. This was Susan B. Anthony's defense when prosecuted for casting a ballot in a federal election in 1872, but it was rejected by lower federal court. The Court, then, dashed the hopes of another woman seeking to vote in a Missouri election. *Minor v. Happersett,* 21 Wall. (88 U.S.) 162 (1875), held that "the Constitution of the United States does not confer the right of suffrage upon anyone." Two more cases the following year rejected the argument that the Fifteenth Amendment affirmatively grants voting rights.[7]

Women had somewhat greater success in winning the right to vote in the states. In 1870, Wyoming's territorial legislature extended the right to them. Still, by 1913 only nine states allowed women to vote. In 1912, however, the Progressive party of Theodore Roosevelt supported woman's suffrage. Political pressure continued to mount during World War I as larger numbers of women entered the work force and contributed to the war effort. In 1918, President Woodrow Wilson endorsed women's suffrage and the next year Congress submitted a constitutional amendment to the states. The Nineteenth Amendment was ratified in 1920.

Although blacks were guaranteed the right to vote by the Fourteenth and Fifteenth Amendments, and were elected to office in the South during the Reconstruction, barriers of various sorts soon emerged. Poll taxes, literacy tests, and other obstacles (discussed in section C of this chapter) effectively disenfranchised blacks by the turn of this century. Breedlove v. Suttles, 302 U.S. 277 (1937), held that poll taxes did not violate the Fourteenth and Fifteenth Amendments. That ruling sparked a campaign in the 1940s and 1950s to get the states and Congress to abolish poll taxes. The campaign had considerable success in the states; by 1960 only Alabama, Arkansas, Mississippi, Texas, and Virginia retained poll taxes. Congress finally banned poll taxes in federal elections with the Twenty-fourth Amendment (ratified in 1964). When the powerful Harry Byrd political machine sought to evade the law by requiring voters to either pay a poll tax or file a certificate of residency at least six months before an election, it was rebuffed in *Harman v. Forssenius,* 380 U.S. 578 (1965). The Warren Court went even further in *Harper v. Virginia State Board of Elections,* 383 U.S. 663 (1966), ruling that, while the Twenty-fourth Amendment barred poll taxes in *federal* elections, the Fourteenth Amendment equal protection clause forbade poll taxes in *state* elections, and thereby overturned *Breedlove.*

Among the goals of the civil rights movement in the 1950s and 1960s was the elimination of all barriers to black voting rights. Martin Luther King, Jr., launched voter-registration drives in the South, where there was wide-spread resistence and often violence. Congress had passed Civil Rights Acts in 1957 and 1960, but they proved ineffective in placing the burden of eliminating voter discrimination on federal district court judges.

CONSTITUTIONAL HISTORY
President Lyndon B. Johnson's Address to Congress on the Importance of Passing the Voting Rights Act of 1965, March 15, 1965

Many of the issues of civil rights are very complex and most difficult. But about this there can and should be no argument. Every American citizen must have an equal right to vote. There is no reason which can excuse the denial of that right. There is no duty which weighs more heavily on us than the duty we have to ensure that right.

Yet the harsh fact is that in many places in this country men and women are kept from voting simply because they are Negroes.

Every device of which human ingenuity is capable has been used to deny this right. The Negro citizen may go to register only to be told that the day is wrong, or the hour is late, or the official in charge is absent. And if he persists and if he manages to present himself to the registrar, he may be disqualified because he did not spell out his middle name or because he abbreviated a word on the application. And if he manages to fill out an application, he is given a test. The registrar is the sole judge of whether he passes this test. He may be asked to recite the entire constitution, or explain the most complex provisions of state laws. And even a college degree cannot be used to prove that he can read and write.

For the fact is that the only way to pass these barriers is to show a white skin. . . .

This time, on this issue, there must be no delay, or no hesitation or no compromise with our purpose.

We cannot, we must not refuse to protect the right of every American to vote in every election that he may desire to participate in. And we ought not, we must not wait another eight months before we get a bill. We have already waited a hundred years and more and the time for waiting is gone. . . .

As a man whose roots go deeply into Southern soil I know how agonizing racial feelings are. I know how difficult it is to reshape the attitudes and the structure of our society.

But a century has passed, more than a hundred years, since the Negro was freed. And he is not fully free tonight.

It was more than a hundred years ago that Abraham Lincoln, the great President of the Northern party, signed the Emancipation Proclamation, but emancipation is a proclamation and not a fact.

A century has passed, more than a hundred years since equality was promised. And yet the Negro is not equal.

Finally, on the authority of Section 2 of the Fifteenth Amendment, which gives Congress the power to enforce "by appropriate legislation" the amendment's prohibition against racial discrimination in voting, Congress passed the Voting Rights Act of 1965. It outlaws any "voting qualification or prerequisite to voting" that denies the right to vote on account of race or color. Specifically banned are literacy tests,[8] tests for educational achievement and understanding,[9] proofs of "good moral character," and vouchers for the qualifications of registered voters. Such tests were banned in any state or subdivision where less than 50 percent of the persons of voting age were registered on November 1, 1964, or voted in that November's election. Moreover, where the above voting qualifications are suspended, the act provides that states and localities must receive the approval of the district court of the District of Columbia or the U.S. attorney general prior to implementing any changes in election laws. In addition, the law authorizes the U.S. Civil Service Commission to appoint federal voting-examiners to register voters where the attorney general deemed that was necessary to the enforcement of the Fifteenth Amendment.

The Voting Rights Act of 1965 remains controversial. The Court, though, affirmed its constitutionality in *South Carolina v. Katzenbach* (1966) (see page 662).[10] In 1970 the act, which had a five-year limitation, was extended and amended to ban all literacy tests and modified the factors triggering the attorney general's preclearance of changes in states' voting laws. The law was again extended in 1975 for seven more years.

Despite some resistence from within the Reagan administration, the law was further extended in 1982 for twenty-five years. The principal controversy revolved around the standards for determining whether states or localities had discriminatory voting practices. In *City of Mobile v. Bolden*, 446 U.S. 55 (1980), the Burger Court (six to three) upheld Mobile's system of electing a three-member city commission with at-large elections. At-large elections may work to the disadvantage of blacks and other minorities, and in Mobile, although 40 percent of the city were black, no black had ever been elected to the commission.[11] Civil rights organizations contended that Congress should ban election systems that "result" in discrimination. But opponents countered that a "results test" would eventually lead to proportional elections. In the end, the Voting Rights Act of 1982 provides that in cases challenging electoral discrimination judges should look at "the totality of circumstances," the process and results of an election.

When amending the Voting Rights Act in 1970, Congress also enacted a provision forbidding in any local, state, and federal

THE DEVELOPMENT OF LAW
Other Rulings Interpreting the Voting Rights Act

Case	Vote	Ruling
Gaston County v. United States, 395 U.S. 285 (1969)	7:1	Because of past racial discrimination in electoral system, the Court held that "impartial" administration of literary tests would serve only to "perpetuate these [past] inequities in a different form".
Perkins v. Matthews, 400 U.S. 379 (1971)	7:2	Localities covered by the Voting Rights Act may not annex territory or relocate polling places without prior federal approval.
City of Richmond, Virginia v. United States, 422 U.S. 358 (1975)	6:3	Upheld the annexation of twenty-three square miles of the county of Richmond that resulted in a black population of 42 percent rather than 52 percent prior to annexation; no violation of the Voting Rights Act.
Beer v. United States, 425 U.S. 130 (1976)	5:3	The Voting Rights Act does not require redrawing district lines to give black voters proportional representation; the act only bars dilution of the black vote and any "retrogression in the position of racial minorities with respect to their effective exercise of the electoral franchise".
United Jewish Organizations v. Carey, 430 (1976)	8:0	Held that the Fourteenth and Fifteenth Amendments and the Civil Rights Act were not violated by reapportionment plan that diluted the votes of Hasidic Jews by splitting their community into two assembly districts to secure several predominantly nonwhite voting districts.

Case	Vote	Ruling
United States v. Board of Commissioners of Sheffield, Alabama, 435 U.S. 110 (1978)	6:3	Held that the Voting Rights Act requirement for preclearance by the Department of Justice of changes in election laws applies to all elections; here, to the municipal election of city councilmen.
City of Mobile, Alabama v. Bolden, 446 U.S. 55 (1980)	6:3	At-large elections did not violate black voting rights.
City of Rome v. United States, 446 U.S. 156 (1980)	7:2	Annexation violated the Voting Rights Act.
Rogers v. Lodge, 458 U.S. 613 (1982)	6:3	Held that "intent" is necessary to show that changes in election law result in invidious voting dilution.
City of Lockhart v. United States, 460 U.S. 125 (1983)	6:3	City's election plan subject to preclearance.
Thornburg v. Gingles, 478 U.S. 30 (1986)	6:3	Held that (1) the use of multimember districts does not impede minority voters to elect representatives, unless a block of majority voters usually defeats minority candidates; (2) minority voters who challenge the use of multimember districts must demonstrate impermissible vote dilution; and (3) concluded that in the last six elections there was proportionate representation of blacks.

election the denial of the right to vote "on account of age if such citizen is eighteen years or older." Although opposing the lowering of the voting age at a time when there was wide-spread opposition among college students to the Vietnam War, President Nixon signed the act into law but directed Attorney General John Mitchell to challenge its constitutionality. In *Oregon v. Mitchell,* 400 U.S. 112 (1970), the Court was sharply split over

Congress's power to extend the franchise in *state* as well as national elections. Four justices thought Congress had the power; four justices disagreed. Justice Hugo Black cast the deciding vote, holding that Congress could lower the voting age in national but not state and local election. Congress immediately responded to that decision, and within six months the states ratified the Twenty-sixth Amendment (1971).

NOTES

1. Letters of the Federal Farmer, in *The Complete Anti-Federalist*, Vol. 2, ed. Herbert J. Storing (Chicago: University of Chicago Press, 1980), 287–288.

2. Republicus, in *The Complete Anti-Federalist*, Vol. 5, ed. Herbert J. Storing (Chicago: University of Chicago Press, 1980), 167.

3. Alexander Hamilton, in *The Records of the Federal Convention of 1787*, Vol. 2, ed. Max Farrand (New Haven, CT: Yale University Press, 1937), 298–299.

4. John Adams to James Sullivan, May 26, 1776, in *The Founders' Constitution*, Vol. 1, ed. Philip Kurland and Ralph Lerner (Chicago: University of Chicago Press, 1987), 394–395.

5. Benjamin Franklin, *The Records of the Federal Convention of 1787*, Vol. 2, ed. Max Farrand (New Haven, CT: Yale University Press, 1974), 204.

6. Thomas Jefferson, *Notes on the State of Virginia* (Chapell Hill: University of North Carolina Press, 1954), 118–119.

7. See *United States v. Reese*, 92 U.S. 214 (1876); and *United States v. Cruikshank*, 92 U.S. 542 (1876). The Court, however, reconsidered these rulings with respect to black, although not female, voting rights in *Ex Parte Yarbrough*, 110 U.S. 651 (1884).

8. The Court upheld literacy tests in *Guinn v. United States*, 23 U.S. 347 (1915); and *Lassiter v. Northhampton County Board of Elections*, 360 U.S. 45 (1959).

9. The Court upheld tests for whether potential voters understood their state and federal constitution in *Williams v. Mississippi*, 170 U.S. 213 (1898).

10. See also *Allen v. State Board of Elections*, 393 U.S. 544 (1969); *Perkins v. Matthews*, 400 U.S. 379 (1971); *Georgia v. United States*, 411 U.S. 526 (1973); *City of Rome v. United States*, 446 U.S. 156 (1980); and the discussion in section B of this chapter.

11. The Court struck down at-large elections where it found invidious discrimination. See *Rogers v. Herman Lodge*, 458 U.S. 613 (1982). But held that there was no voter discrimination in *City of Lockhart v. United States*, 460 U.S. 125 (1983). See also *Thornburg v. Gingles*, 478 U.S. 30 (1986).

SELECTED BIBLIOGRAPHY

Ball, Howard, Krane, Dale, and Lauth, Thomas P. *Compromised Compliance; Implementation of the 1965 Voting Rights Act.* Westport, CT: Greenwood Press, 1982.
Hamilton, Charles. *The Bench and the Ballot: Southern Federal Judges and Black Voters.* New York: Oxford University Press, 1973.

South Carolina v. Katzenbach
383 U.S. 301, 86 S.Ct. 803 (1966)

Shortly after the passage of the Voting Rights Act of 1965, South Carolina filed suit in the Supreme Court, under its original jurisdiction, seeking a declaration of the unconstitutionality of several sections of the law and an order refraining Nicholas Katzenbach, the attorney general, from enforcing its provisions. South Carolina contended that the act violated the Tenth Amendment and the principle of equal treatment of the states. Katzenbach defended the law as appropriate legislation pursuant to the enforcement of the Fifteenth Amendment.

Chief Justice WARREN delivers the opinion of the Court.

The Voting Rights Act was designed by Congress to banish the blight of racial discrimination in voting, which has infected the electoral process in parts of our country for nearly a century. The Act creates stringent new remedies for voting discrimination where it persists on a pervasive scale, and in addition the statute strengthens existing remedies for pockets of voting discrimination elsewhere in the country. Congress assumed the power to prescribe these remedies from § 2 of the Fifteenth Amendment, which authorizes the National Legislature to effectuate by "appropriate" measures the constitutional prohibition against racial discrimination in voting. We hold that the sections of the Act which are properly before us are an appropriate means for carrying out Congress' constitutional responsibilities and are consonant with all other provisions of the Constitution. We therefore deny South Carolina's request that enforcement of these sections of the Act be enjoined.

The constitutional propriety of the Voting Rights Act of 1965 must be judged with reference to the historical experience which it reflects. Before enacting the measure, Congress explored with great care the problem of racial discrimination in voting. The House and Senate Committees on the Judiciary each held hearings for nine days and received testimony from a total of 67 witnesses. More than three full days were consumed discussing the bill on the floor of the House, while the debate in the Senate covered 26 days in all. At the close of these deliberations, the verdict of both chambers was overwhelming. The House approved the bill by a vote of 328–74, and the measure passed the Senate by a margin of 79–18.

Two points emerge vividly from the voluminous legislative history of the Act contained in the committee hearings and floor debates. First: Congress felt itself confronted by an insidious and pervasive evil which had been perpetuated in certain parts of our country through unremitting and ingenious defiance of the Constitution. Second: Congress concluded that the unsuccessful remedies which it had prescribed in the past would have to be replaced by sterner and more elaborate measures in order to satisfy the clear commands of the Fifteenth Amendment. We pause here to summarize the majority reports of the House and Senate Committees, which document in considerable detail the factual basis for these reactions by Congress. See H. R. Rep. No. 439, 89th Cong., 1st Sess., 8–16 (hereinafter cited as House Report); S.Rep. No. 162, pt. 3, 89th Cong., 1st Sess., 3–16, U.S. Code Congressional and Administrative News, p. 2437 (hereinafter cited as Senate Report).

The Fifteenth Amendment to the Constitution was ratified in 1870. Promptly thereafter Congress passed the Enforcement Act of 1870, which made it a crime for public officers and private persons to obstruct exercise of the right to vote. The statute was amended in the following year to provide for detailed federal supervision of the electoral process, from registration to the certification of returns. As the years passed and fervor for racial equality waned, enforcement of the laws became spotty and ineffective, and most of their provisions were repealed in 1894. The remnants have had little significance in the recently renewed battle against voting discrimination.

Meanwhile, beginning in 1890, the States of Alabama, Georgia, Louisiana, Mississippi, North Carolina, South Carolina, and Virginia enacted tests still in use which were specifically designed to prevent Negroes from voting. Typically, they made the ability to read and write a registration qualification and also required completion of a registration form. These laws were based on the fact that as of 1890 in each of the named States, more than two-thirds of the adult Negroes were illiterate while less than one-quarter of the adult whites were unable to read or write. At the same time, alternate tests were prescribed in all of the named States to assure that white illiterates would not be deprived of the franchise. These included grandfather clauses, property qualifications, "good character" tests, and the requirement that registrants "understand" or "interpret" certain matter.

The course of subsequent Fifteenth Amendment litigation in this Court demonstrates the variety and persistence of these and similar institutions designed to deprive Negroes of the right to vote. Grandfather clauses were invalidated in *Guinn v. United States,* 238 U.S. 347 [1915]; and *Myers v. Anderson,* 238 U.S. 368 [1915]. Procedural hurdles were struck down in *Lane v. Wilson,* 307 U.S. 268 [1939]. The white primary was outlawed in *Smith v. Allwright,* 321 U.S. 649 [1944]; and *Terry v. Adams,* 345 U.S. 461 [1953]. Improper challenges were nullified in *United States v. Thomas,* 362 U.S. 58 [1960]. Racial gerrymandering was forbidden by *Gomillion v. Lightfoot,* 364 U.S. 339 [1960]. Finally, discriminatory application of voting tests was condemned in *Schnell v. Davis,* 336 U.S. 933 [1949]; *Alabama v. United States,* 371 U.S. 37 [1962]; and *Louisiana v. United States,* 380 U.S. 145 [1965].

According to the evidence in recent Justice Department voting suits, the latter stratagem is now the principal method used to bar Negroes from the polls. Discriminatory administration of voting qualifications has been found in all eight Alabama cases, in all nine Louisiana cases, and in all nine Mississippi cases which have gone to final judgment. Moreover, in almost all of these cases, the courts have held that the discrimination was pursuant to a widespread "pattern or practice." White applicants for registration have often been excused altogether from the literacy and understanding tests or have been given easy versions, have received extensive help from voting officials, and have been registered despite serious errors in their answers. Negroes, on the other hand, have typically been required to pass difficult versions of all the tests, without any outside assistance and without the slightest error. The good-morals requirement is so vague and subjective that it has constituted an open invitation to abuse at the hands of voting officials. Negroes obliged to obtain vouchers from registered voters have found it virtually impossible to comply in areas where almost no Negroes are on the rolls.

In recent years, Congress has repeatedly tried to cope with the problem by facilitating case-by-case litigation against voting discrimination. The Civil Rights Act of 1957 authorized the Attorney General to seek injunctions against public and private interference with the right to vote on racial grounds. Perfecting amendments in the Civil Rights Act of 1960 permitted the joinder of States as parties defendant, gave the Attorney General access to local voting records, and authorized courts to register voters in areas of systematic discrimination. Title I of the Civil Rights Act of 1964 expedited the hearing of voting cases before three-judge courts and outlawed some of the tactics used to disqualify Negroes from voting in federal elections.

Despite the earnest efforts of the Justice Department and of many federal judges, these new laws have done little to cure the problem of voting discrimination. According to estimates by the Attorney General during hearings on the Act, registration of voting-age Negroes in Alabama rose only from 14.2% to 19.4% between 1958 and 1964; in Louisiana it barely inched ahead from 31.7% to 31.8% between 1956 and 1965; and in Mississippi it increased only from 4.4% to 6.4% between 1954 and 1964. In each instance, registration of voting-age whites ran roughly 50 percentage points or more ahead of Negro registration.

The previous legislation has proved ineffective for a number of reasons. Voting suits are unusually onerous to prepare, sometimes requiring as many as 6,000 man-hours spent combing through registration records in preparation for trial. Litigation has been exceedingly slow, in part because of the ample opportunities for delay afforded voting officials and others involved in the proceedings. Even when favorable decisions have finally been obtained, some of the States affected have merely switched to discriminatory devices not covered by the federal decrees or have enacted difficult new tests designed to prolong the existing disparity between white and Negro registration. Alternatively, certain local officials have defied and evaded court orders or have simply closed their registration offices to freeze the voting rolls. The provision of the 1960 law authorizing registration by federal officers has had little impact on local maladministration because of its procedural complexities. . . .

The Voting Rights Act of 1965 reflects Congress' firm intention to rid the country of racial discrimination in voting. The heart of the Act is a complex scheme of stringent remedies aimed at areas where voting discrimination has been most flagrant. Section 4 (a)–(d) lays down a formula defining the States and political subdivisions to which these new remedies apply. The first of the remedies, contained in § 4 (a), is the suspension of literacy tests and similar voting qualifications for a period of five years from the last occurrence of substantial voting discrimination. Section 5 prescribes a second remedy, the suspension of all new voting regulations pending review by federal authorities to determine whether their use would perpetuate voting discrimination. The third remedy, covered in § § 6(b), 7, 9, and 13(a), is the assignment of federal examiners on certification by the Attorney General to list qualified applicants who are thereafter entitled to vote in all elections.

Other provisions of the Act prescribe subsidiary cures for persistent voting discrimination. Section 8 authorizes the appointment of federal poll-watchers in places to which federal examiners have already been assigned. Section 10(d) excuses those made eligible to vote in sections of the country covered by § 4 (b) of the Act from paying accumulated past poll taxes for state and local elections. Section 12(e) provides for balloting by persons denied access to the polls in areas where federal examiners have been appointed.

The remaining remedial portions of the Act are aimed at voting discrimination in any area of the country where it may occur. Section 2 broadly prohibits the use of voting rules to abridge exercise of the franchise on racial grounds. Sections 3, 6(a), and 13(b) strengthen existing procedures for attacking voting discrimination by means of litigation. Section 4(e) excuses citizens educated in American schools conducted in a foreign language from passing English-language literacy tests. Section 10(a)–(c) facilitates constitutional litigation challenging the imposition of all poll taxes for state and local elections. Sections 11 and 12(a)–(d) authorize civil and criminal sanctions against interference with the exercise of rights guaranteed by the Act. . . .

These provisions of the Voting Rights Act of 1965 are challenged on the fundamental ground that they exceed the powers of Congress and encroach on an area reserved to the States by the Constitution. South Carolina and certain of the *amici curiae* also attack specific sections of the Act for more particular reasons. They argue that the coverage formula prescribed in § 4(a)–(d) violates the principle of the equality of States, denies due process by employing an invalid presumption and by barring judicial review of administrative findings, constitutes a forbidden bill of attainder, and impairs the separation of powers by adjudicating guilt through legislation. They claim that the review of new voting rules required in § 5 infringes Article III by directing the District Court to issue advisory opinions. They contend that the assignment of federal examiners authorized in § 6(b) abridges due process by precluding judicial review of administrative findings and impairs the separation of powers by giving the Attorney General judicial functions; also that the challenge procedure prescribed in § 9 denies due process on account of its speed. Finally, South Carolina and certain of the *amici curiae* maintain that §§ 4(a) and 5, buttressed by § 14(b) of the Act, abridge due process by limiting litigation to a distant forum.

Some of these contentions may be dismissed at the outset. The word "person" in the context of the Due Process Clause of the Fifth Amendment cannot, by any reasonable mode of interpretation, be expanded to encompass the States of the Union, and to our knowledge this has never been done by any court. . . . Likewise, courts have consistently regarded the Bill of Attainder Clause of Article I and the principle of the separation of powers only as protections for individual persons and private groups, those who are peculiarly vulnerable to non-judicial determinations of guilt. Nor does a State have standing as the parent of its citizens to invoke these constitutional provisions against the Federal Government, the ultimate *parens patriae* of every American citizen. The objections to the Act which are raised under these provisions may therefore be considered only as additional aspects of the basic question presented by the case: Has Congress exercised its powers under the Fifteenth Amendment in an appropriate manner with relation to the States?

The ground rules for resolving this question are clear. The language and purpose of the Fifteenth Amendment, the prior decisions construing its several provisions, and the general doctrines of constitutional interpretation, all point to one fundamental principle. As against the reserved powers of the States, Congress may use any rational means to effectuate the constitutional prohibition of racial discrimination in voting. . . .

The basic test to be applied in a case involving § 2 of the Fifteenth Amendment is the same as in all cases concerning the express powers of Congress with relation to the reserved powers of the States. Chief Justice MARSHALL laid down the classic formulation, 50 years before the Fifteenth Amendment was ratified:

> "Let the end be legitimate, let it be within the scope of the constitution, and all means which are appropriate, which are plainly adapted to that end, which are not prohibited, but consist with the letter and spirit of the constitution, are constitutional." *McCulloch v. Maryland,* 4 Wheat. 316 [1819]. . . .

We therefore reject South Carolina's argument that Congress may appropriately do no more than to forbid violations of the Fifteenth Amendment in general terms—that the task of fashioning specific remedies or of applying them to particular localities must necessarily be left entirely to the courts. Congress is not circumscribed by any such artificial rules under § 2 of the Fifteenth Amendment. In the oft-repeated words of Chief Justice MARSHALL, referring to another specific legislative authorization in the Constitution, "This power, like all others vested in Congress, is complete in itself, may be exercised to its utmost extent, and acknowledges no limitations, other than are prescribed in the constitution." *Gibbons v. Ogden,* 9 Wheat. 1 [1824]. . . .

After enduring nearly a century of widespread resistance to the Fifteenth Amendment, Congress has marshalled an array of potent weapons against the evil, with authority in the Attorney General to employ them effectively. Many of the areas directly affected by this development have indicated their willingness to abide by any restraints legitimately imposed upon them. We here hold that the portions of the Voting Rights Act properly before us are a valid means for carrying out the commands of the Fifteenth Amendment. Hopefully, millions of non-white Americans will now be able to participate for the first time on an equal basis in the government under which they live. We may finally look forward to the day when truly "[t]he right of citizens of the United States to vote shall not be denied or abridged by the United States or by any State on account of race, color, or previous condition of servitude."

The bill of complaint is dismissed.

Bill dismissed.

Justice BLACK concurring in part.

Though . . . I agree with most of the Court's conclusions, I dissent from its holding that every part of § 5 of the Act is constitutional. Section 4(a), to which § 5 is linked, suspends for five years all literacy tests and similar devices in those States coming within the formula of § 4(b). Section 5 goes on to provide that a State covered by § 4(b) can in no way amend its constitution or laws relating to voting without first trying to persuade the Attorney General of the United States or the Federal District Court for the District of Columbia that the new proposed laws do not have the purpose and will not have the effect of denying the right to vote to citizens on account of their race or color. I think this section is unconstitutional on at least two grounds. . . .

[I]t is hard for me to believe that a justiciable controversy can arise in the constitutional sense from a desire by the United States Government or some of its officials to determine in advance what legislative provisions a State may enact or what constitutional amendments it may adopt. If this dispute between the Federal Government and the States amounts to a case or controversy it is a far cry from the traditional constitutional notion of a case or controversy as a dispute over the meaning of enforceable laws or the manner in which they are applied. And if by this section Congress has created a case or controversy, and I do not believe it has, then it seems to me that the most appropriate judicial forum for settling these important questions is this Court acting under its original Art. III, § 2, jurisdiction to try cases in which a State is a party. At least a trial in this Court would treat the States with the dignity to which they should be entitled as constituent members of our Federal Union. . . .

My second and more basic objection to §5 is that Congress has here exercised its power under §2 of the Fifteenth Amendment through the adoption of means that conflict with the most basic principles of the Constitution. . . . Section 5, by providing that some of the States cannot pass state laws or adopt state constitutional amendments without first being compelled to beg federal authorities to approve their policies, so distorts our constitutional structure of government as to render any distinction drawn in the Constitution between state and federal power almost meaningless. One of the most basic premises upon which our structure of government was founded was that the Federal Government was to have certain specific and limited powers and no others, and all other power was to be reserved either "to the States respectively, or to the people." Certainly if all the provisions of our Constitution which limit the power of the Federal Government and reserve other power to the States are to mean anything, they mean at least that the States have power to pass laws and amend their constitutions without first sending their officials hundreds of miles away to beg federal authorities to approve them. Moreover, it seems to me that § 5 which gives federal officials power to veto state laws they do not like is in direct conflict with the clear command of our Constitution that "The United States shall guarantee to every State in this Union a Republican Form of Government." I cannot help but believe that the inevitable effect of any such law which forces any one of the States to entreat federal authorities in faraway places for approval of local laws before they can become effective is to create the impression that the State or States treated in this way are little more than conquered provinces. And if one law concerning voting can make the States plead for this approval by a distant federal court or the United States Attorney General, other laws on different subjects can force the States to seek the advance approval not only of the Attorney General but of the President himself or any other chosen members of his staff. It is inconceivable to me that such a radical degradation of state power was intended in any of the provisions of our Constitution or its Amendments. Of course I do not mean to cast any doubt whatever upon the indisputable power of the Federal Government to invalidate a state law once enacted and operative on the ground that it intrudes into the area of supreme federal power. But the Federal Government has heretofore always been content to exercise this power to protect federal supremacy by authorizing its agents to bring lawsuits against state officials once an operative state law has created an actual case and controversy. A federal law which assumes the power to compel the States to submit in advance any proposed legislation they have for approval by federal agents approaches dangerously near to wiping the States out as useful and effective units in the government of our country. I cannot agree to any constitutional interpretation that leads inevitably to such a result. . . .

In this and other prior Acts Congress has quite properly vested the Attorney General with extremely broad power to protect voting rights of citizens against discrimination on account of race or color. Section 5 viewed in this context is of very minor importance and in my judgment is likely to serve more as an irritant to the States than as an aid to the enforcement of the Act. I would hold § 5 invalid for the reasons stated above with full confidence that the Attorney General has ample power to give vigorous, expeditious and effective protection to the voting rights of all citizens.

B. VOTING RIGHTS AND THE
REAPPORTIONMENT REVOLUTION

Despite disenfranchisement of large segments of the population in the nineteenth century, Congress and the states by-and-large adhered to the principle of representation based on equal population. In the Northwest Ordinance of 1787, for example, Congress provided that representation in territorial legislatures was to be based on population. And as discussed in Chapter 5, from 1842 to 1929 Congress required that members of the House of Representatives be elected from "contiguous, equal districts." Between 1790 and 1889, no state was admitted into the union that did not guarantee representation in its state legislature based on population. And thirty-six of the original state constitutions required that representation in state houses be based primarily on population.

But in the late nineteenth and early twentieth centuries, with the influx of immigrants and the emergence of large urban areas due to the Industrial Revolution, many states bowed to political pressures and refused to reapportion state legislative districts. As a result, votes in rural areas greatly outweighed that in urban areas. As discussed in Chapter 2, the Court held in *Colegrove v. Green,* 328 U.S. 549 (1946), that reapportionment was a "political question" for Congress and state legislatures, not the Court, to decide. In that case, Illinois had not redrawn its electoral district lines since 1901 and the voting inequalities were as great as nine to one in some districts. But Illinois was by no means unique in failing to reapportion its legislative houses. In 1910, 41.9 million people lived in urban areas, while 49.9 lived in rural areas. Fifty years later, in 1960, 125.2 million lived in urban areas, whereas only 54 million lived in rural areas.

In 1960, the Warren Court confronted the related issue of racial malapportionment. In *Gomillion v. Lightfoot* (1960) (see page 679), the Court rebuffed an attempt by Tuskegee, Alabama, to redraw its electoral lines so as to exclude virtually all black voters from within the city's limits.

Finally, in *Baker v. Carr,* 369 U.S. 186 (1962) (see page 131), the Court responded to the malapportionment controversy, reversing *Colegrove* and holding that reapportionment was no longer a nonjusticiable controversy. Years later, after leaving the bench, Chief Justice Earl Warren explained in a television interview that *Baker* was more important than the Court's landmark school desegregation ruling:

[I]n my mind the most important case we have had in all those years was the case of *Baker v. Carr,* which is what we might call the parent case of the one man, one vote doctrine, which guarantees to every

American citizen participating in government an equal value of his vote to that of any other vote that is cast in the particular election. And the reason I say that is not because it decided any particular issue at the time but the courts had vascillated on that question for a great many years and there were decisions that ended up three, three, three, without a majority of the vote in any of them. And which were, the net result of which were to stratify the situation in states where the legislature was grossly malapportioned, and some places it remained that way for sixty or seventy years and there was no way that the people of the state could get a constitutional amendment on which to vote, because the people who were [in] the malapportioned legislatures wouldn't submit that kind of an amendment to them, and there was no way under their state government for the people to initiate such a measure. . . . [W]e held in *Baker v. Carr* that it was a judicial question, and that the courts, therefore, had jurisdiction. . . . And I believe that if we had had the decision shortly after the Fourteenth Amendment was adopted, that most of these problems that are confronting us today, particularly the racial problems, would have been solved by the political process where they should have been decided, rather than through the courts acting only under the bare bones of the Constitution. And if Blacks and everybody else could vote, the people who were in the majority in these various states had an opportunity to elect their people instead of having some district with large votes that were just about like the old so-called rotten boroughs over in England.[1]

While *Baker* announced the coming of the "reapportionment revolution" by inviting litigation challenging malapportioned legislatures, it did not address head-on the merits of the reapportionment controversy. Not until the following year did Justice Douglas announce the principle of "one person, one vote." When striking down Georgia's county-unit system of primary elections for state offices for diluting the votes of urbanites in *Gray v. Sanders,* 372 U.S. 368 (1963), Douglas declared that "[t]he conception of political equality from the Declaration of Independence, to Lincoln's Gettysburg address, to the Fifteenth, Seventeenth, and Nineteenth Amendments can mean only one thing—one person, one vote."

The next year, the Warren Court handed down fourteen reapportionment rulings. In the two leading cases, with Justices Clark, Harlan, and Stewart dissenting, Chief Justice Warren upheld the principle of one person, one vote as the "essence of self-government" when extending it to malapportioned congressional districts, in *Wesberry v. Sanders* (1964) (see page 681), and to state legislative districts in *Reynolds v. Sims* (1964) (see page 690).

The Court's 1964 reapportionment rulings far from settled the controversy or put an end to litigation. The Court's rulings affected the apportionment of forty-eight states and there were already challenges to forty-one states' apportionment in the lower federal courts.

The Court also further extended the principle of one person, one vote to most elections for local offices, although not all.[2]

In *Hadley v. Junior College District of Metropolitan Kansas City, Missouri*, 397 U.S. 50 (1970), Justice Black underscored the Court's determination to apply the principle of one person, one vote to virtually every election:

We . . . hold today that as a general rule, whenever a state or local government decides to select persons by popular election or perform government functions, the equal protection clause of the Fourteenth Amendment requires that each qualified voter must be given an equal opportunity to participate in that election, and when members of an elected body are chosen from separate districts, each district must be established on a basis which will insure, as far as practicable, that equal numbers of voters can vote for proportionally equal numbers of officials.

THE DEVELOPMENT OF LAW
Rulings Extending the Principle of One Person, One Vote to Local Governments

Case	Vote	Ruling
Avery v. Midland County, Texas, 390 U.S. 474 (1968)	6:3	Held district lines for voting for county commissioners were disproportionate and diluted local votes.
Kramer v. Union Free School District, 395 U.S. 621 (1969)	6:3	Held New York statute limiting voting in school district elections to homeowners violated the Fourteenth Amendment.
Hadley v. Junior College District of Metropolitan Kansas City, 397 U.S. 50 (1970)	6:3	Found that the selection of junior college trustees was based on disproportionate voting and held that virtually all state and local elections must abide by the principle of one person, one vote.
Board of Estimate of City of New York v. United States, 109 S.Ct. 1433 (1989)	9:0	Applied principle of "one person, one vote" to New York Board of Estimate.

The Court also continued to confront controversies arising from the use of multimember districts. These districts have been attacked, and sometimes adopted, for aiming to dilute the vote of minorities by expanding the size of a district. The Court held that multimember districts are not unconstitutional per se.[3] *Whitcomb v. Chavis*, 403 U.S. 124 (1971), upheld the use of multimember districts, despite considerable evidence that the votes of blacks and poor were diluted. Although the Court has expressed a preferance for single-member districts,[4] *City of Mobile v. Bolden*, 446 U.S. 55 (1980), reaffirmed that vote dilution in multimember districts is unconstitutional only if there is evidence an "intent" to discriminate. But as already noted, Congress responded to that ruling in the Voting Rights Act of 1982 by rejecting an "intent" standard and substituting a "totality of circumstances" standard for determining whether an electoral system is discriminatory. In *Rogers v. Herman Lodge*, 458 U.S. 613 (1982), the Burger Court ordered the establishment of single-member districts as a remedy for invidious discrimination in the at-large electoral system in Burke County, Georgia.[5]

The Court continues as well to confront litigation challenging the disparity in the weight of votes in electoral systems. The following two tables summarize the rulings, respectively, of the Warren Court and those of the later Burger Court. Note that in more than two decades the Court has continued to grapple

The Warren Court made sweeping changes in constitutional law and politics. But with the exception of the Court's 1954 landmark ruling on school desegregation, a solid majority on the Warren Court did not emerge until after the appointments of Justice Byron White and Arthur Goldberg in 1962. Seated, left to right, are Justices Tom C. Clark and Hugo L. Black, Chief Justice Earl Warren, and Justices William O. Douglas and James Byrnes. Standing, left to right, are Justices Byron R. White, William J. Brennan, Jr., Potter Stewart and Arthur J. Goldberg. *Collection of the Supreme Court of the United States*

with the line-drawing problem created by the Warren Court's holding that mathematical exactitude is not necessary to ensure the principle of one person, one vote, but rather "honest and good faith effort[s] to construct districts . . . as nearly of equal population as is practicable." But the Burger Court has been more willing to permit deviations from a rigid application of the principle of one person, one vote.

THE DEVELOPMENT OF LAW

Other Warren Court Rulings Implementing the Principle of One Person, One Vote

Case	Vote	Ruling
WMCA, Inc. v. Lomenzo, 377 U.S. 633 (1964)	7:2	Held New York's apportionment was not substantially based on population; its ten most-urban districts, with 75.3 percent of the population, had only 64.9 percent of the state senate seats and 61.3 percent of the assembly seats.
Maryland Committee for Fair Representation v. Towes, 377 U.S. 656 (1964)	7:2	Maryland state legislature not sufficiently based on population.
Davis v. Mann, 377 U.S. 679 (1964)	7:2	Virginia's apportionment violates the equal protection clause because districts with 41.1 percent of the state's population elected a majority of state senate, and residents of one urban city were 30 percent underrepresented, while one rural district was 38 percent overrepresented.
Roman v. Sincock, 377 U.S. 685 (1964)	7:2	Delaware's state senate was malapportioned because a majority of its seats were elected by only twenty-one percent of the state's population, and its state house districts had a ratio of one to twelve between the most- and least-populous areas.

Case	Vote	Ruling
Lucas v. 44th-General Assembly of Colorado, 377 U.S. 713 (1964)	6:3	Held Colorado's legislative apportionment violated the Fourteenth Amendment.
Fortson v. Dorsey, 379 U.S. 433 (1965)	8:1	Upheld Georgia's multimember districts for urban areas.
Burns v. Richardson, 384 U.S. 73 (1966)	8:0	Upheld use of multimember state senatoral district as not *ipso facto* invidious discrimination.
Swann v. Adams, 385 U.S. 440 (1967)	7:2	Ruled "*De minimis* deviations are unavoidable, but variations of 30% among state districts and 40% among house districts can hardly be deemed *de minimis* and none of our cases suggests that differences of this magnitude will be approved without a satisfactory explanation grounded on acceptable state policy."
Kilgarlin v. Hill, 386 U.S. 120 (1967)	6:3	Invalidated apportionment of state congressional districts with a ratio of 1.31 to 1
Kirkpatrick v. Preisler, 394 U.S. (1969)	6:3	Held that a variance of 3.3 percent between Missouri's largest and smallest congressional districts impermissible; reapportionment plan did not satisfy the "good faith effort . . . nearly as practicable . . . precise mathematical equality" standard.
Wells v. Rockefeller, 304 U.S. 542 (1969)	6:3	Struck down New York's apportionment as unjustified departure from absolute equality of all districts because thirty-one of the state's forty-one districts were based on seven homogeneous regions.

THE DEVELOPMENT OF LAW

Other Rulings of the Burger Court Implementing the Principle of One Person, One Vote

Case	Vote	Ruling
Ely v. Klair, 403 U.S. 108 (1971)	9:0	Held federal district court did not improperly permit the 1970 election to be held even though apportionment had not been adjusted in light of census changes.
67th Minnesota State Senate v. Beens, 406 U.S. 187 (1972)	8:1	Held district exceeded its authority in devising a reapportionment that reduced size of state senate from 67 to 35 and that of the state house from 135 to 105.
Mahan v. Howell, 410 U.S. 315 (1973)	5:3	Held that states may apply one person, one vote principle more flexibly when drawing new state legislative districts than when drawing congressional district lines; here, allowed a 16 percent deviation in population among Virginia's state districts.
Gaffney v. Cummings, 412 U.S. 735 (1973)	5:3	Allowed 1.9 percent deviation from absolute equality among districts and held that states within tolerable limits may undertake "not to minimize or eliminate the political strength of any group or party, but to recognize it and, through districting, provide a rough sort of proportional representation in the legislative halls of the State."
White v. Regester, 412 U.S. 755 (1973)	6:3	Held that Texas's apportionment with an average deviation of 1.82 percent was not invidious discrimination, and

Case	Vote	Ruling
		that deviation of up to 10 percent require no justification.
Connor v. Finch, 431 U.S. 407 (1977)	8:1	Mississippi's reapportionment violated the equal protection clause because of population deviations of 16.5 percent in senate districts and 19.3 percent in house districts.
Karcher v. Daggett, 462 U.S. 725 (1983)	5:4	Struck down New Jersey's congressional apportionment plan that had an average district variance from perfect equality of 0.6984 percent, but reaffirmed that there is no fixed standard for justifying deviations and acceptability of justification depends on the circumstances of each case.

Finally, as the tables indicate, since the appointment of Chief Justice Burger and as the Court's composition has further changed since 1969, the justices have been more willing to allow various kinds of justifications for deviations from the principle of one person, one vote, especially in *Mahan v. Howell*, 410 U.S. 315 (1973), holding that states have greater flexibility in departing from the principle of one person, one vote in state legislative redistricting than when drawing new district lines for congressional districts. Consequently and perhaps inexorably, the Court was put into the position of confronting challenges to the practice of political gerrymandering. *Gerrymandering* is a term describing efforts to draw district lines to preserve partisan power. It originated in Massachusetts in 1812, where the state legislature produced a salamander-shaped district, named after the governor, Elbridge Gerry. Since then it has been commonplace in the politics of congressional and state legislative districting. Gerrymandering is principally used to either safeguard incumbents' seats or, more recently, to create districts in urban areas that will ensure the election of an ethnic or racial minority. The Warren Court repeatedly rejected opportunities to supervise this practice, except in cases like *Gomillion* involving gerrymandering aimed at disenfrachising minorities. In *United Jewish Organizations v. Carey*, 430 U.S. 144 (1977), the Burger Court likewise dismissed the

The Original Gerrymander in 1812,
with Head, Wings, and Claws by Gibert Stuart. *The
Granger Collection*

claims of Hasidic Jews, who challenged the constitutionality of
New York's redistricting plan that divided their community,
thereby diluting their voting power, to establish several predominately nonwhite voting districts. However, in Chief Justice Burger's last term on the Court, in *Davis v. Bandemer* (1986) (see
page 698), the Court held that political gerrymandering was a
justiciable controversy. Whether and how far the Rehnquist
Court assumes the task of supervising political gerrymandering
remains to be seen.

NOTES

1. "A Conversation with Earl Warren," WGBH-TV (Boston) Education Foundation (1972), transcript pp. 15–16.

2. The approved a system for electing the board of directors of a
water district that limited the electorate to landowners and weighted
their votes in *Salyer Land Company v. Tulare Water Storage District*, 410

U.S. 719 (1973). See also *Gordon v. Lance*, 403 U.S. U.S. 1 (1971); *Holt Civic Club v. City of Tuscaloosa*, 439 U.S. 60 (1978); and *Ball v. James*, 451 U.S. 355 (1981).

3. See *Fortson v. Dorsey*, 379 U.S. 433 (1965); and *Burns v. Richardson*, 384 U.S. 73 (1966).

4. See *Connor v. Johnson*, 402 U.S. 690 (1971); *Chapman v. Meier*, 420 U.S. 1 (1975); and *East Carrol Parish School Board v. Marshall*, 424 U.S. 636 (1976).

5. But see *Thornburg v. Gingles*, 478 U.S. 30 (1986), in the table in section A of this chapter.

6. See also *Rockefeller v. Wright*, 376 U.S. 169 (1964); and *Gaffney v. Cummings*, 412 U.S. 735 (1973).

SELECTED BIBLIOGRAPHY

Baker, Gordon. *The Reapportionment Revolution.* New York: Random House, 1966.

Dixon, Robert. *Democratic Representation: Reapportionment in Law and Politics.* New York: Oxford University Press, 1968.

Elliott, Ward. *The Rise of Guardian Democracy.* Cambridge, MA: Harvard University Press, 1974.

Grofman, Bernard, Lijohart, Arend, McKay, Robert, and Scarrow, Howard, eds. *Representation and Redistricting Issues.* Lexington, MA: D. C. Heath, 1982.

Polsby, Nelson, ed. *Reapportionment in the 1970s.* Berkeley: University of California Press, 1971.

Gomillion v. Lightfoot
364 U.S. 339, 81 S.Ct. 125 (1960)

Charles Gomillion and several other black voters sued Phil Lightfoot, the mayor of Tuskegee, Alabama, for denying their voting rights as guaranteed under the Fifteenth Amendment. In 1957, Alabama's legislature redrew the boundaries of Tuskegee's electoral district from a square shape to that of figure with twenty-eight sides. The redistricting placed virtually all black voters outside of the city limits and in a district that had no whites. (See Figure 8.2, which the Court included in an appendix to its opinion.) A federal district court dismissed the suit, and a court of appeals affirmed that ruling. Gomillion then appealed to the Supreme Court, which granted review.

TUSKEGEE, ALABAMA, BEFORE AND AFTER ACT 140

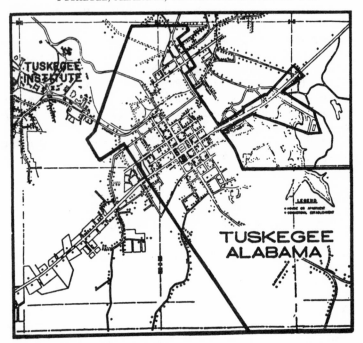

The entire area of the square comprised the city prior to Act 140. The irregular black-bordered figure within the square represents the postenactment city.

Justice FRANKFURTER delivers the opinion of the Court.

The complaint amply alleges a claim of racial discrimination. Against this claim the respondents have never suggested, either in their brief or in oral argument, any countervailing municipal function which Act 140 is designed to serve. The respondents invoke generalities expressing the State's unrestricted power— unlimited, that is, by the United States Constitution—to establish, destroy, or reorganize by contraction or expansion its political subdivisions, to wit, cities, counties, and other local units. We freely recognize the breadth and importance of this aspect of the State's political power. . . .

In no case involving unequal weight in voting distribution that has come before the Court did the decision sanction a differentiation on racial lines whereby approval was given to unequivocal withdrawal of the vote solely from colored citizens. Apart from all else, these considerations lift this controversy out of the so-called "political" arena and into the conventional sphere of constitutional litigation. . . .

When a State exercises power wholly within the domain of state interest, it is insulated from federal judicial review. But such insulation is not carried over when state power is used as an instrument for circumventing a federally protected right. This principle has had many applications. It has long been recognized in cases which have prohibited a State from exploiting a power acknowledged to be absolute in an isolated context to justify the imposition of an "unconstitutional condition." What the Court has said in those cases is equally applicable here, viz., that "Acts generally lawful may become unlawful when done to accomplish an unlawful end, *United States v. Reading Co.,* 226 U.S. 324 [1913], and a constitutional power cannot be used by way of condition to attain an unconstitutional result." *Western Union Telegraph Co. v. Foster,* 247 U.S. 105. [1918]. The petitioners are entitled to prove their allegations at trial.

For these reasons, the principal conclusions of the District Court and the Court of Appeals are clearly erroneous and the decision below must be reversed.

Reversed.

Baker v. Carr
369 U.S. 186, 82 S.Ct. 691 (1962)

This watershed case inaugurated the "reapportionment revolution," in holding that federal courts had jurisdiction and reapportionment controversies were justiciable, and not "political questions" to be decided by the other branches of government. Although *Baker* did not address the merits of the reapportionment dispute, it is no less important to this chapter. Pertinent parts of this case are reprinted on page 131.

Wesberry v. Sanders
376 U.S. 1, 84 S.Ct. 526 (1964)

James Wesberry, Jr., and several other registered voters filed a suit in federal district court, asking it to declare unconstitutional Georgia's statute prescribing congressional districts. The 1931 statute created ten districts. But according to the 1960 census, the Fifth Congressional District had a population of 823,680, while the average population of the ten districts was 394,312, less than half of the Fifth District's population. Moreover, the

Ninth District had a population of only 272,154, less than one-third as many as the Fifth District. Wesberry contended that because there was only one congressman for each district, the Fifth District's congressman had to represent from two to three times as many people as other congressmen. A three-judge federal district court, however, dismissed the suit and an appellate court affirmed. Wesberry then appealed to the Supreme Court.

Justice BLACK delivers the opinion of the Court.

We agree with the District Court that the 1931 Georgia apportionment grossly discriminates against voters in the Fifth Congressional District. A single Congressman represents from two to three times as many Fifth District voters as are represented by each of the Congressmen from the other Georgia congressional districts. The apportionment statute thus contracts the value of some votes and expands that of others. If the Federal Constitution intends that when qualified voters elect members of Congress each vote be given as much weight as any other vote, then this statute cannot stand.

We hold that, construed in its historical context, the command of Art. I, § 2, that Representatives be chosen "by the People of the several States" means that as nearly as is practicable one man's vote in a congressional election is to be worth as much as another's. This rule is followed automatically, of course, when Representatives are chosen as a group on a statewide basis, as was a widespread practice in the first 50 years of our Nation's history. It would be extraordinary to suggest that in such statewide elections the votes of inhabitants of some parts of a State, for example, Georgia's thinly populated Ninth District, could be weighted at two or three times the value of the votes of people living in more populous parts of the State, for example, the Fifth District around Atlanta. Cf. *Gray v. Sanders,* 372 U.S. 368 [1963]. We do not believe that the Framers of the Constitution intended to permit the same vote-diluting discrimination to be accomplished through the device of districts containing widely varied numbers of inhabitants. To say that a vote is worth more in one district than in another would not only run counter to our fundamental ideas of democratic government, it would cast aside the principle of a House of Representatives elected "by the People," a principle tenaciously fought for and established at the Constitutional Convention. The history of the Constitution, particularly that part of it relating to the adoption of Art. I, § 2, reveals that those who framed the Constitution meant that, no matter what the mechanics of an election, whether statewide or by districts, it was population which was to be the basis of the House of Representatives.

During the Revolutionary War the rebelling colonies were

loosely allied in the Continental Congress, a body with authority to do little more than pass resolutions and issue requests for men and supplies. Before the war ended the Congress had proposed and secured the ratification by the States of a somewhat closer association under the Articles of Confederation. Though the Articles established a central government for the United States, as the former colonies were even then called, the States retained most of their sovereignty, like independent nations bound together only by treaties. There were no separate judicial or executive branches: only a Congress consisting of a single house. Like the members of an ancient Greek league, each State, without regard to size or population, was given only one vote in that house. It soon became clear that the Confederation was without adequate power to collect needed revenues or to enforce the rules its Congress adopted. Farsighted men felt that a closer union was necessary if the States were to be saved from foreign and domestic dangers.

The result was the Constitutional Convention of 1787, called for "the sole and express purpose of revising the Articles of Confederation. . . ." When the Convention met in May, this modest purpose was soon abandoned for the greater challenge of creating a new and closer form of government than was possible under the Confederation. Soon after the Convention assembled, Edmund Randolph of Virginia presented a plan not merely to amend the Articles of Confederation but to create an entirely new National Government with a National Executive, National Judiciary, and a National Legislature of two Houses, one house to be elected by "the people," the second house to be elected by the first.

The question of how the legislature should be constituted precipitated the most bitter controversy of the Convention. One principle was uppermost in the minds of many delegates: that, no matter where he lived, each voter should have a voice equal to that of every other in electing members of Congress. In support of this principle, George Mason of Virginia

"argued strongly for an election of the larger branch by the people. It was to be the grand depository of the democratic principle of the Govt."

James Madison agreed, saying "If the power is not immediately derived from the people, in proportion to their numbers, we may make a paper confederacy, but that will be all.". . .

Some delegates opposed election by the people. The sharpest objection arose out of the fear on the part of small States like Delaware that if population were to be the only basis of representation the populous States like Virginia would elect a large enough number of representatives to wield overwhelming power in the National Government. Arguing that the Convention had no authority to depart from the plan of the Articles of Confederation which gave each State an equal vote in the National Congress, William Paterson of New Jersey said, "If the sovereignty of the States is to be maintained, the Representatives must be drawn immediately from the States, not from the people: and we have no power to vary the idea of equal sovereignty." To this end he proposed a single legislative chamber in which each State, as in the Confederation, was to have an equal vote. A number of delegates supported this plan.

The delegates who wanted every man's vote to count alike were sharp in their criticism of giving each State, regardless of population, the same voice in the National Legislature. Madison entreated the Convention "to renounce a principle wch. was confessedly unjust," and Rufus King of Massachusetts "was prepared for every event, rather than sit down under a Govt. founded in a vicious principle of representation and which must be as short-lived as it would be unjust."

The dispute came near ending the Convention without a Constitution. Both sides seemed for a time to be hopelessly obstinate. Some delegations threatened to withdraw from the Convention if they did not get their way. Seeing the controversy growing sharper and emotions rising, the wise and highly respected Benjamin Franklin arose and pleaded with the delegates on both sides to "part with some of their demands, in order that they may join in some accomodating proposition." At last those who supported representation of the people in both houses and those who supported it in neither were brought together, some expressing the fear that if they did not reconcile their differences, "some foreign sword will probably do the work for us." The deadlock was finally broken when a majority of the States agreed to what has been called the Great Compromise, based on a proposal which had been repeatedly advanced by Roger Sherman and other delegates from Connecticut. It provided on the one hand that each State, including little Delaware and Rhode Island, was to have two Senators. As a further guarantee that these Senators would be considered state emissaries, they were to be elected by the state legislatures, Art. I, § 3, and it was specially provided in Article V that no State should ever be deprived of its equal representation in the Senate. The other side of the compromise was that, as provided in Art. I, § 2, members of the House of Representatives should be chosen "by the People of the several States" and should be "apportioned among the several States . . . according to their respective Numbers." While those who wanted both houses to represent the people had yielded on the Senate, they had not yielded on the House of Representatives. William Samuel Johnson of Connecticut had summed it up well: "in *one* branch the *people,* ought to be represented; in the *other,* the *States.*"

The debates at the Convention make at least one fact abundantly clear: that when the delegates agreed that the House should represent "people" they intended that in allocating Congressmen the number assigned to each State should be determined solely by the number of the State's inhabitants. . . .

It would defeat the principle solemnly embodied in the Great Compromise—equal representation in the House for equal numbers of people—for us to hold that, within the States, legislatures may draw the lines of congressional districts in such a way as to give some voters a greater voice in choosing a Congressman than others. The House of Representatives, the Convention agreed, was to represent the people as individuals, and on a basis of complete equality for each voter. The delegates were quite aware of what Madison called the "vicious representation" in Great Britain whereby "rotten boroughs" with few inhabitants were represented in Parliament on or almost on a par with cities of greater population. Wilson urged that people must be represented as individuals, so that America would escape the evils of the English system under which one man could send two members to Parliament to represent the borough of Old Sarum while London's million people sent but four. The delegates referred to rotten borough apportionments in some of the state legislatures as the kind of objectionable governmental action that the Constitution should not tolerate in the election of congressional representatives. . . .

It is in the light of such history that we must construe Art. I, § 2, of the Constitution, which, carrying out the ideas of Madison and those of like views, provides that Representatives shall be chosen "by the People of the several States" and shall be "apportioned among the several States . . . according to their respective Numbers." It is not surprising that our Court has held that this Article gives persons qualified to vote a constitutional right to vote and to have their votes counted. *United States v. Mosley,* 238 U.S. 383, [1915]. *Ex parte Yarbrough,* 110 U.S. 651 [1884]. Not only can this right to vote not be denied outright, it cannot, consistently with Article I, be destroyed by alteration of ballots, see *United States v. Classic,* 313 U.S. 299 [1941], or diluted by stuffing of the ballot box, see *United States v. Saylor,* 322 U.S. 385 [1944]. No right is more precious in a free country than that of having a voice in the election of those who make the laws under which, as good citizens, we must live. Other rights, even the most basic, are illusory if the right to vote is undermined. Our Constitution leaves no room for classification of people in a way that unnecessarily abridges this right. In urging the people to adopt the Constitution, Madison said in No. 57 of The Federalist:

> "Who are to be the electors of the Federal Representatives? Not the rich more than the poor; not the learned more than the ignorant; not the haughty heirs of distinguished names,

more than the humble sons of obscure and unpropitious fortune. The electors are to be the great body of the people of the United States. . . ."

Readers surely could have fairly taken this to mean, "one person, one vote." Cf. *Gray v. Sanders,* . . .

While it may not be possible to draw congressional districts with mathematical precision, that is no excuse for ignoring our Constitution's plain objective of making equal representation for equal numbers of people the fundamental goal for the House of Representatives. That is the high standard of justice and common sense which the Founders set for us.

Reversed and remanded.

Justice CLARK concurring in part and dissenting in part.

Unfortunately I can join neither the opinion of the Court nor the dissent of my Brother HARLAN. It is true that the opening sentence of Art. I, § 2, of the Constitution provides that Representatives are to be chosen "by the People of the several States. . . ." However, in my view, Brother HARLAN has clearly demonstrated that both the historical background and language preclude a finding that Art. I, § 2, lays down the *ipse dixit* "one person, one vote" in congressional elections.

On the other hand, I agree with the majority that congressional districting is subject to judicial scrutiny. This Court has so held ever since *Smiley v. Holm,* 285 U.S. 355 [1932].

I therefore cannot agree with Brother HARLAN that the supervisory power granted to Congress under Art. I, § 4, is the exclusive remedy.

I would examine the Georgia congressional districts against the requirements of the Equal Protection Clause of the Fourteenth Amendment. As my Brother BLACK said in his dissent in *Colegrove v. Green,* [328 U.S. 549 (1946)], the "equal protection clause of the Fourteenth Amendment forbids . . . discrimination. It does not permit the states to pick out certain qualified citizens or groups of citizens and deny them the right to vote at all. . . . No one would deny that the equal protection clause would also prohibit a law that would expressly give certain citizens a half-vote and others a full vote. . . . Such discriminatory legislation seems to me exactly the kind that the equal protection clause was intended to prohibit.". . .

The trial court, however, did not pass upon the merits of the case, although it does appear that it did make a finding that the Fifth District of Georgia was "grossly out of balance" with other congressional districts of the State. Instead of proceeding on the merits, the court dismissed the case for lack of equity. I believe that the court erred in so doing. In my view we should therefore vacate this judgment and remand the case for a hearing on the merits. At that hearing the court should apply the standards laid down in *Baker v. Carr*.

Justice HARLAN dissenting.

I had not expected to witness the day when the Supreme Court of the United States would render a decision which casts grave doubt on the constitutionality of the composition of the House of Representatives. It is not an exaggeration to say that such is the effect of today's decision. The Court's holding that the Constitution requires States to select Representatives either by elections at large or by elections in districts composed "as nearly as is practicable" of equal population places in jeopardy the seats of almost all the members of the present House of Representatives. . . .

Although the Court finds necessity for its artificial construction of Article I in the undoubted importance of the right to vote, that right is not involved in this case. All of the appellants do vote. The Court's talk about "debasement" and "dilution" of the vote is a model of circular reasoning, in which the premises of the argument feed on the conclusion. Moreover, by focusing exclusively on numbers in disregard of the area and shape of a congressional district as well as party affiliations within the district, the Court deals in abstractions which will be recognized even by the politically unsophisticated to have little relevance to the realities of political life.

In any event, the very sentence of Art. I, § 2, on which the Court exclusively relies confers the right to vote for Representatives only on those whom *the State* has found qualified to vote for members of "the most numerous Branch of the State Legislature." So far as Article I is concerned, it is within the State's power to confer that right only on persons of wealth or of a particular sex or, if the State chose, living in specified areas of the State. Were Georgia to find the residents of the Fifth District unqualified to vote for Representatives to the State House of Representatives, they could not vote for Representatives to Congress, according to the express words of Art. I, § 2. Other provisions of the Constitution would, of course, be relevant, *but, so far as Art. I, § 2, is concerned,* the disqualification would be within Georgia's power. How can it be, then, that this very same sentence prevents Georgia from apportioning its Representatives as it chooses? The truth is that it does not.

The Court purports to find support for its position in the third paragraph of Art. I, § 2, which provides for the apportionment of Representatives among the States. The appearance of support in that section derives from the Court's confusion of two issues:

direct election of Representatives within the States and the apportionment of Representatives among the States. Those issues are distinct, and were separately treated in the Constitution. The fallacy of the Court's reasoning in this regard is illustrated by its slide, obscured by intervening discussion from the intention of the delegates at the Philadelphia Convention "that in allocating Congressmen the number assigned to each State should be determined solely by the number of the State's inhabitants," to a "principle solemnly embodied in the Great Compromise—equal representation in the House for equal numbers of people." The delegates did have the former intention and made clear provision for it. Although many, perhaps most, of them also believed generally—but assuredly not in the precise, formalistic way of the majority of the Court—that within the States representation should be based on population, they did not surreptitiously slip their belief into the Constitution in the phrase "by the People," to be discovered 175 years later like a Shakespearian anagram.

Far from supporting the Court, the apportionment of Representatives among the States shows how blindly the Court has marched to its decision. Representatives were to be apportioned among the States on the basis of free population plus three-fifths of the slave population. Since no slave voted, the inclusion of three-fifths of their number in the basis of apportionment gave the favored States representation far in excess of their voting population. If, then, slaves were intended to be without representation. Article I did exactly what the Court now says it prohibited: it "weighted" the vote of voters in the slave States. Alternatively, it might have been thought that Representatives elected by free men of a State would speak also for the slaves. But since the slaves added to the representation only of their own State, Representatives from the slave States could have been thought to speak only for the slaves of their own States, indicating both that the Convention believed it possible for a Representative elected by one group to speak for another nonvoting group and that Representatives were in large degree still thought of as speaking for the whole population *of a State*.

There is a further basis for demonstrating the hollowness of the Court's assertion that Article I requires "one man's vote in a congressional election . . . to be worth as much as another's." Nothing that the Court does today will disturb the fact that although in 1960 the population of an average congressional district was 410,481, the States of Alaska, Nevada, and Wyoming each have a Representative in Congress, although their respective populations are 226,167,285,278, and 330,066. In entire disregard of population, Art. I, § 2, guarantees each of these States and every other State "at Least one Representative." It is whimsical to assert in the face of this guarantee that an absolute principle of "equal representation in the House for equal numbers of people" is "solemnly embodied" in Article I. All that there is is a provision which bases representation in the House, generally but not entirely, on the population of the States. The provision for representation of *each State* in the House of Representatives is not a mere exception to the principle framed by the majority; it shows that no such principle is to be found.

Finally in this array of hurdles to its decision which the Court surmounts only by knocking them down is § 4 of Art. I which states simply:

> "The Times, Places and *Manner* of holding Elections for Senators and Representatives, shall be prescribed in each State by the Legislature thereof; but the Congress may at any time by Law make or alter such Regulations, except as to the Places of chusing Senators." (Emphasis added.)

The delegates were well aware of the problem of "rotten boroughs," as material cited by the Court and hereafter makes plain. It cannot be supposed that delegates to the Convention would have labored to establish a principle of equal representation only to bury it, one would have thought beyond discovery, in § 2, and omit all mention of it from § 4, which deals explicitly with the conduct of elections. Section 4 states without qualification that the state legislatures shall prescribe regulations for the conduct of elections for Representatives and, equally without qualification, that Congress may make or alter such regulations. There is nothing to indicate any limitation whatsoever on this grant of plenary initial and supervisory power. The Court's holding is, of course, derogatory not only of the power of the state legislatures but also of the power of Congress, both theoretically and as they have actually exercised their power. It freezes upon both, for no reason other than that it seems wise to the majority of the present Court, a particular political theory for the selection of Representatives. . . .

The upshot of all this is that the language of Art. I, §§ 2 and 4, the surrounding text, and the relevant history are all in strong and consistent direct contradiction of the Court's holding. The constitutional scheme vests in the States plenary power to regulate the conduct of elections for Representatives, and, in order to protect the Federal Government, provides for congressional supervision of the States' exercise of their power. Within this scheme, the appellants do not have the right which they assert, in the absence of provision for equal districts by the Georgia Legislature or the Congress. The constitutional right which the Court creates is manufactured out of whole cloth.

The unstated premise of the Court's conclusion quite obviously is that the Congress has not dealt, and the Court believes it will not deal, with the problem of congressional apportionment in accordance with what the Court believes to be sound political principles. Laying aside for the moment the validity of such a consideration as a factor in constitutional interpretation, it becomes relevant to examine the history of congressional action under Art. I, § 4. This history reveals that the Court is not simply undertaking to exercise a power which the Constitution reserves to the Congress; it is also overruling congressional judgment. . . .

This Court, no less than all other branches of the Government, is bound by the Constitution. The Constitution does not confer on the Court blanket authority to step into every situation where the political branch may be thought to have fallen short. The stability of this institution ultimately depends not only upon its being alert to keep the other branches of government within constitutional bounds but equally upon recognition of the limitations on the Court's own functions in the constitutional system.

What is done today saps the political process. The promise of judicial intervention in matters of this sort cannot but encourage popular inertia in efforts for political reform through the political process, with the inevitable result that the process is itself weakened. By yielding to the demand for a judicial remedy in this instance, the Court in my view does a disservice both to itself and to the broader values of our system of government.

Believing that the complaint fails to disclose a constitutional claim, I would affirm the judgment below dismissing the complaint.

Justice STEWART disagreed with Justice HARLAN on the justiciability of the controversy, but otherwise joined his opinion.

Reynolds v. Sims
377 U.S. 533, 84 S.Ct. 1362 (1964)

M. O. Sims and several other voters sued state and party officials in federal district court, alleging that Alabama's legislature was malapportioned and denied them an equal voting right. Although the state's constitution provided for a reapportionment every ten years, none had been undertaken since 1901. As a result, about one-fourth of the state's population could elect a majority of the state senators and representatives. The ratios of people to legislators varied by as much as fourteen to one in senate districts and up to sixteen to one in the lower house. The district court judge agreed that Sims's rights under the Fourteenth Amendment equal protection clause were violated and ordered the state to undertake reapportionment plans. Alabama's legislature came up with two plans but neither was based strictly on population. And the district court declared them unconstitutional. At that, B. A. Reynolds and several other state officials appealed to the Supreme Court.

Chief Justice WARREN delivers the opinion of the Court.

A predominant consideration in determining whether a State's legislative apportionment scheme constitutes an invidious discrimination violative of rights asserted under the Equal Protection Clause is that the rights allegedly impaired are individual and personal in nature. As stated by the Court in *United States v. Bathgate*, 246 U.S. 220 [1918], "[t]he right to vote is personal. . . . ." While the result of a court decision in a state legislative apportionment controversy may be to require the restructuring of the geographical distribution of seats in a state legislature, the judicial focus must be concentrated upon ascertaining whether there has been any discrimination against certain of the State's citizens which constitutes an impermissible impairment of their constitutionally protected right to vote. Like *Skinner v. Oklahoma*, 316 U.S. 535 [1942], such a case "touches a sensitive and important area of human rights," and "involves one of the basic civil rights of man," presenting questions of alleged "invidious discriminations . . . against groups or types of individuals in violation of the constitutional guaranty of just and equal laws." Undoubtedly, the right of suffrage is a fundamental matter in a free and democratic society. Especially since the right to exercise the franchise in a free and unimpaired manner is preservative of other basic civil and political rights, any alleged infringement of the right of citizens to vote must be carefully and meticulously scrutinized. . . .

Legislators represent people, not trees or acres. Legislators are elected by voters, not farms or cities or economic interests. As long as ours is a representative form of government, and our legislatures are those instruments of government elected directly by and directly representative of the people, the right to elect legislators in a free and unimpaired fashion is a bedrock of our political system. It could hardly be gainsaid that a constitutional claim had been asserted by an allegation that certain otherwise qualified voters had been entirely prohibited from voting for members of their state legislature. And, if a State should provide that the votes of citizens in one part of the State should be given two times, or five times, or 10 times the weight of votes of citizens in another part of the State, it could hardly be contended that the right to vote of those residing in the disfavored areas had not been effectively diluted. It would appear extraordinary to suggest that a State could be constitutionally permitted to enact a law providing that certain of the State's voters could vote two, five, or 10 times for their legislative representatives, while voters living elsewhere could vote only once. And it is inconceivable that a state law to the effect that, in counting votes for legislators, the votes of citizens in one part of the State would be multiplied by two, five, or 10, while the votes of persons in another area would be counted only at face value, could be constitutionally sustainable. Of course, the effect of state legislative districting schemes which give the same number of representatives to unequal numbers of constituents is identical. . . .

Logically, in a society ostensibly grounded on representative government, it would seem reasonable that a majority of the people of a State could elect a majority of that State's legislators. To conclude differently, and to sanction minority control of state legislative bodies, would appear to deny majority rights in a way that far surpasses any possible denial of minority rights that might otherwise be thought to result. Since legislatures are responsible for enacting laws by which all citizens are to be governed, they should be bodies which are collectively responsive to the popular will. And the concept of equal protection has been traditionally viewed as requiring the uniform treatment of persons standing in the same relation to the governmental action questioned or challenged. With respect to the allocation of legislative representation, all voters, as citizens of a State, stand in the same relation regardless of where they live. Any suggested criteria for the differentiation of citizens are insufficient to justify any discrimination, as to the weight of their votes, unless relevant to the permissible purposes of legislative apportionment. Since the achieving of fair and effective representation for all citizens is concededly the basic aim of legislative apportionment, we conclude that the Equal Protection Clause guarantees the opportunity for equal participation by all voters in the election of state legislators. Diluting the weight of votes because of place of residence impairs basic constitutional rights under the Fourteenth Amendment. . . .

We are told that the matter of apportioning representation in a state legislature is a complex and many-faceted one. We are advised that States can rationally consider factors other than population in apportioning legislative representation. We are admonished not to restrict the power of the States to impose differing views as to political philosophy on their citizens. We are cautioned about the dangers of entering into political thickets and mathematical quagmires. Our answer is this: a denial of constitutionally protected rights demands judicial protection; our oath and our office require no less of us. . . . To the extent that a citizen's right to vote is debased, he is that much less a citizen. The fact that an individual lives here or there is not a legitimate reason for overweighting or diluting the efficacy of his vote. The complexions of societies and civilizations change, often with amazing rapidity. A nation once primarily rural in character becomes predominantly urban. Representation schemes once fair and equitable become archaic and outdated. But the basic principle of representative government remains, and must remain, unchanged—the weight of a citizen's vote cannot be made to depend on where he lives. . . .

We hold that, as a basic constitutional standard, the Equal Protection Clause requires that the seats in both houses of a bicameral state legislature must be apportioned on a population basis. Simply stated, an individual's right to vote for state legislators is unconstitutionally impaired when its weight is in a substantial fashion diluted when compared with votes of citizens living in other parts of the State. . . .

Much has been written since our decision in *Baker v. Carr* about the applicability of the so-called federal analogy to state legislative apportionment arrangements. After considering the matter, the court below concluded that no conceivable analogy could be drawn between the federal scheme and the apportionment of seats in the Alabama Legislature under the proposed constitutional amendment. We agree with the District Court, and find the federal analogy inapposite and irrelevant to state legislative districting schemes. Attempted reliance on the federal analogy appears often to be little more than an after-the-fact rationalization offered in defense of maladjusted state apportionment arrangements. The original constitutions of 36 of our States provided that representation in both houses of the state legislatures would be based completely, or predominantly, on population. And the Founding Fathers clearly had no intention of establishing a pattern or model for the apportionment of seats in state legislatures when the system of representation in the Federal Congress was adopted. Demonstrative of this is the fact that the Northwest Ordinance, adopted in the same year, 1787, as the Federal Constitution, provided for the apportionment of seats in territorial legislatures solely on the basis of population.

The system of representation in the two Houses of the Federal Congress is one ingrained in our Constitution, as part of the law of the land. It is one conceived out of compromise and concession indispensable to the establishment of our federal republic. Arising from unique historical circumstances, it is based on the consideration that in establishing our type of federalism a group of formerly independent States bound themselves together under one national government. Admittedly, the original 13 States surrendered some of their sovereignty in agreeing to join together "to form a more perfect Union." But at the heart of our constitutional system remains the concept of separate and distinct governmental entities which have delegated some, but not all, of their formerly held powers to the single national government. . . .

Political subdivisions of States—counties, cities, or whatever—never were and never have been considered as sovereign entities. Rather, they have been traditionally regarded as subordinate governmental instrumentalities created by the State to assist in the carrying out of state governmental functions. . . . The relationship of the States to the Federal Government could hardly be less analogous. . . .

Since we find the so-called federal analogy inapposite to a consideration of the constitutional validity of state legislative apportionment schemes, we necessarily hold that the Equal Protection Clause requires both houses of a state legislature to be apportioned on a population basis. The right of a citizen to equal representation and to have his vote weighted equally with those of all other citizens in the election of members of one house of a bicameral state legislature would amount to little if States could effectively submerge the equal-population principle in the apportionment of seats in the other house. . . .

By holding that as a federal constitutional requisite both houses of a state legislature must be apportioned on a population basis, we mean that the Equal Protection Clause requires that a State make an honest and good faith effort to construct districts, in both houses of its legislature, as nearly of equal population as is practicable. We realize that it is a practical impossibility to arrange legislative districts so that each one has an identical number of residents, or citizens, or voters. Mathematical exactness or precision is hardly a workable constitutional requirement.

In *Wesberry v. Sanders*, the Court stated that congressional representation must be based on population as nearly as is practicable. In implementing the basic constitutional principle of representative government as enunciated by the Court in Wesberry—equality of population among districts—some distinctions may well be made between congressional and state legislative representation. Since, almost invariably, there is a significantly larger number of seats in state legislative bodies to be distributed within a State than congressional seats, it may be feasible to use political subdivision lines to a greater extent in establishing state legislative districts than in congressional districting while still affording adequate representation to all parts of the State. To do so would be constitutionally valid, so long as the resulting apportionment was one based substantially on population and the equal-population principle was not diluted in any significant way. . . .

So long as the divergences from a strict population standard are based on legitimate considerations incident to the effectuation of a rational state policy, some deviations from the equal-population principle are constitutionally permissible with respect to the apportionment of seats in either or both of the two houses of a bicameral state legislature. But neither history alone, nor economic or other sorts of group interests, are permissible factors in attempting to justify disparities from population-based representation. Citizens, not history or economic interests, cast votes. Considerations of area alone provide an insufficient justification for deviations from the equal-population principle. Again, people, not land or trees or pastures, vote. Modern developments and improvements in transportation and communications make rather hollow, in the mid-1960's, most claims that deviations from population-based representation can validly be based solely on geographical considerations. Arguments for allowing such deviations in order to insure effective representation for sparsely settled areas and to prevent legislative districts from becoming so large that the availability of access of citizens to their representatives is impaired are today, for the most part, unconvincing.

A consideration that appears to be of more substance in justifying some deviations from population-based representation in state legislatures is that of insuring some voice to political subdivisions, as political subdivisions. Several factors make more than insubstantial claims that a State can rationally consider according political subdivisions some independent representation in at least one body of the state legislature, as long as the basic standard of equality of population among districts is maintained. Local governmental entities are frequently charged with various responsibilities incident to the operation of state government. In many States much of the legislature's activity involves the enactment of so-called local legislation, directed only to the concerns of particular political subdivisions. And a State may legitimately desire to construct districts along political subdivision lines to deter the possibilities of gerrymandering. However, permitting deviations from population-based representation does not mean that each local governmental unit or political subdivision can be given separate representation, regardless of population. Carried too far, a scheme of giving at least one seat in one house to each political subdivision (for example, to each county) could easily result, in many States, in a total subversion of the equal-population principle in that legislative body. This would be especially true in a State where the number of counties is large and many of them are sparsely populated, and the number of seats in the legislative body being apportioned does not significantly exceed the number of counties. Such a result, we conclude, would be constitutionally impermissible. And careful judicial scrutiny must of course be given, in evaluating state apportionment schemes, to the character as well as the degree of deviations from a strict population basis. But if, even as a result of a clearly rational state policy of according some legislative representation to political subdivisions, population is submerged as the controlling consideration in the apportionment of seats in the particular legislative body, then the right of all of the State's citizens to cast an effective and adequately weighted vote would be unconstitutionally impaired. . . .

Affirmed and remanded.

Justice CLARK concurring.

In my judgment, today's decisions are refuted by the language of the Amendment which they construe and by the inference fairly to be drawn from subsequently enacted Amendments. They are unequivocally refuted by history and by consistent theory and practice from the time of the adoption of the Fourteenth Amendment until today.

The Court's elaboration of its new "constitutional" doctrine indicates how far—and how unwisely—it has strayed from the appropriate bounds of its authority. The consequence of today's decision is that in all but the handful of States which may already satisfy the new requirements the local District Court or, it may be, the state courts, are given blanket authority and the constitutional duty to supervise apportionment of the State Legislatures. It is difficult to imagine a more intolerable and inappropriate interference by the judiciary with the independent legislatures of the States. . . .

Although the Court—necessarily, as I believe—provides only generalities in elaboration of its main thesis, its opinion nevertheless fully demonstrates how far removed these problems are from fields of judicial competence. Recognizing that "indiscriminate districting" is an invitation to "partisan gerrymandering," the Court nevertheless excludes virtually every basis for the formation of electoral districts other than "indiscriminate districting." In one or another of today's opinions, the Court declares it unconstitutional for a State to give effective consideration to any of the following in establishing legislative districts:

(1) history;

(2) "economic or other sorts of group interests";

(3) area;

(4) geographical considerations;

(5) a desire "to insure effective representation for sparsely settled areas";

(6) "availability of access of citizens to their representatives";

(7) theories of bicameralism (except those approved by the Court);

(8) occupation;

(9) "an attempt to balance urban and rural power."

(10) the preference of a majority of voters in the State.

So far as presently appears, the *only* factor which a State may consider, apart from numbers, is political subdivisions. But even "a clearly rational state policy" recognizing this factor is unconstitutional if "population is submerged as the controlling consideration. . . ."

I know of no principle of logic or practical or theoretical politics, still less any constitutional principle, which establishes all or any of these exclusions. Certain it is that the Court's opinion does not establish them. So far as the Court says anything at all on this score, it says only that "legislators represent people, not trees or acres"; that "citizens, not history or economic interests, cast votes," that "people, not land or trees or pastures, vote". All this may be conceded. But it is surely equally obvious, and, in the context of elections, more meaningful to note that people are not ciphers and that legislators can represent their electors only by speaking for their interests—economic, social, political— many of which do reflect the place where the electors live. The Court does not establish, or indeed even attempt to make a case for the proposition that conflicting interests within a State can only be adjusted by disregarding them when voters are grouped for purposes of representation. . . .

These decisions also cut deeply into the fabric of our federalism. What must follow from them may eventually appear to be the product of state legislatures. Nevertheless, no thinking person can fail to recognize that the aftermath of these cases, however desirable it may be thought in itself, will have been achieved at the cost of a radical alteration in the relationship between the States and the Federal Government, more particularly the Federal Judiciary. Only one who has an overbearing impatience with the federal system and its political processes will believe that that cost was not too high or was inevitable.

Finally, these decisions give support to a current mistaken view of the Constitution and the constitutional function of this Court. This view, in a nutshell, is that every major social ill in this country can find its cure in some constitutional "principle," and that this Court should "take the lead" in promoting reform when other branches of government fail to act. The Constitution is not a panacea for every blot upon the public welfare, nor should this Court, ordained as a judicial body, be thought of as a general haven for reform movements. The Constitution is an instrument of government, fundamental to which is the premise that in a diffusion of governmental authority lies the greatest promise that this Nation will realize liberty for all its citizens. This Court, limited in function in accordance with that premise, does not serve its high purpose when it exceeds its authority, even to satisfy justified impatience with the slow workings of the political process. For when, in the name of constitutional interpretation, the Court *adds* something to the Constitution that was deliberately excluded from it, the Court in reality substitutes its view of what should be so for the amending process. . . .

Davis v. Bandemer
478 U.S. 109, 106 S.Ct. 2797 (1986)

Following the 1980 federal census, an Indiana legislative conference committee began setting new boundaries for legislative districts. As in the past, all members on the committee were Republicans, the majority party. Furthermore, a Republican computer
firm assisted in drawing the district maps. Democrats served as
advisers but had no committee vote or access to the computer-
generated data and the committee's deliberations.

The conference committee unveiled its plan for redistricting
two days before the legislative session was to adjourn. The plan
established fifty senate districts and seventy-seven house districts,
including sixteen multimember districts and several noncontigu-
ous districts. Both houses adopted the plan, voting along party
lines. On January 12, 1982, Irwin Bandemer and other Indiana
Democrats sued to enjoin Susan Davis and other members of
the Indiana State Election Board from using the plan.

A three-judge district court struck down the plan after determining that although Democratic candidates for the House received 51.9 percent of the statewide vote, only forty-three Democrats were elected to the 100 available seats. The court also found
that in the state senate, where 25 seats were at stake, the Democrats won 13 seats despite having won 53.1 percent of the statewide vote. Conceding that the districts met the requirements
of one person, one vote, the court found "no conceivable justification" for the shapes of some of the districts and rejected various
justifications offered by the drafters of the plan. That court's
ruling was then appealed by Davis to the Supreme Court, which
granted review.

Justice WHITE announces the judgment of the Court and
delivers the opinion of the Court as to Part II and an opinion
in which Justice BRENNAN, Justice MARSHALL, and Justice
BLACKMUN join as to Parts I, III, and IV.

II

The outlines of the political question doctrine were described
and to a large extent defined in *Baker v. Carr* [369 U.S. 1962)]. . . .

In *Baker* . . . the Court concluded that none of the identifying
characteristics of a political question were present:

"The question here is the consistency of state action with the
Federal Constitution. We have no question decided, or to be
decided, by a political branch of government coequal with this

Court. Nor do we risk embarrassment of our government abroad, or grave disturbance at home if we take issue with Tennessee as to the constitutionality of her action here challenged. Nor need the appellants, in order to succeed in this action, ask the Court to enter upon policy determinations for which judicially manageable standards are lacking. Judicial standards under the Equal Protection Clause are well developed and familiar, and it has been open to courts since the enactment of the Fourteenth Amendment to determine, if on the particular facts they must, that a discrimination reflects *no* policy, but simply arbitrary and capricious action.". . .

This analysis applies equally to the question now before us. Disposition of this question does not involve us in a matter more properly decided by a coequal branch of our Government. There is no risk of foreign or domestic disturbance, and in light of our cases since *Baker* we are not persuaded that there are no judicially discernible and manageable standards by which political gerrymander cases are to be decided.

It is true that the type of claim that was presented in *Baker v. Carr* was subsequently resolved in this Court by the formulation of the "one person, one vote" rule. See, *e.g., Reynolds v. Sims.* The mere fact, however, that we may not now similarly perceive a likely arithmetic presumption in the instant context does not compel a conclusion that the claims presented here are non-justiciable. The one person, one vote principle had not yet been developed when *Baker* was decided. At that time, the Court did not rely on the potential for such a rule in finding justiciability. Instead, as the language quoted above clearly indicates, the Court contemplated simply that legislative line-drawing in the districting context would be susceptible of adjudication under the applicable constitutional criteria.

Furthermore, in formulating the one-person, one-vote formula, the Court characterized the question posed by election districts of disparate size as an issue of fair representation. In such cases, it is not that anyone is deprived of a vote or that any person's vote is not counted. Rather, it is that one electoral district elects a single representative and another district of the same size elects two or more—the elector's vote in the former district having less weight in the sense that he may vote for and his district be represented by only one legislator, while his neighbor in the adjoining district votes for and is represented by two or more. . . .

The issue here is of course different from that adjudicated in *Reynolds.* It does not concern districts of unequal size. Not only does everyone have the right to vote and to have his vote counted, but each elector may vote for and be represented by the same number of lawmakers. Rather, the claim is that each political group in a State should have the same chance to elect representatives of its choice as any other political group. Nevertheless, the issue is one of representation, and we decline to hold that such claims are never justiciable.

Our racial gerrymander cases such as *White v. Regester* [412 U.S. 755 (1973) and *Whitcomb v. Chavis* [403 U.S. 124 (1927)] indicate as much. In those cases, there was no population variation among the districts, and no one was precluded from voting. The claim instead was that an identifiable racial or ethnic group had an insufficient chance to elect a representative of its choice and that district lines should be redrawn to remedy this alleged defect. In both cases, we adjudicated the merits of such claims, rejecting the claim in *Whitcomb* and sustaining it in *Regester*. . . .

These decisions support a conclusion that this case is justiciable. . . .

In fact, Justice O'CONNOR'S attempt to distinguish this political gerrymandering claim from the racial gerrymandering claims that we have consistently adjudicated demonstrates the futility of such an effort. Her conclusion that the claim in this case is not justiciable seems to rest on a dual concern that no judicially manageable standards exist and that adjudication of such claims requires an initial policy decision that the judiciary should not make. Yet she does not point out how the standards that we set forth here for adjudicating this political gerrymandering claim are less manageable than the standards that have been developed for racial gerrymandering claims. Nor does she demonstrate what initial policy decision—regarding, for example, the desirability of fair group representation—we have made here that we have not made in the race cases. She merely asserts that because race has historically been a suspect classification individual minority voters' rights are more immediately related to a racial minority group's voting strength. This, in combination with "the greater warrant the Equal Protection Clause gives the federal courts to intervene for protection against racial discrimination, suffice to render racial gerrymandering claims justiciable." (O'CONNOR, J., concurring in judgment).

Reliance on these assertions to determine justiciability would transform the narrow categories of "political questions" that *Baker v. Carr* carefully defined into an ad hoc litmus test of this Court's reactions to the desirability of and need for judicial application of constitutional or statutory standards to a given type of claim. Justice O'CONNOR'S own discussion seems to reflect such an approach: She concludes that because political gerrymandering may be a "self-limiting enterprise" there is no need for judicial intervention. She also expresses concern that our decision today will lead to "political instability and judicial malaise," because nothing will prevent members of other identifiable groups from bringing similar claims. To begin with, Justice O'CONNOR'S factual assumptions are by no means obviously correct: It is not clear that political gerrymandering *is* a self-limiting enterprise or that other groups will have any great incentive to bring gerrymandering claims, given the requirement of a showing of discriminatory intent. At a more fundamental level, however, Justice O'CONNOR'S analysis is flawed because it focuses on the perceived need for judicial review and on the potential practical problems with allowing such review. Validation of the consideration of such amorphous and wide-ranging factors in assessing justiciability would alter substantially the analysis the Court enunciated in *Baker v. Carr,* and we decline Justice O'CONNOR'S implicit invitation to rethink that approach.

III

Having determined that the political gerrymandering claim in this case is justiciable, we turn to the question whether the District Court erred in holding that appellees had alleged and proved a violation of the Equal Protection Clause. . . .

We also agree with the District Court that in order to succeed the Bandemer plaintiffs were required to prove both intentional discrimination against an identifiable political group and an actual discriminatory effect on that group. Further, we are confident that if the law challenged here had discriminatory effects on Democrats, this record would support a finding that the discrimination was intentional. Thus, we decline to overturn the District Court's finding of discriminatory intent as clearly erroneous.

Indeed, quite aside from the anecdotal evidence, the shape of the House and Senate Districts, and the alleged disregard for political boundaries, we think it most likely that whenever a legislature redistricts, those responsible for the legislation will know the likely political composition of the new districts and will have a prediction as to whether a particular district is a safe one for a Democratic or Republican candidate or is a competitive district that either candidate might win. . . .

We do not accept, however, the District Court's legal and factual bases for concluding that the 1981 Act visited a sufficiently adverse effect on the appellees' constitutionally protected rights to make out a violation of the Equal Protection Clause. The District Court held that because any apportionment scheme that purposely prevents proportional representation is unconstitutional, Democratic voters need only show that their proportionate voting influence has been adversely affected. Our cases, however, clearly foreclose any claim that the Constitution requires proportional representation or that legislatures in reapportioning must draw district lines to come as near as possible to allocating seats to the contending parties in proportion to what their anticipated statewide vote will be. . . .

To draw district lines to maximize the representation of each major party would require creating as many safe seats for each party as the demographic and predicted political characteristics of the State would permit. This in turn would leave the minority in each safe district without a representative of its choice. We upheld this "political fairness" approach in *Gaffney v. Cummings*, [412 U.S. 735 (1973)], despite its tendency to deny safe district minorities any realistic chance to elect their own representatives. . . .

In cases involving individual multi-member districts, we have required a substantially greater showing of adverse effects than a mere lack of proportional representation to support a finding of unconstitutional vote dilution. Only where there is evidence that excluded groups have "less opportunity to participate in the political processes and to elect candidates of their choice" have we refused to approve the use of multi-member districts. *Rogers v. Lodge*, 458 U.S., [418 U.S. 613 (1982)]. See also *United Jewish Organizations of Williamsburgh, Inc. v. Carey*. [430 U.S. 144 (1977)]. In these cases, we have also noted the lack of responsiveness by those elected to the concerns of the relevant groups. . . .

These holdings rest on a conviction that the mere fact that a particular apportionment scheme makes it more difficult for a particular group in a particular district to elect the representatives of its choice does not render that scheme constitutionally infirm. This conviction, in turn, stems from a perception that the power to influence the political process is not limited to winning elections. An individual or a group of individuals who votes for a losing candidate is usually deemed to be adequately represented by the winning candidate and to have as much opportunity to influence that candidate as other voters in the district. We cannot presume in such a situation, without actual proof to the contrary, that the candidate elected will entirely ignore the interests of those voters. This is true even in a safe district where the losing group loses election after election. Thus, a group's electoral power is not unconstitutionally diminished by the simple fact of an apportionment scheme that makes winning elections more difficult, and a failure of proportional representation alone does not constitute impermissible discrimination under the Equal Protection Clause.

As with individual districts, where unconstitutional vote dilution is alleged in the form of statewide political gerrymandering, the mere lack of proportional representation will not be sufficient to prove unconstitutional discrimination. Again, without specific supporting evidence, a court cannot presume in such a case that those who are elected will disregard the disproportionately underrepresented group. Rather, unconstitutional discrimination occurs only when the electoral system is arranged in a manner that will consistently degrade a voter's or a group of voters' influence on the political process as a whole.

Although this is a somewhat different formulation than we have previously used in describing unconstitutional vote dilution in an individual district, the focus of both of these inquiries is essentially the same. In both contexts, the question is whether a particular group has been unconstitutionally denied its chance to effectively influence the political process. In a challenge to an individual district, this inquiry focuses on the opportunity of members of the group to participate in party deliberations in the slating and nomination of candidates, their opportunity to register and vote, and hence their chance to directly influence the election returns and to secure the attention of the winning candidate. Statewide, however, the inquiry centers on the voters' direct or indirect influence on the elections of the state legislature as a whole. And, as in individual district cases, an equal protection violation may be found only where the electoral system substantially disadvantages certain voters in their opportunity to influence the political process effectively. In this context, such a finding of unconstitutionality must be supported by evidence of continued frustration of the will of a majority of the voters or effective denial to a minority of voters of a fair chance to influence the political process.

Based on these views, we would reject the District Court's apparent holding that *any* interference with an opportunity to elect a representative of one's choice would be sufficient to allege or make out an equal protection violation, unless justified by some acceptable state interest that the State would be required to demonstrate. In addition to being contrary to the above-described conception of an unconstitutional political gerrymander, such a low threshold for legal action would invite attack on all or almost all reapportionment statutes. District-based elections hardly ever produce a perfect fit between votes and representation. The one-person, one-vote imperative often mandates departure from this result as does the no-retrogression rule required by § 5 of the Voting Rights Act. Inviting attack on minor departures from some supposed norm would too much embroil the judiciary in second-guessing what has consistently been referred to as a political task for the legislature, a task that should not be monitored too closely unless the express or tacit goal is to effect its removal from legislative halls. We decline to take a major step toward that end, which would be so much at odds with our history and experience.

The view that a prima facie case of illegal discrimination in reapportionment requires a showing of more than a *de minimis* effect is not unprecedented. Reapportionment cases involving the one-person, one-vote principle such as *Gaffney v. Cummings* and *White v. Regester* provide support for such a requirement. In the present, considerably more complex context, it is also appropriate to require allegations and proof that the challenged legislative plan has had or will have effects that are sufficiently serious to require intervention by the federal courts in state reapportionment decisions.

The District Court's findings do not satisfy this threshold condition to stating and proving a cause of action. In reaching its conclusion, the District Court relied primarily on the results of the 1982 elections: Democratic candidates for the State House of Representatives had received 51.9% of the votes cast statewide and Republican candidates 48.1%; yet, out of the 100 seats to be filled, Republican candidates won 57 and Democrats 43. In the Senate, 53.1% of the votes were cast for Democratic candidates and 46.9% for Republicans; of the 25 Senate seats to be filled, Republicans won 12 and Democrats 13. The court also relied upon the use of multi-member districts in Marion and Allen counties, where Democrats or those inclined to vote Democratic in 1982 amounted to 46.6% of the population of those counties but Republicans won 86 percent—18 of 21—seats allocated to the districts in those counties. These disparities were enough to require a neutral justification by the State, which in the eyes of the District Court was not forthcoming.

Relying on a single election to prove unconstitutional discrimination is unsatisfactory. The District Court observed, and the parties do not disagree, that Indiana is a swing State. Voters sometimes prefer Democratic candidates, and sometimes Republican. The District Court did not find that because of the 1981 Act the Democrats could not in one of the next few elections secure a sufficient vote to take control of the assembly. Indeed, the District Court declined to hold that the 1982 election results were the predictable consequences of the 1981 Act and expressly refused to hold that those results were a reliable prediction of future ones. The District Court did not ask by what percentage the statewide Democratic vote would have had to increase to control either the House or the Senate. The appellants argue here, without a persuasive response from appellees, that had the Democratic candidates received an additional few percentage points of the votes cast statewide, they would have obtained a majority of the seats in both houses. Nor was there any finding that the 1981 reapportionment would consign the Democrats to a minority status in the Assembly throughout the 1980's or that the Democrats would have no hope of doing any better in the reapportionment that would occur after the 1990 census. Without findings of this nature, the District Court erred in concluding that the 1981 Act violated the Equal Protection Clause. . . .

This requirement of more than a showing of possibly transitory results is where we appear to depart from Justice POWELL. Stripped of its "factors" verbiage, Justice POWELL'S analysis turns on a determination that a lack of proportionate election results can support a finding of an equal protection violation, at least in some circumstances. Here, the only concrete effect on the Democrats in Indiana in terms of election results that the District Court had before it was one election in which the percentage of Democrats elected was lower than the percentage of total Democratic votes cast. In Justice POWELL's view, this disproportionality, when combined with clearly discriminatory intent on the part of the 1981 General Assembly and the manipulation of district lines in the apportionment process, is sufficient to conclude that fair representation has been denied.

The factors other than disproportionate election results, however, do not contribute to a finding that Democratic voters have been disadvantaged in fact. They support a finding that an intention to discriminate was present and that districts were drawn in accordance with that intention, but they do not show any actual disadvantage beyond that shown by the election results: It surely cannot be an actual disadvantage in terms of fair representation on a group level just to be placed in a district with a supermajority of other Democratic voters or a district that departs from preexisting political boundaries. Only when such placement affects election results and political power statewide has an actual disadvantage occurred.

Consequently, Justice POWELL'S view would allow a constitutional violation to be found where the only proven effect on a political party's electoral power was disproportionate results in one (or possibly two) elections. This view, however, contains no explanation of why a lack of proportionate election results should suffice in these political gerrymandering cases while it does not in the cases involving racial gerrymandering. In fact, Justice POWELL'S opinion is silent as to the relevance of the substantive standard developed in the multi-member district cases to these political gerrymandering cases.

In rejecting Justice POWELL'S approach, we do not mean to intimate that the factors he considers are entirely irrelevant. The election results obviously are relevant to a showing of the effects required to prove a political gerrymandering claim under our view. And the district configurations may be combined with vote projections to predict future election results, which are also relevant to the effects showing. The other factors, even if not relevant to the effects issue, might well be relevant to an equal protection claim. The equal protection argument would proceed along the following lines: If there were a discriminatory effect and a discriminatory intent, then the legislation would be examined for valid underpinnings. Thus, evidence of exclusive legislative process and deliberate drawing of district lines in accordance with accepted gerrymandering principles would be relevant to intent, and evidence of valid and invalid configuration would be relevant to whether the districting plan met legitimate state interests.

This course is consistent with our equal protection cases generally and is the course we follow here: We assumed that there was discriminatory intent, found that there was insufficient discriminatory effect to constitute an equal protection violation, and therefore did not reach the question of the state interests (legitimate or otherwise) served by the particular districts as they were created by the legislature. Consequently, the valid or invalid configuration of the districts was an issue we did not need to consider.

It seems inappropriate, however, to view these separate components of an equal protection analysis as "factors" to be considered together without regard for their separate functions or meaning. This undifferentiated consideration of the various factors confuses the import of each factor and disguises the essential conclusion of Justice POWELL'S opinion: that disproportionate election results alone are a sufficient effect to support a finding of a constitutional violation.

In sum, we decline to adopt the approach enunciated by Justice POWELL. In our view, that approach departs from our past cases and invites judicial interference in legislative districting whenever a political party suffers at the polls. We recognize that our own view may be difficult of application. Determining when an electoral system has been "arranged in a manner that will consistently degrade a voter's or a group of voters' influence on the political process as a whole" is of necessity a difficult inquiry. Nevertheless, we believe that it recognizes the delicacy of intruding on this most political of legislative functions and is at the same time consistent with our prior cases regarding individual multi-member districts, which have formulated a parallel standard.

IV

In sum, we hold that political gerrymandering cases are properly justiciable under the Equal Protection Clause. We also conclude, however, that a threshold showing of discriminatory vote dilution is required for a prima facie case of an equal protection violation. In this case, the findings made by the District Court of an adverse effect on the appellees do not surmount the threshold requirement. Consequently, the judgment of the District Court is

Reversed.

Justice O'CONNOR, with whom the CHIEF JUSTICE and Justice REHNQUIST join, concurring.

Today the Court holds that claims of political gerrymandering lodged by members of one of the political parties that make up our two-party system are justiciable under the Equal Protection Clause of the Fourteenth Amendment. Nothing in our precedents compels us to take this step, and there is every reason not to do so. I would hold that the partisan gerrymandering claims of major political parties raise a nonjusticiable political question that the judiciary should leave to the legislative branch as the Framers of the Constitution unquestionably intended. Accordingly, I would reverse the District Court's judgment on the grounds that appellees' claim is nonjusticiable.

There can be little doubt that the emergence of a strong and stable two-party system in this country has contributed enormously to sound and effective government. The preservation and health of our political institutions, state and federal, depends to no small extent on the continued vitality of our two-party system, which permits both stability and measured change. The opportunity to control the drawing of electoral boundaries through the legislative process of apportionment is a critical and traditional part of politics in the United States, and one that plays no small role in fostering active participation in the political parties at every level. Thus, the legislative business of apportionment is fundamentally a political affair, and challenges to the manner in which an apportionment has been carried out—by the very parties that are responsible for this process—present a political question in the truest sense of the term.

To turn these matters over to the federal judiciary is to inject the courts into the most heated partisan issues. It is predictable that the courts will respond by moving away from the nebulous standard a plurality of the Court fashions today and toward some form of rough proportional representation for all political groups. The consequences of this shift will be as immense as they are unfortunate. I do not believe, and the Court offers not a shred of evidence to suggest, that the Framers of the Constitution intended the judicial power to encompass the making of such fundamental choices about how this Nation is to be governed. Nor do I believe that the proportional representation towards which the Court's expansion of equal protection doctrine will lead is consistent with our history, our traditions, or our political institutions. . . .

[T]he Court fails to explain why a bipartisan gerrymander— which is what was approved in *Gaffney*—affects individuals any differently than a partisan gerrymander, which the Court makes vulnerable to constitutional challenge today. In *Gaffney*, Connecticut, as part of a bipartisan effort, had drawn up a plan intended to "provide a rough sort of proportional representation" for the two major political parties. The Court declined to invalidate this plan, which undertook "not to minimize or eliminate the political strength of any group or party, but to recognize it" and suggested that "judicial interest should be at its lowest ebb when a State purports fairly to allocate political power to the parties in accordance with their voting strength and, within quite tolerable limits, succeeds in doing so."

A bipartisan gerrymander employs the same technique, and has the same effect on individual voters, as does a partisan gerrymander. In each instance, groups of individuals are assigned to districts with an eye towards promoting the ends of a political party and its incumbent legislators. Some groups within each party will lose any chance to elect a representative who belongs to their party, because they have been assigned to a district in which the opposing party holds an overwhelming advantage. Independent voters may lose any chance to influence the outcome of elections in their district, if one party has a sufficiently strong majority. As the plurality acknowledges, the scheme upheld in *Gaffney* tended to "deny safe district minorities any realistic chance to elect their own representatives." If this bipartisan arrangement between two groups of self-interested legislators is constitutionally permissible, as I believe and as the Court held in *Gaffney*, then—in terms of the rights of individuals—it should be equally permissible for a legislative majority to employ the same means to pursue its own interests over the opposition of the other party.

The Court's determination to treat the claims of mainstream political parties as justiciable thus emerges as precisely the sort of "initial policy determination of a kind clearly for nonjudicial discretion" that *Baker v. Carr* recognized as characteristic of political questions. The Court has in effect decided that it is constitutionally acceptable for both parties to "waste" the votes of individuals through a bipartisan gerrymander, so long as the *parties* themselves are not deprived of their group voting strength to an extent that will exceed the plurality's threshold requirement. This choice confers greater rights on powerful political groups than on individuals; that cannot be the meaning of the Equal Protection Clause. . . .

Under the plurality's approach, where it is shown that under a challenged apportionment plan one party will consistently fail to gain control of the legislature even if it wins a majority of the votes, a court would be justified in finding the "threshold showing" met, at which point "the legislation would be examined for valid underpinnings." It may fairly be doubted that this last step is anything more than a formality, except perhaps in the case of bipartisan gerrymanders that have proved unexpectedly favorable to one party. Consequently, although the plurality criticizes Justice POWELL for effectively concluding "that disproportionate short-term election results alone are a sufficient effect to support a finding of a constitutional violation," the plurality itself arrives at the conclusion that foreseeable, disproportionate *long-term* election results suffice to prove a constitutional violation.

Thus, the plurality opinion ultimately rests on a political preference for proportionality—not an outright claim that proportional results are required, but a conviction that the greater the departure from proportionality, the more suspect an apportionment plan becomes. This preference for proportionality is in serious tension with essential features of state legislative elections. Districting itself represents a middle ground between winner-take-all statewide elections and proportional representation for political parties. If there is a constitutional preference for proportionality, the legitimacy of districting itself is called into question: the voting strength of less evenly distributed groups will invariably be diminished by districting as compared to at-large proportional systems for electing representatives. Moreover, one implication of the districting system is that voters cast votes for candidates in their districts, not for a statewide slate of legislative candidates put forward by the parties. Consequently, efforts to determine party voting strength presuppose a norm that does not exist—statewide elections for representatives along party lines.

The plurality's theory is also internally inconsistent. The plurality recognizes that, given a normal dispersion of party strength and winner-take-all district-based elections, it is likely that even a narrow statewide preference for one party will give that party a disproportionately large majority in the legislature. The plurality is prepared to tolerate this effect, because not to do so would spell the end of district-based elections, or require reverse gerrymandering to ensure greater proportionality for the minority party. But this means that the plurality would extend greater protection to a party that can command a majority of the statewide vote than to a party that cannot: the explanation, once again, is that the plurality has made a political judgment—in this instance, that district-based elections must be taken as a given. . . .

I would avoid the difficulties generated by the plurality's efforts to confine the effects of a generalized group right to equal representation by not recognizing such a right in the first instance. To allow district courts to strike down apportionment plans on the basis of their prognostications as to the outcome of future elections or future apportionments invites "findings" on matters as to which neither judges nor anyone else can have any confidence. Once it is conceded that "a group's electoral power is not unconstitutionally diminished by the simple fact of an apportionment scheme that makes winning elections more difficult," the virtual impossibility of reliably predicting how difficult it will be to win an election in 2, or 4, or 10 years should, in my view, weigh in favor of holding such challenges nonjusticiable. Racial gerrymandering should remain justiciable, for the harms it engenders run counter to the central thrust of the Fourteenth Amendment. But no such justification can be given for judicial intervention on behalf of mainstream political parties, and the risks such intervention poses to our political institutions are unacceptable. "Political affiliation is the keystone of the political trade. Race, ideally, is not." *United Jewish Organizations of Williamsburgh, Inc. v. Carey,* 430 U.S. 144 (1977) (BRENNAN, J., concurring).

Justice POWELL, with whom Justice STEVENS joins, concurring in Part II and dissenting.

I believe that the plurality's opinion is seriously flawed in several respects. First, apparently to avoid the forceful evidence that some district lines indisputably were designed to and did discriminate against Democrats, the plurality describes appellees' claim as alleging that "Democratic voters over the State as a whole, not Democratic voters in particular districts, have been subjected to unconstitutional discrimination." This characterization is not inconsistent with appellees' proof, and the District Court's finding, of statewide discriminatory effect resulting from "individual districting" that "exemplif[ies] this discrimination." If Democratic voters in a number of critical districts are the focus of unconstitutional discrimination, as the District Court found, the *effect* of that discrimination will be felt over the State as a whole.

The plurality also erroneously characterizes the harm members of the losing party suffer as a group when they are deprived, through deliberate and arbitrary distortion of district boundaries, of the opportunity to elect representatives of their choosing. It may be, as the plurality suggests, that representatives will not "entirely ignore the interests" of opposition voters. But it defies political reality to suppose that members of a losing party have as much political influence over state government as do members of the victorious party. Even the most conscientious state legislators do not disregard opportunities to reward persons or groups who were active supporters in their election campaigns. Similarly, no one doubts that partisan considerations play a major role in the passage of legislation and the appointment of state officers. Not surprisingly, therefore, the District Court expressly found that "[c]ontrol of the General Assembly is crucial" to members of the major political parties in Indiana. In light of those findings, I cannot accept the plurality's apparent conclusion that loss of this "crucial" position is constitutionally insignificant as long as the losers are not "entirely ignored" by the winners.

The plurality relies almost exclusively on the "one person, one vote" standard to reject appellees' convincing proof that the redistricting plan had a seriously discriminatory effect on their voting strength in particular districts. The plurality properly describes the claim in this case as a denial of fair and effective "representation" but it does not provide any explanation of how complying with "one person, one vote" deters or identifies a gerrymander that unconstitutionally discriminates against a cognizable group of voters. While that standard affords some protection to the voting rights of individuals, "it protects groups only indirectly at best," *Karcher v. Daggett*, [462 U.S. 725 (1983)] (STEVENS J., concurring), even when the group's identity is determined solely by reference to the fact that its members reside in a particular voting district. "One person, one vote" alone does not protect the voting rights of a group made up of persons affiliated with a particular political party who seek to achieve representation through their combined voting strength. Thus, the facts that the legislature permitted each Democratic voter to cast his or her one vote, erected no direct barriers to Democratic voters' exercise of the franchise, and drew districts of equal population, are irrelevant to a claim that district lines were drawn for the purpose and with the effect of substantially debasing the strength of votes cast by Democrats as a group.

The final and most basic flaw in the plurality's opinion is its failure to enunciate any standard that affords guidance to legislatures and courts. Legislators and judges are left to wonder whether compliance with "one person, one vote" completely insulates a partisan gerrymander from constitutional scrutiny, or whether a fairer but as yet undefined standard applies. The failure to articulate clear doctrine in this area places the plurality in the curious position of inviting further litigation even as it appears to signal the "constitutional green light" to would-be gerrymanderers. . . .

A court should look first to the legislative process by which the challenged plan was adopted. Here, the District Court found that the procedures used in redistricting Indiana were carefully designed to exclude Democrats from participating in the legislative process. In February 1981, both houses of the General Assembly passed reapportionment bills with no substantive content and referred them to the other chamber where conflicting amendments were made. The purpose of this process was to send "vehicle bills" to a Conference Committee whose task was to apportion representation. Four conferees and four advisors served on the Committee. The conferees, all Republicans, were responsible for designing the voting districts and were entitled to vote on the result of their own efforts. The advisors, Democrats, were excluded from the mapmaking process and were given no committee vote. . . .

The legislative process consisted of nothing more than the majority party's private application of computer technology to mapmaking. The Republican State Committee engaged the services of a computer firm to aid the conferees in their task. According to the Conference Committee chairman, the only data used in the computer program were precinct population, race of precinct citizens, precinct political complexion, and statewide party voting trends. Access to the mapmaking process was strictly limited. No member of the Democratic party and no member of the public was provided with any of the information used in or generated by the computer program. When questioned about the lack of minority party participation in the redistricting process, the chairman of the Conference Committee stated that the Democrats would "have the privilege to offer a minority map. But I will advise you in advance that it will not be accepted."

Republicans promised to hold public hearings on redistricting. No hearing was held during the mapmaking process, the only time during which voters' views could be expected to influence their legislators.

Two days before the end of the General Assembly's regular

session, during the first and only public hearing on reapportionment, the Conference Committee revealed for the first time the result of its mapmaking effort. This timing gave the Democrats but 40 hours in which to review the districting of more than 4,000 precincts. On the last day of the session, April 30, 1981, the Conference Committee report was introduced for a vote and was adopted by party line vote in both houses of the General Assembly. . . .

In addition to the foregoing findings that apply to both the House and Senate plans, the District Court also noted the substantial evidence that appellants were motivated solely by partisan considerations. There is no evidence that the public interest in a fair electoral process was given any consideration by appellants. Indeed, as noted above, the mapmakers' partisan goals were made explicitly clear by contemporaneous statements of Republican leaders who openly acknowledged that their goal was to disadvantage Democratic voters. . . .

In conclusion, I want to make clear the limits of the standard that I believe the Equal Protection Clause imposes on legislators engaged in redistricting. Traditionally, the determination of electoral districts within a State has been a matter left to the legislative branch of the state government. Apart from the doctrine of separation of powers and the federal system prescribed by the Constitution, federal judges are ill-equipped generally to review legislative decisions respecting redistricting. As the plurality opinion makes clear, however, our precedents hold that a colorable claim of discriminatory gerrymandering presents a justiciable controversy under the Equal Protection Clause. Federal courts in exercising their duty to adjudicate such claims should impose a heavy burden of proof on those who allege that a redistricting plan violates the Constitution. In light of *Baker v. Carr, Reynolds v. Sims,* and their progeny, including such comparatively recent decisions as *Gaffney v. Cummings,* this case presents a paradigm example of unconstitutional discrimination against the members of a political party that happened to be out of power. The well-grounded findings of the District Court to this effect have not been, and I believe cannot be, held clearly erroneous.

C. CAMPAIGNS AND ELECTIONS

Since the 1960s, the Supreme Court has increasingly assumed a supervisory role in overseeing the electoral process. This is only partially due to the reapportionment revolution and the Court's duty to ensure compliance with the Voting Rights Act. In addition, the Court has applied the Fourteenth Amendment equal protection clause to bar invidious forms of discrimination in the electoral process and interpreted the First Amendment guarantee for freedom of association to protect some aspects of political parties, campaigns, and elections.

Besides striking down poll taxes and literacy tests,[1] the Court has limited the power of states to control access to elections through residency requirements for voters. The Voting Rights Act of 1970 limited residency requirements to a thirty-day registration period for presidential elections. While the Court in *Dunn v. Blumstein*, 405 U.S. 330 (1972), indicated that that period of time appeared "ample" for state elections as well, fifty-day registration periods were subsequently upheld.[2] The Court also ruled that states may not bar military personnel, or others in a federal enclave, from voting in state elections.[3] States may deny convicted felons of the right to vote, but *O'Brien v. Kinner*, 414 U.S. 524 (1974), held that persons in jail awaiting trial must be provided with absentee ballots or an alternative means of voting.

Under the Fourteenth Amendment equal protection clause, the Court strictly scrutinizes electoral systems for discriminating against minorities and the poor by imposing special burdens on their running for office and voting. In *Newberry v. United States*, 256 U.S. 232 (1921), however, the Court took the view that primaries were "in no real sense part of the manner of holding [an] election." Consequently, some southern states sought to discriminate against blacks at this stage of the electoral process.

But *Nixon v. Herndon*, 273 U.S. 536 (1927), invalidated Texas's prohibition on blacks voting in primary elections as a denial of the Fourteenth Amendment equal protection clause. *Nixon v. Condon*, 286 U.S. 73 (1932), then, struck down another attempt by Texas to disenfranchise blacks by authorizing political parties to specify the qualifications of voters in primary elections. Following that ruling and in the absence of state legislation, the Texas Democratic party voted to deny the participation of blacks in its primary elections. The Court upheld this practice in *Grovey v. Townsend*, 295 U.S. 45 (1935), on *Newberry*'s theory that primaries are exempt from the constitutional restraints that bind official state action. Six years later, though, the Hughes Court ruled that primaries are "an integral part" of the political process, when sustaining the convictions of several Louisiana officials who tampered with primary ballots in a congressional election. Finally, in *Smith v. Allwright*, 321 U.S. 649 (1944), *Newberry* and *Grovey* were abandoned. There the Court held that primaries and political parties, which are in various ways subject to state regulation, are integral to the operation of state and local governments and as such constitute "an agent of the state" subject to the proscriptions of the Fourteenth and Fifteenth Amendments. *Terry v. Adams*, 345 U.S. 461 (1953), extended this ruling to unofficial primaries in Texas run by the Jaybird party, a Democratic county organization that excluded blacks. In the Court's words, the "Jaybird primary has become an integral part, indeed the only effective part, of the elective process that determines who shall rule and govern in the county." As such, the Jaybird party primary was invalid under the Fifteenth Amendment.

The Court has also stood against other attempts by states to keep third-party candidates off the ballot. *Williams v. Rhodes,* 393 U.S. 23 (1968), for example, invalidated an Ohio law requiring third parties (although not established political parties) to file petitions with more than 400,000 signatures of registered voters to have a candidate's name placed on the ballot. In several other cases the Court struck down similar state requirements for the submission of petitions and early filing deadlines as a precondition for a candidate being placed on the ballot.[4] *Communist Party of Indiana v. Whitcomb,* 414 U.S. 441 (1974), overturned a law requiring loyalty oaths of candidates of minority parties as an infringement of the First Amendment right of free speech and association (see Vol. 2, Ch. 5). A series of other rulings invalidated state laws imposing exorbitant filing fees for getting on the ballot.[5]

THE DEVELOPMENT OF LAW

Other Rulings on Campaigns and Elections

Case	Vote	Ruling
Williams v. Rhodes, 393 U.S. 23 (1968)	8:1	Struck down an Ohio law precluding the Socialist Labor party from being placed on the ballot.
Gordon v. Lance, 403 U.S. 1 (1971)	9:0	Upheld West Virginia law allowing 60 percent of voters in a referendum to approve tax increases.
Jenneas v. Fortson, 403 U.S. 431 (1971)	9:0	Upheld Georgia's requirement that any political organization other than those receiving 20 percent or more in last gubernatorial election must file a nominating petition with not less than 15 percent of eligible voters signing it within 180 days of filing deadline for candidates in primaries.

Case	Vote	Ruling
Roudebush v. Hartke, 405 U.S. 15 (1972)	5:2	Constitutional provision that each house will judge elections does not prohibit Indiana from conducting a recount of 1970 election ballots.
Rosario v. Rockefeller, 410 U.S. 752 (1973)	5:4	State does not violate First Amendment right of freedom of association by requiring that voters in primary elections enroll in the party at least thirty days before the last general election.
Kusper v. Pontikes, 414 U.S. 51 (1973)	7:2	States impermissibly abridge First Amendment by forbidding citizens to vote in the primary of one party if they have voted in that of another party in the preceding twenty-three months.
Storer v. Brown and Frommhagen v. Brown, 415 U.S. 724 (1974)	6:3	States may require that independent candidates disassociate themselves from an established party at least one year before the primary election of the year in which they plan to run for office.
American Party of Texas v. White, U.S. 767 (1974)	8:1	A state's compelling interest in protecting the integrity of the nominating process may require new and minority parties to secure a certain number of voter signatures on petitions, excluding those who voted in a party primary in the same year, to place candidate's name on the ballot.
Anderson v. United States, 417 U.S. 211 (1974)	7:2	State and local officials may be prosecuted under federal law for tampering with ballots in local election because voters have an unimpeded right to vote in congressional and sen-

Case	Vote	Ruling
		atorial primaries held at the same time.
Hill v. Stone, 421 U.S. 709 (1974)	5:3	Struck down section of Texas election code limiting the right to vote in city bond issues to property owners; held that only age, residence and citizenship distinctions may be made.
Richardson v. Ramirez, 418 U.S. 24 (1974)	6:3	Held that state may disenfranchise convicted felons who have completed their prison sentences.
Town of Lockport v. Citizens for Community Action, 430 U.S. 259 (1977)	9:0	Upheld a New York law requiring that new county charters go into effect only approved by concurrent majorities of voters living within cities in the county and voters living outside of the cities.
Hunter v. Underwood, 471 U.S. 222 (1985)	9:0	Held that Alabama constitution disenfranchising people convicted of crimes of moral turpitude violated the Fourteenth Amendment's equal protection clause.
Tashjian v. Republican Party of Connecticut, 107 S.Ct. 544 (1986)	5:4	Connecticut's primary statute, allowing unaffiliated voters to participate in elections, violated political party's First Amendment right of association.
Eu v. San Francisco County Democratic Central Committee, 109 S.Ct. 1013 (1989)	8:0	Struck down an ordinance forbidding primary endorsement of political parties and restrictions on the organization and composition of official governing bodies of state political parties.

The Court has dealt as well with a number of controversies arising from political parties' organization, conventions, and campaigns. After a couple of contradictory rulings on the seating of delegates at party conventions, *Cousins v. Wigoda,* 419 U.S. 477 (1975), held that the national party convention has the power to decide the credentials of convention delegates and how delegates from state political parties will be seated at a national convention. There the Court affirmed political parties' freedom to determine the composition of its convention as protected by First Amendment right of association. *Democratic Party v. LaFollette,* 450 U.S. 107 (1981), further ruled that states could not mandate that state delegates to a national political convention cast their votes for the winner of the state's presidential primary. However, *Marchioro v. Chaney,* 442 U.S. 191 (1979), allowed that states could demand that state political parties have at least two persons from each county in the state.

Controversies over campaign finance have increasingly come to the Court since Congress passed the Federal Election Campaign Act of 1971. That law limits the amount of money individuals and groups may contribute to candidates and political parties, imposes spending limits and reporting requirements, and created an eight-member commission to oversee the law's implementation. The Court was badly split in *Buckley v. Valeo* (1976) (see page 720), when upholding limitations on political contributions but overturning restrictions on campaign spending. In *Brown v. Socialist Workers 74 Campaign Committee,* 459 U.S. 87 (1982), requirements for the disclosure of lists of contributors as applied to the Socialist Workers party were deemed to violate the First Amendment right of freedom of association (see Vol. 2, Ch. 5). Subsequently, *Federal Election Commission v. National Conservative Political Action Committee (NCPAC)* (1985) (see page 735) invalidated the law's restrictions on campaign expenditures by political action committees. In both *Buckley* and *NCPAC,* the Court balanced the First Amendment right of association against Congress's interest in eliminating corruption in campaigns and electoral politics.

Other issues affecting campaigns and elections have been dealt with under the First Amendment's safeguards for freedom of speech and press. In *CBS, Inc. v. Federal Communications Commission,* 453 U.S. 367 (1981), for instance, affirmed an FCC order that CBS, Inc. sell airtime for advertisements for candidates' running in the 1980 presidential election.[6]

Under the First Amendment commercial speech doctrine (see Vol. 2, Ch. 5), the Court has struck down state laws restricting the political expenditures and advertising of corporations. *First National Bank of Boston v. Bellotti,* 435 U.S. 765 (1978), overturned

THE DEVELOPMENT OF LAW
Other Rulings on Campaign Finance

Case	Vote	Ruling
Citizens Against Rent Control/ Coalition for Fair Housing v. Berkeley, California, 454 U.S. 290 (1981)	8:1	Declared unconstitutional a California ordinance imposing a $250 ceiling on each contributor to organizations supporting or opposing issues placed on referendums, as an infringement of the First Amendment right of association.
Brown v. Hartlage, 456 U.S. 45 (1982)	9:0	Overturned as an infringement of the First Amendment the application of Kentucky's Corrupt Practices Act as applied to a candidate for the office of county commissioner who pledged to lower commissioners' salaries if elected.
Federal Election Commission v. Massachusetts Citizens for Life, Inc., 479 U.S. 238 (1986)	5:4	Held a section of the Federal Election Campaign Act, banning corporate expenditures for endorsing particular candidates for public office, to violate the First Amendment freedom of expression.
Meyer v. Grant, 108 S.Ct. 1886 (1988)	9:0	Held unconstitutional a ban on paying circulators of petitions for signatures of registered voters supporting the placement of a referendum on the ballot.
Austin v. Michigan Chamber of Commerce, 110 S.Ct. 1392 (1990)	6:3	Held that States may ban corporations, even nonprofit corporations, from making independent financial expenditures in support or opposition of political candidates.

Massachusetts's law forbidding corporations from publicizing its views on an income-tax referendum and making campaign contributions. *Consolidated Edison Company of New York v. Public Service Commission of the State of New York,* 447 U.S. 530 (1980), and *Pacific Gas & Electric v. Public Utilities Commission of California,* 475 U.S. 1 (1986), held that states may not force a public utilities companies to include in their newsletters and billing statements the materials of third parties addressing controversial issues of public policy with which the companies disagree.

Finally, in a highly controversial ruling in *Elrod v. Burns* 427 U.S. 347 (1976), the justices, voting five to three, with Justice Stevens not participating, struck down the practice of patronage dismissals as an unconstitutional restriction on city employees' First Amendment freedoms. The controversy and struggle within the Court over the permissibility of political patronage continued in *Branti v. Finkel,* 445 U.S. 507 (1980). There the justices, six to three, with Stewart, Powell, and Rehnquist dissenting, ruled that the First Amendment protects district attorneys from being discharged for expressing their political views. But after Justice Stewart retired in 1981 and was replaced by Justice O'Connor, the Court held five to four (with Brennan, Blackmun, Marshall, and Stevens now dissenting), in *Connick v. Myers,* 461 U.S. 138 (1983), that the firing of state attorneys general for political reasons does not violate the First Amendment. But in *Rutan v. Republican Party of Illinois* (1990) (see page 740), Justice Brennan pulled together a bare majority for sharply limiting political patronage in the hiring, promoting, and transferring of most public employees.

NOTES

1. In addition, the Court struck down so-called grandfather clauses, which exempted persons from literacy tests if their ancestors were entitled to vote at some specified time. See *Guinn v. United States,* 238 U.S. 347 (1915); and *Lane v. Wilson,* 307 U.S. 268 (1939).

2. *Marston v. Lewis,* 410 U.S. 679 (1973); and *Burns v. Fortson,* 410 U.S. 686 (1973).

3. See *Carrington v. Rash,* 380 U.S. 89 (1965); and *Evans v. Cornman,* 398 U.S. 419 (1970).

4. See *Moore v. Ogilvie,* 394 U.S. 814 (1969), overturning Illinois's requirement that candidates to get on the ballot, file petitions signed by 25,000 registered voters, and the Court's earlier ruling in *MacDougall v. Green,* 335 U.S. 281 (1948). *Anderson v. Celebrezze,* 460 U.S. 780 (1983), struck down Ohio's early filing deadline for candidates not belonging to a major political party.

5. See *Bullock v. Carter*, 405 U.S. 134 (1972), striking down a Texas law requiring a filing fee of up to $8,900; and *Lubin v. Parish*, 415 U.S. 709 (1974), finding that California's filing fees (of $701.50) for candidates was not unreasonable but, because there were no alternative ways of getting on the ballot, the requirement was discriminatory. See also *Illinois State Board of Elections v. Socialist Workers Party*, 440 U.S. 173 (1979).

6. But see also *CBS v. Democratic National Committee*, 412 U.S. 94 (1973), approving of CBS's policy of refusing paid editorial advertisements (see Vol. 2, Ch. 5).

SELECTED BIBLIOGRAPHY

Claude, Richard. *The Supreme Court and the Electoral Process.* Baltimore, MD: Johns Hopkins University Press, 1970.

Gillette, William. *The Right to Vote: Politics and the Passage of the Fifteenth Amendment.* Baltimore, MD: Johns Hopkins University Press, 1965.

Buckley v. Valeo

424 U.S. 1, 96 S.Ct. 612 (1976)

In 1971, Congress enacted the Federal Election Campaign Act to safeguard against corruption in federal elections. The act, as amended in 1974, among other things, provides that

1. Political contributions by individuals and groups are limited to $1,000 each and by political committees to $5,000 for any single candidate in an election, with an annual limit of $25,000 on any individual contributor.
2. Independent spending by an individual or group "relative to a clearly identified candidate" was limited to $1,000 per election.
3. Personal contributions by both the candidate and relatives toward a campaign were limited according to the office being sought.
4. Overall expenditures by a candidate in an election were limited according to the office being sought.
5. Political committees were required to keep records on contributions and expenditures, publicly disclose the identity of contributors and the reason for expenditures above a certain amount.

6. An eight-member commission was created to oversee enforcement of the law.
7. The Internal Revenue Code was amended to provide for public financing of primary and general elections with major party candidates receiving "full" funding and "minor" or "new" party candidates receiving a reduced proportion of funding on a dollar-matching basis.

Republican Senator James Buckley and former Democratic senator and presidential candidate Eugene McCarthy, among others, sued Francis Valeo, the secretary of the Senate, the clerk of the House of Representatives, and others. Buckley contended that various provisions of the law were unconstitutional and in violation of the appointments clause of Article II, Section 2, Clause 2, and the First and Fifth Amendments. The Court of Appeals for the District of Columbia Circuit, however, rejected most of Buckley's arguments, and he appealed to the Supreme Court.

PER CURIAM

These appeals present constitutional challenges to the key provisions of the Federal Election Campaign Act of 1971 as amended in 1974. . . .

The Act, summarized in broad terms, contains the following provisions: (a) individual political contributions are limited to $1,000 to any single candidate per election, with an overall annual limitation of $25,000 by any contributor; independent expenditures by individuals and groups "relative to a clearly identified candidate" are limited to $1,000 a year; campaign spending by candidates for various federal offices and spending for national conventions by political parties are subject to prescribed limits; (b) contributions and expenditures above certain threshold levels must be reported and publicly disclosed; (c) a system for public funding of Presidential campaign activities is established by Subtitle H of the Internal Revenue Code; and (d) a Federal Election Commission is established to administer and enforce the Act. . . .

In this Court, appellants argue that the Court of Appeals failed to give this legislation the critical scrutiny demanded under accepted First Amendment and equal protection principles. In appellants' view, limiting the use of money for political purposes constitutes a restriction on communication violative of the First Amendment, since virtually all meaningful political communications in the modern setting involve the expenditure of money. Further, they argue that the reporting and disclosure provisions of the Act unconstitutionally impinge on their right to freedom of association. Appellants also view the federal subsidy provisions of Subtitle H as violative of the General Welfare Clause, and as inconsistent with the First and Fifth Amendments. Finally, appellants renew their attack on the Commission's composition and powers. . . .

I. CONTRIBUTION AND EXPENDITURE LIMITATIONS

The intricate statutory scheme adopted by Congress to regulate federal election campaigns includes restrictions on political contributions and expenditures that apply broadly to all phases of and all participants in the election process. The major contribution and expenditure limitations in the Act prohibit individuals from contributing more than $25,000 in a single year or more than $1,000 to any single candidate for an election campaign and from spending more than $1,000 a year "relative to a clearly identified candidate." Other provisions restrict a candidate's use of personal and family resources in his campaign and limit the overall amount that can be spent by a candidate in campaigning for federal office. . . .

A. *General Principles* The Act's contribution and expenditure limitations operate in an area of the most fundamental First Amendment activities. Discussion of public issues and debate on the qualifications of candidates are integral to the operation of the system of government established by our Constitution. . . .

In upholding the constitutional validity of the Act's contribution and expenditure provisions on the ground that those provisions should be viewed as regulating conduct not speech, the Court of Appeals relied upon *United States v. O'Brien,* 391 U.S. 367 (1968) The *O'Brien* case involved a defendant's claim that the First Amendment prohibited his prosecution for burning his draft card because his act was "symbolic speech" engaged in as a " 'demonstration against the war and against the draft.' ". . .

We cannot share the view that the present Act's contribution and expenditure limitations are comparable to the restrictions on conduct upheld in *O'Brien.* The expenditure of money simply cannot be equated with such conduct as destruction of a draft card. Some forms of communication made possible by the giving and spending of money involve speech alone, some involve conduct primarily, and some involve a combination of the two. Yet this Court has never suggested that the dependence of a communication on the expenditure of money operates itself to introduce a nonspeech element or to reduce the exacting scrutiny required by the First Amendment. . . .

Even if the categorization of the expenditure of money as conduct were accepted, the limitations challenged here would not meet the *O'Brien* test because the governmental interests advanced in support of the Act involve "suppressing communication." The interests served by the Act include restricting the voices of people and interest groups who have money to spend and reducing the overall scope of federal election campaigns. Although the Act

does not focus on the ideas expressed by persons or groups subjected to its regulations, it is aimed in part at equalizing the relative
ability of all voters to affect electoral outcomes by placing a ceiling
on expenditures for political expression by citizens and groups.
Unlike *O'Brien*, where the Selective Service System's administrative
interest in the preservation of draft cards was wholly unrelated
to their use as a means of communication, it is beyond dispute
that the interest in regulating the alleged "conduct" of giving
or spending money "arises in some measure because the communication allegedly integral to the conduct is itself thought to be
harmful.". . .

Nor can the Act's contribution and expenditure limitations be
sustained, as some of the parties suggest, by reference to the
constitutional principles reflected in such decisions as *Cox v. Louisiana* [379 U.S. 536 (1965)], *Adderley v. Florida*, 385 U.S. 39, (1966),
and *Kovacs v. Cooper*, 336 U.S. 77 (1949). Those cases stand for
the proposition that the government may adopt reasonable time,
place, and manner regulations, which do not discriminate between
speakers or ideas, in order to further an important governmental
interest unrelated to the restriction of communication. In contrast
to *O'Brien*, where the method of expression was held to be subject
to prohibition, *Cox, Adderley,* and *Kovacs* involved place or manner
restrictions on legitimate modes of expression—picketing, parad-
ing, demonstrating, and using a soundtruck. The critical difference between this case and those time, place and manner cases
is that the present Act's contribution and expenditure limitations
impose direct quantity restrictions on political communication
and association by persons, groups, candidates and political parties
in addition to any reasonable time, place, and manner regulations
otherwise imposed.

A restriction on the amount of money a person or group can
spend on political communication during a campaign necessarily
reduces the quantity of expression by restricting the number of
issues discussed, the depth of their exploration, and the size of
the audience reached. This is because virtually every means of
communicating ideas in today's mass society requires the expenditure of money. The distribution of the humblest handbill or leaflet
entails printing, paper, and circulation costs. Speeches and rallies
generally necessitate hiring a hall and publicizing the event. The
electorate's increasing dependence on television, radio, and other
mass media for news and information has made these expensive
modes of communication indispensible instruments of effective
political speech.

The expenditure limitations contained in the Act represent
substantial rather than merely theoretical restraints on the quantity and diversity of political speech. The $1,000 ceiling on spend-
ing "relative to a clearly identified candidate," 18 U.S.C.
§ 608(e)(1), would appear to exclude all citizens and groups except

candidates, political parties and the institutional press from any significant use of the most effective modes of communication. Although the Act's limitations on expenditures by campaign organizations and political parties provide substantially greater room for discussion and debate, they would have required restrictions in the scope of a number of past congressional and Presidential campaigns and would operate to constrain campaigning by candidates who raise sums in excess of the spending ceiling.

By contrast with a limitation upon expenditures for political expression, a limitation upon the amount that any one person or group may contribute to a candidate or political committee entails only a marginal restriction upon the contributor's ability to engage in free communication. A contribution serves as a general expression of support for the candidate and his views, but does not communicate the underlying basis for the support. The quantity of communication by the contributor does not increase perceptibly with the size of his contribution, since the expression rests solely on the undifferentiated, symbolic act of contributing. At most, the size of the contribution provides a very rough index of the intensity of the contributor's support for the candidate. A limitation on the amount of money a person may give to a candidate or campaign organization thus involves little direct restraint on his political communication, for it permits the symbolic expression of support evidenced by a contribution but does not in any way infringe the contributor's freedom to discuss candidates and issues. While contributions may result in political expression if spent by a candidate or an association to present views to the voters, the transformation of contributions into political debate involves speech by someone other than the contributor.

Given the important role of contributions in financing political campaigns, contribution restrictions could have a severe impact on political dialogue if the limitations prevented candidates and political committees from amassing the resources necessary for effective advocacy. There is no indication, however, that the contribution limitations imposed by the Act would have any dramatic adverse effect on the funding of campaigns and political associations. The overall effect of the Act's contribution ceilings is merely to require candidates and political committees to raise funds from a greater number of persons and to compel people who would otherwise contribute amounts greater than the statutory limits to expend such funds on direct political expression, rather than to reduce the total amount of money potentially available to promote political expression. . . .

In sum, although the Act's contribution and expenditure limitations both implicate fundamental First Amendment interests, its expenditure ceilings impose significantly more severe restrictions on protected freedoms of political expression and association than do its limitations on financial contributions.

Section 608(b) provides, with certain limited exceptions, that "no person shall make contributions to any candidate with respect to any election for Federal office which, in the aggregate, exceeds $1,000.". . .

[T]he primary First Amendment problem raised by the Act's contribution limitations is their restriction of one aspect of the contributor's freedom of political association. The Court's decisions involving associational freedoms establish that the right of association is a "basic constitutional freedom" that is "closely allied to freedom of speech and a right which, like free speech, lies at the foundation of a free society." In view of the fundamental nature of the right to associate, governmental "action which may have the effect of curtailing the freedom to associate is subject to the closest scrutiny." *NAACP v. Alabama* [377 U.S. 288 (1968)]. Yet, it is clear that "[n]either the right to associate nor the right to participate in political activities is absolute." Even a " 'significant interference' with protected rights of political association" may be sustained if the State demonstrates a sufficiently important interest and employs means closely drawn to avoid unnecessary abridgment of associational freedoms. . . .

It is unnecessary to look beyond the Act's primary purpose— to limit the actuality and appearance of corruption resulting from large individual financial contributions—in order to find a constitutionally sufficient justification for the $1,000 contribution limitation. Under a system of private financing of elections, a candidate lacking immense personal or family wealth must depend on financial contributions from others to provide the resources necessary to conduct a successful campaign. The increasing importance of the communications media and sophisticated mass mailing and polling operations to effective campaigning make the raising of large sums of money an ever more essential ingredient of an effective candidacy. To the extent that large contributions are given to secure political *quid pro quos* from current and potential office holders, the integrity of our system of representative democracy is undermined. . . .

Of almost equal concern as the danger of actual *quid pro quo* arrangements is the impact of the appearance of corruption stemming from public awareness of the opportunities for abuse inherent in a regime of large individual financial contributions. . . . Congress could legitimately conclude that the avoidance of the appearance of improper influence "is also critical . . . if confidence in the system of representative Government is not to be eroded. . . ."

Appellants contend that the contribution limitations must be invalidated because bribery laws and narrowly drawn disclosure requirements constituted a less restrictive means of dealing with "proven and suspected *quid pro quo* arrangements." But laws making criminal the giving and taking of bribes deal with only the most blatant and specific attempts of those with money to influenced governmental action. And while disclosure requirements serve the many salutary purposes discussed elsewhere in the opinion, Congress was surely entitled to conclude that disclosure was only a partial measure, and that contribution ceilings were a necessary legislative concomitant to deal with the reality or appearance of corruption inherent in a system permitting unlimited financial contributions, even when the identities of the contributors and the amounts of their contributions are fully disclosed. . . .

We find that, under the rigorous standard of review established by our prior decisions, the weighty interests served by restricting the size of financial contributions to political candidates are sufficient to justify the limited effect upon First Amendment freedoms caused by the $1,000 contribution ceiling. . . .

Apart from these First Amendment concerns, appellants argue that the contribution limitations work such an invidious discrimination between incumbents and challengers that the statutory provisions must be declared unconstitutional on their face. . . .

[But t]here is no . . . evidence to support the claim that the contribution limitations in themselves discriminate against major-party challengers to incumbents. Challengers can and often do defeat incumbents in federal elections. Major-party challengers in federal elections are usually men and women who are well known and influential in their community or State. Often such challengers are themselves incumbents in important local, state, or federal offices. Statistics in the record indicate that major-party challengers as well as incumbents are capable of raising large sums for campaigning. Indeed, a small but nonetheless significant number of challengers have in recent elections outspent their incumbent rivals. And, to the extent that incumbents generally are more likely than challengers to attract very large contributions, the Act's $1,000 ceiling has the practical effect of benefiting challengers as a class. Contrary to the broad generalization drawn by the appellants, the practical impact of the contribution ceilings in any given election will clearly depend upon the amounts in excess of the ceilings that, for various reasons, the candidates in that election would otherwise have received and the utility of these additional amounts to the candidates. . . .

In view of these considerations, we conclude that the impact of the Act's $1,000 contribution limitation on major-party challengers and on minor-party candidates does not render the provision unconstitutional on its face. . . .

Section 608(b)(2) of Title 18 permits certain committees, designated as "political committees," to contribute up to $5,000 to any candidate with respect to any election for federal office. In order to qualify for the higher contribution ceiling, a group must have been registered with the Commission as a political committee under 2 U.S.C. § 433 for not less than 6 months, have received contributions from more than 50 persons and, except for state political party organizations, have contributed to five or more candidates for federal office. Appellants argue that these qualifications unconstitutionally discriminate against ad hoc organizations in favor of established interest groups and impermissibly burden free association. The argument is without merit. Rather than undermining freedom of association, the basic provision enhances the opportunity of bona fide groups to participate in the election process, and the registration, contribution, and candidate conditions serve the permissible purpose of preventing individuals from evading the applicable contribution limitations by labeling themselves committees. . . .

C. Expenditure Limitations The Act's expenditure ceilings impose, direct and substantial restraints on the quantity of political speech. The most drastic of the limitations restricts individuals and groups, including political parties that fail to place a candidate on the ballot, to an expenditure of $1,000 "relative to a clearly identified candidate during a calendar year." § 608(e)(1). Other expenditure ceilings limit spending by candidates, § 608(a), their campaigns, § 608(c), and political parties in connection with election campaigns, § 608(f). It is clear that a primary effect of these expenditure limitations is to restrict the quantity of campaign speech by individuals, groups, and candidates. The restrictions, while neutral as to the ideas expressed, limit political expression "at the core of our electoral process and of the First Amendment freedoms.". . .

1. The $1,000 Limitation on Expenditures "Relative to a Clearly Identified Candidate"

Section 608(e)(1) provides that "[n]o person may make any expenditure . . . relative to a clearly identified candidate during a calendar year which, when added to all other expenditures made by such person during the year advocating the election or defeat of such candidate, exceeds $1,000." The plain effect of § 608(e)(1) is to prohibit all individuals, who are neither candidates nor owners of institutional press facilities, and all groups, except political parties and campaign organizations, from voicing their views "relative to a clearly identified candidate" through means that entail aggregate expenditures of more than $1,000 during a calendar year. The provision, for example, would make it a federal criminal offense for a person or association to place a single one-quarter page advertisement "relative to a clearly identified candidate" in a major metropolitan newspaper. . . .

We turn then to the basic First Amendment question—whether § 608(c)(1), even as thus narrowly a explicitly construed, impermissibly burdens the constitutional right of free expression. . . .

The discussion, *supra,* explains why the Act's expenditure limitations impose far greater restraints on the freedom of speech and association than do its contribution limitations. . . .

We find that the governments interest in preventing corruption and the appearance of corruption is inadequate to justify § 608(e)(1)'s ceiling on independent expenditures. First . . . § 608(e)(1) prevents only some large expenditures. So long as persons and groups eschew expenditures that in express terms advocate the election or defeat of a clearly identified candidates they are free to spend as much as they want to promote the candidate and their views. The exacting interpretation of the statutory language necessary to avoid unconsitutional vagueness that undermines the limitation's effectiveness as a loophole-closing provision by facilitating circumvention by those seeking to exert improper influence upon a candidate or office-holder. . . .

Second . . . parties defending § 608(e)(1) contend that it is necessary to prevent would-be contributors from avoiding the contribution limitations by the simple expedient of paying directly for media advertisements or for other portions of the candidate's campaign activities. They argue that expenditures controlled by or coordinated with the candidate and his campaign might well have virtually the same value to the candidate as a contribution and would pose similar dangers of abuse. Yet such controlled or coordinated expenditures are treated as contributions rather than expenditures under the Act. Section 608(b)'s contribution ceilings rather than § 608(e)(1)'s independent expenditure limitation prevent attempts to circumvent the Act through prearranged or coordinated expenditures amounting to disguised contributions. By contrast § 608(e)(1) limits expenditures for express advocacy of candidates made totally independently of the candidate and his campaign. Unlike contributions, such independent expenditures may well provide little assistance to the candidate's campaign and indeed may prove counter-productive. The absence of prearrangement and coordination of an expenditure with the candidate or his agent not only undermines the value of the expenditure to the candidate, but also alleviates the danger that expenditures will be given as a *quid pro quo* for improper commitments from the candidate. Rather than preventing circumvention of the contribution limitations, § 608(e)(1) severely restricts all independent advocacy despite its substantially diminished potential for abuse. . . .

It is argued, however, that the ancillary governmental interest in equalizing the relative ability of individuals and groups to influence the outcome of elections serves to justify the limitation on express advocacy of the election or defeat of candidates imposed by § 608(e)(1)'s expenditure ceiling. But the concept that government may restrict the speech of some elements of our society in order to enhance the relative voice of others is wholly foreign to the First Amendment, which was designed "to secure 'the widest possible dissemination of information from diverse and antagonistic sources,' " and " 'to assure unfettered interchange of ideas for the bringing about of political and social changes desired by the people.' " *New York Times Co. v. Sullivan* [376 U.S. 254 (1964)]. The First Amendment's protection against governmental abridgement of free expression cannot properly be made to depend on a person's financial ability to engage in public discussion. . . .

For the reasons stated, we conclude that § 608(e)(1)'s independent expenditure limitation is unconstitutional under the First Amendment.

2. Limitation on Expenditures by Candidates from Personal or Family Resources

The Act also sets limits on expenditures by a candidate "from his personal funds, or the personal funds of his immediate family, in connection with his campaigns during any calendar year.". . .

The ceiling on personal expenditures by candidates on their own behalf, like the limitations on independent expenditures contained in § 608(e)(1), imposes a substantial restraint on the ability of persons to engage in protected First Amendment expression. The candidate, no less than any other person, has a First Amendment right to engage in the discussion of public issues and vigorously and tirelessly to advocate his own election and the election of other candidates. . . . Section 608(a)'s ceiling on personal expenditures by a candidate in furtherance of his own candidacy thus clearly and directly interferes with constitutionally protected freedoms. . . .

3. Limitations on Campaign Expenditures

Section 608(c) of the Act places limitations on overall campaign expenditures by candidates seeking nomination for election and election to federal office. Presidential candidates may spend $10,000,000 in seeking nomination for office and an additional $20,000,000 in the general election campaign. § 608(c)(1)(A), (B). The ceiling on Senate campaigns is pegged to the size of the voting age population of the State with minimum dollar amounts applicable to campaigns in States with small populations. . . .

No governmental interest that has been suggested is sufficient to justify the restriction on the quantity of political expression imposed by § 608(c)'s campaign expenditure limitations. The major evil associated with rapidly increasing campaign expenditures is the danger of candidate dependence on large contributions. The interest in alleviating the corrupting influence of large contributions is served by the Act's contribution limitations and disclosure provisions rather than by § 608(c)'s campaign expenditure ceilings. The Court of Appeal's assertion that the expenditure restrictions are necessary to reduce the incentive to circumvent direct contribution limits is not persuasive. There is no indication that the substantial criminal penalties for violating the contribution ceilings combined with the political repercussion of such violations will be insufficient to police the contribution provisions. Extensive reporting, auditing, and disclosure requirements applicable to both contributions and expenditures by political campaigns are designed to facilitate the detection of illegal contributions. . . .

The interest in equalizing the financial resources of candidates competing for federal office is no more convincing a justification for restricting the scope of federal election campaigns. Given the limitation on the size of outside contributions, the financial resources available to a candidate's campaign, like the number of volunteers recruited, will normally vary with the size and intensity of the candidate's support. . . .

In any event, the mere growth in the cost of federal election campaigns in and itself provides no basis for government restrictions on the quantity of campaign spending and the resulting limitation on the scope of federal campaigns. The First Amendment denies government the power to determine that spending to promote one's political views is wasteful, excessive, or unwise. In the free society ordained by our Constitution it is not to government but the people—individually as citizens and candidates and collectively as associations and political committees—who must retain control over the quantity and range of debate on public issues in a political campaign.

For these reasons we hold that § 608(c) is constitutionally invalid.

In sum, the provisions of the A that impose a $1,000 limitation on contributions to a single candidate, § 608(b)(2) a $5,000 limitation on contributions by political committee to a single candidate § 608(b)(2), and a $25,000 limitation of total contributions by an individual during any calendar year, § 608(b)(3), and constitutionally valid. These limitations along with the disclosure provisions, constitute the Act's primary weapons against the reality or appearance of improper influence stemming from the dependence of candidates on large campaign contributions. The contribution ceilings thus serve the basic governmental interest in safeguarding the integrity of the electoral process without directly impinging upon the rights of individual citizens and candidates to engage in political debate and discussion. By contrast, the First Amendment requires the invalidation of the Act's independent of expenditure ceiling, § 608(e)(1), its limitation on a candidate's expenditures from his own personal funds, § 608(a), and ceilings on overall campaign expenditures, § 608(c). These provisions place substantial and direct restrictions on the ability of candidates, citizens, and associations to engage in protected political expression, restrictions that the First Amendment cannot tolerate. . . .

CONCLUSION

In summary, we sustain the individual contribution limits, the disclosure and reporting provisions, and the public financing scheme. We conclude, however, that the limitations on campaign expenditures, on independent expentirues by individuals and groups, and on expenditures by a candidate from his personal funds are constitutionally infirm.

Justice STEVENS did not participate in the consideration or decision of these cases.

Chief Justice BURGER concurring in part and dissenting in part.

I dissent from those parts of the Court's holding sustaining the Act's provisions (a) for disclosure of small contributions, (b) for limitations on contributions, and (c) for public financing of Presidential campaigns. In my view, the Act's disclosure scheme is impermissibly broad and violative of the First Amendment as it relates to reporting $10 and $100 contributions. . . .

For me contributions and expenditures are two sides of the same First Amendment coin. . . .

The Court's attempt to distinguish the communication inherent in political *contributions* from the speech aspects of political *expenditures* simply will not wash. We do little but engage in word games unless we recognize that people—candidates and contributors—spend money on political activity because they wish to communicate ideas, and their constitutional interest in doing so is precisely the same whether they or someone else utter the words.

The Court attempts to make the Act seem less restrictive by casting the problem as one that goes to freedom of association rather than freedom of speech. I have long thought freedom of association and freedom of expression were two peas from the same pod. . . .

At any rate, the contribution limits are a far more severe restriction on First Amendment activity than the sort of "chilling" legislation for which the Court has shown such extraordinary concern in the past. . . . If such restraints can be justified at all, they must be justified by the very strongest of state interests.

Justice WHITE concurring in part and dissenting in part.

I dissent . . . from the Court's view that the expenditure limitations of 18 U.S.C. § 608(c) and (e) violate the First Amendment. . . .

The congressional judgment, which I would also accept, was that . . . steps must be taken to counter the corrosive effects of money in federal election campaigns. One of these steps is § 608(e), which, aside from those funds that are given to the candidate or spent at his request or with his approval or cooperation limits what a contributor may independently spend in support or denigration of one running for federal office. Congress was plainly of the view that these expenditures also have corruptive potential; but the Court strikes down the provision, strangely enough claiming more insight as to what may improperly influence candidates than is possessed by the majority of Congress that passed this Bill and the President who signed it. . . .

I would take the word of those who know—that limiting independent expenditures is essential to prevent transparent and widespread evasion of the contribution limits. . . .

The Court also rejects Congress' judgment manifested in § 608(c) that the federal interest in limiting total campaign expenditures by individual candidates justifies the incidental effect on their opportunity for effective political speech. I disagree both with the Court's assessment of the impact on speech and with its narrow view of the values the limitations will serve. . . .

[T]he argument that money is speech and that limiting the flow of money to the speaker violates the First Amendment proves entirely too much. Compulsory bargaining and the right to strike, both provided for or protected by federal law, inevitably have increased the labor costs of those who publish newspapers, which are in turn an important factor in the recent disappearance of many daily papers. . . . But it has not been suggested, nor could it be successfully, that these laws, and many others, are invalid because they siphon off or prevent the accumulation of large sums that would otherwise be available for communicative activities.

In any event, as it should be unnecessary to point out, money is not always equivalent to or used for speech, even in the context of political campaigns. . . .

The record before us no more supports the conclusion that the communicative efforts of congressional and Presidential candidates will be crippled by the expenditure limitations than it supports the contrary. The judgment of Congress was that reasonably effective campaigns could be conducted within the limits established by the Act and that the communicative efforts of these campaigns would not seriously suffer. In this posture of the case, there is no sound basis for invalidating the expenditure limitations, so long as the purposes they serve are legitimate and sufficiently substantial, which in my view they are.

In the first place, expenditure ceilings reinforce the contribution limits and help eradicate the hazard of corruption. . . .

Without limits on total expenditures, campaign costs will inevitably and endlessly escalate. Pressure to raise funds will constantly build and with it the temptation to resort in "emergencies" to those sources of large sums, who, history shows, are sufficiently confident of not being caught to risk flouting contribution limits. Congress would save the candidate from this predicament by establishing a reasonable ceiling on all candidates. This is a major consideration in favor of the limitation. It should be added that many successful candidates will also be saved from large, over-hanging campaign debts which must be paid off with money raised while holding public office and at a time when they are already preparing or thinking about the next campaign. The danger to the public interest in such situations is self-evident.

Besides backing up the contribution provisions, which are aimed at preventing untoward influence on candidates that are elected, expenditure limits have their own potential for preventing the corruption of federal elections themselves. . . . One would be blind to history to deny that unlimited money tempts people to spend it on *whatever* money can buy to influence an election. On the assumption that financing illegal activities is low on the campaign organization's priority list, the expenditure limits could play a substantial role in preventing unethical practices. There just wouldn't be enough of "that kind of money" to go around. . . .

It is also important to restore and maintain public confidence in federal elections. It is critical to obviate or dispel the impression that federal elections are purely and simply a function of money, that federal offices are bought and sold or that political races are reserved for those who have the facility—and the stomach—for doing whatever it takes to bring together those interests, groups and individuals that can raise or contribute large fortunes in order to prevail at the polls.

The ceiling on candidate expenditures represents the considered judgment of Congress that elections are to be decided among candidates none of whom have overpowering advantage by reason of a huge campaign war chest. At least so long as the ceiling placed upon the candidates is not plainly too low, elections are not to turn on the difference in the amounts of money that candidates have to spend. This seems an acceptable purpose and the means chosen a common sense way to achieve it. . . .

[T]he wealthy candidate's immediate access to a substantial personal fortune may give him an initial advantage that his less wealthy opponent can never overcome. And even if the advantage can be overcome, the perception that personal wealth wins elections may not only discourage potential candidates without significant personal wealth from entering the political arena, but also undermine public confidence in the integrity of the electoral process.

The concern that candidacy for public office not become, or

appear to become, the exclusive province of the wealthy assumes heightened significance when one considers the impact of § 608(b), which the Court today upholds. That provision prohibits contributions from individuals and groups to candidates in excess of $1,000, and contributions from political committees in excess of $5,000. While the limitations on contributions are neutral in the sense that all candidates are foreclosed from accepting large contributions, there can be no question that large contributions generally mean more to the candidate without a substantial personal fortune to spend on his campaign. Large contributions are the less wealthy candidate's only hope of countering the wealthy candidate's immediate access to substantial sums of money. With that option removed, the less wealthy candidate is without the means to match the large initial expenditures of money of which the wealthy candidate is capable. In short, the limitations on contributions put a premium on a candidate's personal wealth.

In view of § 608(b)'s limitations on contributions, then, § 608(2) emerges not simply as a device to reduce the natural advantage of the wealthy candidate, but as a provision providing some symmetry to a regulatory scheme that otherwise enhances the natural advantage of the wealthy. . . .

I therefore respectfully dissent from the Court's invalidation of § 608(a).

Justice BLACKMUN concurring in part and dissenting in part.

I am not persuaded that the Court makes, or indeed is able to make, a principled constitutional distinction between the contribution limitations, on the one hand, and the expenditure limitations on the other, that are involved here. I therefore do not join [all] of the Court's opinion . . . [and] dissent [in part].

Justice REHNQUIST concurred in part and dissented in part.

Justice MARSHALL concurring in part and dissenting in part.

The Court invalidates § 608(a) as violative of the candidate's First Amendment rights. "[T]he First Amendment," the Court explains, "simply cannot tolerate § 608(a)'s restriction upon the freedom of a candidate to speak without legislative limit on behalf of his own candidacy.". . . I disagree.

Federal Election Commission v. National Conservative Political Action Committee (NCPAC)

and

Democratic Party of the United States v. National Conservative Political Action Committee (NCPAC)
470 U.S. 480, 105 S.Ct. 1459 (1985)

The Court's ruling in *Buckley v. Valeo* did not put an end to the controversies surrounding the Federal Election Campaign Act. Under the act, if presidential candidates accept public financing for their election campaigns, independent political action committees (PACs) may not spend more than $1,000 to support the election of their presidential candidate. In 1975, the National Conservative Political Action Committee (NCPAC) was formed to help promote the election of political conservatives. When the Federal Election Commission, which monitors campaign contributions for federal elections, and the Democratic Party of the United States charged that NCPAC was violating the provisions of the Federal Election Campaign Act, NCPAC countered that the law violated its First Amendment rights of freedom of speech and association. A federal district court agreed that the restrictions on PAC's campaign contributions ran afoul of the First Amendment. The Federal Election Commission and the Democratic Party of the United States appealed that decision to the Supreme Court. Justice William H. Rehnquist further discusses the pertinent facts in his opinion announcing the decision of the Court.

Justice REHNQUIST delivers the opinion of the Court.

The Presidential Election Campaign Fund Act (Fund Act), 26 U.S.C. § 9001 *et seq.*, offers the Presidential candidates of major political parties the option of receiving public financing for their general election campaigns. If a Presidential candidate elects public financing, § 9012(f) makes it a criminal offense for independent "political committees," such as appellees National Conservative Political Action Committee (NCPAC) and Fund For A Conservative Majority (FCM), to expend more than $1,000 to further that candidate's election. A three-judge District Court for the Eastern District of Pennsylvania, in companion lawsuits brought respectively by the Federal Election Commission (FEC) and by the Democratic Party of the United States and the Democratic National Committee (DNC), held § 9012(f) unconstitutional on its face because it violated the First Amendment to the United States Constitution. . . . [We now affirm the lower court's ruling.]

NCPAC is a nonprofit, nonmembership corporation formed under the District of Columbia Nonprofit Corporation Act in August 1975 and registered with the FEC as a political committee. Its primary purpose is to attempt to influence directly or indirectly the election or defeat of candidates for federal, state, and local offices by making contributions and by making its own expenditures. It is governed by a three-member board of directors which is elected annually by the existing board. The board's chairman and the other two members make all decisions concerning which candidates to support or oppose, the strategy and methods to employ, and the amounts of money to spend. Its contributors have no role in these decisions. It raises money by general and specific direct mail solicitations. It does not maintain separate accounts for the receipts from its general and specific solicitations, nor is it required by law to do so.

FCM is incorporated under the laws of Virginia and is registered with the FEC as a multicandidate political committee. In all material respects it is identical to NCPAC.

Both NCPAC and FCM are self-described ideological organizations with a conservative political philosophy. They solicited funds in support of President Reagan's 1980 campaign, and they spent money on such means as radio and television advertisements to encourage voters to elect him President. On the record before us, these expenditures were "independent" in that they were not made at the request of or in coordination with the official Reagan election campaign committee or any of its agents. . . .

In this case we consider provisions of the Fund Act that make it a criminal offense for political committees such as NCPAC and FCM to make independent expenditures in support of a candidate who has elected to accept public financing. . . .

There is no question that NCPAC and FCM are political committees and that President Reagan was a qualified candidate, and it seems plain enough that the PACs' expenditures fall within the term "qualified campaign expense." The PACs have argued in this Court, though apparently not below, that § 9012(f) was not intended to cover truly independent expenditures such as theirs, but only coordinated expenditures. But "expenditures in cooperation, consultation, or concert, with, or at the request or suggestion of, a candidate, his authorized political committees, or their agents," are considered "contributions" under the FECA and as such are already subject to FECA's $1,000 and $5,000 limitations in §§ 441a(a)(1), (2). Also, as noted above, one of the requirements for public funding is the candidate's agreement not to accept such contributions. Under the PACs' construction, § 9012(f) would be wholly superfluous, and we find no support for that construction in the legislative history. We conclude that the PACs' independent expenditures at issue in this case are squarely prohibited by § 9012(f), and we proceed to consider whether that prohibition violates the First Amendment.

There can be no doubt that the expenditures at issue in this case produce speech at the core of the First Amendment. . . .

The PACs in this case, of course, are not lone pamphleteers or street corner orators in the Tom Paine mold; they spend substantial amounts of money in order to communicate their political ideas through sophisticated media advertisements. . . . But for purposes of presenting political views in connection with a nationwide Presidential election, allowing the presentation of views while forbidding the expenditure of more than $1,000 to present them is much like allowing a speaker in a public hall to express his views while denying him the use of an amplifying system. . . .

We also reject the notion that the PACs' form of organization or method of solicitation diminishes their entitlement to First Amendment protection. The First Amendment freedom of association is squarely implicated in this case. NCPAC and FCM are mechanisms by which large numbers of individuals of modest means can join together in organizations which serve to "amplif[y] the voice of their adherents." *Buckley v. Valeo.* . . .

Having concluded that the PAC expenditures are entitled to full First Amendment protection, we now look to see if there is a sufficiently strong governmental interest served by § 9012(f)'s restriction on them and whether the section is narrowly tailored to the evil that may legitimately be regulated. . . .

Corruption is a subversion of the political process. Elected officials are influenced to act contrary to their obligations of office by the prospect of financial gain to themselves or infusions of money into their campaigns. The hallmark of corruption is the financial *quid pro quo:* dollars for political favors. But here the conduct proscribed is not contributions to the candidate, but independent expenditures in support of the candidate. The amounts given to the PACs are overwhelmingly small contributions, well under the $1,000 limit on contributions upheld in *Buckley;* and the contributions are by definition not coordinated with the campaign of the candidate. The Court concluded in *Buckley* that there was a fundamental constitutional difference between money spent to advertise one's views independently of the candidate's campaign and money contributed to the candidate to be spent on his campaign. . . .

We think the same conclusion must follow here. It is contended that, because the PACs may by the breadth of their organizations spend larger amounts than the individuals in *Buckley*, the potential for corruption is greater. But precisely what the "corruption" may consist of we are never told with assurance. The fact that candidates and elected officials may alter or reaffirm their own positions on issues in response to political messages paid for by the PACs can hardly be called corruption, for one of the essential features of democracy is the presentation to the electorate of varying points of view.

Justice STEVENS concurred in part and dissented in part on a question of standing to sue.

Justice WHITE, with whom Justice BRENNAN and Justice MARSHALL join, dissenting.

Section 9012(f) of the Internal Revenue Code limits to $1000 the annual independent expenditures a PAC can make to further the election of a candidate receiving public funds. Because these expenditures "produce speech at the core of the First Amendment," *ante,* at 1467, the majority concludes that they can only be regulated in order to avoid real or apparent corruption. Perceiving no such danger, since the money does not go directly to political candidates or their committees, it strikes down § 9012(f).

My disagreements with this analysis, which continues this Court's dismemberment of congressional efforts to regulate campaign financing, are many. First, I continue to believe that *Buckley v. Valeo* (1976), was wrongly decided. Congressional regulation of the amassing and spending of money in political campaigns without doubt involves First Amendment concerns, but restrictions such as the one at issue here are supported by governmental interests—including, but not limited to, the need to avoid real or apparent corruption—sufficiently compelling to withstand scrutiny. Second, even were *Buckley* correct, I consider today's holding a mistaken application of that precedent. The provision challenged here more closely resembles the contribution limitations that were upheld in *Buckley*, and later cases, than the limitations on uncoordinated individual expenditures that were struck down. Finally, even if *Buckley* requires that in general PACs be allowed to make independent expenditures, I do not think that that proposition applies to § 9012(f). As part of an integrated and complex system of public funding for presidential campaigns, § 9012(f) is supported by governmental interests that were absent in *Buckley*, which was premised on a system of private campaign financing. . . .

In short, as I said in *Buckley*, I cannot accept the cynic's "money talks" as a proposition of constitutional law. Today's holding also rests on a second aspect of the *Buckley* holding with which I disagree, *viz.*, its distinction between "independent" and "coordinated" expenditures. The Court was willing to accept that expenditures undertaken in consultation with a candidate or his committee should be viewed as contributions. But it rejected Congress' judgment that independent expenditures were matters of equal concern, concluding that they did not pose the danger of real or apparent corruption that supported limits on contributions. . . . The distinction is not tenable. "Independent" PAC expenditures function as contributions. Indeed, a significant portion of them no doubt would be direct contributions to campaigns had the FECA not limited such contributions to $5,000. . . .

The credulous acceptance of the formal distinction between coordinated and independent expenditures blinks political reality. That the PACs' expenditures are not formally "coordinated" is too slender a reed on which to distinguish them from actual contributions to the campaign. The candidate cannot help but know of the extensive efforts "independently" undertaken on his behalf. In this realm of possible tacit understandings and implied agreements, I see no reason not to accept the congressional judgment that so-called independent expenditures must be closely regulated.

The PACs do not operate in an anonymous vacuum. There are significant contacts between an organization like NCPAC and candidates for, and holders of, public office. In addition, personnel may move between the staffs of candidates or officeholders and those of PACs. This is not to say that there has in the past been any improper coordination or political favors. We need not evaluate the accuracy of reports of such activities, or of the perception that large-scale independent PAC expenditures mean "the return of the big spenders whose money talks and whose gifts are not forgotten." It is enough to note that there is ample support for the congressional determination that the corrosive effects of large campaign contributions—not least among these a public perception of business as usual—are not eliminated solely because the "contribution" takes the form of an "independent expenditure.". . .

[Furthermore, the] majority never explicitly identifies whose First Amendment interests it believes it is protecting. However, its concern for rights of association and the effective political speech of those of modest means indicates that it is concerned with the interests of the PACs' contributors. But the "contributors" are exactly that—contributors, rather than speakers. Every reason the majority gives for treating § 9012(f) as a restraint on speech relates to the effectiveness with which the donors can make their voices heard. In other words, what the majority purports to protect is the right of the contributors to make contributions.

But the contributors are not engaging in speech; at least, they are not engaging in speech to any greater extent than are those who contribute directly to political campaigns. *Buckley* explicitly distinguished between, on the one hand, using one's own money to express one's views, and, on the other, giving money to someone else in the expectation that that person will use the money to express views with which one is in agreement. This case falls within the latter category. . . .

By striking down one portion of an integrated and comprehensive statute, the Court has once again transformed a coherent regulatory scheme into a nonsensical, loophole-ridden patchwork. As The CHIEF JUSTICE pointed out with regard to the similar outcome in *Buckley,* "[b]y dissecting the Act bit by bit, and casting off vital parts, the Court fails to recognize that the whole of this Act is greater than the sum of its parts." Without § 9012(f), presidential candidates enjoy extensive public financing while those who would otherwise have worked for or contributed to a campaign had there been no such funding will pursue the same ends through "independent" expenditures. The result is that the old system remains essentially intact, but that much more money is being spent. In overzealous protection of attenuated First Amendment values, the Court has once again managed to assure us the worst of both worlds. I respectfully dissent.

Justice MARSHALL dissenting.

Although I joined the portion of the *Buckley per curiam* that distinguished contributions from independent expenditures for First Amendment purposes, I now believe that the distinction has no constitutional significance. . . .

I disagree that the limitations on contributions and expenditures have significantly different impacts on First Amendment freedoms. First, the underlying rights at issue—freedom of speech and freedom of association—are both core First Amendment rights. Second, in both cases the regulation is of the same form: It concerns the amount of money that can be spent for political activity. Thus, I do not see how one interest can be deemed more compelling than the other. . . .

Rutan v. Republican Party of Illinois
110 S.Ct. 2729 (1990)

In 1980, Illinois's Republican Governor James Thompson issued an executive order freezing all hiring of state employees and placing virtually all of the state's 62,000 civil service positions under the jurisdiction of his personnel office. Cynthia Rutan and several other public employees who had never supported the Republican party were subsequently denied promotions. Rutan contended that her promotion was denied simply for partisan reasons and that that violated her First Amendment rights to freedom of speech and association. In his opinion announcing the decision of the Court, Justice Brennan further discusses the facts in this case.

Justice BRENNAN delivers the opinion of the Court.

To the victor belong only those spoils that may be constitutionally obtained. *Elrod v. Burns,* 427 U. S. 347 (1976), and *Branti v. Finkel,* 445 U. S. 507 (1980), decided that the First Amendment forbids government officials to discharge or threaten to discharge public employees solely for not being supporters of the political party in power, unless party affiliation is an appropriate requirement for the position involved. Today we are asked to decide the constitutionality of several related political patronage practices—whether promotion, transfer, recall, and hiring decisions involving low-level public employees may be constitutionally based on party affiliation and support. We hold that they may not. . . .

In *Elrod,* we decided that a newly elected Democratic sheriff could not constitutionally engage in the patronage practice of replacing certain office staff with members of his own party "when the existing employees lack or fail to obtain requisite support from, or fail to affiliate with, that party.". . .

Four years later, in *Branti,* we decided that the First Amendment prohibited a newly appointed public defender, who was a Democrat, from discharging assistant public defenders because they did not have the support of the Democratic Party. . . .

Respondents urge us to view *Elrod* and *Branti* as inapplicable because the patronage dismissals at issue in those cases are different in kind from failure to promote, failure to transfer, and failure to recall after layoff. Respondents initially contend that the employee petitioners' First Amendment rights have not been infringed because they have no entitlement to promotion, transfer, or rehire. We rejected just such an argument in *Elrod.* . . .

Respondents next argue that the employment decisions at issue here do not violate the First Amendment because the decisions are not punitive, do not in any way adversely affect the terms of employment, and therefore do not chill the exercise of protected belief and association by public employees. This is not credible. Employees who find themselves in dead-end positions due to their political backgrounds *are* adversely affected. They will feel a significant obligation to support political positions held by their superiors, and to refrain from acting on the political views they actually hold, in order to progress up the career ladder. Employees denied transfers to workplaces reasonably close to their homes until they join and work for the Republican Party will feel a daily pressure from their long commutes to do so. And employees who have been laid off may well feel compelled to engage in whatever political activity is necessary to regain regular paychecks and positions corresponding to their skill and experience.

The same First Amendment concerns that underlay our decisions in *Elrod,* and *Branti,* are implicated here. Employees who do not compromise their beliefs stand to lose the considerable increases in pay and job satisfaction attendant to promotions, the hours and maintenance expenses that are consumed by long daily commutes, and even their jobs if they are not rehired after a "temporary" layoff. These are significant penalties and are imposed for the exercise of rights guaranteed by the First Amendment. Unless these patronage practices are narrowly tailored to further vital government interests, we must conclude that they impermissibly encroach on First Amendment freedoms. . . .

We hold that the rule of *Elrod* and *Branti* extends to promotion, transfer, recall, and hiring decisions based on party affiliation and support and that all of the petitioners and cross-respondents have stated claims upon which relief may be granted. We affirm the Seventh Circuit insofar as it remanded Rutan's, Taylor's, Standefer's, and O'Brien's claims. However, we reverse the Circuit Court's decision to uphold the dismissal of Moore's claim. All five claims are remanded for proceedings consistent with his opinion.

It is so ordered.

Justice STEVENS, concurred in a separate opinion.

Justice SCALIA, with whom the Chief Justice and Justice KENNEDY join, and with whom Justice O'CONNOR joins as to Parts II and III, dissenting.

Today the Court establishes the constitutional principle that party membership is not a permissible factor in the dispensation of government jobs, except those jobs for the performance of which party affiliation is an "appropriate requirement." It is hard to say precisely (or even generally) what that exception means, but if there is any category of jobs for whose performance party affiliation is not an appropriate requirement, it is the job of being a judge, where partisanship is not only unneeded but positively undesirable. It is, however, rare that a federal administration of one party will appoint a judge from another party. And it has always been rare. See *Marbury v. Madison,* 1 Cranch 137 (1803). Thus, the new principle that the Court today announces will be enforced by a corps of judges (the Members of this Court included) who overwhelmingly owe their office to its violation. Something must be wrong here, and I suggest it is the Court.

The merit principle for government employment is probably the most favored in modern America, having been widely adopted by civil-service legislation at both the state and federal levels. But there is another point of view, described in characteristically Jacksonian fashion by an eminent practitioner of the patronage system, George Washington Plunkitt of Tammany Hall:

"I ain't up on sillygisms, but I can give you some arguments that nobody can answer.

"First, this great and glorious country was built up by political parties; second, parties can't hold together if their workers don't get offices when they win; third, if the parties go to pieces, the government they built up must go to pieces, too; fourth, then there'll be hell to pay." W. Riordon, Plunkitt of Tammany Hall 13 (1963).

It may well be that the Good Government Leagues of America were right, and that Plunkitt, James Michael Curley and their ilk were wrong; but that is not entirely certain. As the merit principle has been extended and its effects increasingly felt; as the Boss Tweeds, the Tammany Halls, the Pendergast Machines, the Byrd Machines and the Daley Machines have faded into history; we find that political leaders at all levels increasingly complain of the helplessness of elected government, unprotected by "party discipline," before the demands of small and cohesive interest-groups.

The choice between patronage and the merit principle—or, to be more realistic about it, the choice between the desirable mix of merit and patronage principles in widely varying federal, state, and local political contexts—is not so clear that I would be prepared, as an original matter, to chisel a single, inflexible prescription into the Constitution. Fourteen years ago, in *Elrod v. Burns,* (1976), the Court did that. *Elrod* was limited however, as was the later decision of *Branti v. Finkel,* (1980), to patronage firings, leaving it to state and federal legislatures to determine when and where political affiliation could be taken into account in hirings and promotions. Today the Court makes its constitutional civil-service reform absolute, extending to all decisions regarding government employment. Because the First Amendment has never been thought to require this disposition, which may well have disastrous consequences for our political system, I dissent.

I

The restrictions that the Constitution places upon the government in its capacity as lawmaker, *i.e.,* as the regulator of private conduct, are not the same as the restrictions that it places upon the government in its capacity as employer. We have recognized this in many contexts, with respect to many different constitutional guarantees. Private citizens perhaps cannot be prevented from wearing long hair, but policemen can. *Kelley v. Johnson,* 425 U.S. 238 (1976). Private citizens cannot have their property searched without probable cause, but in many circumstances government employees can. *O'Connor v. Ortega,* 480 U.S. 709 (1987). Private citizens cannot be punished for refusing to provide the government information that may incriminate them, but government employees can be dismissed when the incriminating information that they refuse to provide relates to the performance of their job. *Gardner v. Broderick,* 392 U.S. 273 (1968). With regard to freedom of speech in particular: Private citizens cannot be punished for speech of merely private concern, but government employees can be fired for that reason. *Connick v. Myers,* 461 U.S. 138, (1983). Private citizens cannot be punished for partisan political activity, but federal and state employees can be dismissed and otherwise punished for that reason. *Public Workers v. Mitchell,* 330 U.S. 75 (1947); *CSC v. Letter Carriers,* 413 U.S. 548 (1973); *Broadrick v. Oklahoma,* 413 U.S. 601 (1973).

Once it is acknowledged that the Constitution's prohibition against laws "abridging the freedom of speech" does not apply to laws enacted in the government's capacity as employer the same way it does to laws enacted in the government's capacity as regulator of private conduct, it may sometimes be difficult to assess what employment practices are permissible and what are not. That seems to me not a difficult question, however, in the present context. The provisions of the Bill of Rights were designed to restrain transient majorities from impairing long-recognized personal liberties. They did not create by implication novel individual rights overturning accepted political norms. Thus, when a practice not expressly prohibited by the text of the Bill of Rights bears the endorsement of a long tradition of open, widespread, and unchallenged use that dates back to the beginning of the Republic, we have no proper basis for striking it down. Such a venerable and accepted tradition is not to be laid on the examining table and scrutinized for its conformity to some abstract principle of First-Amendment adjudication devised by this Court. To the contrary, such traditions are themselves the stuff out of which the Court's principles are to be formed. They are, in these uncertain areas, the very points of reference by which the legitimacy or illegitimacy of *other* practices are to be figured out. When it appears that the latest "rule," or "three-part test," or "balancing test" devised by the Court has placed us on a collision course with such a landmark practice, it is the former that must be recalculated by us, and not the latter that must be abandoned by our citizens. I know of no other way to formulate a constitutional jurisprudence that reflects, as it should, the principles adhered to, over time, by the American people, rather than those favored by the personal (and necessarily shifting) philosophical dispositions of a majority of this Court. . . .

II

Even accepting the Court's own mode of analysis, however, and engaging in "balancing" a tradition that ought to be part of the scales, *Elrod, Branti,* and today's extension of them seem to me wrong.

A

The Court limits patronage on the ground that the individual's interest in uncoerced belief and expression outweighs the systemic interests invoked to justify the practice. The opinion indicates that the government may prevail only if it proves that the practice is "narrowly tailored to further vital government interests."

That strict-scrutiny standard finds no support in our cases. Although our decisions establish that government employees do not lose all constitutional rights, we have consistently applied a lower level of scrutiny when "the governmental function operating . . . [is] not the power to regulate or license, as lawmaker, an entire trade or profession, or to control an entire branch of private business, but, rather, as proprietor, to manage [its] internal operatio[ns] . . . ." *Cafeteria & Restaurant Workers v. McElroy*, 367 U.S. 886 (1961). When dealing with its own employees, the government may not act in a manner that is "patently arbitrary or discriminatory," but its regulations are valid if they bear a "rational connection" to the governmental end sought to be served, *Kelley v. Johnson*. . . .

Because the restriction on speech is more attenuated when the government conditions employment than when it imposes criminal penalties, and because "government offices could not function if every employment decision became a constitutional matter," *Connick v. Myers*, we have held that government employment decisions taken on the basis of an employee's speech do not "abridg[e] the freedom of speech," merely because they fail the narrow-tailoring and compelling-interest tests applicable to direct regulation of speech. We have not subjected such decisions to strict scrutiny, but have accorded "a wide degree of deference to the employer's judgment" that an employee's speech will interfere with close working relationships.

When the government takes adverse action against an employee on the basis of his political affiliation (an interest whose constitutional protection is derived from the interest in speech), the same analysis applies. . . .

The whole point of my dissent is that the desirability of patronage is a policy question to be decided by the people's representatives; I do not mean, therefore, to endorse that system. But in order to demonstrate that a legislature could reasonably determine that its benefits outweigh its "coercive" effects, I must describe those benefits as the proponents of patronage see them: As Justice Powell discussed at length in his *Elrod* dissent, patronage stabilizes political parties and prevents excessive political fragmentation— both of which are results in which States have a strong governmental interest. Party strength requires the efforts of the rank-and-file, especially in "the dull periods between elections," to perform such tasks as organizing precincts, registering new voters, and providing constituent services. Even the most enthusiastic supporter of a party's program will shrink before such drudgery, and it is folly to think that ideological conviction alone will motivate sufficient numbers to keep the party going through the off-years. . . .

The Court simply refuses to acknowledge the link between patronage and party discipline, and between that and party success. . .

It is self-evident that eliminating patronage will significantly undermine party discipline; and that as party discipline wanes, so will the strength of the two-party system. But, says the Court, "[p]olitical parties have already survived the substantial decline in patronage employment practices in this century." This is almost verbatim what was said in *Elrod.* Fourteen years later it seems much less convincing. Indeed, now that we have witnessed, in 18 of the last 22 years, an Executive Branch of the Federal Government under the control of one party while the Congress is entirely or (for two years) partially within the control of the other party; now that we have undergone the most recent federal election, in which 98% of the incumbents, of whatever party, were returned to office; and now that we have seen elected officials changing their political affiliation with unprecedented readiness, the statement that "political parties have already survived" has a positively whistling-in-the-graveyard character to it. Parties have assuredly survived—but as what? As the forges upon which many of the essential compromises of American political life are hammered out? Or merely as convenient vehicles for the conducting of national presidential elections?

The patronage system does not, of course, merely foster political parties in general; it fosters the two-party system in particular. When getting a job, as opposed to effectuating a particular substantive policy, is an available incentive for party-workers, those attracted by that incentive are likely to work for the party that has the best chance of displacing the "ins," rather than for some splinter group that has a more attractive political philosophy but little hope of success. Not only is a two-party system more likely to emerge, but the differences between those parties are more likely to be moderated, as each has a relatively greater interest in appealing to a majority of the electorate and a relatively lesser interest in furthering philosophies or programs that are far from the mainstream. The stabilizing effects of such a system are obvious. . . .

Equally apparent is the relatively destabilizing nature of a system in which candidates cannot rely upon patronage-based party loyalty for their campaign support, but must attract workers and raise funds by appealing to various interest-groups. There is little doubt that our decisions in *Elrod* and *Branti,* by contributing to the decline of party strength, have also contributed to the growth of interest-group politics in the last decade. Our decision today will greatly accelerate the trend. It is not only campaigns that are affected, of course, but the subsequent behavior of politicians once they are in power. The replacement of a system firmly based in party discipline with one in which each office-holder comes to his own accommodation with competing interest groups produces "a dispersior of political influence that may inhibit a political party from enacting its programs into law."

Patronage, moreover, has been a powerful means of achieving the social and political integration of excluded groups. By supporting and ultimately dominating a particular party "machine," racial and ethnic minorities have—on the basis of their politics rather than their race or ethnicity—acquired the patronage awards the machine had power to confer. No one disputes the historical accuracy of this observation, and there is no reason to think that patronage can no longer serve that function. The abolition of patronage, however, prevents groups that have only recently obtained political power, especially blacks, from following this path to economic and social advancement. . . .

While the patronage system has the benefits argued for above, it also has undoubted disadvantages. It facilitates financial corruption, such as salary kickbacks and partisan political activity on government-paid time. It reduces the efficiency of government, because it creates incentives to hire more and less-qualified workers and because highly qualified workers are reluctant to accept jobs that may only last until the next election. And, of course, it applies some greater or lesser inducement for individuals to join and work for the party in power.

To hear the Court tell it, this last is the greatest evil. That is not my view, and it has not historically been the view of the American people. Corruption and inefficiency, rather than abridgement of liberty, have been the major criticisms leading to enactment of the civil-service laws—for the very good reason that the patronage system does not have as harsh an effect upon conscience, expression, and association as the Court suggests. As described above, it is the nature of the pragmatic, patronage-based, two-party system to build alliances and to suppress rather than foster ideological tests for participation in the division of political "spoils." What the patronage system ordinarily demands of the party worker is loyalty to, and activity on behalf of, the organization itself rather than a set of political beliefs. He is generally free to urge *within the organization* the adoption of any political position; but if that position is rejected he must vote and work for the party nonetheless. The diversity of political expression (other than expression of party loyalty) is channeled, in other words, to a different stage—to the contests for party endorsement rather than the partisan elections. It is undeniable, of course, that the patronage system entails some constraint upon the expression of views, particularly at the partisan-election stage, and considerable constraint upon the employee's right to associate with the other party. It greatly exaggerates these, however, to describe them as a general " 'coercion of belief,' " quoting *Branti*. Indeed, it greatly exaggerates them to call them "coercion" at all, since we generally make a distinction between inducement and compulsion. The public official offered a bribe is not "coerced" to violate the law, and the private citizen offered a patronage job is not "coerced" to work for the party. In sum, I do not deny that the patronage system influences or redirects, perhaps to a substantial degree, individual political expression and political association. But like the many generations of Americans that have preceded us, I do not consider that a signifiant impairment of free speech or free association. . . .

Even were I not convinced that *Elrod* and *Branti* were wrongly decided, I would hold that they should not be extended beyond their facts, viz., actual discharge of employees for their political affiliation. Those cases invalidated patronage firing in order to prevent the "restraint it places on freedoms of belief and association." The loss of one's current livelihood is an appreciably greater constraint than such other disappointments as the failure to obtain a promotion or selection for an uncongenial transfer. Even if the "coercive" effect of the former has been always to outweigh the benefits of party-based employment decisions, the "coercive" effect of the latter should not be. We have drawn a line between firing and other employment decisions in other contexts, see *Wygant v. Jackson Bd. of Education*, 476 U.S. 267 (1986) and should do so here as well. . . . If *Elrod* and *Branti* are not to be reconsidered in light of their demonstrably unsatisfactory consequences, I would go no further than to allow a cause of action when the employee has lost his position, that is, his formal title and salary. That narrow ground alone is enough to resolve the constitutional claims in the present case. . . .

The Court's opinion, of course, not only declines to confine *Elrod* and *Branti* to dismissals in the narrow sense I have proposed, but, unlike the Seventh Circuit, even extends those opinions beyond "constructive" dismissals—indeed, even beyond adverse treatment of current employees—to all hiring decisions. In the long run there may be cause to rejoice in that extension. When the courts are flooded with litigation under that most unmanageable of standards (*Branti*) brought by that most persistent and tenacious of suitors (the disappointed office-seeker) we may be moved to reconsider our intrusion into this entire field.

In the meantime, I dissent.

MEMBERS OF
THE SUPREME COURT
OF THE UNITED STATES

	Appointing President	Dates of Service
CHIEF JUSTICES		
Jay, John	Washington	1789–1795
Rutledge, John	Washington	1795–1795
Ellsworth, Oliver	Washington	1796–1800
Marshall, John	Adams, J.	1801–1835
Taney, Roger Brooke	Jackson	1836–1864
Chase, Salmon Portland	Lincoln	1864–1873
Waite, Morrison Remick	Grant	1874–1888
Fuller, Melville Weston	Cleveland	1888–1910
White, Edward Douglass	Taft	1910–1921
Taft, William Howard	Harding	1921–1930
Hughes, Charles Evans	Hoover	1930–1941
Stone, Harlan Fiske	Roosevelt, F.	1941–1946
Vinson, Frederick Moore	Truman	1946–1953
Warren, Earl	Eisenhower	1953–1969
Burger, Warren Earl	Nixon	1969–1986
Rehnquist, William Hubbs	Reagan	1986–
ASSOCIATE JUSTICES		
Rutledge, John	Washington	1790–1791
Cushing, William	Washington	1790–1810
Wilson, James	Washington	1789–1798

	Appointing President	Dates of Service
Blair, John	Washington	1790–1796
Iredell, James	Washington	1790–1799
Johnson, Thomas	Washington	1792–1793
Paterson, William	Washington	1793–1806
Chase, Samuel	Washington	1796–1811
Washington, Bushrod	Adams, J.	1799–1829
Moore, Alfred	Adams, J.	1800–1804
Johnson, William	Jefferson	1804–1834
Livingston, Henry Brockholst	Jefferson	1807–1823
Todd, Thomas	Jefferson	1807–1826
Duvall, Gabriel	Madison	1811–1835
Story, Joseph	Madison	1812–1845
Thompson, Smith	Monroe	1823–1843
Trimble, Robert	Adams, J. Q.	1826–1828
McLean, John	Jackson	1830–1861
Baldwin, Henry	Jackson	1830–1844
Wayne, James Moore	Jackson	1835–1867
Barbour, Philip Pendleton	Jackson	1836–1841
Catron, John	Van Buren	1837–1865
McKinley, John	Van Buren	1838–1852
Daniel, Peter Vivian	Van Buren	1842–1860
Nelson, Samuel	Tyler	1845–1872
Woodbury, Levi	Polk	1845–1851
Grier, Robert Cooper	Polk	1846–1870
Curtis, Benjamin Robbins	Fillmore	1851–1857
Campbell, John Archibald	Pierce	1853–1861
Clifford, Nathan	Buchanan	1858–1881
Swayne, Noah Haynes	Lincoln	1862–1881
Miller, Samuel Freeman	Lincoln	1862–1890
Davis, David	Lincoln	1862–1877
Field, Stephen Johnson	Lincoln	1863–1897
Strong, William	Grant	1870–1880
Bradley, Joseph P.	Grant	1870–1892
Hunt, Ward	Grant	1873–1882
Harlan, John Marshall	Hayes	1877–1911
Woods, William Burnham	Hayes	1881–1887
Matthews, Stanley	Garfield	1881–1889
Gray, Horace	Arthur	1882–1902
Blatchford, Samuel	Arthur	1882–1893
Lamar, Lucius Quintus C.	Cleveland	1888–1893
Brewer, David Josiah	Harrison	1890–1910
Brown, Henry Billings	Harrison	1891–1906

	Appointing President	Dates of Service
Shiras, George, Jr.	Harrison	1892–1903
Jackson, Howell Edmunds	Harrison	1893–1895
White, Edward Douglass	Cleveland	1894–1910
Peckham Rufus Wheeler	Cleveland	1896–1909
McKenna, Joseph	McKinley	1898–1925
Holmes, Oliver Wendell	Roosevelt, T.	1902–1932
Day, William Rufus	Roosevelt, T.	1903–1922
Moody, William Henry	Roosevelt, T.	1906–1910
Lurton, Horace Harmon	Taft	1910–1914
Hughes, Charles Evans	Taft	1910–1916
Van Devanter, Willis	Taft	1911–1937
Lamar, Joseph Rucker	Taft	1911–1916
Pitney, Mahlon	Taft	1912–1922
McReynolds, James Clark	Wilson	1914–1941
Brandeis, Louis Dembitz	Wilson	1916–1939
Clarke, John Hessin	Wilson	1916–1922
Sutherland, George	Harding	1911–1938
Butler, Pierce	Harding	1923–1939
Sanford, Edward Terry	Harding	1923–1930
Stone, Harlan Fiske	Coolidge	1925–1941
Roberts, Owen Josephus	Hoover	1930–1945
Cardozo, Benjamin Nathan	Hoover	1932–1938
Black, Hugo Lafayette	Roosevelt, F.	1937–1971
Reed, Stanley Forman	Roosevelt, F.	1938–1957
Frankfurter, Felix	Roosevelt, F.	1939–1962
Douglas, William Orville	Roosevelt, F.	1939–1975
Murphy, Frank	Roosevelt, F.	1940–1949
Byrnes, James Francis	Roosevelt, F.	1941–1942
Jackson, Robert Houghwout	Roosevelt, F.	1941–1954
Rutledge, Wiley Blount	Roosevelt, F.	1943–1949
Burton, Harold Hitz	Truman	1945–1958
Clark, Thomas Campbell	Truman	1949–1967
Minton, Sherman	Truman	1949–1956
Harlan, John Marshall	Eisenhower	1955–1971
Brennan, William Joseph, Jr.	Eisenhower	1956–1990
Whittaker, Charles Evans	Eisenhower	1957–1962
Stewart, Potter	Eisenhower	1958–1981
White, Byron Raymond	Kennedy	1962–
Goldberg, Arthur Joseph	Kennedy	1962–1965
Fortas, Abe	Johnson, L.	1965–1969
Marshall, Thurgood	Johnson, L.	1967–
Blackmun, Harry A.	Nixon	1970–

	Appointing President	Dates of Service
Powell, Lewis Franklin, Jr.	Nixon	1972–1986
Rehnquist, William Hubbs	Nixon	1972–
Stevens, John Paul	Ford	1975–
O'Connor, Sandra Day	Reagan	1981–
Scalia, Antonin	Reagan	1986–
Kennedy, Anthony	Reagan	1988–
Souter, David Hackett	Bush	1990–

GLOSSARY

Advisory opinion.   An opinion or interpretation of law that does not have binding effect. The Court does not give advisory opinions, for example, on hypothetical disputes; it decides only actual cases or controversies.

Affirm.   In an appellate court, to reach a decision that agrees with the result reached in a case by the lower court.

Affirmative action programs.   Programs required by federal or state laws designed to remedy discriminatory practices by hiring minority-group persons and/or women.

Amicus curiae.   A friend of the court, a person not a party to litigation, who volunteers or is invited by the court to give his views on a case.

Appeal.   To take a case to a higher court for review. Generally, a party losing in a trial court may appeal once to an appellate court as a matter of right. If the party loses in the appellate court, appeal to a higher court is within the discretion of the higher court. Most appeals to the Supreme Court are within its discretion to deny or grant a hearing.

Appellant.   The party that appeals a lower-court decision to a higher court.

Appellee.   One who has an interest in upholding the decision of a lower court and is compelled to respond when the case is appealed to a higher court by the appellant.

Brief.   A document prepared by counsel to serve as the basis for an argument in court, setting out the facts and legal arguments in support of his case.

Case.   A general term for an action, cause, suit, or controversy, at law or equity; a question contested before a court.

Case law. The law as defined by previously decided cases, distinct from statutes and other sources of law.

Certification, writ of. A method of taking a case from appellate court to the Supreme Court in which the lower court asks that some question or interpretation of law be certified, clarified, and made more certain.

Certiorari, writ of. A writ issued from the Supreme Court, at its discretion and at the request of a petitioner, to order a lower court to send the record of a case to the Court for its review.

Civil Law. The body of law dealing with the private rights of individuals, as distinguished from criminal law.

Class action. A lawsuit brought by one person or group on behalf of all persons similarly situated.

Comity. Courtesy, respect; referring to the deference federal courts pay to state court decisions that are based on state law.

Common law. The collection of principles and rules, particularly from unwritten English law, that derive their authority from long-standing usage and custom or from courts recognizing and enforcing those customs.

Compelling state interest. A test used to uphold state action against First Amendment and equal protection challenges because of the serious need for government action.

Concurring opinion. An opinion by a justice that agrees with the result reached by the Court in a case but disagrees with the Court's rationale or reasoning for its decision.

Contempt (civil and criminal). Civil contempt is the failure to do something for the benefit of another party after being ordered to do so by a court. Criminal contempt occurs when a person exhibits disrespect for a court or obstructs the administration of justice.

Controversies. *See* Justiciable controversy.

Criminal law. The body of law that deals with the enforcement of laws and the punishment of persons who, by breaking laws, commit crimes against the state.

Declaratory Judgment. A court pronouncement declaring a legal right or interpretation but not ordering a special action.

De facto. In fact, in reality.

Defendant. In a civil action, the party denying or defending itself against charges brought by a plaintiff. In a criminal action, the person indicted for the commission of a offense.

De jure. As a result of law, as a result of official action.

Dicta. *See* Obiter dictim.

Discretionary jurisdiction. Jurisdiction that a court may accept or reject in particular cases. The Supreme Court has discretionary jurisdiction in over 90 percent of the cases that come to it.

Dismissal. An order diposing of a case without a hearing or trial.

Dissenting opinion. An opinion by a justice that disagrees with the result reached by the Court in a case.

Docket. All cases filed in a court.

Due process. Fair and regular procedure. The Fifth and Fourteenth Amendments guarantee persons that they will not be deprived of life, liberty, or property by the government until fair and usual procedures have been followed.

Error, writ of. A writ issued from an appeals court to a lower court requiring that it send the record of a case so that it may review it for error.

Exclusionary rule. This rule commands that evidence obtained in violation of the rights guaranteed by the Fourth and Fifth Amendments must be excluded at trial.

Executive agreement. A treatylike agreement with another country made by the president.

Executive privilege. Exemption from the disclosure requirements for ordinary citizens because of the executive's need for confidentiality in discharging highly important governmental functions.

Ex parte. From, or on, only on side. Application to a court for some ruling or action on behalf of only one party.

Federalism. The interrelationships among the states and the relationship between the states and the national government.

Federal preemption. The federal government's exclusive power over certain matters such as interstate commerce and sedition to the exclusion of state jurisdiction and law.

Grand jury. A jury of twelve to twenty-three persons that hears in private evidence for serving an indictment.

Habeas corpus. Literally, "you have the body"; a writ issued to inquire whether a person is lawfully imprisoned or detained. The writ demands that the persons holding the prisoner justify his detention or release him.

Immunity. A grant of exemption from prosecution in return for evidence by testimony.

In camera. "In chambers," referring to court hearings in private without spectators.

Indictment. A formal charge of offenses based on evidence presented by a prosecutor from a grand jury.

In forma pauperis. In the manner of a pauper, without liability for the costs of filing cases before a court.

Information. A written set of charges, similar to an indictment, filed by a prosecutor but without a grand jury's consideration of evidence.

Inherent powers. Powers originating from the structure of government or sovereignty that go beyond those expressly granted or which could be construed to have been implied from those expressly granted.

Injunction. A court order prohibiting a person from performing a particular act.

In re. In the affair of, concerning; often used in judicial procedings where there is no adversary but where the matter (such as a bankrupt's estate) requires judicial action.

Judgment. The official decision of a court.

Judicial review. The power to review and strike down any legislation or other government action that is inconsistent with federal or state constitutions. The Supreme Court reviews government action only under the Constitution of the United States and federal laws.

Jurisdiction. The power of a court to hear a case or controversy, which exists when the proper parties are present and when the point to be decided is among the issues authorized to be handled by a particular court.

Justiciable controversy. A controversy in which a claim of right is asserted against another who has an interest in contesting it. Courts will consider only justiciable controversies, as distinguished from hypothetical disputes.

Majority opinion. An opinion in a case that is subscribed to by a majority of the justices who participated in the decision.

Mandamus, writ of. "We command"; an order issued from a superior court directing a lower court or other government authority to perform a particular act.

Mandatory jurisdiction. Jurisdiction that a court must accept. The Supreme Court must decide cases coming under its appellate jurisdiction, though it may avoid giving them plenary consideration.

Moot. Unsettled, undecided. A moot question is also one that is no longer material, or that has already been resolved, and has become hypothetical.

Motion. A written or oral application to a court or judge to obtain a rule or order.

Natural rights. Rights based on the nature of man and independent of those rights secured by positive laws.

Obiter dictum. A statement by a judge or justices expressing an opinion and included with, but not essential to, an opinion resolving a case before the court. Dicta are not necessarily binding in later cases.

Opinion for the court. The opinion announcing the decision of a court.

Original jurisdiction. The jurisdiction of a court of first instance, or trial court. The Supreme Court has original jurisdiction under Article III of the Constitution.

Per curiam. "By the court"; an unsigned opinion of the court.

Petitioner. One who files a petition with a court seeking action or relief, including the plaintiff or appellant. When a writ of certiorari is granted by the Supreme Court, the party seeking review is called the petitioner, and the party responding is called the respondent.

Petit jury. A trial jury, traditionally a common law jury of twelve persons, but since 1970 the Supreme Court has permitted states to use juries composed of less than twelve persons.

Plenary consideration. Full consideration. When the Supreme Court grants a case review, it may give it full consideration, permitting the parties to submit briefs on the merits of the case and to present oral arguments, before the Court reaches its decision.

Plurality opinion. An opinion announcing the decision of the Court, but which has the support of less than a majority of the Court.

Political question. Questions that courts refuse to decide because they are deemed to be essentially political in nature, or because their determination would involve an intrusion on the powers of the executive or legislature, or because courts could not provide a judicial remedy.

Probable cause. Reasonable cause, having more evidence for, rather than against, when establishing the basis for obtaining a search warrant, for example.

Rational basis test. A test used by appellate courts to uphold legislation if there is evidence of a rational basis for the law's enactment.

Reapportment. A realignment or change in electoral districts due to changes in population.

Remand. To send back. After a decision in a case, the case is often sent back by a higher court to the court from which it came for further action in light of its decision.

Respondent. The party that is compelled to answer the claims or questions posed in a court by a petitioner.

Reverse. In an appellate court, to reach a decision that disagrees with the result reached in a case by a lower court.

Ripeness. When a case is ready for adjudication and decision; the issues presented must not be hypothetical, and the parties must have exhausted other avenues of appeal.

Search warrant. An order issued by a judge or magistrate directing a law enforcement official to search and seize evidence of the commission of a crime, contraband, the fruits of crime, or things otherwise unlawfully possessed.

Separation of powers. The division of the powers of the national government according to the three branches of government: the legislative, which is empowered to make laws; the executive, which is required to carry out the laws; and the judicial, which has the power to interpret and adjudicate disputes under the law.

Seriatim. Separately, individually, one by one. The Court's practice was once to have each justice give his opinion on a case separately.

Sovereignty. Supreme political authority; the absolute and uncontrollable power by which an independent nation-state is governed.

Standing. Having the appropriate characteristics to bring or participate in a case; in particular, having a personal interest and stake in the outcome.

Stare Decisis. "Let the decision stand." The principle of adherence to settled cases, the doctrine that principles of law established in earlier cases should be accepted as authoritative in similar subsequent cases.

State action. Actions undertaken by a state government and those done "under the color of state law"; that is, those actions required or sanctioned by a state.

Statute. A written law enacted by a legislature.

Subpoena. An order to present oneself before a grand jury, court, or legislative hearing.

Subpoena duces tecum. An order to produce specified documents or papers.

Summary decision. A decision in a case that does not give it full consideration; when the Court decides a case without having the parties submit briefs on the merits of the case or present oral arguments before the Court.

Tort. An inury or wrong to the person or property of another.

Transactional immunity. Immunity granted a person in exchange for evidence or testimony, which protects that person from prosecution, regardless of independent evidence against him; *see* Use immunity.

Treaties.   A compact made between two or more independent nations; treaties are made in the United States by the president with the advice and consent of the Senate.

Use immunity.   Immunity granted a person in exchange for evidence or testimony but that only protects that person from prosecution based on the use of his own testimony.

Vacate.   To make void, annul, or rescind the decision of a lower court.

War power.   The power of the national government to wage war; Congress has the power to declare war, while the president, as commander in chief, has authority over the conduct of war.

Writ.   An order commanding someone to perform or not perform acts specified in the order.

INDEX OF CASES

GENERAL INDEX

abortion issue, 34, 36, 75, 108, 166, 168, 175–76
absolutism (literalism), 77–78
Act to Improve the Administration of Justice of 1988, 104, 152
"adequate state grounds" doctrine, 648–49
administrative agencies, federal:
  delegation of powers to, 249, 288, 340–43, 344, 351
  Nixon's misuse charged, 371
admiralty cases, 36–37
adverseness of parties requirement, 98
advisory opinions, 98–99
affirmative action, 107
African-Americans. *See* Blacks; racial discrimination
Agricultural Adjustment Act of 1938, 493, 494, 508
Alien and Sedition Acts of 1798, 31, 32, 41, 217, 544
ambulatory retroactivity, doctrine of, 169
Americans United for Separation of Church and State, 125
Anti-Federalists, 25–26, 29, 45, 83, 87, 446–47, 542–43, 545, 579, 653
antitrust cases, 103, 104, 478, 480, 482, 494, 496*n.8*
appeal(s), 103, 114
  avenues of, *fig.* 97
  direct, 96, 103
  filing, 98, 150
  limited length of, 98
  mandatory, decrease of, 103, 104, 114, 150, 151, 152
appeals courts, federal, *fig.* 97, *map* 100, 102
Appellate Docket, 151

appellate jurisdiction of Supreme Court, 96, *fig.* 97, 102, 114, 151, 152, 173, 600
appointment and removal powers, 190, 196, 249, 250, 284–89, 302–3, 306
  independent counsel, 318–19
appointment of federal judges, 176, 284
  congressional influence over, 172, 173, 190
  1801 midnight judges, 45, 171
  nominees rejected by Senate, *table* 285
  senatorial courtesy in, 284–86
  to Supreme Court, average frequency of, 176
apportionment, legislative, 35, 111–12, 131–32, 386–87, 670–77
  one person, one vote principle, 387, 651–52, 653, 670–77
  see also districting, legislative; reapportionment cases
appropriations laws, 443
Article I, US Constitution, 190, 217, 249, 340, 369, 370, 385, 387–88, 443–44, 522, 546, 654–55
Article II, US Constitution, 190, 191, 220, 284, 285, 367, 370, 371
Article III, US Constitution, 24–25, 27, 32, 96, 173, 546, 600
Article IV, US Constitution, 111, 546
Article V, US Constitution, 385, 546
Article VI, US Constitution, 546–47, 551, 555, 600, 601
Article VII, US Constitution, 542
Articles of Confederation, 191, 197, 443–44, 541, 542, 549, 654
Articles of Impeachment against President Richard M. Nixon, 381–84